HISTORY OF WORLD WAR I

HISTORY OF WORLD WAR I

Editor-in-Chief
A J P Taylor

Compiled by
S L Mayer

Octopus Books

CONTENTS

First published 1974 by
Octopus Books Limited
59 Grosvenor Street, London W1

Distributed in USA by
Galahad Books
A division of A & W Promotional Book Corp.
95 Madison Avenue, New York, New York 10016

Distributed in Australia by
Rigby Limited
30 North Terrace, Kent Town
Adelaide, South Australia 5067

ISBN 0 7064 0398 3

© 1968/69/70 BPC Publishing Ltd.
© 1973/74 Phoebus Publishing Company

This book is adapted from "The History of
the 20th Century". It has been produced by
Phoebus Publishing Company in
co-operation with Octopus Books Limited

Printed in England by
Jarrold & Sons Limited, Norwich

THE GREAT WAR

Introduction

For those who lived through the First World War, it was known as, and is still considered to be, the Great War. It was the cataclysm of a century, perhaps of all time. That is certainly the way it seemed then. A great war among the European powers had been feared for decades, but it was assumed that at the final moment, they would stop short of the brink, and major war could be averted.

In July 1914, however, it was different. When the diplomats stumbled and armies mobilized, the long dormant fear of a major war rose and, surprisingly, was welcomed on all sides. Within every European state social forces were pressing for change. In Russia, electoral, industrial and social reform on a broad front was being demanded by every stratum of society, from the nobility right through the middle classes and the peasantry. In Britain the Irish question was tearing at the fabric of the nation and causing great rifts among the politicians of the majority party, the Liberals. Trade unions were demanding shorter hours, higher pay and better working conditions throughout Western Europe. Women were demanding the franchise. By 1912 the Social Democratic Party had become the majority party in the German lower house, the *Reichstag*. The monarchs of Central and Eastern Europe had held back the tide of nationalism in Poland and the Balkans for decades. The more democratic, more highly industrialized states of Western Europe had held off the demands of the working classes in the factories for decades too. All demanded change. Each group thought that a war might bring about these changes faster. Thus, even those parties which had previously been anti-militaristic, like the German social democrats, now accepted and supported the war, for the

call of nationalism was too strong to resist.

Ironically, those who resisted social change also supported the idea of war, as they believed it would divert attention from social, economic and electoral reform in a great national effort that would unite, rather than divide, class against class. When war came, therefore, it was accompanied by an outburst of enthusiasm and relief from every social class in every major European nation. German helmets were festooned with flowers, placed there by the women who cheered as their troops, their husbands and sons, marched off to the front. French and British soldiers who boarded the trains taking them to war, and many to their deaths, were cheered with equal enthusiasm. An outburst of nationalistic pride and fierce chauvinism gripped Europe in August 1914. It would, of course, be a short war. The boys would be home by Christmas.

It is difficult to pinpoint the reasons why war, which had been feared and avoided for so long, should break out because of the killing of an Austrian archduke and his wife. Why should world war have broken out over the Sarajevo Incident, and not over the many, seemingly more important crises, which had taken place earlier? The answer lies in the power of Great Britain relative to her European rivals. After the defeat of Napoleon, Britain was unrivalled as a major world power. On the seas Britannia ruled without peer; her colonial empire expanded when and as British interests determined it should. But in the most important area of all, industrial power and technological superiority, Britain was decades ahead of even France, potentially her greatest continental rival. As the 19th century went on, however, this once yawning industrial and technological gap perceptibly narrowed.

By 1870, when Prussia had expanded to

create the German Empire, the Second Reich, proclaimed in the Hall of Mirrors of the Palace of Versailles after the defeat of France in January 1871, Britain still maintained her once seemingly insurmountable lead. But now a rival worthy of her potential loomed across the North Sea, then called the German Ocean. Although never a serious rival as a naval or colonial power in the 19th century, Bismarck, the German Chancellor, sought to pit Britain against France and Russia in a naval armaments race and a scramble for colonial territory which heretofore Britain had been content to influence, but not necessarily rule. Meanwhile, Bismarck saw to it that Germany's industrial strength increased in the only continent which mattered to him, Europe. By 1900 it was clear that the industrial gap had narrowed markedly between Britain and Germany, and at this stage Kaiser Wilhelm II, who had sacked Bismarck ten years before, sought to challenge Britain in a naval arms race as well. Although most of the Eastern Hemisphere had been divided into colonies or spheres of influence between Britain and France and a few other states, the Kaiser sought to provoke Britain in the colonial world, demanding a 'place in the sun', more colonial influence, and above all, greater prestige for Germany in consonance with her increased industrial strength.

Britain took this challenge seriously. But by 1914 Germany had passed Britain in many crucial areas. Certain key indices pointed to a German supremacy which had already been established. German production of pig iron was 40 per cent greater than Britain's; in steel production Germany was far ahead, her annual total over double that of Britain. Germany was almost an equal to Britain in coal production. Furthermore,

Germany was far more self-sufficient in foodstuffs than a Britain which had increasingly come to depend on her colonies and the United States for the food she consumed. Markets which had once been British for industrial goods—the Low Countries, Scandinavia—were now increasingly within German orbit. Given time, Germany would surely have outstripped Britain in the rest of Europe.

Given time, Germany's increasing naval strength would have been a major challenge on the seas which Britain had come to regard as her own. If Germany was to be stopped, the time was now—in 1914. Britain could not afford to give Germany more time. The Kaiser's bellicose pronouncements, his aggressive stance, his celebrated or infamous blank cheque to Austria to do with Serbia what she would, made it easy for Britain, urged on by France, to meet the German challenge. Diplomacy failed in 1914 because the Great Powers deliberately let it fail. Ironically, the Kaiser, who most stood to gain by maintaining a fragile European peace, did more than most to provoke the war which could deny Germany the hegemony in Europe which Bismarck and Wilhelm II had sought for so long.

But even the Kaiser realized that only a short war could bring victory to Germany. Britain's command of the seas would bring her the foodstuffs and industrial supplies from abroad which she would require in a long conflict. Thus, for many years Germany planned on striking a knockout blow against France within the first six weeks of the war, before France's ally, Russia, had time to mobilize her armed forces. Then German military might could be brought to bear upon Russia, thereby forcing a peace on her two greatest continental rivals regardless of what Britain did. So it can be argued that the war was lost for Germany at the First Battle of the Marne in early September, when the French and British Expeditionary Force stopped the great German sweep across Belgium and France short of Paris.

By the end of the autumn a line of trenches was dug from the English Channel to Switzerland. The war of attrition on the Western Front had set in. The boys would not be home by Christmas. It was going to be a long war.

On the Eastern Front Germany did rather better. After the humiliation inflicted upon Russia at Tannenberg, German soldiers slowly pushed into Russian Poland. By the end of 1914 German troops had occupied practically all of Belgium, much of northern France, and parts of western Russia. The Allies had been driven from German soil. The Allies, like the Germans, still hoped to bring an end to the war by one sudden breakthrough, even though it became increasingly apparent, to the men at the front at least, that such a breakthrough would cost too many lives and was, in the circumstances, impossible.

Unable to win on the Western Front, the Allies hoped to achieve victory by starving Germany to death through a blockade of her coasts and seizing colonial territory from Germany and her ally, the Ottoman Empire. By 1915 the German flag had been rung down over the few colonies she possessed in Africa and Asia, save in Tanganyika, German East Africa, where von Lettow-Vorbeck fought on, clinging to a part of the colony by an intensive and cleverly fought semi-guerrilla campaign. Japan and Australia had partitioned German possessions in Asia, and France and Britain and her dominion of South Africa had taken what Germany once held in Africa. The pressing concern for the Allies in early 1915 was to bring assistance to Russia, who was unable to maintain a line of defence against Germany and Austria-Hungary, who continued to press the Russians back. The Gallipoli campaign, the purpose of which was to force the Dardanelles and bring Turkey to her knees, thereby giving the Allies access to the Black Sea to bring arms to Russia unharassed on a year-round basis, was one of the major disasters of the war for the Allies. The landings on the Gallipoli peninsula south of Constantinople were mishandled. Turkish forces, aided by German arms and military advisers, like Liman von Sanders, stiffened. Partly due to Allied errors, partly to Turkish resistance, the Allies were thrown back. Gallipoli was a fiasco.

The time had come for the Allies to seek further assistance. A deal was struck with Italy, heretofore neutral in the war and to one extent or other allied to both sides, to give her portions of Austrian and Turkish territory if she declared war against the Central Powers. It was hoped that Italian pressure on Austria-Hungary would sap the strength of the Central Powers, thereby stopping the advance into Russia and preventing a German breakthrough on the Western Front. The Italian declaration of war in the spring of 1915 did not accomplish this aim. First of all, Italy declared war only against Austria-Hungary. She did not declare war against Germany until 1916, and in any event, could do nothing directly against German territory. The war in Italy went badly for the Allies, who ironically had to send troops and munitions to prevent a collapse of the Italian front.

It was clear that further help was needed for an Allied breakthrough. By now most of Europe was in the war, and those nations that were not were not terribly significant in broad terms. Although the Scandinavian countries and the Netherlands remained neutral, the British blockade saw to it that few goods from the Americas and elsewhere were able to filter through these states to Germany as they had done at the outset of the war. Of the Great Powers in the world, only one remained outside the conflict by 1915; the United States. There was little fear that the US would enter the conflict, if they did so at all, on the German side. But if America could be brought into the war in support of the Allies, it could make all the difference. The sinking of the British liner *Lusitania* helped Allied propaganda in the United States immeasurably. Although the Germans had warned any Americans travelling aboard the *Lusitania* that they were travelling at their own risk into a war zone around Britain which Germany had filled with submarines in order to break the Allied blockade, the American public reaction was one of shock and horror when it became known that 128 Americans, some of them quite prominent, had lost their lives when the liner was sunk off the coast of Ireland.

President Woodrow Wilson insisted that the unrestricted submarine warfare the Germans were waging be brought to an end. Otherwise Germany ran the risk of bringing the US into the war. Unrestricted submarine warfare did end after a time, but a significant shift in American public opinion had taken place. Although it is now known that the *Lusitania* carried considerable amounts of arms and other contraband, and therefore Germany was within her rights under international law to sink her, British propaganda in the States utilized this event to the full. Like the death of Edith Cavell, a British nurse who was acting as a spy behind German lines in Belgium and who, when caught, received the treatment that any captured spy in wartime can expect, the sinking of the *Lusitania* made Americans feel that the Germans were brutes, inhuman and worthy of contempt, outside the community of civilized nations. It has even been argued that Winston Churchill, the driving force behind Gallipoli, who was sacked because of its failure, contrived to have the *Lusitania* sunk because it would bring the United States nearer to intervention on the Allied side. But America steadfastly remained neutral, although she did loan Britain billions of dollars and continued to ship foodstuffs and other goods to Britain even though she was now virtually unable to trade with Germany. If an Allied breakthrough was to take place in 1915, it would have to be without American help.

The diplomatic illusions of the old Europe were shattered when the troop trains started rolling in August 1914. The military illusions of the general staffs had expired in the bloody trenches of Gallipoli and Neuve-Chapelle. The first two chapters take us to that point where the combatants realized that Europe's 'Great War' was a conflict far beyond the confines of any previous experience. The stage was set for the mass battles of 1916, the waging of Total War . . .

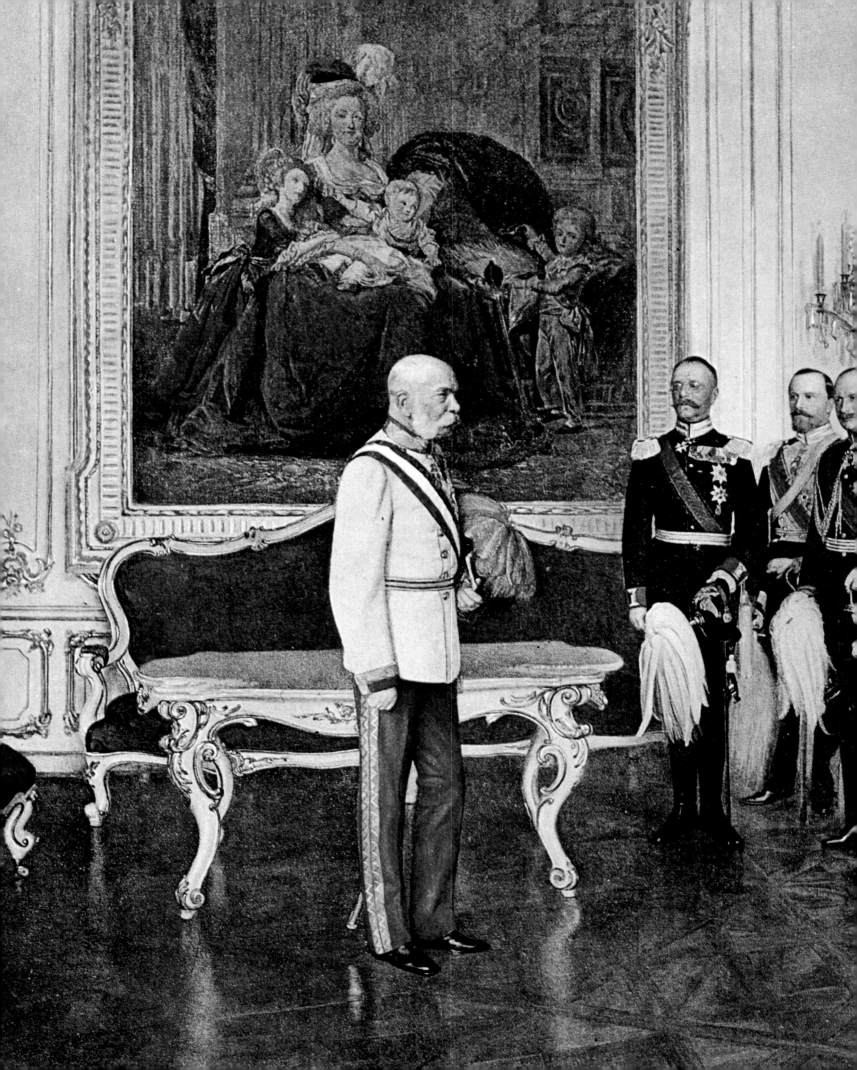

1 THE GREAT WAR BEGINS

Why Europe Went to War

In 1911 G. P. Gooch, an English historian who had, until the previous year, been a Liberal MP, published a little book called *History of our Time 1885-1911*. It is still worth reading, not least because its closing sentences show an optimism about international affairs which has now all but disappeared. Although, the author noted, five million men were at that moment under arms in Europe, nevertheless he said, 'we can now look forward with something like confidence to the time when war between civilized nations will be considered as antiquated as a duel, and when the peacemakers shall be called the children of God'.

In those words spoke the proud, confident, liberal, humanitarian Europe which had been built over the previous halfcentury. Less than three years later it was blown to the winds, and we have never quite recovered it.

It is worthwhile to recall just how great a blow was given to this confidence by the scale of what followed. The war which began on 1st August 1914, when Germany declared war on Russia, was the first of several wars which were later to be lumped together as one—the 'Great War'. The struggle between Austria-Hungary and Serbia—the expression of a deeper conflict soon to erupt between Austria-Hungary and Russia—and the war between France and Germany which quickly followed had little logic to connect them: what had Vienna to do with Alsace, or Frenchmen with the fate of Serbia? That the British, too, should then join in seemed odd to many people on both sides of the Channel. And this was only the beginning. Japan, Tur-

Left: Franz-Josef of Austria-Hungary – symbol of the old order

key, China, Siam—the list of those at war was to grow until it included every major state and left unrepresented no part of the globe. Thirty-two 'victorious' nations were to be represented at the Peace Conference in 1919; some of them did not even exist in 1914 and twenty-two of them were non-European. By then, Baluchis and Vietnamese had been brought to fight in France, Americans and Japanese had gone to Vladivostok, Canadians to Archangel and Australians to Palestine, while Germans and British had slaughtered one another across the oceans of the world from the coasts of Chile to the Western Approaches. The fighting only ended when, in 1922, Greeks and Turks at last made peace.

This extraordinary explosion of violence was hardly foreseen in 1914. Though many people by then feared war, few envisaged so colossal a holocaust. In part, this was because, once started, the struggle developed its own, unforeseeable logic. The two sides were nearly balanced in strength at the outset and this led to efforts to mobilize a margin of superiority which would guarantee victory and to find new allies: this intensified and spread the war. Yet much of what followed was implicit in the state of the world and, above all, of its centre, Europe, on the eve of the outbreak.

The shock of the war soon provoked a hunt for those who were guilty of starting it. This was the earliest form of the search to explain so astonishing an event. It was to go on for many years. It came out most crudely in popular catch-phrases: 'Hang the Kaiser' in Great Britain had its equivalents in other countries. But some looked for guilty men at home. Even before 1914 radicals and pacifists were attacking the Liberal government and its foreign secretary, Sir Edward Grey, for

committing the country to the side of France without authorization from Parliament. Another personal, but different, criticism was made of Grey by Germans: if only he had been more explicit (it was said), if only it had been made clear that Great Britain would enter a war between France and Germany, the German government would not have gone to war.

Some people preferred to blame whole groups of men. Germans blamed the British who, they said, grudged them their place in the sun; the British detected in Germans and German history a domineering tendency. Radicals and socialists attacked rather vaguely defined 'capitalists' who, it was alleged, either by so manipulating foreign policies as to safeguard their overseas investments and trade, or by encouraging the armaments which kept their factories working and paying large dividends, had pushed the world towards war. Whatever plausibility such arguments once had, historians have swung away both from them, and from large, schematic interpretations of the origins of the war in terms of economic interest.

We now prefer to place less emphasis on personal responsibility and policy except in the case of a few, clearly identifiable and delimited, crucial decisions. We need not go so far as to say that no one was ever personally responsible for anything decisive; the actions of Wilhelm II and his military advisers would by themselves make nonsense of such a view. Nevertheless, we admit that statesmen often have less freedom to act than they think, and that circumstances are as important in shaping their decisions as their own view of what they want. If we approach the world of 1914 in this way, what was there in its nature and structure which now appears, first, to have made war likely, and then so disastrous when it came?

The diplomatic 'system'

The international system itself has been blamed. In an age of so much quarrelling and bickering, it may seem paradoxical to speak of a 'system'. Yet there was enough awareness of common principles and practice to make it possible to use this term. Diplomats everywhere understood one another in a sense in which, perhaps, they do not today, when deep ideological differences may separate them on fundamentals. The concept of national self-interest was the accepted basis of their business. This was tempered by a broad agreement that only vital threats to a nation's self-interest or a violent outrage to its dignity (whose preservation was a part of the national interest) could justify war between great powers. If war came, it was assumed, no power would ever seek to modify fundamentally the institutions of another – there would be, that is to say, no appeal to revolution as a weapon, and peace would eventually be made on the basis of a new adjustment of enduring interests.

This framework of common assumptions was reinforced by the fact that diplomatic business was then almost exclusively the affair of professional diplomats, who had evolved a very effective *esprit de corps* and skill. In 1914 they could look back to a long succession of tragedies averted and crises survived as evidence of the success of their methods. One towering fact stood out above all: since 1871 there had been no war between two European great powers and in this sense the Continent had enjoyed its longest period of peace since the Reformation.

The 'concert of Europe', as it had been called in the 19th century, was still a reality in that the European great powers had recently still tended to act in concert to avert threats to peace. They had done this successfully many times and, of course, to most statesmen it was only the European great powers which really mattered. This was not unreasonable. Portents of a very different future could already be discerned: there *had* been a war between Russia and Japan, and the United States *had* stripped Spain of her Caribbean and Pacific possessions. But these hints of a new era of global politics did not invalidate the achievement of the diplomats in Europe, because in 1914 it was still Europe which determined the fate of the world.

Yet this traditional diplomatic system has itself been blamed for the disaster. In one sense, this is a truism: war did break out in 1914 and the old diplomacy did not stop it. Many students of the crisis have concluded that the statesmen who were trying to deal with the crisis were too much imprisoned by their conventional assumption and too unwilling to step outside their usual framework of ideas to be able to dominate affairs as, perhaps, a Bismarck might have done. This is a charge which it is easier to make than to prove or disprove. What may fairly be observed is that conventional diplomacy assumed that the aims of the great powers were rational and moderate enough for negotiation to bring about their reconciliation one with another – and this was no longer possible when some of these powers had come to believe, as they had done by 1914, that their very existence was at stake.

Yet it is not usually on this basis that the old diplomacy has been attacked. More usually, it has been asserted that there was a defect in the international machine itself which made conflict in the end inevitable,

and this has been identified as the 'nightmare of alliances' which Bismarck had so feared and which was an almost all-embracing reality in 1914. It had by then long been pointed out that the alliances introduced a dangerously mechanical and deterministic element into international life: once one cog began to turn, would not, in the end, the whole machine have to follow? Those who feared this thought mainly of two alliances: the Franco-Russian, signed in 1894, and the Triple Alliance of Germany, Austria-Hungary, and Italy, formed in 1882 and later modified and adhered to by Rumania. By them, it was said, Europe was divided into two armed camps, and the chance of war was immeasurably increased.

This is too simple. Qualifications are needed. The Triple Alliance, for example, was far from firm. Italy was not to enter the war on her allies' side in 1914 and by then it was well known in Vienna and

Berlin that Rumania could not be depended upon. Both countries eventually went to war – but on the other side. The Franco-Russian treaty, too, had originally been made as a basis for co-operation against Great Britain. Its terms, so far as they concerned Germany, were consequential upon German action. Only if Germany attacked Russia was France to come to the aid of her ally; in the end the alliance never came into action at all because the Germans settled the question of France's involvement by attacking her. Similarly, the *entente cordiale* by no means pointed irresistibly towards a Franco-British alliance against Germany. In 1911, Agadir had certainly aroused feeling and had strengthened the informal ties between London and Paris. Yet this, too, was a paradoxical outcome, since the French government of the day

*Europe's heads of state in 1914. **1** Franz Josef of Austria-Hungary at a family wedding. **2** Kaiser Wilhelm II with the French General Foch. **3** Kaiser Wilhelm and George V of Great Britain. **4** President Poincaré (centre) of France visits Russia in 1914*

was one which had hoped to cultivate better relations with Germany. By 1914 the British had got over their alarm at the Germans' battleship-building, and down almost to the eve of the war Anglo-German relations were better than they had been for twenty years.

Nor did European alliances determine the extent of the conflict. Although the Great War was to be focused on Europe and make its impact on world history through the damage it did to Europe, it was to be a world-wide war. Great Britain's participation made this inevitable, but there were other reasons for it, too. Tradition, geography, and domestic politics all made it inconceivable that the United States should join in European quarrels in 1914, but two other non-European states – Japan and Turkey – did become involved.

Japan's position in 1914 cut right across the pattern of European alliances. She was the only formal ally of the British, who had turned to her because of their traditional fear of Russia in Asia and the threat to their interests posed by the seeming break-up of China. The alliance was crowned by the Japanese victory over Russia in 1905. Two years later, an Anglo-Russian convention attempted to clear up some of the delicate problems which still divided London and St Petersburg. Yet by 1914 the two states were bickering over Persia much as they had always done. It was not, in other words, formal alliances which brought about the paradoxical situation at the end of August 1914 in which Great Britain, Japan, and Russia stood on the same side as allies against Germany.

Struggle for the Balkans

Turkey, too, was involved fundamentally and perhaps inevitably in the war, but hardly because of formal diplomacy. One possible name for the Great War would be the last war of the Turkish succession; eastern European history since the 17th century had been the story of attempts to allocate the booty and fill the vacuum left behind by the slow rolling-back of a Turkish power which had once embraced Hungary and lapped at the very walls of Vienna. The last stage in the dissolution of Turkey's European empire had opened in the Balkan Wars of 1912. The second Balkan War made it clear that among the claimants to the Turkish succession – the 'new nations' which had appeared in the Balkans in the 19th century – quarrels were just as likely as between the Habsburg and Romanov dynasties which had for so long suspiciously watched one another's advances at Turkish expense.

Here, indeed, was a true seed of the war. Two great states sought power and influence in an area abandoned to feeble and bickering small states by the Turkish retreat. Inevitably, they had favourites and satellites. But Vienna and St Petersburg managed to co-operate or avoid conflict until the annexation of Bosnia-Herzegovina in 1908. Thereafter, to concern about prestige and influence in the Balkans was added fear for the Habsburg empire itself. Serbia, a Russian protégé, drew like a magnet the loyalty of the South Slav subjects of the Dual Monarchy in the recently annexed provinces. A reckoning with Serbia would have to come, it was felt

in Vienna, and felt all the more strongly when Serbia gained more than a million and a half new subjects in the Balkan Wars. If the reckoning came, Russia would not be likely to leave Serbia unsupported in a second humiliation like that of 1909, when she had to recognize the Austro-Hungarian annexation.

Yet, Turkey's involvement at this level was remote and indirect: she was only to enter the war for very different reasons. Since 1900 German commercial and military influence had grown greatly in Constantinople. The Russians became more and more alarmed at the prospect of a re-invigorated Turkey under German influence. The old historic link between Berlin and St Petersburg, based on their common guilt in holding down the Poles, had begun to give way when Bismarck's successors decided to support the Dual Monarchy unconditionally against Russia (a crucial specific decision). It was killed by the fear of German power at the Straits. Russian hostility led the Turks to an alliance with Germany on 2nd August, 1914, the day after Germany declared war on Russia. It still took two months and the arrival of a German battle-cruiser (which guaranteed naval supremacy in the Black Sea) before Turkey took the plunge. And that meant the extension of the war to Egypt, Mesopotamia, and the Caucasus – theatres far from the provinces of Alsace and Lorraine, which had once seemed the greatest threat to European peace.

Thus, the part played in 1914 by formal alliances was small. The striking fact about the actual outbreak of war was the extent to which policy, in the end, was subordinated to questions of technique. What mattered were military plans and time-tables. In the end, the Franco-Russian alliance

The Great War Begins

never came into operation at all, the entente proved too weak to take Great Britain into the war without the German invasion of Belgium, Germany's allies, Italy and Rumania, felt greater grievances against Vienna than against the entente and so stayed out, and, by a crowning irony, the contingency upon which the German-Austrian alliance had rested—a war between Russia and the Dual Monarchy—was the last and most superfluous link of all in the main chain of events. It was not until 6th August that those two empires went to war.

The failure of the diplomats, therefore, though real enough, was not pre-determined by the irresistible working of an alliance system which trapped them. Much in the traditional system, indeed, worked in precisely the opposite way in the twenty years before 1914. Not only had the well-tried resources of diplomacy avoided war over Fashoda, Morocco, Bosnia, and Agadir; they had also partitioned Africa peacefully and demarcated the interests of the powers in China. Even the aftermath of the Balkan Wars had again shown how the great powers could, if they wished, impose their will on the troublesome small.

The failure of Liberalism

If we accept the fact that the alliances did not lead men willy-nilly into conflict, but that many different forces brought about this, we have a problem at a different level. When we have isolated the facts which made the last crucial decisions probable, and can understand the logic of the military and logistical planning which dominated the last weeks, it still remains astonishing that so many Europeans dreaded war so little and did so little to avert it. We have to explain why the comparatively few people who worked the machine should have felt so confident that their action would be endorsed by the millions they commanded.

This is all the harder to understand because the first years of this century were, for many people, the culmination of an era of liberal civilization and idealism. It had been marked by great optimism about the progressive enlightenment of international society. It was evidence of this which encouraged such men as Gooch—and there were many like him. The Hague Conferences had seemed to be the first steps towards disarmament and they had actually done something to regulate the conduct of war between civilized nations. An international peace movement existed and carried on a vigorous propaganda. The practice of international arbitration of disputes between two states had become more and more common. And even those who felt sceptical about such things could still comfort themselves with the thought that

commercial and other economic ties made the disruption of international life by war between two major states almost unthinkable. Even the socialists felt confident: did not governments know that the workers of all countries would act, if necessary by strike action, to stop them going to war?

Or so it was hoped. Little attention was paid to what factors might qualify this optimism. The Second International, for example, could not actually organize collective action against war. All it could do was to conceal divisions between the socialists of different countries by vague formulae. In 1914 they meant nothing. One British socialist minister left the government and the Serbian and Russian socialists condemned the war. But that was all. As the German chancellor, Bethmann Hollweg, had hoped, Russian mobilization swung the SPD into line behind the imperial government. The socialist failure was, in a measure, symptomatic; it was only the most disillusioning of all the evidences of the helplessness of the pacifist and progressive forces so confident only a few years before. The force which overwhelmed them was old-fashioned patriotism.

This century, much more than the last, has been the great age of nationalism. More new countries have appeared since 1914 than ever before, and have been accepted as possessing the right to exist. The Great War was in this sense a great triumph of nationalism; it broke up historic and dynastic Europe to provide the new nations of the 1920's. But national feeling had already played a big part in mobilizing the psychological and emotional support which in some cases sustained and in some cases trapped governments in 1914. In every capital immense crowds greeted with enthusiasm the news that many of them were to be sent off to be killed.

Of course, the actual outbreak was a moment of excitement. Clearly, too, they did not know what was to come. By 1916 'war-weariness' and casualties would take the steam out of patriotic enthusiasm everywhere. Yet even then there was little support anywhere for a peace that was less than victory. In retrospect this seems astonishing; no nation, after all, faced in the Great War what seemed to face Great Britain or Russia if they were defeated in 1940 or 1941. The explanation of desperation born of fear, therefore, is not enough. The strength of nationalism is the key to the inner nature of the Great War, the most popular war in history when it started, and the most democratic yet seen in the efforts it called forth as it went on.

This had not been easy to foresee. The behaviour of representative bodies is not a clear guide. The attitude of the Reichstag is not good evidence for the views of the German people and it is notable that the

elections of 1914 in France (the only European great power where universal male suffrage actually worked) produced a chamber very hostile to the law of 1913 which imposed three years military service. On the other hand, the British Liberal government had more trouble with its internal and parliamentary critics than with the electorate when it undertook its great ship-building programmes.

The difficulty of knowing how to interpret such evidence as there is of mass opinion before 1914 has led to some attempts to blame the more strident examples of nationalism at that time on conscious propaganda. Some weight can be given to this, it is true. The British Navy League and the German *Flottenverein* had done much to excite popular interest in naval rivalry, for example. Winston Churchill's account of the years before 1914 in *The World Crisis* shows how wide an influence this exercised. Germans were encouraged by the publicity campaigns of their admiralty to believe that only a fleet could guarantee them British respect. This made Englishmen who had hardly given a thought to naval strategy uneasy; figures of comparative battleship strengths seemed easy to comprehend and were easy to dramatize. In turn, British spokesmen used violent language which aroused in Germans fear of an attempt to 'Copenhagen' (the modern expression would be 'Pearl Harbor') the German fleet: that the British Admiralty might have similar fears was neither here nor there. Fear, indeed, some of it consciously inspired, must come high on the list of explanations of what happened in 1914. Fear of the consequences of a Russian victory provided the excuse German Social Democrats needed to fight for capitalist and imperialist Germany in 1914. But fear need not be the only source of acts of collective madness.

National feeling and xenophobia were, after all, not new. They had been shown more violently by the French against the British at the time of Fashoda and the Boer War than they were by the British against the Germans in 1914. What was new—or comparatively new—was the social context of nationalist feeling before 1914. Patriotism and jingoism were now widely shared, thanks to new technical and institutional facts. One of the most fundamental, paradoxically, was the immense spread of popular education since the mid-19th century. This had two important results. The first was that most education, because it was provided by the state, led to the spread of common attitudes and assumptions, many of them intimately linked with the nation and its symbols. Whether elementary education brought to the mass of the population the reading of patriotic poems and the singing of patriotic

Below: This was, at its outset, perhaps the most popular war in history. Here, a German crowd greets the declaration of war by singing a patriotic song. Was one of the most enthusiastic members of the crowd Adolf Hitler (see inset face)? Certainly, like many others, he lost himself happily in a surge of warlike enthusiasm

songs as in France and Germany, rituals about the national flag as in the United States, celebration of royal birthdays or glorification of the national past as in Great Britain, it was probably the most single powerful agency in spreading a conscious sense of national identity. And nations, traditionally, glorified their prowess in war.

The second important result was the spread of the ability to read. It is no accident that the sensational newspaper appeared in about 1900 in most western European countries as well as in the United States. Its pre-condition was a mass readership, and by that time this had been created by mass education. It was quickly associated with a stridently patriotic style of journalism, whose first-fruits were the excitement of American opinion against Spain in 1898 and the British hysteria over Mafeking. They could arouse popular excitement over international affairs, which had previously interested only a relatively small governing class.

One curious reflection of changing popular mentality was the growth of a new class of popular books about imaginary future wars. An able recent study has shown that between 1900, when there appeared *How the Germans Took London*, and 1914, when Conan Doyle's *Danger* gave a prescient account of the threat unrestricted submarine warfare would pose to Great Bri-

tain, there were something like 180 books published in the main European languages on this topic. This was roughly double the rate of the fourteen years before 1900. They were enthusiastically received everywhere. In Germany, *Der Weltkrieg* (1904), which depicted a German conquest of Great Britain, was a best-seller. The greatest success of all was the English book of 1906, William Le Queux's *The Invasion of 1910*, which sold a million copies.

These books had great influence in forming the stereotyped ideas which filled most people's minds when they thought about international affairs. Many were zealously pushed by interested parties; Lord Roberts endorsed Le Queux's book as valuable support for the plea for compulsory military service. They also reflect shifts of opinion. In 1900 the 'enemy' in English books of this sort was still usually French. In 1903 came Erskine Childer's description of a German plan to invade England in *The Riddle of the Sands* and thereafter Germany was usually the danger which threatened. Such books prepared the popular mind for the fears and excitements which were first to sustain the big armament programmes and later to feed the hatreds used by the professional propagandists of the war years.

Another dangerous feature of pre-war society was its familiarity with violence.

Most people saw something of it, if only by report. We must beware of being selective as we look back at the golden age which the years before 1914 sometimes appear to be. As J.M.Keynes, the economist, was to remark when the war was over, and the truth of his observation was obvious, the crust of civilization was very thin. In many countries there was a deep fear of revolution, which was strengthened by the social violence so common in the decade before the war. A great individual disturbance like the *Semana Trágica* in Barcelona in 1909, or the massacres attending the Russian revolution of 1905, did much to encourage such fears, but they were fed almost every day by a running current of social unrest and violence. Giovanni Giolitti, the liberal Italian prime minister, was accounted a great humanitarian idealist (or, alternatively, a poltroon) because he suggested that there might be some better way of dealing with Italy's social troubles than by force. Clemenceau made himself hated by French socialists by his ruthless strike-breaking long before he was famous as the saviour of France. Even in Great Britain, the use of soldiers in support of the civil power was common in the years before the war.

Nor did all the violence or potential violence which faced governments come from social or economic grievance. The

The Great War Begins

terrorism which broke out at Sarajevo had been for years a threat to the Habsburg empire. In Poland young revolutionaries held up post offices to obtain money for their cause. Nationalism, wherever state and nation did not coincide, was a far more violently disruptive force than class hatred. In 1914 the most striking example, indeed, was in Great Britain where the irreconcilability of two communities, the southern Irish and the Ulstermen, brought the country to the verge of civil war in 1914 and presented the world with the astonishing spectacle of leaders of the Conservative Party abetting armed resistance to laws made by Parliament.

Fear of revolution
It has sometimes been suggested that fears and tensions arising from such sources led some people to welcome war as a means of avoiding revolution. There is something in this; certainly the Ulster crisis evaporated almost overnight when the outbreak of war removed the threat of Home Rule. It is also true that many people welcomed war through ignorance of what it would mean. This is not merely a matter of ignorance of what the results of the war would be but also of what its nature would be while it was going on. Soldiers, sailors, civilians alike all assumed, for example, that war would be short. Hardly any foresaw the destructive power of modern weapons and the casualties they would impose. That the internal combustion engine, barbed-wire, the machine-gun, and the aeroplane might revolutionize tactics was almost equally unforeseen. Above all, as the literature of imaginary wars shows, the inhumanity of 20th-century war was undreamed of. Only one writer, a Swiss, I.S.Bloch, correctly outlined the nature of the next war (one other writer, a man of genius, H.G.Wells, saw even farther ahead, and in 1913 already wrote about 'atomic bombs'). Most people assumed that war would be a sharp but short struggle of the armies and fleets.

Such ignorance made it easier for politicians to think war a simplifying release from problems otherwise almost insoluble. Revolutionaries in eastern Europe, too, sensing the damage war could do to the great empires they hated, thought the same. But it was not only ignorance of what war would bring that prepared people to accept it. One of the most surprising features of the reception of the news of the war was the enthusiasm shown not only by the half-educated and xenophobic masses, but by intellectuals, too. It was a German economist and future minister of the Weimar republic, Walter Rathenau, who, even in 1918, remembered the outbreak as 'the ringing opening chord for an immortal song of sacrifice, loyalty, and heroism' and a great historian, Meinecke,

who later looked back on it as a moment of 'profoundest joy'. A famous English example was the poet, Rupert Brooke. His enthusiastic and second-rate poem, 'Now, God be thanked Who has matched us with His hour', expresses an attitude shared by many of his contemporaries in all countries. In Italy many felt dismay at the prospect of neutrality.

Running through such responses to the war was a significant trait in pre-war culture which has too often been ignored. When it has been recognized, it has been explained as the creation of, rather than part of the background to, the Great War. This is the deliberate cultivation of values and qualities directly opposed to those of the dominant liberal civilization of the day. To the belief in reason inherited from the Enlightenment was opposed the glorification of unreason as the source of man's greatest triumphs; to liberal eulogies of the virtues of co-operation and negotiation as social techniques was opposed the teaching of those who saw conflict and violence as the dynamo of progress.

The roots of such cultural currents are very deep. The teachings of Karl Marx and Charles Darwin about the social and biological role of conflict must be counted among them. The much misunderstood but also much quoted writings of Friedrich Nietzsche were another. Some of the pioneers of the irrationalist wave, too, were not themselves aware of all the implications of what they were doing: Sigmund Freud's great onslaught on the primacy of reason was conducted in the name of scientific enquiry and therapeutic technique, and William James, whose philosophy of 'Pragmatism' won admirers in Europe in the early years of this century, was pursuing a healthy attempt to bring philosophy down to the firm earth of commonsense experience. Yet such sources fed a current deeply destructive of the assumptions of liberal civilization which made their work possible.

This came out clearly and explicitly in attempts to justify violence and irrationalism in moral or aesthetic terms. One spectacular example was the French engineer-turned-philosopher, Georges Sorel. His work, *Reflections on Violence* (1908), justified industrial action by the workers by a view of history which attributed all great achievements to violence and the heroic attitudes which were fed by struggle and myth. He despised the intellectuals and parliamentarians of his day who emasculated their civilization by directing its attention to material goals and to the rational settlement of disputes. In this he was like the Italian poet, Gabriele d'Annunzio, later to be identified by Lenin as the only true revolutionary in Italy. D'Annunzio had himself done very well out of the material goods of bourgeois society,

but had joined the violent Italian nationalists to urge forward his countrymen to the invasion of Tripoli in 1911 as a step towards national regeneration by heroism and sacrifice.

A taste for violence was shared by other Italians. One of the oddest was the painter and poet, Marinetti, leader of the 'Futurists', who had already begun that attack on accepted aesthetic standards which culminated in Surrealism. The Tripoli adventure of 1911, he claimed, showed that the Italian government had at last become Futurist and his cultural pre-occupations increasingly drew him towards political themes. One Futurist's invention of the early weeks of the war, 'anti-neutralist' clothing, was, perhaps, only comic, but even such gestures as this registered the bankruptcy of traditional culture and traditional authority in the eyes of many of the young. The great liberal platitudes seemed to them to be cramping and stifling: they could not believe in them and strove to smash them. *'Merde à Versailles Pompei Bruges Oxford Nuremberg Toledo Benares!'* proclaimed the French poet, Apollinaire, in a Futurist pamphlet. Cultural revolutionaries, like political ones, welcomed a war that promised to destroy the *status quo*.

Many middle-class people had expressed dissatisfaction with the materially satisfying but morally uninspiring world of the early 20th century. William James once said that humanity needed to find a 'moral equivalent of war' – an experience which promised the same demand for heroism, the same possibility of release from the humdrum and the conventional. In 1914 the behaviour even of thinking men throughout Europe showed how little progress had been made towards this elusive goal. The tiredness and the stuffiness of liberal civilization turned men against it, just as, paradoxically, did its material success.

It is not, therefore, in the diplomatic documents or the plans of the war offices that the whole story of the origins of the war can be found. When they have been ransacked, there still remain important questions about mass psychology and spiritual weariness to be answered before we can confidently say how so great a cataclysm came about. One participant, Winston Churchill, sketched briefly his own diagnosis in 1914 when he wrote: 'There was a strange temper in the air. Unsatisfied by material prosperity the nations turned restlessly towards strife internal or external'. It is only in this context that the automaton-like movements of the great military machines in the last crucial days can be understood, for it was only this temper that had prepared men, slowly, subtly, to accept such machines at all.

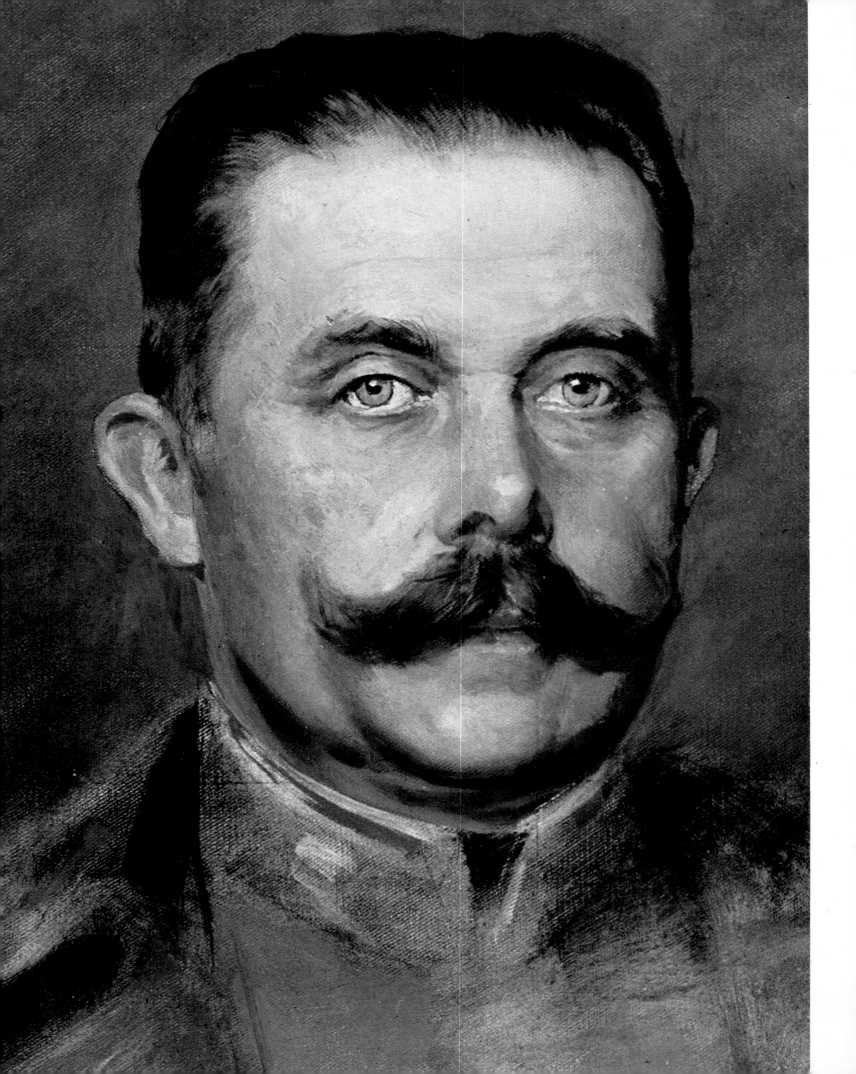

Sarajevo

No other political assassination in modern history has had such momentous consequences as the shooting of Archduke Franz Ferdinand, heir apparent to the Habsburg empire, in Sarajevo, the capital of the turbulent provinces of Bosnia-Herzegovina, on 28th June 1914.

The Sarajevo murder was an incident which, under more normal international circumstances, could not have provoked such historical upheavals. But in the early summer of 1914 relations between the great European powers were so tense that the killing of the archduke by a Bosnian student, named Gavrilo Princip, led to the outbreak of the First World War through a series of quick and irreversible steps—the Austrian ultimatum to Serbia on 23rd July, her declaration of war on 28th July, Russian mobilization, Germany's declaration of war on Russia on 1st August, and on France on 3rd August, and Great Britain's declaration of war against Germany on 4th August.

The murder in Sarajevo was one of the most amateurish assassinations carried out in modern times. The assassins were students, most of them in their teens. They belonged to a secret society called *Young Bosnia,* one of the many clandestine organizations among the South Slavs within the Habsburg monarchy. Although between 1910 and 1914 there had been six attempts against the lives of the Habsburg dignitaries, organized by the South Slav revolutionary movement, and a dozen conspiracies which did not materialize, the plot of 28th June 1914 was very badly conceived. It succeeded only through sheer luck and the negligence of the authorities.

Precautions left to providence

The Habsburg police did not take any serious measures to protect the archduke and the imperial party when they entered Sarajevo. However, warnings against the archduke's visit to Sarajevo had been numerous and they had come from all sides, from Sarajevo, Vienna, Budapest, Berlin, and even from the United States (the secret societies of the Americans of South Slav descent plotted for years against Archduke Franz Ferdinand, and the secret agents of the Habsburg police in New York suspected a distinguished professor of the Columbia University of Serbian origin of being a member of the leading group among the conspirators).

The archduke was a brave man and sometimes had a fatalistic attitude towards the warnings he had been receiving. Two

months before his violent death, while he was at Miramare, near Trieste, he decided on the spur of the moment to take a short excursion. Somebody mentioned the question of security and the archduke answered: 'Precautions? Security measures? . . . I do not care the tiniest bit about this. Everywhere one is in God's hands. Look, out of this bush, here at the right some chap could jump at me . . . Fears and precautions paralyze one's life. To fear is always a dangerous business.'

The archduke's wife, the Duchess of Hohenberg, was in great fear for his life on the journey to Sarajevo and she expressed doubts on the necessity of the visit on several occasions. The archduke persuaded her, however, that they should go to Bosnia. According to the memoirs of the archduke's eldest son, Dr Max Hohenberg, even Emperor Franz Josef tried to convince the archduke not to go to Bosnia: 'The High Command decided that the great manoeuvres should take place that year in Bosnia. The choice of this country, recently annexed by Austria, where a muffled rebellion persisted, was deplorable. We were distressed to learn that the old Emperor Franz Josef—who only by a miracle escaped an attempt on his life during the visit to Sarajevo—advised our father against going to the great manoeuvres. Would we thus be deprived of this treat? Our joy returned when we learned that our father had scoffed at the Emperor's prudent advice. One evening he said at the table: "I am Inspector-General of the Austro-Hungarian armed forces. I must go to Sarajevo. The soldiers would never be able to explain my absence." '

The Emperor Franz Josef had many reasons to be afraid for the life of his heir apparent. The resentment at Habsburg rule in Bosnia-Herzegovina was strong, particularly among the Serbs. The archduke had deliberately chosen to visit Sarajevo on 28th June, the greatest Serbian festival, St Vitus' Day, *Vidovdan.* This day has been celebrated among the Serbs since 28th June 1389, when at the battle of Kosovo, an Ottoman army commanded by Sultan Murad annihilated the Serbian feudal army led by Prince Lazar. Both warlords were killed—the Ottoman Sultan by a Serbian nobleman called Miloš Obilić who penetrated by ruse into the Turkish ranks and ripped the Sultan's stomach with his dagger. The Serbians lost the battle, and this defeat marked the end of the independence of the medieval Serbian state, and the beginning of more than four

Above: Front page of a special edition of the Bosnian Post. *The headline was: 'The Attacks'. The cross-headings read (starting in the left-hand column): 'Messages of sympathy'; 'To the second attack'; 'An unexploded bomb'; 'The assassination the work of a long arm?' (meaning Serbia); 'The effect of the catastrophe'. Left: Archduke Franz Ferdinand—victim of one of the most amateur assassinations of modern times*

The Great War Begins

centuries of harsh rule by the Ottomans over the Serbs and South Slavs.

The archduke's decision to visit Sarajevo on the Kosovo day festival, 28th June, 1914, was as bold as if, for instance, King George V had decided to visit Dublin on St Patrick's day in 1917!

Despite this explosive situation, the security precautions on the day of the archduke's assassination were almost non-existent, particularly in comparison with the police protection provided for Emperor Franz Josef on his visit to Sarajevo in June 1910. For the Emperor's visit the route through which he was passing had been lined with a double cordon of soldiers, while for the archduke there were no soldiers on the streets, although 70,000 of them were just outside Sarajevo. When the Emperor came, hundreds of suspected citizens were ordered not to leave their homes, but no such measures were taken on the occasion of Franz Ferdinand's visit.

The police officials of Sarajevo defended themselves and put the blame on General Oskar Potiorek, the military governor of Bosnia, and on the military committee for the archduke's reception. They prepared a special report on the activities of the Young Bosnians, but were rebuked 'for having a fear of children'. On the eve of 28th June they again warned that the archduke should not visit Sarajevo on St Vitus' Day. However, the chief of the committee, an army officer, rejected the warning by saying: 'Do not worry. These lesser breeds would not dare to do anything.'

'Security measures on 28th June will be in the hands of Providence' was the answer of one police official. On their own initiative, the police issued orders to their 120 men, reinforced by a few detectives from Budapest and Trieste, to turn their faces toward the crowd during the passage of the imperial party. But 120 could not do much on a route of about four miles.

The deed is done

In the activities of the local police there was a lot of *Schlamperei* (sloppiness). Most of the policemen, seeing six automobiles with the Habsburg noblemen, lost their heads. They were overwhelmed by the sight of the great spectacle. But the conspirators stuck to their job. Nedeljko Cabrinovic asked a policeman who was standing by him to tell him which car the archduke was in. The excited detective pointed in the right direction, and a few seconds later the assassin knocked the cap off a hand grenade and hurled it at the archduke's car. The bomb wounded twenty people, among them three of the imperial party. The Duchess of Hohenberg was slightly injured, too: the skin of her neck was grazed.

After the first attempt, the fateful decision was made that the archduke should continue his drive through the streets of Sarajevo. General Potiorek lost his head and not only issued new orders for security on the streets, but to the explicit question of the archduke, 'What about these bombs, and will it happen again?' answered: 'Your Imperial Highness, you can travel quite happily. I take the responsibility.'

Princip (front row, centre) and other conspirators on trial

The only change in the route of the imperial procession was made at the wish of the archduke so that he could visit one of the wounded officers, but no one informed the drivers of the cars. Who made this mistake, and whether it was deliberate or accidental, is a controversial point. The Czech driver of the archduke's car was about to follow the first two cars in which were detectives and local chiefs, when General Potiorek shouted angrily at him: 'What is this? Stop! You are going the wrong way!'

Stepping hard on the brake, the driver stopped the car just in front of a shop, close to the crowded pavement, where the chief assassin Gavrilo Princip, the best sharp-shooter among them, was waiting. At that very instant he took out his revolver. A policeman saw the danger and was on the point of grabbing his hand, when he was struck by someone standing nearby, presumably a friend of the killer. Pistol shots were heard. Princip was only a few steps from the target. The duchess died first. A bullet aimed at General Potiorek had penetrated the side of the car, her corset, and her right side. The archduke outlived her for a few moments. A bullet had pierced the right side of his coat collar, severed the jugular vein and come to stop in the spine.

All was over at 11.30 am 28th June 1914. The imperial couple lay dead in the governor's residence, the *Konak*, a building dating from Turkish times. The archduke's collar was open, and a gold chain from which hung seven amulets, with frames of gold and platinum, could be seen. Each of them was worn as protection against a different type of evil. His sleeves were rolled up, and on his left arm could be seen a Chinese dragon tattooed in colours. Around the neck of the duchess was a golden chain with a scapular containing holy relics guarding her from ill health.

The gift from Mars

For the Viennese war party, the tragic event in Sarajevo was a godsend, a gift from Mars. Although this powerful group lost its leader, Archduke Franz Ferdinand, its grip in Vienna was strengthened. General Franz Conrad von Hötzendorf, the chief of the Austro-Hungarian general staff, and the late archduke's right-hand man, had for years advocated aggression against Serbia. According to his own memoirs, in the seventeen months from 1st January 1913 to 1st June 1914 he had urged a war against Serbia no less than twenty-five times. For Conrad and other members of his group the Sarajevo assassination was the long-sought excuse for the settling of the accounts with Serbia. He wrote: 'This is not the crime of a single fanatic; assassination represents Serbia's declaration of war on Austria-Hungary . . . If we miss this occasion, the monarchy will be exposed to new explosions of South Slav, Czech, Russian, Rumanian, and Italian aspirations . . . Austria-Hungary must wage war for political reasons.'

On his return from Sarajevo, Conrad found that the foreign minister, Count Leopold von Berchtold, and the Austrian government shared his opinion. The Hungarian prime minister, Count Stephan Tisza, had some scruples about a rash punitive action against Serbia. Conrad and Berchtold at first had the idea of attacking Serbia without warning. Tisza's attitude forced them to prepare an ultimatum to Serbia, which was purely a formality since the decision to declare war on Serbia had already been taken in the first days of July.

Germany's attitude in the crucial days after 28th June was decisive. Of all the great powers Germany had the most advanced military preparations. Since October 1913 a common understanding had grown up between Berlin and Vienna over the Balkan policies of the two Germanic empires. After 28th June 1914 Berlin gave Vienna the green light to settle accounts with Serbia by force, and on several occasions in the first weeks of July urged that Austria-Hungary should not lose this opportunity. As the documents from the German state archives show, Berlin was aware that the Austro-Hungarian attack on Serbia might drag Russia into the war.

However, Great Britain's behaviour in the decisive weeks of July was rather ambiguous. Berlin's interpretation of this was that London was not much interested in the conflict between Austria-Hungary and Serbia. It is true that the mutiny of the militant Protestant settlers in Ulster threatened the unity of the British armed forces and that Sir Edward Grey, the foreign secretary, had to take the wishes of the pacifists within the Liberal government into account, but there was an overall impression that Grey's attitude encouraged German aggressiveness.

In fact London was well informed about Vienna's real intentions against Serbia since the very beginning of July. The first warning to Belgrade about Vienna's warlike preparations came from the Serbian minister in London!

During the previous two great international confrontations, over Agadir in 1911 and the First Balkan War in 1912, for instance, the British government made its position to Berlin very clear by stating that in the case of a general conflict, Great Britain would come to France's aid. But for the first three weeks of July 1914 Sir Edward Grey was noncommittal.

Vienna, however, did its best to hide its preparations for the aggression against Serbia. Berchtold told Conrad that 'it would be a good thing if you and the minister of war would go on vacation for a time. In such a way an appearance would be kept up that nothing is going on'.

The Black Hand

What at that time was the Serbian government's position and was it in any way involved in the Sarajevo conspiracy?

As has already been mentioned, the Young Bosnians were one of the many South Slav secret societies operating against the Habsburg rule. They had contacts with similar organizations in Slovenia (the secret society *Preporod),* Croatia, and Dalmatia as well as with secret societies in Serbia, particularly with the *Ujedinjenje ili smrt* ('Union or Death', better known as the *Black Hand*). It was headed by Colonel Dragutin Dimitrijević-Apis, the chief of the intelligence department of the Serbian general staff.

Although the Sarajevo assassins were Bosnians and Austro-Hungarian citizens, and although they had plotted against the Habsburg dignitaries for years, three leading members of the conspiracy, Princip, Čabrinović, and Grabež came to Sarajevo from Belgrade, armed with pistols and bombs which they had obtained through some Bosnian youth from Major Vojislav Tankosić, a leader of the Black Hand.

The common goal of the Young Bosnians and the Black Hand was national liberation. Despite this they differed in their philosophy and in their approach to the internal problems of South Slav society. Colonel Apis was a militarist and a pan-Serb, who wanted for Serbia among the South Slav lands a privileged position, something like Prussia's position in the German empire. The Young Bosnians were rebels not only against a foreign rule, but against their own society. They were a kind of anarchist group, atheists; they were for a South Slav federation in the fullest sense of the word.

On the eve of 28th June 1914 the Black Hand was in a life and death struggle with the Serbian government. Prime Minister Pašić regarded Colonel Apis and his group as a sort of praetorian guard that was threatening the whole political system of Serbia. Colonel Apis had planned a *coup d'état* against the government in the spring of 1914, but the conspiracy was discovered in time to prevent it.

The Serbian government had no reasons to provoke any conflicts with Austria-Hungary in 1914. After two Balkan wars and an uprising in neighbouring Albania which, when the insurgents raided Oebar and Ohrid, compelled the Serbs to mobilize and invade, the Serbian army was decimated and had neither enough weapons nor ammunition. The country badly needed peace. The Serbian government did its best to stop any incident during the archduke's visit to Bosnia, as recently discovered Serbian documents prove. The Serbian government was informed by the civilian authorities at the border that some members of the Black Hand were smuggling arms into Austro-Hungarian territory. An investigation was opened at once against Colonel Apis, but he denied that his men were involved in these operations.

There is a theory that it was the power struggle between Pašić and Apis that led Apis to approve Tankosić's delivery of the arms to the Sarajevo assassins. It seems that Apis did not expect that Princip and his accomplices would succeed in killing the archduke, but that he did think their efforts might further strain relations between Pašić and the Vienna government and that such complications would further weaken Pašić's position in relation to Apis. This thesis was strengthened by Tankosić's statement when he was arrested after the delivery of the Austrian ultimatum to Serbia. A general present at the arrest asked: 'Why have you done this?' Tankosić replied: 'To spite Pašić.'

The investigation in Sarajevo provided no proof of the Serbian government's responsibility. A special emissary of the Viennese foreign ministry, Friedrich von Wiesner, went to Sarajevo on 10th July 1914 to study the investigation material and find out whether the Serbian government had in any way been responsible for the

The Great War Begins

Top: Austrian stamp commemorating the victims. Above: Uniform (with bloodstains) worn by the Archduke at Sarajevo

assassination. On 13th July Wiesner telegraphed: 'There is nothing to show the complicity of the Serbian government in the direction of the assassination or its preparations or in supplying of weapons. Nor is there anything to lead one even to conjecture such a thing. On the contrary, there is evidence that would appear to show complicity is out of the question . . . If the intentions prevailing at my departure still exist, demands might be extended for:

(a) Suppression of complicity of Serbian government officials in smuggling persons and material across the frontier; (b) Dismissal of Serbian frontier officers at Šabax and Loznica in smuggling persons and materials across the frontier; (c) Criminal proceedings against Ciganović and Tankosić.'

It is interesting that German authorities came to a similar conclusion. The former chancellor Bernhard von Bülow wrote in his memoirs: 'Although the horrible murder was the work of a Serbian society with branches all over the country, many details prove that the Serbian government had neither instigated nor desired it. The Serbs were exhausted by two wars. The most hotheaded among them might have paused at the thought of war with Austria-Hungary, so overwhelmingly superior especially since, in Serbia's rear, were rancorous Bulgarians and untrustworthy Rumanians. Thus at least did Herr von Griesinger, our minister in Belgrade, sum up the position, as also did the Belgrade correspondents of every important German newspaper.'

Nevertheless, in its note and ultimatum to Serbia, on 23rd July 1914, the Austro-Hungarian government chose to draw quite different conclusions and asserted that the Serbian government had tolerated the machinations of various societies and associations directed against the monarchy, unrestrained language on the part of the press, glorification of the perpetrators of outrages, participation of officers and officials in subversive agitation, and so on.

The Austro-Hungarian government asked the Serbian government to undertake specifically these ten points:

1. To suppress all publications inciting to hatred of Austria-Hungary and directed against her territorial integrity;

2. To dissolve forthwith the *Narodna odbrana* society and to 'confiscate all its means of propaganda'; to treat similarly all societies engaged in propaganda against Austria-Hungary, and to prevent their revival in some other form;

3. To eliminate from the Serbian educational system anything which might foment such propaganda;

4. To dismiss all officers or officials guilty of such propaganda, whose names might be subsequently communicated by Vienna;

5. To accept 'the collaboration in Serbia' of Austro-Hungarian officials in suppressing 'this subversive movement against the monarchy's territorial integrity';

6. To open a judicial inquiry against those implicated in the murder, and to allow delegates of Austria-Hungary to take part in this;

7. To arrest without delay Major Tankosić and Milan Ciganović, implicated by the Sarajevo inquiry;

8. To put an effectual stop to Serbian frontier officials sharing in the 'illicit traffic in arms and explosives', and to dismiss certain officials at Šabac and Loznica who had helped the murderers to cross over;

9. To give explanations regarding the 'unjustifiable' language used by high Serbian officials after the murder;

10. To notify Vienna without delay of the execution of all the above measures.'

The fateful telegram

The Serbian government informed the Austro-Hungarian minister on 25th July that it accepted all the demands, except point 6, which would be a violation of the Serbian Constitution and of the Law of Criminal Procedure. The Serbian government stressed also that if the Austro-Hungarian government was not satisfied with the reply, it was 'ready, as always, to accept a peaceful agreement, by referring this question to the Hague Court, or to the great powers which took part in drawing up the declaration made by the Serbian government on 31st March, 1909'.

The Serbian government made this decision despite the fact that the Russian government advised Serbia that it should not offer any resistance in the event of an Austro-Hungarian invasion and place its future in the hands of great powers. But the decision of the Russian government to mobilize its troops in military regions close to Austria-Hungary gave hopes to the Serbs that Russia would defend them if Austria-Hungary attacked.

Although, even in some circles in Berlin, the Serbian answer was regarded as favourable, Austria-Hungary declared war on Serbia, on 28th July, at 11 am. The Viennese foreign office for the first time in history sent a declaration of war by telegram, which reached the Serbian government in Niš, a town in central east Serbia, at about 1 pm. At that very moment, the Serbian prime minister, Pašić, was at lunch. Sibe Miličić, a poet from Dalmatia, and a junior official in the Serbian ministry of foreign affairs, described thus the historical event of the receipt of the Austro-Hungarian declaration of war:

'I was having lunch in Hotel "Europa" in Niš. The dining-hall was crowded with people from Belgrade. Between twelve and one o'clock a postman entered and handed something to Mr Pašić, who was eating not far from me, about two tables away. Pašić read what the postman handed to him, and then stood up and said in a deadly silence: "Austria has declared war on us. Our cause is just. God will help us!"'

When Pašić hurriedly returned to his office, he learned that the Serbian supreme command had received an identical telegram from Vienna. He started doubting the authenticity of the telegram. His suspicion was further strengthened by the fact that at 3 pm, on the same day, when he asked the German minister for news, he was told that the German legation knew nothing. Pašić immediately sent cables to London, Paris, and St Petersburg about the strange telegram, asking whether Austria-Hungary had really declared war on Serbia.

However, his doubts were cleared even before he got the answers to his cables. The news came from Belgrade that the Austro-Hungarian guns had started bombarding the capital of Serbia. The last hopes that war would be avoided were shattered; the biggest slaughter in the history that mankind had yet experienced was beginning.

War by Time-table

It was often said before 1914 that one day the weapons of war would go off by themselves. In 1914 this happened. Though there were no doubt deep-seated reasons for disputes between the great powers, the actual outbreak of the First World War was provoked almost entirely by the rival plans for mobilization. Events moved so fast that there was no time for diplomatic negotiations or political decisions. On 28th July the great powers were at peace. On 4th August all except Italy were at war. They were dragged into war by their armies, instead of using the armies to further their policies.

The great powers had been elaborating plans for mobilizing mass armies ever since the Franco-German war of 1870-71. As usual, men prepared for the last war instead of for the next one. The general staffs all assumed that the coming war would be decided by the first engagements on the frontiers, as had happened in 1870, and each general staff aimed to get its blow in first. Yet they were all terrified that the other side might beat them to it. Each one of them attributed to others a speed and flexibility which they knew they did not possess themselves. The deterrent of the overwhelming blow put the generals in a panic instead of giving them security. Such is the usual way with deterrents.

The plans for mobilization were all based on elaborate railway time-tables, precisely calculated over the years. The moment the signal was given, millions of men would report at their barracks. Thousands of trains would be assembled and would proceed day after day to their allotted places. The time-tables were rigid and could not be altered without months of preparation. Germany and France both had only one plan for mobilization—each directed, of course, against the other. Russia and Austria-Hungary had alternative plans: the Russian either for general mobilization against both Germany and Austria-Hungary or for partial mobilization against Austria-Hungary alone; the Austrian against Serbia, Italy, or Russia. If one of these plans began to operate, it would make the switch to an alternative plan impossible. The time-tables could not be changed overnight.

None of the plans had been rehearsed. No great power had mobilized since the Congress of Berlin in 1878, except for Russia during the Russo-Japanese war, and that was irrelevant to European conditions. The plans existed only on paper and were the more rigid on that account. No general staff had the experience of extemporizing plans as it went along. Moreover the plans had been worked out in academic secrecy. The generals did not tell the statesmen what they were doing or, if they did, the statesmen did not take it in. Count Leopold von Berchtold, the Austro-Hungarian foreign minister, thought he could threaten Serbia without losing his freedom of action against Russia. Sergei Sazonov, the Russian foreign minister, thought he could threaten Austria-Hungary without losing his freedom of action against Germany. Bethmann Hollweg, the German chancellor, thought he could threaten Russia without losing his freedom of action against France. Sir Edward Grey, the British foreign secretary, thought that he could protect Belgium without becoming necessarily committed to France. They were all wrong. When they learned their respective mistakes, they surrendered helplessly to the dictates of the military time-tables.

The statesmen had not been unduly alarmed by the assassination of Archduke Franz Ferdinand at Sarajevo. They were used to troubles in the Balkans and assumed that this trouble would end as earlier ones had done—with alarms, threats, and ultimately negotiations. They recognized that Austria-Hungary had grievances against Serbia and believed in any case that, as a great power, she was entitled to get most of her own way. Even Sir Edward Grey held that Serbia, being a small country, must pay the price for peace, however unjust that might be. But there was nothing Europe could do until Austria-Hungary formulated her demands. These demands, when they came, were excessive. For this very reason, they seemed to offer all the more opening for negotiation and compromise.

The Austrians, however, were determined not to be dragged before a European conference. They wished to keep their dispute with Serbia as a private quarrel. Hence they first broke off relations and then on 28th July declared war. Even now the other European statesmen were not dismayed. Bethmann Hollweg, Sazonov, and Grey all arrived independently at the same solution. This was the Halt in Belgrade. The Austrians would occupy Belgrade and thus vindicate their military prowess. Then they would declare their willingness to halt and would hold Belgrade as a pledge during negotiations. There would be a compromise, very much at Serbia's expense, but she would remain an independent country, and hence the prestige of Russia, Serbia's patron, would be vindicated also.

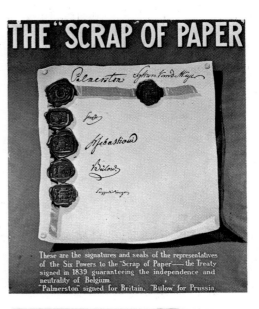

THE "SCRAP OF PAPER"

These are the signatures and seals of the representatives of the Six Powers to the "Scrap of Paper"—the Treaty signed in 1839 guaranteeing the independence and neutrality of Belgium. *Palmerston signed for Britain. *Bülow for Prussia.

Top: British poster illustrating the treaty that guaranteed Belgian neutrality, described by Bethmann Hollweg as a 'scrap of paper'. Above: Kaiser Wilhelm and Moltke pore over plans for the invasion of the west

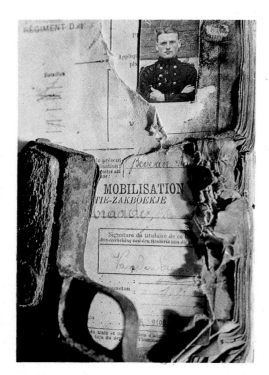

Belgian relics of Germany's assault: a page from a book of mobilization records and a pistol, now in the Royal Army Museum in Brussels

This ingenious proposal broke down for an unexpected and most extraordinary reason. Though Austria-Hungary claimed to be a great power, her army was in no condition to occupy Belgrade and so could not halt there. Mobilization, even against Serbia, would take some weeks. In any case, the Austrian general staff dared not mobilize against Serbia unless it were first assured of Russian neutrality, for, if it did so, it could not switch over to the alternative plan for mobilizing against Russia. Hence the Austrian general staff preferred to do nothing. As a little extra twist of irony, the Serbs had decided not to defend Belgrade, which could therefore have been occupied by a single Austro-Hungarian company, and the Halt in Belgrade would really have been possible after all.

Just as the Austrians knew nothing of the Serbian plans, so the Russians knew nothing of the Austrian plans, or lack of them. The tsar and his ministers assumed that Austria-Hungary would attack Serbia almost at once. The Russians were resolved that they would not leave Serbia in the lurch as they had done during the Bosnian crisis of 1908-09. Somehow they had to assert Russia's interest in the Austro-Serbian conflict. They could no longer claim to be included in negotiations. These, as between Austria-Hungary and Serbia, were over. Direct negotiations between Russia

and Austria-Hungary could be initiated only if Russia answered the Austro-Hungarian gesture of declaring war against Serbia by some corresponding gesture of her own. Sazonov, the Russian foreign minister, thought he knew the answer. The Russian army should begin a partial mobilization directed solely against Austria-Hungary. In this way, he imagined, there would be no Russian challenge to Germany. Now the time-tables interfered again. The Russian generals were horrified at Sazonov's proposal. A partial mobilization, they insisted, would rule out any general mobilization against Germany for months to come. Russia would be helpless, at Germany's mercy.

Sazonov might have persisted if he had been confident of German neutrality. Exactly the opposite was the case. Bethmann Hollweg and Kaiser Wilhelm had promised to support Austria-Hungary against Russia and believed that threats were the best way of doing this. Moreover the German generals took alarm at the rumour of even a partial Russian mobilization. Far from recognizing that this would cripple Russia in any activity against Germany, they believed that it was a preliminary to general mobilization and thus a sinister device for stealing a march on the German time-table. On 29th July therefore the German ambassador warned Sazonov that any Russian mobilization, however partial, would provoke German mobilization—and war. Sazonov believed the first part of the warning. He still could not believe that any power would proceed from threatening gestures to the real thing.

Decision lay with Nicholas II, the Russian tsar. By nature, he was a retiring family man, who preferred tennis and sea-bathing to the affairs of state. But he had inherited a unique position as an absolute monarch, and he dutifully discharged his trust. Now he had to show that Imperial Russia was a power of the first rank. Throughout 29th and 30th July he debated with Sazonov and with the minister of war. Or rather he sat lackadaisically by while the two ministers argued. The orders for partial and for general mobilization both lay on his desk. Really there was little to discuss. The only object of partial mobilization had been to appease Germany, and, now that the Germans had refused to be appeased, there was no sense left in it. The only alternatives were general mobilization or nothing, and to do nothing would be to abdicate as a great power.

In the evening of 29th July the tsar agreed to general mobilization. Half an hour later he changed his mind. The order was cancelled. The next day the discussion began again. One of the generals said: 'It is hard to decide.' Nicholas II was provoked. He answered roughly: 'I will decide,' and

signed the order for general mobilization. This time there was no going back. The red notices of call-up were soon displayed all over Russia. The troop-trains began to gather. Nicholas wrote in his diary: 'I went for a walk by myself. The weather was hot. Had a delightful bathe in the sea.' The decision had been made without consulting either France, Russia's ally, or Great Britain, Russia's friend. Later on, British and French statesmen were criticized and condemned for failing to warn Russia against this grave step. What held them back was fear that, if they did so, Russia might break with them and go over to the German side. As well, the British and French statesmen, just like the Russian, did not realize exactly how grave the consequences would be. They appreciated that a general Russian mobilization would increase the tension, but they also supposed that for this very reason it would speed up the opening of negotiations between the great powers. They still envisaged some sort of European conference and had no idea that in German eyes Russia's mobilization made war inevitable.

Here was the strongest factor in 1914, and one which proved catastrophic. All the great powers had carefully-prepared plans for general mobilization which would put them in a better position for fighting a great war. These plans would take some time to mature, and even then the mobilized armies could be held on the frontiers in suspense. For all of them there was a margin, though a thin one, between mobilization and war. For all of them, that is, except Germany. The Germans had no plans for general mobilization as such. The German general staff had wrestled for twenty years with the problem how they were to win a two-front war against France and Russia with one army. Their answer was to defeat France before the Russian army was ready. The French frontier itself was too strongly fortified for a successful attack to be possible. Hence Count von Schlieffen, who had been chief of the German general staff from 1891 to 1908, devised a plan for encircling the French armies by marching through Belgium.

This was a difficult operation. There were only eighty miles between the supposedly-impassable Ardennes and the Dutch frontier. Through this gap four armies, 840,000 men, had to be pumped. All of them had to go through the single railway junction of Aachen. The troop trains could not pile up at Aachen, however much its marshalling yards were extended. They had to go on so as to clear the lines for more trains behind. Hence, in the German plans for mobilization, there was no stopping at the frontier. The advance into Belgium was an integral part of the mobilization. Schlieffen never reflected that Germany might want to make a show of strength without actually starting a war. He was a technician pure and simple. Helmuth von Moltke, his successor, had no gift for strategy. He accepted the plan just as Schlieffen had left it. Or rather he gave no thought to the question until the news of Russia's mobilization. Then he opened the drawer of his desk and followed Schlieffen's instructions.

Kaiser Wilhelm and Bethmann Hollweg, with whom the political decisions rested, had no idea how restricted they were by the military plans. They never asked, and the general staff never told them. They went on dreaming that they could rattle the sword, as other European rulers did, without actually drawing it. Now on the morning of 31st July, Moltke appeared with the news that Russia was mobilizing. He insisted that the German armies must mobilize at once and invade Belgium. Bethmann Hollweg asked whether there were no lesser alternative. There was none. Bethmann Hollweg bowed to the dictates of strategy. The preliminary orders for mobilization were sent out. An ultimatum was dispatched to St Petersburg, demanding that Russia should arrest her mobilization within twenty-four hours.

The demand was of course refused. On 1st August the German ambassador handed to Sazonov Germany's declaration of war. The Kaiser, wearing full Guards uniform, drove in an open carriage from Potsdam to his palace in Berlin. Surrounded by glittering generals, he was keyed up to sign the order for general mobilization. Bethmann Hollweg appeared with startling news from London. Sir Edward Grey had stated that Great Britain would remain neutral, if Germany would refrain from attacking France. The Kaiser was delighted: 'This calls for champagne. We must halt the march to the west.' Moltke changed colour. Eleven thousand trains would have to be stopped in their tracks. He said in a trembling voice: 'It is impossible. The whole army would be thrown into confusion.' Once more the time-tables dictated policy. Wilhelm acquiesced and signed the mobilization orders.

The streets were crowded with cheering people. It appeared to simple Germans that they were threatened with attack by Russia's Mongol hordes. Until this moment the German Socialists had been contemplating, somewhat glumly, their pledge to declare a general strike against war. Now they rallied to the defence of European civilization against the barbaric East. The Reichstag passed the war-credits unanimously. The parties declared a political truce for the duration of the war. Inspired by this unity, Wilhelm declared: 'I see no parties any more. I see only Germans.'

War had started between Russia and Germany, though neither power was in a con-

dition to fight it. All Germany's offensive power was directed against France, with whom as yet she had no ostensible cause of quarrel. A pretext had to be found. On 1st August the German ambassador called on René Viviani, the French premier and foreign minister, and demanded a promise of French neutrality. If Viviani had agreed, the ambassador would have gone on to demand the surrender of Toul and Verdun as a pledge. Viviani cut the discussion short: 'France will act according to her interests.' The Germans did not renew their demand. It occurred to them that France might agree and then their offensive plans would be ruined. Instead German aeroplanes dropped a few bombs on Nuremberg. The Germans announced that these aeroplanes were French, and with this pretext declared war on 3rd August. The French statesmen had been somewhat worried how they were to explain their secret obligations under the Franco-Russian alliance. Now they did not need to do so. France, too, was fighting a war of national defence. The French troops' trains also began to roll towards the frontiers.

Thus Germany, Russia, and France were brought to war by Schlieffen's time-table. Two great powers, Great Britain and Italy, were not included in the schedule. Italy, though allied to Germany and Austria-Hungary, was determined not to fight on their side. She badgered her allies for approval that she should remain neutral. At the same time, she badgered them for the rewards she would have received if she had not stayed neutral. This complicated double-play ended by missing on both counts.

The British government was technically uncommitted. It had friends, but no allies. Some Englishmen, mainly Conservatives, believed that Great Britain should at once

rush to the aid of Russia and France. Others, mainly radicals and Labour, thought that Great Britain should remain strictly aloof. As one radical paper said: 'We care as little for Belgrade as Belgrade does for Manchester.' Grey, the foreign secretary, felt that he was committed to France, but tried to avoid saying so. He waited for his hand to be forced. As he wrote later: 'Circumstances and events were compelling decision.' On 30th July he refused to give Russia any promise of support. On 1st August he even suggested that Great Britain would stay neutral if France were not attacked—though it is uncertain whether he meant what he said. On 2nd August the leaders of the Conservative opposition delivered a letter to Asquith, the prime minister, urging support for France and Russia. The Liberal cabinet took no notice. Instead they resolved that they would not allow the German fleet to enter the Channel and attack the French

Britain's French (1); France's Lanrezac (2), Galliéni (3), and Franchet d'Esperey (4)

Germany's Ludendorff (1), Hindenburg (2) and Kluck (3); and Serbia's Putnik (4)   *Russia's Duke Nicholas (1), Rennenkampf (2); Austria's Conrad (3), Potiorek (4)*

The Great War Begins

Right: Britain's 'Daily Mirror' echoes the nation's commitment. Below: The time-tables triumph: German troops about to depart for the front

ports. This was not a decision for war. It was a decision for armed neutrality, and the Germans were delighted with it: keeping out of the Channel was a cheap price for keeping Great Britain out of the war.

The crux – Belgian neutrality

The British government had one little worry. It was determined to protect the neutrality of Belgium, as its great predecessor Gladstone had done in 1870. Then a request that both France and Germany respect Belgian neutrality had kept Great Britain out of war. So why not now? On Sunday, 2nd August, the cabinet resolved that 'any substantial violation of Belgian neutrality would compel us to take action'. The neutralists in the cabinet regarded this as a victory. Like everyone else, they did not grasp that Germany's strategy revolved on the invasion of Belgium. The Belgian people also did not grasp this. They spent that Sunday enjoying a sunny neutral afternoon. The same evening the German ambassador presented the demand that German troops should be allowed to pass through Belgium. The Belgian government deliberated until the early morning and resolved that the German demand should be refused. It still hoped that resolute opposition would deter the Germans and therefore appealed to the British government only for 'diplomatic intervention'.

Monday, 3rd August, was a Bank Holiday in England. There were cheering crowds in the streets of London, as there had been in Paris and Berlin. Lloyd George, the chancellor of the exchequer, who had previously been against the war, was much affected by the display of wartime enthusiasm. In the afternoon, Grey explained to the House of Commons the equivocal entanglements with France and Russia into which he had drifted. Fortunately, he was able to tack on the news about Belgium, and this united practically all the members of the House of Commons. Later in the evening, the cabinet decided that a polite message should be sent to the Germans, requesting them to leave Belgium alone. Grey apparently did not think there was any urgency. At any rate he did not send the message until the next morning, when German troops were already in Belgium.

About midday, the news reached London, though there was as yet no Belgian appeal for help. However, the news stirred Grey into firmer action. Without consulting the cabinet, he sent off an ultimatum to Germany, demanding by midnight a promise to respect Belgian neutrality. At 7 pm Bethmann Hollweg refused to make any such promise. He complained that Great Britain was going to war 'just for a scrap of paper'. Did he use these very words? Did he speak in English or German? We shall never know. But a fortnight earlier there had been amateur theatricals at the British Embassy in Berlin. The piece by Sardou was entitled *A Scrap of Paper*. No message from Berlin reached London. Asquith and other cabinet ministers sat round, perhaps still half-hoping for a favourable reply. Someone unknown ingeni-

ously pointed out that midnight in Berlin was 11 pm in London. Hence they could declare war an hour early and get off to bed. The declaration of war was in fact handed to the German ambassador at 11.5 pm. The time-tables had won another triumph.

There was a final twist. The British had gone to war in order to protect Belgian neutrality. But when Asquith met his generals on 5th August, he learned that time-tables dictated even to the small British army. There was a prepared plan for placing this army on the left flank of the French. There was no plan for sending it to the aid of Belgium. Thus Great Britain found herself a full ally of France after all.

The British declaration of war committed the entire British Empire also, including the Dominions and India. Only the Canadian parliament subsequently expressed independent approval. The one country still tailing behind was the one which had started the race: Austria-Hungary. On 6th August Austria-Hungary declared war on Russia. On 12th August, after complaints from Russia, Great Britain and France declared war on Austria-Hungary. Every country claimed to be fighting a war of self-defence, and so in a sense they were. But all of them believed that attack was the only form of defence. Hence, in order to defend themselves, they attacked each other. The general staffs, who had given the signal for war, proved wrong on every count. The war was not short; there were no quick victories; defence turned out to be the best form of defence.

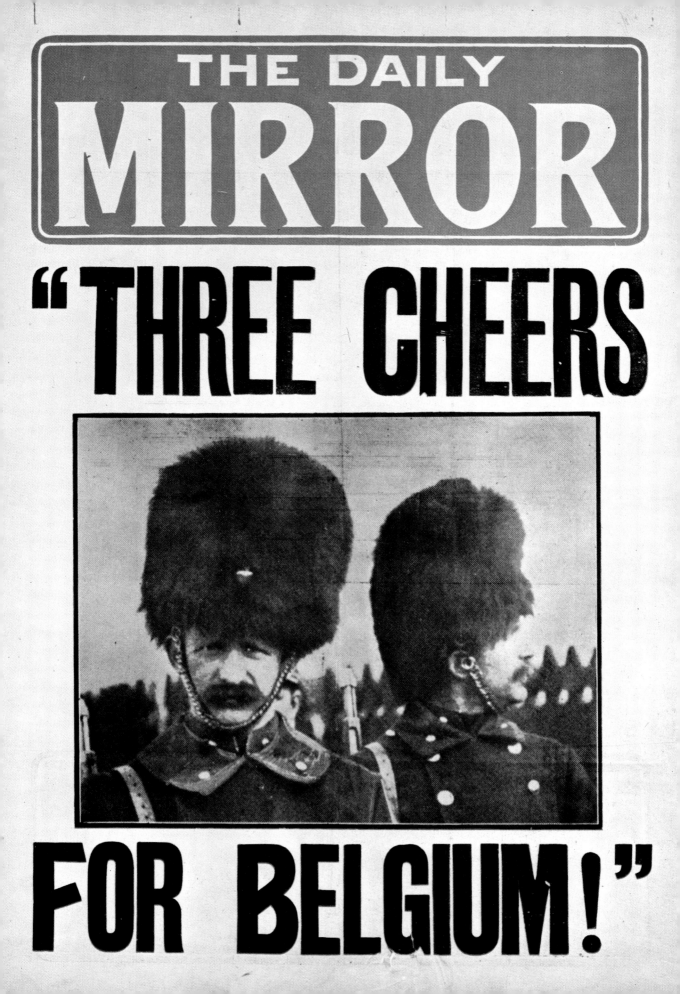

The Military Balance

George Stephenson and General Lazare Carnot could well be called the grandfathers, or perhaps the great grandfathers, of the European military system of 1914. From the French Revolution and from Carnot, who had built the armies Napoleon used, came the concept of the nation in arms – so-called, though it would be more accurate to call it the concept of 'the whole manpower of the nation in the army'. Under Napoleon this system had overwhelmed the armies of the old regime. To save themselves the other great continental powers had been forced to adopt it, but once peace was re-established, a military as well as a political reaction had set in, and armies had reverted to traditionalism and long-service professionalism.

In 1857 Prince Wilhelm, Regent of Prussia, appointed General Helmuth von Moltke chief of general staff of his army, and, in 1859, another reforming general, Albrecht von Roon, minister for war. Meeting bitter political opposition to army reform, Roon suggested the appointment of Bismarck as minister-president. Under these four, Wilhelm, soon King of Prussia, Bismarck, Moltke, and Roon, the nation in arms idea re-appeared in Prussia and there reached its prime. In 1866 the Prussians quickly and decisively defeated the old-style Austrian army, then, in 1870 at the head of the North German Confederation, overwhelmed the French.

Roon in 1870 put 1,183,400 officers and men into the field. Moltke had been a pupil of Clausewitz, but he could not have handled effectively and rapidly an army of this size if there had not been two vital technical advances. First, the development of agriculture and industry had provided the means to feed, arm, and equip great numbers, and indeed produced the larger populations from which they sprang. Second, railways could now assemble this massed manpower along frontiers, supply it, and effect further strategic movements as needed. Deeply impressed by the events of 1866 and 1870, the armies of continental Europe made haste to imitate the Prussian model.

The weapons of 1870 were a marked advance on those used in the Napoleonic Wars. By 1914 weapons had been further developed. Not at the pace to which we are accustomed today, but faster than at any previous time in history. The magazine rifle, the machine-gun, and the breech-loading quick-firing field gun, especially,

had been perfected since 1870. But, partly because the internal combustion engine was still in its childhood, and much more because soldiers and statesmen in power are inherently prejudiced against change, no new military system had appeared. Strategy remained a strategy dependent on railways. Movement at the 15-20 mph of the troop train became movement at the age-old 15-20 miles a day, normal march for men and horsedrawn transport, as soon as contact with the enemy became likely. Tactical theory, recoiling from the ugly lessons of 1870 and of the American Civil War of 1861-65, had gone into reverse, and reflected ideas that had already started to be out of date in the days of muzzle-loaders.

The German Aufmarsch

The German empire, proclaimed in the Hall of Mirrors, Versailles in 1871, had in 1914 a population of over 65,000,000. In theory, except for the small number required by the navy, all fit men of military age belonged to the army. Called up each year, from the age of seventeen to twenty they were enrolled in the *Landsturm*, Class I. At twenty those who were fit joined the active army for two-years' service, or the cavalry and horse artillery for three. Afterwards they went into the Reserve for five years (in the case of the cavalry and horse artillery for four years). In practice, the active army could only take about half the annual call-up, and the surplus, together with those excused for other reasons, was enrolled in the *Ersatz* Reserve, receiving, at best, very limited training. From the age of twenty-seven to thirty-nine, all served in the *Landwehr*, then from thirty-nine to forty-five in the *Landsturm*, Class II.

The active army of twenty-five and a half army corps – each of two divisions – and eleven cavalry divisions was maintained at fifty to sixty per cent war strength. In addition, there were thirty-two reserve, seven *Ersatz* reserve and the equivalent of sixteen *Landwehr* divisions.

Mobilization was a vast and critical operation, during which the army would be largely ineffective as a fighting machine. Nor did it end there, for the army must be deployed, which in 1914 meant deployment by rail. This operation, the *Auf-marsch*, was vital and planned with at least as much care as mobilization itself, for on it would hang the success of the opening campaign and, it was thought, of

Top: Troops of Belgium's neglected and poorly trained army. Above: Austrian cavalry officers, the 'élite' of the Habsburg army. Left: Kaiser Wilhelm II (fourth from right), surrounded by German generals

the war. Mobilization must be ordered in time so that the enemy could not establish a lead, and once ordered it led inevitably to the *Aufmarsch*. The armies could perhaps then be halted on the frontier, but the possibility was not seriously canvassed, and in 1914 mobilization spelled war.

Schlieffen's strategy

To this pattern, almost standard in Europe, the Germans had made two exceptions. Seeking to achieve crushing superiority for a quick victory against France in a war on two fronts, General von Schlieffen, chief of the general staff from 1892 to 1905, had planned to use reserve and *Ersatz* reserve divisions in the opening battles, relying on the well-trained regular and reserve officers and on strong cadres of regular non-commissioned officers to make good the reserves' deficiencies of training. Secondly, six infantry brigades with attached cavalry, artillery, and pioneers were maintained in peace at war strength and quartered close to the Belgian frontier, ready to seize the Liége forts and open the way through Belgium to northern France as soon as war was declared.

The peacetime strength of the army in 1914 was 856,000. On mobilization, trained reserves would bring it up to 3,800,000, but in emergency a maximum of 8,500,000 could be called to the colours. Against France seven armies would be deployed, totalling thirty-four army corps—of which eleven were reserve formations—and four cavalry corps. In the east, the VIII Army—four army corps of which one was a reserve corps with cavalry and some *Landwehr*—comprised some 200,000 and would hold off the Russians as best it could. There were other garrisons, depots, and reserves, and in Schleswig-Holstein a reserve army corps was held back in case the British attempted a landing.

Despite their defeat in 1870, the French had given the Germans more than one sharp lesson about the power of the breech-loading rifle against men in the open, and in their training afterwards the Germans took modern fire power seriously. When the machine-gun was perfected, the Germans took it up more seriously than other armies. Schlieffen's strategic plan to envelop the French armies by a massive advance through Belgium stemmed from his realization that frontal attack would be costly and indecisive. Watching the German manoeuvres of 1895, an expert British observer wrote that the soldiers '. . . act like intelligent beings, who thoroughly understand their duty, and the fact speaks volumes for the way in which even privates are taught to use their initiative'.

But as the years passed, memories of 1870 faded and traditionalism and arrogance asserted themselves. The Germans remained good soldiers, but of the manoeuvres of 1911, Colonel Repington of *The Times* wrote, 'there is insufficient test of the initiative of commanders of any units large or small . . . The infantry lack dash and display no knowledge of the ground . . . offer vulnerable targets at medium ranges . . . are not trained to understand the connection between fire and movement and seem totally unaware of the effect of modern fire'.

In theory the vain and unstable Wilhelm II would be commander in war, and until 1908 he frequently spoke of actually doing so. He lacked his grandfather's serious interest in military affairs, revelling in display rather than warlike efficiency. Schlieffen pandered to him with military spectacle, cavalry charges, and unrealistic victories in manoeuvres and war games. General von Moltke, nephew of the great Moltke and also a Helmuth, who became chief of general staff at the beginning of 1906, refused to do so. Artistic, doubting his own military ability, obsessed by fear of revolution, he had accepted the appointment in the belief that he would not be called upon to command in war. Lacking the conviction and force of character needed to carry through the Schlieffen Plan, he tampered with it, weakening the enveloping right wing, strengthening the holding left and the Eastern Front. In war games he accepted frontal offensives as practicable. In 1914 he was sixty-six, in poor health, past the work to which he had never been equal.

Below him came the army commanders: on the vital right wing, commanding the I, II and III Armies respectively, a trio of sixty-eight-year-olds, Generals von Kluck, von Bülow, and von Hausen, hard men, drivers—especially Kluck, brutal, a little brittle in crisis. Next came a trio of royals: the Duke of Württemberg commanding the IV Army; the Crown Prince, the V; Prince Rupprecht of Bavaria, the VI; then finally von Heeringen, sixty-four, ex-minister for war, the VII. In the Prussian tradition their chiefs of staff supported them with authority almost equal to theirs. Commanding the VIII Army in East Prussia was General von Prittwitz und Gaffron, sixty-six, fat, self-important, indolent, with connections so far proof against Moltke's wish to remove him. Major-General Ludendorff, forty-nine—his name was unadorned with the aristocratic von—was assistant chief of staff of the II Army, having lost the key post of head of the deployment section under Moltke for too much insistence on increasing the intake of the army.

The populations of France and the North German Confederation had in 1870 been approximately equal, but by 1914, while the population of the German empire had risen to over 65,000,000, that of France was still under 40,000,000. The disparity dominated French strategic thinking, and, with tragic irony, led in the end to a military creed savagely extravagant of human life.

France had astonished the world with the speed of her recovery after 1870. She had re-organized her army on the Prussian model with short service and a powerful general staff. Where the loss of Alsace and Lorraine had laid open her eastern frontier, she had built a strong fortified line stretching from Belfort to Verdun. At the turn of the century the army had been racked and discredited by the Dreyfus Affair's outcome. In 1905 military service had been cut down to two years. Confronted with the rising menace of Germany, the prestige of the army and willingness to serve in it recovered, and in 1913 service was restored to three years. After that men served in the Reserve, the Territorial Army and the Territorial Reserve for varying periods up to the age of forty-eight.

In July 1914 the peace strength of the French army was 736,000. On mobilization it rose to 3,500,000, of which some 1,700,000 were in the field army of five armies, in all twenty-one army corps, plus two colonial, three independent, ten cavalry, and twenty-five reserve divisions, the rest in territorials, garrisons, and depots. The five armies stretched from the Swiss frontier, where the 1st Army had its right at Belfort, to a third of the way along the Belgian frontier, where the left of the 5th was near Hirson. Beyond that was a cavalry corps of three divisions. A German offensive from Metz would thus be covered, but one through Belgium would meet only a weak cavalry screen.

French élan

The French, however, had no intention of waiting for any offensive to develop, for the army had persuaded itself that the disasters of 1870 had been due to lack of offensive spirit on their side. Looking back to Napoleonic and even earlier battles, the army had become imbued with mystical faith in the attack, pressed home regardless of cost, as the answer to all military problems. To ensure its *élan,* when the Germans went sensibly into field grey, the French had retained the traditional long blue coats and bright red trousers of their infantry. More practical matters were neglected, and the French infantryman wore his long coat and heavy military underwear even in the heat of August, his boots were hard, and a load of sixty-six pounds was piled on him compared to the German's fifty-six.

For fire power, the French relied on the rifle and the 75-mm field gun, an outstanding weapon produced in large numbers. Machine-guns were neglected. As for tactics, 'Success depends,' said the

	Great Britain	France	Russia	Germany	Austria-Hungary	Turkey
Population	46,407,037	39,601,509	167,000,000	65,000,000	49,882,231	21,373,900
Soldiers available on mobilization	711,000[1]	3,500,000+	4,423,000[2]	8,500,000[3]	3,000,000+	360,000
Merchant fleet (net steam tonnage)	11,538,000	1,098,000	(1913) 486,914	3,096,000	(1912) 559,784	(1911) 66,878
Battleships (built and being built)	64	28	16	40	16	
Cruisers	121	34	14	57	12	
Submarines	64	73	29	23	6	
Annual value of foreign trade (£)	1,223,152,000	424,000,000	190,247,000	1,030,380,000	198,712,000	67,472,000
Annual steel production (tons)	6,903,000	4,333,000	4,416,000	17,024,000	2,642,000	
Railway mileage	23,441	25,471	46,573	39,439	27,545	3,882

[1] Including empire [2] Immediate mobilization [3] Emergency maximum

manual of 1913, 'far more on forcefulness and tenacity than upon tactical skill.' Luckily the French soldier was not only brave but also adaptable and able to learn quickly, while the colonial empire, which during the war would supply 500,000 men, was available to replace some of the first shattering losses.

General Joffre, sixty-two, was vice-president of the war council, earmarked as commander-in-chief on an outbreak of war. He had been appointed in 1911, largely because the disciples of attack wished to get rid of his predecessor. Ponderous, very taciturn but a good listener, veteran of colonial service, he had no strong views on strategy or tactics, but was an engineer, and expert in military movement. He was to prove imperturbable and able in crisis, but did nothing before the war to check the ideas and plans that made crisis inevitable when war came. Galliéni, Joffre's superior in the colonies, more alert and realistic, had refused the appointment, and was now without military employment.

Of the army commanders, Lanrezac of the 5th Army, brilliant, pessimistic, impatient, and outspoken, was thought of by many as Joffre's eventual successor. Foch, responsible as commandant of the staff college for spreading the doctrine of attack, was a corps commander. Like Joffre he would be strong in crisis, and had in Weygand a chief of staff who could translate his wishes into clear orders. Pétain, out of favour for his realistic belief in fire power, commanded a division.

Neutral Belgians: British 'mercenaries'
Standing in the path of the main German thrust, Belgium deployed a field army of six infantry divisions totalling some 117,000 men, and three fortress garrisons, Antwerp, Liége, and Namur. Because Belgium was neutral, two infantry divisions faced France, one at Antwerp, Great Britain, one at Liége, Germany, with the rest in central reserve.

Relying on her neutrality, Belgium had neglected her army. Service in it was unpopular, training severely limited, morale poor, the officer corps seriously disunited. The fortresses were obsolete, improvements planned in 1882 were still incomplete and had by now been themselves overtaken by weapon development. There was one bright spot, however. King Albert, thirty-nine, was intelligent and brave, and he had great personal integrity. He did not control the army in peace, but when war came he was obliged by the constitution to command it.

The British, as is their habit, were in two minds about sending an army to the Continent at all. In 1908 Haldane had reorganized the British army, forming the units at home into an Expeditionary Force,

six infantry and one cavalry division totalling some 160,000 men, capable of supporting either the garrisons of the empire or a Continental ally. In 1905 staff talks with the French had been authorized, but had languished until, early in 1911, the francophile Major-General Henry Wilson had come to the War Office as director of military operations. That August the crisis over Agadir had revealed an alarming divergence of war plans between the War Office, where Wilson had made detailed arrangements with the French for the deployment of the Expeditionary Force on the left of the 5th Army, and the Admiralty, which strongly opposed continental commitment of the army, though it did not have a properly worked out proposal to put in place of Henry Wilson's. The Council of Imperial Defence had deferred formal decision, but allowed the War Office to continue planning with the French.

When in 1914 war was declared, there were those who thought that the Expeditionary Force should remain in Great Britain, or should go direct to Belgium in fulfilment of the British guarantee of neutrality, but it was too late now to change, and on 6th August the cabinet decided that it should go to France as planned, but without two of its divisions which would for the present remain in Great Britain.

Although small, the British army was well-trained and equipped. On the South African veldt Boer bullets had taught it something of the reality of fire power. Now the marksmanship of the infantry was in an entirely different class from that of continental armies. The cavalry, too, were armed with a proper rifle, not the neglected carbine of continental cavalry, and knew how to use it, but there peacetime reaction was setting in and the glamorous, futile charge coming back into fashion.

Called by the Germans an army of

mercenaries and, more flatteringly, a perfect thing apart, the British army was recruited from volunteers, who enlisted for seven years followed by five in the reserve. Each battalion at home found drafts for another in the overseas empire, so that its men were often raw and its numbers short. There were experienced men in the divisions that went to France, but to see them all as hardened professionals is a mistake; some were young soldiers, others reservists grown soft in civil life.

Continuing an old tradition in modern shape, the Territorial Force and the Yeomanry had been organized by Haldane into a second-line army of fourteen divisions, far from fully trained or equipped, but a good deal more effective than many realized. Beyond that there were the older reservists and the militia for replacements, and the distant imperial garrisons and armies of India and the dominions.

Field Marshal Sir John French, commander-in-chief, British Expeditionary Force, had been a successful cavalry commander in South Africa, but at sixty-two was showing his age. Lieutenant-General Sir Douglas Haig, commanding the 1st Corps, French's chief-of-staff in South Africa and Haldane's assistant in the subsequent reforms, was able and ambitious, but inflexible and wedded to cavalry doctrine. Kitchener, now secretary of state for war, a tremendous national figure, had flashes of insight amounting almost to

1 The imperturbable, ponderous, and taciturn Joffre—the French commander-in-chief. 2 Moltke—the German commander-in-chief. He was artistic, lacked force of character, and doubted his military ability. 3 French military dress of 1914: cavalry helmet, bayonets, képis, and bright red trousers

genius but little appreciation of staff organization or civilian control. In general, British officers were efficient and devoted but narrow in outlook. However, a far higher proportion of them than of officers in France and Germany had experienced the reality of war.

The armies in the East

With the main German strength committed in the west, the clash in the east would be between Austria-Hungary and Russia. Austria had been worsted by the French in 1859, and in 1866 trounced by Prussia. Since then the army had been reformed on the Prussian model, but not for forty-eight years tested in war.

The population, 50,000,000 in 1914, was a complex racial mixture. Germans were the ruling group in Austria, Magyars in Hungary; Poles in Austria and Croats in Hungary had special privileges; Ruthenes, Czechs, Slovaks, Slovenes, Serbs, Italians, and Rumanians were potentially disaffected. Languages, literacy, religions, and racial characteristics differed widely. Slav races formed two-thirds of the infantry, and the Germans in charge notoriously lacked the high martial seriousness of the Prussians. Yet, if the sottish chaos described by Jaroslav Hašek, a Czech writer, in *The Good Soldier Schweik,* typified one side of the coin, there was another: to many the army was an ideal of the empire as a supra-national society.

At the beginning of 1914 the peace strength of the Austro-Hungarian army was some 450,000. On mobilization it rose to over 3,000,000, of which some 1,800,000 formed the field army of six armies, in all sixteen army corps—mostly of three divisions, some of them reserve divisions—and eleven cavalry divisions. In a war against Serbia, the III, V, and VI

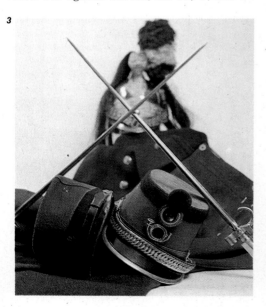

3

Armies would be deployed in the south, according to Plan B (Balkans); but in a war against Russia and Serbia, Plan R, the III Army would be deployed northeast with I, II, and IV in the Galician plain beyond the Carpathian mountains. By ordering partial mobilization on 25th July the army was committed to Plan B, until the III Army could be recalled from the Serbian front.

General Conrad von Hötzendorf, chief of general staff, sixty-two, a cavalryman, hard working, spartan, a writer on tactics and training, was, like Foch, a firm apostle of the offensive. His recipe for victory against Russia was an early attack before the vast manpower of the enemy could be brought into action, but that plan was now seriously compromised by partial mobilization. Conrad would command the northern armies, General Potiorek, another spartan, keen, vain, incompetent, with powerful court connections, responsible for the muddle that had given the Sarajevo assassins their chance, would command against Serbia.

Although Russia went to war to rescue Serbia, the Serbian army, under Marshal Putnik, 190,000 strong, organized in three armies each little stronger than an Austrian corps, was in grave danger of being overwhelmed before help could become effective. Leaving delaying detachments on the frontier, it assembled in north Serbia, ready to deploy wherever the attack came. It had fought in the bitter Balkan Wars of 1912 and 1913. Its men were seasoned, inspired by fierce patriotism, and looked back undaunted on generations of relentless warfare. The prospect of engaging it in its native mountains might have given pause to better soldiers than Conrad and Potiorek.

The Russian masses

For Russia, whose population numbered 167,000,000, manpower seemed the least of her problems. Bad roads, scant railways, low industrial capacity, poor standards of education and literacy, and a grudging treasury limited the size and effectiveness of her army. Later it would appear that so much of the Russian economy depended on sheer manual labour, that it would suffer disproportionately from withdrawal of manpower. For the moment, the great distances and bad communications slowed mobilization. Officer and non-commissioned officer cadres were weak in numbers and education, weapons, and equipment were in short supply, ammunition reserves set low, manufacture severely restricted.

Russia had fought Japan in Manchuria in 1904-05 and been badly worsted. Since then efforts had been made with the aid of large loans from France to modernize the army, but the combination of vast numbers

and restricted resources had prevented it reaching the standard of Western armies of the day. In such choice as there was between quantity and quality, Russia had chosen quantity, instinctively believing that sheer numbers would bring victory. While a Russian division had sixteen battalions against a German division's twelve, its fighting power was only about half that of the German.

The peace strength of the Russian army was 1,423,000. On mobilization, three million men were called up at once, with 3,500,000 more to follow before the end of November. There were thirty-seven corps, mostly of two divisions, and in all seventy first-line divisions, nineteen independent brigades, thirty-five reserve divisions, twenty-four cavalry and Cossack divisions with twelve reserve.

It was planned to deploy thirty corps—ninety-five infantry and thirty-seven cavalry divisions, some 2,700,000 men—against Germany and Austria, but of these only fifty-two divisions could appear by the twenty-third day of mobilization (22nd August). Two armies, the 1st and 2nd, would face East Prussia; three, the 5th, 3rd and 8th, Austria. Another, the 4th, would deploy against Germany (Plan G), if the main German strength came east, or against Austria (Plan A), if it struck west against France. Two more armies watched the Baltic and Caucasian flanks. General mobilization was ordered on 29th July, and on 6th August, deployment on Plan A.

General Sukhomlinov, minister for war since 1909, had been an energetic reorganizer, backed by the Tsar; he was corrupt, possibly pro-German, and a military reactionary, boasting that he had not read a manual for twenty-five years. Grand Duke Nicholas, commander-in-chief, fifty-eight, an imposing figure six-foot-six tall, was a champion of reform and opposed by Sukhomlinov. The jealousy of his nephew, the Tsar, had kept him from the Russo-Japanese War, depriving him of the chance to prove his worth as a commander, but also keeping him free of blame for the defeat. General Zhilinsky, commanding against East Prussia, had visited France in 1912 when chief of general staff, and had absorbed Foch's military beliefs, while also becoming personally committed to Russia's undertaking for an early advance against Germany.

Almost from the moment of declaration of war, France began to urge Russia to make this advance quickly and in strength. Russia responded gallantly, sacrificing her chance of massive deployment before action. Perhaps it need hardly be added that in Russia, as elsewhere, progressives and reactionaries were agreed on one thing, their faith in the offensive.

2 THE SHOCK OF ARMS

The Battle for Northern France

At the outbreak of the First World War both the German and the French general staffs looked forward to a quick war—'home before the leaves fall'. After all, the last two major European wars, the Austro-Prussian (1866) and the Franco-Prussian (1870-71), had been quick, decisive wars of 'movement'. Few foretold anything different on 3rd August 1914. And, indeed, the opening phase of the war, the struggle for northern France, began in traditional style. For Germany a knock-out blow, as prescribed by the Schlieffen Plan, was essential if she were to avoid a two-front war against France and Russia. The French hoped that the pattern of offensives called for by Plan 17 would bring a quick recovery of the lost provinces, Alsace and Lorraine.

But the battle did not proceed according to plan. That was hardly surprising in so far as France was concerned, since Plan 17, based on wishful thinking, made assumptions which were wholly unjustifiable. It was considered that even should the Germans violate Belgian neutrality, they would not be able to extend their offensive dispositions north of Luxembourg. This deduction led the French to concentrate their five armies between Belfort and Mézières (see map, p. 39), leaving a gap of 125 miles between their left and the sea. Nor can this be excused by saying that they counted on the British Expeditionary Force and the Belgians to hold this gap, for no arrangements could be made with neutral Belgium, while the BEF was to arrive in France in total ignorance of its allies' intentions. In defence of Plan 17 it should be pointed out that a move westward to the Sambre, about

Left: The Canadians at Second Ypres

eighty-five miles from the sea, was envisaged in the plan—and anyway, a concentration of forces on the Belgian frontier would have looked very curious in peacetime. Even so, at the tactical level, the French doctrine was thoroughly unsound. The *'offensive à outrance'*—all-out attack with the bayonet—was the ideal, but it was a system which had not even worked in the days when Wellington's line used to shatter Napoleon's column by its concentrated fire. There had been no war with Germany for forty-four years and it is understandable that training should have become unrealistic. Still, a careful study of the South African and Russo-Japanese campaigns might well have saved the lives of many of the 300,000 Frenchmen who fell in August 1914. But whatever their disadvantages the French had one great asset: the monumental calm of their phlegmatic commander, General Joffre.

The German plan, calling for a great enveloping movement round the French left wing, seemed far from being unrealistic. By including twelve reserve corps in their order of battle the Germans were able to deceive the French as to their numbers, and had the younger Moltke, the chief of the general staff, had anything of the genius for war displayed by his uncle, the victor of 1866 and 1870, the campaign of 1914 might well have ended in the fall of Paris and the rout of the French armies. The unprincipled decision to invade Belgium added the BEF and the Belgian army to Joffre's order of battle and went some way towards redressing the balance of numbers. But these reinforcements were far from being sufficient to turn the tide against the Germans. In truth, they had no worse enemy than their elderly commander, who besides continually tinkering with the

Schlieffen Plan, never had that firm control of the battle which is the hallmark of military greatness. It may also be that the Germans paid insufficient attention to the problem of supplying their strong right wing.

At the tactical level the Germans were certainly superior to the French, handling their machine-guns and heavy artillery to much better effect. Their infantry were rather inclined to bunch, a fault which had not been sufficiently checked at manoeuvres, and therefore paid a heavy price for their advances.

Army commanders on both sides, except for the princes among them, were rather elderly by modern standards, and two at least—Moltke, and French, in command of the BEF, who had suffered a mild stroke —should never have passed the doctor.

The strategic moves of both sides were governed by their relative slowness once they were beyond the railways. When a corps could make only fifteen to twenty miles in a day, and had no motor transport to lift it, it behoved the staff to see that they really marched them to the right place. False moves were paid for by the exhaustion of the men, and a decline in morale. To many the *pavé* roads of northern France were far more terrible than a brisk skirmish.

Few military plans survive the opening phases of a battle, since commanders have to improvise as their opponents' moves interfere with their cherished combinations. In 1914 the Germans managed to adhere to their plan for considerably longer than their enemies, for the French plan came unstuck in about five days.

The Germans were first off the mark. On 5th August Kluck's I Army attacked the Belgian fortress of Liége, whose reduction

was a necessary preliminary to the deployment south and south-west across Belgium of the two northernmost German armies. The Belgian garrison under Lieutenant-General Leman put up a spirited resistance. Unfortunately, however, the forts, built twenty years earlier, had not been connected by a trench system as planned by their constructor, the famous engineer, Brialmont. As a result the Germans penetrated the line by a night attack and took the city. This daring exploit very nearly went wrong, but General Ludendorff took command of a lost brigade and seized the citadel on 7th August. The forts had still to be reduced, but they were smashed by the huge Austrian 42-cm. Skoda howitzers, and by 14th August the German columns were pouring through the city. The last fort fell on the 16th.

The French wings had begun to probe forward as early as 6th August. On the left General Sordet's cavalry corps got within nine miles of Liége, but did little to dispel the fog of war, because the area was as yet unoccupied by the Germans.

By 16th August it was clear at Joffre's headquarters that seven or eight German corps and four cavalry divisions were pushing westwards between Givet and Brussels 'and even beyond these points'. It was thought that there were six or seven corps and two or three cavalry divisions between Bastogne and Thionville. South of Metz the Germans appeared to be acting on the defensive. While this intelligence was not inaccurate the presence of reserve corps had not yet been discovered.

Joffre now planned to take the offensive, intending to break the German centre, and then to fall upon their advanced right wing. His plan was decidedly optimistic. He had no reason to suppose that his centre outnumbered Moltke's and, therefore, he should not have counted on a break-through.

The French offensive opened in the south where for several days Prince Rupprecht of Bavaria fell back according to plan, until early on the 20th he counter-attacked in the battles of Sarrebourg and Morhange. The French 2nd Army was driven back and the 1st conformed to its movement, though it struck back on the 25th and checked the pursuit. Eventually the front became stabilized just inside the French frontier.

The ill success of his right wing was not enough to alert Joffre, whose early service had been in the engineers, to the shortcomings of French infantry training. On 21st August the 3rd and 4th Armies crossed the frontier and after an advance of some ten or fifteen miles the heads of their columns ran broadside on into the German armies of the Crown Prince and the aged

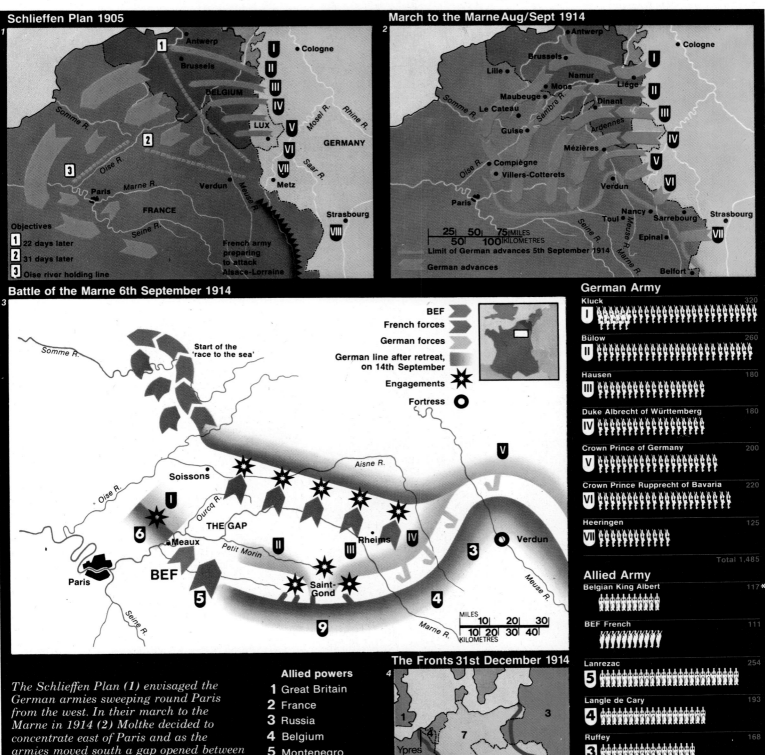

Schlieffen Plan 1905

Objectives
1 22 days later
2 31 days later
3 Oise river holding line

French army preparing to attack Alsace-Lorraine

March to the Marne Aug/Sept 1914

25 50 75 MILES
50 100 KILOMETRES

Limit of German advances 5th September 1914

German advances

Battle of the Marne 6th September 1914

BEF
French forces
German forces
German line after retreat, on 14th September
Engagements
Fortress

Start of the 'race to the sea'

THE GAP

MILES 10 20 30
10 20 30 40 KILOMETRES

German Army

I	Kluck	320
II	Bülow	260
III	Hausen	180
IV	Duke Albrecht of Württemberg	180
V	Crown Prince of Germany	200
VI	Crown Prince Rupprecht of Bavaria	220
VII	Heeringen	125

Total 1,485

Allied Army

	Belgian King Albert	117 *
	BEF French	111
5	Lanrezac	254
4	Langle de Cary	193
3	Ruffey	168
2	Castelnau	200
1	Dubail	256

figures in thousands   Total 1,299

* excluding fortress and reserve troops

The Fronts 31st December 1914

Allied powers
1 Great Britain
2 France
3 Russia
4 Belgium
5 Montenegro
6 Serbia

Central powers
7 Germany
8 Austria-Hungary
9 Turkey

The Schlieffen Plan (1) envisaged the German armies sweeping round Paris from the west. In their march to the Marne in 1914 (2) Moltke decided to concentrate east of Paris and as the armies moved south a gap opened between the I and II armies, through which the BEF and French 5th Army penetrated (3). After the battle of the Marne the Germans withdrew. They resisted the British and French on the Aisne, after which 'the race to the sea' began. At the end of the year the fronts in the west stabilized. The map of Europe (4) shows the situation on all fronts at the end of 1914

1914: on all fronts
a war of movement

In both east and west during 1914, the fortunes of the war ebbed and flowed to an extent perhaps unparalleled except in 1918. The Germans, having reached the Marne, were driven back into northernmost France and this was matched by the short-lived inroads of the Russians onto the 'sacred soil' of East Prussia and the unsuccessful Austrian attack on Serbia.

1 A panorama (in which the perspective has been distorted) of the battle of the Marne. In the left-hand panel, the BEF (in three wedges in the centre of the picture) can be seen advancing through the gap between Kluck's and Bülow's armies. The long column (in the upper right section of the panel) is Kluck's retreating army. The centre panel shows Foch's army (bottom left) recouping to attack the German III Army. The right-hand panel shows Langle de Cary's army shelling the German IV Army in the Argonne. 2 German troops on the Eastern Front. 3 Austro-Hungarian troops attacking a village in Serbia

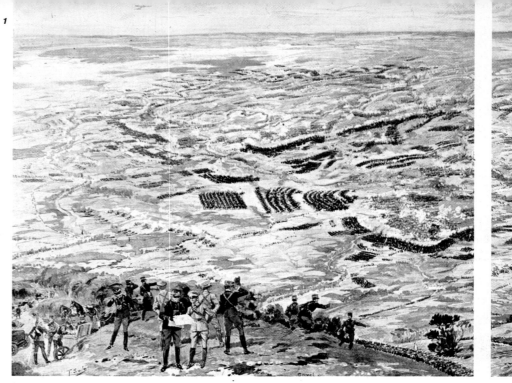

3

The Shock of Arms

Duke of Württemberg in slightly superior force, which were crossing their front. In the actions at Virton, Tintigny, Rossignol, and Neufchateau they were defeated with heavy loss especially in officers – it was a point of honour with the latest 'promotion' from St Cyr to wear white gloves and their full-dress shakos for their 'baptism of fire'. It is understandable that, caught in the narrow wooded defiles of the Ardennes, the French had been unable to employ their artillery to much purpose. They fell back to the Meuse. Joffre's bid to break the German centre had collapsed.

The real trouble was that the infantry ignored the basic tactical principle known as 'fire and movement', by which, even in those distant days, sub-units helped each other forward, engaging the enemy with aimed fire. Here the unreasoning belief in the bayonet took its toll of French manhood. Had it not been for a premature attempt at an enveloping movement by the Crown Prince the disaster to the French might have been still worse. German casualties were also heavy, especially when their columns exposed themselves to the fire of the 75s.

BEF goes into action

On 21st August the BEF, which had begun to mobilize on the 5th and had crossed the Channel without the least interruption from the German navy, was approaching the Mons-Condé Canal. By this time the situation was that the Belgian field army had been driven back into the fortress of Antwerp, though not before inflicting considerable delay on the Germans, notably in the action at Haelen on 18th August, a check which may account for the undue caution of the German cavalry in the fighting that followed.

Of the Allied armies only those under Lanrezac and French had so far escaped a mauling. The Allies' strategic situation was hardly brilliant at the moment when the BEF stepped upon the stage. The Schlieffen Plan was unrolling itself with something like clockwork precision. The only real hitch had been the failure to drive the Belgian field army away from Antwerp. This had compelled them to employ two corps in investing that city. Victory was within Moltke's grasp. Without the four divisions of the BEF which lay that night (21st August) with its outposts overlooking Marlborough's old battlefield of Malplaquet (1709) Joffre, for all his iron nerve and relentless will, could never have turned the tide which was running so strongly against him.

The BEF was in action next day. From the first, British musketry asserted its superiority. In a skirmish that same afternoon the Scots Greys inflicted thirty or forty casualties for the loss of one officer

wounded. This superiority was to be a factor of prime importance until the campaign died out in the damp November woods round Ypres.

While the BEF was moving up French had on 17th August visited Lanrezac to confer as to their future co-operation. Neither understood the other's language, Lanrezac, tense with anxiety, was needlessly rude, and the interview, so far from doing good left the two army commanders in a state of profound mutual distrust. Lanrezac told Joffre that the British would not be ready until the 24th at the earliest, that their cavalry were to be employed as mounted infantry and could be counted upon for no other purpose. More significant still, he raised the question of possible confusion if the British used the same roads 'in the event of retirement'. It was a considerable shock to Joffre to find that Lanrezac, who, in peacetime had been 'a veritable lion', not only had made no attempt to join in the great French advance, but was now thinking of withdrawal.

On 23rd August the long-awaited storm broke over Lanrezac's army when Bülow attacked him with four corps on the line of the Sambre. 'It rained shells,' was all that one French soldier could remember of that day's fighting. An Algerian battalion, 1,030 strong, charged a German battery, bayoneted the gunners, and returned, it is said, with only two men unhit! Everywhere the French suffered terrible losses especially in officers. One corps was compelled to fall back.

During the night Hausen brought four corps, supported by 340 guns against Lanrezac's line on the Meuse, gaining bridgeheads west of the river. Here they were up against a great soldier General Franchet d'Esperey ('desperate Frankie' to his British allies), the commander of 1st Corps. D'Esperey had actually made his men dig in, but this was simple prudence not over-caution. His corps counterattacked and pitched the Saxons back across the river.

Through the long day Lanrezac remained at his headquarters, Philippeville, a 'prey to extreme anxiety'. Well he might be. He received no guidance from Joffre, merely demands for his opinion of the situation. At noon came the well-nigh incredible news that the Belgians were evacuating Namur, the great fortress hinge of the Sambre-Meuse line. He received no information from Langle on his right, but on his left French, while declining to attack Bülow's right, guaranteed to hold the Mons Canal for twenty-four hours.

While Lanrezac watched the endless column of Belgian refugees drifting through the square at Philippeville, his staff opportuned him with vain demands for a counter-attack. Lanrezac ordered no

such thing. Perhaps he was pusillanimous as his critics assert: he was certainly correct. Late in the day came news of Langle's retreat, which left the Meuse unguarded between Lanrezac's right and Sedan, where the French had met with disaster in 1870, as they were to do again in 1940. The day ended with another splendid counter-attack on d'Esperey's front, when General Mangin's brigade drove the Saxons out of their bridgehead at Onhaye. But this did not alter the fact that Lanrezac's position was untenable. At the risk of being taken for a 'catastrophard' he ordered a general retreat. To one of his staff he remarked 'We have been beaten but the evil is reparable. As long as the 5th Army lives, France is not lost.'

Mons and the retreat

This was the situation when on 23rd August the BEF fought its first serious action in the coalfields round Mons, on a line about nine miles northward of Lanrezac's main position and with both flanks in the air. For a loss of about 1,600 casualties and two guns the 2nd Corps, under General Smith-Dorrien, delayed Kluck's advance for a whole day and inflicted very severe losses on three of his corps (III, IV, and IX). A German account frankly describes the fighting: 'Well entrenched and completely hidden, the enemy opened a murderous fire . . . the casualties increased . . . the rushes became shorter, and finally the whole advance stopped . . . with bloody losses, the attack gradually came to an end.' The XII Brandenburg Grenadiers (III Corps) attacking the 1st Battalion Royal West Kent lost twenty-five officers and over 500 men. The 75th Bremen Regiment (IX Corps) lost five officers and 376 men in one attack. Frontal attack was worse than useless against British troops dug in in such a position. Only a flanking movement could turn them out and this – belatedly – Kluck realized.

Lanrezac neither consulted nor warned French before retreating, and it was not until 11 pm on the 23rd that Sir John was told of it by his liaison officer, Lieutenant Spears. With the BEF left in the air its temperamental commander was beset with gloom, and in a letter to Kitchener next day hinted that he was contemplating departure, 'I think immediate attention should be directed to the defence of Havre.'

By this time the BEF, to the astonishment of the Brandenburger captain, Bloem, who had seen his men slaughtered the previous day, was in full retreat. By the 24th even the placid Joffre recognized that his army was 'condemned to a defensive posture' and must hold out, making use of its fortified lines, wear down the enemy, and await the favourable moment for a counter-attack. The evident lack of success so far he attributed not to any fault of his own, but to 'grave shortcomings on the part of commanders'. That some had broken cannot be denied. During the Ardennes battle one divisional commander had actually committed suicide. Joffre sacked the weaklings ruthlessly. There was some recognition of French tactical failings and on the 24th Joffre issued a training instruction emphasizing the need for collaboration between infantry and artillery in the capture of *'points d'appui'* ('strongpoints'): 'Every time that the infantry has been launched to the attack from too great a distance before the artillery has made its effect felt, the infantry has fallen under the fire of machine-guns and suffered losses which might have been avoided.

'When a *point d'appui* has been captured it must be organized immediately, the troops must entrench, and artillery must be brought up.'

'Reign of terror'

Joffre's lesson on tactics would have seemed pretty elementary stuff to the officers of the BEF – or to the Germans for that matter. But they, too, had their troubles. The British after long marches up the *pavé* in the August sun, had won a victory, and were now, incomprehensibly, invited to march back the way they had come. They felt they were being 'messed about'. The Germans had a special nightmare of their own: the *franc tireur* (guerrilla). Captain Bloem records that on a day when his company marched twenty-eight miles not a man fell out: 'the thought of falling into the hands of the Walloons was worse than sore feet.'

To orderly German minds the thought of civilians intervening as snipers, albeit for

---

GOUVERNEMENT MILITAIRE DE PARIS

Armée de Paris, Habitants de Paris,

Les Membres du Gouvernement de la République ont quitté Paris pour donner une impulsion nouvelle à la défense nationale.

J'ai reçu le mandat de défendre Paris contre l'envahisseur.

Ce mandat, je le remplirai jusqu'au bout.

Paris, le 3 Septembre 1914.

Le Gouverneur Militaire de Paris,
Commandant l'Armée de Paris,

GALLIÉNI

Above: Galliéni's pledge to defend Paris 'until the end'

---

hearth and home, was utterly repugnant. Princess Blücher was told that there were thirty German officers in hospital at Aachen, their eyes gouged out by Belgian women and children. Atrocities, even imaginary ones, breed reprisals, and *Shrecklichkeit* (Frightfulness) was a matter of deliberate policy with the German high command which did not mean to detach strong forces to guard the lines of communication. Had not the great Clausewitz laid it down that terror was the proper way to shorten war? Only by making the civilian population feel its effects could the leaders be made to change their minds, and sue for peace. In Belgium the first important massacre was at Andenne where Bülow had 211 people shot on 20th and 21st August. At Tamines, sacked on the 21st, 400 were executed in the main square. The Saxons pillaged and burnt Dinant on the 23rd, leaving their aged commander, Hausen, 'profoundly moved', but indignant against the Belgian government which 'approved this perfidious street fighting contrary to international law'. The sack of Louvain – sparked off, apparently by German soldiers firing on each other in panic after a Belgian sortie from Antwerp – was the worst episode of this reign of terror. If anything these atrocities served to stiffen the resolution of the Belgians and their allies.

The retreat continued, but with five German armies carving their way into France, Joffre never despaired of resuming the offensive. By this time he had realized that the forces of his left wing were insufficient to stop the German onrush. On 25th August he ordered the formation of a new French army, the 6th under Maunoury. Its divisions were to be found from the now static front in Lorraine, and it was to take its position on the left of the BEF.

Moltke's fatal error

On the 25th Moltke also was taking men from the Western Front, not, however, from Lorraine where they could perhaps have been spared, but from his right wing! And this at a time when Kluck was detaching one of his corps to invest Maubeuge. Moltke was worried by the Russian threat to East Prussia and determined to reinforce the latter with two corps, though, ironically enough, they were not to arrive until the Germans had won their decisive victory at Tannenberg. Beyond question this was fatal alteration to the Schlieffen Plan at a moment when decisive victory lay within his grasp. The trouble was that by the 24th the Germans thought that they only had beaten men before them. That this was not so was forcibly demonstrated by the BEF at Le Cateau on the following day.

Late on the night of the 25th Smith-

Dorrien (2nd Corps) realized that, with some of his units only just coming in, and with many scattered and exhausted, it was not possible to carry out French's orders to continue the retreat. He decided to stand and fight.

Battle of Le Cateau

Kluck had nine divisions within reach of the battlefield at dawn, but only managed to bring two of them, with three cavalry divisions, into action against Smith-Dorrien's three. Kluck had, however, a tremendous concentration of artillery, and it was really this which made the British stand difficult. The German infantry came on in bunches, firing from the hip, and suffered severely. Kluck's strong right wing (two corps) allowed itself to be engaged by Sordet's cavalry corps and a French territorial division. The corps on his left, marching and counter-marching, covered eleven miles without intervening in the fight. In consequence Smith-Dorrien managed to extricate himself with a loss of some 8,000 men and thirty-eight guns. Mons and Le Cateau left Kluck with a profound respect for the BEF – 'it was an incomparable army', he told British officers after the war. Its rapid rifle fire had convinced many Germans that the BEF had twenty-eight machine-guns per battalion when in fact they had two.

While the battle of Le Cateau was in progress Joffre held a conference with French and Lanrezac at St Quentin in order to explain his latest plans. General Order No. 2 had reached GHQ the previous night, but there had not yet been time to study it. Joffre was shocked by French's excited complaints. He was threatened with envelopment by superior numbers and his right had been left in the air by Lanrezac's sudden withdrawal. His men were too tired to go over to the offensive.

After this uncomfortable meeting Joffre departed, suspecting that the BEF had lost its cohesion. The truth was that GHQ had lost touch with the army it was supposed to control, and things were not as gloomy as French thought. Kluck for his part saw things in much the same light as Sir John. On the 27th he hoped to 'cut off the British who were in full flight westwards'. With Namur in his hands and Bülow pressing Lanrezac's broken troops Moltke was feeling the 'universal sense of victory' that now pervaded the German army. But already things were going wrong. In three days furious fighting (24th-27th August) Rupprecht's twenty-six divisions had been hurled back from Toul, Nancy, and Epinal by Castelnau and Dubail. On the Meuse Langle held up the Duke of Württemberg from the 26th to the 28th.

On the 29th Bülow's army, astride the river Oise, blundered head-on into Lanrezac's columns, which were crossing their front, and suffered a severe check. In the battles of Guise and St Quentin Lanrezac was counter-attacking, most reluctantly, on direct orders from Joffre, who stayed with him and watched him for three hours of the battle. Had French permitted Haig's corps, which was still practically intact, to co-operate, the Germans might have suffered a severe defeat. Once more a counter-attack by d'Esperey's corps sustained the right wing at the moment of crisis. It was a magnificent spectacle. Bands playing, colours flying, the French infantry, covered by the fire of the 75s, swept eagerly forward and the Germans gave way. That night the 5th Army withdrew unimpeded.

The pursuit continued, though thanks to the absence of five corps — practically the equivalent of an army — awkward gaps were beginning to appear in the German right wing. On 31st August Kluck abandoned his pursuit of the British who had disappeared south of Compiègne, and wheeled south to strike at Lanrezac. On 1st September he crossed the Oise reaching Crépy-en-Valois and Villers-Cotterets, a bare thirty miles from Paris. The same day a stormy interview took place in the British embassy in Paris, when Kitchener, in his field-marshal's uniform, made it clear to the sulking French that he was to keep the BEF in the line and conform to the movements of his allies.

'We must strike'

Moltke was now attracted by the idea of driving the French south-east and thus cutting them off from Paris. He ordered Kluck to cover this movement in the direction of Paris, 'remaining in the rear of the Second Army'. The independent-minded Kluck, whose army was the farthest forward and the best placed to attack the French 5th Army, did not see this. Nor did he anticipate any danger from Paris. On the evening of the 2nd he gave orders to cross the Marne next day, leaving only one weak corps as a flank guard. That night the French government left Paris for Bordeaux. Next morning General Galliéni, the governor, still thought the Germans were marching on the capital. When at noon an airman reported their columns moving east towards the south-east, Maunoury's staff refused to credit it, but at 7 pm it was confirmed. 'We must strike!' cried Galliéni, and having given warning orders, asked Joffre's permission. At 8 am on the 4th one of his officers reached Joffre's headquarters at Bar-sur-Aube, and the intelligence staff traced Kluck's latest moves on the wall map. 'But we have

them,' they exclaimed. 'We must stop the retreat and seize our heaven-sent chance at once.'

Joffre himself appeared. 'A remarkable situation,' was his comment. 'The Paris army and the British are in a good position to deliver a flank attack on the Germans as they are marching on the Marne.' It remained to convince Sir John French.

D'Esperey, who had replaced Lanrezac, was ready with proposals for an attack on the 6th. These he had drawn up in concert with Major-General Wilson, French's deputy chief-of-staff. Galliéni pointed out that by the 7th the Germans would have

German cartoon, October 1914. Grey, the British foreign secretary, having buried Belgium, is now burying France

scented the danger threatening them from the direction of Paris.

Meanwhile, Moltke's mood of elation was deteriorating through a period of deepening panic towards complete nervous breakdown. Despite the pictures painted by his generals, there were still no masses of prisoners, no parks of captured guns. The French and British had refused to admit defeat, Kluck was following his own devices, and French reinforcements were approaching Paris from the east. At 6 pm on the 4th he sent out the following order

by wireless: 'I and II Armies will remain facing Paris, I Army between Oise and Marne, II Army between Marne and Seine.' This order did not reach Kluck until next day, by which time he had crossed the Marne. He gave the order to advance towards the Seine on the 5th, leaving only one corps behind the Marne.

On the afternoon of the 5th Joffre visited French's headquarters at Melun in order to ensure British co-operation. Later he wrote: 'I put my whole soul into convincing French that the decisive hour had come and that an English abstention would be severely judged by history. Finally, striking the table with my fist, I cried: *"Monsieur le Maréchal.* The honour of England is at stake!" French blushed, and murmured with emotion, "I will do all that is possible", and for me that was the equivalent of an oath.'

The battle of the Marne

The battle of the Marne was in effect a series of disjointed combats. It began on the afternoon of the 5th when the French 6th Army moving up to its start line on the river Ourcq unexpectedly ran into Kluck's flank guard, IV Reserve Corps, in the hills north of Meaux.

During the evening an emissary from Moltke, who was still running the campaign by remote control from Luxembourg, arrived at Kluck's HQ. This was Lieutenant-Colonel Hentsch, chief of intelligence branch, whose mission was to explain the real situation and in effect to bring him to heel. Kluck resigned himself to a withdrawal, but as yet unaware of the action on the Ourcq, contented himself with a leisurely retrograde move which left most of his army south of the Marne.

The three armies on the Allied left made a little progress on the 6th. Until the previous day the BEF and the 5th Army had continued the retreat, and the sudden change left them in cautious mood. The 6th Army was held up some six miles short of the Ourcq. The River Marne and a gap of eight miles separated its right from the BEF. In the south the 1st and 2nd French Armies successfully resisted the German VII and VI under Rupprecht, and on the 8th Moltke finally abandoned the unprofitable Lorraine offensive. The 3rd French Army, now under General Sarrail, and the 4th Army held their own well against the German V and IV Armies. But where Hausen's Saxons threatened Foch's much weaker 9th Army there was serious cause for disquiet.

On the 7th, Gronau reinforced by two more of Kluck's corps recalled from farther south, had little difficulty in holding Maunoury west of the Ourcq. The aggressive Kluck now conceived the notion of attacking the 6th Army from the north, hoping to drive it back on Paris and enter the capital on its heels. For this master-stroke he switched his two remaining corps with astonishing speed from south of the Marne to his northern wing. By so doing he opened a gap of some twenty miles between himself and Bülow, a gap which was masked by a fairly strong screen of nine infantry battalions (eight being *Jäger*) and two cavalry corps on the Petit Morin.

German retreat

If the British were slow to exploit this advantage the fault lay with GHQ rather than the men, who were in good spirits now that they were going forward once more. D'Esperey's progress on the 7th was comparable with that of the BEF, but by this time Foch, under severe pressure, was being driven south from the marshes of Saint-Gond. It was on the 8th that he sent the legendary report to Joffre: 'My centre is yielding, my right wing is giving way. An excellent situation. I attack tomorrow.' But the Germans no longer hoped for a break-through; rather it was their aim to extricate Bülow and close the gap. Shortly before 9 am on the 9th an aviator reported to Bülow that there were five British columns with their heads on or across the Marne. Another had already reported that there were no German troops in the path of the BEF's advance. Warning Kluck of his intention, Bülow issued orders for a retirement. Almost simultaneously Kluck also gave orders for a withdrawal in the general direction of Soissons. It was about 5.30 pm before it became evident to the British that the Germans were abandoning the battlefield. Their success had not been particularly costly; between 6th and 10th September the BEF's casualties numbered no more than 1,701.

The battle of the Marne, in which, it has been calculated, some fifty-seven Allied divisions (eight cavalry) turned back fifty-three German (seven cavalry) was over, and with it died the famous Schlieffen Plan. Tactically its results were disappointing, for it was not fought to the bitter end. Strategically it was of profound importance, for it meant that all hope of a swift knockout blow was over. As in 1940 the Germans counted on a swift *blitzkrieg* to defeat their semi-mobilized enemies and win the war. Could they have won? The two corps sent to East Prussia would have been more than sufficient to close that famous gap.

Joffre is not generally numbered among the great captains, but he had won one of the strategically decisive battles of all time.

By the morning of the 10th the Germans had vanished, Kluck retiring to the Aisne

at Soissons and Bülow to the Vesle at Rheims. In general it cannot be said that the pursuit was vigorous, though much transport, some forty guns and about 14,000 prisoners were taken. Bad weather prevented air reconnaissance and the French, whose men and horses were tired, could only average six or seven miles a day. There was still a gap between the German I and II Armies, but this was not evident to the Allies. On the 13th the VII reserve corps, released by the fall of Maubeuge, arrived in the nick of time to close the gap. By a forced march of forty miles in twenty-four hours it just succeeded in forestalling Haig's corps.

A dead French soldier. The French soon found that élan *was of very little help against the enemy's concentrated firepower*

The offensive had left one-tenth of France, with much of her coal and iron, in German hands. The failure of the Schlieffen Plan had brought Moltke's secret replacement by General Erich von Falkenhayn, the minister of war, who at fifty-three was a mere boy compared to most of the army commanders on the Western Front. Neither he nor Joffre quite despaired of a speedy decision in a war of movement. When the battle of the Aisne began to crystallize into the trench warfare of the next four years, both improvised

plans to outflank the other's northern flank, between the Oise and the sea. With the Belgian field army, 65,000 strong, ensconced in Antwerp, the Allies had some hopes of a success in Flanders. Winston Churchill, the First Lord of the Admiralty, did his best to stiffen the garrison with a naval division, 12,000 strong (30th October), but two-thirds of these men were neither well-trained nor properly equipped. The Germans began to bombard the city on the 7th and General Deguise, the fortress commander, made no attempt to hold out to the last. The north-eastern forts were tamely surrendered without bombardment or attack, but the field army escaped westwards to the River Yser.

Meanwhile, Joffre had agreed that the six British divisions on the Aisne should be transferred to Flanders and they began to detrain near Abbeville on 9th October. On the same day the 7th Division landed at Ostend, and, since Antwerp had fallen, became part of the BEF.

First battle of Ypres

With Antwerp in his hands Falkenhayn had a fleeting chance of a break-through, for he had five reserve corps available for instant action. They were not the best troops in the world for 'the men were too young and the officers too old', but they showed the most determined bravery in the first battle of Ypres, which raged between Arras and the sea in that autumn (12th October to 11th November).

The fighting opened well enough for the Allies but by 21st October the Germans had won the initiative, and battered away at the Allied line for the next three weeks. The Kaiser himself appeared in the battle area to witness the break-through. The climax of the battle came on the 31st when the Germans broke into the British line at Gheluvelt.

In an astonishing counter-attack, inspired by Brigadier-General Fitzclarence, the 368 survivors of the 2/Worcestershires threw them out. Eventually, the storm died out with the repulse of the Prussian Guard on 11th November.

The BEF had, it is estimated, lost over 50,000 men, and the Germans at least twice as many, including about half the infantry engaged.

The Western Front now ran from Switzerland to the sea, following the line of the Vosges, the Moselle, the Meuse hills, the Argonne, the Chemin des Dames, the Aisne, until by way of Armentières and Ypres it reached Dixmude. There were still those who believed that with the spring would come the return of open warfare. But the line was not to move more than ten miles either way for the next three years.

The Eastern Front

Within a week of the German invasion of Belgium, 800 miles to the east the battle lines of the 'Eastern Front', running from the gloomy East Prussian marches in the north to the high Carpathians in the south, were already drawn up and the several armies swarming on them, the Russian, the Austro-Hungarian and the German, were on the point of being set in full motion. The Russians, though mobilization had so far brought only one-third of their available manpower into the field, were intent on breaking into East Prussia: the Germans concentrated to defend it. In southern Poland and Galicia the Austro-Hungarians, their army a multi-national patchwork stitched out of Germans, Slavs, and Magyars, prepared to strike at the Russians, while the Russians proposed to launch their main attack against Austria-Hungary. The result was soon a whirlpool of battles which sucked in whole armies to destruction, crippling the Austrians, battering the Russians, and straining the Germans. Wild as the fighting was, with the masses of Austrian and Russian peasant soldiers lumbering about, the Eastern Front impinged directly on operations in the west when, at a crucial stage in the flailing German offensive against 'the Franco-English Army', the German command drew off men and speeded them eastwards to hold sacred German soil, the sanctum of Prussia, against the Slav intruder, the historical image of whose 'frightfulness' fevered the German mind. The rival armies in the east each played their special supporting parts: Russia marched on East Prussia at France's urgent request, Austria-Hungary, battling with Serbia, lunged across the Russian frontiers at Germany's prompting. For Germany, the two-front war had materialized, not in military mathematics, but as gunfire on its own frontiers.

The armies which rolled upon each other in the east did so in accordance with the war plans upon which the respective general staffs had prepared long before the actual clash. German planners wrestled with the intractabilities of a two-front war; early planning variants (relying on the lengthy period which they presumed Russian mobilization would take) stripped East Prussia of men, but subsequent signs of waxing Russian strength caused a revision; according to the new plan the VIII Army was to be stationed in East Prussia, its role essentially defensive. Austria-

Hungary nurtured two war plans. The first, Plan B, envisaged war against Serbia only, against whom three armies would be committed while the other three held Galicia against the Russians; the second, Plan R, related to war with Serbia and Russia: two armies would march on Serbia and four against Russia. Russia, meanwhile, developed two war plans of its own, one defensive, Plan G, the other offensive, Plan A. Plan G assumed a primary German effort against Russia, in which contingency the North-Western and South-Western Army Groups would first retire, and then the Russians would make a counteroffensive. Plan A prescribed an offensive when the German blow was directed against France: Russian armies would strike at East Prussia and Galicia, the bulk of Russian strength (four armies) falling on the Austrians, with two driving into East Prussia.

This military calculus was based, not only upon guesses about what would happen, but also upon the possibilities (and the restrictions) of the supposed 'front'. Overshadowing all else was the giant Russian salient—Russian Poland—which jutted out to the west, its tip not 200 miles from Berlin. The salient was both a springboard and a trap for the Russians; from it they could leap into Silesia, but they could be militarily entombed if German troops from East Prussia and Austrian troops from Galicia struck from north and south to crumple the salient. East Prussia was unmistakably exposed but, thanks to German attention to interior communications, eminently defensible. In terms of plans, Germany determined to hold East Prussia: Russia, at France's insistence, opted for Plan A: Austria-Hungary, having first set in motion Plan B, suddenly switched to Plan R (which meant pulling the whole II Army back from Serbia).

The Russians take the field
At daylight on 12th August 1914, under a calm morning sky, the first units from Rennenkampf's 1st Army—cavalry squadrons and a rifle regiment—crossed the frontier into East Prussia. The Russian invasion had begun, a converging attack mounted with two armies of General Zhilinsky's North-Western Group: Rennenkampf's 1st Army was to strike from the east, Samsonov's 2nd Army from the southeast, two claws digging into East Prussia

Eastern Front 1914

RUSSIAN FORCES
GERMAN AND AUSTRIAN FORCES

100 MILES
150 KILOMETRES

Kovno
Gumbinnen
Danzig
EAST PRUSSIA
GERMANY
Masurian Lakes
Vistula R.
Tannenberg
RUSSIA
Warsaw
Łódź
SILESIA
Lublin
RUSSIAN POLAND
Breslau
Kraków
Przemyśl Lemberg
AUSTRIA-HUNGARY
GALICIA

Left: Russian machine-gunners bitterly resist the German advance at the battle of Tannenberg. A realistic film-still.
Above and below: The campaign and orders of battle on the Eastern Front, August to December 1914

German and Russian order of battle:
East Prussia, August 1914

German	Russian (North Western Group)
VIII Army (Prittwitz Hindenburg)	1st Army (Rennenkampf) 2, 3, 4, 20 Corps
I, I Reserve XVII, XX Corps	2nd Army (Samsonov) 1, 6, 13, 15, 23 Corps

Austro-Hungarian and Russian order of battle:
Galicia, August 1914

Austro-Hungarian	Russian (South Western Group)
I Army (Dankl)	4th Army (Salza)
IV Army (Auffenburg)	5th Army (Plehve)
III Army (Bruderman)	3rd Army (Ruszki)
II Army (moved from Serbia) (Ermolli)	8th Army (Brusilov)

German, Austrian, and Russian order of battle:
late November, 1914 (battle of Łódź)

German	Russian
VIII Army	10th Army
IX Army	1st Army
	2nd Army (Łódź)
Austrian	5th Army
I Army	4th Army
IV Army	9th Army
III Army	3rd Army
II Army	8th Army

to crumple and destroy it. On the German side, Lieutenant-General von Prittwitz had already begun to deploy the four corps of the VIII Army assigned to defend East Prussia: to block the Russian drive from the east, three corps took positions along the line of the river Angerapp and a fourth was deployed to the south, amid the lakes and forests of Tannenberg, barring the way to the Russian army moving from the south-east. Deliberately, taking advantage of excellent internal communications —and with substantial knowledge of Russian movements, thanks to an appalling carelessness shown by the Russians in transmitting orders *en clair* for much of the time—Prittwitz drew up his corps and made his plans: he would deal with one Russian army at a time, striking first at Rennenkampf and then at Samsonov. Though the alarm bells were beginning to ring through Prussia, there seemed to be a margin of time and therefore an assurance of safety.

Certainly the Imperial Russian Army was—at France's entreaty—rushing into the attack; as a consequence it was incompletely mobilized. Yet this was not its basic weakness. The real defects lay deeper. To shortcomings in organization, training, equipment, and supply were added the fatal flaws of a corrupt, ruinously inefficient society where no institution could respond to 'the concentrated demands of wartime'. In addition, the Russian army was fearfully short of fire-power: even where the guns did exist, the available ammunition often ran out. The Russian Plan A nevertheless went into operation, and the attack on East Prussia slowly ground into gear. On 17th August Rennenkampf's 1st Army moving from the east, its columns separated and its northern flank dangerously bare, crossed the frontier in force. Samsonov in the south-east was not due to move off for another five days.

Meanwhile, farther south, Austro-Hungarian troops had crossed the Russian frontier on 10th August. Following the dictates of Plan R, Field-Marshal Conrad von Hötzendorf launched the Austro-Hungarian armies from Austrian Poland (Galicia) towards the north to engage the main Russian forces, which he assumed lay in this direction. The field-marshal's assumption proved to be totally wrong; Russian strength lay in yet another direction, to the south-east, and this again was due to the mistaken anticipation by the Russian command of Austrian intentions. General Ivanov, South-Western Group commander, expected the Austrians to strike from the direction of Lemberg (Lwów) and it was here that he proposed to make his own maximum effort. These initial misconceptions, therefore, played a major role in producing a lop-sided battle-front, with the Austrians flailing away in the north and the Russians loosing a massive attack in the south.

At first, Austrian and Russian armies blundered into each other along the Austrian line of advance to the north (in the direction of Lublin-Kholm), though after 23rd August heavy fighting developed. Vastly encouraged by the first results, Conrad reinforced his left flank and ordered the III Army into the attack east of Lemberg—where the Russians were ready and waiting: and having switched from Plan B to Plan R, Conrad brought II Army shuttling up from Serbia. On 26th August Ivanov opened his own offensive with two armies (3rd and 8th) which smashed into the depleted, struggling Austrian III Army: the III Army fell back in disorder on Lemberg. Late in August Conrad was facing a confused though by no means desperate situation—the gleam of success in the north, the spurt of danger in the south. The field-marshal decided to fight for his Lemberg front, not of itself a disastrous decision, but the manner in which he implemented it finally provided Ivanov with the opportunity to rip the whole Austrian front wide open.

The Russians are trapped

Though Russian armies were on the verge of a vast triumph in Galicia, the invasion of East Prussia had come to terrible grief. From its first set-piece arrangement, the battle for East Prussia rapidly developed into a rolling, lurching, savage affair, pitching into violent motion when the impetuous commander of the German I Corps, General François, brought Rennenkampf to battle ahead of the line chosen by Prittwitz. But the undiscerning Rennenkampf ploughed on, thereby helping to restore reality to German plans. On 20th August Samsonov began his advance from the south-east, a signal for Rennenkampf to halt calmly so that Samsonov might catch up in time and space. Prittwitz determined to act, proposing to launch a counter-blow at Rennenkampf, much to the disgust of his chief operations officer, Max Hoffmann, for it meant unravelling the German line. General François once again led the I Corps against Rennenkampf and other corps engaged in the 'battle of Gumbinnen', a wild, swirling encounter in which the German XVII Corps was badly mauled. News of this, intelligence of Samsonov's advance, and panic that the Russians might burst through the Insterburg Gap, splitting the VIII Army apart, caused Prittwitz to lose what little nerve he possessed. He decided on precipitate retreat to the Vistula, to the consternation of his commanders. Adamant about withdrawal, Prittwitz proceeded to petrify the high

Top: Postcard illustration of Austro-Hungarian artillery men. Above: Russian howitzer—primitive looking weapon, but the Russians could have done with more

command with the details of disaster he retailed by telephone to Helmuth von Moltke (the German chief of general staff) at Coblenz—the Vistula it had to be, and Prittwitz doubted that he could hold this line without reinforcement.

This wailing from the east cut across the gigantic battle raging in the west. Moltke wasted no time. He despatched Major-General Erich Ludendorff as chief-of-staff and General Paul von Hindenburg (hitherto on the retired list) as the new commander of the VIII Army. Prittwitz was brushed aside. The idea of hasty withdrawal had already been abandoned in the east and Hoffmann devised a plan to draw off troops facing Rennenkampf to pit them against Samsonov. Rennenkampf failed to follow through after Gumbinnen; he hung poised in the north, an undoubted threat but a stationary one. Samsonov inched his way along, arguing all the way with Zhilinsky. The VIII Army command faced one crucial question: was there time to knock out Samsonov before Rennenkampf came down from the north? On the morning of 25th August that problem received swift, if startling resolution; uncloaked by code, Rennenkampf broadcast his line of advance and its distance. The Russian 1st Army would not, on this evidence, strike into the rear of the VIII Army. As for Samsonov, imagining himself to be pursuing a broken enemy, he proposed to rest his troops on 25th August. It seemed as if the Russians were inviting their own destruction. Further news from their own command, however, brought disquiet to the Germans; at Coblenz, Moltke had decided to pull out three corps and a division from the Western Front – where every unit was needed – as reinforcement for the east. Two corps and a cavalry division were already detached on 26th August, an action Moltke justified by arguing that 'the decision' in the west had already been gained. Yet three corps, loaded as they were on troop trains and trundling over Germany, could not 'save' East Prussia and remained lost to the German right wing on the Western Front.

Meanwhile the VIII Army, speeded along internal railway lines, shifted its weight to the south. The Russian 'pincers' waved in the air: at the *Stavka* (Russian GHQ) concern mounted at Rennenkampf's dawdling. Zhilinsky did nothing to urge Rennenkampf to close with Samsonov, whom he thought to be in no danger. On 26th August Samsonov's 2nd Army resumed its advance, the Russian centre moving all unsuspecting into a German trap ringed with four corps: the full weight of VIII Army – all but one division, which was holding Rennenkampf in the north – crashed on Samsonov's hungry, ill-clad men. The 'battle of Tannenberg', running its course for three agonizing days, snared three Russian corps (13th, 15th, and 23rd) in the German net: German guns lashed the Russian divisions, the Russians broke and the fight continued in the woods and across the marshes. On 29th August Samsonov knew the extent of the catastrophe; that evening he spent huddled in a clearing in the forest. Shortly after midnight he drew aside and shot himself. The Germans took over 100,000 prisoners and large quantities of guns. Two Russian corps (13th and 15th) were obliterated, another (23rd) drastically thinned, and the two flank corps reduced to the strength of mere divisions.

With the defeat of Samsonov, the killing was but half done. Rennenkampf in the north was now marked down for destruc-tion and the VIII Army, coiling across East Prussia like a spring and strengthened by reinforcement arriving from the west, regrouped to attack once more. On 5th September the German drive on Rennenkampf's left flank opened, and 'the battle of the Masurian Lakes' began; at the centre Rennenkampf held off the German assault, but in so doing weakened the whole of the 1st Army. On 9th September Rennenkampf ordered a general withdrawal to pull the 1st Army out of the trap closing on it, and also launched one stabbing attack with two divisions – enough to slow down the German right wing. The Russian infantrymen trudged eastwards: Rennenkampf made the journey in the comfort of his car, back to and over the Russian frontier. His army did escape, but had suffered a grievous mauling, with 100,000 men lost. The invasion of Prussia, which cost the Russians almost a quarter of a million men, had failed. Zhilinsky tried – unsuccessfully – to unload the blame on Rennenkampf: Rennenkampf (whose conduct incurred suspicions of treason) stayed and Zhilinsky was dismissed.

The rout of the Austrians

9th September 1914: the Germans had failed on the Marne: Samsonov was dead, Rennenkampf in retreat: the Russians were defeated in East Prussia, and almost triumphant in Galicia. Conrad, in trying to cover himself at Lemberg, opened a gap in the north and the Russian 5th Army came bursting through. To escape encirclement, the Austrian command ordered a general withdrawal, and withdrawal degenerated into pell-mell flight. The whole Austro-Hungarian front quivered and collapsed, caving in to a depth of a hundred miles and immolating over 300,000 men in the Galician catastrophe. Russian troops took Lemberg and swept on to cut off the great fortress of Przemyśl, bottling up 100,000 more men. In this whole *débâcle,* the Austro-Hungarian armies suffered a loss not even suggested by numbers, for many of the cadre 'Austrian' officers, the hard core of the army, were lost or captured. The rout of the Austrians in Galicia, for it was nothing short of that, brought fresh dangers to Germany: the Russians were already opening a pathway into Silesia. The situation called for German troops, but Erich von Falkenhayn (who replaced Moltke after the first battle of the Marne) would let none go from the Western Front. Hindenburg therefore stripped East Prussia of four of its six corps to form a new German army in the east, the IX, which began to deploy at Czestochowa late in September, closing with the Austrian I Army. Both sides – Russian and German – were at this stage planning to attack and a phase of fierce, formidable battles in the east was about to begin. The Russians found themselves once more under pressure from the French to mount a major attack, this time in the direction of the German industrial base in Silesia; the Russian threat to Cracow did itself involve the security of Silesia – and Hindenburg had hurried to close the most staring gap – but an offensive along the Warsaw-Posen axis by Russian armies would mean great and growing danger for Germany. Towards the end of September, Russian armies were regrouping for this new offensive.

Hindenburg, however, struck first, using his new IX Army and aiming straight at the huge Russian base of Warsaw, the attack for which the Austrians had pleaded at the end of August. For the first time the Russians learned of the existence of the IX Army and rushed every available man to the Vistula to hold off the German advance: Austrian troops also started an attack towards the line of the river San. Late in September the IX Army rolled forward and by 9th October Hindenburg was on the Vistula. Three days later German troops began their advance on Warsaw. To hold the city the Russian command speeded up the movement of Siberian regiments from the Far East, troops released for service in European Russia at the end of August when Japan entered the war against Germany and Russia had no further fear of a clash with Japan. At the end of a month's journey, the Far Eastern regiments detrained in Warsaw and went straight into action, fighting savage bouts with the bayonet under the walls of the city.

By mid-October, with two Russian armies (1st and 2nd) piling up on his northern flank, Hindenburg deemed it prudent to withdraw; the IX Army began to fall back, the Austrians were floundering to the south and by the end of the month German and Austrian troops were back in the positions they had occupied towards the close of September. It was now the turn of the Russian command to take the offensive, to launch an invasion of Silesia with four armies while a fifth (1st Army, still under the command of Rennenkampf) protected the Russian northern flank from its positions on the Vistula. Once again, with staggering negligence, the Russians blared their movements over the air and once again the Russian command failed to take speedy German redeployment into account. The German IX Army, formidable and efficient, was already on the move, speeding along good rail communications to its new concentration area, a blocking position between Posen and Thorn; the place of IX Army in the German-Austrian line was taken by the Austrian II Army which had been moved up from the Carpathians.

1△

The scene was almost set for the fiercest round fought so far, without the grand tragedy of East Prussia or the massive confusion of Galicia, but a test of arms of a very decisive nature, itself connected with a subtle but profound change which was overtaking the war in the east—at least from the German side. Hindenburg and Ludendorff now assumed over-all command of German troops in the east. They were already the inseparable martial pair, twinned by the triumphs of East Prussia and set upon that rise which took them finally to supreme military control of Germany's destiny. In the east the German army fought a war of mobility and also in the east Ludendorff sought to realize Schlieffen's idea of victory—not attained in the west—that true victory must be wholly and utterly decisive. Ludendorff was therefore embarked on his search for 'a decision' in the east, which inevitably brought a clash over the claims of the west: it meant conflict with Falkenhayn, and it required reinforcements, the addition of strength to mobility.

To fend off the Russians, the German command determined to pre-empt their attack. With the IX Army drawn up in its new operational area, now under General von Mackensen's command, the German plan envisaged an operation timed for 11th November and designed to crumple the

Russian drive into Silesia by driving between the 1st and 2nd Russian Armies. On the Western Front Falkenhayn was fighting the last great battle of 1914 at Ypres, and having broken through the British lines to the south-east, he espied eventual victory: no men could be spared for the east. Hindenburg and Ludendorff, however, could not afford to wait, being persuaded—correctly—of the gravity of the Russian threat. On 11th November, as planned, the IX Army attacked on a front west and north-west of Łódź, closing on the 1st and 2nd Russian armies. This did not prevent the Russians from loosing their armies in a westerly drive towards Silesia three days later, but within forty-eight hours the Russian offensive was brought to an abrupt halt. The German IX Army had crashed straight into the junction of 1st and 2nd Armies—and the fault this time lay unambiguously with Rennenkampf in charge of the 1st Army. On 16th November the enormity of the situation finally broke over the Russian command, who had been waiting for the IX Army to be crushed between the two Russian armies—a Russian Tannenberg where the IX Army would march to its doom. But Mackensen tossed Rennenkampf's corps aside—badly strung out as they were—and then ripped into the right flank of the Russian 2nd Army, which the Germans intended to

encircle, the second time that this unfortunate army was to be done to death.

With the grip of winter tightening each day, the fight for Łódź and for the life or death of the 2nd Army lasted until early in December. Furious fighting flared as the Germans closed in and as the Russians beat them off. The Russian 5th Army was ordered to close with the 2nd: two Russian corps, driven along in forced marches, managed to press the right flank of the IX Army back. The left flank of the IX Army lapped right round to the south-east of Łódź, giving the Russians the chance to spring a trap of their own, though late in November the German corps fought its way out. In the end neither the German nor the Russian trap had closed fully, but early in December Russian troops began withdrawing from Łódź, whereupon German troops immediately entered the city in their wake. After his showing in these battles, Rennenkampf was finally dragged out of his command of the 1st Army; the new commander, General Litvinov, quickly ordered a withdrawal to the Bzura and Rawka river lines where the army wintered. The battle of Łódź, even if it enjoyed none of the fame of Tannenberg, nevertheless had a decisiveness all its own: frustrated though they were in their tactical designs, Hindenburg and Ludendorff had throttled completely the Russian offensive.

1 and 2 German and Russian troops (right) in action during the fighting on the Eastern Front. 3 General Samsonov, who shot himself after the battle of Tannenberg. 4 After the battle, Samsonov's wife searches for her husband. 5 Austro-Hungarian troops in Galicia tend one of their wounded. The early months of the war brought a shattering defeat for Austria-Hungary

Russia licks her wounds

For the rest of December the Eastern Front remained quiet. Four months of fighting, however, had wrought some fearful changes. Russian armies had been dreadfully mauled in East Prussia: Austria-Hungary suffered calamitous losses in Galicia and a motley army lost much of its irreplaceable 'Austrian' cadre. The Russian triumph in Galicia could momentarily blot out disaster in East Prussia, but Tannenberg inflicted a deep and terrible wound: worse, it stood as a sinister portent. The Russian infantryman, ill-equipped and under-fed, performed prodigies of endurance and raw, unflinching courage, but manpower could not continually match a murderous enemy firepower: German superiority in artillery mangled the Imperial Russian Army. Within a month of the opening of the war Russian armies were chronically starved of ammunition and the gun-batteries, insufficient as they were, remained all but bereft of shells. The war minister, Sukhomlinov, 'an empty and slovenly man', bore most of the responsibility for this disgraceful state of affairs, but it was the regime itself which allowed men like Sukhomlinov to grow fat on inefficiency and to flourish on calamity. The Russian high command showed mostly its ineptitudes: the Imperial Army took the field inadequately trained,

indifferently and incompetently led, badly supplied—and for all this the peasant soldier had to pay in blood.

At the end of 1914, though Russian losses were already grievous—shocking enough to promote feelings that a settlement with Germany would be the best course, or that again Russia was shouldering an unfairly heavy burden—Russian armies still covered Warsaw, the front was advantageously shortened in western Poland and much of Galicia was in Russian hands. The Russian command had plunged from the outset into the offensive in fulfilment of their agreement with the French, even though only a third of the Imperial Army was mobilized and deployed: Tannenberg and then the disaster at the Masurian Lakes had followed. 'The first days of war were the first days of disgrace,' branding a sense of helplessness, of ineradicable inferiority into Russian consciousness in the face of a German war-machine which clicked, whirred, and roared to command. The German success in the east was huge and enlarged by the developing myth of Hindenburg-Ludendorff; the German command waged a relentless, fierce war, applying the principle of mobility and maximum concentration against the weakest point with devastating effect.

It was also a brutal war: if 'the flames of Louvain' blazed in the west, so did 'the

flames of Kalisz' crackle in the east. For a moment, when the fat, trembling Prittwitz had the telephone to Moltke in his hand, disaster seemed to loom, but massed German guns, the speeding German trains, the tactical ingenuity of the command swept this away. Yet, almost ironically, the very magnitude of German successes in the east conjured up problems of a singular order for the military leaders; the critical issue was not that some German formations had moved from west to east during a particular battle, but that the idea burgeoned of winning the war by actions in the east. German victory in this theatre itself contributed directly to sustaining hopes for speedy, 'total' victory—and the prospect of knocking an enfeebled, bumbling Russia out of the war seemed glittering. General Falkenhayn was not so very greatly impressed (nor, for the moment, was Russia's military prospect utterly critical); Falkenhayn, committed to guarding the gains in the west and launching limited offensives to tear at the enemy, was firmly of the opinion that 'no decision in the east . . . could spare us from fighting to a conclusion in the west'. Hindenburg and Ludendorff perforce argued that Germany could not afford—if for no other reason because of the need to hold up a tottering Austria-Hungary—to defer or avoid seeking a decision in the east.

5 ▽

The Spreading War

On a fine autumn day of 1914 Colonel Hankey, secretary of the British pre-war Council of Imperial Defence and now of the smaller War Council, crossing the South Downs near Lewes, stopped to watch the men of Kitchener's army marching and drilling, scattered across the usually deserted downland. Still in civilian clothes, for uniforms and rifles could not yet be provided for them, they had in hundreds of thousands answered the call for voluntary enlistment, overwhelming the creaking military machine. That winter, as Hankey listened to ministers, admirals, and generals, he was to think of that scene and the drilling men, the flower of Great Britain's manhood. It was their fate that had to be decided.

On the Western Front the German army had been stopped on the Marne. After that had come the so-called race to the sea, as the opposing forces tried to out-flank each other to the north, only to crash head-on again, as each attempted the same manoeuvre. When in mid-November the last desperate German attacks failed against an equally desperate defence at Ypres, no vulnerable flank remained. Frontal attack, then, it must be, but frontal attack had already failed repeatedly with shattering losses. By the spring the armies would be firmly entrenched, with deep barbed-wire entanglements and ever growing numbers of machine-guns.

On the Eastern Front the Germans had crushed the Russians invading East Prussia at Tannenberg and the Masurian Lakes, but in the great, complex series of battles around Lemberg (Lwów)—which happened almost at the same time as that of the Marne—the Russians had thrown the invading Austro-Hungarians back to the Carpathian passes. Here, too, November had seen a second round as the Germans came to the aid of their allies, defeating the Russians at Łódz. Halted by the eastern European winter, the battered armies licked their wounds, but here, in the vast eastern plains, as no longer in the west, room still remained for armies to man-oeuvre against each other.

In the south the heroic Serbian army still surprisingly survived, having in-flicted galling defeats on the Austro-Hungarians. Now it was exhausted, weakened by casualties, short of supplies. Typhus raged in its ranks. Bulgaria, nursing deep injuries from the Second Balkan War but still undecided, threatened its flank. Austria-Hungary, too, was threatened by new enemies, for Italy and Rumania were discussing with the Allies the terms on which they might join them.

At sea the German High Seas Fleet, having refused to give battle to the stronger British Grand Fleet, was penned in the south-eastern corner of the North Sea. Raiding cruisers, a serious nuisance in the wide Atlantic and Pacific, had, by the end of 1914, mostly been rounded up. Submarines had given the Grand Fleet a scare, but so far they had hardly threatened the laden merchant ships whose protection or destruction is, in the last analysis, the purpose of fleets.

Turkey—the ramshackle empire

At the beginning of November Turkey entered the war against the Allies. The ramshackle Ottoman empire had been crumbling for fifty years when, in 1908, the revolutionary Young Turks Committee had seized power, getting rid of Sultan Abdul Hamid with startling ease. Further defeats had followed: in 1911 by Italy in Tripoli, and in 1912 in the First Balkan War. Although the Turks regained some territory in the Second Balkan War, the army, exhausted by six years' fighting, was by then close to collapse, often hungry and in rags, its pay in arrears, its administration broken down. Since then a strong German mission had been at work, energetically organizing and training. The Turks knew, at least, the realities of war, and in the Turkish units—some of the divisions were Arab and resented Turkish dominance—there burned a fierce, resentful, wolf-like pride, which would, on the battlefield make Turkish soldiers as stubborn and bitter fighters as any in the world.

Cut off by Bulgaria, still neutral, from her northern allies, Turkey could receive from them the much needed military supplies only by subterfuge. Within her own territories, the new railway being built by German engineers still had breaks either side of the Gulf of Alexandretta, where it crossed the Taurus and Amanus mountains on its way to Aleppo. There it branched one way towards Baghdad, but stopped 380 miles short of the Tigris, and the other towards Amman and Medina. It was 250 miles from the Russian Caucasus frontier at its nearest point.

The army, something over a million strong with thirty-six regular divisions, was distributed in the I, II, III, and IV Armies, which were respectively in Turkey-in-Europe, western Anatolia, Erzurum near the Russian frontier, and Syria. In addition there were two regular divisions each in the Yemen, central Arabia, and Mesopotamia (modern Iraq).

Above: Prisoners of a world strategy— Germans under guard in distant East Africa. Although a colonial 'sideshow', the war the British Empire fought to eradicate von Lettow-Vorbeck's German guerillas cost her three times the lives that she had lost in the Boer War, and the campaign left the Germans undefeated in November 1918.
Left: Field Marshal Lord Kitchener.
Below: The East African campaign. The British advanced from British East Africa, South Africa, and Rhodesia (as the arrows show). The Germans withdrew, making a brief stand whenever there was an opportunity to inflict heavy casualties. By September 1916 the British and South Africans had cooped the Germans up in fifteen per cent of the territory—but the army remained for another two years

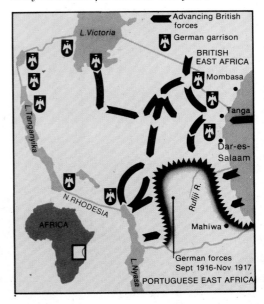

The Shock of Arms

Enver Pasha, minister for war, who with Talat Bey, minister for the interior, dominated the cabinet, took command of the III Army, about 150,000 strong, and in mid-December sent his ill-equipped soldiers across the mountains into the Caucasus against the smaller Russian 7th Army. Overtaken by winter blizzards, the timing of the arrival of the three corps was thrown out, and they attacked piecemeal. But the hungry, exhausted soldiers fought fiercely, and the Russian command was alarmed. Then, defeated around Sarikamish, the Turks faced the choice of surrender or retreat through the icy passes. Only 12,000 got back to Erzurum. One entire corps laid down its arms, and the Russians counted 30,000 frozen bodies in the mountains.

In February the IV Army sent 20,000 men across the Sinai peninsula to cut the Suez Canal. Egypt, still in 1914 nominally a part of the Ottoman empire but since 1882 controlled and occupied by Great Britain, had been declared a British protectorate when Turkey entered the war. It was garrisoned by one British Territorial and two Indian divisions, and the two-division Australia and New Zealand Army Corps was assembling and training there. The Turks were thrown back with ease. In the years that followed, the British turned to the attack across Sinai, at first clumsily and tentatively, then in 1917 under Allenby brilliantly and overwhelmingly, taking Jerusalem in December 1917.

Farther east the British took the initiative early against the Turks. A brigade from India landed at the head of the Persian Gulf in October 1914, followed by the rest of a division intended to guard the Anglo-Persian oilfields and prevent enemy incursions into the Indian Ocean. It quickly took Basra and gained some distance up the Euphrates.

By far the most important Turkish contribution to the Austro-German cause was, however, the immediate one, made in October 1914 by closing the Dardanelles and Bosphorus to Allied shipping. This, by cutting off Russia's Black Sea ports, brought her great corn exporting trade to an end, and closing her most important gateway for supplies from the outside world. At a blow her exports fell by ninety-eight per cent and her imports by ninety-five per cent, figures crippling to any nation, likely to be fatal to Russia with her vast population and flimsy industrial base. It imposed powerful strategic and moral obligations on her Allies to come to her aid.

Germany's empire seized

On the African coast of the Indian Ocean lay German East Africa (modern Tanzania), bordered to the north by British East Africa (Kenya) and to the west by the Belgian Congo, 400 miles from north to south, 600 miles inland to Lake Tanganyika, mostly uncultivated bush, varying from grassland to deep jungle. Here von Lettow-Vorbeck successfully resisted the British attempts to dislodge him.

Across equatorial Africa, on its western coast, were two more German colonies. The Cameroons, 200 miles of coastline, extending 500 miles inland and reaching a width of 600, bordered by the British colony Nigeria and French Equatorial Africa, was garrisoned by 200 German and 3,300 African soldiers and armed police. A small Franco-British force landed from the sea and took the port, Douala, on 27th September 1914, but the Germans withdrew inland across the swampy coastal belt to the capital, Yaoundé. Columns sent across the undeveloped grass hinterland from Nigeria and French Equatorial Africa took Yaoundé on 1st December 1915, and the garrison slipped back through the coastal belt to internment in Spanish Guinea. Togoland, with ninety miles of coastline, 300 miles deep, between the British Gold Coast and French Dahomey, was quickly occupied in August 1914.

Finally, between the South Atlantic and the Kalahari Desert lay German-South West Africa (subsequently mandated to South Africa), with 800 miles of coastline, reaching in the north 600 miles inland, mostly high, sandy desert. It had two harbours, Lüderitz Bay and, facing the British enclave at Walvis Bay, Swakopmund, with the capital and wireless station at Windhoek. It was garrisoned by 2,000 German soldiers backed by 5,000 male German civilians. Its African population had risen in 1904 and had been brutally suppressed.

Now the Germans hoped for a rising of the South African Dutch against the British, but South Africa had become a self-governing dominion in 1910, and on 10th August 1914 the last British troops left Cape Town for France, leaving South Africa, under the general cover of British seapower, to handle her own defence. A small South African force took Lüderitz Bay, but then a rising of some 11,000 pro-German South Africans brought operations to a standstill until the end of January 1915. After that Swakopmund was quickly occupied. Windhoek fell on 12th May 1915, and on 6th July the German commander capitulated, freeing South African forces for German East Africa and for France.

Of the scattered islands and harbours of the Pacific, the second area where her belated colonial activity had taken her, Germany held the Marianas Islands, the Marshall Islands, the Caroline Islands with Yap and Truk, the Palau Islands, the Bismarck Archipelago with Rabaul, the eastern half of New Guinea with Port Moresby, and Samoa—names familiar in the Second World War as the scenes of battles between American and Japanese fast carrier groups, amphibious forces, and island bases—and, on the Chinese mainland, a concession on the Shantung peninsula, Kiaochow Bay, with the port of Tsingtao. Such strategic value as these had was, in 1914, as potential lying-up places for raiders and as bargaining counters in peace negotiations.

At the outbreak of war, small Australian and New Zealand forces took German New Guinea and Samoa, while the Royal Navy destroyed the wireless stations at Yap and Nauru. On 23rd August 1914 Japan declared war on Germany and occupied the Palaus, Carolines, and Marshalls, then, early in September, landed a division, to which one British and one Indian battalion was attached, to take Tsingtao. On 31st October Japanese 11-inch howitzers began to bombard the recently completed fortifications, and on the night of the 6th November the infantry assault went in with the determination that characterized the Japanese in a later war. Early next morning the Germans surrendered.

Back in London, in 1914 at the turn of the year, the choices still lay open which, wisely taken, could shape the war. On Boxing Day Hankey submitted a long and able paper to the war council. It began: 'The remarkable deadlock which has occurred in the western theatre of war invites consideration of the question whether some other outlet can be found for the employment of the greater forces of which we shall be able to dispose in a few months' time.' It suggested the development of new armoured devices to overcome the siege warfare conditions of the Western Front, and went on to recommend the use of British seapower to open a new flank or front. Discarding attack on the German coast as requiring the violation of Dutch and Danish neutrality, Hankey turned to the Mediterranean to suggest that an attack on Turkey, or through the Balkans on Austria-Hungary should be considered, and to the German overseas empire, already, as we have seen, being taken over.

Almost simultaneously, on New Year's Day, Lloyd George, chancellor of the exchequer and a member of the war council, circulated a memorandum, which reasoned similarly. He suggested either an attack on Austria-Hungary in conjunction with the Greeks and Rumanians, who might be rallied to the Allied cause, and Serbia, or an attack on Turkey by a landing in Syria after the Turks had got themselves involved in Sinai. 'Unless we are prepared for some project of this character, I frankly despair of our achieving any success in this war,' he wrote. 'Germany and Austria have between them 3,000,000 young men quite as well trained as the men of the Kitchener Armies, ready to take the place of the men now in the trenches when these fall.'

Winston Churchill, first lord of the Admiralty, had during the autumn conferred with Sir John French on the possibility of an amphibious operation against the German northern flank. On 29th December he wrote to Asquith, the prime minister: 'I think it is quite possible that neither side will have the strength to penetrate the other's lines in the Western theatre . . . although no doubt several hundred thousand men will be spent to satisfy the military mind on that point.' He still mentioned the Admiralty's pre-war plan to seize islands off the German coast and open the Baltic, but his mind was turning to the Dardanelles. Admiral Lord Fisher, first sea lord, still thought of the Baltic, but the reality of war and its risks were beginning to make him cautious.

Kitchener, who had for some time been sounding French, wrote to him on 2nd January that if the French army could not break the German front, 'then the German lines in France may be looked upon as a fortress that cannot be carried by assault, and also cannot be completely invested—with the result that the lines can only be held by an investing force, while operations proceed elsewhere'. Sir John replied, claiming that, given more guns, more shells and, of course, more men, the Germans could be beaten in France in 1915. At this juncture a message came from the British ambassador in Petrograd forwarding an urgent appeal from Grand Duke Nicholas for a naval or military demonstration to relieve Turkish pressure in the Caucasus.

The War Council met under Asquith on the 7th and 8th January to consider the situation. Sir John's project for an attack along the Flanders coast met a chilly reception, but it was agreed that he should be allowed to continue his preparations and be sent additional divisions, subject to final approval for the attack itself. Consequently when, on the second day, the council turned to the situation in the eastern Mediterranean, Kitchener had to inform it that the Anzacs in Egypt were not yet trained and he had nothing available for any action there. As the council, stale from two days discussion, contemplated this unwelcome information, Churchill introduced the idea of a naval attack on the Dardanelles, which would require no considerable military force, and could be easily abandoned if it did not succeed.

The idea caught on, and it was finally agreed that in addition to French's offensive in Flanders, preparations should be made for a naval expedition in February 'to bombard and take the Gallipoli peninsula, with Constantinople as its objective'. A final proviso said that 'if the position in the western theatre becomes in the spring a stalemate, British troops should be despatched to another theatre and objective'.

The sentence of death

This, although it perhaps reads like an attempt to please everyone, was at this stage sound enough, calling as it did for full investigation of two of the proposed operations, and leaving the way open for others. In 1915, however, nothing comparable to the chiefs-of-staff committee and joint planning staff of the Second World War existed, and the necessary staff studies and reference back for considered decision were not undertaken. Kitchener, with whom Churchill continued to confer, and Fisher, who after momentarily backing the Dardanelles increasingly gave way to rather senile fits of temperament, would by later standards have been responsible for this neglect, but both had spent their lives in the days of arbitrary decision by senior officers and no argument.

So the protagonists pursued their separate projects, and Churchill was able to push through the ill-fated naval attack on the Dardanelles.

The Balkan project put forward by Lloyd George found, rather surprisingly, influential support in France. By coincidence Galliéni had on 1st January made a similar proposal to M.Briand, the war minister, and M.Viviani, the premier. 'One cannot break through on the Western Front,' he said; 'therefore we must find another way.' Joffre, who on 20th December had begun another attack which was to cost him 90,000 casualties to little advantage, had supported French against Kitchener. When Galliéni's proposal was referred to him, he said it was unsound and refused to part with divisions for it. Two were, however, scraped up, and sent to take part in the Gallipoli expedition, and later others were found to form with the British the Army of the East under the French General Sarrail. On 5th October 1915, one British and one French division landed by secret agreement with the Greek prime minister, Venizelos, at Salonika—a Greek port recently acquired from Turkey in the Balkan Wars—to go up the Vardar valley to Serbia. By then Bulgaria was mobilizing against Serbia, King Constantine of the Hellenes was ready to dismiss Venizelos, and the chance to rally the Balkans to the Allies, if it ever existed, had passed.

French's offensive, meanwhile, began in March; as might have been expected, it had little result other than to create new and higher piles of bodies between the trenches, at greater and greater cost.

At the beginning of 1915 Germany, too, faced an east versus west decision. In September 1914, when it became clear that the battle of the Marne was lost, General Falkenhayn, minister for war, was called by the Kaiser to take Moltke's place as chief of general staff, retaining his old appointment as well. Realizing, after the battles of November, more clearly than the French and British generals opposed to him, that the war had become static, he gave orders to husband German strength by the systematic application of trench warfare methods, by intensifying the manufacture of guns, machine-guns, and ammunition, and by improving railways by which reserves could be quickly moved where required. By these means, and by raising four new corps with experienced cadres, he planned to have available in the spring of 1915 a powerful central reserve, to strike a concentrated, decisive blow in the west.

Ludendorff v. Falkenhayn

Like the Allied statesmen, however, the German chancellor and foreign minister called for action in the east, where they were working to bring Bulgaria, Rumania, and Italy into the war on their side. Rather desperately the Austrians supported them. Conrad von Hötzendorf telegraphed Falkenhayn on 27th December: 'Complete success in the eastern theatre is still, as hitherto, decisive for the general situation and extremely urgent.'

The German general staff was quite capable of turning a deaf ear to the chancellor and Conrad, but now Falkenhayn was faced with a powerful opponent within his own military system. On the favoured Western Front the events of 1914 had been indecisive and bitterly disappointing, but in the east, starved of means, Hindenburg and Ludendorff had won a series of spectacular victories. They now confronted Falkenhayn with the proposition that the war could be won in the east, if a great new effort were made, but not in the west, and demanded that he send them the central reserve. On New Year's Day Falkenhayn, Conrad, and Ludendorff met in Berlin, and Falkenhayn gave his decision for the west. Hindenburg then approached the chancellor asking for Falkenhayn's removal. On the 4th Conrad, hearing that Italy was about to join the Allies, telegraphed Falkenhayn and Hindenburg for German divisions. Falkenhayn refused them, only to find that Hindenburg, without consulting him, had promised them to the Austrians.

As chief of general staff and minister for war, Falkenhayn was Hindenburg's superior, and this was defiance, but the prestige of the Hindenburg-Ludendorff combination was far too high for them to be dismissed. It had to go to the Kaiser, and he decided for the east, but kept on Falkenhayn. So in 1915 the Germans would defend in the west, and attack in the east with disastrous results for the Allies.

The Sea-raiders

Until at least the 1890's, as an Englishman once said to Grand Admiral von Tirpitz, Germany 'was not a sea-going nation'. Plans for a navy, inspired as much by nationalism as by strategic needs, stagnated in disputes between the competing authorities, the admiralty, executive command, and the naval cabinet, between the Kaiser and the general staff. Even after Tirpitz gained the Kaiser's favour in 1892 and began to create the nucleus of the German navy, there remained the dilemma of what sort of force it should be. Was there to be a High Seas Fleet to wear down Great Britain (because there was never any doubt of the ultimate naval enemy) from a strong centralized position as Great Britain herself had done in the Napoleonic Wars? Or should they build fast cruisers, like 18th-century privateers, to destroy the enemy's trade and distract their main fleet as well?

German naval authorities argued about this crucial decision for ten years after 1895 —the year in which Tirpitz resigned because his battle fleet was being subordinated to the political arguments for cruiser warfare. Colonial ambition was proving a strong argument in favour of a far seas strategy. Not only were the new fast cruisers to fly the German flag in every port of the world, reinforcing pro-German sympathies in South America, Africa, and Asia, but they provided the defence of the scattered islands and territories proudly called the German 'empire'. Frequently they were the reason for acquiring them: Tirpitz himself negotiated the acquisition of the last of the treaty ports in China, Tsingtao, as a base for the East Asia Squadron.

The primacy given to cruiser warfare faded after Tirpitz returned. The second Navy Bill of 1900 outlined the need for a strong home fleet. But as a *quid pro quo* to the cruiser strategists, it also attempted to define an important role for the warships in the far seas: 'to represent the German navy abroad . . . and to gather fruits which have ripened as a result of the naval strength of the Reich embodied in the Home Battle Fleet'.

Until 1910 this policy backed a programme of building fast, well-armed cruisers and light cruisers, capable of from 24 to 27 knots and fitted with 4.1-inch and 6-inch guns which were, at that date, the most accurate for their size in the world. When, under the pressure of the race to build larger and larger capital ships, the emphasis changed, and all new cruisers

were kept for the battle fleet, it was the cruisers of the period 1905-10 which were assigned to foreign stations. They were superior both in speed and gunnery to the equivalent British ships, although this was not obvious to either side before hostilities began. They were intended, however, not for direct action against warships, but to draw away vital units from the British Grand Fleet and leave the North Sea open to a blow from the German North Sea Fleet.

British strategy did not rely on a counterpart to the German cruisers. It was hard enough to get money to build battleships— even the dreadnoughts—and only enough new cruisers were laid down for home waters. This left a fair number of County Class cruisers, built in a period of bad naval design between 1895 and 1905, too costly to scrap, whose failings in speed and armaments were not shown until they were actually under fire. To make up these deficiencies, and to guard her immensely long trade routes and communications, Great Britain relied on the alliance with Japan— whose fleet could blockade Tsingtao, Germany's only effective Asiatic port—and on the combined forces of Australia and New Zealand, which were to neutralize Germany's Pacific colonies. No specific defences were provided for the Indian Ocean, which was felt to be a British preserve.

When war was declared, the main German strength lay in the East Asia Squadron, commanded by Vice-Admiral von Spee, which consisted of the heavy cruisers *Scharnhorst* and *Gneisenau* and three light cruisers *Emden, Leipzig,* and *Nürnberg*. In the Caribbean were two of the fastest light cruisers, *Karlsruhe* and *Dresden,* and in the Indian Ocean, based on German East Africa, *Königsberg*. In the Mediterranean there was *Goeben,* one of the finest battle-cruisers in the German navy, and *Breslau*. Finally, mainly in American or German ports, there were the great liners of the passenger fleet, ships of over 20,000 tons, capable of 25 knots, fitted with gun mountings, waiting for the signal to rendezvous with warships and collect their armaments.

The Allied defences appeared far greater on paper than they were in practice because of the immense distances to be covered. Eastern command was based in Hong Kong and Singapore and combined with the small, but modern, Australian fleet. The North Pacific was left to the Japanese; three cruiser squadrons and one French squadron defended the Atlantic; two obsolete squadrons in the Indian Ocean

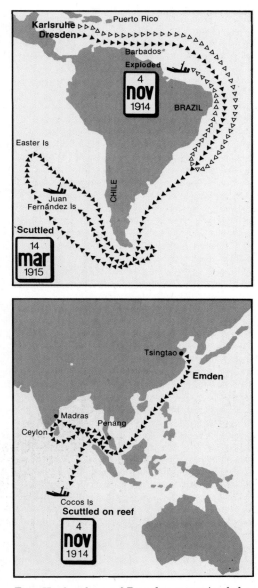

Top: Karlsruhe and Dresden *terrorized the coast of Brazil. When Spee summoned* Dresden *to meet him in the Pacific,* Karlsruhe *turned north. She was making for the rich British colony of Barbados, when, unaccountably, she blew up.*
Above: Emden *wrought havoc in the Indian Ocean, once regarded as a British preserve. She sailed from Tsingtao through the Sumatra channel, sank nine ships, bombarded Madras, sank another ten ships near Ceylon, sailed into Penang harbour to sink more ships. Eventually, chased by* Sydney, *her captain ran her aground off the Cocos Islands.*
Left: The Emden *ablaze*

completed the preparations in the far seas. Churchill, the first lord of the Admiralty, and his staff were aware that the line was thin—they did not realize how severely it was to be tested.

Impressive initial successes

Immediately after the declaration of war, Germany chalked up an impressive list of successes. *Goeben* bombarded the French bases of Bône and Philippeville in North Africa and, with bewildering speed, evaded the French and British fleets in the Mediterranean. She succeeded in reaching Constantinople where she was sold to the ostensibly neutral Turkish government. The persuasive force of her presence in Constantinople and, even more, the intrigues of her powerful commander Admiral Souchon, helped materially to bring Turkey into the war on the side of Germany in the autumn of 1914. Meanwhile, in early August, *Königsberg* sank the *City of Winchester* with most of the Ceylon tea crop on board, off the coast of Aden, and threatened the safety of the Suez route to India. Two armed liners escaped through the North Sea and another, *Kronprinz Wilhelm,* ran the blockade of the American ports, while *Karlsruhe* sank her first merchant ship in the Caribbean.

Before the British Admiralty had time to react to these threats, the necessities of the war on the Western Front made the job more difficult. After the retreat from Mons the demand for more power rose dramatically. As the front extended itself from the Channel to Verdun, Kitchener, the secretary of state for war, summoned the reserves, subordinating the Admiralty's other plans in order to escort home the vital battalions of the British army in India. Added to this were the divisions from Australia and New Zealand which, with *Königsberg* at large, would need to be escorted at least through the Red Sea. For weeks half the far seas squadrons were diverted from chasing the German cruisers

But what might have been a great opportunity for the raiders was lost. One of the decisive battles of the war, the minor engagement in the North Sea off Heligoland on 28th August, in which the Germans lost three light cruisers, so disturbed the Kaiser that he shrank from endangering his cherished fleet again. A defensive strategy took the place of that worked out before 1914; a defective one as far as cruiser warfare was concerned. Instead of ordering immediate strikes at vulnerable points, German planning took account of the imminent loss of her Pacific bases, Samoa, Nauru, New Guinea, and Tsingtao, and the difficulties of supplying and coaling

The Königsberg, *which was to prove her superior speed and guns in the Indian Ocean*

the raiders, rather than of their immense potential. Tirpitz wanted to order Spee home, but such was the atmosphere in Berlin that no orders were sent at all: Pohl, the chief of naval staff, said: 'it is impossible to tell from here whether the squadron will be able to choose against whom it will deal its dying blows'. Within a month of hostilities, the German admiralty had entirely abandoned the preparation of years, the network of colliers and supply ships, communications, and neutral sympathizers. The successes of the raiders in the autumn were obtained without even moral support from home.

The raiders harried two main areas, both vital to the British war effort: the mid-Atlantic and the Indian Ocean. The most vital British interests in August were the troop convoys from India through the Suez Canal. None of these were safe until the whereabouts of *Königsberg* were known. But Captain Looff and his ship had disappeared; he had gone back to German East Africa and did not emerge until 20th September when at dawn he attacked the quiet harbour of Zanzibar, shelled the port, and sank the British light cruiser *Pegasus*. In these anxious months, the calm of the waters between Australia and India, so long a British preserve, was shattered by the foremost raider of all, *Emden*.

'There are great prizes to be won'
Admiral von Spee had left Tsingtao on manoeuvres before war broke out and he was soon deprived of his base by the Japanese blockade. He foresaw the dilemma of his squadron: that if he stayed in the Pacific he must ultimately run out of coal or be destroyed by the Singapore and Japanese squadrons. Instead, he chose to sail round Cape Horn, break through the Atlantic defences, and run for home through the North Sea. But Karl von Müller, captain of *Emden,* asked permission to raid in the Indian Ocean. Spee wrote: 'A single light cruiser can coal from captured vessels and maintain herself for longer . . . as there are great prizes to be won there, I despatched the fastest light cruiser.'

Heavily disguised, with a false funnel, *Emden* crept through the Sumatra channel and began her raiding career on 7th September by sinking nine ships in a week. When the news reached London it produced consternation and a steep rise in insurance rates; and Australia and New Zealand demanded a strong escort for the Anzac troop convoy. Nothing could be given because of the war office priority for the Indian convoys endangered by *Königsberg*. On 21st September Müller carried the war on to enemy territory and bombarded the city of Madras by night, setting fire to the great oil tanks and, by the light of the blaze, destroying the harbour installations. He

then turned south and in the seas around Ceylon, impudently within range of the defences of Colombo, captured or sunk another ten merchant ships. Loss of confidence and prestige caused bitter questions—what was the Admiralty doing? Australia and New Zealand bluntly postponed the convoy for three weeks.

Emden did not strike again until mid-October—just when the convoy, with an escort, was ready, and at a time when the war in South Africa against the German-backed rebels under Christian de Wet was at its most dangerous. Several more sinkings preceded one of the boldest strokes of the war: Müller sailed into the harbour of Penang on the Malay peninsula and sank the Russian light cruiser *Zhemchug* and a French destroyer. Combined with the steady toll taken in the Atlantic by *Karlsruhe* and the armed liners, and Spee's attack on the French colony of Tahiti, the raiders were achieving their object of distracting the enemy. By the end of October they had captured or sunk more than forty Allied ships.

Karlsruhe alone had accounted for nearly 100,000 tons of shipping. She had nearly been caught by Admiral Cradock's squadron in the Caribbean in early August, but she refuelled from the armed liner *Kronprinz Wilhelm* and escaped to Puerto Rico with almost empty bunkers. But thereafter Captain Kohler could easily evade pursuit in his 27½-knot ship, as Cradock wearily traversed the mid-Atlantic. In concert with *Dresden* during August and September, the two raiders terrorized the waters off the coast of Brazil where all the trade routes to South America converged. They held up cargoes of frozen meat in Argentine ports and gave a strong stimulus to pro-German feeling among neutral Latin American countries.

Then Spee summoned *Dresden* to meet him in the Pacific, luring Cradock south and leaving the West Indies open to *Karlsruhe* —a chance which Kohler did not miss. He drew his information about the sailings of merchant vessels from German intelligence in Brazil, the Argentine, and Chile, and waited for them to arrive. Working with *Kronprinz Wilhelm* he sank twenty ships in late September, taking what he needed from their cargoes.

The extent of this damage was only realized when he landed 400 prisoners, and the pursuit was not fully organized until 14th October, when Admiral Stoddart was given overall command of the mid- and North Atlantic and the modern cruiser *Defence*. But Kohler was warned in advance; he sank two more rich cargoes and turned north, planning a spectacular blow to Allied morale in the heart of the West Indies, by destroying Barbados and Fort de France in Martinique.

So far, the only British successes had been the sinking of two armed liners, *Kaiser Wilhelm der Grosse* on the African coast, and *Cap Trafalgar* (by another armed liner, the Cunard *Carmania*) which disrupted supplies of coal to *Karlsruhe*. In the Pacific, all the German bases had been captured by combined operations with the dominions and Japanese. But the main danger was the unknown, powerful squadron of Spee, of which Admiral Cradock, now commanding the South Atlantic, was more aware than the British Admiralty. No one could know that Spee had decided to bring his ships home, if possible, intact. If he passed Cape Horn, Cradock reasoned, he could attack Capetown or even cross to head off the Anzac convoy. It was this which led him, at loggerheads with the Admiralty, to seek out Spee on the Pacific coast—and to the disastrous battle of Coronel. The first British naval engagement for a century ended on 1st November in almost total disaster for the British.

At once the strategic picture changed. Spee must be destroyed. Two battle-cruisers were withdrawn from Jellicoe's Grand Fleet and despatched with such urgency that the fitters were left on board. A great concentration took place off the Brazilian coast and a net of steel was stretched on either side of Cape Horn. The Japanese and Australian fleets cut off the retreat to the Pacific. The urgency of the war in Europe was at last transferred to the far seas and finally ended the careers of the raiders: only as a result of a major humiliation was Pohl's gloomy prophecy fulfilled.

End of the 'Swan of the East'
After two months of unparalleled havoc in the Indian Ocean, pursued by the game but ineffective Captain Grant in *Yarmouth*, *Emden*'s luck changed. Müller decided to attack the wireless station in the Cocos Islands to cut the trunk cables to Australia and South Africa, and ran straight into the path of the Anzac convoy which, heavily escorted, had at last left Perth. HMAS *Sydney,* under Captain Glossop, was detached in pursuit, and after a long running battle, Müller ran the ruined shell of *Emden,* the 'Swan of the East', on the coral reefs of the Cocos Islands. He was taken prisoner and, in unusual recognition, allowed to keep his sword.

Captain Kohler was meanwhile steaming towards Barbados. With all the Atlantic warships to the south, nothing could have saved the unsuspecting colony, but on a clear day, for no known reason, *Karlsruhe* suddenly exploded and was torn in two, sinking at once with the loss of her captain and most of the crew. It was ironic that, on the same day, the German admiralty cabled: 'Return home, your work is done.'

The Shock of Arms

The end of a glorious career — Emden, the 'Swan of the East', now a battered shell, on the coral reefs off the Cocos Islands

The danger of armed liners was also largely over. They had been, at best, an extravagant form of raider, fast but requiring immense quantities of coal. An organization for supplying them existed, run by Captain Boy-Ed of the German embassy in Washington, but the British warships waiting outside US territorial waters were too great a deterrent and the majority were interned. Only *Kronprinz Wilhelm* had a successful raiding career, sinking in six months some 60,000 tons of shipping. But although her speed was 25 knots she had to spend valuable weeks coaling at sea from captured colliers and, after November, was largely disregarded by the British forces concentrating on the threat at Cape Horn.

On 9th December came the news of the battle of the Falkland Islands in which Admiral Sturdee destroyed the whole of Spee's squadron except the raider *Dresden*. This was, practically speaking, the end of the war in the far seas. *Dresden* escaped along the myriad inlets of the Chilean coast but remained a hunted vagrant, finally tracked down and scuttled at Juan Fernández. The German colliers still slipped out from Brazilian ports to supply *Kronprinz Wilhelm* and another armed liner, *Prinz Eitel Friedrich,* which had escaped before the battle of the Falklands. Between them they took eighteen merchant ships during the winter but in March, for lack of coal, unable to undertake the long voyage home, they both ran in to Newport harbour in the United States and were interned. Six months later the recall of Captain Boy-Ed was demanded by the American government. His activities probably did more to swing American opinion against Germany than to create any lasting advantage for German seapower.

Königsberg alone remained. After the successful raid on Zanzibar Captain Looff had returned to his secret base, charted before the war, in the intricate muddy channels of the Rufiji river in German East Africa

where he was tracked down and bottled in by a strong British squadron commanded by Captain Drury-Lowe. But *Königsberg* was out of range and hidden behind the forests and mangrove swamps, while her men were entrenched in efficient land defences. Supplies reached them from the interior. One of the channels was blocked by sinking an old collier, but others were open: *Königsberg* posed a unique problem and tied down three modern cruisers.

Primitive aircraft brought by ship from Capetown were able to locate her, but tropical rain and heat made them unusable. Both sides settled down to stalemate and nothing happened until March, when the German admiralty sent the collier *Rubens* to refuel the raider and give Looff the chance to break for the open sea and return home. After circling the north of Scotland and running down past the Cape, *Rubens* was sunk within a day's sail of the Rufiji. Looff sent half his men inland to help General von Lettow-Vorbeck in the war on Lake Tanganyika and abandoned hope of escaping. But *Königsberg* was still indestructible. More aircraft were sent out, and finally two monitors — flat gun emplacements, drawing only five feet of water. In the first air-sea operation ever mounted they steamed up river, firing indirectly at *Königsberg*, the fall of shot spotted from the air. At the first attack they were withdrawn, severely damaged. But the Germans were short of ammunition and the next assault, a week later, succeeded. The last of the German raiders was left, a riddled hulk on a mosquito-plagued shore, nearly a year after the start of the war.

The daring of the privateers

The raiders inherited the tradition of 18th-century privateers. Their orders debarred them from attacking warships except in emergency. German planning of bases, supplies of coal, and repairs was as efficient as the scattered nature of her colonies and the benevolence of neutrals

would allow. But because of reverses in Europe, there was no subsequent strategy except, at the end, the order for recall. Yet, in the North Sea, few of the raiders would have had a use comparable to their value abroad. Events called in question the whole conception of far seas strategy. The German cruisers were superior in speed and gunnery to their British counterparts. *Karlsruhe* could have taken on Cradock's whole squadron and escaped — and if Spee, instead of turning away to preserve his ships had sailed straight into Port Stanley itself, he would have caught a fleet half at anchor, and sunk or severely damaged some of the best units in the British fleet, 6,000 miles from a British port. The German admiralty seems to have been dominated by calculations of sheer number. If the staff really believed the cruisers were doomed, they could have sent them down in crippling attacks on troop convoys or even harbours like Hong Kong. The courage and dash came from the raiders themselves, Müller and Kohler, not Berlin.

The war of movement took both sides by surprise. The effectiveness of the raiders, the daring of *Emden* and *Karlsruhe,* had not been foreseen. The needs of the army in Flanders overrode naval advice and it took Coronel to galvanize the British defences. Then the truth became clear: surface raiders had only a limited life. Submarines, two years later, were needed to bring Great Britain to the edge of starvation.

But the raiders meant something more. They pointed the contrast between war in the far seas and the struggles on the Western Front and the stagnation of embittered fleets facing each other across the North Sea. The raiders hit the headlines and the imagination. The gamekeeper's pursuit of the poacher did not. To German soldiers in Europe and in the snowbound trenches of the Russian Front the names of *Emden, Karlsruhe, Dresden,* and *Königsberg* brought pride and, above all, hope for the future, as operations contracted, grimly, to the war of attrition.

Revenge at Sea

At the outbreak of war, the German East Asia Squadron under Vice-Admiral Graf Maximilian von Spee had been widely dispersed; but by 12th October all the most powerful ships, the *Scharnhorst, Gneisenau, Nürnberg* and *Leipzig* were gathered at Easter Island where they were joined by the light cruiser *Dresden,* which brought news of the British reaction to Spee's exploits to date, and thus gave him some idea of the forces being ranged against him.

These did not amount to much. If what *Dresden*'s captain told Spee was correct, the only British ships west of Cape Horn were the old armoured cruiser *Monmouth,* the modern light cruiser *Glasgow,* and the armed merchantman *Otranto,* while just east of the Horn at the British coaling base at Port Stanley on the Falkland Islands, the admiral commanding this tatterdemalion collection of ships, Vice-Admiral Sir Christopher Cradock, waited—presumably for more effective reinforcement—in the armoured cruiser *Good Hope.*

If this were all the naval opposition ranged for the moment against him, there was obviously no point in further delay; Spee coaled his squadron from colliers carefully collected beforehand at Easter Island, and on 18th October left—first for Más Afuera and then for the Chilean coast. He and his ships were forty miles off Valparaiso late on the afternoon of 30th October, and the following evening he learned that the British light cruiser *Glasgow* was at Coronel, 250 miles to the south.

Detaching *Nürnberg* to pick up mail in Valparaiso, Spee took his squadron south in order to cut off the British cruiser, and perhaps to meet other British ships in company. By 1600 on Sunday, 1st November 1914, his ships were off Coronel, and at 1625 his lookouts sighted two ships away to the south-west; they were *Glasgow* and *Monmouth* and shortly afterwards these two were joined by *Good Hope* flying the flag of Admiral Cradock, and the armed merchantman *Otranto.* The two forces had found each other at last, and the first battle began in which ships of the German navy were ranged in line of battle against ships of the Royal Navy.

Everything favoured the German ships.

By 1800 the two battle lines were formed, and briefly there did appear some small advantage for the British: the setting sun was behind them, blinding the German gunners but lighting up the German ships into perfect targets. But the range was not

close enough for the out-dated British guns, so at 1804 Cradock turned his ships four points towards his enemy—who with superior speed and room to manoeuvre turned away and kept out of range. Grimly, the British re-formed their battle line and assessed the odds against them—now shown up with ominous clarity; *Scharnhorst* and *Gneisenau* riding powerfully over the seas, the details of their high-placed heavy armament picked out by the westering sun, the seas racing along the towering sides and occasionally sweeping the foredecks.

Behind them came the light cruisers *Leipzig* and *Dresden,* and radio signals warned that *Nürnberg* was coming down fast from the north—but most fatal of all for the British, evening slowly crept over the sea from the east and touched the German battleline, greying it into the sea and the sky beyond. As twilight thickened, the moon came up behind heavy clouds, to show fleetingly through them, briefly outlining the German ships—and at last it seemed that *Scharnhorst* and *Gneisenau* were closing in. To the west, the afterglow of the sun made a fiery, yellow-shot tapestry of the windswept sky, against which the British ships now stood out in black, hard-edged clarity; nothing would help them tonight but their courage and the long tradition of the Royal Navy.

The massacre begins

At 1904 on Sunday, 1st November 1914, the 8·2-inch guns of the German East Asia Squadron at last opened fire on the British ships, at a range of 12,000 yards.

From the bridge of *Glasgow* were seen two lines of orange flashes from *Scharnhorst* and *Gneisenau,* and as the thunder of *Good Hope*'s 9·2s answered, grey-white mushrooms blossomed from the sea 500 yards short of the British ships, beautifully aimed, beautifully grouped.

Glasgow's pair of modern 6-inch guns fired experimentally into the darkness, but even while the gun controller was vainly searching the east for fall of shot, the orange lines sparkled again and then again—lengthened now as *Leipzig* and *Dresden* opened fire. Shell splinters whined shrilly overhead, the seas erupted around the British ships, *Monmouth* steamed ahead through a forest of water and *Good Hope*'s foredeck exploded in a sheet of flame which twisted the forward 9·2-inch gun into a hopeless knot of steel protruding from a turret like a blazing cauldron, and abruptly halved the British chance of

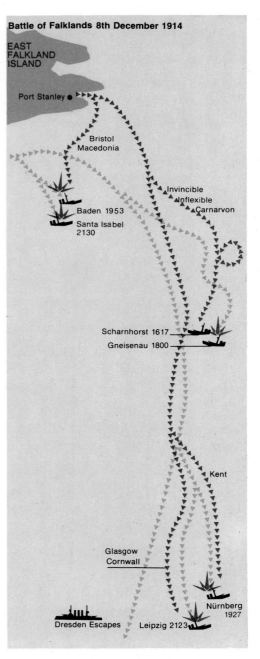

The battle of the Falkland Islands, showing when the German ships sank. *Baden and* Santa Isabel *were supply ships mopped up during the battle*

harming the enemy at anything but short range. Before the mind could react, the next salvo arrived.

Monmouth's foredeck flared in hard-edged flame and black smoke billowed from sudden, sharp fires along her starboard side; *Good Hope*'s deck amidships threw up a fan of sparks, her upper bridge, masthead, and foretop glowed redly as *Scharnhorst*'s high-explosive burst between them, and as the glow faded cordite flared on the deck, and stacked ammunition exploded whitely along the gun-flats.

Intent on closing the range and thus bringing his secondary armament into action, Cradock now led the British ships directly towards the German line — but Spee expertly held the range to his own advantage so that his ships remained unscathed while Cradock's took a dreadful punishment. *Monmouth*, especially, received the full attention of the guns of the *Gneisenau* — which had won the Kaiser's Gold Cup only months before — and began slowly to sag out of line as though beaten away by sheer weight of metal. Flames belched from her quarterdeck, water flooded through gaping holes in her bows, she listed badly to port and as darkness increased she disappeared to the south and her guns lapsed into silence.

Except for the endless flashes from their batteries, the German ships were now quite invisible from the British decks. Not so *Good Hope*; she flared like a beacon.

Since action had commenced the British flagship had received the undivided attention of the gunners aboard *Scharnhorst*, who were to prove as efficient as their colleagues aboard *Gneisenau*. At 1940, *Good Hope* was seen to slow and stagger under the rain of blows; her foredeck was ablaze, clouds of steam and smoke billowed around her, glowing sullenly, and her ports glowed redly from the fires in her crowded flats.

Then at 1942, as if in contempt for her own condition, *Good Hope* seemed to gather up her remaining strength, turn directly towards her antagonists and charge them. Abruptly, *Scharnhorst* and *Gneisenau* changed course slightly and shortened range to bring their full broadsides to bear — and, blanketed under a dreadful fire, *Good Hope* was at last brought to a halt and her last desperate throw defeated.

As though stunned, she drifted down silently between the lines.

Then the fires reached a main magazine and at 1953 — fifty minutes after the first salvo had been fired at her — *Good Hope* was shattered by an explosion which still lives in the memories of those who witnessed it. A broad column of flame rose upwards from between her main and after funnels until it towered two hundred feet above her decks, and in its awful light jagged and incongruous shapes soared up

and away into the darkness, twisting and weaving in the blast, tumbling in the sudden vacuums.

Then the waves took the blazing hulk farther off into the darkness, the flames dwindled and all that now remained of Cradock and his men drifted out of the battle. This was virtually the end of the battle of Coronel. *Otranto* had already left the battleline — ordered away by Cradock — and now *Glasgow*, after a vain attempt to succour *Monmouth*, fled to the south. At 2035, *Nürnberg* found *Monmouth* painfully making her way towards the Chilean coast and as the British ship made no attempt to strike her colours, had little choice but to reopen the action and finally sink her. At 2058 the waves finally closed over the stern of the British cruiser. There were no survivors — and none from the *Good Hope*, which was never seen again after she drifted from the battle. In two hours the Royal Navy had lost two ships and over 1,000 men and boys.

When the news reached Great Britain, the reaction was immediate and drastic. The first lord of the Admiralty, Winston Churchill, learned of the disaster at 1900 on 4th November, and immediately convened a meeting with the sea lords. As it happened, the position of first sea lord had just been taken over (for the second time) by Lord Fisher, and this doughty old man

Dresden, tracked down, shows the white flag

had no time for half measures — a characteristic which endeared him to Churchill.

Within a week the two battle-cruisers *Invincible* and *Inflexible* (as superior in speed and armament to *Scharnhorst* and *Gneisenau* as the German ships had been to *Good Hope* and *Monmouth*) had sailed from Devonport for the Falkland Islands, and they were joined on their voyage south by the County Class cruisers *Carnarvon*, *Cornwall*, and *Kent*, and the light cruisers *Bristol* and *Glasgow* (hurriedly patched up after her escape from Coronel in the dry dock at Rio). The squadron was under command of Vice-Admiral Sir Frederick Doveton Sturdee, and as it moved farther and farther south — searching all the time for Spee's ships in case they had already come around the Horn — his search line was lengthened every day by the addition of a

host of colliers together with the armed merchantman *Orama*, and eventually by another cruiser, *Macedonia*.

Sturdee's augmented squadron reached the Falkland Islands on 7th December, and he ordered concentration in Port Stanley and the outer bay at Port William for coaling. After their long voyage, some of the ships needed to draw their fires for boiler examination, but *Glasgow* and *Carnarvon* coaled through the night, *Macedonia* patrolled outside the harbour, and at dawn on 8th December the colliers went alongside the battle-cruisers to begin filling their enormous demands for fuel.

To Sturdee, it thus seemed that within ten or twelve hours — twenty-four at the most — his entire squadron would be ready for sea again, to take up the search for the elusive German ships. This, of course, was his great problem, for with the enormous power at his disposal, there could be no doubt as to the outcome of a battle with the East Asia Squadron, once they were sighted. It was a problem rapidly solved.

Shortly after 0830 on the morning after his arrival at Port Stanley — while his capital ships were still coaling and two of his cruisers carrying out boiler examination — Sir Frederick was interrupted while shaving with the news that *Gneisenau* and *Nürnberg* were approaching the island and about twenty miles off, and the smoke from the other ships of Spee's command was visible on the horizon astern of them. It says much for the Vice-Admiral's *sang-froid* that his only comment was the classic 'Then send the men to breakfast'.

Spee's critical error

There is no way of being certain why Spee chose to attack the Falkland Islands, but there is little doubt about the fact that had he ordered an immediate attack on the British squadron as they lay at anchor in the two bays, he could have inflicted on them a defeat of staggering proportions — though probably at the cost of his own ships and certainly at the cost of using up all his remaining ammunition.

Fortunately for Sturdee, however, as soon as the captain of the *Gneisenau* reported the presence of a large number of British warships, Spee issued the order: 'Do not accept action. Concentrate on course east by south. Proceed at full speed.'

In doing so, the German admiral signed his own death-warrant and condemned his squadron to annihilation — though this fact did not become apparent to him or his men until 1000 when, to the dismay and astonishment of the observers aboard *Leipzig*, two pairs of tripod masts — the recognition mark of battle-cruisers were seen above the low-lying spit, proceeding towards Port William harbour.

From the British point of view, every

advantage favoured them. A long summer day stretched ahead, visibility was at its maximum, the sea calm, the sky clear and pale. By 1048 the whole squadron was at sea in a long line stretching eastwards from Port William – *Glasgow* in the lead, *Inflexible* and *Invincible* three miles astern, *Kent* two miles astern of them and *Cornwall* and *Carnarvon* as much again. The squadron's speed was 19 knots, the enemy were some twelve miles ahead and their calculated speed was only 15 knots.

The distance between the two adversaries inexorably lessened and at 1257 *Inflexible* fired the first shot of the battle of the Falkland Islands – at *Leipzig,* the lame duck of the German squadron. The shell fell well short, and only occasional sighting shots were fired during the next thirty minutes; then at 1320, Spee hoisted the signal: 'Light cruisers part company and endeavour to escape.' And the two armoured cruisers bravely turned to accept action from their formidable opponents.

As at Coronel by six o'clock in the evening, the main forces were now ranging broadside against broadside – but this was half past one in the afternoon, there were still eight hours of daylight left, and no mounting seas or storm clouds to complicate the hazards of war. *Invincible* opened fire against *Gneisenau*; *Inflexible* against *Scharnhorst*.

By this time, the British light and County Class cruisers had swung away from the main battle to chase the escaping German light cruisers, and Captain Allen aboard *Kent,* later wrote this description of the scene:

With the sun still shining on them, the German ships looked as if they had been painted for the occasion. They fired as if they had but eight minutes in which to make a record battle-practice score and never have I seen heavy guns fired with such rapidity and yet with such control. Flash after flash travelled down their sides from head to stern, all their six and eight-inch guns firing every salvo.

Of the British battle-cruisers less could be seen as their smoke drifted from them across the range and not only obscured their own view but also the spectator's view of them. Nevertheless, they seemed to be firing incessantly, their shells hitting the German ships at intervals whereas all that could be seen of the German fire was that it straddled the British ships. Four or five times in the first twenty minutes the white puff of bursting shell could be seen among the clouds of brown cordite smoke in Gneisenau, *and she was seen to be on fire near her mainmast, but this soon disappeared.* (By permission of *Naval Review.)*

In addition to the greater weight of broadside and greater range of guns, the battle-cruisers had a further advantage – they were firing, for the first time in a naval battle, lyddite shell, and this new explosive wreaked dreadful havoc aboard the German ships. However Spee might seek to twist and turn, hoping for some sudden squall or mist patch in which to escape, the British battle-cruisers hung grimly on, unhurried but implacable, inexorably smashing his ships to pieces. All through the afternoon the battle continued, and aboard the British ships great admiration was felt for the perfect timing and grouping of the German gunnery, despite the chaos visible on the German decks.

By 1545 clouds of steam gushed upwards from *Scharnhorst*'s decks, the first and second funnels were leaning against each other, an enormous livid rent had been torn in the side-plating below her quarter-deck and she was blazing fore and aft – but still her starboard batteries fired.

Her masts were gone, her bridge was wrecked, her magazines must have been almost empty, but still her ensign fluttered from a jury mast above the after control station. Then suddenly, just before 1600 her batteries ceased fire as though they had been switched off, and she was seen to turn eight points to starboard and come staggering across the seas towards her powerful antagonists. Behind her, *Gneisenau* swung across still firing rapidly, and as *Inflexible* re-engaged the farther ship, *Invincible* turned and headed for Spee's flagship. Less than 10,000 yards separated the two admirals, but it was soon evident that they would never meet, for *Scharnhorst*'s decks were a sea of fire, her speed fell away and she listed badly.

Just before 1610 her list took her deck-rails under, water flooded inboard to quench the flames and she rolled on to her beams end. Through rents in her plating a few figures climbed laboriously and stood on her side-plates watching the battle-cruisers and the cold, impartial sea. Seven minutes later, *Scharnhorst*'s bows suddenly dipped, her stern came up, steam and smoke wreathed about her and with her flag still flying, she slid quickly under water and was gone, leaving only a huge yellow patch on the surface of the sea.

Fifteen minutes later, *Carnarvon* reached the spot and steamed directly through the stained waters. Neither survivors nor wreckage were visible.

By this time, *Invincible* had rejoined *Inflexible* and the two battle-cruisers turned their attention on *Gneisenau*.

The end was now a foregone conclusion, and as Sturdee had no intention of sustaining avoidable damage to either of his ships, he ordered them to stand off and take their time. Thus *Gneisenau*'s agony was protracted for another hour, by which time the destruction aboard beggared description.

Between the masts, her decks were beaten down to the armoured deck, and soon even this was torn open by plummeting shells. Her after-turret was jammed at ninety degrees, all the starboard casemate guns blown into the sea or pounded into shapeless masses of metal. Half her crew were dead or wounded, and shells had ended much suffering by exploding in the sick-bay and in the stokers' bathrooms where an emergency bay had been set up.

Then a shell from *Carnarvon* caused jamming of *Gneisenau*'s helm so that she slowly came round and, almost for the first time, the port batteries could come into action – though there was little enough ammunition left to fire. But there was some – enough to sting the battle-cruisers into re-opening fire and finishing *Gneisenau* as a fighting ship. Just before 1730 she lay almost motionless in the water, listing so badly that the seas flooded inboard through the lower gun ports.

Yet she was not sinking – and in order to ensure that nothing of value would fall into British hands, her captain gave the order for explosive charges between the inner and outer hull skins to be blown, and the stern torpedoes to be fired with the sluice gates left open. At a few minutes to six in the evening, *Gneisenau* seemed to shake herself and come fractionally out of the water; then she lay over at about ten degrees and began to settle. Her crew – what was left of them – gave three cheers for the Kaiser and then clambered across the decks to drop down into the icy waters alongside; and at two minutes after six, *Gneisenau*'s bows came up, keel uppermost, then slid down out of sight, leaving the seas littered with debris and struggling men. Only 187 of these, including seventeen officers but not *Gneisenau*'s captain, were picked up by British boats.

Of the remaining ships of Spee's command, *Nürnberg* was chased, caught, and sunk by *Kent* at 1927, *Leipzig* fought gallantly until 2123, against both *Cornwall* and *Glasgow*; and *Dresden* escaped for the moment. She reached Punta Arenas three days after the battle, passed through the Magellan Straits and played hide and seek with British pursuers until the morning of 14th March 1915, when she was found by *Glasgow* and *Kent* sheltering in Cumberland Bay on Juan Fernández Island.

But there was no battle. Tamely, her captain ran up a white flag, evacuated the crew ashore and then blew up the main magazine – and *Dresden*'s wreck still lies in the bay. After the fire and fury of the two battles, this was something of an anticlimax, but it should be remembered that *Dresden* was not an original member of the East Asia Squadron. Spee's captains all fought to the end, and went down with their ships.

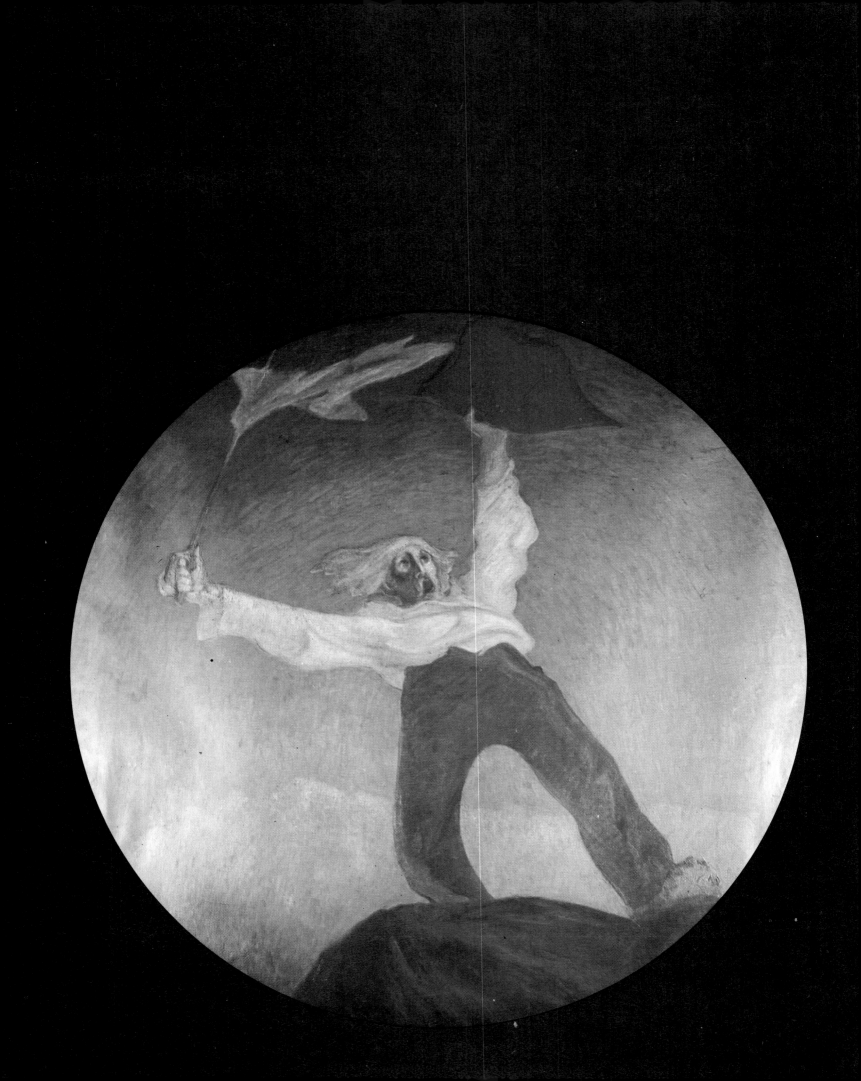

Italy Goes to War

In July 1914 Italy had for thirty years been allied (by the Triple Alliance of 1882) to the central European empires of Austria-Hungary and Germany. Ten months later Italy, forced by circumstances, entered the war against Austria-Hungary. No one in July could have foreseen this.

Italian Nationalists were ever ready to theorize on the inevitability of war, but even after the fatal revolver shots of Sarajevo, they still predicted that there would be a long period of peace for the Habsburg monarchy, troubled though it was by its own domestic problems.

If the Nationalists thought this, there were others who thought so too. On the morning of the 25th July, just after the news broke that Austria-Hungary had delivered her ultimatum to Serbia, there was much excitement among the passengers on the Milan-Venice express. On board the train was the president of the Trento and Trieste Irredentist Association. (Irrendentism was a movement which worked for the union of various Italian-speaking districts, mainly those ruled by Austria-Hungary, with Italy.) In the course of their conversation the president's travelling companion, Giuseppe Volpi, authoritatively declared that 'everything will be settled as usual by an international conference . . . And so, no war? No, certainly not. Europe has other things to think about. . . .'

Volpi was a high financier, a diplomat, and an expert in Balkan affairs. But Claudio Treves, one of the leaders of the Italian Socialist Party, reasoned along nearly the same lines as Volpi. On the eve of the war he placed his hopes for peace in two forces: 'high finance and socialism, the bank and the proletariat'. Above all he pinned his faith on Great Britain, in particular on the diplomacy of Sir Edward Grey, the 'spokesman of capitalist preoccupations'. Treves belonged to the moderate wing of the party; the revolutionaries, however, echoed his words, or else trusted completely in a rebellion of the masses who might be dragged to the slaughter. Luigi Luzzatti, the former prime minister (1910-11), believed that 'the destruction of lives, wealth, culture, civilization, whoever was victorious and whoever was conquered, would debase and debilitate Europe, so benefiting another continent, America, and would provide a pretext for a future Asiatic invasion'. Giovanni Giolitti, the most influential man in Italy, the Liberal 'dictator' of Italian politics, was, in the vital last weeks of July, abroad. He too, right up to

the end, refused to believe that the governments of civilized Europe could fall prey to the folly of war. It took the German ultimatum to Russia and France to make him change his mind. He was afterwards frequently to recall his extremely bitter disappointment at the 'monstrous war'.

In this atmosphere of dismay it was clear that if Italy had to take up a position in favour of one side or the other, she would follow the policy mapped out in the past. Besides, after the Libyan affair, the introduction of universal suffrage, and the bloody disturbances of the 'Red Week', Italian political parties were divided into two great blocks. There were the parties of law and order (in fact, of the 'establishment'): Liberals, Liberal-Conservatives, Catholics, and Nationalists; and there were the popular parties: Radicals, Social Reformists, the Italian Socialist Party (PSI), Republicans, Syndicalists, and Anarchists. This very division strengthened the tendencies of the parties of order (who had a majority in parliament) not to stray from traditional paths in either foreign or domestic policy.

The 'irredentists' and the Triple Alliance

In Trieste itself and in several small towns in Venezia Giulia many Italian irredentists (supporters of the Liberal National party and of Nationalist currents) thought along similar lines. On 29th July 1914 the Italian consul in Trieste reported that 'last night a great procession of Austrian patriotic societies and constitutional elements marched on the consulate, cheering Italy, the war, and the Triple Alliance'. From the end of the 19th century the Italian irredentists had seen Slav pressure grow, politically, economically, socially, and culturally. They could not disregard it. They wanted to become part of Italy; but they were, nevertheless, also willing to fight a war for the Triple Alliance.

When it became certain that there would be a European war the Nationalists, therefore, had few doubts. They wanted Italy to enter the war on the side of Austria-Hungary and Germany. They admired Germany and considered the Habsburg empire a great bulwark against the Slav advance. And they were concerned more about the Mediterranean and the colonies than about the Balkans. The real enemy for them was Italy's 'Latin sister', France, who had usurped the position of a great power, while she was becoming ever weaker on account of her democratic misgovernment.

The Liberals supported the Triple

Top: The right-wing Salandra who committed Italy to her Adriatic war. *Above:* General Cadorna who was to command her army. He favoured a war against the French in a German alliance. Although he undertook war against the Central Powers enthusiastically he was later dismissed for incompetence. *Left:* 'The Intervention', an ironic painting by Aldo Carpi. The red flag of socialism and the white flag of reaction greet Italy's entry into the war against her former partner in the Triple Alliance

Headlines of two Italian socialist papers—November 1914—show the political struggle developing around the defence of neutrality. Benito Mussolini, founder of Italian Fascism, starts his political journey to the extreme right wing by quitting as editor of the socialist Avanti! *(below) and founding the interventionist* Il Popolo d'Italia *(above). In the headline shown above,* Avanti! *attacks its former editor*

Alliance for rather different reasons. The Liberals, who still considered themselves the true 'governing party', prided themselves on being cautious and realistic, and for that very reason were unwilling to break old ties. One could see this simply by reading their mass-circulation newspapers, whether Giolittian or anti-Giolittian, northern or southern. *La Stampa, La Tribuna, Il Giornale d'Italia, Il Mattino,* and *Il Resto del Carlino,* all predicted, or at least admitted, that Italy would intervene on the side of the Central powers. They may have been frightened at the prospect of Great Britain entering the war, but what they feared more was isolation. They regarded the Triple Alliance as a means by which Italy could assert itself. There were some exceptions, but even Luigi Albertini, editor of the *Corriere della Sera,* who regretted the Austrian ultimatum and its result, did not exclude the possibility of Italy entering the war on the side of her ancient allies.

Then there were the Catholics who, for the most part, made the arguments of the Liberals their own. They felt a special sympathy with Austria, the great Catholic state and bulwark against the Orthodox Christian Slavs. Everyone—Nationalists, Liberals, Catholics, at any rate—severely judged the popular parties which, at a moment's notice, organized meetings and demonstrations against the war. The government alone had the right to the last say: the state must be strong and disciplined. Memories of the 'Red Week' lingered on, aggravating the differences between the parties.

The view of the popular parties

Even among the popular parties there were some who, like Arturo Labriola, the tireless spokesman of revolutionary syndicalism, were in favour of Italy's intervention on the side of the Central powers. Some influential Radical parliamentarians were of the same opinion but, on the whole, the popular parties were against war. They revived their past preoccupations: opposition to the Triple Alliance, sympathy for France, distrust for the monarchy, the antimilitarism which had been growing since 1911, internationalism and pacifism. They organized demonstrations and took up again their traditional catchphrases 'against Austrian militarism which had erected gallows and gibbets in Italy'. 'No blood, no money, no complicity with the Habsburgs'. 'Let governments of all Europe set light to the fuse; the explosion will blow them up and them only'. But events took the popular parties by surprise and their various moves were badly coordinated. News from beyond the Alps of the international proletariat's trial of strength (to prevent war) was dishearteningly bad. Moreover, there was bad blood between revolutionaries, Social Reformists, and Radicals. The popular parties, while seeking a decision in favour of neutrality, were already showing their weaknesses.

These party divisions gave the government a fairly free hand, but it did not find it easy to orientate itself. The right-wing Liberal-Conservative, Antonio Salandra, had replaced Giolitti as prime minister in March. Giolitti cabled from Paris in favour of neutrality, but Sidney Sonnino, the old political friend of Salandra, the real leader of the Liberal-Conservative wing, insisted on fighting with Italy's allies. And for his part the chief of general staff, General Cadorna, had on 29th July already taken military measures to strengthen defences against France. Two days later he even suggested to the King that half the Italian army should be transferred to the Rhine to help the Germans. Nevertheless, the government was increasingly favouring the course of neutrality and on 2nd August the Italian government declared itself neutral. Nothing in the Triple Alliance compelled Italy to mobilize, and Austria-Hungary was opposed to any discussion on the 'compensations' foreseen by the treaty. The Italian government therefore reasserted its freedom of action. But there were many alternatives. San Giuliano, the foreign minister, was soon to consider war against Austria, though without excluding other eventualities: 'it suits us to make every effort to maintain good relations for after the war with the allies', he wrote to Salandra on 4th August. Later he confided to his friends, 'The ideal for us would be for Austria to be defeated on one side and France on the other'. Despite everything, the legacy of the Triple Alliance was still strong. And it is here that we have the key to our understanding of the events.

Only a few days after the declaration of neutrality the Nationalists made a *volte face.* They now argued that Italy should enter the war against Austria-Hungary. The leap was certainly enormous. Nevertheless, the Nationalists did not try to disclaim the attitude they had held earlier. They still wanted Italy to become a really great power. But the Central powers, they argued, had left Italy in the lurch, and the Triple Alliance no longer served any purpose. It was better, therefore, to gain supremacy in the Adriatic. Italy had to wage 'her own war', the 'Italian War', and conquer Trento, Trieste, and Dalmatia. Italy had no interests in common with France, Great Britain, or Russia. Her natural alliances were not with these powers; and once the war was over she would have to reconstruct them. Austria-Hungary, the Nationalists thought, should be reduced but should not disappear, Germany would be conquered but still powerful. Some time in the future, Italy would march again hand in hand with the Central powers for the great conflict, which would take place in the Mediterranean.

For the Nationalists in particular, an alliance between Italy and Germany, nations who had come recently into being as unified states at the same time inspired by the same national enthusiasm, obeyed the laws of history.

The Nationalists (Corradini, Federzoni,

Rocco, and others) were few in number, and had only three representatives in parliament (ten if one includes their allies). But they spoke a great deal and got themselves talked about even more. They had the sympathy of many Liberal-Conservatives and Catholics. In order to strengthen their position, they were prepared to come to an agreement even with the interventionists from the popular parties. The Nationalists intended to use them, not to serve them. The war, they thought, would mark the triumph of the authority of true values: tradition, hierarchy, discipline, 'in place of the three false ideals—innovation, equality, and liberty'. The Nationalists, in fact, wanted as always to drag in the other parties of order, and, unfortunately, they met no insuperable obstacles.

The Liberal reaction

The Liberals remained the largest party, but now they seemed unequal to the gravity of the situation. They were split into neutralists and interventionists. Perhaps it was not so much this that mattered but rather that they no longer shared the ideas of the Nationalists, without managing to find any realistic alternatives. Whether neutralists or interventionists, it was on the whole difficult for them to go beyond their programme: to negotiate with

Right: Giolitti, 'the old wizard', who for once misjudged the situation and lost control. Below: Mussolini, arrested after an intervention rally which became a riot

Austria-Hungary (for Trentino and part of Venezia-Giulia) or to declare 'our war'.

The Liberals were also deeply reluctant to abandon completely the July 1914 position. Those who tended to favour war wanted first to discover whether Vienna would concede any of the Italian districts in Austrian possession. Those inclined towards neutrality wanted to be sure that it would not imperil Italy's position. They would stay neutral, but only at a price—which they were prepared to make Austria-Hungary pay. In other words, they were prepared for a purely 'Italian War', one that would not involve them too much with the Entente powers and would not, if possible, mean an irreparable break with

Germany. They had their own views undoubtedly; but it was almost impossible to stand in the way of the Nationalists.

Giolitti, 'the old wizard' of Italian politics, was for once in danger of failing to produce the magic formula to calm the tempest. He was still the head of the majority party, but he brushed aside the advice of friends to bring down the Salandra government. He preferred to influence affairs from the outside. Salandra, prime minister mainly because of Giolitti's support, was a Liberal-Conservative, and an old enemy; but the Liberal-Conservatives in fact were hesitating, inclined towards neutrality, but neutrality 'with profit and with honour'. This almost coincided with Giolitti's policy. With his experience, with his hidden but deep faith in the liberal state, Giolitti tried to study the problem deeply, but he did not this time manage to find a clear-cut solution. All too often he measured events with a pre-war yardstick. He thought, in spite of everything, that the real friction was between Great Britain and Russia in the Dardanelles and in Asia, and that in any case the Entente between Great Britain, France, and Russia was not stable.

In the spring of 1915 *La Stampa,* the great Giolittian newspaper, let it be understood that Italy's real hope for the future would consist in an Anglo-German-Italian agreement. Italy, as long as she could, would have to move between Great Britain and Germany.

Certainly, for the moment at least, it was hard to separate Germany from Austria-Hungary. Giolitti felt that hostility against Austria-Hungary would automatically mean hostility against Germany, and this seemed to him a very strong argument in favour of neutrality. But at moments Giolitti appeared to share the idea that Germany would leave Austria at her hour of need to her own destiny and that Italy could declare war against Austria with Germany's agreement or connivance. Just as in May 1915, one of his followers was later to reveal, Giolitti still hoped that some secret factor would be found which could justify the government's decision—that secret factor being an agreement with Germany at Austria-Hungary's expense. Giolitti considered that Italy was still too weak, and that one had to weigh things carefully before exposing her to war.

In January 1915 Giolitti published a famous letter, in which he declared himself in favour of negotiations with Vienna. Giolitti, as usual, was thinking of Trentino, of part of Venezia-Giulia, of Trieste Free City—all territories he seriously wanted to obtain. 'If the war ends without our gaining any advantage there will be trouble. Even present neutralists will throw stones,' he confided to his friends.

Giolitti was a relative neutralist; and so, in the main, were the business community and the organized Catholics. So too was the Holy See, which took it for granted that Italy should obtain part of the unredeemed territory from Austria—otherwise intervention was inevitable. Such was the predominant mood in Italy.

The popular parties and intervention

No serious guarantee of neutrality was possible. The PSI, a number of Syndicalists, and Anarchists tried to ensure it, but in vain. The masses, in particular the large peasant masses, were calm. As many Prefects reported, they were quite resigned. In the event of intervention against Austria-Hungary, there would be no serious disorders.

The defence of neutrality did not allow any effective political initiative. Many revolutionaries (Socialists, Republicans, Anarchists, and Syndicalists) were soon convinced of this. Benito Mussolini, editor of the Socialist newspaper *Avanti!,* was one of these.

Those of the revolutionaries who favoured intervention on the side of the Entente powers considered that, from the beginning, the government's position of neutrality had been equivocal. The parties of order, they thought, were beating about the bush, were still aiming at some kind of compromise with the feudal authoritarian Central powers. The revolutionary interventionists felt that the war was a 'revolution of the people' – against the establishment, against the old ruling class, against the monarchy, and for a revolutionary cause and for international democracy. They wanted to bring to a happy end the *Risorgimento* (the 19th-century

The debates of the politicians ended.
For thousands of Italians it meant farewell
to their families and off to the war

wars in which Italy threw off the Austrian yoke), and secure the triumph of a vague 'proletarian nationalism'.

In reality there was a great deal of confusion in these ideas. Popular leaders like Bissolati, Salvemini, and Battisti tried to clarify the situation. They were the leaders of another form of interventionism, which was openly democratic. They wanted to see the disappearance of Austria-Hungary and the triumph of the principle of 'nationality'. Intervention, participation in the 'democratic war', had, they thought, become a duty as well as a necessity. But they failed to convince even all their own followers; and they succeeded even less in convincing the parties of order.

In fact, as when Italy declared herself neutral, in August, the final word was again left to the government, which had to resolve the dilemma: negotiations with Austria or an 'Italian war'.

Giolitti was in agreement; but this time he had committed two errors: he had not taken into account Austria-Hungary's habit of always arriving 'an hour late' at the appointments of history. Furthermore, he had not fully realized what leaving a free hand to the government in power, principally to the key men, might involve – particularly when the key men were men like Salandra and Sonnino, who became foreign minister in November 1914, after

San Giuliano's death. The consequences of these two errors, when added to one another, were irreparable. Salandra and Sonnino, of course, started serious negotiations in Vienna, and also in Rome with Bülow, the former German chancellor. But when Austria hesitated and procrastinated about considering territorial concessions, Salandra and Sonnino, much more readily than Giolitti, embraced the idea of war. Salandra and Sonnino were not warmongers; they suppressed mass demonstrations of the interventionists. But as good Liberal-Conservatives they reasoned differently from Giolitti. In Italy they thought there was a need to reinforce the authority of the state, to strengthen traditional institutions, to improve the prestige of both crown and army. A victorious war – which, as many thought at the time, would last six months or a year at the most – could be just what was needed.

At the beginning of March they opened negotiations with the Entente powers; on 26th April 1915 they signed the Treaty of London. Sonnino, who in 1914 had so decisively supported intervention on the side of Austria-Hungary and Germany, had now taken the plunge. But he did not abandon all his ideas. By the treaty Italy was to obtain south Tyrol (Trentino), Trieste, Venezia-Giulia, and northern Dalmatia together with several islands, in order to guarantee Italian supremacy in the Adriatic against the Slavs. In short, the treaty corresponded to the 'Italian War' concept. Moreover, the treaty did not say in so many words that relations with Germany would irreparably be broken off. At least that is what Salandra and Sonnino relied on. And it was not to be until the middle of 1916 that Italy declared war against Germany.

Nevertheless, there was more than enough in this treaty to trouble Giolitti and the majority of Liberals and Catholics. When the news broke there were also several Liberal-Conservatives who thought that Salandra and Sonnino had jumped the gun. Giolitti returned to Rome, and soon afterwards, on 13th May, the ministry resigned.

It was the last but one act of the drama. Salandra and Sonnino were really quite willing to cede power or to accept Giolitti's advice: to re-open negotiations with Vienna. They interpreted the Treaty of London as an agreement between governments and not between states, especially as military plans were still unsettled. And the recent Austro-German victory at Gorlice-Tarnów (2nd May) caused anxiety. But it was now too late to reappraise the situation.

Passions had been roused little by little; interventionists, once united, organized demonstration after demonstration at which d'Annunzio made his inspiring calls

to rebellion, to war, and to violence; the neutralists, uncertain and passive, were as usual not keeping up with events. Giolitti himself did not want to take back the reins of power. The situation was getting too hot to handle, and the risk of failure after having advised resumption of negotiations, was too great.

Italy declares war

The King had, meanwhile, refused to accept the resignation of the Salandra ministry. On the 24th May 1915 Italy entered the war against Austria-Hungary, Salandra invoking what he called *sacro egoismo* – the sacred demands of self-interest – to justify this action. But the situation was by no means clear. The old ruling class was by now split. The interventionists once again started squabbling among themselves. The Socialists had lost the initiative. Economic preparations were inadequate, and were arranged from day to day. Moreover, the country in a large measure was passive. This assuredly was not a good start for the terrible ordeal to come.

Foreign policy encountered far more serious difficulties. During the negotiations with Austria-Hungary, and during those which led up to the Treaty of London, the aims of national unity for the 'unredeemed territories' had certainly established the directive throughout. But between *realpolitik* and nationalism the liberal aim of the 19th century had now dispersed itself. In 1914-15 the myth of the 'last war of the *Risorgimento*' was still alive, but had little or at least only indirect, influence on the ruling classes.

What is more, with Italy's intervention, the problem created by the Habsburgs' rule over many widely differing nationalities had been put into the 'melting pot'. But Italy, under the Treaty of London, could not co-operate with the other oppressed nationalities of the Habsburg empire. The possibilities of a happy solution were more remote than ever.

The army was also in difficulties. Much money had been spent on it, but military preparations had followed old-fashioned methods. Moreover – it is the only conclusion which could be deduced from the fighting which had already taken place in the war – tactical and strategic plans were based on the theory that frontal attack on the enemy troops would be the best method of fighting. The battles and the massacres of the Isonzo were not far off. That the chief of staff, the army commander in the war, should be the very same Cadorna who in July 1914 had made the suggestion that half the Italian army should be mobilized on the Rhine against France, seemed at the moment only an ironical symbol of the troubled thinking which had led Italy into the war.

The Dardanelles Campaign

It is doubtful whether any single campaign of either of the two World Wars has aroused more attention and controversy than the ill-fated venture to force the Dardanelles in 1915. 'Nothing so distorted perspective, disturbed impartial judgement, and impaired the sense of strategic values as the operations on Gallipoli,' Sir Edward Grey has written. Lord Slim – who fought at Gallipoli, and was seriously wounded – has described the Gallipoli commanders in scathing terms as the worst since the Crimean War. The defenders of the enterprise – notably Winston Churchill, Sir Roger Keyes, and General Sir Ian Hamilton – have been no less vehement and there have been other commentators who have thrown a romantic pall over the campaign. 'The drama of the Gallipoli campaign,' wrote the British official historian, 'by reason of the beauty of its setting, the grandeur of its theme, and the unhappiness of its ending, will always rank amongst the world's classic tragedies.' He then went on to quote Aeschylus's words: 'What need to repine at fortune's frowns? The gain hath the advantage, and the loss does not bear down the scale.'

Today, more than fifty years later, the Gallipoli controversies still rumble sulphurously, and the passions that the campaign aroused have not yet been stilled.

Amateurs in council

Few major campaigns have been initiated under stranger circumstances. The opening months of the war had imposed a strain upon the Liberal government from which it never really recovered. Asquith's leadership at the outbreak of war had been firm and decisive, but subsequently – whether from ill-health, as has been recently suggested by Lord Salter, or from other causes is immaterial in this narrative – his influence had been flaccid and irresolute. The creation of a War Council in November had not met the essential problem; the council met irregularly, its Service members were silent, and its manner of doing business was amateurish and unimpressive. As Winston Churchill commented in a memorandum circulated in July 1915: 'The governing instrument here has been unable to make up its mind except by very lengthy processes of argument and exhaustion, and that the divisions of opinion to be overcome, and the number of persons of consequence to be convinced, caused delays and compromises. We have always sent two-thirds of what was necessary a month too late.'

The military situation itself played a crucial part in what developed. The first fury of the war had been spent, and the opposing lines writhed from the Channel to the Swiss frontier; Russia had reeled back from her advance on East Prussia; everywhere, the belligerents had failed to secure their primary objectives. Already, the character of the battle on the Western Front had become grimly evident, and by the end of 1914 Churchill (first lord of the Admiralty), Lord Fisher (first sea lord), Lloyd George (chancellor of the exchequer), and Sir Maurice Hankey (secretary to the War Council) were thinking in terms of using British force – and particularly sea power – in another sphere.

It was Churchill who emerged with the most attractive proposal. Since the early weeks of the war his restlessness had been unconcealed, and he had already proposed, at the first meeting of the War Council on 25th November, a naval attack on the Dardanelles, with the ultimate object of destroying the German warships, *Goeben* and *Breslau,* whose escape from British squadrons in the Mediterranean in August had been a decisive factor in bringing Turkey into the war at the beginning of November on the side of the Germans. The suggestion had been shelved, but the idea had been put forward, and Hankey is not alone in stressing the significance of this first airing of the plan.

Impatience with the lack of progress on the Western Front was now buttressed by an appeal from Russia for a 'demonstration' against Turkey, after a large Turkish army had advanced into the Caucasus. (By the time the appeal was received, the Turks had been defeated, but this was not known for some time in London.) Churchill at once revived the idea of an assault on the Dardanelles, and telegraphed to the British admiral – Carden – in command of the squadron standing off the western entrance of the Dardanelles about the possibilities of a purely naval assault. Admiral Carden replied cautiously to the effect that a gradual attack might succeed; Churchill pushed the issue, and Carden was instructed to submit his detailed plans; when these arrived, Churchill put the matter before the War Council.

The extent to which Churchill's service colleagues at the Admiralty were alarmed at this speed was not communicated to the ministers on the council, a fact which to a large degree absolves them from their collective responsibility. Churchill's account was brilliant and exciting, and on 15th January the War Council agreed that 'the Admiralty should prepare for a naval ex-

Top: Assault by British Royal Naval Division on the Turkish lines. **Above:** *HMS Cornwallis in action*

pedition in February to bombard and take the Gallipoli peninsula, with Constantinople as its object'. Churchill took this as a definite decision; Asquith, however, considered that it was 'merely provisional, to prepare, but nothing more'; Admiral Sir Arthur Wilson, a member of the council, subsequently said that 'it was not my business. I was not in any way connected with the question, and it had never in any way officially been put before me'. Churchill's naval secretary considered that the naval members of the council 'only agreed to a purely naval operation on the understanding that we could always draw back – that there should be no question of what is known as forcing the Dardanelles'. Fisher, by this stage, was very alarmed indeed.

Quite apart from the matter of whether the navy had sufficient reserve of men and ships – even old ships, which was a major part of Churchill's scheme – to afford such an operation, the forcing of the Dardanelles had for long been regarded with apprehension by the navy, and Churchill himself had written in 1911 that 'it should be remembered that it is no longer possible to force the Dardanelles, and nobody would expose a modern fleet to such peril'. But Churchill – as his evidence to the Dardanelles Commission, only recently available for examination, clearly reveals – had been profoundly impressed by the effects of German artillery bombardments on the Belgian forts, and it was evident that the Turkish batteries were conspicuously sited, exposed, and equipped with obsolete equipment. And Churchill was not alone in rating Turkish military competence low. The admirals' doubts were put aside, Fisher swallowed his misgivings, and Carden prepared for the assault.

All this represented a considerable

achievement for Churchill. There is no doubt that he forced the pace, that the initiative was solely his, and that his subsequent account in *The World Crisis* must be approached with great caution. A case in point is his version of the negotiations to persuade Lord Kitchener (secretary of state for war) to release the Regular 29th Division for the Eastern Mediterranean. The recently revealed minutes of the War Council make it plain that Churchill had no intention of using the troops for the attack on the Dardanelles, but to employ them subsequently 'to reinforce our diplomacy' and garrison Constantinople. It was not surprising that Kitchener did not agree to send the division until March 10th.

The plans for the naval attack continued, and the British and Dominion (Australian and New Zealand) troops in Egypt were put on the alert. Carden opened his attack on 19th February, and had no difficulty in suppressing the outer forts at Sedd-el-Bahr and Kum Kale. The difficulties really began when the warships entered the Straits.

The intermediate and inner defences consisted of gun emplacements on the Gallipoli and Asiatic shores. These were supplemented by batteries capable of causing damage only to lightly armoured ships, and by mobile batteries. The Straits had been mined since the beginning of the war, but it was only in February and March that the lines of mines represented a serious menace. The attempts of the British minesweepers – East Coast fishing trawlers manned by civilian crews and commanded by a naval officer with no experience whatever of minesweeping – ended in complete failure. Marines went ashore at Kum Kale and Sedd-el-Bahr on several occasions, but early in March the resistance to these operations increased sharply.

Bad weather made the tasks of the warships and the hapless trawlers – barely able to make headway against the fierce Dardanelles current, operating under fire in wholly unfamiliar circumstances – even more difficult. Carden was an ailing man. The warships – with the exception of the brand-new battleship *Queen Elizabeth* – were old and in many cases in need of a refit. The standard of the officers was mixed. The Turkish resistance was more strenuous with every day that passed. The momentum of the advance faltered.

Urged on by Churchill, Carden decided to reverse his tactics; the fleet would silence the guns to allow the sweepers to clear the minefields. On the eve of the attack Carden collapsed and was replaced by Rear-Admiral Robeck.

By now, the soldiers were on the scene. Lieutenant-General Birdwood, a former military secretary to Kitchener now commanding the Anzacs in Egypt, had been sent by Kitchener to the Dardanelles to report on the situation. His reports were to the effect that military support was essential. Slowly a military force was gathered together, and General Sir Ian Hamilton was appointed commander-in-chief of what was called the Mediterranean Expeditionary Force, and which consisted at that moment of some 70,000 British, Dominion, and French troops. Hamilton was informed of his new appointment on 12th March; he left the next day – Friday, 13th March – with a scratch staff hastily gathered together, a series of instructions from Kitchener, and some meagre scraps of information about the area and the Turks. He arrived just in time for the *débâcle* of 18th March. Robeck lost three battleships sunk, and three crippled, out of nine; the minefields had not been touched.

Much ink has subsequently been spilled on the subject of what Robeck ought to have done. He did not know, of course, that the Turkish lack of heavy shells made their situation desperate. Even if he had, the fact remained that it was the mobile and minor batteries that were holding up the minesweepers. Roger Keyes's plan of using destroyers as minesweepers and storming the minefields was the only one that had a real chance of success, and it would have taken some time to prepare them.

The soldiers, however, were very willing to take over. On 22nd March Hamilton and Robeck agreed on a combined operation, and Hamilton sailed off to Alexandria to re-organize his scattered forces. 'No formal decision to make a land attack was even noted in the records of the Cabinet or the War Council,' as Churchill has written. '. . . This silent plunge into this vast military venture must be regarded as an extraordinary episode.' It was, however, no more extraordinary than the events that had

Hamilton – 'He should have really taken command, which he has never yet done'

Liman von Sanders – he committed several major errors which might have been fatal

The landing at Suvla Bay, Gallipoli, 1915, painted by subaltern R.C.Lewis during the action, using the dye from cigarette packets

preceded the crucial conference of 22nd March. Attempts by Hankey to obtain better information and an agreed assessment of the situation made no progress. 'The military operation appears, therefore, to be to a certain extent a gamble upon the supposed shortage of supplies and inferior fighting qualities of the Turkish armies,' he wrote in one of a series of prescient memoranda. But the War Council did not meet from the middle of March until two months later.

What subsequently happened was the direct result of the manner in which the British drifted haphazardly into a highly difficult amphibious operation. No calculation had been made of whether the British had the resources to undertake this operation. As Hankey wrote at the end of March: 'Up to the present time . . . no attempt has been made to estimate what force is required. We have merely said that so many troops are available and that they ought to be enough.' The state of affairs was subsequently well summarized by Sir William Robertson: 'The Secretary of State for War was aiming for decisive results on the Western Front. The First Lord of the Admiralty was advocating a military expedition to the Dardanelles. The Secretary of State for India was devoting his attention to a campaign in Mesopotamia. The Secretary of State for the Colonies was occupying himself with several small wars in Africa. And the Chancellor of the Exchequer was attempting to secure the removal of a large part of the British army from France to some Eastern Mediterranean theatre.'

One can sympathize with the cry of the GOC Egypt, Sir John Maxwell: 'Who is co-ordinating and directing this great combine?'

Furthermore, there was divided command in the eastern Mediterranean. Maxwell was in command in Egypt; Hamilton had his army; Robeck his ships. Before the campaign ended, there were further complications. Each commander fought for his own force and his own projects, and the limited supplies of men and material were distributed on an *ad hoc* and uncoordinated basis.

To all these difficulties, Hamilton added some of his own. His refusal to bring his administrative staff into the initial planning – and, indeed, into anything at all so long as· he was commander-in-chief – had some easily foreseeable results. Security was non-existent. 'The attack was heralded as few have ever been,' the Australian military historian has written. 'No condition designed to proclaim it seems to have been omitted.' This was not Hamilton's fault, yet his protests were wholly ineffective.

His plan for landing on Gallipoli – Asia he ruled out entirely, over the strong arguments of Birdwood and Hunter-Weston, commanding the 29th Division – was imaginative and daring. The 29th Division was to land at five small beaches at the southern end of the peninsula; the Anzacs were to land farther to the north on the western shore, just above the jutting promontory of Gaba Tepe, and then to push overland to the eminence of Mal Tepe, overlooking the narrows. There were to be feint landings at Bulair, at the 'neck' of the peninsula, and (by the French) at Besika Bay, opposite the island of Tenedos. The French were also to make a real, but temporary, landing at Kum Kale, to protect the landing of the 29th Division.

Meanwhile, the Turks had been having their own problems. Until March the Turkish forces in the area had been scattered and few in number. In spite of the urgency of the situation, the Turks acted lethargically. When, on the morning of 26th March, General Liman von Sanders arrived to take command of the troops at the Dardanelles, the situation that faced him was grim indeed. In short, his task was to defend a coast-line of some 150 miles with a total force of 84,000 men, but an actual fighting strength of only about 62,000. His army had no aircraft, and was seriously deficient in artillery and equipment. The men themselves, for so long used to defeat, were the despair of the German officers, and it would have been difficult to see in these poorly equipped and ragged formations the army that was to rise to such heights of valour and resource.

Sanders has been fortunate to have been treated at his own valuation by the majority of British commentators. In fact, he committed several major errors which might have been fatal. He placed two divisions at the neck of the peninsula, two on the Asiatic shore, one to defend the entire southern Gallipoli peninsula, and a final division in reserve near Mal Tepe. The entire area south of the bald, dominant height of Achi Baba was defended by one regiment and one field battery, with the reserves placed several hours' marching away to the north. To the dismay of the Turkish officers, Sanders drew his forces back from the beaches and concentrated them inland. This, the Turks argued, overlooked the fact that on the whole of the peninsula there were barely half a dozen beaches on which the British could land; Sanders, like Hamilton, over-estimated the effects of naval bombardment on well dug-in troops. He was saved by the epic courage of the Turkish troops, good luck, and mismanagement by the enemy from losing the entire campaign on the first day.

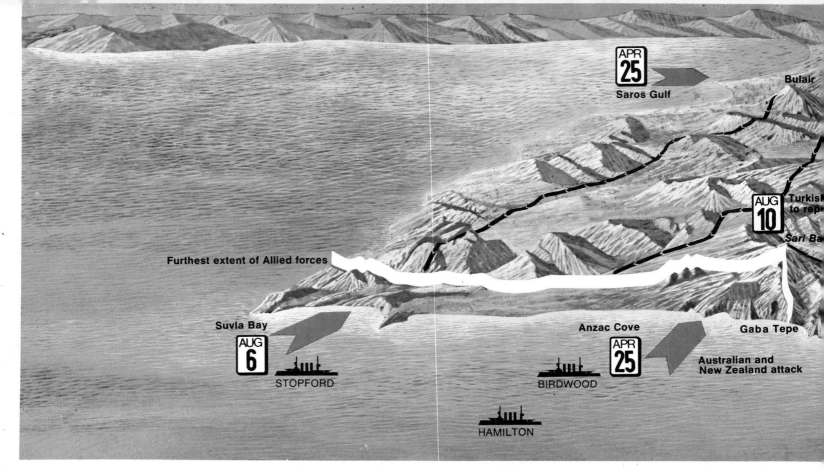

Labels on the map:
APR 25 — Saros Gulf
AUG 10 — Turkish [to rep...]
Sari Ba[...]
Bulair
Furthest extent of Allied forces
Suvla Bay — AUG 6 — STOPFORD
Anzac Cove — APR 25 — BIRDWOOD — Gaba Tepe
Australian and New Zealand attack
HAMILTON

The Gallipoli peninsula, seen from the west. On the map are marked the naval attack on 18th March, the landings on 25th April, the landing at Suvla Bay on 6th August, and the farthest extent of the Allied advances. The broken black lines show the direction of the Turkish thrusts against the Allies. The generals directed operations from ships offshore

It is impossible, even now, to contemplate the events of 25th April 1915, without emotion. The British and Dominion troops sailed from Mudros Harbour, in the island of Lemnos, in a blaze of excitement and ardour. 'Courage our youth will always have,' Lord Slim has written, 'but those young men had a vision strangely medieval, never, I think, to be renewed.' It was the baptism of fire for the Anzacs. It was also, in a real sense, the day on which Turkey began her emergence as a modern nation.

Three of the British landings at Helles were virtually unopposed. One was resisted, but the enemy defeated. But the fifth, at Sedd-el-Bahr, was a catastrophe. As the British came ashore, a torrent of fire was poured upon them as they waded through the water or sat helplessly jammed in open boats; others who attempted to land from a converted collier, the *River Clyde,* fared no better. In this crisis Hunter-Weston did not show himself to advantage. He was in a cruiser, barely five minutes' sailing from the disastrous beach, yet it was not until the day was well advanced that he was aware of what had occurred. The day ended with the British, exhausted and shaken, clinging to their positions.

The Anzacs had had a day of very mixed fortunes. They had been landed over a mile to the north of their intended position, in some confusion, to be faced with precipitous

cliffs and plunging, scrub-covered gorges. As the first men moved inland, congestion built up at the tiny beach — Anzac Cove — which had to cope with all reinforcements and supplies. Only one battery of field artillery was landed all day, and units became hopelessly intermingled. As in the south, the maps were dangerously inaccurate. By mid-morning the Turks had begun to counter-attack and, spurred on by the then unknown Colonel Mustapha Kemal, these attacks developed in fury throughout the day. By evening, the Anzacs were pushed back to a firing-line which extended only a thousand yards inland at the farthest point; casualties had been heavy, and Birdwood's divisional commanders advised evacuation. In the event, although Birdwood reluctantly agreed, Hamilton ordered him to hang on. This was virtually the only initiative taken by Hamilton — on board the *Queen Elizabeth* — throughout the day. As Birdwood wrote — some months later, 'he should have taken much more personal charge and *insisted* on things being done and really taken command, which he has never yet done'. Thus began the epic defence of Anzac, a fragment of cliff and gorge, overlooked by the enemy.

Hamilton pressed on at Helles, but although a limited advance was made, it was apparent by 8th May that the initial effort of his troops was spent. Casualties had been horrific — over 20,000 (of whom over 6,000 had been killed) out of a total force of 70,000 — and the medical and supply arrangements had completely collapsed under the wholly unexpected demands. The arrival of a German submarine and the sinking of three battleships — one by a Turkish torpedo-boat attack — deprived the army of the physical and psychological sup-

port of the guns of the fleet. Thus ended the first phase of the Gallipoli Campaign.

A week later the Liberal government fell, the first major casualty of the campaign, although there were other important contributory causes. Asquith formed a new coalition government in which Balfour, the former Conservative leader, replaced Churchill as first lord of the Admiralty. An inner cabinet, from 7th June called the Dardanelles Committee, took over the conduct of operations, and a ministry of munitions was established. The new government resolved to support Hamilton, and more troops were dispatched. Hamilton continued to batter away at Helles throughout May and July until, in the memorable words of a British corporal, the battlefield 'looked like a midden and smelt like an opened cemetery'. Achi Baba still stood defiantly uncaptured, and the army was incapable of further sustained effort. To the shelling, the heat, and the harsh life of the trenches was now added the scourge of dysentery.

Hamilton now swung his assault north. A daring scheme for capturing the commanding heights of the Sari Bair range had been worked out at Anzac. Unfortunately, as in April, other schemes were added to this basic project, until it developed into a joint operation as complex and dangerous as the first. The Anzacs, with British and Indian reinforcements, would break out of the Anzac position to the north, and scale the incredibly tangled gullies and ridges to the summit of the Sari Bair range by night after diversionary attacks at the south of the Anzac position and at Helles. At dawn on 6th August, a new Army Corps would be landed in Suvla Bay, which was thought to be sparsely defended and which lay to the north of Anzac, and,

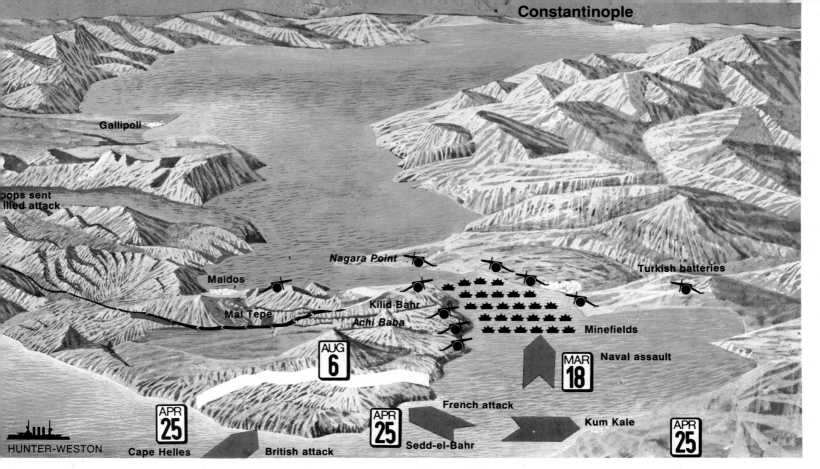

Gallipoli

oops sent
lied attack

Nagara Point

Maidos

Turkish batteries

Mal Tepe

Kilid Bahr

Achi Baba

Minefields

AUG 6

MAR 18 Naval assault

French attack

APR 25

APR 25 Kum Kale

HUNTER-WESTON

Cape Helles   British attack   Sedd-el-Bahr

APR 25

at first light, the Turkish positions at Anzac would be assaulted from front and rear. Some 63,000 Allied troops would be attacking an area defended by well under 30,000 Turks.

This time, the veil of secrecy that descended on the operation was so complete that senior commanders were not informed until very late. Sir Frederick Stopford, the commander of the 9th Corps, which was to land at Suvla, was allowed to amend his instructions so that his task was merely to get ashore and capture the bay. There was no co-ordination between General Stopford and Birdwood at Anzac, either before or during the action. Hamilton stayed at his headquarters for two vital days.

In the circumstances, the marvel was that the operation came so close to success. Sanders, once again, was outwitted by Hamilton. The night march from Anzac was a chaotic and frightening business, but by dawn on August 7th the New Zealanders were within a fraction of seizing the vital summit. The Suvla landing, although opposed by small units and something of a shambles in other respects, was successful. By the morning of August 7th the Turkish situation at Sari Bair was desperate, but the heat, the exhaustion and inexperience of the British, and dilatoriness by their commanders, saved Sanders; the Turks, as always, fought with frenzy and unheeding valour. It developed into a weird, ghastly battle. At Suvla, 9th Corps remained glued to the shore, and advanced only with timidity. At Anzac, the failures in advance planning and command meant that everything depended on the courage and initiative of the troops and their immediate officers; neither were lacking, and the fighting was intensely bitter, even by Gallipoli standards; but they were insufficient. Sanders gave

command of the entire area to Kemal, who checked the British at Suvla just as they were making a positive forward movement on the urgent commands of Hamilton, and at Sari Bair he launched a desperate attack at first light on August 10th that swept the Allies from the positions that had been won and held at a severely high cost. One British officer, commanding men of the 1/6th Gurkhas, had a glimpse of the Dardanelles.

The rest was aftermath. Hamilton launched one last abortive attack at Suvla which was in terms of numbers the biggest battle of the campaign, but the issue had already been decided. At home, the many opponents of the venture became more vociferous and urgent; a new army was sent to Salonika; the Gallipoli fronts subsided into trench warfare; the weather got colder, and the decision of Bulgaria to enter the war meant that Austrian guns began to shell the exposed British lines with a new accuracy. In October Hamilton was recalled. His successor was Sir Charles Monro, a man of a very different stamp, who recommended evacuation. Bluntly faced with the grim implications, the government became irresolute again. Kitchener went out to investigate, and was eventually persuaded of the necessity of withdrawal. Birdwood was in charge of the evacuation of Suvla and Anzac, which was brilliantly conducted, without a single casualty, on 19th-20th December.

The evacuation of Helles was now inevitable, and this was accomplished on 8th-9th January, again without loss of men, although that of stores and equipment was extensive. Thus, the campaign ended with a substantial triumph, an indication of what might have been achieved earlier.

The casualties were substantial. The

first was the Asquith government, and, in particular, Churchill, whose removal from the Admiralty in May was a *sine qua non* for Conservative participation in the new coalition; it was many years before the shadow of Gallipoli was lifted from his reputation. Asquith's own prestige and position were badly shaken, as were those of Kitchener. The dream of a Balkan alliance against Germany was shattered, and Italy was the only Mediterranean nation that—in mid-May—joined the Allied cause. The British had acquired another vast commitment in Salonika. The Russian warm-sea outlet was irretrievably blocked. Compared with this last strategical disaster, the actual losses in battle or through disease—which are difficult to calculate on the Allied side but which were certainly over 200,000 (the Turkish are unknown, but must have been considerably greater, with a higher proportion of dead)—were perhaps of lesser significance. But, at the time, these loomed largest of all, and what appeared to many to be the futility of such sacrifice when the real battle was being fought almost within sight of the shores of Great Britain had an enduring effect. On 28th December the cabinet formally resolved that the Western Front would be the decisive theatre of the war. The stage was set for the vast killing-matches to come.

Had it all been loss? The enterprise came near to success on several occasions, but it is questionable whether even the capture of Gallipoli and the Straits would have had the decisive effects that appeared at the time. The entire operation grimly justified words written by Lloyd George before it had even been seriously considered: 'Expeditions which are decided upon and organised with insufficient care generally end disastrously.'

1915: Disasters for the Allies

A majority of the Allied leaders, both military and political, suffered in the opening months of 1915 from the delusion that the war would be won that year.

The generals, British and French, believed that this victory would follow from a reversion to 'open' warfare. They had seen their enemy elude them (as it appeared) by 'digging in' after the battle of the Marne. If the key could be found to unlock this barrier the character of the fighting would alter, and the Allies would have the advantage.

The first of these propositions is incontestable, the second highly dubious. The science of military analysis was not much heeded by the French generals, still less by the British, both preferring the doctrine of their own infallibility—which was good for morale. It seems that they interpreted the German adoption of trench warfare as an admission of weakness, a form of cowardice it could be said, by an enemy who feared the outcome of a 'real' battle. It is probable also that they drew encouragement from the east, where a combination of space, limited firepower, and enormous bodies of cavalry endowed the campaign with the appearance of something in a different epoch from that of the close-fought positional battles in the west.

But if the setting was different, the principles of grand strategy were immutable, and in due course the Russians had been caught by their application. The bloody defeat of Samsonov's army at Tannenberg effectively halted the Russian steamroller, and eliminated the threat to East Prussia. Furthermore, it showed to Falkenhayn, the chief of the German general staff, that although the Schlieffen plan had failed its purpose might still be attained because the scale of forces needed to defeat the Tsar was not—on account of the tactical clumsiness and ineptitude of the Russian commanders—irreconcilable with an active, though necessarily defensive, Western Front.

Accordingly, in his appreciation for 1915, Falkenhayn recommended a defensive posture in France and concentration of strength in the east. After some vacillation the Kaiser had agreed and the necessary redeployment (which also entailed taking divisions from Hindenburg and Ludendorff in Silesia) was put in motion. Headquarters, and the imperial train, moved to the east, carrying the German centre of gravity with it.

All this took time, and during those weeks the southern wing of the Russian armies continued to batter away at the Austro-Hungarians, taking the famous fortress town of Przemyśl in March. Friction began to develop between the German commanders. Ludendorff had his own, more radical scheme for defeating the Russians by a wide outflanking stroke from the north, and resented being held in check while Falkenhayn concentrated for a direct approach on the Galician front.

To the Allies, therefore, appearance augured better than reality. The Germans appeared to be standing on the defensive in France from fear of their opponent, while in the east they were still in retreat. Considerations of grand strategy vied with those of national—and personal—prestige to make a Western contribution to this giant 'pincer' urgently desirable.

Joffre was intending to mount the French offensive in May. But there were private reasons which made the British commanders in the field keen to stage a 'demonstration' at a much earlier date. Lord Kitchener, the secretary of state (who enjoyed poor relations with the commander of the British Expeditionary Force, Sir John French), favoured using the new units which had been formed during the winter for an amphibious assault on Ostend and Zeebrugge in Belgium. Both Sir John, and Douglas Haig, his subordinate, saw that this would entail restricting the size and resources of the BEF—perhaps indefinitely—in favour of a new army which would come under the command of Kitchener or his nominee. Accordingly they planned to attack the enemy themselves as soon as weather permitted.

The area selected was the German salient which protruded around the village of Neuve-Chapelle. It was lightly defended, by some six companies who disposed of twelve machine-guns between them, set out in a line of shallow sand-bag breastworks (the ground was too waterlogged for a proper trench system). Against this 'position'—in effect little more than a screen—Haig threw no fewer than forty-eight battalions supported by sixty batteries of field artillery, and a hundred and twenty heavy siege pieces. In several places the attackers broke right through, into open country—a feat which they were not to repeat for two and a half years. But the expected 'open' warfare never materialized. To hesitant leadership, at every level, was added poor communications and a cumbersome chain of command.

During the night the troops who had broken through milled about aimlessly on the edge of certain natural barriers that were very lightly held by some scratch

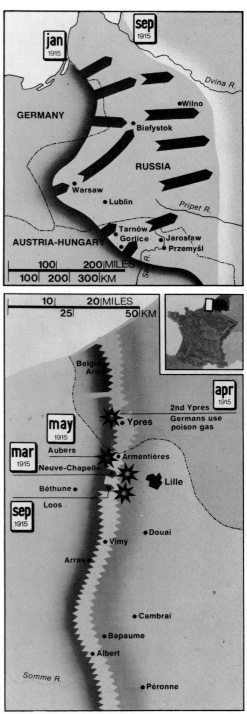

Above: The campaigns of 1915. In the west it was a story of failed offensives, and in the east of massive German victories and advances. Left: Two French grenadiers wearing gas masks. Poison gas, used for the first time this year, had added a new horror to warfare

groups of enemy infantry, in the belief that it was the German 'second line'. In fact, the Germans had no second line, but they energetically improvised one, with two companies of bicycle-mounted sharpshooters, during the early hours of the morning. On the second day less than a dozen machine-guns held up the whole British army, whose artillery had practically no ammunition left to deal with them. However, the British numerical superiority was still more than seven to one and Haig, the army commander, ordered that 'attacks are to be pressed regardless of loss'. Loss, not surprisingly, was the only result.

The battle of Neuve-Chapelle exemplifies the way in which the relation of attack to defence remained constant – though the degree of force applied on either side was to escalate violently throughout the war. Ammunition shortage had lulled the Germans into underestimating the power of the British artillery, hence their feeble, lightly-manned defence works. If the British had disposed of the firepower which the French enjoyed they might well have broken through at their second attempt; if the German line had included the deep concrete *Wohngraben* shelters which they began hastily to dig after digesting the shock of the Neuve-Chapelle attack, the British would never have got across no man's land – as was to be painfully demonstrated in the Aubers offensive two months later. In point of fact the two forces remained in balance (which meant of course that the defence prevailed) all the way up to the ten-day barrages and concrete pillbox chains of Passchendaele in November of 1917.

Both sides drew their conclusions from the failure to exploit the initial breakthrough at Neuve-Chapelle. Falkenhayn expressed the view that 'the English troops, in spite of undeniable bravery and endurance on the part of the men, have proved so clumsy in action that they offer no prospect of accomplishing anything decisive against the German Army in the immediate future'.

But the British staff took a different view. A GHQ memorandum, dated the 18th April, concludes the 'lessons' of Neuve-Chapelle with the assertion that '. . . by means of careful preparation as regards details it appears that a section of the enemy's front line can be captured with comparatively little loss'.

And this was a judgement which Joffre regarded as needlessly conservative. Of his own prospects, he confided to Sir Henry Wilson (the liaison officer at French HQ) that 'he was bringing up even more troops and really thought he would break the line past mending, and that it might be, and ought to be, the beginning of the end'.

The new German soldier. A cartoon drawn by Raemaekers in 1915, shortly after the experimental poison gas attack at Ypres

Poison gas

Meanwhile, time was running out for the Russian armies in south Poland, as Falkenhayn gradually accumulated fresh German divisions behind the depleted Austrian line in readiness for his counter-offensive. The Germans planned to reinforce their local numerical superiority (fourteen divisions against two) by tactical surprise (the use of a new weapon – poison gas). However, the commanders responsible for mounting the gas attack had insisted that the new weapon should first be tried under actual battle conditions, and it was decided to stage the dress rehearsal in the west.

The area selected was a quiet four-mile stretch of front at the northern corner of the Ypres salient. The line was held by French colonial troops whose erratic tactics and discipline had been a source of friction between the British and French commanders for some weeks. Ill-fitted to resist a determined conventional attack, they collapsed immediately under the impact of this new and frightening weapon. This time it was the Germans who broke right through the trench line (they, too,

would have to wait almost three years before they could repeat the performance) and it was their turn to be surprised by the opportunity which offered. The gas had been used without any particular objective, even at tactical level, in mind. The German Corps commander quickly tried to improvise an operation which might pinch out the whole Ypres salient from the north, but he was frustrated by his own meagre resources and by the extraordinary heroism of small detachments of Canadian and British troops who placed themselves across his advance.

Once the German impetus had died away Sir John French staged a series of ill-managed and extravagant counter-attacks against the new enemy positions (the British troops were told to protect themselves against gas by dipping their handkerchiefs in a solution of water and Boric acid, and tying them across their mouths). These achieved little except the destruction of two brigades of the Indian army and the dismissal of Sir Horace Smith-Dorrien, the first – and last – senior commander to protest against the cost in casualties of repetitive frontal attacks.

The experience of 'Second Ypres' (as the April battles in the salient were called) confirmed the lesson that the fighting soldier was fatally vulnerable to accurate – but remote – artillery and isolated machine-gunners under conditions of 'open' warfare. In fact, his only defence was to dig, as fast and as deep as he could. But the senior Allied commanders continued to regard a break-up of the trench system as their goal, and held the view that this could be attained by the application of the same formula; though in heavier and heavier concentrations. In any case it was now too late to alter the plans for the next British offensive, to be launched against the Aubers ridge on the 9th May, timed to coincide with Joffre's own, delayed, attack farther to the south.

This time the British artillery was weaker than at Neuve-Chapelle, the German defences stronger. As the first wave went over the top the Germans were amazed to see that '. . . there could never before in war have been a more perfect target than this solid wall of khaki men side-by-side. There was only one possible order to give – "Fire! Until the barrels burst!"' The attack was stopped dead. But the men who had been moved up to 'exploit' it now congested the forward trenches, and they too were ordered to attack – in exactly the same place, and with the same result. There could be no thought of working round the enemy flank. It was a point of honour to advance directly on to his guns. Two days later there were no shells left, and very few men. In some gloom (and unusual candour) an officer at Haig's headquarters wrote that '. . . Our attack has failed, and failed badly, and with heavy casualties. That is the bald and most unpleasant fact.'

Soon after the failure at Aubers news began to seep back to the western capitals of a terrible disaster in Poland. Falkenhayn's long delayed offensive had burst upon the Russian right flank, and four German Army Corps were pouring through the gap. Within a week they had advanced seventy miles; a fortnight passed and the San, the great river barrier in the Russian rear, had been forced at Jaroslaw; a month, and Przemyśl had been recaptured—all those fortress towns whose fall had cheered the Allied press in the winter months of 1914 were now abandoned by the fleeing Tsarist armies.

The Russian collapse

There was much to distract the British public—the Dardanelles, the 'Shells Scandal' (the British lack of shells was fiercely attacked in the press), the cabinet changes. But the hard facts remained. While the Allies licked their wounds impotently on the Western Front the Russian collapse became daily more serious. If she should be forced out of the war, the German strategic purpose—the original motive of the Schlieffen plan—would be achieved and the whole weight of the German army could be shifted to France.

How was it that the front, on either side, could so often be broken in the east, so seldom in the west? Why was it that gains in Poland were measured in hundreds of miles, in France in yards?

The force-to-space ratio (force being an amalgam of numbers and firepower) was widely different between the two theatres. In France the ratio was very high and steadily increasing. But in Russia the front was four times as long, the number of men engaged little higher than in the west, their scale of armament very much lower. Wheeling cavalry formations encountering the odd machine-gun could simply gallop off into the steppe, out of range. The Russians were short even of rifles, and those equipped with them seldom had more than twenty rounds per man. Many of the Austrian rifles were not even magazine-fed.

Across this sprawling, under-manned battlefield the well-led, well-equipped Germans cut a deep swathe: following his victory at Gorlice-Tarnów on 2nd May, Falkenhayn at last allowed the impatient Ludendorff to debouch from East Prussia and seize the vital rail junction of Bialystok in July. Under this double threat the Russian armies, plagued by desperate munition shortages, stumbled back to the shelter of the Dvina and the Pripet. By the middle of August they had lost 750,000 prisoners.

Now the Allied motives swung right round; so far indeed, that the solution, seen from the opposite pole, seemed identical. Massive attacks in the west were urgently necessary, no longer as part of a victorious pincer movement but as succour for the failing Russian strength, a desperate attempt to draw the bulk of the German army back across Poland to the west.

Joffre, as always, was optimistic; his British colleagues less so. The French were to attack in Champagne, the British at Loos. The British did not yet have enough artillery to support the whole of their attack frontage and so Haig decided to use gas on a large scale. This immediately put

The first gas masks—respirators which were issued in May 1915. When gas was first used the British troops were told to protect themselves by dipping handkerchiefs in a solution of water and boracic acid and tying them across their mouths. A German wrote: 'The effects of the successful gas-attack were horrible . . . All the men lie on their backs, with clenched fists; the whole field is yellow'

The Shock of Arms

his men at a disadvantage as gas depends for its effectiveness on a favourable prevailing wind (which could not, naturally, be guaranteed at H-hour) nor, by itself, will it cut barbed wire. In addition, the British and French sections were too far apart to give mutual support. For some weeks the British procrastinated and all the time the news from the east got worse. Finally, the date was fixed, for 25th September—ironically, a week after Falkenhayn had ordered that offensive operations in the east were to be halted, and the divisions transferred to France.

No one had much confidence in the prospects. The ground had been selected, not by the British themselves, but by Joffre. As the hour approached Sir John French's nerve began to fail and he sent a message (effectively calling the whole operation off) that he '. . . would assist according to

ammunition'. There was uproar at French HQ. 'Sir John had better walk warily,' growled Henry Wilson into his diary. Joffre himself complained to Kitchener, darkly hinting that he had been made personally responsible for securing English co-operation and that if he should be sacked the politicians might make a separate peace. Haig, meanwhile, had recovered his own confidence and believed that the attack would be successful. Under this double pressure, from above and below, Sir John could do nothing but go along with the plan. All that could be hoped was that by committing everything, including two raw volunteer divisions that had just arrived in France, something might be achieved—even if it was only to impress our Allies with our 'sincerity'.

Winston Churchill has described how, back in London, '. . . The Private Secretary

informed me that Lord Kitchener wished to see me. He ('K') looked at me sideways with a very odd expression on his face. I saw he had some disclosure of importance to make, and waited. After appreciable hesitation he told me that he had agreed with the French to a great offensive in France. I said at once that there was no chance of success. He said that the scale would restore everything, including of course the Dardanelles. He had an air of suppressed excitement, like a man who has taken a great decision of terrible uncertainty, and is about to put it into execution'.

In the event, the battle of Loos was a miserable defeat. Like Neuve-Chapelle in its clumsy repetition of frontal attacks and disdain for the indirect approach, it differed when the attackers came to the enemy second line. This time they were ordered straight at it, without any preparation, artillery or reconnaissance or even—in the case of the two fresh volunteer divisions—being given a meal. A German Regimental war diary records how: 'Ten columns of extended line could clearly be distinguished, each one estimated at more than a thousand men, and offering such a target as had never been seen before, or even thought possible. Never had the machine-gunners such straightforward work to do nor done it so effectively. They traversed to and fro along the enemy's ranks unceasingly. As the entire field of fire was covered with the enemy's infantry the effect was devastating . . .'

Nothing, at either strategic or tactical level, was achieved by the Loos offensive. Nor can anything be said to have been learned from it. But its effects were highly important. Sir John French was dismissed; Haig was promoted; Robertson, a close personal associate of Haig's, was transferred to London where, as chief of the imperial general staff, he controlled the strategic direction of the war.

Kitchener, whose deep Imperial vision and gloomy assessment of the Western Front obstructed all those commanders whose ambition resided there, was left without real power and henceforth the strategic decisions were taken by the Haig-Robertson duumvirate, a combination irrevocably committed to the continental strategy, the massive land force on the Western Front, and to a rejection of the imperial strategic principles of William Pitt, which had stood inviolate for a hundred and fifty years.

German cartoon, 1915. Russia's commander-in-chief, Grand Duke Nicholas, is depicted as Macbeth 'in blood Stepp'd in so far that, should I wade no more, Returning were as tedious as go o'er'

The Sinking of the Lusitania

The last of the Lusitania, *drawn by an Englishman who survived the disaster. He was fortunate. 1,198 of the* Lusitania's *passengers and crew, 128 of them American, were swallowed up by the waves*

The New York passenger dock was more than usually crowded with newspaper reporters, cameramen, and sightseers when the *Lusitania* sailed on 1st May 1915. Their interest was prompted by an advertisement in the travel pages of the morning editions warning Atlantic travellers that British and Allied ships on route from the United States were liable to be attacked if they entered the European war zone. The notice was paid for by the German embassy and in some papers it appeared next to a Cunard list of departure dates which included a prominent reference to the *Lusitania,* the 'fastest and largest steamer now in Atlantic service. . . .'

The newshounds quickly added two and two together and came up with the obvious answer. Cunard's proudest vessel was marked as a potential victim of Germany's submarine patrol. By sailing time the rumour had strengthened to the extent that many passengers were receiving anonymous telegrams urging them to cancel their bookings. Yet few were noticeably perturbed by the excitement on shore. After all, the *Lusitania* was known to have the steam power to outpace almost any vessel above or below the water. But more important was the irresistible feeling that a floating luxury hotel could not be regarded as a worthwhile target for a German

The Shock of Arms

1 *The nurses on board the* Lusitania. *Few of those who travelled on her were alarmed by the German warnings.* 2 *Captain Turner: 'What in God's name have I done to deserve this?'* 3 *A medal struck by a German craftsman. It was intended as a satire on the Anglo-American cupidity which allowed the* Lusitania *to sail despite German warnings, but the British reproduced it in large quantities as proof that the German government was exulting over the death of the passengers. One side (left) shows 'The great steamer* Lusitania *sunk by a German submarine, 7th May 1915'. The inscription above reads 'No contraband'. The other side of the medal shows Death selling tickets in the Cunard office under the motto 'Business before everything'.* 4 *British poster on the sinking of the* Lusitania. *The sword of justice is proffered to America*

U-boat—particularly when it was crowded with neutral Americans whose good will the Kaiser could not lightly afford to lose. Any last-minute doubts were finally settled when the celebrities came on board. Their names read like an extract from an American *Who's Who*. There was Alfred Vanderbilt, multi-millionaire; Charles Frohman, theatrical producer; George Kessler, wine merchant and 'Champagne King'; Rita Jolivet, actress; and Elbert Hubbard, whose mid-west brand of homespun philosophy made him one of the best known newspaper and magazine writers in the United States. Surely, said the humbler passengers, if there was any danger these VIPs would know enough to save their valuable necks. There were one or two cancellations, but no more than were normal on any voyage.

The Lusitania *sets out*

As the 32,000-ton liner edged its way out of New York harbour, and its occupants turned their attention to the pleasures of an ocean cruise, unpleasant stories of the European conflict were forgotten. A British girl later recalled: 'I don't think we thought of war. It was too beautiful a passage to think of anything like war.'

A more realistic attitude might have prevailed, if the travellers had known that the cargo list included an item that could be regarded only as war material. Stacked in the holds of the *Lusitania* were 4,200 cases of small arms ammunition—not, perhaps, a vitally significant contribution to a campaign in which millions of rounds were expended in a single battle, but the Germans, who were already suffering from a blockade that seriously impeded their military supplies, were in no mood to make allowances for a minor breach of the rules. All ships carrying war contraband were legitimate naval targets if they were caught in the waters surrounding Great

Britain and Ireland. As if to underline the warning, the *Gulflight*, a tanker flying the American flag, was torpedoed on the day the *Lusitania* sailed from New York. Three Americans, including the captain, were killed.

In May 1915 there were about fifteen German submarines on the prowl, out of a total force of not more than twenty-five. Their captains, like contemporary aeroplane pilots, were a small, select company, publicized as larger-than-life heroes whose spirit of gallantry somewhat humanized their destructive powers. For instance, it was customary to warn crews on merchant ships to get clear before the torpedoes were launched and, later in the war, one U-boat captain even provided a tow for two lifeboats stranded some distance from land.

The underwater pirates were immediately successful and, faced with the prospect of greater losses, the British Admiralty ordered merchant ships to be armed, and worked out a procedure for ramming U-boats if they surfaced. The rate of destruction of cargo vessels continued to increase, but submarine commanders were inclined to act less generously towards their potential victims.

The *Lusitania* crossed the half-way line on the night of 4th May. A few hours later the U 20 appeared off the Old Head of Kinsale on the south coast of Ireland. Kapitänleutnant Schwieger had not achieved a single kill in the five days since he and his crew had sailed from Emden. He attacked one merchant vessel, but allowed it to escape when he saw that it was flying the Danish flag.

Ireland offered slightly better prospects. An old three-masted schooner on its leisurely way to Liverpool with a small cargo of food was halted by the U 20. As the crew pushed away in their life-boat, shells splintered the brittle timbers and she

slumped over on her side. It made a pathetic sight: the latest and most terrible weapon of war exercising her superiority over a tired veteran.

On 6th May the U20 sank the *Candidate*, a medium-sized liner bound for Jamaica, and the *Centurion*, on route to South Africa. In neither case were there any casualties among the passengers or crew, who managed to get clear despite Schwieger's natural refusal to give advance warning. At 7.50 pm Captain Turner, on board the *Lusitania*, received the first Admiralty confirmation of U-boat activity off the south coast of Ireland. Forty minutes later an urgent radio message advised all British ships in the area to avoid headlands, pass harbours at full speed, and steer a mid-channel course. The appeal was repeated at intervals throughout the night. Safety precautions were checked, the life-boats swung out, and some of the watertight bulkheads closed. Shortly after midday on 7th May, when the morning fog had dispersed, the *Lusitania* was in sight of the Irish coast. Turner was disturbed by the total absence of patrol boats or, for that matter, any other type of vessel. His concern might have been all the greater had he known that twenty-three merchant ships had been torpedoed in the area during the past week. At 1.40 pm he sighted a friendly landmark—the Old Head of Kinsale. Kapitänleutnant Schwieger, who at that moment was searching the horizon through his periscope, experienced the same thrill of welcome discovery. He had sighted the *Lusitania*.

The torpedo was fired at 2.09 pm. A starboard lookout was the first to see it. Captain Turner heard the warning shout and caught a glimpse of the trail of white foam on the water. At 2.10 pm Schwieger noted: '. . . shot hits starboard side right behind bridge. An unusually heavy detonation

TAKE UP THE SWORD OF JUSTICE

follows with a very strong explosion cloud. . . .'

The passengers did not know it, but they had only eighteen minutes to escape from the sinking liner. A general feeling of security, based on the knowledge that the coastline was within ten miles, gave way to near panic as the ship listed sharply to the starboard side. The first life-boats were swung out, but even without engine power the *Lusitania* was moving too fast for a safe launching. The order to stop lowering was immediately obeyed but not soon enough to save one boat which had dropped heavily at one end, spilling its occupants into the water. By this time the starboard list was so pronounced that boats on the port side either fell on the deck when released or were gashed open as they slithered down the ship's plates.

Passengers rushed this way and that, searching for their lifebelts and fitting them with inexpert hands. One or two jumped overboard and more followed as the water inched up to the starboard deck. A few of the remaining boats plopped safely into the sea but many others were left dangling uselessly at the end of their ropes. Women screamed, children cried, seamen swore, and three Irish girls sang 'There is a Green Hill Far Away' in cracked voices. Chairs, tables, crockery, trunks, and all objects not fastened to the boards slid across the ship in destructive confusion.

From his unique vantage point, the commander of the U 20 recorded in his log: '. . . great confusion on board . . . they must have lost their heads.' Schwieger was convinced that the *Lusitania* was about to capsize.

In fact the massive liner tilted down at the bows and, as the remaining passengers and crew scrambled up the deck, the propellers and rudder—which moments before had been hidden beneath the water

—rose steeply into the air. Briefly the ship remained in this position as her bows penetrated the mud three hundred feet below the surface. Then her stern gradually settled and with a roar that to some survivors sounded like an anguished wail, the *Lusitania* disappeared. Bodies, debris, swimmers, and boats covered an area half a mile across. As the rescue ships steamed into sight those who stayed afloat must have silently expressed the bewildered sentiment of Captain Turner, who was holding on to an upturned boat: 'What in God's name have I done to deserve this?'

'Piratical murderers!'

One thousand, one hundred and ninety-eight passengers and crew drowned with the *Lusitania*. One hundred and twenty-eight of them were Americans. The *Frankfurter Zeitung* described the sinking as 'an extraordinary success' for the German navy, but Allied journals referred to 'piratical murderers' who attacked 'innocent and defenceless people without fear of retaliation'. It is often thought that the torpedo which destroyed the *Lusitania* was chiefly responsible for bringing the United States into the war, and certainly a flood of propaganda was directed to this end. Commemorative medals said to have been issued by the German government were reproduced by the Foreign Office who distributed them at home and abroad to show what devilish practices the enemy were happy to approve. A *Times* editorial was directed at the 'doubters and indifferent' who ignored 'the hideous policy of indiscriminate brutality which has placed the whole German race outside the pale'. With his readers across the Atlantic very much in mind the writer continued: 'The only way to restore peace to the world, and to shatter the brutal menace, is to carry the war throughout the length and breadth of

Germany. Unless Berlin is entered, all the blood which has been shed will have flowed in vain.' But the United States remained neutral for two more years and by that time other factors, including the German offer to help Mexico reclaim New Mexico, had robbed the sinking of the *Lusitania* of its dramatic impact.

If the propaganda experts failed to win a powerful ally for Great Britain, they could at least congratulate themselves on effectively smothering those features of the story that might have set a limit to anti-German feeling. The official inquiry skirted the fact that the *Lusitania* was carrying war material and concluded that a second explosion was caused not by the ammunition but by a second torpedo. Leslie Morton, an able seaman on the *Lusitania* who is now a retired captain, maintains that he saw two torpedoes running right into the point of contact between numbers 2, 3, and 4 funnels. But all other evidence, including the submarine log, suggests that the damage caused by one shot from the U 20 was greatly aggravated by the accidental detonation of the war cargo. That is why the *Lusitania* sank in eighteen minutes.

Other embarrassing questions were left unanswered. For instance, why was the *Lusitania* not diverted around the north coast of Ireland when submarine activity was first detected? At the very least, why was she not provided with an escort? Why did the patrol boats remain in Queenstown harbour until it was too late for them to do anything except lend a hand with the rescue work?

The sinking of the *Lusitania* was a stupid error of judgement which the Germans could ill afford; but those who died were perhaps the victims of Admiralty carelessness as well as the victims of ruthless fighters.

3 TOTAL WAR

Introduction

The second and third years of the war were trying for both sides. The myth that the war would be short was finally laid to rest. But many misconceptions, born in the enthusiasm of the summer of 1914, were still maintained. The dream of imminent breakthrough on the Western Front alternated with the despair born of mass slaughter and the impasse which led some to believe that breakthrough was impossible; either peace must be secured with no decision either way, or victory, out of the grasp of the Allies and the Central Powers, could be obtained some other way. For the Germans and Austrians, the impasse in Flanders and France led them to hope for either a breakthrough on the Eastern Front and in the Balkans or victory at sea. The conquest of Serbia, after almost a year and a half of conflict, came at last to Austria-Hungary. Further advances into Russian territory by the German army gave only temporary hope to the Kaiser.

It became clear by 1916 that victory in the Balkans would have only a peripheral effect on the fighting capacity of Britain and France, and no matter how much Russian territory was occupied, the Russians had an age-old advantage; they could sell space to gain time. And there was a lot of space. True enough, one of the principal German war aims, as announced in Chancellor Bethmann Hollweg's September Programme in 1914, was to create a series of puppet states in Eastern Europe economically, and thus, ultimately, politically tied to the Second Reich. That end was clearly being accomplished. A nascent Polish state was being created, and as the German armies pushed into the Baltic provinces of Russia, efforts toward creating Lithuanian and Latvian

Left: Mackensen, German conqueror of Serbia

states were similarly made. But these advances brought the end of the war no nearer. Thus, any effort to win the war for Germany outside Western Europe had to be made on the seas.

Britain's lifeline had always been her sea routes, protected by the superiority of the British fleet. As early as 1915 this superiority was being challenged by Germany in a new way. Submarine warfare plagued Allied shipping. For Britain this was a matter of life or death. Food was required in Britain, and something like half of it had to come from overseas, particularly wheat and other grains, mostly from Canada and the United States. Germany estimated that by sinking an average of 600,000 tons of shipping per month for five or six months they could bring Britain to her knees. The upshot of the *Lusitania* disaster was the suspension of unrestricted submarine warfare. Even at that, caused by Woodrow Wilson's insistence that it stop, an average of 300,000 tons of shipping per month was being sunk. If British naval superiority could effectively be challenged, Germany could win the war. The greatest sea battle of the war, the Battle of Jutland in 1916, helped to destroy this dream.

Jutland was the meeting of giants, the heavyweight championship of the naval world, when the two giant navies clashed for the one and only time during the war. The German High Seas Fleet, equipped with more modern dreadnoughts and submarines than the British Grand Fleet, was, on the whole, numerically far inferior. From 1915 on it had languished in port, bottled up by the Allied blockade.

The Germans decided to mass their forces in the North Sea off the Danish peninsula of Jutland. When the battle was over it was clear that in numerical terms, the Germans

had won. The British lost almost twice as much tonnage and over twice the number of men. But the High Seas Fleet was a spent force. It was a classic example of winning the battle and losing the war. Never again did the High Seas Fleet venture far from harbour. The threat of German naval power was swept from even the North Sea. If Germany was to break the blockade it would have to be done through submarine activity, made all the more difficult now because of the fear that a renewal of unrestricted warfare would bring America into the conflict on the British side, perhaps tipping the finely balanced scales of power against the Germans. The introduction of the convoy to safeguard the seaways across the Atlantic reduced the effectiveness of submarine warfare as well. Throughout 1916 Germany was frustrated, unable to break through on either the Western Front, the blockade, or the Eastern Front. The Brusilov Offensive indicated that Russia was not quite a spent force, and these albeit temporary setbacks for Germany in the East did not increase the confidence of the Central Powers in 1916.

It was becoming clear to both sides that if the war was to be won or lost, it would have to be done the hard way, on the trench-lined Western Front. Throughout 1916 two battles were fought which must be considered among the greatest blood-lettings in history. The German attempt to seize the fortress of Verdun and the British attempt to relieve the fortress by an attack on the Somme literally cost hundreds of thousands of lives on both sides. The French, British and Germans were still labouring under one of the great myths of the Great War: that with one gigantic effort, with sufficient élan, a breakthrough could be achieved if only one persevered and continued to throw more troops into the fray. Both sides were

War in the trenches: Germans have occupied an Allied trench and auxiliaries run up to strengthen its defences against counter-attack

less convinced of this after Verdun and the Somme. On the first day of the Somme offensive, 1st July 1916, 60,000 British lives were lost. Although General Haig was still convinced that with just one more push the 'Boche' would cave in, some of his superiors in London were less willing to sacrifice the lives of a generation. It was as true in Britain as it was in France, Russia and Germany: how much longer could this slaughter go on without the most disastrous social upheavals at home? But how could any government face its people with a peace without victory, merely the cessation of hostilities, which Woodrow Wilson and even the Pope called for?

Yet, although the situation looked increasingly grim for Germany and Austria-Hungary, by 1916, deprived of the charismatic leadership of their old Emperor Franz Joseph who finally died after 68 years of rule over the Habsburg Empire, it was not remarkably better for the Allies. The social upheavals which the war was supposed to postpone or prevent began to break out when the Irish, who had pressed for home rule for two generations, decided to take matters into their own hands in the Easter Week rebellion of 1916, which began a civil war within the United Kingdom for the next six years. Forced to introduce conscription for the first time in its modern history in 1915, with women earning their right to vote by filling the empty places in factories and offices vacated by men in France and elsewhere, the British government now had to divert some of her troops to quell the Irish rebellion, while continuing to conduct the European war. Nationalism was as dangerous a movement to unleash in the British Empire as it was in the Habsburg domains. If the Habsburgs ruled over at least ten different language groups and nationalities, the British ruled over hundreds. While Ireland was in turmoil, India began to question British imperialism. Yet Britain herself used anti-imperialist sentiments when, through the intercession of T.E.Lawrence, she championed Arab

nationalism against the Ottoman Empire in the Arabian peninsula and the Levant.

Implying that national self-determination would be granted to the Arabs if they supported the British invasion of Palestine and Mesopotamia, while at the same time partitioning the area with France in the Sykes-Picot agreement of 1916, the British placated influential Jewish families like the Rothschilds, who helped to underwrite the costs of the war effort, by promising the Jews a 'national homeland' in Palestine after the war was over.

These conflicting promises did not prevent Britain from gaining the support she needed to destroy the Turkish Empire from the Arabs, and from 1916 on steady progress was made in overthrowing Ottoman power in the Levant and replacing it with British troops. While British imperialism was being questioned in Ireland and India, it was clearly on the march in the Middle East.

While neither side was capable of breaking the impasse which the war had reached in 1916, both sought the aid of new weapons which would bring the breakthrough which men could not achieve. Three new weapons were introduced, but none of them was able to achieve victory. Submarines harassed but did not break the blockade. Planes, first used for reconnaissance, later for bombing and dog-fighting in the skies over France, were colourful yet ultimately ineffectual in winning the war. Aerial bombing of Britain by Zeppelins frightened the British population but caused little fundamental damage either to the British fighting spirit or British industry, against which they were aimed. But the introduction of the tank into the fighting on the Western Front in 1916 was the development that was hoped would win the war. Like the introduction of gas warfare into the trenches in 1915, tanks tended to neutralize each other, and were not powerful or numerous enough to have much effect at that time. Gas warfare, however, made life in the trenches even more hellish, cost more lives, but hardly affected

the progress of either of the two sides. Technology, which was assumed to be able to achieve anything, had failed as the armies themselves had failed. As Germany moved even closer to military rule, as Russia edged towards the precipice of revolution, as Austria-Hungary's nationalities demanded more liberty, the French and British populations were tiring of war. Yet, since neither side would accept a peace without victory, victory had to be achieved. British efforts redoubled to bring the United States into the war to tip the scales, while Germany hoped that the long-awaited collapse of Russia would end the two-front war so that she could achieve the last big push in Flanders and France which would secure the victory she almost won before Paris in September 1914.

Germany had one last throw of the dice. As the power of Chancellor Bethmann Hollweg waned, his supremacy over the General Staff weakening with every passing month and with no sign of victory, Falkenhayn, Hindenburg and Ludendorff, supported widely by German public opinion, pressed for the resumption of unrestricted submarine warfare. The calculations of the *Kriegsmarine* that Britain could be brought to her knees within six months of the resumption prevailed. Since war could not be won in any other foreseeable way in early 1917, and since the peace overtures of 1916 had come to nothing, Germany took the gamble: to defeat Britain at once in the hope that America would not enter the war, and that even if she did, she could not bring her potential to bear upon Europe until 1918. By then, Germany hoped, it would be too late. After the submarines were unleashed on 1st February 1917, all eyes turned to the United States. Would Wilson act? And if he did, would American aid come in time to prevent German victory?

The chapter 'Total War' brings us to the point where Allied hopes turned in desperation to the United States, and her millions to fill the ranks of the men who had fallen at Verdun and the Somme . . .

Serbia Overwhelmed

Throughout the spring and summer of 1915, while the great guns scarred the Gallipoli peninsula and gas-clouds drifted over the Flanders trenches, the war along the Danube seemed to hang fire, remote and curiously irrelevant to the issues being decided on other fronts. In December 1914 the Serbs had ejected the Austro-Hungarian invaders from their kingdom and liberated their capital city of Belgrade, and there had been talk in London and Paris of sending aid to Serbia through neutral Greece. But the inexorable demands of the commanders in the west and the frustrations of Gallipoli soon pushed all strategic diversions to the back of men's minds; and for ten months the Serbs and Austrians faced each other over the broad river, reluctant to resume a conflict for which neither side had men or material. The only assistance to reach Serbia was a small naval force (which converted Danube launches into improvised torpedo-boats) and seven surgical hospital units sent to combat the scourge of typhus which was carrying off a thousand victims a day in the overcrowded towns of Niš, Kragujevac, and Skoplje. The cumulative effect of this epidemic and the casualties in the earlier battles was that, after a year of war, the Serbs could put into the field rather less than 200,000 combatants, only half as many as they mobilized in the previous summer.

The decision to eliminate Serbia as a military unit was taken by General Falkenhayn at German headquarters in Pless at the start of August 1915. His prime strategic motive was to strengthen the bonds between the Central powers and their Turkish partner: only by sweeping aside the Serbian obstacle from the middle Danube would it be possible for German troops and supplies to move freely along the trans-European railways, so as to make Turkey an effective ally. The assault on the Serbian positions was to be undertaken by German and Austrian units which would cross the Danube and the Sava under the command of General Mackensen. Within a week this force would receive assistance from two Bulgarian armies advancing from the east, on Niš and Skoplje respectively, so as to cut the links between central Serbia and Salonika along the Morava-Vardar valleys. As a reward for participation in the campaign Bulgaria would secure the areas in Macedonia which she had sought in vain during the Balkan Wars. It was assumed that, before the coming of the full rigours of a Balkan winter, the Serbs would be

trapped at the foot of the savage mountains and destroyed.

The Serbs discovered that the Germans had made overtures to Bulgaria for a military alliance in the middle of September. Immediately Pašič, the Serbian prime minister, telegraphed to Paris an appeal for 150,000 Allied soldiers to be sent to Salonika so as to safeguard the vital railway up the Vardar. The British and French found Venizelos, the prime minister of Greece, not unsympathetic to the landing of Allied troops on Greek soil, but they could not raise so large an army as Pašič had requested. By diverting units from Gallipoli they gathered together a scratch force of 13,000 men, who disembarked at Salonika on 5th October. This Allied response to Serbia's appeal was, however, both too slight and too late. That very day King Constantine of Greece, the Kaiser's brother-in-law, forced Venizelos to resign and installed a new Greek government which was strictly neutralist, if not pro-German. Fifteen hours later, nearly three hundred miles to the north of Salonika, Mackensen's guns opened up on Belgrade and the German and Austrian troops moved through mist and rain to their advanced positions. With the Greek authorities sullenly unco-operative and with three ranges of mountains separating the defenders of Belgrade from the Salonika force, it seemed unlikely that the Allies could bring effective succour to the Serbs.

The initial stages of Mackensen's offensive were a masterpiece of strategic planning, conceived in secrecy and executed with meticulous precision. Falkenhayn had issued a directive that the troops should have 'practically nothing to do but march up and proceed instantly with the crossing'. Concentrated artillery fire ensured that Falkenhayn's orders were carried out to the letter. Within two days Belgrade had fallen, even though the Serbs defended it street by street. Despite a treacherous wind, a bridge was soon thrown across the Danube so that a quarter of a million men were able to begin an advance on Kragujevac within ten days of the start of operations. The Bulgarians duly declared war on 14th October and despatched the I Army in the general direction of Niš, the temporary capital of Serbia and a vital railway-junction only forty-five miles from the Bulgarian frontier.

Mackensen's plan was to break the Serbian army somewhere along the seventy miles which separated Niš itself from Kragujevac. Putnik, the Serbian chief-

Top: Austrian monitor (gunboat) on the Danube bombards Belgrade. *Above:* 'The Last Day of Resistance of Belgrade', a painting by Oscar Laske. The Serbs defended their capital street by street, but with German artillery stiffening their resolve, Mackensen's Austro-German force blasted their way to the heart of the city and crossed the Danube within two days

Total War

of-staff, knew that conditions were desperate but hoped to delay the enemy advance long enough for aid to reach him from the Franco-British force which General Maurice Sarrail was concentrating in Salonika. On 22nd October news reached Putnik that French infantry had thrown back a Bulgarian column near Strumica. The skirmish had taken place more than two hundred miles south of Kragujevac, but it heartened the Serbs. In Niš the citizens decorated the streets with bunting

so as to welcome the French force. The bedraggled flags were still flying mournfully in the rain when the Bulgarians entered the town on 5th November.

The Germans and Austrians failed to trap the Serbs at Kragujevac. The constant rain delayed their advance while the Bulgarians, to the south-east, were held up by the stubborn defenders of the small fortress of Pirot. But the loss of Kragujevac on 31st October was a hard blow for the Serbs. If they were to fall back towards the mountains they had to abandon their stores and supplies. As Mackensen's troops entered the town, flames shot high into the sky and a roar of explosions marked the destruction of Serbia's arsenal.

For another fortnight Putnik's men continued to retreat into the mountainous plateau bordering Albania. Once, and once only, there seemed a chance that Sarrail's army might break through to the Serbs. The French pressed up the Vardar to Negotin, within twenty-five miles of the Serbian outposts at Veles. But at Negotin the French were delayed by an unforeseen obstacle, a bridge left unrepaired from the time of the Balkan Wars. By the time they had crossed the river, Veles had fallen to the Bulgarians and, although they were able to harry the Bulgarian flank, they

86

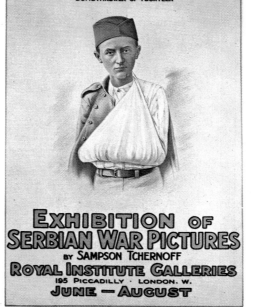

Above: British sympathy—an exhibition held in London in 1915. But the help the Allies sent was too slight and too late. *Left:* Map showing the stages in which the German and Austrian army overran Serbia. *Below:* A Bulgarian anti-aircraft company in Macedonia

could not prevent Mackensen tightening his noose around the retreating Serbs.

A nation on the march

By the middle of November the remnants of the Serbian army were on the plateau of Kosovo, where the medieval Serbian kingdom had fought its final valiant battle against the Turks in 1389. With three of the four escape routes in enemy hands and with a blizzard sweeping in from the east, Putnik decided to make one last bid for safety. Ordering the remaining trucks and guns to be destroyed, he split his force into four columns which were to force their way through the Albanian mountains to the Adriatic, where it was hoped that Allied naval vessels would be at hand to evacuate survivors. On 23rd November the Serbian horde—for it could hardly now be termed an army—took to the mountains.

The Serbian retreat across Albania is an epic of courage and tragedy unique in the chronicle of the First World War. No one knows for certain how many refugees perished in the narrow defiles between the mountain peaks, famished and frozen, as Napoleon's Grand Army had been as it stumbled from the Berezina to the Niemen in 1812. In one contingent alone twenty thousand men and women died during the three weeks which they were forced to spend in the mountains; most were killed by the terrible conditions, but typhus continued to claim its victims and some were butchered by Albanian tribesmen. This was the march of a nation, rather than the withdrawal of a fighting unit from battle. There were men over seventy and boys of twelve and thirteen in the long columns which wound their way slowly towards the coast. King Peter, aged seventy-one, had first fought the Turks in these wild mountains half a century ago; now he trudged along beside his peasant soldiers until, too sick to continue the march, they bore

him with them down to the plain. Prince-Regent Alexander, his son and the eventual King of Yugoslavia, was only twenty-seven, but throughout the march he suffered agonies from a stomach ulcer and underwent an operation before reaching the Adriatic. Putnik, the veteran chief-of-staff, was also a sick man; he was carried across the mountains, barely conscious, in an improvised sedan-chair. Among those on the retreat were Austrian prisoners, captured in the previous campaign, and a group of British nurses—mostly Scottish—who had come to Serbia with the medical units earlier in the year under the auspices of the Women's Suffrage Federation.

For three weeks after the withdrawal from Kosovo there was hardly any news of the Serbs. The enemy was not so rash as to pursue them through the snow, although the Bulgarian VIII Division advanced cautiously into eastern Albania in the middle of December. Sarrail's troops and the British 10th Division (which had been caught by the blizzard along the Bulgaro-Greek frontier) fell back on Salonika where work started on the construction of a fortified camp. The Bulgarians, for the moment, halted on the border of Greece and Serbia.

On 15th December the first Serbian units reached the plain around Scutari, at the northernmost tip of Albania. Many men had trudged for over a hundred miles through the mountains. At Scutari they seemed momentarily safe, protected from the Austrian enemy by their Montenegrin allies to the north. During the following fortnight other groups struggled down from the mountains. But, in reality, the Serbs were still far from safety. At the beginning of January, 1916, the Austrian forces launched an offensive from their Dalmatian bases on Montenegro and

forced the Montenegrins, too, to seek refuge in flight.

Scutari soon became untenable and fell to the Austrians on 22nd January. Once more the Serbs were on the move. This time they found shelter at Durazzo, fifty miles to the south and within the Italian sphere of influence in Albania. There the older men were taken off by sea to Italy or to recuperate in Bizerta. But Durazzo was no resting place. The Austrians approached so rapidly that it was impossible, with such inadequate harbour facilities, to get all the Serbian troops embarked; and, after one last skirmish with the Austrians, the Serbian survivors resumed their southward trek on 10th February down the coast to

Valona, the best port in Albania, 130 miles away. Ships of the Royal Navy escorted fifteen Italian and fourteen French transports from Valona down the ninety-mile channel to Corfu which, although a Greek island, had been occupied by the French in January 1916, despite loud protests from King Constantine in Athens.

That spring hundreds of Serbs lay for weeks in hospital tents on Corfu, recuperating from the rigours of the retreat and the long march south. Perhaps as many as 10,000 died in Corfu or on the small islands off its coast. But others recovered quickly under the warm Ionian sun. Their country was in enemy hands but their spirit remained unbroken. At Salonika, Sarrail was

gathering a cosmopolitan force which, by the end of May 1916, was to number more than 300,000 men. More than a third of this 'Army of the Orient' consisted of veterans from Serbia, re-equipped by the French and transported in convoys from Corfu through the submarine-infested waters around the Cyclades so as to resume the fight. And by the end of November 1916 they were again on Serbian soil, with the town of Monastir in their hands and the confidence that, in time, they would sweep the invaders back to the Danube and beyond.

The retreat—Serbian columns make their way through the mountains

The Naval Blockade

Warring states have from the earliest times endeavoured to deprive their enemies of seaborne supplies. But blockade in its modern form dates only from the beginning of the 17th century when Hugo Grotius, the famous Dutch jurist, put forward the claim for *'Mare Liberum'* – the Freedom of the Seas. This meant that ships flying the flag of a neutral nation, and the goods they carried, should be exempt from seizure by belligerents. The British reply was that he who commanded the sea automatically acquired the right to control all traffic passing over it, regardless of nationality. Thus was born the claim to 'Belligerent Rights', which remained a cardinal feature of British maritime policy for more than two centuries, but was always very unpopular with neutral nations.

In 1856 the Declaration of Paris, an appendage to the treaty ending the Crimean War, was signed. It abolished privateering, from which Great Britain had suffered serious losses in earlier wars; but as it exempted the property of a belligerent state from capture, except in the case of contraband, it went a long way towards accepting Grotius's doctrine. The situation remained unchanged until the winter of 1908-09 when, shortly after the conclusion of the second Hague conference, the principal naval powers met in London and formulated the Declaration of London. This document attempted to define contraband of war by dividing commodities into three classes – absolute contraband, conditional contraband, and free goods. Though it accepted that foodstuffs carried in neutral ships might be declared contraband, such commodities as oil, raw cotton, and rubber were classed as free goods.

Though the Bill giving the Declaration of London the force of law was passed by the Liberal majority in the House of Commons it was thrown out by the House of Lords. Nonetheless, shortly after the outbreak of war in 1914, the Asquith government announced its intention of adhering to its terms. This seemingly short-sighted and gratuitous acceptance of a self-imposed handicap probably arose from the desire to placate opinion in neutral countries, and especially the USA. But it is also true to say that no nation realized at the time that in total war between industrialized countries economic pressure would prove an extremely powerful, perhaps decisive weapon.

There are two types of blockade – usually described as naval blockade and commercial (or economic) blockade. The two types, however, nearly always overlap – that is to say a naval blockade also has commercial implications, and *vice versa*. A naval blockade is enforced by stationing warships off an enemy port with the object of preventing his warships coming out, or of engaging them if they do try to escape. This form of blockade was brought to a fine art by the Royal Navy in the Napoleonic War, and contributed greatly to the defeat of imperial France.

A commercial blockade, on the other hand, aims to cripple the enemy's economy and starve his people into submission by seizing all goods destined to him, even if they are consigned to a neutral nation in the first place, and regardless of the ownership of the ship carrying the goods. The procedure followed begins with the recognized right of a belligerent to 'visit and search' a ship on the high seas, continues with the detention of the cargo if it is believed to be contraband, and ends with the condemnation of the cargo, and possibly of the ship as well, before a nationally constituted Prize Court.

Prior to the Agadir crisis of July 1911 the Asquith government, preoccupied as it was by a far-reaching programme for social and electoral reform, paid comparatively little attention to defence policy or to the strategy to be employed should the threat of war with Germany and her allies (Austria-Hungary and Italy) materialize. But shortly after the crisis, Winston Churchill became first lord of the Admiralty, and under his vigorous direction naval policy and plans became a live issue. The Committee of Imperial Defence (CID), an advisory body of which the prime minister was chairman, began to meet more frequently, and one of its subcommittees reviewed the susceptibility of the Central European powers to the economic pressure of a blockade, and the means required to apply such pressure.

At about the same time, the Admiralty considered the strategy to be employed against the powerful German High Seas Fleet, based in the southern North Sea, and the detached squadrons of cruisers which the German navy had stationed overseas – especially in the Mediterranean and the Pacific. Although the 1908 War Orders had reaffirmed the ancient principle that the Royal Navy's primary function was 'to bring the main German fleet to decisive action', and so secure command of all the seas and oceans, the Admiralty recognized that the High Seas Fleet might well not fall in with such a purpose. Therefore that fleet must be neutralized by a naval blockade of its home bases. The same

Top: Dutch cartoonist Raemaekers shows the Kaiser under pressure of the Royal Navy's blockade. Above: Germany nursing her latest offspring, a submarine, while the Kaiser and Admiral Tirpitz smile down benignly from their portraits. Left: A painting of British dazzle-ships by Edward Wadsworth. The camouflage was intended to confuse German attackers

principle applied to the much less well developed bases used by the detached cruisers, such as Tsingtao on the north east coast of China and the Austrian bases in the Adriatic.

By the early years of the 20th century technical progress, and especially the development of the mine, the submarine, the torpedo, and aircraft had obviously made the old concept of close blockade on the Napoleonic War model totally obsolete. Nonetheless, there was in British naval circles a good deal of hesitation about abandoning what was regarded as a well-tried and provenly effective strategy. Not until the middle of 1912 was close blockade replaced by what was called an 'observational blockade' of the Heligoland Bight. This was to be enforced by a line of cruisers and destroyers patrolling the North Sea from the south-west coast of Norway to the Dutch coast, with heavy squadrons from the main fleet in support to the north and west. But this idea proved short-lived, since it was plainly impossible to patrol a 300-mile-long line effectively, by night and day, in winter and summer.

The blockade plan laid down

A month before the outbreak of war the observational blockade was therefore abandoned in favour of a 'distant blockade' designed to control the exits from the North Sea. This was made possible by the geographical chance which has placed the British Isles like a breakwater across the passages leading from the outer oceans to the German seaports and naval bases on their North Sea and Baltic coasts. The British plan was that the Channel Fleet, based chiefly on the Thames estuary ports, Dover, and Portsmouth, would close the Straits of Dover, while the much more powerful Grand Fleet would be based on Scapa Flow in the Orkneys and would throw out a line of cruisers or armed merchant cruisers (called the Northern Patrol) to watch the remote and stormy waters between the Shetland Islands, Norway, and Iceland. Such was, in brief outline, the final naval blockade plan which was brought into force in August 1914.

But recent technical developments had a much wider influence than merely to render the concept of close blockade obsolete. They all, but especially the mine, proved potent instruments of blockade in their own right, and both sides laid large numbers of mines, and disposed submarines in the approaches to the other side's ports and bases for this purpose. Unfortunately, the early British mines, like their torpedoes, were extremely inefficient, and it was not until 1917, when an exact copy of the German mine was produced in quantity, that the Royal Navy was provided with an efficient mine.

The Admiralty always expected that the enemy's reply to the British blockade would, as in all earlier wars, take the form of an attack on commerce by cruisers and armed merchantmen. This was a perfectly legal form of warfare, subject to the regulations incorporated in the Hague Conventions regarding the safety of the crews of captured merchant ships; and the German surface raiders in fact showed humanity in their observance of those regulations. Before the war the CID reviewed the measures necessary to keep shipping moving despite the possibility of capture, and recommended that the State should receive eighty per cent

of the insurance premiums required to cover war risks on merchant ships and stand eighty per cent of the losses. The Treasury, however, was not at first willing to accept such an intrusion into the field of private enterprise, and the War Risks Insurance scheme did not actually come into force until the outbreak of war.

By July 1915 all the German raiders which had been at sea at the beginning of the war had in fact been destroyed. Allied (mainly British) seapower so dominated the outer seas and oceans that German trade had been brought to an almost complete halt immediately war broke out — except in the Baltic. Many German merchant ships sought refuge in neutral ports, and the transfer of cargoes destined for Germany to neutral ships began at once. Freight rates rose very sharply, and the neutral nations began to reap enormous profits. These developments stimulated

British concern over the emasculation of Belligerent Rights by the Declarations of Paris and London. The first step taken to restore the earlier state of affairs was to issue Orders in Council transferring various commodities from the 'free goods' to the contraband list, and in 1915 the distinction between conditional and absolute contraband was all but wiped out.

On 20th November 1914 a small British merchant ship was sunk by a German submarine in the North Sea and the crew left in the boats — contrary to the Hague Conventions. Other sinkings by submarines soon followed, and thus was ushered in an entirely new element in the German attack on trade — and one for which the Royal Navy was almost totally unprepared. Plainly the implications were very serious. On 11th March 1915 the British government issued an Order in Council, generally referred to as the 'Reprisals Order', since it was made in reprisal for the illegal use of submarines. It declared that goods which could be shown to be destined for Germany were liable to seizure, even though the vessel carrying them was bound for a neutral port.

This led to strong protests from the neutrals, and especially from the USA, regarding interference with what they regarded as legitimate — and of course highly profitable — trade. The USA never moved from the position that the Reprisals Order was illegal — until they themselves were at war. But the real reason for the issue of the order was that the British government

was aware that the Scandinavian countries and Holland were importing vastly greater quantities of goods which were on the British contraband list than they had taken before the war. Obviously the surplus was being passed direct to Germany, and the shipping services of the neutral nations were thus replacing the immobilized German merchant fleet. The leak through the blockade via Italy was never serious, and when she entered the war on the Allied side in May 1915 it stopped altogether. But with the Scandinavian countries and Holland the leak was very large indeed, and it did not prove easy to stop it.

In home waters the British blockade was operated through contraband control stations in the Orkneys and the Downs (the anchorage in the Channel between the Goodwin Sands and the coast), and ships intercepted were sent into one or other

1 A German submarine detains a merchant vessel at sea. 2 German raider Möwe. A disguised merchantman, it made two cruises and sank 122,000 tons of shipping. 3 Armed tanker burning after attack by German U-boat

unless their cargoes were above suspicion. In 1915 the Northern Patrol cruisers intercepted 3,098 ships, and in the following year 3,388. Those sent in for examination totalled 743 and 889 respectively. Many neutral ships called voluntarily at the examination stations, and they were given priority for clearance; but there were always some to whom the prospect of high profits outweighed the risks involved in not conforming with the British regulations. When flagrant cases came to light a series of seizures in prize would probably be organized. For example the very high shipments of lard from USA to Scandinavia were stopped by the seizure of four cargoes in October and November 1914.

Ruffled neutral feathers

On the outbreak of war the CID set up a 'Trading with the Enemy Committee' to control imports through neutral countries; but its procedure proved too slow and cumbrous, and its functions were therefore taken over in March 1915 by the War Trade Intelligence Department, which collected evidence regarding consignees, studied the scale of neutral imports of all

commodities and generally 'acted as a clearing house for the collection, analysis, and dissemination of economic data relating to enemy and neutral trade'. The Exports Control Committee under the Intelligence Department was responsible for issuing import and export licences to shippers, and ruffled neutral feathers were often smoothed by purchasing detained cargoes instead of seizing them in prize.

Nonetheless, difficulties with neutral nations sometimes became acute. Intercepted ships were often subject to long delays, and sometimes they were sunk while being taken into port under British armed guard. After the war the British government paid full value plus five percent accrued interest on all ships sunk in such circumstances. Because of neutral susceptibilities the British government had to move with caution and moderation, especially in dealings with the USA, where the anti-British lobby was powerful and vociferous. The process of keeping American public opinion sweet was, however, aided by German ruthlessness – notably over the sinking of the Cunard liner *Lusitania* on 7th May 1915 with a heavy loss of lives.

The German reply to the tightening British blockade was to declare on 4th February 1915 the whole of the waters around the British Isles a 'War Zone' in which any ship might be sunk without warning. Thus began the first unrestricted submarine campaign. It lasted until August, when the rising tide of neutral protests caused the German government to order a return to less flagrantly illegal methods. However, the substantial tonnage sunk by submarines in that phase (748,914 tons in the whole of 1915) caused great anxiety in Allied circles, and should have provided an opportunity to find the proper antidote – namely convoy. Such, however, was not the case, since the Admiralty remained stubbornly opposed to convoy.

The winter of 1915-16 saw a revival of German surface ship raiders; but this time disguised merchantmen instead of warships were employed. Altogether five such ships were sent out, and one of them (the *Möwe*) made two cruises and sank 122,000 tons of shipping. Two were caught right at the beginning of their careers, but the others proved skilful and elusive enemies. Like their predecessors of the cruiser period they caused considerable delay and dislocation to shipping, and the last of them was not eliminated until early in 1918.

Despite the success achieved by the first unrestricted submarine campaign, the situation as regards the blockade and counterblockade at the end of 1915 was not unfavourable to the Allies. This was the more fortunate because in all theatres of military operations that year was one of unmitigated defeat and disaster for their

British Q ship B2. Posing as unarmed merchantmen, Q ships sailed in submarine-infested waters shelling unwary German submarines with their concealed guns

cause. It was true there was a shortage of shipping, caused partly by excessive requisitioning by the service departments; but the flow of supplies of all kinds had been kept up, and losses of merchant ships, which had totalled 855,721 tons during the year, had been replaced by newly built and captured vessels.

With complete deadlock prevailing on the Western Front, the commercial blockade of Germany had obviously gained in importance. Accordingly in February 1916 the British government set up a new Ministry of Blockade under Lord Robert Cecil to co-ordinate the political and administrative measures necessary to cripple the Central powers' resources. The new ministry, working closely with the War Trade Intelligence Department, gradually built up world-wide control over the movement of all merchant ships and the shipment of cargoes. Consular shipping control officers were installed in all important ports, and they transmitted to London a stream of information regarding the true shippers and consignees of cargoes. With this knowledge in hand the ministry was able to compile a list of firms known to be trading with the enemy, and great ingenuity was shown in exerting pressure to curb their activities. Because bunkering facilities in many overseas ports were British-controlled it was possible to deprive ships of coal and other essential supplies when they called. The location of the greater part of the world's banking and insurance business in London enabled credit and insurance cover to be refused to firms whose activities were not above suspicion. And British control over most of the world's wireless and cable communications made it improbable that such activities would long remain un-

covered. Finally, if a ship did sail with an illicit cargo, the Admiralty would be asked to take special steps to intercept it; and if that succeeded condemnation in prize was virtually certain.

But the Ministry of Blockade did not only work to prevent shipment of contraband cargoes. Neutral nations' imports were rationed with increasing stringency at a figure no greater than they had taken before the war; and goods which were particularly vital to the enemy war effort, such as the special minerals (wolfram and tungsten, for example) used in weapon and armour plate manufacture, were controlled by the pre-emptive purchase of the whole available supply.

One of the first actions of the Ministry of Blockade was to issue (29th February 1916) a 'Statutory Black List' of firms in neutral countries with whom all transactions were forbidden. This aroused strong American protests — since a number of the firms were American. In the following month a system known as 'Letters of Assurance' for approved shippers was introduced. These were always referred to as 'Navicerts' (from the code word used in cables referring to them), and possession of such a letter ensured a ship unhindered passage through the blockade. Encouragement was given to shippers to arrange with London for advance booking of cargoes, which would then be approved or disapproved by the Contraband Committee.

Neutral shipowners were also given every encouragement to order their ships to call in voluntarily for examination at Scapa Flow and the Downs or at Halifax, Alexandria, and Gibraltar where additional stations were set up. In 1916 no less than 1,878 neutral vessels called in voluntarily, 950 were intercepted and sent

in, and only 155 (some five per cent of the total) successfully ran the blockade. New Orders in Council were issued to increase the stringency of the blockade — notably that of 7th July 1916 which repealed the Declaration of London Order in Council of August 1914. Throughout 1916 the effectiveness of the Allied machinery of commercial blockade steadily increased.

The Germans did not, of course, take this escalation of Allied blockade measures lying down. In March 1916 they renewed the unrestricted submarine campaign, and again quickly achieved a fairly high rate of sinkings — 126,000 tons in April. However, they once again caused the loss of American lives, and the resultant protests produced a temporary lull. In September they tried again, and despite the wide variety of measures introduced by the Admiralty to combat the submarine menace — minefields, nets, surface patrols, and the much advertised 'mystery' or 'Q-ships' — German submarines sank nearly 147,000 tons of shipping in October. The implications were plainly very serious, since if the upward trend continued the loss to be anticipated in 1917 would exceed 2,000,000 tons. Furthermore the total Allied shipping losses in 1916 amounted to 1,237,634 tons, which was nearly fifty per cent higher than in the previous year; and, finally, the rate of sinking of U-boats had not been satisfactory in relation to the speed at which new ones were built. From the beginning of the war to the end of 1916 only forty-six had been sunk.

But if the closing months of 1916 brought little comfort to those responsible for maintaining the flow of Allied supplies, to the German people the implication of that year's developments were far more threatening. Though their armed forces had not suffered appreciably, since they were given priority for all available supplies, the condition of the civilian population was beginning to deteriorate seriously. The 1915 and 1916 harvests had been bad, due chiefly to lack of imported fertilizers, the conquered territories in eastern Europe had failed to replace supplies from overseas, home producers of foodstuffs were withholding their produce or selling it on the extensive black market, the calorific value of the civilian ration was falling steadily, and the shortage of clothing was becoming increasingly acute. With the winter of 1916-17 approaching — it was to be remembered in Germany as the 'Turnip Winter' — the outlook was grim indeed.

Such was the state of affairs that led the German government to adopt the desperate expedient of renewed submarine warfare on merchant shipping in February 1917; and that led to the entry of the USA into the war, and so to the utter defeat of the Central powers.

The Battle of Jutland

The British view

With the arrival of spring 1916, the First World War was eighteen months old. On land a decision had eluded the opposing armies; they had settled into a war of attrition bleeding both sides white. At sea the two most powerful fleets the world had ever seen faced each other across the North Sea, each eager to engage the other, but neither able to bring about an en-counter on terms favourable to itself.

The British Grand Fleet, under Admiral Sir John Jellicoe, was concentrated at Scapa Flow, in the Orkneys, whence, it was calculated, the northern exit from the North Sea could be closed to the enemy, while the German fleet could still be inter-cepted and brought to battle should it threaten the British coasts. The British ability to read German coded radio mes-

Signals before the battle. 31st May 1916: the greatest battle fleet the world had ever seen steams into the North Sea to meet its German rival

Total War

Overleaf: HMS Lion *leads cruisers* Warrior *and* Defence *into action (left) and battle-cruisers* Princess Royal, Tiger, *and* New Zealand *(right). Painted by W. Wyllie RA (Reproduced by permission of Earl Beatty)*

sages enabled them to obtain warning of any impending moves.

The German High Seas Fleet, numerically much inferior to its opponent, could contemplate battle with only a portion of the British Grand Fleet. From almost the beginning of the war its strategy had been aimed at forcing the British to divide their strength so that this might be brought about. Raids by the German battle-cruiser force, commanded by Rear-Admiral Hipper, on English east coast towns had been mounted. The failure of the Grand Fleet to intercept these had resulted in the Grand Fleet's battle-cruiser force, under Vice-Admiral Sir David Beatty, being based at Rosyth; and when Hipper again sortied in January 1915 he had been intercepted. In the battle of Dogger Bank which had followed, the German armoured cruiser *Blücher* had been sunk and the battle-cruiser *Seydlitz* had narrowly escaped destruction when a shell penetrated her after turret, starting a conflagration among the ammunition. Only flooding the magazine had saved her.

Further adventures by the High Seas Fleet had been forbidden by the Kaiser and the Germans had launched their first unrestricted U-boat campaign against Allied merchant shipping. For the rest of 1915 the High Seas Fleet had languished in port, chafing against its inaction.

But in January 1916, its command had been taken over by Admiral Reinhard Scheer who had at once set about reanimating it. Raids on the English coast were resumed. As before, the Grand Fleet, in spite of the warnings received through radio interception, had been unable to reach the scene from Scapa Flow in time to interfere. Jellicoe was forced to agree to his 5th Battle Squadron—the fast and powerful Queen Elizabeth-class ships—joining Beatty's Battle-cruiser Fleet at Rosyth.

When in May 1916, the U-boat campaign was called off at the threat of American intervention on the Allied side and the submarines recalled, Scheer had the conditions necessary for his ambition to bring about a fleet action on favourable terms by bringing the three arms of the fleet simultaneously into play. His surface forces were to sortie for a bombardment of Sunderland and lure the enemy to sea where his U-boats could ambush them, while his Zeppelin airships would scout far afield and so enable him to avoid any confrontation with a superior enemy concentration.

Plans were drawn up for the latter part of May; the actual date, to be decided at the last moment, would depend upon when the fleet was brought up to full strength by the return of the battle-cruiser *Seydlitz* from repairs caused by mine damage during a previous sortie, and upon suitable weather for the airships to reconnoitre

efficiently. Meanwhile the U-boats, sixteen in number, sailed on 17th May for their stations off Scapa, Cromarty, and the Firth of Forth. Their endurance made the 30th the latest possible date. The *Seydlitz* did not rejoin until the 28th, however, and then a period of hazy weather set in, unsuitable for air reconnaissance.

Against such a development, an alternative plan had been prepared. Hipper's battle-cruiser force was to go north from the Heligoland Bight and 'trail its shirt' off the Norwegian coast where it would be duly reported to the British. Beatty's battle-cruiser fleet from Rosyth would come racing eastwards to fall into the trap of the High Seas Fleet battle squadrons, waiting some forty miles to the southward of Hipper, before the Grand Fleet from Scapa could intervene.

The trap is set

Such a plan—assuming an unlikely credulity on the part of the British—was naïve, to say the least, even allowing for the fact that the British ability to read German wireless signals was not realized. Nevertheless, when the thick weather persisted throughout the 28th and 29th, it was decided to employ it. On the afternoon of 30th May, the brief signal went out to the High Seas Fleet assembled in the Schillig Roads—31GG2490, which signified 'Carry out Secret Instruction 2490 on 31st May'.

This was duly picked up by the Admiralty's monitoring stations and though its meaning was not known, it was clear from various indications that some major operation by the German fleet was impending. At once the organization for getting the Grand Fleet to sea swung into action; the main body under the commander-in-chief, with his flag in the *Iron Duke,* including the three battle-cruisers of the 3rd Battle-Cruiser Squadron, who had been detached there from Rosyth for gunnery practice, sailed from Scapa Flow; from the Cromarty Firth sailed the 2nd Battle Squadron, the 1st Cruiser Squadron, and a flotilla of destroyers. These two forces were to rendezvous the following morning (31st) in a position some ninety miles west of Norway's southerly point. When joined, they would comprise a force of no less than 24 dreadnought battleships, 3 battle-cruisers, 8 armoured cruisers, 12 light cruisers, and 51 destroyers. Beatty's Battle-Cruiser Fleet—6 battle-cruisers, the four 15-inch-gun, fast Queen Elizabeth-class battleships, 12 light cruisers, 28 destroyers, and a seaplane carrier—was to steer from the Firth of Forth directly to reach a position some 120 miles west of the Jutland Bank at 1400 on the 31st, which would place him some sixty-nine miles ahead of the Grand Fleet as it steered towards the Heligoland Bight. If Beatty had sighted

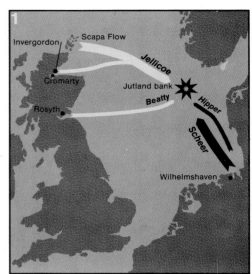

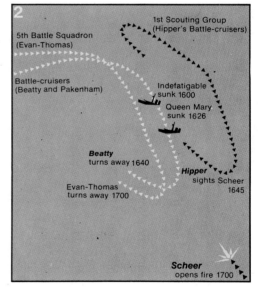

1 The titans weigh anchor and steam to battle stations on the Jutland Bank, 31st May 1916. 2 Battle-cruiser action, 1415-1800, 31st May. Lacking flash-tight magazines and betrayed by inadequate armour protection, Indefatigable *and* Queen Mary *exploded under a hail of fire from Hipper's ships. 3 First fleet action, 1815-1835. Scheer had manoeuvred into the worst possible situation for a fleet action. Only by ordering a simultaneous 'about turn' could he extricate himself from the trap so brilliantly sprung by Jellicoe. 4 Second fleet action, 1912-1926. The British battle fleet opened fire at 1912 but the engagement was broken off when Scheer executed a second 'about turn', at the same time launching a massed torpedo attack. Jellicoe promptly countered by turning his own battle line. 5 Loss of contact during the night of 31st May-1st June, 2100-0300. Scheer eluded Jellicoe and ran for home.*

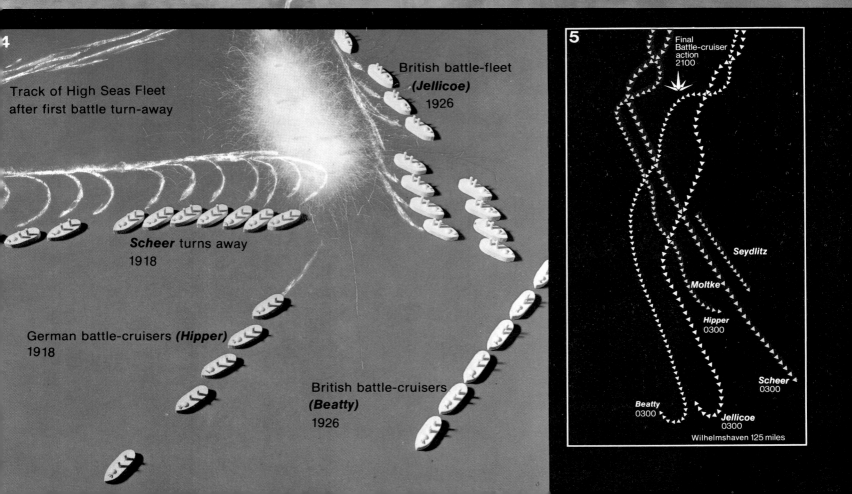

Jellicoe deploys battle-fleet into line of battle
1815

5th Battle Squadron
(Evan-Thomas)

Warspite disabled
1826

British battle-cruisers
(Beatty, Hood,
and **Pakenham)**

Scheer executes battle turn-away
1835

German battle-cruisers **(Hipper)**
1835

Track of High Seas Fleet
after first battle turn-away

British battle-fleet
(Jellicoe)
1926

Scheer turns away
1918

German battle-cruisers **(Hipper)**
1918

British battle-cruisers
(Beatty)
1926

Final
Battle-cruiser
action
2100

Seydlitz

Moltke

Hipper
0300

Scheer
0300

Beatty
0300

Jellicoe
0300

Wilhelmshaven 125 miles

'Some Sea Officers, 1914-1918' painted by Sir Arthur S.Cope RA. Among them, left to right, are Beatty who led the battle-cruiser fleet at Jutland (left foreground), Sturdee (seated centre right), and Jellicoe, who was the commander-in-chief at Jutland (far right)

no enemy by that time, he was to turn north to meet Jellicoe.

Thus, long before the first moves of Scheer's plan to lure Beatty out had been made, the whole vast strength of the British fleet was at sea. The schemer was liable to have the tables turned on him. The first aim of Scheer's project had already been missed. His U-boats had failed to deliver any successful attacks on the British squadrons as they sortied; furthermore their reports of what they had seen added up only to various isolated squadrons at sea and gave no warning that the Grand Fleet was at sea in strength.

At 0100 on 31st May, therefore, the first ships of Hipper's force — five battle-cruisers of the 1st Scouting Group (*Lützow* (flagship), *Derfflinger, Seydlitz, Moltke, Von der Tann*), four light cruisers of the 2nd Scouting Group, and 33 destroyers led by another light cruiser — weighed anchor and steered north past Heligoland and through the swept channels, leaving the Horn Reef light vessel to the eastward of them. They were followed, fifty miles astern, by Scheer, his flag in the *Friedrich der Grosse*, leading 16 dreadnought battleships, 6 predreadnoughts, and accompanied by 5 light cruisers of the 4th Scouting Group and 39 destroyers led by a light cruiser.

By 1400 Hipper was abreast the Jutland Bank off the Danish coast — his scouting light cruisers spread on an arc extending from ahead to either beam, some seven to ten miles from the battle-cruisers. It was a clear, calm, summer day with visibility extreme but likely to become hazy as the afternoon wore on. Unknown to Hipper and equally ignorant of his presence, Beatty was fifty miles to the north-westward, zigzagging at 19 knots on a mean course of east and approaching the eastward limit set for his advance, with his light cruisers scouting ahead in pairs. The signal to turn north was made at 1415 and was obeyed by all except the light cruiser *Galatea*

which held on to investigate smoke on the eastern horizon. This came from a Danish merchantman and was simultaneously being investigated by the western-most of Hipper's light cruisers, the *Elbing*. The two warships thus came in sight of one another, reported, and fired the opening shots of the battle of Jutland.

The two battle-cruiser admirals turned at once towards the sound of the guns which soon brought them in sight of one another on opposite courses, when Hipper altered course to the southward to lead his opponents towards the advancing German battle squadrons. That these were at sea was still unknown to either Beatty or Jellicoe. The British radio monitoring stations had been led to believe that the High Seas Fleet was still in harbour, misled by an arrangement on the part of Scheer's staff which transferred the flagship's call-sign to a shore station so that the commander-in-chief would not be distracted by administrative matters.

The battle-cruisers open fire

The *Lion*, leading *Princess Royal, Queen Mary, Tiger, New Zealand* and *Indefatigable* (in that order), turned on a parallel course and at 1548 each side opened fire. Hipper was outnumbered, six ships to five. He would have been even more, perhaps disastrously, inferior, but for Beatty's impetuosity in racing at full speed into action without waiting for the 5th Battle Squadron, which was not only initially six miles farther from the enemy but, owing to signal confusion, failed to conform at once to Beatty's movements. By the time it did so, it was ten miles astern, and it was not until twenty-seven minutes after action had been joined that the 15-inch guns of the British battleships could open fire.

In the interval much had happened. Hipper's ships had quickly displayed a gunnery superiority over their opponents who were very slow to find the range. The *Lion,*

Princess Royal, and *Tiger* had all been heavily hit before a single German ship had suffered; though the *Seydlitz, Derfflinger,* and *Lützow* were then each hit hard, the advantage had continued to lie with Hipper's ships and at 1600 Beatty's rear ship, *Indefatigable,* had blown up and sunk as shells plunged through into her magazines. Almost simultaneously the *Lion* had been only saved from a similar fate by flooding the magazine of her mid-ship turret when it was penetrated by a shell from the *Lützow*.

But now, at last, the 5th Battle Squadron (*Barham, Valiant, Warspite, Malaya,* lying in that order) was able to get into action. Their gunnery was magnificent. The two rear ships of Hipper's line were quickly hit. Disaster must have overwhelmed him but for a defect of the British shells, some of which broke up on impact instead of penetrating the armour. Nevertheless, it seemed impossible Hipper could survive long enough for Scheer's battle-squadrons, still over the horizon, to come to his rescue. In spite of this the German battle-cruisers continued to shoot with deadly accuracy and at 1626 the *Queen Mary,* betrayed, like the *Indefatigable,* by her inadequate armour, blew up.

Meanwhile, a destroyer battle had been raging between the lines, the flotillas on each side moving out to attack with torpedoes and meeting to fight it out with guns. Of all the torpedoes fired, one only, from the British *Petard,* found a billet in the *Seydlitz,* but did not damage her enough to put her out of action. Two British destroyers were sunk.

The fast-moving battle had left the majority of Beatty's scouting cruisers behind, except for Commodore Goodenough's 2nd Light Cruiser Squadron which by 1633 had succeeded in getting two miles ahead of the *Lion*. At that moment to Goodenough's astonished gaze the top masts of a long line of battleships hove in sight.

The battle-cruiser Seydlitz, *one of the five ships in Hipper's 1st Scouting Group, on fire during the Battle of Jutland. Although she was heavily damaged both by the torpedo from the* Petard *and by shellfire, she was not put out of action*

In the radio rooms of the ships of the British fleet, the message, which all had almost despaired of ever hearing, was taken in: 'Have sighted enemy battle fleet, bearing SE. Enemy's course North.'

Hipper had been saved in the nick of time, and his task of luring Beatty brilliantly achieved. Goodenough's timely warning, however, enabled the latter to escape the trap. Before the enemy battle fleet came within range, Beatty reversed course to the northward. The 5th Battle Squadron held on for a while to cover the damaged battle-cruisers' retreat. By the time they turned back themselves they came under heavy fire from the German battle squadrons and *Malaya*, in particular, received damaging hits. In reply they did heavy damage to the *Lützow, Derfflinger,* and *Seydlitz,* as well as hitting the leading German battleships.

The situation had now been reversed, with Beatty drawing the enemy after him towards a superior force the latter knew nothing of—the Grand Fleet, pressing southwards at its best speed of 20 knots. Jellicoe's twenty-four battleships were in the compact cruising formation of six columns abeam of each other, with the fleet flagship leading the more easterly of the two centre columns. Before encountering the enemy they would have to be deployed into a single battle line to allow all ships to bring their guns to bear. If deployment was delayed too long, the consequences could be disastrous. To make a deployment by the right method, it was essential to know the bearing on which the approaching enemy would appear.

For various reasons—discrepancy between the calculated positions of the two portions of the fleet and communication failures—this was just what Jellicoe did not know. And, meanwhile, the two fleets were racing towards each other at a combined speed of nearly 40 knots. Even though Beatty's light cruisers had made

visual contact with Jellicoe's advanced screen of armoured cruisers at 1630, though the thunder of distant gun-fire had been audible for some time before the *Marlborough,* leading the starboard column of the Grand Fleet battleships, sighted gun-flashes through the gathering haze and funnel smoke ahead at 1750, and six minutes later Beatty's battle-cruisers were sighted from the *Iron Duke* racing across the line of Jellicoe's advance—and incidentally spreading a further pall of black smoke—it was not until nearly 1815 that at last, in the nick of time, the vital piece of information reached the commander-in-chief from the *Lion:* 'Enemy battle fleet bearing south-west.'

Jellicoe's vital decision

During the next minute or so, through the mind of Jellicoe as he stood gazing at the compass in its binnacle on the bridge of the *Iron Duke,* sped the many considerations on the accurate interpretation of which, at this moment of supreme crisis, the correct deployment and all chances of victory depended. The decision Jellicoe made—to deploy on his port wing column on a course south-east by east—has been damned and lauded by opposing critics in the controversy that was later to develop.

To the appalled Scheer, as out of the smoke and haze ahead of him, between him and retreat to his base, loomed an interminable line of dim grey shapes from which rippled the flash of heavy gunfire, and a storm of shell splashes began to fall round the leading ships of his line, there was no doubt. His 'T' had been crossed—the worst situation possible in a fleet action. Fortunately for him a counter to such a calamity, a simultaneous 'about turn' by every ship of the battle columns—a manoeuvre not lightly undertaken by a mass of the unwieldy battleships of the day—had been practised and perfected by the High Seas Fleet. He ordered it now,

and so, behind a smoke screen laid by his destroyers extricated himself from the trap so brilliantly sprung by Jellicoe.

His escape was only temporary, nevertheless. Between him and his base was a force whose full strength he had been unable as yet to determine, which he must either fight or somehow evade.

While the trap was thus being sprung on Scheer, some final spectacular successes had been achieved by the Germans. Of the 5th Battle Squadron, the *Warspite,* with her helm jammed, had charged towards Scheer's battle line and before she could be got under control again, had been severely damaged and forced out of action. Jellicoe's advanced screen of armoured cruisers had been caught at short range by Hipper's battle-cruisers and the leading German battleships as they emerged from the smoke haze. The *Defence* had been overwhelmed and blown up, the *Warrior* so heavily damaged that she staggered out of action to sink on her way back to harbour. Then the German battle-cruisers had encountered the three battle-cruisers attached to the Grand Fleet. In a brief gun duel at short range, the Germans had suffered many hits and further damage; but in reply had sunk the *Invincible*.

This was the last major success for the Germans, however. They had fought magnificently and, with the aid of superior ship design and ammunition, had had much the better of the exchanges, though the *Lützow* was by now fatally crippled, limping painfully off the scene, and only the stout construction and well-designed compartmentation of the other battle-cruisers was saving them from a similar state. But Scheer was now desperately on the defensive, though he had not yet realized that it was the whole Grand Fleet he had encountered. As soon as his initial retreat brought relief from the concentration of fire on his van, he reversed course once again in the hope of being able to cut

Above: Battle-cruiser Indefatigable *going into action at Jutland. **Below:** Battleship* Warspite *laid up in dry dock*

Above: *Battleship* Malaya *of the 5th Battle Squadron. **Below:** Battle-cruiser* Invincible. *Blew up like* Indefatigable

through astern of the enemy to gain a clear escape route to the Horn Reef lightship and safety behind his own minefields. Once again he ran up against the immense line of dreadnoughts of which all he could see in the poor visibility to the eastward was the flickering orange light of their broadsides. Once again he had hastily to retire or be annihilated.

While he was extricating himself he launched his much-tried battle-cruisers on a rearguard thrust and his destroyer flotillas to deliver a massed torpedo attack. The former miraculously survived a further hammering before being recalled. The latter launched a total of twenty-eight torpedoes at the British line. More than any other single factor they were to save the High Seas Fleet from disaster, robbing Jellicoe of the fruits of the strategic masterpiece he had brought about.

The counter to the massed torpedo attack by destroyers, which could be backed by long-range torpedo fire from retreating battleships, had been carefully studied. There were several alternatives; the only one sufficiently effective in Jellicoe's opinion, was a simultaneous turn away by his own battle line. This was promptly carried out—a turn of 45 degrees.

Contact lost

The two battle fleets were now on widely diverging courses and rapidly ran out of range and sight of one another. By the time the twenty-eight torpedoes had been avoided—not one scored a hit—and the British battle line turned back to regain contact, more than fifteen miles separated Jellicoe and Scheer. Sunset was barely half an hour away. Yet there was time in the long summer twilight ahead for the battle to be renewed on greatly advantageous terms for Jellicoe if he turned at once to an interception course. That he did not do so until too late for various reasons, not the least of which was the failure of his scouting forces to keep him informed of the enemy's position and movements, was to be the central feature of much criticism.

The van of the German battle fleet came, in fact, briefly into view from the nearest British battleship division at the moment that Jellicoe, who was not willing to accept the uncertain fortunes of a night action, ordered a turn away and the adoption of a compact night cruising disposition. The opportunity was let slip, never to return.

Nevertheless, at this stage, as night settled down over a calm sea, the outlook for Scheer was bleak, indeed. Between him and his base was an overwhelming enemy force. Unless he could get past it during the night, the battle must be resumed at daybreak and, with a long summer day ahead, it could only spell annihilation for him. He decided his only hope was to try

to bludgeon his way through, regardless of consequences. To his fleet he signalled the course for the Horn Reef Light at a speed of 16 knots, adding the instruction that this course was to be maintained at all costs.

Jellicoe, having formed his night disposition and ordered his flotillas (many of whom had not yet been in action) to the rear, was steering a course slightly converging with that of Scheer but at a knot faster. From Jellicoe's point of view, Scheer had the choice of two routes—to the entrance of the channels which began at the Horn Reef Light or southward into the German Bight before turning eastward round the mined areas. The extra knot would keep the Grand Fleet between Scheer and the latter. If he chose the former he must pass astern of Jellicoe's battle squadrons, where he would encounter the massed British flotillas which could be counted on to inflict severe losses and to keep Jellicoe informed.

In the event the British flotillas failed to do either of these things. The pre-dreadnought battleship *Pommern* and a light cruiser were their sole victims in a series of night encounters, and they passed no information of the position and course of the enemy. On the other hand Scheer's message to his fleet was intercepted by the Admiralty and was passed to Jellicoe, though a further message in which Scheer asked for airship reconnaissance of the Horn Reef area at dawn which would have clinched the matter, was withheld.

In the absence of certain knowledge of the enemy's movements, Jellicoe held on through the night. Scheer crossed astern of him and by daylight was safe, a development which seemed little short of miraculous to the German admiral.

The battle of Jutland was over. Controversy as to its outcome was to rage for decades. The bald facts, of which German publicity made the most in claiming a great victory, while the British Admiralty's communiqué did nothing to explain or qualify them, showed that a superior British force had lost three capital ships, three cruisers, and a number of destroyers against one battle-cruiser, a pre-dreadnought battleship, four cruisers, and some destroyers sunk on the German side.

Even to-day more than fifty years since the battle, it is not easy to strike a balance sheet of victory and defeat. British losses were largely the result of inferior armour protection in their battle-cruisers, which had been accepted in favour of mounting bigger guns, the advantage of which had been lost through faulty design of armour-piercing shells. Even so, one of the surviving German battle-cruisers only reached harbour in a sinking condition, another was a hideous shambles with 200 casualties, bearing witness to the pounding they had received even from defective shells.

The High Seas Fleet was no longer fit for battle on the morning of the 1st June 1916 and could only make for harbour and repairs, fortunately close at hand. The Grand Fleet was largely intact and ready to renew the fight. Jellicoe may be said, perhaps, to have lost the battle of Jutland. Scheer can hardly be judged to have won anything but an escape from annihilation.

So much for the immediate results of the encounter. They do not add up to a victory for either side. In the larger context of the war at sea as a whole, it is no easier to weigh the results. When Scheer led the High Seas Fleet out once again in August 1916 (except for *Seydlitz* and *Derfflinger*, still under repair), he narrowly escaped being caught in a second Jutland trap, with no safe base under his lee this time, in spite of Zeppelin reconnaissance aloft. Both Scheer and the Kaiser's general head-quarters were finally convinced that the risks to be faced in attempting to bring about a sea fight were unacceptable. The High Seas Fleet, built at such cost to challenge Great Britain's seapower, was ordered back on to the defensive. The fatal decision was taken to revert to the un-restricted submarine warfare which was to bring America into the war.

It is true, of course, that the High Seas Fleet kept 'in being', forced the continued maintenance of the huge Grand Fleet, ab-sorbing many thousands of trained seamen and a hundred destroyers which could have been more profitably employed combating the U-boats. On the other hand, that same High Seas Fleet, its ships lying idle in harbour, the morale of its crews sinking, degenerated into a centre of discontent and revolution. In August 1917 Scheer had to quell an open mutiny. A year later, when ordered to sea by its new commander, Hipper, it flared into revolt and led the disintegration of the Kaiser's Germany. This, too, can be accounted one of the con-sequences of Jutland – perhaps the most important when reviewing the war as a whole.

The German view

Jutland was the last of many naval battles fought by long lines of closely spaced big ships with heavy guns. Its tactical details are well-known, for each ship kept a log. Its results were inconclusive. It was the climax of the Anglo-German naval rivalry, with the scuttling of the German fleet at Scapa Flow three years later as the anti-climax.

This rivalry, which cost both nations dearly, was at least partly caused by the fact that the Germans did not fully realize the implications of seapower. In their difficult position in central Europe they needed a navy of some strength to balance the fleets of the Franco-Russian alliance. But from their inferior strategic position in the south-eastern corner of the North Sea they could neither protect their over-seas trade nor attack the sea routes vital to Great Britain. When war broke out in 1914 the Royal Navy was not compelled to attack the German bases but could content itself on the whole with a distant blockade from Scapa Flow.

In the first two years of the war there were a number of operations and clashes in the North Sea which did not change the situation, since neither side wanted to give battle too far from their own bases. In 1916 this changed to some extent. Admiral Reinhard Scheer, the new commander-in-chief of the German High Seas Fleet, was more aggressive than his predecessors. On the Allied side, the Russians felt the blockade heavily and clamoured for the British to force the Baltic so that they might receive ammunition and raw materials which they needed desperately. An operation of that kind had no prospects of success, however, as long as the High Seas Fleet was intact. Therefore it was decided that stronger efforts should be made to bring it to battle. The Grand Fleet under Admiral Sir John Jellicoe had been considerably reinforced by new ships. In spring 1916 it was almost twice as strong as the German fleet.

Early in March, the German fleet made a sortie into the southern North Sea and came within sixty miles of Lowestoft. On 25th March British light forces operated south of Horn Reef, and aircraft from a sea-plane-carrier tried to bombard airship sheds. Bad weather prevented contact of the heavy ships. On 25th April German battle-cruisers bombarded Lowestoft. Early in May the British repeated the attempt to attack airship sheds. Both fleets were at sea, but no contact was established.

For the second half of May, Admiral Scheer planned an operation with all his forces. The battle-cruisers were to bom-bard Sunderland, and twelve submarines were stationed off the British bases to attack the squadrons of the Grand Fleet when they put to sea. Scouting by airships was necessary for the German fleet to avoid being cut off by superior forces. When the time ran out for his submarines after two weeks at sea and the weather remained unfavourable, Scheer compro-mised on a sweep of his light forces through the Skagerrak backed up by the battle fleet. Shortly after midnight of 30th to 31st May 1916 the German scouting forces (5 battle-cruisers, 5 light cruisers, and 30 destroyers under Rear-Admiral Hipper) left Schillig Roads near Wilhelmshaven, soon followed by the battle fleet (16 new and 6 old battleships, 6 light cruisers, and 33 destroyers).

Above: German cruiser Blücher *sinking in battle of Dogger Bank, January 1915.*
Below: Iron Duke, *Jellicoe's flagship*

Above: Beatty's flagship Lion *firing first shots in the battle. Below:* Derfflinger, *the battle-cruiser that sank* Invincible

Total War

The Grand Fleet at sea

At that time the Grand Fleet was already at sea, course set for the Skagerrak, too. The bombardment of Lowestoft had roused public opinion, the situation of the Russians had deteriorated, and Jellicoe now planned to set a trap for the German fleet. Light cruisers were to sweep through the Skagerrak deep into the Kattegat; in the meantime the main forces would take up position near Horn Reef to meet the Germans who were sure to come out in order to intercept the British cruisers operating in the Kattegat.

In the early afternoon of 31st May occurred the first of the incidents which greatly changed the course of the events. The British battle-cruiser fleet, under Vice-Admiral Sir David Beatty in *Lion*, changed course from east to north to rendezvous with the battle fleet under Admiral Jellicoe in *Iron Duke*. At 1430 *Lützow*, flying Admiral Hipper's flag, was only forty-five miles east of *Lion* steering a slightly converging course. Contact would have been made considerably later but for a small Danish steamer plodding along between the two forces. Two German destroyers and a British light cruiser were dispatched to examine her. Soon the first salvoes were fired; the first hit (a dud) was made by *Elbing* on *Galatea*.

Within minutes wireless messages informed the admirals of the situation. Signals went up, Hipper swung his force round, and Beatty soon followed suit. The crews were alerted by bugles sounding action stations, guns and powder rooms were manned, steam was raised in reserve boilers, and damage parties assembled deep down in the ships. The gunnery officers climbed to their elevated positions, received ready reports from turrets, range-finders, and fire-control-stations, and then reported their batteries ready for action to their captains. Now a hush of expectancy fell over the great ships while the distance decreased by nearly a mile a minute.

At first, sight was obscured by the smoke of the cruisers. Then these fell back on their battle-cruisers, and the huge shapes of the adversaries came into each other's sight, but only for the few men whose duty was to watch the enemy. Almost all the technical personnel and most of the sailors fought without seeing an enemy ship.

Hipper faced heavy odds, ten ships with heavier guns against his five. His plan was simple: to draw the enemy to Scheer's battle fleet, which was following at a distance of fifty miles. His smaller calibres (11- and 12-inch as against 12-, 13-, and 15-inch in the British ships) made it imperative for him to get comparatively close before opening fire. He offered battle on a north-westerly course, reversed course

when Beatty tried to cut his force off, and with a few terse signals coolly manoeuvred his fine ships through the danger zone. At 1548 they were at the right distance (16,500 yards) and in perfect order. The *Lützow* opened fire.

Beatty's ships started answering quickly but they were not yet in formation to use all their guns. Because of delays in signalling, the four powerful and fast battleships of the Queen Elizabeth-class had fallen astern and were out of range. Conditions for a gunnery duel were perfect: visibility was good, especially to the west, and there was hardly any seaway.

First blood to the Germans

The first salvoes all appear to have fallen wide, perhaps because the range-takers were more interested in the details of their foes than in measuring the distance exactly. After three minutes the Germans obtained hits on *Lion*, *Princess Royal*, and *Tiger*. Because the first target in sight had been light cruisers, the gunnery officer of *Lützow* had given orders to load shells detonating on impact. For reasons of ballistics he did not change over to armour-piercing shells. *Lion* was hit twelve times and suffered heavy casualties, but minor injuries only, except for one shell which penetrated the roof of a turret, killed the gun crews, and ignited powder-bags. The turret-commander, Major Harvey of the Royal Marines, was fatally wounded but before he died he ordered the magazines to be flooded and thus saved the ship.

Now disaster struck the rear of the British line. Here *Indefatigable* and *Von der Tann* fought an even match. At 1604, *Indefatigable*, hit by two salvoes in quick succession, erupted in a violent explosion, turned over to port and disappeared in the waves. *Von der Tann* had fired fifty-two 11-inch shells in all. Twenty minutes later a similar fate overtook *Queen Mary* who had come under the concentrated fire of *Derfflinger* and *Seydlitz*. After vehement detonations she capsized and went down with her propellers still turning. *Tiger*, the next astern, barely avoided crashing into the wreck.

In spite of these losses the situation now eased for the British. The magnificent 5th Battle Squadron, ably handled by Rear-Admiral Evan-Thomas, came up and took the rear ships of the German line under fire. When one of the projectiles, weighing almost a ton, struck *Von der Tann* far aft, the whole ship vibrated like a gigantic tuning-fork. Hipper increased speed and distance and sent his destroyers to the attack. They were met by British destroyers, and in the ensuing mêlée *Nomad* and two Germans were sunk. At the same time 1630 the 2nd Light Cruiser Squadron under Commodore Goodenough

sighted smoke to the south-east and, soon after, a seemingly endless column of heavy ships surrounded by light cruisers and destroyers.

Now the tables were turned. Under heavy fire Beatty reversed course and steered to the north to draw the High Seas Fleet to the British Battle Fleet. *Barham* and *Malaya* received several hits which did not, however, impair their speed, but, *Nestor*, attacking the German van with some other destroyers, was sunk. When her boatswain was rescued with other survivors he was mainly disgusted at the smallness and squalor of the coal-burning torpedo-boat which had picked him up.

All through these events the British Battle Fleet had been steadily drawing nearer, in cruising formation with its twenty-four battleships in six divisions, these in line abreast, screened by armoured and light cruisers and destroyers. The 3rd Battle-Cruiser Squadron, under Rear-Admiral Hood in *Invincible*, was twenty-five miles ahead and far to the east of its calculated position. Jellicoe, 'the only man who could lose the war in an afternoon', was now faced with the decision on which course to form his divisions into single line ahead. In all war games and exercises the rule had been 'towards Heligoland'. Yet the reports he received were incomplete and contradictory, it was impossible to get a clear picture of the situation. At the last moment, when Beatty's battle-cruisers came in sight, Jellicoe ordered his division to turn together to port to the north-east. In this way he gained a favourable position for crossing the enemy's T. He was unintentionally assisted by the 3rd Battle-Cruiser Squadron, which almost missed the Germans, but now closed in from the east and brought the German van between two fires. The light cruiser *Wiesbaden* soon lay dead in the water. For hours the battle raged around her, she was fired upon by many British ships, but did not sink until 0200 on 1st June. Only one survivor was picked up, two days later.

The delay in forming the line of battle put part of the screen and the 5th Battle Squadron in a difficult situation at what was later called 'Windy Corner'. Making room for Beatty's battle-cruisers to go to the van of the line, some armoured cruisers came into range of the German battleships. *Defence* blew up in view of both fleets; *Warrior* was saved a similar fate by the chance intervention of *Warspite*. The 5th Battle Squadron was forced to countermarch and came under the fire of several battleships. After a hit *Warspite*'s rudder jammed; she turned towards the German line, thus masking *Warrior*, who was able to creep away, but sank on the next morning. *Warspite* almost collided with *Valiant*

Left: Fatally wounded, with the gun's crew dead and dying around him, Boy 1st Class John Travers Cornwell (aged 16) remains at his post on HMS Chester *during the battle of Jutland and earns a posthumous VC. From the painting by Sir Frank Salisbury*

and made two full circles at high speed before her rudder was in working order again. Heavily damaged she was ordered home and reached Rosyth after evading the attack of a German submarine.

Visibility was now generally decreasing and greatly varying as a result of masses of funnel and artificial smoke. For the commanders-in-chief it was most difficult to gain a reliable picture of the actual situation from their own limited observations (radar was not yet invented) and the reports of their subordinates. For a few moments Scheer toyed with the idea of splitting his line to take Windy Corner under two fires. However, there was no battle signal for this promising but unusual procedure, his van was evidently hard pressed, and so he continued with his battleships in line ahead. With the loss of the destroyer *Shark* the 3rd Battle-Cruiser Squadron had inflicted heavy damage on the Germans and now took up station at the head of the British line followed by Beatty's battle-cruisers.

For more than half an hour the German ships could see no more than the flashes of the enemy guns. Then at 1830 visibility suddenly improved, *Lützow* and *Derfflinger* sighted *Invincible,* the leading ship, at a distance of 9,500 yards and sank her in a few minutes. There were only six survivors, among them the gunnery officer who, as he said, 'merely stepped from the foretop into the water'.

At that time Scheer ordered a battle turn reversing course to get his ships out of the overwhelming enemy fire. Beginning from the rear the heavy ships had to turn to starboard in quick succession until single line ahead was formed on the opposite course. Light cruiser squadrons and destroyer flotillas had to conform. This manoeuvre was all the more difficult because the fleet was now disposed almost in a semi-circle, but it was successful, supported by a destroyer attack on the centre of the British line. The fleets drew apart, and the fire slackened and then ceased altogether. A German destroyer was crippled and sank later, and the battleship *Marlborough* received a torpedo-hit which reduced her speed.

The German fleet now steamed to the west south-west, and the British fleet slowly hauled round to the south. With its higher speed it had a good chance of cutting off the Germans from their bases. Scheer sensed this even though contact had been lost completely. Therefore he ordered another battle turn to the old course with the express intention to deal the enemy a heavy blow, to surprise and confuse him, to bring the destroyers to the attack, to facilitate disengaging for the night, and, if possible, to rescue the crew of the *Wiesbaden*. The execution of this plan has been criticized but there is no doubt that Scheer succeeded in getting his fleet out of a difficult situation although his van suffered heavily.

The German thrust was directed against the British centre. The attacking ships soon came under heavy fire without being able to reply effectively because visibility was better to the west and favoured the British gunnery. Scheer saw his fleet rush into a wide arc of gun flashes and decided to support the destroyer attack by the battle-cruisers while the battle fleet executed its third battle turn. To the battle-cruisers he made the well-known signal, 'Ran' ('At them'), which meant charging regardless of consequences. *Lützow* could not take part because after twenty-three hits she was far down by the bow and could steam no more than 15 knots. So *Derfflinger* led that death ride. Her captain transmitted Scheer's signal to all battle stations and was answered by a thundering roar, gun crews shouting, stokers banging their shovels against bulkheads. The destroyers went in, fired torpedoes, and retreated, the battle-cruisers then turned after receiving numerous hits. Not a single torpedo reached a target, for Jellicoe turned away. Contact ceased again and a lull in the battle followed. Both fleets hauled round to the south until their courses converged. The Germans proceeded in inversed order and in several columns, the British in single line ahead, sixteen miles long.

At sunset (2020) the terribly mauled battle-cruisers again came under the fire of the leading British battleships, the old ships of the II Battle Squadron under that of the British battle-cruisers. The Germans were silhouetted against the western horizon, their opponents were hardly visible to them. As a British officer later wrote: 'I sighted an obsolete German battleship firing in a desultory way at apparently nothing.' All the German columns turned to the west; the British did not follow but took up night-cruising order, the battleships in divisions abreast, destroyer flotillas following in their wake, course south-east, speed 17 knots. Jellicoe intended to put himself between the Germans and their bases and to renew the battle at daylight. Scheer collected his units practically on the same course which took some time, and at 2300 headed southeast for Horn Reef, speed 16 knots. Because of the heavy odds against him, he wanted to fight a renewed battle nearer to his bases. It was another whim of fate that, as a consequence, the German main body crashed through the British flotillas which were not looking for the enemy but were waiting for the day battle. In contrast the German destroyers searched in vain for the heavy ships of the enemy.

The night actions

During the short northern summer night there were numerous clashes. They started with a furious fight between light cruisers at short distance. *Dublin* and *Southampton* suffered heavy damage and casualties; the obsolete *Frauenlob* was hit by a torpedo and sank with most of her crew. Next the 4th Destroyer Flotilla, led by *Tipperary*, converged upon the German van, came under the fire of half a dozen battleships, and turned away in disorder firing torpedoes and leaving *Tipperary*, burning fiercely, behind. When the battleships turned to starboard to avoid the torpedoes, the light cruiser *Elbing* was rammed and remained stopped with flooded enginerooms. The battleship *Nassau* tried to ram the destroyer *Spitfire*: they collided on nearly opposite courses, and the destroyer bounced off the side armour of her robust opponent leaving part of her bridge behind. With her forecastle a shambles, *Spitfire* succeeded in limping home.

Both sides resumed course and soon met again. In the intense fire *Broke*, and immediately afterwards *Contest*, rammed *Sparrowhawk*, which kept afloat to the morning. This time a torpedo crippled the light cruiser *Rostock*. Half an hour later, shortly after midnight, the unlucky 4th Flotilla encountered the same ships for the third time and lost *Fortune* and *Ardent*. Most of the other destroyers were damaged, it was no more a fighting unit.

A short time later a large ship approached the centre of the German line from port. It was the armoured cruiser *Black Prince*. She had probably been damaged when *Defence* blew up, and had tried to follow the battle fleet. Too late she turned away, and in minutes was a blazing pyre.

These clashes saved the 6th Battle Squadron from an encounter with German battleships. It lagged behind because torpedo damage prevented *Marlborough*, the flagship, from keeping up 17 knots. As it were the German van passed no more than three miles astern at around 0100. A little later it hit the rear of a line of thirteen destroyers belonging to four flotillas. *Turbulent* was sunk, others damaged, the Germans carried on. At early dawn, after a calm of an hour, they were sighted and attacked by the 12th Flotilla. The German ships succeeded in evading a great number of torpedoes but the old battleship *Pommern* was hit and broke in two after several detonations.

The great battle was over. At 0300 the Germans were approaching Horn Reef, the British battle fleet, thirty miles to the south-west, reversed course, neither commander-in-chief was inclined to renew the fight. Jellicoe went north to look for German stragglers. However, *Lützow*, *Elbing*, and *Rostock* had already been scuttled after German destroyers had taken their crews off. Both fleets steered for their bases. The *Ostfriesland* struck a mine in a field laid a few hours earlier by *Abdiel* but reached port without assistance.

The battle changed neither the ratio of strength between the two fleets nor the strategic situation. The British blockade continued, and Russia remained cut off from the supplies she needed urgently. The tactical advantage was with the Germans: they had inflicted about double their own losses on a greatly superior opponent. The fleet was proud of this achievement, and Scheer was willing to go on baiting the British. On 19th August 1916 both fleets were again in the North Sea but missed each other by thirty miles. However, it was evident – and Scheer said so in his reports – that the war could not be decided by this strategy. The situation on the fronts deteriorated after Allied offensives, and lack of food was painfully felt at home. Therefore the German government declared unrestricted submarine warfare two weeks before the Russian revolution broke out. The submarines did great havoc to Allied shipping, but brought the United States into the war.

The losses in battle

	British	German
Battle-cruisers	3	1
Armoured cruisers	3	-
Old battleships	-	1
Light cruisers	-	4
Destroyers	8	5
	tons 112,000	tons 61,000
Killed	6,000	2,500

As to the High Seas Fleet it did not remain inactive in port as has been alleged. In April 1918 it made its last sweep to the latitude of Bergen/Shetlands. But its main duty was now to support the submarine war by protecting the minesweepers and by giving its best young officers and ratings to the submarine arm. Other reasons for the sudden break-up of this efficient fighting force in November 1918 were psychological mistakes, malnutrition, and subversion, aggravated by the hopeless political and military situation of Germany.

The New Warfare

The old warfare meets the new. French cavalry equipped with steel helmets, and gas masks for horse and rider alike

In 1914 the armies marched to the battle-field on foot as they had done for centuries. The only difference was that they were taken part of the way by rail, and that their reserves could be switched from one flank to another by that same mechanical means. The main effect of this change was that such large numbers were poured on to the roads beyond railheads as to impede their own manoeuvre, while a supplementary effect, due to more rapid switching, was that an enemy's manoeuvre could be more easily blocked.

The war gave a tremendous impetus to the growth of mechanical transport, both road and roadless. Motor vehicles multiplied by scores of thousands, but this acceleration of movement only improved the capacity of supply; it did not markedly affect strategy since it could not alter the immobility of fighting troops who had already been driven, by the machine-gun, to bury themselves in trenches. The possibility of moving at 30 mph was of little avail to soldiers who had been reduced by a tactical obstacle to 0 mph.

To resurrect movement in face of fire, the fire-support of the attackers was developed by multiplication—of guns—and by addition—of new weapons, the light machine-gun, the mortar, the grenade, together with gas, smoke, and flame-projectors. Some of them contributed to defence as much as to the attack, and none of them succeeded so far as to revive a war of movement.

Eventually the tracked and armour-clad vehicle, known as the tank, was introduced; this went farther than any other means to overcome the machine-gun obstacle, and by German admission proved the most important military factor in the final phase of the war. But the end came, after a gradual withdrawal, before the tank had been developed far enough to produce more than a local acceleration of movement. In the army that retired, and in the armies that followed it up, a mass of motor vehicles were mingled with a greater mass of horse vehicles.

It is a question whether movement as a whole could have been much quicker even if the machine-gun brake had been lifted. Retardation may have averted confusion. On the other fronts—Bulgarian, Turkish, and Austrian—the brake was less effective, with the consequence that the new air weapon found dense targets. And under its blows the retreating armies dissolved in chaos.

The navies of 1914 showed a greater advance on the past than the armies. They were also less tested. Battleships and cruisers were the natural heirs of the old wooden ships of the line and frigates, but through steam and armour they had been so transformed that their properties were difficult to gauge owing to the paucity of naval actions since the mechanized age of naval warfare had dawned. With the invention of the torpedo they had been confronted with a new menace, at first projected by the torpedo-boat, to which the destroyer, developed as a counter, became a successor.

If the new weapon had a certain likeness to the old fireship, it had much wider possibilities. These were increased by the advent of the submarine, while the movement of fleets suffered a fresh restriction by the development of mines. It was more difficult to estimate the change of conditions because of the controversy that raged round the torpedo. The conflict of enthusiasm and prejudice produced an atmosphere in which scientific study was suffocated—if it was ever possible among a class who were men of action and had never been educated in a scientific way of thought. The natural result was a compromise by which the maintenance of the existing order was mixed with concessions to the new idea. Destroyers were added to the battlefleet, but were tied to its protection rather than applied to an offensive role.

As for submarines, at the outbreak of war in 1914 Germany had only twenty-eight, and by 1917 little more than a hundred, out of which only about a third were operating at any particular time. Yet, even apart from their deadly action against commerce, the effect of their latent menace to battleships was such that by the summer of 1916 the British naval authorities were agreed that the Grand Fleet must be kept out of their reach. To quote the British Official Naval History they had 'so restricted the movements of a fleet of super-Dreadnoughts—each one of which could steam several thousands of miles without refuelling—that the waters opposite one-third of the eastern coastline of Great Britain, and about half of the North Sea, were outside its zone of effective action'.

Farce on horseback

The course of land warfare proved so different from the expectation of the military leaders that a fuller discussion of their pre-war views is necessary.

If there was one feature of the half-century preceding 1914 that would seem impossible to misjudge, it was the increasing advantage of the defensive, due to the growing power of infantry firearms—first the magazine rifle and then the machine-gun. An obvious corollary was the limitation placed on cavalry action. The American Civil War, as it advanced, made these new factors plain. It was not to be expected that European generals would profit by this second-hand experience, since the great Field-Marshal von Moltke dismissed it as no more than 'two armed mobs chasing each other round the country, from which nothing could be learned'. But the Franco-German War, despite its brevity, demonstrated at Gravelotte and elsewhere the same change of conditions. Nevertheless in 1883 we find the German protagonist of the 'Nation in Arms', the future Field-Marshal von der Goltz, declaring that 'the idea of the greater strength of the defensive is a mere delusion'. The Boer War might surely have suggested a doubt of this dictum, yet in 1903 the future Marshal Foch, already acting as the official mould of French military ideas, committed himself to the confident prediction that 'any improvement in firearms is bound to strengthen the offensive'.

He at least had not been a participant in any real test, but the future Field-Marshal Haig, called upon by the royal commission, when fresh from the South African battlefields, to give account of the light that he had gained, was confident that 'cavalry will have a larger sphere of action in future wars'. His forecast might have been more intelligible if he had been thinking merely of mounted troops, which had been necessary to cope with Boer mobility. But he showed that his mind was fixed on the cavalry charge by the stress he laid on mounted *action,* and he confirmed this subsequently by the severe measures he took to curb the tendency to turn cavalry into mounted riflemen.

His view was shared by the military authorities of all the Continental powers, with the result that in 1914 Germany, France, Russia, and Austria-Hungary each deployed over a hundred thousand cavalry. With what result? The French relied for their information mainly on their cavalry, but, as has been officially related: 'This immense mass of cavalry discovered nothing of the enemy's advance . . . and the French Armies were everywhere surprised.' The most important effect that the German cavalry achieved was that, by their reckless destruction of telegraph lines everywhere, they did much to paralyse their own command during the advance into France. The Austrians' advance was 'preceded by a great mass of cavalry'; their official history records that most of them never came within sight of the enemy, owing to their horses being disabled

through sore backs. They at least were luckier than those who did make contact. For since the Russian cavalry stayed behind, the remaining Austrian cavalry bumped into the Russian infantry; poor shots as these were they did not fail to hit such a target, and the Austrian cavalry came back with nothing to compensate their heavy casualties.

This cavalry prelude was overshadowed by the drama that followed, when the main armies clashed, but it was perhaps the hugest farce that has ever been enacted in a theatre of war.

The generals were no more fortunate in gauging the possibilities of newer instruments. Not many years before 1914, when the attention of a member of the British Army Council was drawn to a note on the development of aircraft, he endorsed it thus: 'We are no nearer the solution of the conquest of the air than we were in the days of Montgolfier's Fire Balloon.' A more comprehensive disbelief in change was expressed by General Sukhomlinov, the Russian war minister who warned the in-

structors at the staff college that he could 'not hear the words "modern war" without a feeling of annoyance. As war was, so it remains; all these things are vicious innovations'. Sukhomlinov was disappointed in his ambition to command the Russian armies in the war, but he could at least content himself with having helped to ensure that they marched blind and little better than armless to the slaughter.

Military myopia
Different in form, but fundamentally similar in nature, was the assurance of the French commander-in-chief, Joffre, when on 6th August, 1914, he serenely declared: 'It may be concluded that the Germans are executing a plan of which we have knowledge.' Hence it was with ample confidence that he launched his forces east-

ward into Lorraine, and into a trap, while the Germans swept through Belgium.

The German command thus scored an initial surprise, but they threw away the advantage through an over-confidence that verged on intoxication. They told the Austrians that if the French army took the offensive they counted on attaining a decision 'on the 21st day of mobilization', i.e. 23rd August. If the French army stayed on the defensive behind its frontier defence, they might take a week longer to achieve a decisive victory. They would then transfer their forces to the Russian front where they 'should arrive on the 41st day of mobilization'. The decision had not come when 22nd August came, although that day the French, advancing blindly, ran into the advancing Germans in the Ardennes, and were thrown back. Although mauled, they slipped away. Yet the German command was sufficiently persuaded that the decisive victory had already been won that, on the 25th, it began transferring forces to Russia from the right wing. By the time this reached the Marne, it was much weaker than the forces opposing it. And on the 41st day of mobilization, 11th September, it was in full retreat!

The decisive turn had come with the penetration of the British Expeditionary Force into a thirty-mile gap between the two German armies of the right wing. This gives an ironical turn to the fact that the German command had rebuffed the offer of their navy to interfere with the shipment of the BEF, saying that 'it would be of advantage to settle with the 160,000 British at the same time as the French and Belgians'.

Left: A dazed and wounded German is guided to a stretcher by a comrade, Amiens 1918. Doctors used new skills to aid the victims of the new warfare. Below: German pioneer ascertaining the height of enemy aircraft for anti-aircraft battery

Below: Painting of U-53 on Atlantic patrol by Claus Bergen. The Germans were not slow to appreciate the revolutionary addition of submarines to their naval armoury

The blindness of generalship, especially towards new developments, was not cured by sharp contact with reality—partly, perhaps, because that contact was at second-hand. The German machine-guns had paralysed movement on the battlefield for months when Haig (now commander of the British First Army), resisting a proposal for increasing the British strength in these weapons, remarked that: 'The machine-gun was a much overrated weapon and two per battalion were more than sufficient.' Called upon for his judgment, Field-Marshal Lord Kitchener, now made war minister, conceded that four per battalion might be useful, but anything 'above four may be counted a luxury'. Long before the war ended, there would be a scale of more than forty heavy and light machine-guns per battalion—but that was due to the foresight and forceful pressure of a civilian minister, Lloyd George.

Military myopia likewise prevailed when means were mooted to overcome the defensive barrier formed by the hostile machine-guns. When the project of building tanks was submitted to the British engineer-in-chief in June 1915, he icily remarked: 'Before considering this proposal we should descend from the realms of imagination to solid facts.' Eight months later, when the first tank performed in front of Lord Kitchener, his comment was: 'A pretty mechanical toy.' 'The war,' he added, 'would never be won by such machines.'

Most of the generals were confident that it would be won long before such unnecessary aids could be produced. They had been confident from the earliest months, and they remained so despite constant disproof.

On 13th September, 1914, General Henry Wilson, the right hand of the British commander-in-chief, Sir John French, unwisely noted in his diary a conversation he had had with the guiding brain of the French commander-in-chief: 'Berthelot asked me when I thought we should cross into Germany, and I replied . . . in four weeks. He thought three weeks.' That very day the Allied armies were held up on the line of the Aisne, where they remained for the next four years.

The following June, Poincaré, the French President, pathetically complained to Kitchener: 'Joffre and Sir John told me in November they were going to push the Germans back over the frontier; they gave me the same assurance in December, March, and May. What have they done? The attacks are very costly and end in nothing.'

Lest it might be imagined that these optimistic forecasts were merely, if rashly, uttered to encourage ministerial morale, one must record a few more prophecies in which the generals indulged in their own circle. Thus, in November 1914, Sir John

107

French asserted that all the hard fighting of the war was over; in January 1915, he expressed the opinion that the war would be over by July; in March, Haig felt sure that the Germans would be wanting peace before the end of July; in August, he declared that he would not be surprised to see the enemy give in by November, and that in any case they could not go on after January 1916.

But in September 1915 the great Allied offensive proved a failure, and at the end of a dismal year French was replaced by Haig as British commander-in-chief.

The Allied commanders had by now come to the conclusion that the solution of the entrenched deadlock lay in multiplying artillery, and the weight of the preparatory bombardment – overestimating its potentialities while disregarding the fact that the heavier it became the worse it would tear up the ground over which they were planning to advance.

The main role in the British summer offensive of 1916 was entrusted to the Fourth Army under Rawlinson. Haig and he, as the British Official History records, 'impressed on all, at conferences and other times, that the infantry would only have to walk over and take possession of the enemy trenches'. The opening assault on 1st July was a complete failure on the greater part of the front, with a loss of 60,000 men in a single day. But the offensive was continued, and by November, when it was at last suspended, the British loss had risen to over 400,000 men, while the French had lost 200,000 – the German

loss being about four hundred thousand.

At the end of 1916, continued disappointment led to the replacement of Joffre by Nivelle, who planned a great offensive for 1917, declaring: 'We shall break the German front when we wish.' When his executive subordinate, General Micheler, reported that the enemy were building a new third line of defence out of reach of his artillery, Nivelle lightheartedly retorted: 'Don't be anxious, you won't find a German in those trenches; they only want to be off!' He confidently asserted that he would break through the Germans' first two positions 'with insignificant loss', that in three days at most his armies would be in open country, beginning the great pursuit to the Rhine. The offensive was duly launched and at nightfall had progressed about 600 yards instead of the six miles anticipated in Nivelle's programme; its continuation on subsequent days did little more than increase the loss to a total of 120,000. The chief effect was to strain the morale of the French troops to breaking-point, producing a dangerous series of mutinies in the attack-sickened army. It was crippled for the rest of the summer and had to be nursed for the rest of the war.

Notwithstanding the paralysis of his allies, Haig told the British cabinet in June 1917, that 'if the fighting were kept up at its present intensity for six months Germany would be at the end of her available man-power'. By such assurances he gained a dubious sanction for his own continued offensive at Ypres. On 21st August he reported to the government that 'the

time is fast approaching when Germany will be unable to maintain her armies'. On 8th October, arguing for permission to push deeper into the shell-torn morass there, he declared that the enemy might collapse 'at any moment'. With obvious doubt, as if making a concession to pessimistic politicians, he prefaced his view of 1918 prospects with the remark: 'Even if they hold out until next year.' But even if they did, and were able to transfer troops from the Russian front, he did not contemplate any serious check to his offensive. Not by a single word did he suggest the possibility that the Germans might take the offensive. As late as 7th January, 1918, when he came home to see the cabinet, he expressed the opinion that the Germans would not attack. But on 21st March, they refuted his forecast, by breaking through his overstrained troops and penetrating his front to a depth of nearly forty miles.

While the series of crises that followed were retrieved, and the scales of the war turned, by the arrival of American reinforcements, it was basically the pressure of seapower that undermined Germany's resistance and ensured her collapse. This fact lends significance to the French command's pre-war estimate of the help that the British navy would afford. Colonel Repington, the military critic, had written in *The Times* that it was 'worth 500,000 bayonets to the French'. But Henry Wilson, then the strategic brain of the British War Office, retorted that 'our Navy was not worth 500 bayonets'. After consulting the three leading French soldiers, he wrote:

'Castelnau and Joffre did not value it at one bayonet . . . Foch is of exactly the same opinion.'

Prophets unheard

It is not true to say that the trend of warfare is impossible to gauge – at least of warfare hitherto. Marshal Foch was making an appropriate confession rather than a scientific statement when he declared in 1926: 'The military mind always imagines that the next war will be on the same lines as the last. That has never been the case and never will be.' One can well understand that in retrospect the war looked different to him from anything he had ever conceived, or prophesied of it, beforehand. But the conditions that dumbfounded him and his fellows were only the climax of an evolutionary process which they could have detected, but did not. Every war for half a century, since 1861, had made it plainer. Others did perceive them.

M. Bloch, a civilian banker of Warsaw, gave a remarkably accurate diagnosis of their essential elements in his *War of the Future*, published on the eve of the 20th century, before he had even the data of South Africa and the Russo-Japanese war in Manchuria to confirm his deductions. There were also military minds, even if these belonged to men not in the seats of authority, that foresaw the coming stalemate and pointed out its chain of causation. Captain Mayer, the French military critic, was provoked by Foch's fiery advocacy of the offensive to predict, only too well, the siege war that would engulf generals who

were dreaming of mobile war without the means of mobility. He was boycotted for his audacity. So was the eminent military historian, Lieutenant-Colonel Grouard, when he turned from the past to the future, and forecast in 1911 exactly what would happen if the French command adopted such a plan as they did, in 1914. And, as we have seen, the British military critic, Colonel Repington, had a far wider grasp than either the French or British general staffs of the factors that would influence the issue of the war.

The war was filled with battles, yet the most that the historian can fairly say is that they were a contributory factor – one of many – the main factor in the collapse of Germany being economic pressure. On this point there is Haig's own admission, at the end of October 1918: 'Germany is not broken in a military sense. During the last weeks her armies have withdrawn . . . in excellent order.' The Allied armies were exhausted and needed to be reorganized before they could follow up. But Germany was broken internally by hunger, sickness, and despair. Her breakdown developed directly from military disappointment, from the depression which spread when her own offensive in the spring failed to bring the victory that Ludendorff had promised. But the foundations of her resistance had been undermined by the Allied blockade.

The abortiveness of battle as a means of winning wars can be traced to the declining power of the attack to overcome defence. This condition was due to the growing power of modern firearms, and had been

Air warfare, 1917. The aeroplane, used mostly as an army auxiliary, formed part of the revolutionary growth in mobility

long in evolution. It was first manifest in the American Civil War, where it came to be a standard calculation that one man in a trench was equal to three or four in an assault. In Europe the wars of 1866 and 1870 brought fresh evidence of the paralysing influence of fire, although the brevity of both wars tended to obscure it. Nevertheless, after the second, the winning strategist of those two wars, Moltke, drew the conclusion that his victory could not be repeated, and enunciated the lesson that: 'As a result of the improvement of firearms, the tactical defensive has acquired a great advantage over the offensive. . . . It seems to be more advantageous to proceed to an attack only after having repelled several attacks by the enemy.'

Then came the Russo-Japanese War, a war which foreshadowed nearly all the factors which upset military calculations in 1914 – the paralysing power of machine-guns, the hopelessness of frontal attacks, and the consequent relapse of the armies into trenches. But military optimism was even more impregnable – to the assault of facts. To ardent soldiers war was unthinkable without successful attack, so that they were able to persuade themselves that attacks could succeed. The delusive basis of that faith was quickly exposed when the First World War began, and was made clearer still when the trench deadlock set in – for four years. And it is significant that

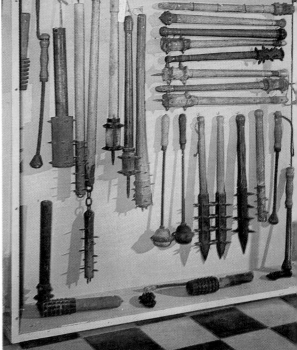

Relics of the Trenches

Millions experienced the new warfare— from the trenches. The weapons and equipment they were given were very varied.

1 German helmet, wire cutters, and spiked club. 2 A fearsome collection of Italian maces. Trench raiding parties armed themselves with clubs and maces for night forays when the ability to deal a swift and silent death was essential. 3 Typical British equipment: steel helmet, gas mask, Mills grenade, ·455 Webley, and trench mirror. 4 Other British trench weaponry: a

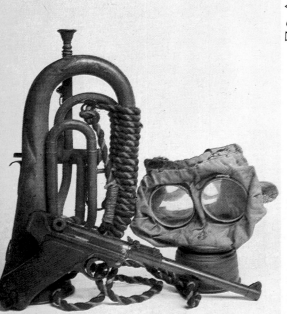

hobnailed cudgel and No. 2 Mk. 1 grenade, together with bullet-proof vest, Mills grenade, ·455 Webley and holster. The Mills grenade or Mills bomb was developed for hand and rifle launching. 5 Austrian bugle, German Navy Luger, and German gas mask. 6 Corroding artifacts. An Italian lamp, meal-box, revolver, and mail vest

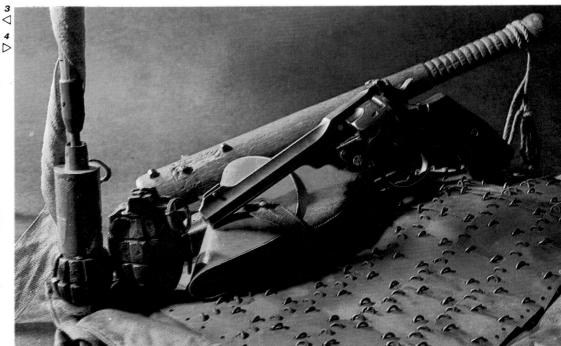

the only great battles which had far-reaching results before morale had broken down were those which took the form of a counter-stroke after the enemy had spent himself in vain attacks – the Allied victories in the first and second battles of the Marne, the German victories at Tannenberg, Gorlice, and Caporetto. Yet none of the commanders at the outset, and hardly any later, showed remembrance of Moltke's advice, or were willing to delay their own offensive dreams until they had dispelled the enemy's.

The historical basis of the belief in the hand-to-hand fight was equally false, and it reacted on the belief in numbers. For a century the military manuals of Europe had continued to emphasize the decisive importance of physical shock, echoing Clausewitz's dictum: 'The close combat, man to man, is plainly to be regarded as the real basis of combat.' The French doctrine of 1914 fervently declared that the object of all attacks was 'to charge the enemy with the bayonet in order to destroy him'. Something might be claimed for it if the emphasis had been on the psychological effect of a close-quarter threat, but the time and attention devoted to bayonet-training showed that the bayonet-fight was regarded as a reality. Yet even in the 18th century a practical soldier like Guibert had remarked its rarity, while Jomini was but one of a number of witnesses of the Napoleonic battles who said that, except in villages and defiles, he had 'never seen two forces cross bayonets'. Half a century later Moltke would point out the fallacy of the French assertion that their victory at Solferino had been won by the bayonet. In 1870 their troops were to pay heavily against Prussian fire for this delusion among their leaders, yet Boguslawski records that in actual fact 'bayonets were never crossed in open fight'.

Only in conditions where shock was a practical possibility could the theory of massing superior numbers be effective. It was difficult to adjust it to conditions where one man with a machine-gun might count for more than a much larger number who were advancing upon him with the bayonet. The fallacy was proved most emphatically of all by the Germans against the Russians; by their superior weapons and technique the Germans discounted the vastly superior numbers of their Eastern Front opponent.

The gradualness of evolution owed much to the stout resistance which the military profession has always offered to novelty. The impetus of science in the 19th century did not suffice to storm these ramparts. The obstruction that the tank had to overcome on paper before it took the field in 1916 is well known; less familiar is the fact that it might have been available before the war began. There was Mr de

Mole's tank, superior in design to the one that was actually produced. But the design had been submitted to the War Office and was there pigeon-holed – until the war was over. There was also the promising idea contained in drawings submitted by a plumber of Nottingham. It also was unearthed after the war; the file bore the brief but decisive verdict: 'The man's mad.' Similar blindness marked the attitude of even the more thoughtful among leading soldiers to the possibilities of the air. When Foch watched the 1910 *Circuit de l'Est,* which proved the reliability of the new invention, he exclaimed: 'That is good sport, but for the Army the aeroplane is no use.'

The lessons of the war

In sum, there were four main features of the 'new warfare' that, developing in the 19th century, came to dominate the course of the First World War from 1914 onwards.

First, was the growth of size. From France under the Revolution and Napoleon, through America in the Civil War and Prussia under Moltke, the armies swelled to the millions of 1914. Yet back in the 18th century Marshal Saxe had foreseen the hindrances of size: 'Multitudes serve only to perplex and embarrass.'

Second, came the growth of fire-power, beginning with the adoption of rifles and breech-loading weapons. This, imposed on size, conduced to a growing paralysis of warfare on land and sea.

Third, was the growth of industrialization. The change from well-distributed agricultural communities to a concentration of population and an interdependence of areas, together with the more complex needs of such a civilization, gave more influence in war to economic objectives. By acting against those, even in the comparatively primitive South, Sherman decided the issue of the American Civil War. Soldiers in Europe, however, remained unable to see much beyond the opposing army. Their eyes were bloodshot. Yet in the end it was the economic pressure, mainly applied by the navy, which decided the issue of the World War.

A fourth was the revolutionary growth of mobility, due in turn to the steam engine and the motor. Paradoxically, its chief effect when added to the other tendencies was to reduce the effective mobility of armies. The railway – which had speed but not flexibility, the other constituent of mobility – fostered the accumulation of masses, and these were hampered not only by their own bulk but by the growth of fire. The road-motor, a much later development, was neglected until the war came and was then at first applied merely to the service of mass. Not until it was embodied in the tank did it begin to assist the recovery of mobility – by making it pos-

sible for men to advance in face of bullets.

The aeroplane likewise began as a mere auxiliary, and to this minor role it was still mainly confined as its numbers grew. Even in the greatest bombing raid on London only thirty-three machines were employed, although four thousand were in use for the narrower duties of army co-operation. But in the last phase of the war, aircraft showed their powers at the expense of armies by frustrating the escape of the defeated Bulgarian, Turkish, and Austrian armies; they turned the ebbing tide into a stagnant shambles.

What were the outstanding lessons of the war along these lines of evolution? The first, certainly, was that the huge conscript armies tended to make war inevitable, just as, when war was engaged, they tended to make it immobile. 'Mobilization means war,' the German ambassador threateningly said to the Russian foreign minister with more profound truth than he intended. For, once the mass of the people were summoned to arms from their normal occupation, an atmosphere was created in which peace-feelers were stifled.

Moreover, these armies were so cumbrous, their movement so complex, that even direction could not be modified. Thus, when the Kaiser, clutching at a report that France might forsake Russia's side and remain neutral, said to Moltke the younger, who had now been appointed to his famous uncle's place as chief of the German general staff: 'We march, then, only towards the East?' Moltke replied that this was 'impossible. The advance of armies formed of millions of men was the result of years of intricate work. Once planned it could not possibly be changed'. So the millions went forward.

But when they reached the battlefield, they were stopped by the machine-guns, few as these were. Back in 1884, a military prophet had acclaimed the machine-gun as 'concentrated essence of infantry'. Military authorities had paid little attention to such prophecies – until the war came in 1914. Then it was shown that one man sitting behind a machine-gun was equal to ten, a hundred, even a thousand, who were rushing on him with the bayonet. The generals were puzzled. They had always counted strength by count of heads.

It was the machine-gun that made infantry advance hopeless and cavalry futile. The next four years were spent in trying to overcome this obstacle.

First, the generals, true to their theory of mass, tried masses of artillery. This method achieved poor results in proportion to the effort. It made a short advance possible but forbade a long one – by ploughing up the ground over which the advance had to be made.

A new method dawned in 1915 – the use

of tanks. Reluctantly accepted by authority, it did not receive a real opportunity in the field until the last year of the war. Then it produced longer and quicker advances than had hitherto been made, and proved, by German admission, the most effective land weapon yet employed.

The Germans had also tried, in 1915, a new means to overcome the barrier. This was gas. Luckily for the Allies, the German soldiers thwarted the German chemists, and the best chance of a decisive result was forfeited. Still, by ringing the changes on various types, gas continued to play an important part. The most effective, by far, was mustard gas, which disabled by blistering the skin and took effect even after a long interval. The strategic effect, however, was more in hampering an enemy's attack than in assisting one's own. Thus it tended to increase the paralysis in which the war was already gripped.

One possibility of overcoming machine-guns was largely neglected – the advance in obscurity. Night attacks were rare, for fear of confusion – although this was a lesser risk than a daylight advance in face of defending machine-guns. Smoke screens were never fully developed. When first suggested in 1914, Kitchener had emphatically declared that they 'would be of no use for land operations'! Yet in 1918, it was under cover of fog – nature's smoke – that the Germans repeatedly broke through the Allied front. When fog was lacking, they failed. It is strange that neither side sought to produce artificial fog on a great scale.

At sea likewise the same lines of evolution led to the same conclusion – a state of general paralysis. The traditional purpose of destroying the enemy's main forces in battle was never fulfilled, and although the fleets were once within range of each other, at Jutland, analysis of that tactically ineffective encounter tends to emphasize the factors that made for paralysis.

Naval development had been marked by swelling as on land, although this elephantiasis at sea affected the size of individual ships rather than the numbers of a fleet. Battleships became so large, and hence so few compared with Nelson's day, that admirals became more reluctant to risk them. And the growth of fire-power tended to keep the fleets apart; fighting at long ranges made a decision more difficult. To this check was added that of a new weapon, the torpedo; if it did not attain the results in sea fighting that had been anticipated by the prophets, this was largely because the fear of it made the admirals shy of pursuing an offensive movement – and thereby exposed the ineffectiveness of a battle-fleet. The lighter craft, too, were in consequence diverted to the unprofitable duty of chaperoning their big sisters. The British official

history candidly confesses: 'The Grand Fleet could only put to sea with an escort of nearly one hundred destroyers . . . the German U-boats had hampered our squadrons to an extent which the most expert and far-sighted naval officer had never foreseen.' A few months after the 'victory' of Jutland, the danger of a German invasion of Denmark loomed on the horizon of the British government; after examination by the Admiralty, the conclusion was reached that 'for naval reasons it would be almost impossible to support the Danes at all'. What a humiliating confession of impotence: The shadow of the German submarine was longer than the shadow of Nelson's column.

Nor was that all. The growth of industrialization had made nations, Great Britain above all, more dependent on overseas supply. By multiplying commerce it had multiplied the targets for indirect attack. While British destroyers were chaperoning battleships, the German submarines were sinking British mercantile shipping – until Great Britain herself was in sight of collapse. When part of the destroyers were diverted to protect commerce, the Grand Fleet had to be practically locked up for its own safety! It was history's most ironical case of 'protective arrest'.

The Germans' paucity of submarines led in turn to the self-imprisonment of their fleet when the available submarines were wanted for the new unrestricted campaign against merchant shipping. The farcical result was thus reached that 'for the future the two great battle-fleets could but lie inactive, watching one another across a kind of "No Man's Sea", where attack and defence were concerned only with transport and commerce'.

This direct action against the supplies upon which Great Britain depended for her existence, was carried so far that by the following spring, of 1917, she was in sight of collapse before the danger was brought under control – through the introduction of the convoy system, which in turn depended on the additional destroyers provided by America.

This near-fatal menace was created by a comparative handful of submarines, operating under most disadvantageous geographical conditions, and in waters guarded by 3,000 destroyers and light craft – odds of 30 to 1 against the submarines.

As for the growth of mobility, through the supersession of sails by steam, its influence is to be traced throughout the stalemate that prevailed. Its effect was to engender a fundamental immobility. In the case of the outer and greater naval power this prevented it destroying the enemy's fleet; in the case of the inner and weaker, Germany, it ensured her ultimate collapse from pernicious anaemia.

In a painting by Gilbert Rogers, Royal Army Medical Corps personnel move among captured trenches comforting the dying and removing the wounded during the battle of Messines Ridge, June 1917. Trenches were often morasses of reeking mud, but some of the dugouts were remarkably snug

Verdun and the Somme

The year 1916 was the watershed of the First World War. Beyond it all rivers ran in changed directions. It was the year that saw German hopes of outright victory vanish, and the Allied prospects of winning the war with their existing tactics and resources—without the United States—disappear. It was the last year in which Russia would be a powerful military force, and by the end of it Great Britain would have assumed the principal burden on the Western Front. It was also the last year in which the 'Old World' of pre-1914 still had a chance of surviving by means of a negotiated, 'stalemate' peace; it would have been as good a year as any to have ended the war. Finally, 1916 was the year of heavy guns, and—with the exception of the cataclysm of 1918—the year that brought the highest casualty lists.

On land in 1916 there were two battles which more than any others came to symbolize the First World War for the post-war generation: Verdun and the Somme. Verdun was the occasion of Germany's only deviation—between 1915 and 1918—from her profitable strategy of standing on the defensive in the west and letting the Allies waste themselves against an almost impregnable line at unimaginable cost.

By the end of 1915 deadlock had been reached along a static front stretching from Switzerland to the Channel. The Germans had failed, at the Marne battle, to win the war by one sledge-hammer blow against their numerically superior enemies, while suffering three-quarters of a million casualties. In attempting to repulse them from her soil, France had lost 300,000 killed and another 600,000 wounded, captured, and missing. Great Britain's naval might had proved impotent to wrest the Dardanelles from Turkey. Isolated Russia staggered on from defeat to defeat, yet still the Central powers could not bring the war to a decision in the limitless spaces of the east.

But on neither side had these early losses and disillusions impaired the will to fight on. Civilian resolution matched military morale. The opposing troops of France and Germany were no longer the green enthusiasts of 1914, nor yet the battle-weary veterans of 1917-18; they represented the best the war was to produce. In the munitions industries of both sides, artillery programmes had also reached a peak. In Great Britain Kitchener's army of conscripts was about to replace the lost 'First Hundred Thousand'.

On 2nd December, 1915, Joffre, the 'vic-tor of the Marne', was appointed supreme commander of French military forces throughout the world. A sixty-three year-old engineer with little experience of handling infantry, he was now incomparably the most powerful figure on the Allied side and his new ascendancy enabled him to concentrate everything on the Western Front. Four days later Joffre held an historic conference of the Allied commanders at his HQ in Chantilly. From it sprang plans for a co-ordinated offensive by all the allies the following summer. By then, for the first time, there would be an abundance of men, heavy guns, and ammunition. The principal component of this offensive would be a Franco-British 'push' astride the river Somme. Forty French and twenty-five British divisions would be involved. There were no strategic objectives behind this sector of the front; Joffre's principal reason for selecting it was his instinct that he could be most assured of full British participation if they went over the top arm in arm with the French—'bras dessus bras dessous'.

Sir Douglas Haig, who had also just taken over command of the British forces in France from General French, would have preferred to attack in Flanders (a preference which was to reassert itself with disastrous consequences a year later). However, after a meeting with Joffre on 29th December, he allowed himself to be won over to the Somme strategy. But on the other side of the lines, the chief of the German general staff, General Erich von Falkenhayn—a strange compound of ruthlessness and indecision—had his own plans. The Germans were to beat the Allies to the draw.

To bleed France white

Prospects would never again seem so bright for German arms as at the close of 1915. In mid-December Falkenhayn prepared a lengthy memorandum for the Kaiser in which he argued that the only way to achieve victory was to cripple the Allies' main instrument, the French army, by luring it into the defence of an indefensible position. Verdun, perched precariously at the tip of a long salient, about 130 air miles south-east of where Joffre intended to attack on the Somme and just 150 miles due east of Paris, fulfilled all of Falkenhayn's requirements.

Verdun's history as a fortified camp stretched back to Roman times, when Attila had found it worth burning. In the 17th century Louis XIV's great martial

Above: French soldier wearing gas mask mounts guard at an entrance to Fort Souville, Verdun. The fort, part of the main French defence line on the east bank of the Meuse, consistently defied capture.
Left: The horror of Verdun. 'Hell', a painting by Georges Leroux

engineer, Vauban, had made Verdun the most powerful fortress in his cordon protecting France; in the Franco-Prussian War of 1870 it had been the last of the great French strongholds to fall, surviving Sedan, Metz, and Strasbourg. After 1870 it had become the key bastion in the chain of fortresses guarding France's frontier with Germany. In 1914, Verdun had provided an unshakable pivot for the French line, and without it Joffre might not have been able to stand on the Marne and save Paris.

From his knowledge both of her history and character, Falkenhayn calculated that France would be forced to defend this semi-sacred citadel to the last man. By menacing Verdun with a modest outlay of only nine divisions, he expected to draw the main weight of the French army into the salient, where German heavy artillery would grind it to pieces from three sides.

In Falkenhayn's own words, France was thus to be 'bled white'. It was a conception totally novel to the history of war and one that, in its very imagery, was symptomatic of that Great War where, in their callousness, leaders could regard human lives as mere corpuscles.

The V Army, commanded by the Kaiser's heir, the Crown Prince, was appointed to conduct the victorious operation. Day and night the great cannon and their copious munition trains now began to flow toward the V Army from all other German fronts. Aided by the railways behind their front and the national genius for organization, preparations moved with astonishing speed and secrecy. By the beginning of February 1916 more than 1,200 guns were in position—for an assault frontage of barely eight miles. More than 500 were 'heavies', including 13 of the 420mm 'Big Bertha mortars', the 'secret weapon' of 1914 which had shattered the supposedly impregnable Belgian forts. Never before had such a concentration of artillery been seen.

Verdun lay less than ten miles up the tortuous Meuse from the German lines. Most of its 15,000 inhabitants had departed when the war reached its gates in 1914, and its streets were now filled with troops, but this was nothing new for a city which had long been a garrison town.

In notable contrast to the featureless open country of Flanders and the Somme, Verdun was surrounded by interlocking patterns of steep hills and ridges which provided immensely strong natural lines of defence. The key heights were studded with three concentric rings of mighty underground forts, totalling no less than twenty major and forty intermediary works.

Each was superbly sited so that its guns could dislodge any enemy infantry appearing on the superstructure of its neighbour. With concrete carapaces eight feet thick,

staunch enough to resist even the German 'Big Berthas', some of the major forts—such as Douaumont—were equipped with heavy artillery and machine-guns firing from retractable steel turrets. Outlying blockhouses linked by subterranean passages made them able to repel an attack from whatever direction it might come, and in their shell-proof cellars each could house as much as a battalion of infantry.

These forts lay between five and ten miles from Verdun itself. Between them and no man's land stretched a protective network of trenches, redoubts, and barbed wire such as was to be found throughout the whole length of the Western Front. Verdun deserved its reputation as the world's most powerful fortress. In theory.

In fact—despite, or perhaps because of, its reputation—by February 1916, Verdun's defences were in a lamentable state. The fate of the Belgian forts had persuaded Joffre to evacuate the infantry garrisons from the Verdun forts, and remove many of their guns. The troops themselves had become slack, lulled by many months spent in so quiet and 'safe' a sector, whose deceptive calm was deepened by the influence of one of the nastiest, rainiest, foggiest, and most enervating climates in France. The French soldier has never been renowned for his ardour for digging in, and the forward lines of trenches at Verdun compared poorly with the immensely deep earthworks the Germans had constructed at their key points on the Western Front. And, in contrast to the seventy-two battalions of elite storm troops, the Crown Prince held ready for the attack, the French trenches were manned by only thirty-four battalions, some of which were second-class units.

One outstanding French officer, Lieutenant Colonel Emile Driant, who commanded two battalions of *chasseurs* in the very tip of the salient, actually warned the French high command of the impending attack and the bad state of the Verdun defences. For this impertinence, his knuckles were severely rapped; the imperturbable Joffre paid little attention.

'Sauve qui peut!'

After a nine-day delay caused by bad weather (the first serious setback to German plans), the bombardment began at dawn on 21st February. For nine appalling hours it continued. Even on the shell-saturated Western Front nothing like it had ever been experienced. The poorly prepared French trenches were obliterated, many of their defenders buried alive. Among the units to bear the brunt of the shelling were Driant's *chasseurs*.

At 4 that afternoon the bombardment lifted and the first German assault troops

moved forward out of their concealed positions. This was, in fact, but a strong patrol action, testing like a dentist's probe for the weakest areas of the French front. In most places it held. The next morning, the brutal bombardment began again. It seemed impossible that any human being could have survived in that methodically worked-over soil. Yet some had, and, with a heroic tenacity that was to immortalize the French defence during the long months ahead, they continued to face the unseen enemy from what remained of their trenches.

On the afternoon of 22nd February the Germans' first main infantry wave went in. The defenders' front line buckled.

General Philippe Pétain in 1916. From warrior-hero he later turned defeatist

Driant was shot through the head while withdrawing the remnants of his *chasseurs*. Of these two battalions, 1,200 strong, a handful of officers and about 500 men, many of them wounded, were all that eventually straggled back to the rear. But the French resistance once again caused the German storm troops to be pulled back, to await a third softening-up bombardment the following morning.

On 23rd February, there were signs of mounting confusion and alarm at the various HQs before Verdun. Telephone lines were cut by the shelling; runners were not getting through; whole units were disappearing from the sight of their commanders. Order and counter-order were followed by the inevitable consequence. One by one the French batteries were falling silent, while others shelled their own positions, in the belief that these had already been abandoned to the enemy.

24th February was the day the dam burst. A fresh division, flung in piecemeal, broke under the bombardment, and the whole of the second line of the French defences fell within a matter of a few hours.

Total War

During that disastrous day, German gains equalled those of the first three days put together. By the evening it looked as if the war had again become one of movement —for the first time since the Marne.

Between the attackers and Verdun, however, there still lay the lines of the forts—above all, Douaumont, the strongest of them all, a solid bulwark of comfort behind the backs of the retreating *poilus*. Then, on 25th February, the Germans pulled off—almost in a fit of absent-mindedness—one of their greatest coups of the entire war. Acting on their own initiative, several small packets of the 24th Brandenburg Regiment, headed by a twenty-four-year-old lieutenant, Eugen Radtke (using infiltration tactics and armed with trench-clubs and pistols), worked their way into Douaumont without losing a man. To their astonishment, they discovered the world's most powerful fort to be virtually undefended.

In Germany church bells rang throughout the country to acclaim the capture of Douaumont. In France its surrender was rightly regarded as a national disaster of the first magnitude (later reckoned to have cost France the equivalent of 100,000 men). Through the streets of Verdun itself survivors of broken units ran shouting, *'Sauve qui peut!'*

At his headquarters in Chantilly even Joffre had at last become impressed by the urgency of events. To take over the imminently threatened sector, he dispatched Henri Philippe Pétain, France's outstanding expert in the art of the defensive. No general possessed the confidence of the *poilu* more than Pétain. Now—in tragic irony—this uniquely humanitarian leader was called upon to subject his men to what was becoming the most inhuman conflict of the whole war. Pétain's orders were to hold Verdun, 'whatever the cost'.

But the German attack was beginning to bog down. Losses had already been far heavier than Falkenhayn had anticipated, many of them inflicted by flanking fire from French guns across the Meuse. The German lines looped across the river to the north of Verdun, and, from the very first, the Crown Prince had urged that his V Army be allowed to attack along both banks simultaneously. But Falkenhayn— determined to keep his own outlay of infantry in the 'bleeding white' strategy down to the barest minimum—had refused, restricting operations to the right bank. Now, to clear the menace of the French artillery, Falkenhayn reluctantly agreed to extend the offensive across to the left bank, releasing for this purpose another army corps from his tightly hoarded reserves. The deadly escalation of Verdun was under way.

Mission of sacrifice
The lull before the next phase of the German offensive enabled Pétain to stabilize the front to an almost miraculous extent. He established a road artery to Verdun, later known as the Voie Sacrée, along which the whole lifeblood of France was to pour, to reinforce the threatened city; during the critical first week of March alone 190,000 men marched up it.

The Crown Prince now launched a new all-out attack along the left bank toward a small ridge called the Mort-Homme, which, with its sinister name, acquired from some long-forgotten tragedy of another age, was to be the centre of the most bitter, see-saw fighting for the better part of the next three months. On this one tiny sector a monotonous, deadly pattern was establishing that continued almost without let-up. It typified the whole battle of Verdun. After hours of saturating bombardment, the German assault troops would surge forward to carry what remained of the French front line. There were no longer any trenches; what the Germans occupied were for the most part clusters of shell holes, where isolated groups of men lived and slept and died defending their 'position' with grenade and pick helve.

'You have a mission of sacrifice,' ran the typical orders that one French colonel gave to his men. 'Here is a post of honour

where they want to attack. Every day you will have casualties . . . On the day they want to, they will massacre you to the last man, and it is your duty to fall.'

At Verdun most fell without ever having seen the enemy, under the murderous non-stop artillery bombardment, which came to characterize this battle perhaps more than any other. 'Verdun is terrible,' wrote French Sergeant-Major César Méléra, who was killed a fortnight before the armistice, 'because man is fighting against material, with the sensation of striking out at empty air . . .' Describing the effects of a bombardment, Paul Dubrulle, a thirty-four-year-old Jesuit serving as an infantry sergeant (also later killed), said: 'The most solid nerves cannot resist for long; the moment arrives where the blood mounts to the head; where fever burns the body and where the nerves, exhausted, become incapable of reacting . . . finally one abandons oneself to it, one has no longer even the strength to cover oneself with one's pack as protection against splinters, and one scarcely still has left the strength to pray to God.'

Despite the heroic sacrifices of Pétain's men, each day brought the sea of *Feldgrau* a few yards closer to Verdun. By the end of March, French losses totalled 89,000; but the attackers had also lost nearly 82,000 men. Even once they had taken the Mort-Homme, the Germans found themselves hamstrung by French guns on the Côte 304, another ridge still farther out on the flank. Like a surgeon treating galloping cancer, Falkenhayn's knife was enticed ever farther from the original point of application. More fresh German divisions were hurled into the battle — this time to seize Côte 304.

Not until May was the German 'clearing' operation on the left bank of the Meuse at last completed. The final push towards Verdun could begin. But the Crown Prince was now for calling off the offensive, and even Falkenhayn's enthusiasm was waning. The strategic significance of Verdun had long since passed out of sight; yet the battle had somehow achieved a demonic existence of its own, far beyond the control of generals of either nation. Honour had become involved to an extent which made disengagement impossible. On the French side, Pétain — affected (too deeply, according to Joffre) by the horrors he had witnessed — was promoted and replaced by two more ferocious figures: General Robert Nivelle and General Charles Mangin, nicknamed 'The Butcher'.

By now men had become almost conditioned to death at Verdun. 'One eats, one drinks beside the dead, one sleeps in the midst of the dying, one laughs and sings in the company of corpses,' wrote Georges Duhamel, the poet and dramatist,

who was serving as a French army doctor. The highly compressed area of the battle-field itself had become a reeking open cemetery where 'you found the dead embedded in the walls of the trenches; heads, legs and half-bodies, just as they had been shovelled out of the way by the picks and shovels of the working party'. Conditions were no longer much better for the attacking Germans; as one soldier wrote home in April under the French counter-bombardment: 'Many would rather endure starvation than make dangerous expeditions for food.'

On 26th May a 'very excited' Joffre visited Haig at his HQ and appealed to him to advance the date of the Somme offensive. When Haig spoke of 15th August, Joffre shouted that 'The French Army would cease to exist if we did nothing by then.' Haig finally agreed to help by attacking on 1st July instead. Although Haig entertained vague hopes of a breakthrough to be exploited by cavalry, neither he nor Rawlinson — whose 4th Army were to fight the battle — had yet arrived at any higher strategic purpose than that of relieving Verdun and 'to kill as many Germans as possible' (Rawlinson).

Meanwhile, at Verdun the beginning of a torrid June brought the deadliest phase in the three-and-a-half-month battle, with the Germans throwing in a weight of attack comparable to that of February — but this time concentrated along a front only three, instead of eight, miles wide. The fighting reached Vaux, the second of the great forts, where 600 men under Major Sylvain Eugène Raynal in an epic defence held up the main thrust of the German V Army for a whole week until thirst forced them to surrender.

The Suicide Club

Then, just as Vaux was falling, the first of the Allied summer offensives was unleashed. In the east, General Brusilov struck at the Austro-Hungarians with forty divisions, achieving a spectacular initial success. Falkenhayn was forced to transfer troops badly needed at Verdun to bolster up his sagging ally. Verdun was reprieved; although in fact it was not until 23rd June that the actual crisis was reached. On that day, using a deadly new gas called phosgene, the Crown Prince (reluctantly) attacked towards Fort Souville, astride the last ridge before Verdun. At one moment, machine-gun bullets were striking the city streets. Still the French held but there were ominous signs that morale was cracking. Just how much could a nation stand?

Two days later, however, the rumble of heavy British guns was heard in Verdun. Haig's five-day preliminary bombardment on the Somme had begun.

French troops attempt to take up position under fire in the Helby defile at Verdun

Because of her crippling losses at Verdun, the French contribution on the Somme had shrunk from forty to sixteen divisions, of which only five actually attacked on 1st July, compared with fourteen British divisions. Thus, for the first time, Great Britain was shouldering the main weight in a Western Front offensive. Of the British first-wave divisions, eleven were either Territorials or from Kitchener's 'New Armies'. Typical of the latter force was one battalion which had only three 'trained officers', including one who was stone deaf, another who suffered from a badly broken leg, and a sixty-three-year-old commanding officer who had retired before the Boer War. These new amateur units of 'civvies' had been trained to advance in rigid parade-ground formations that would have served well at Dettingen — straight lines two to three paces between each man, one hundred yards between each rank in the assault waves. In their rawness, their leaders did not trust them to attempt any of the more sophisticated tactics of infiltration such as the Germans and French had evolved at Verdun — despite a recommendation by Haig himself. French farmers were reluctant to allow their fields to be used for badly needed extra infantry training. But what 'K's' men lacked in expertise, they more than made up for in zeal and courage.

The Somme meanders through a flat, wide, and marshy valley. In the areas where the battle was to be fought, there are few geographical features of any note, except the high ground running south-east from Thiepval to Guillemont. This lay in German hands, and was the principal tactical objective for Rawlinson's 4th Army. The British, therefore, would everywhere be fighting uphill; whereas opposite General Fayolle's 6th Army, the French faced more or less level ground. The Germans had superb observation points gazing down on the British lines, their excellence matched only by the depth of their fortifications.

In the nearly two years that they had sat on the Somme, they had excavated dugouts and vast dormitories out of the chalk

Haig: Architect of the 'Big Push'

as deep as forty feet below ground, comfortably safe from all but the heaviest British shell. Ironically, the British, by their policy of continual 'strafing' (in contrast to the prevalent German and French philosophy of 'live and let live'), had provoked the defenders to dig even deeper. When captured, the German dugouts astonished everybody by their depth and complexity. The German line on the Somme was, claims Churchill, 'undoubtedly the strongest and most perfectly defended position in the world'.

British security surrounding the Somme offensive was by no means perfect. Among other indiscretions, the press reported a speech made by a member of the government, Arthur Henderson, requesting workers in a munitions factory not to

question why the Whitsun Bank Holiday was being suspended. In his diary for 10th June, Crown Prince Rupprecht, the German army group commander, wrote: '. . . This fact should speak volumes. It certainly does so speak, it contains the surest proof that there will be a great British offensive before long. . . .' Abundantly aware of just where the 'Big Push' was coming, for several weeks previously the German defenders had industriously practised rushing their machine-guns up from the dugouts. This had been perfected to a three-minute drill, which would give the Germans an ample margin on 'Z-day' between the lifting of the British barrage and the arrival of the attacking infantry.

For five days Rawlinson's artillery preparation blasted away without let-up (Haig would have preferred a short preliminary bombardment)—thereby dissipating what little element of surprise there still remained. By British standards of the day, it was a bombardment of unprecedented weight. Yet on their much wider front they could mount not nearly half as many heavy guns as the French; and they had nothing to compare with the French 240mm mortars and 400 'super-heavies' with which Foch (French northern army group commander) had equipped Fayolle. A depressing quantity of the British shells turned out to be dud; while defective American ammunition caused so many premature explosions that some of the 4.5 howitzer gun crews nicknamed themselves 'the Suicide Club'. The fire-plan also suffered from the same inflexibility which characterized the training of the new infantry. Through sheer weight of metal, large sections of the German front-line trenches were indeed obliterated, their skeleton outposts killed. But down below in the secure depths of the dugouts, the main body of the German defenders sat playing *Skat* while the shelling raged above.

The worst shortcoming of the five-day bombardment, however, was that it failed in its essential task of breaking up the barbed wire through which the British assault waves were to advance. Divisional commanders appear to have known this, but to have kept the knowledge to themselves. On the eve of the 'Big Push', Haig wrote in his diary with the misguided optimism that was to be found at almost every level prior to 1st July: 'The wire has never been so well cut, nor the Artillery preparation so thorough. I have seen personally all the Corps commanders and one and all are full of confidence. . . .'

At 0245 hours on 1st July a German listening post picked up a message from Rawlinson wishing his 4th Army 'Good Luck'. A little less than five hours later there was suddenly a strange silence as the British bombardment ended. Some-

where near a hundred thousand men left their trenches at this moment and moved forward at a steady walk. On their backs they carried their personal kit—including a spare pair of socks—water bottles, a day's rations, two gas masks, mess tins and field dressings, as well as rifle, bayonet, 220 rounds of ammunition, and an entrenching tool. Some also carried hand grenades or bombs for a trench mortar. The minimum load was 66lb; some men were laden with as much as 85 to 90lb. It was about to become a broiling hot day.

'. . . They got going without delay,' wrote the commanding officer of a battalion of the Royal Inniskilling Fusiliers;

'No fuss, no shouting, no running, everything solid and thorough—just like the men themselves. Here and there a boy would wave his hand to me as I shouted good luck to them through my megaphone. And all had a cheery face . . . Fancy advancing against heavy fire with a big roll of barbed wire on your shoulders! . . .'

Seen from the defenders' point of view, a German recorded that the moment the bombardment lifted:

'. . . Our men at once clambered up the steep shafts leading from the dug-outs to daylight and ran for the nearest shell craters. The machine-guns were pulled out of the dug-outs and hurriedly placed into position, their crews dragging the heavy ammunition boxes up the steps and out to the guns. A rough firing line was thus rapidly established. As soon as in position, a series of extended lines of British infantry were seen moving forward from the British trenches. The first line appeared to continue without end to right and left. It was quickly followed by a second line, then a third and fourth. They came on at a steady easy pace as if expecting to find nothing alive in our front trenches. . . .'

Reading from left to right along the line, the British forces involved in the principal offensive were the 8th, 10th, 3rd, 15th, and 13th Corps, while below them on the river Somme itself came the French 20th and 35th Corps. General Hunter-Weston's 8th Corps had the most difficult task of all—the terrain was particularly difficult—and, because of its inexperience, it was the corps about which Haig had entertained the most doubts. With the 31st Division holding its left flank, the Yorks and Lancs were encouraged to see ahead of them numerous gaps in the wire opened up by the shelling. But at the moment of reaching them, they were scythed down by devastating machine-gun fire from the weapons which the Germans had rushed up from their dug-outs. It was an experience that was to be repeated innumerable times that day. By early afternoon the 31st Division had lost 3,600 officers and men, of whom only eight were prisoners.

Next to it, the 29th Division, recently returned from Gallipoli, had the task of rushing the 'Hawthorn Redoubt' after an immense mine had been detonated under it. But the mine had been timed to go off ten minutes before zero hour; giving the German machine-gunners plenty of time to reoccupy the crater. Moving across no man's land the Royal Fusiliers could see ahead of them the bodies of their first waves festooning the uncut wire; all that came back from this one battalion was 120 men. The divisional commander, in a supreme understatement, noted that his men had been 'temporarily held up by some machine-guns', and pushed up another brigade; one battalion found itself so obstructed by the dead and the endless lines of wounded that it physically could not get forward. Attacking unsuccessfully but with fantastic courage at Beaumont-Hamel, the Newfoundlanders won their greatest battle honour: in a matter of minutes 710 men fell.

Also at Beaumont-Hamel, troops that had captured the Heidenkopf position were tragically shot down by the second wave, unaware that the German strong-point was already in British hands.

By nightfall, the 8th Corps alone had lost 14,000 officers and men without even broaching the main objective. It had taken only twenty-two prisoners. For the 10th, the 3rd, and part of 15th Corps the story of bloody failure was much the same:

'I get up from the ground and whistle,' recalled an officer commanding an Irish battalion in the second wave. 'The others rise. We move off with steady pace. I see rows upon rows of British soldiers lying dead, dying or wounded in no man's land. Here and there I see the hands thrown up and then a body flops on the ground. The bursting shells and smoke make visibility poor. We proceed. Again I look southward from a different angle and perceive heaped up masses of British corpses suspended on the German wire, while live men rush forward in orderly procession to swell the weight of numbers in the spider's web. . . .'

The Highland Light Infantry went into battle behind their pipers. Swiftly their leading companies invested the German trenches, but while they were still exulting at their success, hidden German machine-guns opened fire. Within little more than an hour of the beginning of the attack, half the HLI were killed or wounded, bringing the assault to a sudden halt.

Opposite Thiepval, the 36th (Ulster) Division came tantalizingly, tragically close to achieving success. Better trained than most of Rawlinson's units, the Inniskillings managed to advance a mile in the first hour of the attack, attaining the top of the ridge and capturing the Schwaben Redoubt, an important strongpoint in the

German first-line. But, following the experiences of 1915 when so many field officers had been killed off, it was Haig's orders that no battalion commanding officers or second-in-commands should go in with their men in the first wave. Thus there was no one senior enough to consolidate the Ulstermen's fine success. Communications with the rear were appalling. Runners sent back for fresh orders never returned. Precious time was thrown away, while the Germans recovered their balance. When finally a reserve brigade was sent up to reinforce the Inniskillings, it too had no senior officers with it; with the result it advanced too fast, running into its own artillery barrage, where it lost something like two-thirds of its soldiers. That evening, of the 10th Corps' 9,000 losses, over half came from the Ulster Division—a fact which was long to cause bitterness against the neighbouring English units. The division was left clinging precariously to the German front line.

On the 3rd Corps' front, the 8th Division was another unit to suffer appalling casualties in return for very little progress. It lost a shocking total of 1,927 officers and men killed; one of its battalions, the 2nd Middlesex, lost 22 officers and 601 men, another—the 8th Yorks and Lancs—21 and 576 respectively, out of an average of 27-30 officers and roughly 700 men to a battalion.

Over the whole British front, only Congreve's 13th Corps, next door to the French, registered any notable success that day. Attacking through Montauban, it captured the entire HQ of the German 62nd Regiment; making a total bag of 1,882 prisoners (compared with the 8th Corps' 22). At Montauban, the cellars were found to be filled with German dead; apparently killed by the French heavy mortars.

Fighting in hell

Indeed, for all the incredible fortitude of Kitchener's men, it was the French who won the laurels on 1st July. The terrain opposite them was admittedly much more favourable, the defences weaker; they had more and heavier guns, which had smashed up even some of the deepest enemy dugouts; their infantry moved with greater skill and flexibility; and they had the advantage of a certain degree of surprise. After the losses inflicted at Verdun, German intelligence could not believe that the French were capable of making a serious contribution on the Somme. To reinforce this belief, Foch cleverly delayed the French attack until several hours after the British.

By early afternoon, Fayolle's troops had taken 6,000 prisoners, destroyed the whole of the German 121st Division's artillery, and come close to making a breakthrough. Péronne itself was threatened. General

Balfourier, commanding the 'Iron' (20th) Corps which had saved Verdun in February, urged Congreve on his left to join him in continuing the advance. But Congreve would budge no farther. Above him, Rawlinson was bent more on consolidation than exploitation. Thus Balfourier, with his left flank hanging in the air, was unable to advance either. It was not until 10 o'clock that night that Rawlinson made any attempt to push reserves up to the areas of least resistance. What prospect there had been of capitalizing on any success gained during the 1st July was swiftly lost; the Germans were soon replacing the machine-guns destroyed that day.

When the casualties were counted, the British figures came to 60,000, of which the dead numbered 20,000. Most of the slaughter had been accomplished by perhaps a hundred German machine-gun teams. 1st July was one of the blackest days in British history. Even at Verdun, the total French casualty list for the worst month barely exceeded what Great Britain had lost on that one day. Fayolle lost fewer men than the defending Germans.

Haig had no idea of the full extent of the British losses until 3rd July and neither he nor Rawlinson quite knew why some efforts had succeeded and others failed. On the 3rd Haig ordered Rawlinson to attack again; this time rightly trying to follow up the good results achieved on his southern sector. But the guns were now short of ammunition, and the losses on 1st July greatly reduced the strength of the new blows. That night it rained, and the next day 'walking, let alone fighting, became hellish'.

On 14th July, Rawlinson—chastened by the terrible casualties his army had suffered—decided to try something new. He would attack by night. Describing it caustically as 'an attack organized for amateurs by amateurs', the French predicted disaster. Haig, equally dubious, caused the attack to be postponed twenty-four hours—a delay that diminished the chances of success. Nevertheless, throwing in six brigades which totalled some 22,000 men, Rawlinson after a short hurricane bombardment punched out a salient four miles wide and a thousand yards deep, breaching the Germans' second line—and thereby briefly restoring the element of surprise to the Western Front. A French liaison officer telephoned the sceptical Balfourier: *'Ils ont osé. Ils ont réussi!'*

Once again, however, the fruits of victory were thrown away by poor communications and the painful slowness to react of the British command. As at Gallipoli, there was a horrifying absence of any sense of urgency. The cavalry were waiting in the wings, but too far back to be available to exploit any gains, and not until mid-after-

Total War

British go over the top in the Somme battle. Their dead bodies were to festoon the wire

noon that day was it decided to push up the already battle-weary 7th Infantry Division. Thus nine valuable hours were wasted, and darkness was falling when at last the British cavalry and infantry reserves attacked. By then the shaken Germans had rallied.

Deeply disappointed, Haig now settled for a long-protracted 'battle of attrition'. Writing to the government, he declared his intention 'to maintain a steady pressure on Somme battle . . . proceeding thus, I expect to be able to maintain the offensive well into the Autumn. . . .' All through August and into September the bloody slogging match continued. As seen by the Australian official history, Haig's new technique 'merely appeared to be that of applying a battering-ram ten or fifteen times against the same part of the enemy's battle-front with the intention of penetrating for a mile, or possibly two . . . the claim that it was economic is entirely unjustified'. By the end of the summer, one level-headed Australian officer was writing '. . . we have just come out of a place so terrible that . . . a raving lunatic could never imagine the horror the last thirteen days. . . .'

Meanwhile, however, Verdun had been finally and definitively relieved by the dreadful British sacrifices on the Somme. On 11th July, one last desperate effort was mounted against Verdun, and a handful of Germans momentarily reached a height whence they could actually gaze down on Verdun's citadel. It was the high-water mark of the battle, and—though not apparent at the time—was perhaps the turning point, the Gettysburg of the First World War. Rapidly the tide now receded at Verdun, with Falkenhayn ordering the German army to assume the defensive all along the Western Front.

At the end of August Falkenhayn was replaced by the formidable combination of Hindenburg and Ludendorff.

Visiting the Somme, Ludendorff criticized the inflexibility of the defence there; '. . . Without doubt they fought too dog-gedly, clinging too resolutely to the mere holding of ground, with the result that the losses were heavy. . . . The Field Marshal and I could for the moment only ask that the front line should be held more lightly. . . .' It was a prelude to the strategic withdrawal to the 'Hindenburg Line' in the following spring.

'A pretty mechanical toy'

On the Somme, 15th September was to become a red-letter day in the history of warfare. Haig decided to throw into a third major attack the first fifty newly invented tanks. Rejected by Kitchener as 'a pretty mechanical toy but of very limited military value', the tank had been developed under the greatest secrecy and crews trained with similar security behind a vast secret enclosure near Thetford in Norfolk. Even the name 'tank' was intended to deceive the enemy. Its inventors begged the army not to employ the first machines, however, until they were technically more reliable; while even Asquith visiting the front on 6th September thought it: '. . . a mistake to put them into the battle of the Somme. They were built for the purpose of breaking an ordinary trench system with a normal artillery fire only, whereas on the Somme they will have to penetrate a terrific artillery barrage, and will have to operate in a broken country full of shell-craters . . .'

But Haig was determined. Historians will long continue to argue whether he was right or not; on Haig's side, the Cambrai raid the following year tends to prove that the surprise value of the tank had not entirely been thrown away, and undoubtedly, sooner or later, it would have had to be tried out under battle conditions.

On the day of the attack, only thirty-two of the original fifty tanks reached the assembly area in working order; twenty-four actually went into battle, and most of these broke down, became bogged, or were knocked out. At Flers the tank showed what it could do, and the infantry

*Painters capture the meaning of these sacrificial battles. **Above:** 'Paths of Glory' by C.Nevinson. **Left:** 'Gassed and Wounded' by Eric Kennington*

advanced cheering down the main street of the village behind four solitary machines. But once again poor communications between front and rear gave the Germans a chance to reorganize before success could be exploited. By the evening of the 15th all the tanks were either scattered or destroyed. With them vanished the last of Haig's three opportunities on the Somme; Montauban on 1st July, Rawlinson's night attack on the 14th, and Flers on 15th September.

Now the equinoctial rains turned the battlefield into a slippery bog. But, pressed by Joffre, Haig stuck out his Celtic jaw and soldiered on, in the mystic belief that—somehow, somewhere—an exhausted foe might suddenly break. The British army was equally exhausted. Conditions became even more appalling. In November, a soldier wrote: '. . . Whoever it is we are relieving, they have already gone. The trench is empty . . . Corpses lie along the parados, rotting in the wet; every now and then a booted foot appears jutting over the trench. The mud makes it all but impassable, and now, sunk in it up to the knees, I have the momentary terror of never being able to pull myself out . . . This is the very limit of endurance. . . .'

In a last attack on 13th November, shattered Beaumont-Hamel was finally captured. Having won the bloodily disputed high ground, the British were now fighting their way down into the valley beyond—condemning themselves to spend a winter in flooded trenches. Nothing of any strategic value had been attained. The 'Big Push' was over.

At Verdun in the autumn, Nivelle and Mangin recaptured forts Douaumont and Vaux in a series of brilliant counter-strokes—plus much of the territory gained so painfully by the Crown Prince's men. By Christmas 1916 both battles were finished. After ten terrible months Verdun had been saved. But at what a cost! Half the houses in the city itself had been destroyed by the long-range German guns, and nine of its neighbouring villages had vanished off the face of the earth. When the human casualties came to be added up, the French admitted to having lost 377,231 men, of whom 162,308 were listed as dead or missing. German losses amounted to no less than 337,000. But, in fact, combined casualties may easily have totalled much more than 800,000.

What caused this imprecision about the slaughter at Verdun, as well as giving the battle its particularly atrocious character, was the fact that it all took place in so concentrated an area—little larger than the London parks. Many of the dead were

never found, or are still being discovered to this day. One combatant recalled how 'the shells disinterred the bodies, then reinterred them, chopped them to pieces, played with them as a cat plays with a mouse'. Inside the great sombre *Ossuaire* at Verdun lie the bones of more than 100,000 unknown warriors.

On the Somme, the British had lost some 420,000 men; the French about 200,000 and the Germans probably about 450,000 —although a miasma of mendacity and error still surrounds the exact figures. On the battlefields of Verdun and the Somme, there also expired the last flickers of idealism; yet the war would go on.

The casualties of the two battles included among them the highest warlords on both sides. Falkenhayn had fallen; then Joffre, to be replaced (disastrously) by Nivelle, and Asquith by Lloyd George; a few months later Premier Briand's head would also topple. Because of the appalling extent to which Verdun had 'bled white' his own army, Falkenhayn's grim experiment had failed. Yet, in its longer-range effects, it contained an element of success. As Raymond Jubert, a young French ensign, wrote in prophetic despair before he was killed at Verdun: 'They will not be able to make us do it again another day; that would be to misconstrue the price of our effort. . . .' The excessive sacrifices of the French army at Verdun germinated the seeds of the mutinies that were to sprout in the summer of 1917, thereby making it finally plain that the war could no longer be won without American troops.

In many ways Verdun and Somme were the First World War in microcosm, with all its heroism and futility, its glorious and unspeakable horrors. They were indecisive battles in an indecisive war. Of the two, Verdun undoubtedly had the greater historical significance. Years after the 1918 Armistice this Pyrrhic victory of the 20th century continued to haunt the French nation. From the role the forts at Verdun had played, France's military leaders (headed by Pétain) drew the wrong conclusions, and the Maginot Line—with all its disastrous strategic consequences in 1940—was born.

Spiritually, perhaps, the damage was even greater. More than three-quarters of the whole French army passed through the hell of Verdun—almost an entire generation of Frenchmen. Nobody knew this better than Pétain who, years after the war, remarked that at Verdun 'the constant vision of death had penetrated him (the French soldier) with a resignation which bordered on fatalism'.

For a symbol of what Verdun did to France, one need hardly search beyond the tragic figure of Pétain, the warrior-hero of 1916, the resigned defeatist of 1940.

War in the Air

In the late summer of 1914 western Europe heard the familiar tramp and jingle of men and horses going to the wars. But this time there was a new sound, the hum and drone of a few aeroplanes overhead; a sound that would swell to a mighty roar before the war ended.

It was now eleven years since the Wright brothers had flown a power-driven biplane at Kitty Hawk in North Carolina and long before that event successful experiments had been made with balloons, gliders, man-lifting kites, and small dirigible airships. In its early days aviation was concerned with peaceful uses or sport, and even its first involvements in military affairs were strictly inoffensive. During the siege of Paris in 1870 balloons were used to carry messages and, occasionally, people in and out of the beleaguered city. Captive balloons had been used as high-altitude observation posts, notably by the Italians in the Eritrean War of 1887-88. Man-lifting kites were employed in the South African War, 1899-1902, for reconnaissance—in order to see, as General Sir Edward Swinton said, 'the other side of the hill'.

The first recorded use of aeroplanes in war was by the Italians in the war against Turkey in 1911, and on 23rd October the first wartime flight was carried out by Captain Piazza, who bore the high-sounding title of commander of the air fleet. On 1st November Lieutenant Gavotti made history by dropping four modified 2-kg Swedish hand grenades on a Turkish army camp. Soon afterwards the Turks protested that Italian aeroplanes had bombed a military hospital at Ain Zara. Independent inquiries failed to confirm the existence of a hospital in the camp, but it is possible that some tents were used as a casualty clearing station. The dropping of these diminutive bombs, and the Turkish protest, started a discussion in the press about the ethics of offensive air action, which has continued, more or less vehemently, ever since.

From sport to scouting

At about this time several countries began to form corps of military aviation. In 1911 the British made a start with the Air Battalion, Royal Engineers, which was superseded in July 1912 by the Royal Flying Corps (RFC). This was a joint service, intended to supply the needs of both the navy and the army, with a central flying school at Upavon, Wiltshire, staffed by a mixture of army and naval officers and men. In July 1914 the Royal Navy decided to break away, and the naval wing of the RFC became the Royal Naval Air Service (RNAS). The army wing then reverted to being a corps of the army (RFC).

In Germany the army aviation corps was placed under the inspector-general of military transport, suggesting that it was regarded as a means of conveyance. The naval air service specialized in lighter-than-air craft, and at quite an early date it possessed several large Zeppelin and Schutte-Lanz airships. The range and lifting power of these ships, very great for those days, put them in a class by themselves. Their huge envelopes, however, were filled with hydrogen gas, which made them extremely vulnerable to any form of incendiary attack.

France formed military and naval units of aviation, but gave little thought as to the way in which they were to be used. Indeed Marshal Foch, who had commanded the *Ecole Supérieure de la Guerre,* had no faith in the military value of aviation. He is on record as saying: 'Aviation is good sport, but for the army it is useless.' The United States had an army air arm as early as 1907, but progress was incredibly slow. It was organized as the Aviation Division of the Signal Corps, and even by 1911 it possessed no more than two aeroplanes. Later the American navy set up a small air arm. Not much is known about early Russian military aviation—they were as secretive then as they are now—but little had apparently been done by the outbreak of the First World War.

Unlike most other countries, at the beginning of the First World War Great Britain had a perfectly clear, though very limited, idea of the role of military aviation. It was to be reconnaissance, pure and simple. The navy wanted aircraft to survey large areas of sea, and keep a watch on the enemy's main naval bases, so that they would know at any time the whereabouts of his main sea forces. The army hoped that aircraft would be able to fly over the enemy's rear areas, and provide a stream of up-to-date reports on the location of troops and depots, and the movements of traffic. Such reports would greatly help the intelligence staffs to assess the strength, dispositions, and intentions of the enemy.

For a long time it had been a military maxim that 'information must be fought for', and so long as war was confined to two dimensions this held good. Cavalry patrols

*Top: The planes of the aces, Guynemer's Spad, a fast single-seat French design. **Above:** A Fokker Dr I as flown by von Richthofen taxis under horse-power on a German airfield. **Left:** Air to air combat 1917. The observer of a German Albatros engages British fighters*

Left: French fighters from a camp in Artois beside one of their aircraft, a Nieuport. *Below:* Bombing became a recognized technique of the aerial war. This Italian magazine illustration shows a surprise daylight raid on the Austrian port of Pola. In this raid the Italian pilots, led by an American, Wallis Fitch, succeeded in dropping sixty tons of bombs on Pola

would seek to penetrate into enemy territory, make contact with his forces, and withdraw with their reports. Only such contacts, and the exchange of fire, could establish the presence and probable strength of the enemy's forces at any place.

Experience at the beginning of the First World War seemed to show that this maxim was no longer valid. The ocean of the air is all one, covering both land and sea, and aircraft could fly wherever they wished with no let or hindrance, save for some rather ineffective small-arms fire from the ground. Even when opposing aircraft met they had no means—short of ramming—of injuring each other. As these encounters

became more frequent observers took to carrying fire-arms with them. Since a rifle was an uncommonly awkward thing to handle in a slip-stream of 70 mph or more, the most favoured weapons were revolvers and automatic pistols. But aircraft in motion are difficult targets for such weapons, and usually, after a harmless exchange of shots, aircraft would go on their way with a parting wave of the hand. Before long, however, army field guns were fitted with high-angle mountings, and anti-aircraft shell-fire (AA) became the chief menace to aircraft.

Many ideas were put forward from time to time for mounting machine-guns in aircraft. These fell into two groups: the rigid mounting which required the aircraft itself to be manoeuvred to bring the sights to bear on the target, and the movable gun which was under the control of the observer. The Maxim, Vickers, or Spandau type of gun, heavy, belt-fed, and originally water-cooled, did not lend itself to being fitted in aircraft except in a rigid mounting. But lighter types of automatic weapons, such as the air-cooled Lewis and Hotchkiss guns, using drums or clips of ammunition, were becoming available, and unit workshops in the field produced a great variety of experimental gun-mountings.

The ideal rigid mounting should provide a gun firing directly forward in the line of flight, thus enabling the pilot to point his aircraft straight at the enemy and enjoy the advantage of a 'no-deflection' shot. The difficulty was that if the gun was mounted in the fuselage, so as to be under the control of the pilot for the purpose of reloading, clearing stoppages, and so on, its line of fire was obstructed by the airscrew.

The Germans were the first to solve this problem by inventing an interrupter-gear, which prevented the gun from firing whenever an airscrew blade was in the line of fire. This device was fitted to the Fokker, a small fast monoplane, which thus became the first effective fighter. Its influence was immediately felt. During the winter of 1915-16 it shot down many Allied aircraft and, for the time being, the Germans gained a considerable measure of air supremacy over the Western Front. The old maxim again held good, and information had to be fought for.

The Allies possessed fast single-seater 'scouts', such as the Nieuport, the Morane parasol monoplane, the Martinsyde, and the Bristol Scout. These had been designed for longer-range reconnaissance work, relying on their speed to avoid interception and reduce the danger from AA fire. Various types of gun-mountings had been tried in these scouts, but none was satisfactory in the absence of an interrupter-gear.

The answer to the Fokker was the DH2, and later the FE8. These were single-seater

Total War

'pusher' scouts, with the engine behind the pilot and the normal fuselage replaced by tail-booms. They carried a Lewis gun firing forward in the line of flight, and the absence of an engine in front gave the pilot an uninterrupted view ahead. The DH2 came into service in the spring of 1916, and soon showed itself to be more manoeuvrable than the Fokker. Being a biplane, its short span and light wing-loading gave it a smaller turning-circle and it was more buoyant at high altitudes. These were great advantages in a 'dog-fight', when each aircraft manoeuvred to 'get on to the tail' of its adversary. Very soon the reign of the Fokker was over, and the Allied army co-operation aircraft were able to go about their business again in comparative safety, while the zone of air fighting was pushed eastwards beyond the German front line.

Air fighting became general over the whole of the Western Front, the fighters of each side trying to gain sufficient control of the air to permit their army co-operation aircraft to carry out their routine tasks of reconnaissance, the spotting and control of artillery fire, and some occasional bombing. Before long, however, Great Britain, France, and Germany began to evolve individual patterns of air warfare.

The British adopted a very formal and de-centralized system. Each of the four armies on the Western Front had its own Brigade of the RFC, which included one or more fighter wings. It was British policy to work their army co-operation aircraft continuously from dawn to dusk, and it was therefore necessary for their fighters to patrol the sky over the front during the hours of daylight. This meant that although some fighters were always present, they were never very numerous. This lack of strength was largely offset by the almost incredibly aggressive spirit of the RFC fighter pilots. Neither the French nor the Germans adopted this system of continuous patrol. Both tended to restrict army co-operation work to short periods each day, and put up their main fighter strength to cover it.

It must be understood that the fighter, though strategically defensive, can carry out its task only by means of a sustained tactical offensive. The British pilots would immediately attack any enemy aircraft seen, even if they were outnumbered and in an unfavourable tactical situation. The French and the Germans were more cautious, or maybe more sensible. They seldom attacked except when in superior strength and from a favourable tactical position. They took every advantage of clouds, and the dazzle caused by looking towards the sun, to achieve tactical surprise, a factor of very great importance in air fighting.

During the latter part of 1916 the Germans had produced a new range of faster and more powerful fighters, such as the Pfalz, Albatros, Halberstadt, and Fokker Triplane, and the DH2 and FE8 were definitely outclassed. Their immediate replacements, the DH5, the Sopwith Pup, and the Sopwith 1½ Strutter, were not very successful. Though the Allies now had their own interrupter-gear, the Constantinesco, for fixed guns in tractor aircraft, the performance of these aircraft did not match that of their opponents.

The importance of technical superiority now became apparent. As the Allies gradually lost the air supremacy which they had enjoyed during the spring and summer of 1916, they were forced to realize that no amount of skill, courage, and training could fully compensate for inferior aircraft. A further cause of this decline was the rigidly decentralized organization of the RFC. During the height of the battle of the Somme in the autumn of 1916 the Allies had come perilously near to losing control of the air over the battle zone. The 4th Army, on whose front the battle was fought, had only one RFC brigade (the 4th) allotted to it. The other three brigades were allocated to the relatively disengaged Armies. All attempts by GHQ to induce them to lend fighters to the 4th Brigade were successfully resisted, because they were anxious lest they should lose their squadrons indefinitely, and perhaps in

their turn find themselves short of fighters.

The Germans, operating a much less rigid system, were able to concentrate a high proportion of their air strength where it was most needed, over the battle front. General headquarters then decided to step up air activity, including bombing, on the disengaged army fronts, in the hope of inducing the Germans to disperse their concentrations of fighters opposite the 4th Army. This failed, because the Germans understood their business far too well to do any such thing. Eventually, the situation was largely restored by borrowing eight relatively unemployed fighter squadrons from the RNAS.

At various times fighters were used to escort long-distance photographic reconnaissance missions and bombing raids. This plan never proved very effective, because if the escorting fighters were attacked their only possible defence was to manoeuvre so as to bring their forward-firing guns to bear on the enemy. This brought about a dog-fight, and the aircraft which the fighters were supposed to be protecting were soon lost sight of, and left open to attack by a second wave of enemy fighters. Consequently escorts were largely discontinued in favour of a general fighter cover provided by offensive patrols. As early as 1916 rockets were used in air fighting, especially by French Nieuport

squadrons. They were carried on the interplane struts, and fired electrically. They were, however, difficult to aim and did not prove very successful.

By April 1917 the Allied air-power was at its lowest ebb, and the RFC suffered such heavy casualties that the month has been called 'Bloody April'. Later in the year things improved with the arrival in fair numbers of such excellent fighters as the Sopwith Camel, the SE5 and 5A, the improved Nieuport, and the very fast Spad. A small number of Bristol Fighters, a two-seater fighter-bomber of outstanding worth, also became available. By the end of the year the Allies had overcome their technical inferiority, and the balance was restored.

Quite early in the war the German Zeppelins began night bombing raids on Great Britain. Interception in darkness, even of these huge and relatively slow ships, had proved very difficult. Observer posts were keen and alert enough, but communications were bad, and the division of responsibility between the Admiralty and the War Office caused confusion and delay. Also there were at that time no reliable means of conveying information to aircraft in the air. Public concern grew, but was alleviated when several Zeppelins were brought down in flames, as much by good luck as by good management. The Germans then

German fighters attack a British DH4 flight

started raids by aeroplanes, at first by night and later, more boldly, by day. The climax came in July 1917, with raids by aeroplanes on London in daylight, and public indignation boiled over. It was realized that our air defences were badly organized and largely ineffective. This, and the contrast between the terribly over-stretched RFC and the relatively unemployed RNAS, were the main causes of the unification of our air services in the Royal Air Force, following the Smuts report.

The year 1918 began with the British and French air forces enjoying a good measure of air supremacy. On the Western Front a ding-dong battle went on most of the time, with the Allied fighters, on the whole, just managing to keep the upper hand. By this time the differing national systems of conducting air warfare had become well established. The British maintained their system of continuous activity, covered by fighter patrols, but now in the fourth year of the war they had more and better fighters, and could maintain a stronger effort. A number of pilots, such as Andrew Beauchamp-Proctor, William Bishop, and 'Mick' Mannock attained large scores of enemy aircraft destroyed. In addition, especially able pilots were allowed to carry out lone 'hunting patrols', seeking out enemy aircraft and attempting to take them by surprise, and some of them were very successful at this stalking game. The best known of these were Albert Ball and J.B.McCudden.

The Germans maintained their centralized system, and once or twice a day put up their 'circuses'. These were large formations of fighters, led by their most experienced and successful pilots, such as Ernst Udet, Manfred von Richthofen ('The Red Baron'), and Hermann Goering.

The French system was not unlike that of the Germans, but their concentrations were not so large, and they also encouraged their best pilots to go on lone hunting patrols. The most famous of these pilots were Navarre, Fonck, and Guynemer.

The Americans came into the war too late to play a very significant part in air fighting, and their units were equipped with French or British aircraft. But quite a number of American pilots had voluntarily joined one or other of the Allied air forces, and had given very distinguished service in fighter squadrons. Their best known pilots were Rickenbacker and Vaughn.

These outstandingly successful fighter pilots became known as 'aces'. It was a term of French origin, but was used mainly by the press.

When large formations of fighters met, extensive dog-fights ensued, but casualties were usually fewer than might have been expected from the large numbers engaged. Dog-fighting involved a lot of difficult deflection shots and, even with the help of tracer bullets, many combats were inconclusive. It should be remembered that the amount of ammunition that could be carried in fighters was strictly limited. The DH2, for example, normally carried five double drums, a total of 490 rounds. This was sufficient for about 50 seconds' fire. The later twin-gun fighters, such as the Camel, the SE5A, and the Spad, carried on the average about 500 rounds per gun, also about 50 seconds' fire, though the volume of fire was doubled. Pilots, therefore, especially the inexperienced ones, soon ran out of ammunition in a dog-fight.

In addition to aerial combat, fighter pilots were frequently called upon to shoot down observation balloons, and carry out low 'ground-strafing' attacks against troops or transport. For the attack on balloons and airships incendiary bullets, known as Buckingham, were available. There was also an explosive type, called Pomeroy, but the legality of ammunition of this kind was doubtful, and it was feared that any pilot in possession of it, landing in enemy territory, might have to face trial with the possibility of severe punishment. Pomeroy was hardly used at all, and Buckingham only against balloons, whose occupants always had parachutes, or against

airships that were flying over the fighters' home territory.

When in March 1918 the German armies, reinforced by large numbers transferred from the Eastern Front after the collapse of Russia, broke through the defences of the 5th Army, all available Allied fighters were heavily engaged in ground-strafing attacks in order to stem the German advance. Though costly, these attacks were very successful, and were a major factor in restoring a very serious situation.

The German armies faltered and came to a stop. It was their last great effort, and a general retreat set in. The German air force began at last to decline; the morale of its pilots sank to a low ebb, as the prospect of total military defeat drew closer. In addition, some of its best fighter squadrons had been recalled from the front to defend the homeland against the bombing attacks, by day and by night, of the Independent Air Force. This was a small force of bombers—a development of the GHQ Bombing Wing—which was set up after the formation of the Royal Air Force in April 1918. It never had more than nine operational squadrons, out of a total of nearly 200 on the Western Front, but its attacks on centres of industry and communications in the Rhineland had caused much concern and, at times, consternation among the civic authorities. The German government was compelled to provide a fairly substantial fighter defence. There were many running fights between the day bombers of the Independent Force and the defending fighters. Equipped with the efficient Scarff-ring mounting for the observer's gun, the bombers' losses were not heavy, and they often gave as good as they got. Indeed, bad weather and unreliable engines hampered the bombers as much as did the German fighters. These experiences led, in the inter-war years, to a serious under-estimate of the effectiveness of fighter defences.

In Italy and the Near and Middle East, where the war could neither be lost nor won, all the belligerents—except Turkey, which had no other front—tended to employ their semi-obsolescent aircraft. The pattern of air fighting was much the same as on the Western Front, but at a lower intensity. In the Middle East, since German aircraft were few, and the Turks had not many effective fighters, the Allied fighters were mainly employed in ground-strafing.

The closing months of the war saw the Allies enjoying almost complete air supremacy in all the theatres of war. The Germans were short of aircraft, pilots, fuel, and transport. The war in the air was won.

In the First World War aerial warfare was superimposed on a war conducted in accordance with traditional two-dimensional strategy. It was the last war to be

fought in this way. This meant, however, that almost the whole of the air effort was engaged in the close support of land and sea operations, and the war ended without providing any convincing proof of the offensive power of aircraft as weapons in their own right. It also meant that there was but slight experience of what were to be two of the main tasks of air power in the Second World War—strategic air bombardment and the use of fighters in air defence.

This account would be incomplete without some description of the men who flew the fighters in those early days. The fighter pilots of the Royal Air Force were not untypical of those in all the air forces.

Almost all of them were very young—hardly any were over twenty-five years of age, and a large proportion were under twenty-one—and until the later stages of the war they were very inadequately trained. It was quite common for squadrons on active service to receive pilots with no more than a total of some thirty hours' flying experience, of which perhaps five or six hours might be of the operational type. Most of them had never fired a gun in the air, and had no idea of the tactics of air fighting. There were in those days no operational training units, and all such instruction had to be given by the more experienced pilots of hard-pressed squadrons at the battle front.

Once the first few dangerous weeks were over, the new pilots' chances of survival were greatly increased. The standard of training improved very much in the later stages of the war, especially in the Royal Air Force, where Colonel Smith-Barry's reforms did a great deal to reduce those tragic losses of young inexperienced pilots.

In those days there were no closed cockpits, no heating, no parachutes, and no self-sealing fuel tanks. Pilots on high-altitude patrols in winter were operating in Arctic conditions, and cases of frost-bite were not uncommon.

It was extraordinary how quickly these young men matured and found confidence, many of them leading their flights in the air with great distinction at the age of twenty.

Though constantly engaged in individual combat, and though none could fight harder, they fought cleanly. Untouched by wartime propaganda vilifying the enemy, they felt no personal hatred or bitterness towards their opponents. Indeed, it was always a highly traumatic experience to see an aircraft shot down in flames, and inspired the solemn thought 'There, but for the grace of God, go I'.

In the clear air, high above the mud and blood of the battlefields, a generous feeling of chivalry and fair play was shared by the vast majority of the fighter pilots of all nations involved in the war in the air.

Lawrence and the Arab Revolt

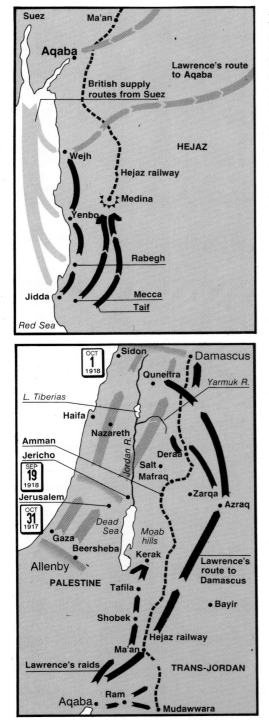

Top: *Mecca to Aqaba, June 1916–July 1917.*
Above: *Aqaba to Damascus, July 1917–October 1918. Damascus fell to Lawrence and Feisal on 1st October 1918*

Arabia, the land with which T.E.Lawrence will always be associated, is reputed to be a harsh and barren mistress, rewarding those who serve her with sickness of the body and distress of the mind. Lawrence's connection with the Arabs brought him at least as much pain as profit, and was in large measure responsible for his decision to retire at an early age from public life, once he judged that his work for the Arabs had been completed.

He is one of the most interesting personalities of his times, as well as one of the most controversial. He possessed the ability to achieve distinction in many fields, and yet, after flashing across the skies like a comet, he chose to become a recluse. Here again he was original, choosing neither the monastery nor the hermit's cave, but the anonymity of life in the ranks as a private soldier, first in the Royal Air Force, then the army, and then once more in the RAF. He believed himself immune from most human weaknesses, renouncing women, drink, and tobacco, but he worshipped speed. A few months after his final retirement from the RAF in 1935, he was riding his motorbike along a Dorset lane when he came upon two cyclists and in a vain attempt to avoid them, crashed and met his death.

A man so varied in accomplishment, so complex in character, so untrammelled by convention, inevitably invited hostile criticism. Richard Aldington, the poet and novelist, sought to destroy the Lawrence legend finally and for ever in his *Lawrence of Arabia* (1955), but he wrecked his case by confusing his facts. Others, too have belittled his contribution to Allenby's victory in Palestine, arguing that Lawrence was at most a gifted leader of guerrillas. Some believed that his desire for anonymity was inspired as much by a clever understanding of the media of publicity as by any genuine desire to withdraw from the hurly-burly of public life. But Lawrence was not an ordinary man. He did not fit, nor did he wish to fit, into the 'establishment'. If fame is a natural ambition, he achieved it, both in the world of action and in letters. If success is to be judged by the acquisition of wealth, he despised it; if it is to be determined by rank or status, he ignored it. The fact that throughout his life he enjoyed the friendship of such men as Churchill, Shaw, Liddell Hart, Wavell, E.M.Forster, and Trenchard is sufficient to demolish the charges brought against him by Aldington. These were not men

who admitted to their friendship the charlatan and the braggart.

The untidy subaltern

Thomas Edward Lawrence was born at Tremadoc in North Wales in 1888. He was the second son of Thomas Chapman, a rather eccentric Anglo-Irishman who later changed his name to Lawrence, and who subsequently inherited a baronetcy. T.E. Lawrence was born out of wedlock, a fact which undoubtedly affected him psychologically, but there is no evidence to suggest that he took the matter as seriously as Aldington has alleged. He discussed his illegitimacy quite openly with his more intimate friends. His father had sufficient private means to live comfortably, but not ostentatiously, and T.E.Lawrence gave early evidence of ability above the average. He learned to read at the age of four, and was learning Latin at six. He contributed towards the cost of his education by winning scholarships, first to Oxford High School, and then to the University. He was an omnivorous reader, with a particular interest in medieval and military history, and archaeology.

While reading history at Jesus College, Lawrence travelled in the Levant visiting Crusaders' castles, and subsequently took a first-class degree. Having been awarded a travelling scholarship, he joined D.G. Hogarth's expedition excavating Carchemish, and also worked with the archaeologist (Sir) Leonard Woolley. This brought him into contact with the Arabs, for whom he discovered he had a natural affinity, and he learned their language and as much as he could about their history and customs. On the outbreak of war in 1914, he tried to join the army, but was rejected at first, because he was below the minimum height of five feet five inches. It was several months before he was given a commission and employed in the intelligence branch of the general staff, where his knowledge of Arabic led to his posting to the 'Arab Bureau' at GHQ in Egypt. He was then a very junior and young-looking subaltern, whose untidiness in uniform and unconcern with the niceties of military protocol were not calculated to endear him to the more orthodox among his superiors.

The war against the Turks was going badly at the time. Their attack on the Suez Canal had been easily repulsed, but the ponderous British advance across Sinai had ground to a halt opposite Gaza. The failure at Gallipoli was fresh in men's

Total War

*Painting of T.E.Lawrence in Arab dress
by Augustus John*

memories, and was soon to be followed by Townshend's surrender at Kut in Mesopotamia (now Iraq). In south-west Arabia the Turks had advanced to the gates of Aden, where they were to remain for the rest of the war. They may have been corrupt and incompetent, but they were not faring too badly against the might of the British empire. It was at this moment, 5th June 1916, that the Hashimite princes of the Hejaz chose to rise against their Turkish overlords. The Arab Revolt, or, as some would prefer it, the Arab Awakening, had begun.

As a military operation, it was no more likely to succeed than some of the more recent military undertakings of the Arabs, in which performance has fallen far short of promise. Mecca, Jidda, and Taif were quickly captured, but the Arabs failed to take Medina, the principal Turkish garrison. The revolt lost impetus, and in the meantime the Turks sent reinforcements down the Hejaz railway, which the Arabs failed to interdict. In October 1916 the British sent Mr (later Sir Ronald) Storrs, accompanied by Lawrence, to investigate the situation at first-hand, and to consult with the Amir Abdullah, second son of Sherif Hussein, ruler of the Hejaz, whose tribal levies had captured Taif the previous month.

After preliminary discussions with Abdullah, Lawrence was dispatched to visit his younger brother, the Amir Feisal, whose tribesmen had been repulsed at Medina, but who was lying up in the hills nearby. The two men established an almost immediate *rapport,* but it was clear to Lawrence that Feisal's ill-disciplined and badly-armed tribesmen were no match for the Turks in conventional positional warfare. Meanwhile, the Turks continued to reinforce Medina, and the unruly bedouin, disappointed in their hopes for loot, began to drift back to their tents in the desert.

Lawrence was completely untrained in military staff work, but he at once appreciated that the key to the strategic situation was the Hejaz railway. So long as this continued operating, the Turks would be able to build up sufficient strength to reconquer the Hejaz. Moreover, the Arabs, although natural guerrillas, lacked the discipline, and even the will, to fight a pitched battle against the Turks, however incompetent the Turkish leadership. Some other use must be made of their natural military qualities and their ability to operate for long periods in the desert, and this could best be done by abandoning the siege of Medina and carrying the campaign into the north, raiding the railway, the Turks' lifeline, and reducing the flow of reinforcements to a trickle. Lawrence was not the first military leader in history to understand the potentialities of guerrilla

warfare when operating against a conventionally-minded enemy, nor has he been the last, for Mao Tse-tung has been equally successful in China, and Giap in Vietnam. But he must at least be given the credit for appreciating how best the Arab Revolt could be harnessed to assist the Allied cause, and at the same time achieve the Arabs' aim, which was to win their independence from foreign rule.

In pursuit of his aim to tie down as many Turks as possible in the Hejaz, Lawrence launched a series of raids against the single-line, wood-burning railway linking Medina with Damascus. He sought not to destroy the railway, but to impede its working, and to compel the Turks to deploy an ever-increasing number of troops to guard it. Fakhri Pasha, the Turkish commander in Medina, lacked initiative, remaining static behind his defences, and clamouring for more and more reinforcements. As they trickled down to him, Lawrence moved steadily farther north, joining forces with the Trans-Jordan tribes, and carrying his raids against the railway nearer to the main British front in Palestine. On 6th July 1917, in company with the famous desert raider, Auda abu Tayi, and his Howeitat tribesmen, he captured Aqaba from the rear, having first overwhelmed a Turkish battalion moving down from Ma'an to reinforce Aqaba.

Feisal then moved his headquarters to Aqaba, which was nearer to the main front than Wejh on the Red Sea, and with Sherif Hussein's permission placed himself under the command of General Allenby, who had taken over command in Palestine. The mainly tribal contingents of Feisal were provided with a stiffening in the shape of armoured cars and light artillery; small detachments of British, French, and Indian troops were sent to Aqaba to support the Arabs; and above all, arms, ammunition, and gold were provided to keep the Arab tribesmen in the field. Allenby intended to employ the Arabs to protect his open flank east of the river Jordan, and to hinder Turkish attempts to reinforce their armies in Palestine. He also realized the political appeal of the Arab Revolt, and planned to harness it to his aim of destroying the Turkish armies, containing as they did large numbers of Arab officers and many thousands of Arab conscripts.

To Damascus

The British attack on the Gaza-Beersheba line was planned for early November 1917. The Arabs were asked to cut beforehand the Damascus-Haifa railway in the Yarmuk gorge, west of the junction of Deraa in Syria, in order to impede the flow of reinforcements to Palestine. The

raid involved an approach march from Aqaba of over 350 miles through the desert, but the final stretch was through cultivated country where the peasants gave the Turks warning. The operation was unsuccessful, and nearly a disaster, but the raiders managed to get away and destroyed sections of the railway north of Amman before retreating to Aqaba. Meanwhile, Allenby had successfully broken through the Turkish defences and was advancing on Jerusalem.

Lawrence was present when Allenby entered Jerusalem on 9th December 1917. He greatly admired Allenby, just as Allenby, at their first meeting, had immediately appreciated Lawrence's qualities. He was also unmoved by Lawrence's preference for wearing Arab dress, a practice that reduced many British regular officers to apoplectic fury. Allenby now required the Arabs to move north from Aqaba, through the hills east of the Jordan valley, and establish contact with the British near Jericho. Lawrence thereupon advanced through the mountains of Moab, fighting a fierce battle at Tafila in January 1918, a masterpiece in minor tactics which resulted in the annihilation of a Turkish battalion. However, a farther advance to Kerak and beyond was prevented by the bitterly cold weather which affected the Arabs' morale.

Allenby crossed the Jordan in the spring of 1918 and attempted to capture Salt on the Trans-Jordan plateau. This failed, as did the Arab attack on Ma'an, intended to coincide with the British attack, but large sections of the railway were permanently destroyed and the Turkish army in the Hejaz was effectively isolated. Lawrence had set off for the north to link up with the British, but this too had failed, and he established himself far out in the desert at the oasis of Azraq. There he waited for the main British offensive to begin.

The British attack was due to start on 19th September 1918. Allenby had asked that it should be preceded by a diversionary attack by the Arabs on the important railway junction of Deraa. This was carried out under Lawrence on 17th September with complete success. When, two days later, Allenby fell with massive strength on the Turkish army, its way of retreat through Deraa to Damascus was blocked. Moreover, Lawrence and Feisal, moving north, had raised the tribes south of Damascus. The Turks gave no quarter, nor did they receive any from the Arabs, as they struggled in hopeless confusion across the Jordan into Syria. Feisal entered Damascus in triumph, and for some weeks Lawrence was responsible for civil and military order in the city. On 31st October 1918 an armistice was concluded with Turkey.

Total War

It has sometimes been said of Lawrence's campaign in the desert that it was 'a side-show within a sideshow'. This may be true if war consists of a counting of heads, or 'cipherin' ', as Robert E.Lee described it, but Wavell, in his semi-official history of the Palestine Campaign, certainly does not underrate the valuable contribution made by the Arabs under Lawrence's leadership to Allenby's victory. He makes it clear that a force of barely 3,000 Arabs tied down 50,000 Turks at a crucial moment, and compelled the Turkish high command to deploy some 150,000 troops 'spread over the rest of the region in a futile effort to stem the tide of the Arab Revolt'. As General Glubb has since written: 'To the student of war, the whole Arab campaign provides a remarkable illustration of the extraordinary results which can be achieved by mobile guerrilla tactics. For the Arabs detained tens of thousands of regular Turkish troops with a force barely capable of engaging a brigade of infantry in a pitched battle.'

Al Auruns

When Lawrence arrived in the Hejaz he was junior in rank and untrained in formal military matters. It is the measure of his strategic insight that he was able to perceive how best the Arab Revolt could be utilized to assist the British strategy in the Middle East, and his understanding of the characteristics of Arab tribesmen enabled him to employ them to the best advantage in the war against the Turks. Whatever may be said to the contrary, and there has recently been published a book by an Arab author which seeks to belittle the part played by Lawrence in the Arab Revolt, anyone with experience of the Arabs as soldiers will know that they would never have chosen such tactics of their own volition. They would have met the Turks head-on, and they would have been defeated.

The way in which Lawrence established his leadership over the Arabs is a fascinating study in itself. He proved to them time and again that he could out-match them in their own hardiness. No people live in a harsher environment than the bedouin tribesmen of Arabia. Lawrence lived in the same fashion as they did, enduring the same hardships, and demanding no favours. He rode his camels harder, and farther, and for longer periods, than his Arab companions were accustomed to do. He trained himself to be patient during the interminable, and often fruitless, discussions around the coffee hearth. He ate their food, and drank their water, and suffered in consequence from a succession of debilitating stomach ailments. He was never a fluent Arabic speaker, like Glubb for example, nor could he hope to pass

himself off as an Arab, as Leachman did in Nejd; his piercing blue eyes, fair hair, and skin would soon have given him away. He could appreciate the Arabs' virtues without overlooking their weaknesses, as some Englishmen have done when subjected to the persuasive charm of the bedouin. No one who has lived with the bedouin can forget the attractive side of their characters, but very few men have possessed the ability to fix their bird-like minds on a stable course. Lawrence succeeded in doing this, and no amount of critical hindsight can detract from the part he played in maintaining the impetus of the Arab Revolt.

His work with the Arabs did not end with the conclusion of the armistice in 1918. He believed passionately that his own honour was committed to obtain for them the independence for which they had fought. He understood the force of Arab nationalism as did few others at that time. The Turks had hopelessly under-estimated the strength of the movement for Arab unity, just as the British and the French were to do in later years. The ramshackle Ottoman empire had no other solution for Arab nationalism than repression, but the Arabs' desire for unity is a burning faith, however distant its fulfilment may seem. Statesmen and politicians in London and Paris might scoff, but Lawrence was a visionary, and he understood the Arabs' longing. He gave himself body and soul to help them in their quest. This brought him into conflict with his own government after the war, since the aim of Great Britain and France was to substitute their influence for Turkey's in the Middle East.

Lawrence accompanied the Arab delegation to the Peace Conference at Versailles as an adviser, and found himself ensnarled in the tortuous negotiations conducted by Great Britain and France earlier in the war to carve up the former Turkish empire in Arabia into respective spheres of influence for themselves. It has been a dirty game, as power politics so often is, and Lawrence was soon to learn that pledges made in the stress of war are as likely to be overlooked as honoured after the peace. His practice of wearing Arab dress aroused hostile comment. It was far too unconventional for British tastes, but it was as good a way as any for Lawrence to demonstrate to the Arabs which side he was backing. Nonetheless, despite all his efforts, the outcome of the negotiations could have been predicted. The French received mandates in Syria and the Lebanon, and they at once ejected Feisal from his throne in Damascus. The British were given mandates in Iraq, and in Palestine and Trans-Jordan. Feisal was in due course to be given a throne in Iraq, and Abdullah in Trans-Jordan, but there had

been left a legacy of bitterness which has soured our relations with the Arabs ever since.

Lawrence was far from fit at the time, either physically or mentally. His physical resistance had been lowered by his years in the desert. He had been scarred mentally by the vicious sexual assault he had suffered at the hands of the Turkish commandant in Deraa, where he had been captured while reconnoitring the town. He had managed to escape, his identity still not suspected, but not until after he had been subjected to appalling indignities and a merciless beating. Exhausted though he was, he fought his hardest for the Arabs at Versailles. After the peace treaty had been concluded, and there was nothing more he could do in an official capacity, he resigned from the army, and in letters and articles in the press sought to persuade the British government to honour its obligations and give the Arabs real, instead of sham, independence.

Adviser to Churchill

His vision of the Commonwealth was years ahead of his time, though he expressed himself in contemporary terms. 'This new Imperialism,' he wrote in *The Round Table* in 1920, 'involves an active side of imposing responsibility on the local peoples. . . . We can only teach them by forcing them to try, while we stand by to give advice. . . . We have to be prepared to see them doing things by methods quite unlike our own, and less well; but on principle it is better that they half do it than that we do it perfectly for them.' Much blood, treasure, and heart-ache would have been saved had the colonial powers understood the truth of this. The Middle East was in a turmoil, while Curzon's policy at the Foreign Office was out of tune with the times, old-fashioned imperialism that had had its day. The situation only improved when the Colonial Office assumed responsibility for the Middle East. Churchill was the minister, and he took Lawrence with him as adviser on Arab affairs to a conference convened in Cairo in 1921.

The outcome of the conference was regarded at the time as being entirely satisfactory, almost universally so among the British, and only to a lesser extent among the Arabs. In Churchill's words in *The Aftermath*, 'The Arabs and Colonel Lawrence were appeased by the enthronement of King Feisal at Baghdad; the British Army, which had been costing thirty millions a year, had been brought home; and complete tranquillity was preserved under the thrifty Trenchard'. Lawrence, writing in 1932 a second inscription in the copy of *The Seven Pillars of Wisdom* he had presented to Churchill, had this to say: 'And eleven years after we set our

T.E.Lawrence in RAF uniform. He was killed in 1935 riding his motorbike along a Dorset lane when, coming upon two cyclists, he crashed in a vain attempt to avoid them

strong meat for some people's tastes.

The newspapers tracked him down, and unwelcome publicity forced him to leave the RAF. He promptly re-enlisted in the Royal Tank Corps under the name of T.E.Shaw, which he later adopted by deed poll, but found himself more suited to the RAF than the army. He wangled himself back into the RAF in 1925, pulling every string he could in order to overcome bureaucratic resistance, and he served in India from 1927 to 1929. After India Lawrence was at first posted to the flying-boat station at Cattewater near Plymouth, before being sent to Calshot on the south coast, where he indulged his love of speed by working with high-speed air-sea rescue launches. He invented his own engine and spent hours tinkering with his motor-cycle to get more power out of it. All this time he was corresponding, as a leading aircrafts-man, with the great in the land, and on every imaginable kind of topic from cabbages to kings. He was a brilliant letter-writer, as the publication of *The Letters of T.E.Lawrence to his Friends* has shown. These friends came from all walks of life, and he devoted as much care to a letter to an old comrade from the ranks as he did to one addressed to Field-Marshal Allenby, or George Bernard Shaw.

It was an extraordinary situation, and it is certainly arguable whether a man so gifted is justified in shutting himself away from the world, and avoiding his responsibilities. 'No man is an island,' wrote Donne, but that is what Lawrence was determined to be. Perhaps he had nearly come to terms with himself by the time his service in the RAF ended early in 1935. He had had time to work the bitter-ness and disillusionment out of his system, and he could hardly have expected to insulate himself from the rapidly-growing menace of Nazism. Had he lived, it is almost certain that Churchill would have sought—even commanded—his services. The two men had high regard for each other. But it was not to be, for he was killed the same year in May. He was only forty-seven.

Nearly twenty years after his death, while I was serving with the Arab Legion in Jordan, I retraced many of his journeys and operations, and sought out those who had ridden with him across the desert with Damascus as their lodestar. They were growing few and far between, and most of those I met had reached the stage where memory fails. But in a bedouin tent I found one elderly sheikh who had ridden with Lawrence to Deraa, and I asked what he had thought of him. For a while he was silent, staring out from the tent into the distance, and then he turned to me and said quietly—'Of all the men I have ever met, *Al Aurens* was the greatest Prince.'

hands to making an honest settlement, all our work still stands: the countries having gone forward, our interests having been saved, and nobody killed, either on our side or the other. To have planned for eleven years is statesmanship.' Unhappily, Anglo-Arab relations, which seemed 'set fair' in 1932, were soon to be wrecked on the rocks of Palestine, and Lawrence was fortunate in being spared witnessing the collapse of all he had striven for.

He had been elected a Fellow of All Souls in 1919, and most of his spare time immediately after the war was devoted to the writing of his book, *The Seven Pillars of Wisdom*. His style is modelled on Doughty's in *Arabia Deserta,* and it is curiously stilted in places, but he manages to catch, and convey, the spirit of Arabia as no other book, apart from the Bible, has succeeded in doing. Whether or not posterity remembers Lawrence as a gifted strategist and brilliant guerrilla leader, his name will live in his epic literary account of the Arab Revolt. But although he wrote un-ashamedly for literary fame, he did not seek fame in other fields. In 1922 he en-listed in the ranks of the RAF, taking the name J.H.Ross, and sought his personal seclusion in the barrack-room. He described his experience in the ranks in *The Mint,* written in 1928, which was rather too

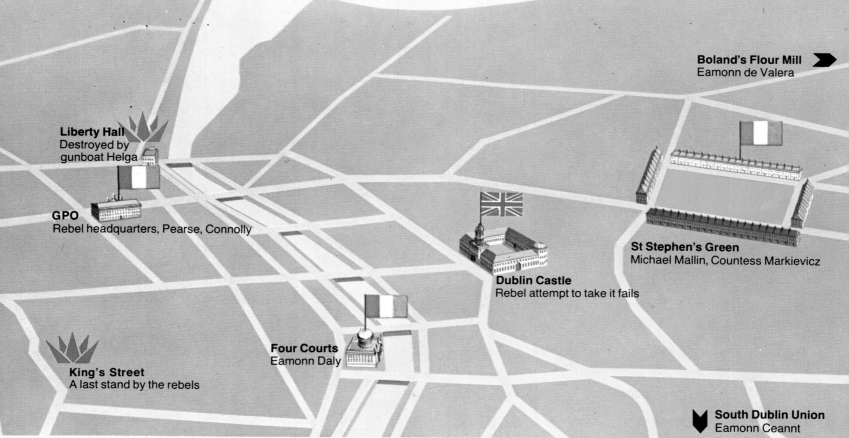

Boland's Flour Mill
Eamonn de Valera

Liberty Hall
Destroyed by
gunboat Helga

GPO
Rebel headquarters, Pearse, Connolly

Dublin Castle
Rebel attempt to take it fails

St Stephen's Green
Michael Mallin, Countess Markievicz

King's Street
A last stand by the rebels

Four Courts
Eamonn Daly

South Dublin Union
Eamonn Ceannt

Above: A bird's eye view of Dublin at the time of the Rising, Easter 1916, showing the principal strong points occupied by the rebels

Below: 'O'Connell Street after the Bombardment' by Joseph McGill. Connolly imagined the British would not shell their own property

The Easter Rising

The circumstances that led to the Irish rebellion of 1916 are of an intense complexity, historical, social, political, and perhaps above all psychological. Sean O'Faolain, that fine Irish writer, has written of his country: 'Most of our physical embodiments of the past are ruins, as most of our songs are songs of lament and defiance.' The Easter Rising was a complete failure, which left large parts of Dublin in ruins; yet without it Ireland might never have been free of English rule. The leaders, alive, had very few supporters even among the Irish patriots; dead, they became and have remained their country's heroes. It was a great historical paradox, and one that to this day the British have perhaps never really understood. Had they understood it, it is conceivable that the British might still have an empire, since the overthrow of British rule in Ireland became the model, the prototype, for the overthrow of imperial British might in Asia, in Africa, and elsewhere.

The historical complexity, from the British point of view, can be traced to a general misunderstanding of the Irish character and of Irish desires. The English were bewildered by the fact that most Irishmen, and all educated Irishmen, spoke English, and wrote it, as well as, and often better than, most Englishmen. They were further bewildered by the fact that a very large proportion of the Irish governing class was of English or Norman ancestry. In 1916, the English had not grasped the fact that for two centuries—since the brutal smashing of the old Irish governing class and the theft of their lands—it was precisely these people, Grattan, Tone, Parnell and so on, who had led the Irish in their longing to be free of alien rule. And the reason for this gross misunderstanding was that the English in England did not realize that the Irish way of life was in many ways—at least in terms of human relationships—culturally superior to the English way, less brutal, less materialistic, more spiritual, more dignified, with infinitely less snobbery and class distinction, directed more towards human happiness than to the acquisition of wealth or objects. Always technologically backward, the Irish were overwhelmed in the course of a thousand and more years by waves of conquerors. If those conquerors remained in Ireland, they became, as the English would and did say, seduced by the ease and pleasure of an Irish attitude that looks for charm, gaiety, and wit rather than for profit: they became 'more Irish than the Irish'.

And this the English, in England, dismissed as fecklessness. The fact that the Irish had different values from their own was regarded as funny—and the 'stage Irishman' was created in London. The fact that English might had always, eventually, crushed Irish rebellion was remembered; the fact that Irishmen had fought with immense distinction in all the major armies of Europe, and not least in that of Great Britain, was often forgotten. From the point of view of Whitehall at the turn of the century Paddy-and-his-pig was an essentially comical, child-like figure. He should know, in English terms, his proper station in life. Perhaps, at a pinch, the Anglo-Irish (an odious and meaningless term) might administer this province of Great Britain, but Paddy, never.

On the other hand, these people were politically troublesome and, furthermore, the English of the late Victorian age were a decent lot on the whole. During the Great Famine of 1846 the English liberals had let Ireland starve in the interests of their *laissez-faire* ideology—to have fed them would have interfered with the workings of the free market so far as corn chandlers were concerned—but later second thoughts prevailed. The Irish were to be given partial sovereignty over their own affairs, and a Home Rule Bill was passed. But then the First World War began. Home Rule was postponed until victory over the Germans should have been achieved. Paddy wouldn't mind, why should he? Paddy would join the British army, as he had always done and as scores of thousands of Irishmen did. Paddy wouldn't understand—and many, perhaps most, did not.

Mounting a revolution

But some Irishmen did understand. The most important of these were the members of the Irish Republican Brotherhood or IRB (which must not be confused with the Irish Republican Army, or IRA, a later creation). The IRB had been formed in 1858. It was a secret society which probably never numbered more than 2,000 including those Irishmen who belonged to it and who lived in England, America, or elsewhere. The majority of its members were what might be loosely called 'intellectuals' and in this, in their determination, and in their secrecy they bore a certain resemblance to their Russian contemporaries, Lenin's small Bolshevik Party. However, their aims were political rather than economic. They were patriots, dedicated to the ideal of national independence, and they were prepared to use all means—including force—to achieve this

*Top: Raging fires silhouette the Dublin skyline. **Centre:** British infantry fire on the Four Courts—a central rebel strongpoint. **Bottom:** After the Rising, rebels in a British gaol. The Irish suffered some thousand casualties in the Rising and hundreds were imprisoned*

Patrick Pearse, in barrister's robe and wig

Above: *MacNeill—attempted to stop Rising*
Below: *Lord Wimborne—lord-lieutenant*

Below: *Countess Markievicz—a socialist*

end. They provided, as it were, the general staff of the mass movement for Irish freedom from British rule, and their fortnightly publication, *Irish Freedom* (founded in 1910), advocated complete republican government for the whole of Ireland. It is significant that all,the men who signed the proclamation of an Irish Republic on Easter Monday were members of the IRB.

When the First World War began, John Redmond, the leader of the Irish Nationalist Party and Parnell's heir, immediately proclaimed his acceptance of the postponement of Home Rule, both for himself and for his followers. These included the Irish Volunteers, perhaps then some 200,000 strong (of whom maybe a couple of thousand were trained and armed). This force had been created in November 1913 as a counter to the Ulster Volunteers, which were originally formed in order to fight against Home Rule. The Ulster Volunteers were also prepared to postpone a struggle that had recently seemed both inevitable and imminent, and from the North of Ireland as from the South scores of thousands of young men went off to fight, and only too often to die, in Flanders. As volunteers. Indeed, Redmond suggested to the government in London that they could remove all British troops from Ireland: his Volunteer force and the Ulster Volunteers were quite capable of seeing that there were no disturbances in Ireland throughout the period of the war.

The IRB had other ideas. At a meeting of their supreme council, as early as August 1914, the decision was taken—in secret of course—that there must be an Irish insurrection before the end of Britain's war with Germany. Until Easter Week 1916 the active members of the IRB were fully occupied in mounting this revolution.

They had at their disposal brains, a fairly considerable amount of money—mostly from Irish Americans—and little else. They had to act through the Irish patriotic organizations, over many of which they had obtained partial control, and if the rising were to be a military success they had to acquire arms, either from British arsenals, or from abroad, which meant in effect from Germany. The balance sheet was roughly as follows: apart from Ulstermen and certain landlords and industrialists, the people of Ireland wanted their freedom from British rule. However, the people were temporarily agreeable to the Home Rule solution, even though the postponed bill gave Ireland less than Dominion status in fiscal and other matters. Furthermore, the farming community, even more important in Ireland then than it is now, was doing very well out of the war. Thus the IRB could rely on very considerable emotional sympathy but little, if any, practical help

from the mass of the people. And since the Irish are in some measure a volatile race, there was no telling how they would react to a rising. Certainly the Roman Catholic Church would be against such a deed: and the parish priests were and are very powerful spokesmen in Ireland.

So far as fighting men went, any insurrection would seem doomed to certain defeat. Redmond's huge numbers of Volunteers were mostly unarmed, or were fighting for the British in France. However, some of those who remained in Ireland and were armed and trained could be relied upon. Their chief-of-staff was the historian Eoin MacNeill, and their commandant a schoolmaster in his early thirties named Patrick Pearse. Both of these men were members of the IRB, but as events will show they did not see eye to eye on tactics. The Volunteers were scattered throughout Ireland.

Resources of David and Goliath

The other para-military force was James Connolly's Irish Citizen Army. Connolly was a socialist who in 1896 had founded the Socialist Republican Party. He was a trained soldier. In 1908 James Larkin had created the Irish Transport and General Workers' Union. When that union organized a strike in 1913, and the strike was broken by strong-arm methods, Connolly decided that a workers' defensive force was needed and created his Citizen Army. It was led by himself and by an ex-British Army officer named Jack White. It has been said that this was the most efficient military force at the disposal of the Republicans. It was, however, very small. When it came to the actual fighting, it was only some 250 men who went out, as opposed to about 1,000 from the Volunteers.

Supporting these was the women's organization. Countess Markievicz—an Irishwoman, born a Gore-Booth, and of aristocratic ancestry—was one of the most prominent. She fought as an officer of the Citizen Army throughout the Easter Rising for she was not only a patriot but a socialist. There were also the so-called 'Fianna Boys', lads who enjoyed the manoeuvring before the Rising, as most boys would, and who also showed guts and resourcefulness when the real thing happened. They were messengers, runners, and so on.

Against them they had what was, on paper at least, a most formidable force.

To maintain their control over Ireland, the British relied primarily on the Royal Irish Constabulary, an armed police force, living largely in barracks, and some 10,000 strong. They were almost all Irishmen, knew their districts thoroughly, and were in 1916, with a very few exceptions, entirely loyal to the Crown. They were well trained, well equipped, only moderately unpopular (the Irish do not love police forces), and well informed. English HQ was Dublin Castle, and 'the Castle' relied on the RIC for its field intelligence.

In Dublin itself the police were not armed, though of course there were arms available. They numbered about 1,000 and were organized on the model of the London police. The Special Branch was concerned with politics. Through its investigations, and general infiltration of Irish republican politics, the Castle was supposed to know what the IRB was planning. The Special Branch did not seem, however, to have been particularly good at this job, nor to have infiltrated the IRB to any great extent. On the other hand the blame may rest with those in the Castle to whom they sent their reports. The evaluation of intelligence is infinitely more important than its accumulation.

And behind those 'occupation' forces there was a large British army in Ireland and what, in wartime and in Irish terms, were almost infinite reserves in Great Britain. If it were a mere question of manpower, the Irish had not a hope.

As for fire-arms, the David and Goliath ratio was even more vivid. Before the outbreak of the First World War the Ulster Volunteers had bought some 35,000 German rifles, the Irish Volunteers about 1,000. And of course the British army had everything, including artillery of all sorts. The Irish made an attempt to rectify this by getting rifles from Germany. Sir Roger Casement, an Irishman with a distinguished past, went to Germany from neutral America. He was to bring the weapons for the Easter Rising that the IRB had agreed on. His mission was a failure. British naval intelligence had broken some German cyphers. The British navy was thus able to intercept the German ship carrying the guns. Casement himself was immediately arrested when he came ashore from a U-boat near Tralee, in County Kerry, on Good Friday. Later the English tried him and hanged him as a traitor. The guns on which the Irish had been relying, even for this forlorn hope, had not arrived. Were they still to go on?

It is here that the different personalities and attitudes become important. We must pause to look at the men, English and Irish, involved; and also at the whole meaning of *Sinn Fein*.

Sinn Fein is usually translated as 'ourselves alone', and this is perhaps the best rendering in English of a complicated Irish concept. It means, first of all and above all, independence from British rule. But since Irish history was in those days so much bound up with contemporary Irish politics, it had a secondary meaning. For many centuries the Irish had been hoping for the help of England's enemies to get rid of the English. The Spaniards and the French had let them down as the Germans were to do in 1916. This was not so much because Britain's enemies lacked the anxiety to defeat Britain in Ireland but because of geographical-military complications (tides, prevailing winds, and so on). Thus *Sinn Fein* also meant that the Irish must rely upon themselves alone in order to rid themselves of their British rulers. For the British, in the years to come, the 'Shinners' were to be the epitome of violent republicanism in Ireland. In fact the party, which only had its first annual convention as late as 1905, was essentially democratic. It had run a parliamentary candidate (who was defeated) in the Leitrim election of 1908. But as time went on it gained an increasing number of the extremists from Redmond's Nationalist Party. Arthur Griffith, its leader and also the editor of the *United Irishmen*, was never a fanatic. He believed in constitutional tactics—and was thus far less of an extremist than many of the IRB leaders—but, unlike Redmond's and Parnell's old party, he no longer trusted the alliance with the Liberal Party in Great Britain. Ourselves alone. To many young men it was a most attractive idea.

The British rulers were, on the whole, a shadowy lot. The Liberal government in London was inevitably devoting almost all its attention to the gigantic struggle on the Continent. Since Ireland appeared so placid in 1916, neither the best politicians nor by any means the best British soldiers were in the country. Augustine Birrell was Chief Secretary. Possessed, it was said, of extreme personal charm, he was a *belle lettrist* whose books, now forgotten, enjoyed in their time considerable esteem. He appears to have regarded his job in Dublin—which might be described as active head of the administration—as something of a sideline to his career as a *littérateur,* and spent a very large proportion of his time being charming in London. His principal Assistant Secretary, responsible for political affairs, was a civil servant experienced in colonial administration, Sir Matthew Nathan. He seems to have had little comprehension of the Irish temperament and to have been happiest behind his desk, dealing with routine paperwork. The general officer commanding the British army in Ireland was a Major-General Field. He, even more, seems to have had no idea of what was going on in Ireland at all. And finally there was Lord Wimborne, the lord-lieutenant and the King's representative, who presided over the British administration as a sort of constitutional monarch with all the powers, and most of the limitations, that that implies. However, he knew Ireland well. He had sponsored the land act of 1903, which had pacified the Irish countrymen by further advantageous changes of the tenant-landlord relationship. He was popular with the Irish governing class, as was Birrell; but, unlike his Chief Secretary, he did not at all care for the situation that was developing.

The British intelligence services had, as we have seen, infiltrated the various Irish 'resistance' movements. The Volunteers, it must be assumed, had few secrets not known to Dublin Castle. And the Castle knew that a rising was planned to take place as soon as possible after the landing of Casement and his German guns. On 21st April 1916, Casement landed and was immediately arrested. Wimborne, who was to have gone to Belfast, cancelled his visit and on Sunday the 23rd, that is to say only a matter of hours before the Rising took place, demanded of Nathan that he immediately arrest 'between sixty and a hundred' of the Irish leaders. Had this been done successfully, it seems unlikely that any Rising would have taken place *at that time*. However, it was probably too late for a mere police action by that date. The men of the Citizen Army and the more militant Volunteers were under arms and ready to fight. As it was, Nathan persuaded his 'constitutional monarch' that there was no need for action. And Birrell was in London.

It would seem probable that Nathan's intelligence service had briefed him as to what was happening within the high command of the Volunteers after the news of Casement's arrest, that he knew Eoin MacNeill had decided that without the guns the Rising must be cancelled or at least postponed. What Nathan presumably did not know was that this decision finally split the Volunteers, and that the IRB was almost solidly behind Patrick Pearse and those other Irish patriots who were prepared to go ahead with the Rising even in these disadvantageous, indeed well-nigh suicidal, circumstances. All this sounds very neat and staff-officerish when put down on paper, but of course the reality was far more chaotic, involving a clash of multiple personalities, orders and counter-orders, and very considerable bitterness. Indeed MacNeill's decision to call off the Rising, and Pearse's to go ahead, was really the death-knell of the Volunteers and of the Nationalist Party whose armed force they were supposed to be. After the Rising, the political leadership of those hostile to British rule in Ireland passed to *Sinn Fein,* while those who fought in Easter week became the nucleus of the Irish Republican Army.

Certainly MacNeill's last-minute proclamation that the Rising be cancelled—he had boys bicycling all over the country, and even announced this supposed non-

Total War

happening in the Sunday papers—cannot possibly have been unknown to Nathan. He must have taken into account the fact that a few hot-heads were likely to ignore this order: he must also have known that the vast bulk of the Volunteers would breathe a sigh of relief and that the clergy —to whom the English have often attached an exaggerated political importance in Ireland owing to their ubiquity and their marked difference from the Anglican clergy in England—would support MacNeill and the mass of his supporters, content with the promise of eventual, diluted Home Rule. The handful of extremists could be dealt with—though not at all as easily as the English thought—by the overwhelming forces arraigned against them. No special precautions were taken, despite Lord Wimborne's fully justified fears. Indeed, on Easter Monday, the first day of the Rising, a great many British officers were at Fairyhouse Races.

The Easter Rising was suicidal. Patrick Pearse was well aware of this. Before ever it happened he said to his mother: 'The day is coming when I shall be shot, swept away, and my colleagues like me.' When his mother enquired about her other son, William, who was also an extreme nationalist, Pearse is reported to have replied: 'Willie? Shot like the others. We'll all be shot.' And James Connolly is said to have remarked: 'The chances against us are a thousand to one.' On the morning of the Rising, when asked by one of his men if there was any hope, he replied, cheerfully: 'None whatever!'

It was hard for the staff officers and colonial administrators of Dublin Castle, accustomed to weighing possibilities so far as their own actions were concerned, to realize that a group of men, perhaps 1,250 strong (the Citizen Army took no notice of MacNeill), was prepared to fight and die in such circumstances. But they should have been wiser in their age: Langemarck was recent, Verdun was going on, the Somme was about to happen. Seldom in history have men been so willing, indeed so eager, to throw away their lives for an ideal, almost any ideal, and the Irish ideal had long roots. The men went out and fought.

Easter week

The essence of the Irish plan was to seize certain key points in the city, and hold these for as long as possible, thus disrupting British control of the capital. It was then hoped that one of three things might happen: the country might rise in sympathy; the British might realize the ultimate impossibility of controlling Ireland and pull out; and last and faintest of hopes, the Germans might somehow come to the rescue of the rebels. Since the rebels had no artillery of any sort, their main

strong-points could only hold out provided that the British did not use their artillery. Connolly and the socialists hoped that the British would, for capitalist reasons, not bombard Dublin and thus destroy their own —or largely their own—property. This, too, was an illusion.

H-hour was 12 noon and since this was a Bank Holiday there were crowds in the streets who witnessed the small bodies of Volunteers and of the Citizen Army marching, armed, through the city to seize their various strongpoints. It went, on the whole, remarkably smoothly. Five major buildings or groups of buildings were seized north of the River Liffey, nine south of it, and some of the railway stations were occupied. Headquarters were established in the massive General Post Office in Sackville Street (now O'Connell Street) from which Irish flags were flown and where Patrick Pearse announced the creation of a provisional government of the new Irish Republic. With him in the Post Office were Connolly as military commander, Joseph Plunkett (a very sick man), The O'Rahilly, Tom Clark, Sean MacDermott, and other leaders. There, too, was a young man named Michael Collins. The rebels immediately set about preparing the Post Office against the attack which they expected almost at once. The four other principal strong-points seized were the South Dublin Union, a congeries of poor-houses and the like (commanded by Eamonn Ceannt); the Four Courts, the headquarters of the legal profession, where heavy law books were used as sandbags (Eamonn Daly); St Stephen's Green, where trenches were dug and barricades of motor-cars erected (Michael Mallin and Countess Markievicz); and Boland's Flour Mill, which covered the approach roads from Kingstown, now Dun Laoghaire, where any reinforcements from England would almost certainly disembark (Eamonn de Valera).

An attempt to seize Dublin Castle failed. An attempt to capture a large quantity of arms and ammunition from the arsenal in Phoenix Park known as the Magazine Fort was only partially successful and merely a few rifles seized. On the other hand, the rebels successfully cut telephone lines, and the Castle was for a time almost isolated. A further success was that a troop of Lancers which attempted to charge down Sackville Street was repulsed with casualties.

The British had been taken by surprise and were now almost completely in the dark. The Castle immediately ordered troops up from the Curragh and other camps outside Dublin and appealed to London for reinforcements. There, Lord French was commander-in-chief. He was an Irishman and an ardent Unionist. He immediately ordered that no less than four divisions be alerted for transfer to Ireland.

British policy was in fact thrown into reverse. Appeasement of the Irish was out; the rebels were to be crushed, rapidly, and massively. But if the British in Dublin were in the dark, so were the rebels. They had no wireless links either between the strong-points they had seized or with the outside world. Communication by runner became difficult and eventually impossible when the fighting reached its peak.

From a military point of view, Tuesday was comparatively calm. The British were closing in cautiously. Their strategy was to throw a cordon around that area of Dublin where the rebels' strong-points were, then cut that area in two, and finally mop up. They moved artillery and troops into Trinity College, a natural fortress which the rebels had failed to seize, though they had planned to do so. The reason was the small number of fighting men available. Looting began by the crowds. Martial law was declared. British reinforcements arrived at Kingstown. A mad British officer, a Captain Bowen-Colthurst, had three harmless journalists shot 'while trying to escape'—a phrase to become hideously familiar, and not only in Ireland. The atrocities had begun.

Dublin burns, Dubliners starve

By Wednesday morning the rebels were outnumbered twenty to one. The British now began to attack in earnest. Their first major action was to destroy Liberty Hall, the headquarters of the Labour Party and of the trade unions, by shellfire from the gunboat *Helga*. As it happened, the rebels had anticipated this, and the building was entirely empty. The British gunfire was inaccurate and many other buildings were hit and many civilians killed. The army also was using artillery: a 9-pounder gun was fired against a single sniper. Dublin began to burn, and the Dubliners to starve, for there was no food coming into the city. This was no longer a police action but full-scale war in which no attempt was made to spare the civilians. Meanwhile, British reinforcements marching in from Kingstown were ambushed by de Valera's men and suffered heavy casualties, but by dint of numbers forced their way through. St Stephen's Green had been cleared of rebels, who retreated into the Royal College of Surgeons, and established a strong-point there.

On Thursday the new British commander-in-chief arrived. Since Ireland was under martial law, he held full powers there. This was General Sir John Maxwell, a soldier of some distinction who had returned the month before from Egypt, where he had been commander-in-chief of the Anglo-Egyptian armies. Although he numbered the Countess Markievicz among his relations, he had no knowledge of the

current political mood in Ireland, and,
indeed, as events were to prove, did more
to undermine British rule in Ireland than
all the rebels put together. He had been
ordered by the British prime minister,
Asquith, to put down the rebellion with all
possible speed. And this he did regardless of
political consequences.

The reinforcements from England were
now in action. These were largely untrained men, and when they discovered
that many of the men of the Irish Republican Army—as the rebels now and henceforth styled themselves—were not in uniform (how could they be?) they began
shooting male civilians on sight.

On that day (Thursday) attacks were
made on Boland's Mill, the men in the
South Dublin Union were forced to give
ground, and there was shelling of the
General Post Office, which began to burn
from the top down. Connolly was wounded
twice. The first wound he hid from his
men: the second was more serious, for one
foot was shattered and he was in great
pain. With the aid of morphia he carried
on, directing the battle as best he could.
The Dublin fires were now great conflagra-
tions. With the streets full of small-arms
fire and the water supplies often cut, these
could not be dealt with. Still, no major
rebel strong-point surrendered.

On Friday Connolly ordered the women
who had fought so bravely to leave the
General Post Office building, which was
now cut off and burning. Later that day he
and Pearse and the remaining rebels escaped from a building that was by now
almost red-hot and about to collapse. They
found temporary refuge nearby, while the
British continued to shell the empty building. All knew that the end was near. A last
battle was fought for King's Street, near
the Four Courts. It took some 5,000 British
soldiers, equipped with armoured cars and
artillery, twenty-eight hours to advance
about 150 yards against some 200 rebels.
It was then that the troops of the South
Staffordshire Regiment bayoneted and shot
civilians hiding in cellars. And now all
was over. On Saturday morning Pearse and
Connolly surrendered unconditionally.

Like so much else about the Easter
Rising, casualties are hard to estimate.
It would seem that those of the British
were about 500; those of the Irish, including
civilians, about twice that figure. Material
damage was estimated at about £2½ million.
Large parts of Dublin lay in ruins.

When, on Sunday, the arrested rebels
were marched across Dublin from one
prison compound to another, they were at
times jeered at and booed by the crowds,
and particularly in the slum areas. The
mass of public opinion had been against the
rebels before the Rising and remained so
until the reprisals began.

On the direct orders of the cabinet in London, reprisals were swift, secret, and brutal. The leaders were tried by court martial and shot: only when they were dead were their deaths announced. Among those thus killed were Willie Pearse, who was no leader and who, it was generally believed in Ireland, was killed because he had followed his famous brother; the invalid Plunkett; and, most disgusting of all to Irish minds, Connolly, who was dying and who had to be propped up in bed for the court martial in his hospital room. He was shot in a chair, since he could not stand. A wave of disgust crossed all Ireland. That wave did not subside when Asquith defended these measures in the Commons; nor when he realized that a mistake had been made, and sacked Maxwell.

When London at last understood that its methods were uniting all Ireland against Britain, there was yet another change of British policy. Many of the three thousand-odd men arrested after the Rising were released from British gaols. They returned to Ireland and began immediately to reorganize a new and more powerful IRA, now with the backing of the people. This was a gesture of appeasement by Lloyd George, the new prime minister, who called an Irish Convention intended to solve 'the Irish problem'. Since *Sinn Fein* boycotted the Convention, it was a complete failure. Again British policy was thrown into reverse, and the leaders of the new independence movement were arrested in the spring of 1918. Michael Collins, however, escaped arrest, though there was a price on his head, dead or alive, which eventually reached the sum of £10,000. He was to be the great guerrilla leader in the next round of the struggle. The Irish leaders, with much backing from the United States, both emotional and financial, set about creating a viable alternative government which could and did take over when the British should have at last seen that they could not win. *Sinn Fein* triumphed, and won most of the Irish seats in the 1918 election. The elected members, however, formed their own 'parliament', *Dail Eireann,* rather than sit in Westminster. Collins drew up a strategy of resistance, first passive, then obstructive, and finally active, which has since been pursued elsewhere against British imperialism, and indeed against the imperialisms of other nations. And in January of 1919 the first shots of the new rebellion were fired in County Tipperary.

The Easter Rising was a total failure. And yet it was a total success. After Easter week 1916 permanent English rule in Ireland became an impossibility. One tragedy was a triumph. Other tragedies were to follow. But the Irish achieved it, and alone.

The Brusilov Offensive

After its great retreat of autumn 1915 the Russian army, which had withdrawn in good order though with great losses, settled down on a new line. This ran from north to south for over 500 miles, from Riga on the Baltic through the Pinsk marshes to the Rumanian frontier. In the north it faced the Germans under Ludendorff, in the south the Austrians under Archduke Frederick. The line was divided into three fronts (army groups). The northernmost of these was the North-West Front, commanded by the same Kuropatkin who in the 1905 Russo-Japanese War had specialized in the tactic of the mis-timed retreat. The next sector was the West Front commanded by General Evert, who was also to manifest a dislike for offensive actions. Finally there was the South-West Front commanded by another master of timidity, General Ivanov.

Major-General Alekseyev who, as chief of staff to the commander-in-chief (Tsar Nicholas), was responsible for the Russian operations, was one of the better generals of the First World War—but his front commanders certainly were not. That men of their outlook held such responsible positions was, on the one hand, an indictment of the Russian political situation: with the Tsar, weak-willed in any case, out of touch at the front, the conduct of affairs at Petrograd (as St Petersburg was now called) was dependent more and more on the intrigues of the Tsarina and her favourites, and this circle tended to oppose the appointment of men of strong character and intellectual energy. On the other hand, there was another reason why so many Russian officers were unaggressive: the victory of 1812 over Napoleon had by now, aided by Tolstoy's dramatic and erroneous interpretation in *War and Peace,* entered the Russian tradition as a victory won by a great general called Kutuzov who had deliberately retreated in order to win the war. Thus there existed a concept—conscious and subconscious—of victory through retreat, which is why so many Russian generals seemed reluctant and over-anxious in attack.

During the winter of 1915-16 the Russian army was slowly restored to fighting condition. The deficiencies in 1915, the lack of rifles, of ammunition, of boots, and of properly-trained soldiers, would not be repeated in 1916. In early 1916 rifles were being produced at the rate of 10,000 per month; most front-line units had their full complement of field and machine-guns; ammunition, except perhaps for the heaviest guns, was being delivered fast

enough to build up stocks for a full summer campaign; the quiet winter months had given time for proper training of recruits—although the shortage of good experienced officers could not be remedied so easily. The Red Cross detachments organized by local civilians were doing much to maintain front-line morale, not least because they made it their business to provide for many of the physical and recreational needs which the war ministry had so obviously neglected.

The last battle of 1915 had been a minor Russian offensive in the south, aimed at helping the Serbian army, which had been driven into retreat when Bulgaria declared war. In the winter an inter-Allied military conference held at Chantilly in France laid plans for the 1916 summer campaign. Russia was to play a relatively small part in these plans, because of the heavy losses she had sustained in 1915: the main Allied offensive was to be on the Somme, and was to be preceded by a small diversionary attack made by the Russian army. However, the Germans disturbed this scheme by their massive attack on Verdun in February: not for the first time—nor the last—Russia was called upon to save her western allies by mounting a hastily-planned offensive to draw German divisions from the west to the east. In March and April a Russian army of the West Front, with artillery support whose intensity surprised the Germans, attacked through the mud of the spring thaw and overcame the German advanced lines. Ludendorff brought up reinforcements, for some reason the Russian GHQ withdrew its heavy artillery and aircraft from the sector, and the Russian soldiers were left almost defenceless in shallow marsh trenches, without gas masks. Unable to withstand the prolonged barrage of gas and high-explosive shells, and sustaining great losses, the Russians, still singing their hymns, were driven back to their start line in one day.

This disaster—the battle of Lake Naroch—was a relatively minor action, and the Russians were already planning bigger things, both to honour their pledge to the Allies (for the Somme operation was still scheduled) and to take pressure off the French, who were bearing heavy losses and in a desperate situation at Verdun. On 14th April the Tsar had presided at a meeting of the front commanders at GHQ. By this time the pessimistic Ivanov had been replaced by General Alexey Brusilov, who as an army commander had distinguished himself in the 1915 retreat even

General Alexey Brusilov. He later claimed that if his fantastically successful offensive had been properly exploited, Russia could have won the war for the Allies. Even if he had not won the war he probably prevented the Allies losing it

though he was a champion of an offensive strategy.

Brusilov risks his reputation

At the 14th April meeting the idea of attacking on the West (Evert's) Front was discussed. Both Evert and Kuropatkin declared that they preferred to stay on the defensive, alleging that there was not enough heavy artillery and shells to start an offensive. Brusilov disagreed, and recommended attacks on all fronts. This latter proposal was made in view of the superior rail communications on the German side of the line. By quickly shifting troops from a quiet sector the German command could easily reinforce that part of its line under threat: if the Russian attack came not at one point but at several this would be more difficult, especially as it would be hard to divine which of the attacks was intended to develop into the main thrust.

It was finally agreed that an offensive would be launched at the end of May, and that Brusilov's South-West Front would make the first move but that the main thrust would in fact start soon afterwards on Evert's West Front and be directed towards Wilno.

As he left this meeting Brusilov was told by a colleague that he had been unwise to risk his reputation by offering to launch an offensive. Unperturbed by this pessimism, he returned to his South-West Front to make the most of his six-week preparation time. He decided not to concentrate his forces but to ask each of the generals commanding his four armies to prepare an attack; with preparations being made at four places on his 200-mile sector of the line the enemy would be unable to anticipate where the main blow would fall. In previous actions, as Brusilov was well aware, both the place and the time of an attack had seemed to produce no surprise, so, in addition to avoiding troop concentrations, he took the precaution of dismissing newspaper correspondents. Also, since he suspected that the Tsarina was a careless talker, he avoided telling her the details of his plan.

The Austro-Hungarian line which Brusilov was preparing to break through was strongly fortified, consisting in most parts of three defensive belts one behind the other at intervals of one or two miles. Each belt had at least three lines of full-depth trenches, with fifty to sixty yards between each trench. There were well-built dugouts, machine-gun nests, sniper hideouts, and as many communication trenches as were needed. Before each belt there was a barbed wire barrier, consisting of about twenty rows of posts to which were attached swathes of barbed wire, some of which was very thick and some electrified or

mined. Brusilov's aircraft had made good photographs of these defences and the information was transferred to large-scale maps so that, as was shown later, the Russian officers had as good maps of the opposing line as had the Austrians. Moreover, although during the preparation period most of the soldiers were kept well behind the line, the officers spent much time in advanced positions studying the terrain over which they would fight. Meanwhile, with odd sighting shots the gunners were able to get the range of their prescribed targets, and shell stocks were building up. Trenches to serve as assembly and jumping-off points were dug near to the front-line Austrian trenches, in some places getting as close as one hundred or even seventy-five yards. Because this was to be a widely dispersed effort and not a conventional hammer-blow attack, no reserves were assembled.

While his four army commanders were each planning the details of their respective attacks, Brusilov was in touch—frequently acrimonious touch—with GHQ on the question of timing. On the one hand, Evert was declaring that his West Front attack, for which Brusilov's was only a preliminary diversion, needed more preparation time. On the other hand, to the urgent situation at Verdun was now added the rout of the Italian army by the Austrians at Trentino: unless Russia could do something to relieve the pressure Italy would be driven out of the war and the Central powers would be able to bring even greater strength against Verdun. In the end, 'Brusilov's Offensive', as it was later called (it was the only victory during the First World War named after a commander) was launched on 4th June.

The Archduke's birthday party

Three of Brusilov's four armies broke through at once, aided by thorough artillery preparation, surprise, and the alacrity with which the Czech elements of the Austro-Hungarian army offered themselves as grateful prisoners of war. Brusilov's main thrust was towards Lutsk and Kovel. The former was taken on the 8th: the Archduke Josef Ferdinand was forced by Russian shells to abandon his birthday party which he was celebrating there. With three deep and wide gaps in their line the Austrians were soon in full and fast retreat. However, the ever-reluctant Evert was still unwilling to start his own attack and on 9th June Brusilov learned that this attack would be postponed until the 18th. By this time Ludendorff was desperately trying to organize a counter-attack, and scraping together German units which he sent south to stiffen the demoralized Austrians. Fortunately for Austria, Brusilov's main thrust, confused by unclear instruc-

tions from GHQ, advanced in two directions at once, and thus lost the chance of capturing Kovel.

On 18th June Evert's promised attack towards Wilno did not materialize. Instead, that general made a minor, ill-prepared, and unsuccessful advance farther south at Baranowicze. By now it was clear that GHQ would do what Brusilov had always opposed: instead of attacking on the West Front it would send Evert's troops to Brusilov, believing that the latter with these reinforcements would be able to exploit his success fully. As Brusilov expected, as soon as the Germans noticed these Russian troop movements they felt able to transfer their own troops southwards and, because they had better railways, got there first. In this way the German command was able to make the best possible use of its scanty resources. Despite a renewed push at the end of July, Brusilov made less and less headway as he found more and more German units opposing him. In general, the Brusilov Offensive came to an end about 10th August, by which time the Austrians had lost not only vast areas of territory but also 375,000 prisoners of war, not to speak of killed and wounded. But Russian casualties already exceeded half a million.

Brusilov later claimed that if his wildly successful offensive had been properly exploited, Russia could have won the war for the Allies. It does seem very possible that if Evert had carried out the main attack as planned (thus occupying those German troops which in fact were sent to help the Austrians) Brusilov would have been able to drive Austria out of the war—which almost certainly would have entailed the surrender of Germany before the end of 1916. In any case, Brusilov's Offensive achieved all the aims which it had been set, and more: Austrian troops in Italy had to abandon their victories and rush north to fight the Russians, and the Germans were forced to end the Verdun operation and transfer no less than thirty-five divisions from France to the Eastern Front. Even if Brusilov had not won the war, he probably stopped the Allies losing it.

Persuading Rumania

In mid-August, just as Brusilov's Offensive was slowing down, it was brought to a definite end by the decision of Rumania to abandon her neutrality and join the Allies, her first step in this direction being to sign a military alliance.

Right from the beginning of the war Allied diplomacy had been busy in Rumania. The Russian effort in this respect was two-pronged and, in view of the Tsar's habit of acting independently of his ministers, it is possible that neither prong knew what the other was doing.

The conventional weapon in this diplomatic campaign was the Russian ambassador in Bucharest, who enjoyed a certain influence in Rumanian political circles. But his talents were well matched by the Rumanian statesman Brătianu, who was long able to postpone a decision. Rumania at this time had well-balanced ties with both Russia and the Central powers, and public opinion was more or less equally

Below: Fund raising for Rumania. British poster depicts a serene King Ferdinand of Rumania warding off the sinister outline of the Kaiser in pickelhaube. *Rumania declared war on Austria on 27th August 1916*

split between those who favoured the Allies and those who supported Germany and Austria. It seems likely that most Rumanians were behind Brătianu in his efforts to delay a decision until the bandwagon of ultimate victory had moved unmistakably in one direction or another.

Russia's second agent in Bucharest was less correct than the ambassador, but may have been more effective in the long run. This was Rear-Admiral Veselkin, who from his miniature flagship *Rus* commanded the Danube Flotilla of the Russian Imperial Navy. This flotilla, directly controlled by GHQ, had been formed in 1914 by arming Danubian steamers and adding a few gunboats from the Black Sea Fleet. Its purpose had been to keep Serbia supplied, but after that nation was overrun it had little to do, apart from engaging in intrigues to push Rumania into war on Russia's side.

Veselkin was a witty, open-hearted, and eloquent officer, popular with his colleagues and, more important, a favourite of the Tsar. Whether he dabbled in genuine cloak-and-dagger activities is doubtful: the mysterious packages which he entrusted to transient Russians for strictly personal delivery to the Tsar contained not secret documents but merely Nicholas's favourite kind of Rumanian smoked sausage. But certainly he devoted all his spare time to the persuasion of the Rumanians. He had been entrusted with two million roubles' worth of jewellery which he distributed as 'gifts' to influential Rumanians and their wives. However, this was little compared to the wealth at the disposal of the German agents (who admittedly needed large sums to bribe railwaymen to turn a blind eye on the thinly-disguised war materials passing through on their way from Germany to Turkey). In mid-1916 it seemed that the pro-German party in Rumania was still strong enough to thwart Russian efforts.

In any case, some influential Russians believed that a neutral Rumania was more advantageous than an allied Rumania. Both the Russian naval and military attachés were sending mournful accounts of Rumania's unpreparedness for any serious war, and other Russian officials had the foresight to realize that an Allied Rumania would ask for help which Russia could not spare. However, a change of Russian foreign ministers was followed by what was virtually an ultimatum setting Rumania a time limit in which to make up her mind: the success of Brusilov's Offensive—then in progress—had encouraged this Russian move while at the same time providing an extra inducement for Rumania to choose the side of the Allies.

Rumania at war

Thus it came about that on 17th August Rumania signed the military alliance which had been pressed upon her, and then immediately began to disprove the belief —still current among the great powers fifty years later—that an ally is inevitably better than a neutral. The Allies had hoped that the more than half-a-million-strong Rumanian army would be sent south against Bulgaria, and then perhaps join up with their own forces at Salonika. However, Rumanian appetites in the direction of Bulgaria had already been satisfied by the Treaty of Bucharest of 1913 which had ended the Second Balkan War. On the other hand, Rumania still had desires (termed 'national aspirations') for Austrian Transylvania. So, on 27th August, to the consternation of friends and enemies alike, Rumania struck north.

Germany, which had been hoping that the Rumanian government would procrastinate just a little longer, was ill-placed to meet this new threat: help had already been sent to Austria to stop Brusilov, the western Allies were starting their Somme offensive at the same time as their forces at Salonika were becoming more active. So at first the Rumanian army carried all before it, capturing the capital of Transylvania in early September. However, by tight organization and by taking great risks in scraping together reinforcements from quiet sectors of other fronts, the German high command did just manage to master the situation. Falkenhayn attacked the Rumanians in Transylvania, while Mackensen went through Bulgaria and attacked the new enemy from the south, forcing the Rumanians to relinquish their Dobrudja territory. It now became evident that the Rumanian army was even worse trained and worse equipped than the pessimists had claimed, and in any case the easy-going Rumanian officers were ill-adapted to modern warfare. The Rumanians called for Russian help, and it was Russian troops which inflicted a temporary check on Mackensen in mid-September. Before the end of the month, despite Russian diversionary pressure farther north, the two German armies were threatening the heart of Rumania. In the south Mackensen drove his enemy over the Danube, while the Rumanian forces which had so cheerfully invaded Transylvania a month previously, were now in full retreat. On 23rd October Mackensen captured the key Black Sea port of Constanta, and in early December Bucharest fell. The Rumanian army was now finished for the time being: it occupied a small part of Rumanian territory around Jassy and was being reorganized by a French general in the hope of better days to come.

By this time two Russian armies were involved in Rumania, and it was not long before a quarter of the Russian army was devoted to this area. The Russian front had now, in effect, been extended to the Black Sea: no longer was there a safely neutral Russo-Rumanian frontier, so that for Petrograd at least the Rumanian alliance had proved to be of negative value. For Germany, once the immediate crisis was over, the entry of Rumania was a blessing: she now occupied the wheatlands and oilfields of that country and had better communications with her ally Turkey. Moreover, rightly or wrongly, the German high command had been anticipating the entry into the war of Holland and Denmark on the Allied side, and the rout of Rumania convinced it that these two countries were now unlikely to risk the same fate.

The Rumanian opportunists did the best they could to retrieve their country's fortunes: they declared peace in May 1918 but rejoined the Allies on the eve of their final victory.

Program for the Peace of the World

By *PRESIDENT WILSON* January 8, 1918

I. Open covenants of peace, openly arrived at, after which there shall be no private international understandings of any kind, but diplomacy shall proceed always frankly and in the public view.

II. Absolute freedom of navigation upon the seas, outside territorial waters, alike in peace and in war, except as the seas may be closed in whole or in part by international action for the enforcement of international covenants.

III. The removal, so far as possible, of all economic barriers and the establishment of an equality of trade conditions among all the nations consenting to the peace and associating themselves for its maintenance.

IV. Adequate guarantees given and taken that national armaments will reduce to the lowest point consistent with domestic safety.

V. Free, open-minded, and absolutely impartial adjustment of all colonial claims, based upon a strict observance of the principle that in determining all such questions of sovereignty the interests of the population concerned must have equal weight with the equitable claims of the government whose title is to be determined.

VI. The evacuation of all Russian territory and such a settlement of all questions affecting Russia as will secure the best and freest coöperation of the other nations of the world in obtaining for her an unhampered and unembarrassed opportunity for the independent determination of her own political development and national policy, and assure her of a sincere welcome into the society of free nations under institutions of her own choosing; and, more than a welcome, assistance also of every kind that she may need and may herself desire. The treatment accorded Russia by her sister nations in the months to come will be the acid test of their good-will, of their comprehension of her needs as distinguished from their own interests, and of their intelligent and unselfish sympathy.

VII. Belgium, the whole world will agree, must be evacuated and restored, without any attempt to limit the sovereignty which she enjoys in common with all other free nations. No other single act will serve as this will serve to restore confidence among the nations in the law which they have themselves set and determined for the government of their relations with one another. Without this healing act the whole structure and validity of international law is forever impaired.

VIII. All French territory should be freed and the invaded portions restored, and the wrong done to France by Prussia in 1871 in the matter of Alsace-Lorraine, which has unsettled the peace of the world for nearly fifty years, should be righted, in order that peace may once more be made secure in the interest of all.

IX. A readjustment of the frontiers of Italy should be effected along clearly recognizable lines of nationality.

X. The people of Austria-Hungary, whose place among the nations we wish to see safeguarded and assured, should be accorded the freest opportunity of autonomous development.

XI. Rumania, Serbia and Montenegro should be evacuated; occupied territories restored; Serbia accorded free and secure access to the sea; and the relations of the several Balkan States to one another determined by friendly counsel along historically established lines of allegiance and nationality; and international guarantees of the political and economic independence and territorial integrity of the several Balkan States should be entered into.

XII. The Turkish portions of the present Ottoman Empire should be assured a secure sovereignty, but the other nationalities which are now under Turkish rule should be assured an undoubted security of life and an absolutely unmolested opportunity of autonomous development, and the Dardanelles should be permanently opened as a free passage to the ships and commerce of all nations under international guarantees.

XIII. An independent Polish State should be erected which should include the territories inhabited by indisputably Polish populations, which should be assured a free and secure access to the sea, and whose political and economic independence and territorial integrity should be guaranteed by international covenant.

XIV. A general association of nations must be formed under specific covenants for the purpose of affording mutual guarantees of political independence and territorial integrity to great and small States alike.

War Weariness and Peace Overtures

Above: *Kühlmann and his wife. He hoped to divide the Allies by negotiating separately with Great Britain. His unauthorized efforts only cemented British support for France and Italy.* **Far left:** *Sceptical German view of Wilson, May 1916. Wilson, a would-be peacemaker, strove to be 'neutral in thought and word'. But, this cartoon points out, Wilson's song of friendship to the German people is drowned by the organ of guns played by America—guns sold to the Allies.* **Left:** *Wilson's 'Fourteen Points' formulated the idealistic principles which Wilson had always felt should dominate peace negotiations. But the interest shown by the other powers in peace proposals was less idealistic.* **Below left:** *'Must Belgium become open territory through which the English army can march on Germany?' German propaganda map showing how in ten days Great Britain could march through Belgium to attack the industrial heart of Germany. Belgium was the main stumbling block in peace negotiations. The Allies insisted that Germany evacuate Belgium: the Germans refused.*

The First World War affected the lives of ordinary men and women to a far greater degree than any war between supposedly civilized powers had ever done before. In the autumn of 1914 the hopes of a quick victory for either side faded, and from that moment the war machine clamoured for more men and more resources, a clamour which continued for almost four years. Millions of men were drafted into the armed forces. More millions, and women also, were directed into work on munitions or other industries essential for war. In most countries, profits and wages were regulated, more or less ineffectively. Prices rose as the governments poured out paper money, and supplies ran short. The free market which had brought prosperity in normal times now broke down. There was rationing of essential goods, particularly of foodstuffs. Very often there was a sharp reduction of the pre-war standard of life, and even so the rations were not supplied in full. Quite apart from the countless dead on the battlefields, the war brought hardship and sometimes starvation to the living.

There was social discontent and political unrest. The surprising thing is how slowly and how late this was translated into war weariness. For much of the period, men were demanding instead that the war should be waged more fiercely and more completely. The demagogues who called for aerial reprisals or the internment of enemy aliens evoked more response than did the few enlightened men who sought a way out. Equally surprising, the rulers of most countries, though usually of a conservative cast, showed little anxiety that the war would shake the fabric of society. On the contrary, they believed that failure to achieve a decisive victory would open the door to revolution. In the last year of the war, the prospect of revolution came to haunt Europe in the shape of Bolshevism, but even this only spurred the governments of the various belligerents to more violent efforts.

In the first two years of the war, peace overtures came from Woodrow Wilson, President of the one great neutral power, and not from any of the countries at war. Wilson strove to be 'neutral in thought and deed'. He refused to judge between the combatants, though his private sympathies were on the Allied side. His sole aim was to bring the belligerent countries to the conference table, and he therefore shrank from propounding terms of peace himself. His overtures were rebuffed by both sides. The Allies and the Central powers remained equally confident of victory, though they did not know how to achieve it. Even the few who advocated compromise were fundamentally in disagreement. Compromise, it was agreed, meant an acceptance of the *status quo,* but each side had a different *status quo* in mind. On the Allied side, the *status quo* meant a return to the frontiers of 1914 with reparation for the devastated areas particularly in Belgium and northern France. For the Germans, the *status quo* meant the actual situation as established after their first victories: Germany would retain all she had conquered or at the very least be generously compensated for any territory from which she withdrew.

A question of territory

Thus there were few peace overtures during this earlier period, because any common ground was lacking. The Germans made some cautious soundings of Russia in the hope of detaching her from the Allied side. Even here they were trapped by their own victories after the campaign of 1915. They would not surrender all the Russian territory they had overrun, and the Tsar Nicholas II was equally determined to liberate the soil of Holy Russia. In the autumn of 1916 the reactionary Russian ministers at last took alarm. They began to fear that war weariness was really beginning in Russia and were ready to respond when the Germans made overtures through Stockholm. At exactly this moment the German high command insisted on a declaration in favour of Polish independence. General Erich Ludendorff, the real director of the German high command, imagined, wrongly, that thousands of Poles would then join the German army. The Poland he proposed to recognize was entirely drawn from Russia's share of the partition. The negotiations with Russia naturally broke down. The Germans lost their chance of ending the war on the Eastern Front.

The topic of peace was first publicly aired in December 1916, though there was no serious intention behind it of ending the war. The impulse came from the renewed demand in German governing circles for unrestricted submarine warfare. The Germans had tried this earlier in 1915 and had then given it up when faced by American protests. Also they did not possess at that time enough submarines to make their threat effective. Now Ludendorff insisted once more. The German attack on Verdun had failed to produce a French collapse. The German armies had been heavily

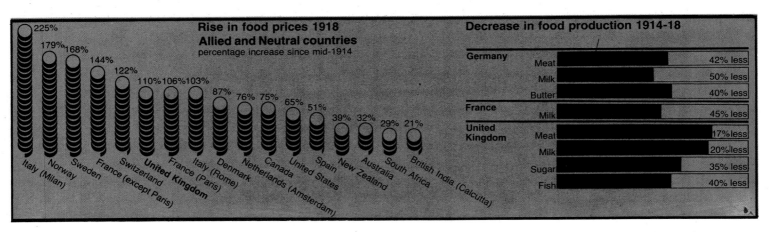

Rise in food prices 1918
Allied and Neutral countries
percentage increase since mid-1914

225% Italy (Milan)
179% Norway
168% Sweden
144% France (except Paris)
122% Switzerland
110% United Kingdom
106% France (Paris)
103% Italy (Rome)
87% Denmark
76% Netherlands (Amsterdam)
75% Canada
65% United States
51% Spain
39% New Zealand
32% Australia
29% South Africa
21% British India (Calcutta)

Decrease in food production 1914-18

Germany		
Meat		42% less
Milk		50% less
Butter		40% less
France		
Milk		45% less
United Kingdom		
Meat		17% less
Milk		20% less
Sugar		35% less
Fish		40% less

strained by the prolonged engagements on the Somme, and Ludendorff did not believe that his armies could achieve a decisive victory in 1917. On the contrary he confessed that the Germans would have to stand on the defensive when he prepared a withdrawal to the Hindenburg Line. Ludendorff accepted, however, the claim of the German naval leaders that unrestricted submarine warfare would bring about the collapse of Great Britain. It might also provoke the United States into entering the war against Germany. Ludendorff did not care. He did not imagine that the Americans could develop any effective military strength, still less that this could be deployed on the European battlefield.

Bethmann's Peace Note
Theobald Bethmann Hollweg, the German chancellor, was less confident. He had seen the brave hopes of German generals and admirals dashed time and again. He was anxious to stave off unrestricted submarine warfare, but this could be done only if he offered a firm prospect of ending the war on Germany's terms. On 12th December 1916 Bethmann therefore issued a Peace Note. This merely announced Germany's willingness to negotiate. There was no indication of the terms Germany would propose. Privately Bethmann intended that they should be those of victory: control of Belgium and north-east France for Germany. Even so, he imagined that war weariness in the Allied countries would produce some sort of favourable response. There had in fact been some discussion behind the scenes in Great Britain whether victory was possible. The people had not been consulted and were still not disillusioned. David Lloyd George, who had just become British prime minister, rejected Bethmann's Peace Note out of hand and answered by demanding the complete defeat of Germany, or, as it was called, the 'Knock Out Blow'.

President Wilson, like Bethmann, wanted to avoid a breach between Germany and the USA. He, too, recognized that negotia-

tions for peace were the only way of achieving this. Despite the failure of Bethmann's Note, Wilson tried much the same tack. On 20th December he invited the contending powers to formulate their war aims: perhaps these 'would not prove irreconcilable'. The Germans failed to answer. They knew that their aims, if openly stated, would outrage Wilson and be the more likely to provoke him into war. The Allies, though offended at being put on the same moral level as the Germans, devised idealistic war aims which could not be denied Wilson's approval. The interchange had not much reality. Both sides were bidding for Wilson's favour, not trying to clear the way for negotiations. The Germans did not bid at all seriously. Even Bethmann had despaired of preventing the renewal of unrestricted submarine warfare and merely kept Wilson in play until the submarines were ready. The Allies picked out the more respectable bits of their aims, but there was a great deal more which they intended to demand and which they did not reveal to Wilson.

Obstacles to peace
These first manoeuvres brought out the obstacles to a negotiated peace then or thereafter. Governments had to display a confidence of future victory in order to keep up the spirits of their peoples. If any country stated the terms which it expected would follow its victory, the opposing side was indignant and spurred to new efforts. If, on the other hand, a country tried to be moderate, the enemy regarded this as a confession that it foresaw defeat. More than this, negotiations were not needed to demonstrate that Belgium was the insuperable obstacle to a negotiated peace. The Germans were in possession and would insist on remaining there more or less openly. They even perversely used their own invasion of Belgium as proof that her neutrality was no protection for the Ruhr. They argued that what they had done in 1914, the British and French would do next time. The British, on their side,

were equally adamant that Belgium must be evacuated and fully restored by the Germans. This was the ostensible reason why Great Britain had entered the war, and the British never wavered from it. The fumbling negotiations, far from making victory unnecessary, showed that nothing could be achieved without it.

Social unrest
Even so, the idea of a compromise peace, however impractical, had been aired for the first time, and this was not without effect on the warring peoples. The early months of 1917 brought the first open signs of war weariness, though rarely in the clear form of a demand to end the war. Living conditions were at their worst during the hard winter of 1916-17. Food, clothes, and fuel ran short. There were strikes everywhere in factories and coal mines. In Germany there was a mutiny among the bored sailors who never left harbour. But there was still a margin for concession. Wages were increased. The trade unions were brought into partnership with government departments and the armed forces. Rationing did something to ensure that the reduced supplies went round more fairly.

In two great countries, the social unrest had political results. In Austria-Hungary, the Emperor Karl, who had succeeded to the throne in November 1916, tried to conciliate the nationalities of his nondescript empire. In Russia, the Tsar, Nicholas II, abdicated and a republic was proclaimed, in the belief that this would provide a government more worthy of the national confidence. It is sometimes said that the first Russian revolution of 1917 was made by the army and was against the war. On the contrary, the army was never in better spirits or better equipped. The revolution came after bread riots in Petrograd and took the army by surprise. The generals and the politicians who most favoured the war at first welcomed the overthrow of the Tsar as a preliminary to waging the war more effectively. Nevertheless, the people of Russia were now given

Left: The cost of continuing the war was hunger and hardship. Food prices rose sharply, even in neutral countries, as trade routes were blocked, men taken from growing food to make or use munitions, and fertile land laid waste. Right: Prague housewives queue for food. Many countries introduced rationing systems – and even so the rations were often not supplied in full. In Germany, where shortages were greatest, civilian deaths exceeded by 760,000 the number which pre-war statistics indicated as probable

a voice, at least in theory, and this voice was soon raised for peace.

The Emperor Karl and the democratic politicians in Russia both recognized that their countries would be ruined unless peace was made in the near future. Both made overtures for peace though they used different ways of doing it. Emperor Karl's way was by secret negotiations, a last splutter of old-style diplomacy. His brother-in-law, Prince Sixte of Bourbon-Parma, approached President Raymond Poincaré of France with terms which he thought the French might accept. Poincaré did not object to them, and Prince Sixte then showed them to Karl as official French demands. The most solid point in them was that France should recover Alsace and Lorraine. To this, Karl on his side made no objection. The British and French governments were now highly excited. They imagined that they were in sight of a separate peace with Austria-Hungary which would deprive Germany of a valuable ally and perhaps even open a backdoor for the invasion of Germany.

In fact the whole affair was a muddle, as usually happens when amateurs dabble in diplomacy. Karl only meant to invite terms which he could show to his German ally. The British and French supposed that he was deserting his ally. There was a further difficulty. Great Britain and France were at war with Austria-Hungary only in theory. Their forces never clashed except for an occasional naval encounter in the Adriatic. Italy was the only Allied power seriously engaged against Austria-Hungary, and the Italian statesmen had no particular interest in securing Alsace and Lorraine for France. The Italians wanted South Tyrol and Trieste. In 1915 the Austrians had accepted war rather than surrender these territories, and their resolve was still unshaken.

However Lloyd George and Alexandre Ribot, the French premier, dangled peace with Austria-Hungary before the Italian foreign minister, Baron Sonnino, though

they did not reveal Emperor Karl's so-called peace offer. Sonnino was unmoved. No peace without victory was his policy as it was that of his allies, except that in his case it was victory over Austria-Hungary, not over Germany, that he wanted. The Austrian peace offer, never very seriously made, ran into the sands. Soon in any case the French decided that they would not welcome a peace which merely benefited Italy, while they went on fighting Germany. Only Lloyd George continued to pursue the dream of a separate peace with Austria-Hungary. General Smuts, for the British war cabinet, and Count Mensdorff, the Austrian diplomat, had long meetings in Switzerland. Their discussions always broke on the same point. Lloyd George wanted to be able to attack Germany through Austrian territory. The Austrians would only abandon their German ally after a general peace had been made. The Habsburg monarchy remained shackled to the war.

Socialist efforts

The Russian search for peace was more open and created more stir in the world. Russia was now theoretically a democracy, and the Provisional Government sought to satisfy the wishes of the Russian people. They abandoned the imperialist aims of tsardom which had been enshrined in the secret treaties and announced a programme of peace without annexations or indemnities. At the same time they remained loyal to their Western allies and desired a general peace, not merely Russia's withdrawal from the war. There were many in the West, particularly among the socialist parties, who desired the same thing. For the first time, public opinion in the West took the talk of peace seriously. Even in Germany there was a pull in the same direction. The moderate Russian socialists thought that peace without annexations or indemnities would prove irresistible, if socialists from all the warring countries combined to support it. They proposed a meeting of European socialists at Stock-

holm. The German socialists agreed to come. British and French socialists also wished to come, though their object was to show that Germany would not agree to the programme and thus to keep Russia in the war, not to secure a real peace. The French government refused to allow their socialists to go. The British government reluctantly gave their socialists permission to attend the Stockholm conference. However, the British seamen, who were furiously anti-German because of the U-boat warfare, refused to convey the socialist delegates. The Stockholm conference was never held.

With this, the hope for a general peace without annexations or indemnities was dead. However, its influence went on rumbling. In Germany, Matthias Erzberger, a leader of the Centre Party, began to doubt whether Germany would win the war. He put forward a peace resolution in the Reichstag, and the Social Democrats supported him. Bethmann also welcomed the peace resolution as a means of restraining the high command. Instead, the high command secured his dismissal. When the peace resolution was passed by the Reichstag, George Michaelis, the new chancellor, endorsed it 'as I understand it'. What he understood was that it would not count as annexation for Germany to keep her present conquests nor would it count as indemnities if she were paid to leave them. When later Germany made peace with Russia and Rumania, it turned out that the Centre and the Social Democrats understood the peace resolution in the same sense. The peace resolution of the Reichstag had no effect in Allied countries. In Germany it helped to stem war weariness. Many Germans believed that the Reichstag had proposed idealistic peace terms and that the Allies had rejected them.

There was another remarkable overture for peace in 1917. The pope – Benedict XV – wanted to save the old order in Europe. Especially he wanted to save the Habsburg monarchy, the last surviving Roman Catholic power. Also he felt the socialist competition for peace. On 12th August 1917 the

Total War

pope proposed peace to the warring powers in much the same vague terms as Woodrow Wilson had used earlier. The papal peace note envisaged a return to the *status quo* of 1914 and even mentioned the restoration of Belgian independence—not terms likely to please the Germans. The Western powers had promised Italy that they would not accept the help of the Vatican in peace negotiations. Arthur Balfour, the British foreign secretary, rashly asked for more precision in regard to Belgium. When France and Italy protested, he withdrew his enquiry. Nevertheless, the Vatican passed the enquiry on to the German government. The Germans, who meant to hang on to Belgium, gave an empty answer. The pope had failed to break the deadlock, like the socialists before him.

The German government was not wholly inactive. Richard von Kühlmann, who became secretary of state on 6th August, doubted whether Germany could win the war and was proud enough of his diplomatic skill to believe that he could end it. His aim was to divide the Allies by negotiating separately with one of them. There had already been some unofficial approaches from French politicians in the same direction. Joseph Caillaux, who had been prime minister before the war, gave repeated hints that he was ready for a separate peace with Germany, though it is uncertain whether he actually attempted to negotiate with German representatives in Rome, while Germany and Italy were still not at war with each other. Aristide Briand, another former prime minister, also fancied that he could make a separate peace and perhaps recover Alsace, or part of it, at the same time. None of this was more than empty talk by out-of-work politicians. The French people, after all their sacrifices, would not accept peace without regaining Alsace and Lorraine. The Germans would not surrender the two provinces unless they were defeated.

Kühlmann thought in any case that it was a waste of time to negotiate with any French politician. In his opinion, it was British resolve which kept the war going. If the British were satisfied, the war would come to an end. Kühlmann therefore approached the British government through the King of Spain. He hinted, quite without authority, that the Germans might withdraw from Belgium if the British made a separate peace. The British, far from wanting to desert their allies, were afraid that France and Italy, both in a shaky position, might desert them. The British answered Kühlmann that they were prepared to discuss peace terms only if their allies were included. Kühlmann announced that Germany would never surrender Alsace and Lorraine. Lloyd George in return pledged that Great Britain would fight by the side of France until Alsace and Lorraine were recovered. The mere attempt to start discussions over peace terms thus, far from bringing understanding, drove the belligerents farther apart.

Pressure from below

The fumblings towards negotiation, which had always been pretty futile, now came to an end and were not seriously resumed until the end of the war. There was, however, considerable pressure from below for some sort of action. Indeed 1917 was the great year of war weariness and even of revolt against war. This went farthest in Russia. Once the Provisional Government had failed to secure a peace without annexations or indemnities, its hold over the Russian people crumbled. It sought permission from its Western allies to make a separate peace. This was refused, for fear of the effect it would have on public opinion in France and Italy. For in these countries war weariness reached the level of action and resistance to war. In both countries discipline was breaking down in the armies, and order was breaking down behind the lines. In France, after the military failures under General Robert Nivelle in April 1917, most of the army refused to obey orders for any new offensive. At one time fifty-four divisions were in a state of mutiny. The more rebellious soldiers talked of marching on Paris and overthrowing the government. In Italy there was less open mutiny, but soldiers deserted their units and went home, where the police dared not arrest them and often did not want to. Thus, by the summer of 1917, the French army was incapable of fighting, and the Italian army was at little more than half its paper strength. The spirit in the factories was little better. In Turin and Milan, the workers were already planning to take over the factories for themselves as they did after the war.

Yet this discontent did not last. The war weariness gradually faded away, and there was a revival of national enthusiasm, though on a more cautious scale. General Henri-Philippe Pétain, who took command of the French armies in May 1917, assured the French soldiers that they would not be flung into more futile offensives and declared his intention of waiting for the Americans. When there was a governmental crisis in November, President Poincaré recognised that he must decide between Caillaux, the man of compromise peace, and Clemenceau, the man of more ruthless war. He chose Clemenceau as premier. From this moment, France was committed to the bitter end. Clemenceau arrested a few so-called pacifist agitators and arraigned Caillaux before the high court for correspondence with the enemy. These gestures were hardly necessary. There was still enough national enthusiasm to sustain Clemenceau, particularly with the Americans just over the horizon.

In Italy the national spirit was actually revived by a catastrophe—the great defeat of Caporetto. As the shattered Italian armies fell back behind the Piave, politicians of all parties rallied to the national cause. Disputes stopped in the factories. Soldiers went back to their units. The war actually became popular in Italy for the first time.

Russian overtures

The Russian army, it seemed, was beyond saving. It began to break up after an unsuccessful offensive in July. The Russian people had become indifferent to the war. There was no mass movement to stop the war, but still less was there any mass support behind the Provisional Government. There was merely indifference, and this indifference enabled the Bolsheviks to seize power in November. Peace was the most urgent point in the Bolshevik programme. Lenin, the Bolshevik leader, believed that the people of every warring country would immediately respond to an appeal for peace if it were made firmly enough. The imperialist governments, as he called them, would have to conform, or they would be swept away by their angry proletariats.

On 8th November 1917 Lenin read the decree on peace to the All-Russian Soviet. It proposed immediate negotiations for 'a just and democratic peace'—with no annexations, no indemnities, and self-determination for every people, however long they had been ruled by another. An armistice of three months should be at once concluded on every front, so that negotiations should proceed. Here was certainly an overture for peace, the most practical and urgent made throughout the war. The German government responded. They welcomed an armistice on the Eastern Front, though they were not moved by the idealistic phrases.

The Western powers were more embarrassed. They wanted the Russians to go on fighting, not to make an armistice. They did not believe that the Germans would ever make peace on Lenin's principles, nor did they intend to do so themselves. Lloyd George and Clemenceau were both symbols of war to the end. If they now compromised, they would be replaced by more sincere peacemakers—Caillaux in France, Lord Lansdowne in England. The old theme was repeated that the only way of saving society and beating off socialist revolution was to carry the war to a victorious resolution. On 29th November the Allied supreme council gave a sharp and final negative to Lenin's Decree on Peace. From this moment the Bolsheviks were denounced as treacherous and disloyal, and their withdrawal was blamed for the continuance of the war.

Below: Bitter Dutch socialist cartoon on the Stockholm conference. Mars: 'I must see to it that the light does not reach him.'
Below centre: *The wounded—victims of Europe's determination to continue the war.*
Bottom: *Swiss cartoon of Lenin, who called for 'open dealings', an end to secret diplomacy, and peace*

At the same time, anyone who proposed a compromise peace or even idealistic terms could be branded as a Bolshevik. This was a convenient arrangement, with rewarding results. War weariness became a symptom of Bolshevism. Most people disapproved of Bolshevism, which was supposed to maintain itself by Chinese methods of torture and to practise among other things the nationalization of women. Most people therefore did their best not to be war weary.

Peace at Brest Litovsk

Peace negotiations between Germany and Soviet Russia were duly held. The Germans interpreted no annexations in the peculiar form that they should keep what they possessed. They also interpreted self-determination to mean that the inhabitants of the Russian territories occupied by German armies did not wish to be put under Bolshevik rule. Trotsky, who led the Soviet delegation, resolved to appeal from the German rulers to the German people. On 10th February 1918 he announced to the astonished conference: 'No war—no peace' and departed. The German and Austrian workers were now supposed to come to the aid of their Russian comrades. So at first they did. There was a renewed outbreak of strikes in both countries. Once more the strikers were mollified by increased wages and more food, itself looted from the Russian land. The strikes died away. On 3rd March 1918 the Soviet government reluctantly concluded with Germany and her allies the Peace of Brest Litovsk. This peace was not based on the principles which Lenin had laid down. The confident hope that idealistic terms would automatically end the war was dispelled.

With this, overtures for peace virtually came to an end. Some vague chat drifted on between British and German spokesmen at The Hague and between British and Austrian in Switzerland. An American, George Heron, also talked interminably to well-meaning Austrian professors who had no influence on their government. In July 1918 Kühlmann said in the Reichstag that the war would ultimately have to be ended by negotiations. For this he was dismissed from office by order of the high command. No one in the Allied countries went even as far as Kühlmann, though Lord Milner and perhaps others had the bright idea of buying Germany out of western Europe by allowing her a free hand to dominate Russia. All such ideas were mere whimsy, another aspect of the anti-Bolshevism with which many Western statesmen were driving themselves demented.

War weariness, strangely enough, also declined. Food supplies improved in both Germany and Austria-Hungary, as the occupied Russian lands were more syste-matically looted. In many parts of Austria-Hungary there was a collapse of public order, or something near it. Deserters formed 'Green bands' and lived by terrorizing the countryside. These disturbances did not reach the industrial areas and had little effect on the Austro-Hungarian armies. In any case, with Russia out of the war, it did not much matter what happened in Austria-Hungary. Her armies in Italy could stand against the Italian forces which were in equally bad shape.

Both Germans and Allied peoples were shored up by the prospect of decisive victory. The Germans were inspired first by Ludendorff's offensives from March to July. During this period there was no war weariness in Germany—a clear indication that it sprang far more from boredom and discouragement than from hardship. During the same period the British and French people were actually stimulated by defeat. From the middle of July onwards they were inspired by victory. After 8th August the Allied armies rolled forwards. War weariness, though still there, was replaced by a confidence that the war would soon be over.

There were now peace overtures of a different kind. The earlier overtures had been political devices with which to embarrass the enemy or sometimes to placate a powerful neutral. At the end of September 1918 both Germany and Austria-Hungary made peace overtures with a genuine intention of ending the war. The two governments imagined that they were still free to choose: if the Allied terms were unsatisfactory, Germany and Austria-Hungary would go on with the war. This was an illusion. The two governments were making peace overtures only because they had lost the war. Moreover, as soon as the peace overtures became known, war weariness burst out. Later it was alleged that the German armies had been stabbed in the back. This was the reverse of the truth. Ludendorff confessed that the war was lost when he insisted on an immediate request for an armistice. Only then did political discontent blaze at home. Similarly, in Austria-Hungary the nationalities staked out their claim to independence only when the imperial government had begged for peace terms from President Wilson.

An ignorant, though rational, observer might assume that war weariness would provoke peace overtures. But, in the First World War, peace overtures, themselves usually a political manoeuvre, provoked war weariness, and when these overtures were rejected, enthusiasm for the war was revived. No doubt the people ought to have demanded an end to the war. In fact fiercer war was from first to last the popular cause.

I WANT YOU
FOR U.S. ARMY
NEAREST RECRUITING STATION

4 AMERICA: THE HOPE IN THE WEST

Introduction

If the First World War had a turning point, it was in the spring of 1917. Two great events took place almost simultaneously which seemed to augur well for both sides. In mid-March the Russian collapse, which the Allies had feared for so long, looked imminent when the Tsar was overthrown, inaugurating the Russian Revolution which could only strengthen German hopes. In April the United States abandoned its neutrality and declared war against Germany, which buoyed up Allied hopes. Neither event fulfilled the hopes and fears which preceded them. Although the revolt in Russia was serious indeed, Russia did not leave the war, and in the summer of 1917 Kerensky, the Russian leader after Tsar Nicholas II was forced to step down, launched a powerful offensive on the Eastern Front which threw the Germans back, if only temporarily. And the resumption of unrestricted submarine warfare did not bring America in at once. Woodrow Wilson still sought peace, and although diplomatic relations with Germany were broken on 3rd February, Wilson still hoped to bring about peace without American intervention. The Zimmermann Note, however, swung American public opinion toward intervention, when, thanks to a British leak of a German diplomatic letter which Britain had intercepted, it was felt that Mexico had been promised huge blocks of American territory in Texas, New Mexico and California by Germany if Mexico joined the war. The American West, until now rather indifferent to the neutrality-submarine issue, clamoured for action. Wilson's hand was forced and the US joined the Allies in April.

Uncle Sam joins the parade. America could bring little immediate help . . . but she could bring hope

But would American aid prevent a German victory in the East and a German breakthrough in the West? American air forces were virtually non-existent in April of 1917. The American army was small and for the first year of intervention, ineffectual. But the American navy, strengthened by the Spanish-American War and the build-up of the American fleet under Theodore Roosevelt in the years after it, could be brought to bear immediately on the war in the Atlantic. The situation was exactly as the Germans had reckoned. Jellicoe, the British First Lord of the Admiralty, told Vice-Admiral W.S.Sims of the US navy in London that it would be impossible for Britain to continue for very long if the losses of merchant shipping continued. Prime Minister David Lloyd George gave Britain another six months.

Germany had miscalculated when she decided to risk American intervention. Six American destroyers arrived in Queenstown (now Cobh), Ireland, on 4th May, and by 5th June there were thirty-four American ships based there to convoy goods across the Atlantic. The more convoys, the fewer the losses to submarines. Meanwhile American men were conscripted in their hundreds of thousands. They could not play a role immediately, but if the combined US and Allied navies could keep Britain going until American soldiers arrived on the Western Front, the war could be won.

The Germans, on the other hand, hoped for a breakthrough in 1917. Morale was cracking in France. Her armies mutinied in the spring of 1917, and there was a real chance that France would be forced to make a separate peace to contain revolution at home. But the mutinies were quelled, despite continuing heavy losses on the Western Front. As 1917 progressed, German hopes were buoyed up by the Italian

collapse at Caporetto and the terrible losses sustained by the British at the Third Battle of Ypres. The Kerensky offensive in the East fizzled out, and by November the Bolsheviks had overthrown the Provisional Government in Russia, thereby inaugurating a civil war which almost certainly meant the withdrawal of Russia. As the Allies worked feverishly on a diplomatic front to keep Russia in the war, the effects of the long conflict were beginning to tell on the civilian populations of France, Britain and Germany. Rationing of certain items was introduced in Britain; shortages of almost every type were having their effect on the German war effort, now taken over completely by the military after the departure of Bethmann Hollweg from the Chancellory. The German gamble had failed. The nucleus of an American army was forming behind the lines in France and in the United States, and the American navy helped keep intact the convoys which kept Britain alive. The war of attrition had reached a new phase. Would Russia be brought to the peace table in time so that Germany could make one final, massive push that would bring her victory on the Western Front? And perhaps more fundamentally, could the nations which were at war maintain order and society at home and stave off the fate already suffered by Russia?

Despite all Allied efforts to the contrary, Russia, under Lenin and Trotsky, decided to make a separate peace with Germany in order to consolidate their position. By the spring of 1918, much of Russia was out of the control of the Bolsheviks. The Czech Legion hostile to Bolshevism controlled most of the Trans-Siberian Railway. British, French, Japanese and American troops began landing at Russian ports, ostensibly to keep Russia in the war, but actually to support the anti-Bolshevik armies who were more anxious to oust Lenin than to force the Germans out of western Russia and the vast territories in the Ukraine and Baltic areas which Germany now occupied. The Treaty of Brest Litovsk removed Russia from the war and satisfied most of Germany's greatest war aims.

German-controlled states dominated the whole of Eastern Europe and huge chunks of Russian territory were separated from her. Russian leaders could then concentrate on winning their civil war, while Germany could now transfer most of her forces on the Eastern Front to make one final push against France and Britain before the force of the American army could be brought to bear. By early 1918, Britain had conquered most of the non-Turkish portions of the Ottoman Empire. Germany had long since effectively lost her colonies. The Allies had won the colonial conflict. The Germans had won the war in the East. Just as von Moltke, von Büllow and the great German military planner, von Schlieffen, had argued before the war, victory would come to Germany only by victory in the West.

As German U-boats were losing the battle on the seas, Erich Ludendorff started his big push in the West. The Michael offensive took German armies almost to the point that they had held in September 1914. The tank now began to play an ever more significant role for both sides, but the initial German offensive was stopped. Germany had pushed forward but had not broken through. By June American troops began to make their appearance near the Marne by throwing the Germans back at Château Thierry. The arrival of the Americans boosted flagging British and French spirits, and war weariness was thrown aside as it became clear that an Allied breakthrough, for so long a seemingly impossible goal, was now within reach. On one final throw, Ludendorff sent waves of Storm Troopers, his élite force, against the Allied lines. On the Black Day of the German Army, 8th August 1918, the Germans were thrown back, many of their best soldiers killed. The Allies pushed forward. German supplies and men were depleted. The blockade had taken its toll. German citizens were going hungry. Only the unfit, overaged or underaged were available to serve the crumbling Second Reich. With manpower weakened and the breakthrough a failure, Ludendorff and Hindenburg approached the Kaiser in September and told him that the war was lost. German salients were being overwhelmed by the Allies. Time was against the Kaiser.

Unless he made a peace of some kind, German positions in France and Belgium would be overrun and Germany herself invaded. By the end of September, as German soldiers fell back, regrouped, and fell back again, the Kaiser appointed Prince Max of Baden as his Chancellor to make the peace on Allied terms that Germany had shunned.

President Wilson had enunciated his plans for a peace with an Allied victory when he addressed Congress in January 1918. His speech, perhaps the most important of any statesman on either side during the war, enumerated the 14 Points upon which America felt a German surrender was acceptable. The 14 Points included a withdrawal of German troops from the territories they occupied in France, Belgium and Russia, an independent Poland with access to the Baltic Sea, a restoration of the disputed territory of Alsace-Lorraine to France and, above all, the principle of national self-determination for the peoples of Europe, particularly those of the Habsburg Empire. Wilson, like so many war-weary people in all countries, hoped that the First World War would be 'a war to end all wars'. Somehow the sacrifice of a generation of men could only be tolerable if, as a result of their sacrifice, peace could be established for all time. Thus, Wilson believed in the establishment of a League of Nations which could maintain the peace, freedom of the seas for all shipping, and a programme of general disarmament.

The Germans could not and did not object to these latter proposals. The loss of the war, which they now accepted as inevitable, would force them to abandon their own war aims and disgorge the territory they had occupied for most of the course of the war. By October the German government felt that the 14 Points were the best basis on which they could make a peace without suffering occupation or, even worse, partition. Germany, after all, was a young state not yet fifty years old. It was a federal state, and separatism, especially in the Catholic south of Germany, was still strong. If the war continued, there was a real possibility of the break-up of Germany into several parts which was a long-desired dream of the French. Germany accepted the 14 Points as a basis of surrender and a cessation of hostilities as the Allies continued to clear France and Belgium of German soldiers. The German Army was cracking. No time could be lost.

In the last weeks of the war Turkey and Bulgaria surrendered, and Austria-Hungary began to disintegrate. On 27th October Austria-Hungary sued for peace. Time was running out on the Second Reich. On 9th November, as armistice negotiations reached their terminal stage, revolution broke out in Berlin and other major German cities while the Kaiser was in the forward military headquarters just inside Belgium, at Spa. Hindenburg reluctantly urged the Kaiser to abdicate and flee to neutral Holland, which he did, as a German Republic was declared by the Social Democrats. Their rather conservative leader, Friedrich Ebert, was named provisional leader of the German nation, and the armistice was signed. The guns ceased to fire in Europe at 11 o'clock in the morning, 11th November 1918. As the shakily established German government formed its new constitution at Weimar, Wilson toured Europe and was ecstatically cheered in France, Italy and Britain, and then settled down in Paris with the other representatives of the victorious allies to make the peace that would end all wars...

If Wilson was most concerned in making a lasting peace, the other leaders of the Great Powers—Orlando, Clemenceau and Lloyd George—were even more anxious to secure and if possible widen the territorial gains they had already made. Britain, France and Belgium quickly agreed to partition the German and Turkish Empires outside Europe among them. But France hoped that if a partition of Germany were not possible, a long-term alliance between France and the Anglo-Americans was the only way she could make sure that another war of revenge would not break out within a generation. The United States was quickly moving towards isolationism, a fact which Wilson ignored, but even Wilson recognized that such an alliance would not be supported by the American people and placed his faith in a general guarantee of frontiers by the League of Nations. The blockade against Germany continued until the spring of 1919, and thousands starved or froze to death. A peace had to be made quickly. The fear that Bolshevism would spread throughout Europe was very real for the diplomats in Paris, and the overthrow of the Bavarian and Hungarian Soviet Republics did not allay their fears. Wilson and Lloyd George were able to contain the most venal of French demands, but the peace imposed upon Germany was far from the ideals of the 14 Points which Germany thought she would get. Disarmament was to begin with the defeated powers. The vanquished were presented with a *fait accompli*. Their choice was small: sign or be occupied. They signed. The Great War had ended.

U-Boats: The Fatal Decision

At long last, on 9th January 1917, Bethmann Hollweg, the German chancellor, at a conference at GHQ, Pless in Upper Silesia, signified his concurrence with the resolution in favour of unrestricted submarine warfare, that is he agreed to the torpedoing of enemy and neutral merchant and passenger ships without warning. His feelings were similar to those which had burdened him during the crisis of July 1914. For him the Pless decision was a leap in the dark, like the action of Austria-Hungary against Serbia in July 1914. On that occasion he realized that any attempt to overthrow Serbia might well lead to a European war. Now he was tormented by anxiety lest the reckless use of the U-boats result in war with the United States. And on both occasions his fears were justified.

In 1914 it was the growing consolidation of the Triple Entente, the increasing strength of Russia, and the critical situation in the Balkans which drove the German government to approve and guarantee the Austro-Hungarian attack on Serbia regardless of the risk of a European war. In 1917 the German government was impelled by the hopelessness of the land war to agree to unrestricted submarine warfare and thereby to run the risk of a conflict with the USA. In 1917, as in 1914, Bethmann Hollweg yielded to the military demands through a mixture of fatalism and a hope that the general situation might be changed by violent action. Bethmann Hollweg's two shattering decisions resembled each other in that each was based on a collapse of political leadership and an excessive regard for the military standpoint.

The arguments about U-boat warfare among the military and political leaders of the German empire had begun as far back as late 1914. The first impulse was given by the unsatisfactory progress of the naval war. At enormous cost a German battle fleet had been built up in sharp naval rivalry with Great Britain. On the outbreak of war, however, any large-scale naval enterprise was discouraged by the government, which needed to maintain the German fleet intact as a political instrument. It was not until 1916 that the naval commanders ventured to engage the Royal Navy, and the battle of Jutland finally showed that Germany had not enough naval power to defeat the great

Below: A U-boat puts out to sea, festooned with garlands, the tribute of the German people's faith in its destructive power. Almost all the press and the people believed, like the high command, that unrestricted submarine warfare could bring Great Britain to her knees

Left: *German approval for the new development 'U-boats go forth'*

British fleet in a battle on the high seas. The pretensions of the German naval leaders were badly injured because of the limited effectiveness of the fleet since 1914, and Germany was driven more and more to rely on submarine warfare against British seaborne commerce. The aim was to destroy the economic life and supply lines of Great Britain and thus force it to sue for peace. But this strategical switch was by no means due solely to the German navy's ambition to play some part in the war. It was forced on the naval leaders by the grim fact that in a few months Great Britain had won complete command of the world's seas and was trying to cut off Germany's overseas imports by a distant blockade. It seemed essential not to accept this gigantic British success meekly but to find some counterstroke in reply. In the first months of the war German U-boats had destroyed several large British warships by underwater torpedo attacks, and these brilliant successes led to an over-estimation of the U-boat weapon, which in fact was still comparatively undeveloped. The chief of the naval staff, Admiral von Pohl, pressed for a blockade of the British coasts as early as the beginning of November 1914. And a little later Admiral von Tirpitz, state secretary of the imperial navy office, gave an interview to Karl von Wiegand, a representative of the American press, in which he drew the world's attention to the possibility of a German blockade of Great Britain by submarines. Among the German people an impression grew that the U-boats were an infallible weapon in the war with Great Britain. The result was a violent public agitation concerning U-boats.

Commercial warfare by U-boat actually began as far back as February 1915 and was consistently carried on in various forms for two years, until January 1917. During this period the German government had time and again to justify the employment of a novel method of warfare in face of the vehement complaints of the European neutrals and, especially, of the United States. Yielding to such opposition, it set its face, until 9th January 1917, against the unrestricted use of the U-boat weapon demanded by the naval authorities. But at the same time, in internal debates, it repeatedly asserted that its negative attitude was not due to consideration of international law but was purely for military and political reasons. When, in January 1917, the ruthless exploitation of U-boat warfare was finally decided upon, Bethmann Hollweg expressly declared that he had never opposed it on principle, but had always been governed by the general situation and the respective strengths of U-boat weapons. In the various deliberations it was the Kaiser Wilhelm II alone

who expressed humanitarian scruples. For him the drowning of innocent passengers was 'a frightful thought'.

As the U-boat was a new weapon, there were in 1914 no international rules regarding its use in commercial warfare. The German government should have striven to obtain international recognition for the new weapon, for both the present and any future war. But instead, the Germans admitted the illegality of U-boat commerce war from the first by describing it as a reprisal measure against the illegal methods adopted by the British in their commercial blockade. For Great Britain, like Germany, had been forced by the advance of weapon technique to break the traditional international rules dealing with blockades. Because of the danger to its naval forces it could not carry on a close blockade of the German coasts—hitherto the only permissible method—but had to engage in a distant blockade directed at neutral as well as German ports. For this purpose the British declared the whole of the North Sea to be a war zone and prescribed for neutral shipping fixed navigational routes which could be supervised by British naval vessels. Moreover, Great Britain extended the regulations about war contraband and the confiscation of cargoes in neutral vessels. Liable to seizure were not only goods useful for the arming and supply of enemy forces, but all foodstuffs and raw materials intended for the Central powers. It was immaterial whether the cargoes were being carried direct to enemy ports or through neutral countries.

The new British contraband regulations initiated an economic and hunger blockade which was aimed at the enemy's civilian population. The German reprisal measure, commercial war by U-boat, was similarly directed against the civilian population. It might therefore be considered as merely a similar measure, by way of reprisal. But in fact there was one great difference. The British blockade was merely a confiscation of material goods, but the German submarine attacks endangered the lives of crews and passengers. When an underwater torpedo was fired without warning, it was impossible to take any steps to save the lives of those on board. And if the ship was attacked from the surface the crew and passengers taking to the lifeboats were exposed to the perils of wind and wave on the open seas, for the U-boat was in no position to pick them up and bring them to a place of safety.

The most difficult thing to justify was the effect of commercial war by U-boat on the neutrals, in whose case there was, of course, no question of reprisal. Instead, the German government demanded that the neutrals submit to submarine warfare as they had submitted to the British block-

ade of the North Sea. But there was only partial justification for this demand. True, neutral shipping used the prescribed routes through the English Channel and submitted to examination of cargoes in British ports. Nevertheless, the European neutrals, in spite of the British blockade, had delivered large food cargoes to Germany down to 1916. On the German side there was no desire to suppress neutral shipping by submarine warfare, but only to drive it out of certain sea areas. In the proclamation of 4th February 1915, which initiated submarine warfare, the waters

Bethmann Hollweg, who struggled in vain against the demands of the high command

around Great Britain and Ireland, including the whole of the English Channel, were declared a war zone. Every enemy merchant ship encountered in the war zone would be destroyed. Neutral ships were advised to avoid it, as attacks on enemy ships might, in the uncertainties of naval warfare, well affect neutral ships also. It was hoped that this warning might frighten neutral shipping off trade with Great Britain. Admiral von Pohl wanted to emphasize this warning by ordering all ships within the war zone to be sunk without distinction, a step which meant unrestricted submarine warfare. He actually wanted a few neutral ships to be sunk without warning at the outset of the U-boat operations so that there should be general uncertainty and neutral trade with Great Britain stopped as soon as possible. In subsequent deliberations the deterrent effect on neutral shipping was an important factor

At the beginning of 1915, and again at the beginning of 1916, such intimidation seemed especially necessary, for Germany at those times was far from possessing enough U-boats to carry on a successful economic war with Great Britain. In February 1915 there were only twenty-one U-boats available for watching the shipping lanes to Great Britain. As the voyage to the war zone, the return journey, and the

America: The Hope in the West

overhaul afterwards, took a considerable time, there were never more than three or four boats operating at any one time on the coasts of Great Britain. Obviously there were not enough of them to inflict any considerable damage to Great Britain's trade by direct action. Thus it was very important to keep neutral ships, and as many enemy ships as possible out of the war zone. But the Germans had no success. Even before the announced U-boat commerce war started on 18th February, very firmly worded notes of protest reached Berlin from the neutral maritime powers affected. Most serious of all, the American government held the German government strictly accountable for all measures that might involve the destruction of any merchant vessel belonging to the United States or for the death of any American subject. The war situation of the Central powers in February 1915 was much too strained to risk complications with powerful neutral states. The chancellor therefore persuaded the Kaiser to order the U-boats to spare neutral ships, especially those belonging to the United States or Italy. The U-boat commerce war began four days late, on 22nd February 1915, in this modified form. In March 1915, out of 5,000 vessels entering and leaving British ports only twenty-one were sunk. Neutral shipping soon resumed trade with Great Britain.

The Lusitania incident

In spite of precautions taken during the period of restricted submarine warfare, a grave incident occurred on 7th May 1915, when a German U-boat sank the British ocean liner *Lusitania* with an underwater torpedo attack. Among the drowned were 128 American citizens. The sinking of the *Lusitania* aroused intense indignation in the United States, and a sharp exchange of notes between the American and German governments ensued. President Wilson had no desire to precipitate an armed conflict with Germany by his *Lusitania* notes, but he feared that a continuation of the U-boat war would one day leave him no other choice. He tried repeatedly to persuade Great Britain to allow food imports into Germany through neutral countries. At the same time he took a firm stand against the contempt for humane principles shown in the kind of warfare used by the U-boats. The first *Lusitania* note of the American government on 15th May 1915 denied the legality in international law of any form of U-boat commerce war, inasmuch as in neither an underwater nor a surface attack could the safety of passengers and crew be guaranteed. In the third *Lusitania* note of 23rd July 1915 Wilson conceded that submarines were a novelty in naval warfare and that no provision could have been made for them in the international regula-

tions. At the same time it was admitted that the German submarine operations of the last two months had complied with the customs of war and had demonstrated the possibility of eliminating the chief causes of offence. This remarkable concession on the part of the Americans was based on the fact that since May 1915 the U-boats had been fitted with deck guns and, owing to the uncertainty of hitting the target with torpedoes, had carried on the commerce war in 'cruiser' style, according to the rules laid down for the taking of prizes. The U-boat came to the surface when attacking a ship and before sinking it allowed the persons on board to take to the boats. All enemy vessels were sunk without exception, but neutral ships were sunk only when they were carrying contraband.

Although this was the actual method of operation during the *Lusitania* crisis, the German naval authorities obstinately opposed any restriction being placed on submarine warfare and especially any attempt to confine U-boats to the rules of 'cruiser' warfare. They maintained that such methods were an intolerable danger to the submarine and its crew. They named as the chief dangers attempts of the merchant ships to ram the submarine, concealed guns on the ships, the use of a neutral flag by British ships, and attacks by enemy warships during the necessarily lengthy searches. The German government was not informed by the navy that in the period May-July 1915 eighty-six per cent of the merchant vessels that were sunk were dealt with according to the cruiser warfare rules, and that from February to July 1915 250 merchant ships carrying a neutral flag were examined and only on three occasions was any misuse of the flag dis-

covered. By its policy of secrecy the navy apparently wanted to avoid being permanently restricted to 'cruiser' warfare and losing for ever the chance of unrestricted submarine warfare. On 6th June 1915 the Kaiser ordered that all large passenger liners, whether enemy or neutral, must be spared. Nevertheless, on 19th August, the British liner, *Arabic*, was sunk without warning, two more American citizens losing their lives. The Kaiser then ordered that no passenger liner was to be sunk until it had been warned and the passengers and crew given a chance to escape. During the arguments about U-boat methods in the summer of 1915 Tirpitz, in order to put pressure on the Kaiser, twice offered his resignation. His offers were abruptly refused. Yet the Kaiser changed his chief of naval staff at the beginning of September. Vice-Admiral Bachmann, a Tirpitz adherent who had held the office since February 1915, was replaced by Admiral von Holtzendorff, who was more amenable to the political views of the chancellor. On 18th September 1915 Holtzendorff gave orders that the U-boat commerce war on the west coast of Great Britain and in the Channel should be carried out on the 'cruiser' system. The naval commanders were not ready for this step and brought the U-boat war around Great Britain to a standstill. Thus ended the first phase of the U-boat war. The *Arabic* case was settled on 6th October by German compliance. The German government did not defend the action of the U-boat commander, which infringed the order of 6th June. The *Lusitania* case remained unsettled. The German government refused to admit that the U-boat attack on the *Lusitania* was contrary to international law, for if it did so future

Arming at sea—a U-boat takes ammunition on board. From May 1915 U-boats were fitted with deck guns as well as with torpedoes, and surfaced before attacking an enemy ship

unrestricted submarine warfare would be impossible.

In 1915 several U-boats, large and small, were sent to the Austro-Hungarian naval base of Pola, and also to Constantinople. These carried on trade war in the Mediterranean and the Black Sea with great success, limiting their actions to the 'cruiser' rules. They restricted the flow of supplies to the Anglo-French forces in the Dardanelles and Salonika. But at the beginning of 1916 U-boat activities were severely handicapped by the progressive arming of the enemy's merchant vessels. The U-boat flotilla at Pola therefore asked the naval staff for permission to sink any armed merchant ship without warning. Holtzendorff granted the request, but with the proviso that passenger ships should continue to be exempt. At the same time he re-opened the trade war around Great Britain by issuing the same orders. A new phase in the submarine war was begun on 29th February 1916 and was termed 'intensified' U-boat war.

The high-ranking officers of the German navy looked on the new measures as a mere transitional phase. Since the beginning of the year the prospects for unrestricted submarine war had considerably improved, for General von Falkenhayn, chief of the army general staff, was now expressly demanding it. Since the autumn of 1914 the German armies, in co-operation with those of Austria-Hungary, Turkey, and Bulgaria, had created firm front lines on enemy territory; they had driven the Russians far back to the east, and by the occupation of Serbia had opened the way to Constantinople. Falkenhayn was at the peak of his military successes. In February 1916 he intended to deliver an all-out offensive on the Western Front, starting with a holding attack on Verdun. In the summer and autumn of 1915 he had firmly advised against the ruthless use of the U-boat weapon because he thought that a break with the United States might produce unfavourable reactions from the European neutrals and in particular might make Bulgarian assistance in the campaign against Serbia doubtful. In 1916, on the other hand, when the Balkan situation had been stabilized, such considerations were no longer valid. He believed that unrestricted submarine warfare directed against Great Britain would help his offensive on the Western Front. The U-boat action was timed to start in the middle of March. Almost the whole of the German press advocated ruthless use of the U-boats. The alliance between Falkenhayn and the navy on this point put Bethmann Hollweg in a very difficult position, and he spent the first weeks of the New Year in a very worried state. He feared that the adoption of un-restricted submarine warfare 'might result in condemnation by the whole civilized world and a sort of crusade against Germany'.

The Charleville conference

In the decisive conference with the Kaiser on 4th March 1916 at GHQ, Charleville, Falkenhayn declared that, in view of the dwindling resistance of the German allies and the German civil population, the war must be brought to an end before the year was out. The only means of achieving this was by unrestricted submarine warfare. On his part Bethmann Hollweg argued that Germany could stand another winter campaign. He would rather have a compromise peace than risk prolonging the war indefinitely by challenging America. In his opinion there were still insufficient U-boats. In the middle of March 1916 there were only fourteen large submarines capable of carrying on a commerce war in British waters.

On 4th March 1916 the Kaiser, unable to make up his mind, postponed his final decision until the beginning of April and then indefinitely. Nevertheless, with the agreement of the chancellor, a further tightening of the U-boat blockade was ordered on 13th March 1916. In the war zone both armed and unarmed merchant ships were to be destroyed without warning. Outside the war zone the previous orders remained in force. Tirpitz, who had not been called to the Charleville conference, reported sick to the Kaiser in protest and on 15th March he agreed to resign. One of Bethmann Hollweg's chief opponents had left the scene.

Whereas the instruction for the sinking of armed merchant ships was made public, the new order of 13th March was kept secret. Its effects, however, were viewed by the neutrals with growing alarm. Washington suspected that Germany had already started unrestricted submarine warfare. A new incident soon gave rise to another German-American crisis. On 24th March 1916 two Americans were injured when the cross-Channel passenger steamer, *Sussex,* was torpedoed without warning. In the erroneous belief that American citizens had lost their lives in the sinking President Wilson sent a note on 18th April threatening to break off diplomatic relations with Germany if it did not abandon its current methods of submarine warfare. Under pressure from this ultimatum the Kaiser gave orders, at Bethmann Hollweg's request, cancelling the tightened-up rules for submarine warfare in the combat zone around Great Britain. The rules of the 'cruiser' system were to be observed until further notice. The commanding officers on the naval front declared that such a procedure was un-

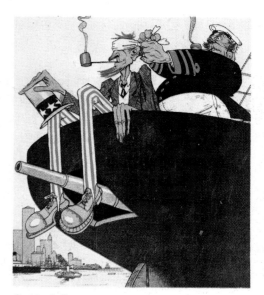

Cynical German cartoon protesting against the outcry over the drowning of passengers – a 'blind' American passenger on an 'unarmed' merchant ship

workable, because of the danger to the U-boats, and they brought the submarine war in British waters to a complete standstill. In the Mediterranean the U-boats continued the campaign according to the new rules.

At the end of April 1916, when the reply to the American note had to be drafted, Falkenhayn again tried to persuade the Kaiser to agree to unrestricted submarine warfare. He asserted that he would have to forego action against Verdun if the U-boat war was suspended. Bethmann Hollweg indignantly rejected such an alternative and after a bitter dispute he once again convinced the Kaiser. In a note dated 4th May 1916 the German government agreed to the demands of the American government and informed it that the German naval forces had been instructed to observe the canons of international law with regard to the stopping, searching, and destruction of merchant vessels. At the same time it expressed its expectation that the United States would now induce the British government to abandon as soon as possible such of its methods of waging naval war as were contrary to international law. The German government reserved its complete freedom to alter its decision if this were not done. Wilson at once protested against the German claim to make respect for the rights of American citizens on the high seas dependent on the behaviour of the British government. Responsibility in such matters was individual not joint, absolute not relative. The two opposing standpoints were thus definitely laid down. If Germany again intensified the submarine war, it was to be expected that the

'This is how your money can fight — turn it into U-boats.' An appeal for war loans. In the background is a sinking enemy ship

United States would promptly enter the war.

It was but a few months after the settlement of the *Sussex* case that the problem of unrestricted submarine warfare once again became acute. During the summer of 1916 the war situation was completely transformed. The Central powers, who had held the initiative for a whole year, were now forced into defensive battles lasting for months by the persistent offensive of the Russians in Volhynia and eastern Galicia and of the British and French on the Somme river, which could only be withstood by enormous efforts and casualties. Falkenhayn had to break off the battle for Verdun, which was bleeding not only France but also Germany to death. His prestige was shattered, and when Rumania entered the war against the Central powers on 27th August 1916 he was replaced by Hindenburg and Ludendorff. Hindenburg, who was the most popular of the German military leaders, became chief of the general staff. Bethmann Hollweg had worked for Hindenburg's appointment to this post during the critical summer months of 1916 because he thought that a moderate peace could be made acceptable to the German people, so misled by exaggerated hopes, only if it were covered by the name of Hindenburg. In other words, Bethmann Hollweg hoped to use the great authority of the field marshal in his efforts towards a peace of understanding. But Hindenburg's authority was fatal to Bethmann Hollweg's policy. Hindenburg and Ludendorff were advocates of unrestricted

submarine warfare. After they had been summoned to take up the highest posts in the army they pleaded for a temporary postponement of this war measure only with respect to the difficult military situation. For at the moment great danger threatened from Rumania, and sufficient troops had to be made available as security against the European neutrals, who might regard unrestricted submarine warfare as a challenge. By the end of December 1916 the Rumanian army was defeated and in the following months military deployments against European neutrals could be initiated.

Bethmann Hollweg had previously been able to stifle the arguments of Falkenhayn and the naval authorities in favour of unrestricted submarine warfare because the war situation in the spring of 1916 did not make such a risky measure absolutely essential. By the summer, however, the war was threatening to become one of attrition of man power and exhaustion of resources. Germany would not be strong enough in 1917 to undertake a large-scale offensive with the land forces available. A weapon that might well win the war was offered by the U-boats.

In these circumstances Bethmann Hollweg, in the latter part of 1916, tried to avoid the necessity of unrestricted submarine warfare by bringing about an early peace of compromise. President Wilson was working for the same end, because he wanted to keep America out of the war. On 12th December 1916 the Central powers made a peace offer to the Allies. On the 21st President Wilson invited the belligerents to state their war aims and announced his willingness to take part in the discussions. Hindenburg and Ludendorff had notified their concurrence with the peace offer of the Central powers, but as soon as the first negative reports began to arrive from the camp of the Allies they demanded, at the end of December 1916, speedy and energetic action at sea.

The prospects for unrestricted submarine warfare at the beginning of 1917 were much better than they had been a year before. Germany now had 105 U-boats, of which 46 large and 23 small vessels were available for the campaign in British waters. In view of the bad world harvests of 1916 unrestricted submarine warfare, if started before the chief overseas transport season began in early February, would foreseeably have a grave effect on Great Britain's grain supplies. Since 6th October 1916 the U-boats had carried on the commerce war in British waters on the 'cruiser' rules. Total sinkings were reckoned at 400,000 tons a month (in actual fact the figure was round about 325,000). By the removal of restrictions one expected an increase to 600,000 tons. The navy esti-

mated that such a figure, enhanced by the consideration that neutral shipping would be frightened away, would in five months reduce the trade with Great Britain by thirty-nine per cent. This would force Great Britain to sue for peace. About the results of an American intervention in the war there was wide difference of opinion. The army thought that any great increase in the supply of American war material to the Allies was impossible, nor did it expect the arrival in Europe of large numbers of American troops. The politicians, however, thought that the American entry would encourage the Allied nations to hold out, would put large financial resources at their disposal, and would bring many American volunteers to join the Allies in Europe.

On the question of U-boat warfare Hindenburg and Ludendorff found their views supported by the vast majority of the German people. The largest party in the Reichstag, the Centre Party, passed a resolution on 7th October 1916 saying that the decision of the chancellor regarding submarine warfare must be based on the views of the supreme army command. As the Conservatives and National Liberals were in any case outright champions of unrestricted submarine warfare, Bethmann Hollweg knew that if he refused to make use of the U-boat weapon in opposition to Hindenburg and Ludendorff he could no longer count on a majority in the Reichstag. The feeling of the people was summed up by Bethmann Hollweg in his memoirs: 'No nation will stand for not winning a war when it is convinced that it can win.' He himself, in spite of his constant resistance to unrestricted submarine warfare, seems at times to have wondered whether, after all, the use of this extreme weapon might not achieve a turn for the better.

For the moment Bethmann Hollweg left the problem unsolved. When on 9th January 1917 he went to Pless to discuss the ever more pressing problem, he found the naval staff and the supreme army command united against him and they had already won over the Kaiser to their side. Hindenburg and Ludendorff saw no possibility of bringing the war to a victorious end unless the U-boats were used without restrictions. They declared themselves ready to shoulder all responsibility for any results caused by this war measure. The chief of the naval staff guaranteed that he could force Great Britain to its knees before the next harvest. Once again Bethmann Hollweg produced all his objections, but after the failure of the Central powers' peace move all hopes for a peace of understanding seemed to have vanished. Bethmann Hollweg could no longer maintain his opposition to the demands of the military and he told the Kaiser that he could not recommend him to oppose the vote of his military advisers. He felt he must refrain from offering his resignation, so as not to expose the inner dissensions in the German leadership to all the world. Until the last moment, however, he continued to doubt the wisdom of the decision of 9th January 1917. When towards the end of the month the prospects for a successful outcome of Wilson's peace efforts seemed more favourable, he tried to secure a postponement of unrestricted submarine warfare, but the naval staff assured him that most of the U-boats had already been despatched.

The beginning of unrestricted submarine warfare on 1st February 1917 was at first countered by Wilson with the rupture of diplomatic relations, whereby he hoped to bring Germany to its senses. The political tension between the two countries was increased at the beginning of March by the publication of a German offer of alliance to Mexico (intercepted by the British intelligence service) should the United States enter the war because of the submarine war. The sinking of seven American merchant ships by U-boats by 21st March finally obliged Wilson to summon Congress, which on 4th and 6th April approved a declaration of war.

At first the figures of sinkings by the U-boats surpassed the forecasts and expectations of the German naval authorities, reaching its maximum in April 1917. But when in the course of the summer merchant ships sailing for Great Britain were assembled in convoys and protected by destroyers the number of successes dwindled. Nevertheless, unrestricted submarine warfare brought Great Britain difficulties which led the British government to begin to take an interest in political solutions. But on the whole the strong urge towards peace that was expected from the U-boat menace failed to materialize. Looking back, it is clear that the German military leaders and politicians regarded the unrestricted submarine warfare as a failure. For from March 1917 onwards the Central powers were relieved of a great burden by the Russian Revolution. Russia dropped out of the war in the winter of 1917-18, and negotiations for a general peace of understanding might have been possible had not the Allies been encouraged to hold on by the prospect of American armed assistance. But the principal effect of unrestricted submarine warfare was on America itself, for it caused the abandonment of America's policy of isolation and its entry into world politics.

'Shelling a merchantman' by H.R.Butler. This U-boat has warned the crew before firing, and they are escaping in lifeboats

Wilson and the Ordeal of Neutrality

The outbreak of war in Europe in August 1914 came, in its suddenness, to President Wilson like a bolt of lightning out of a clear sky. To be sure, Wilson had not been unaware of the possibility of a conflagration, for his confidential adviser and some-time agent, Colonel Edward M.House, writing from Berlin in May 1914, had warned that Europe was a powder keg about to explode. However, House's talks with German and British leaders had raised the tantalizing possibility of an Anglo-American-German entente under Wilson's auspices. No one in Washington (or in European capitals, for that matter) saw that the fuse was burning rapidly after the murder of the heir to the Austrian and Hungarian thrones and his young wife by a Serbian nationalist in Sarajevo on 28th June 1914. Moreover, when the great European powers went over the brink in late July and early August, Wilson was mired in controversy with Congress and in deep despair over the fatal illness of his wife. He could only wait in fascinated horror as Sir Edward Grey, the British foreign minister, wept as he told the American ambassador in London, Walter Page, about the British ultimatum to Germany, and King George exclaimed, 'My God, Mr Page, what else could we do?' One American well expressed what was surely Wilson's reaction when he wrote: 'The horror of it all kept me awake for weeks, nor has the awfulness of it all deserted me, but at first it seemed a horrid dream.'

But Armageddon *had* come. Wilson, as head of the greatest neutral power, whose interests would be vitally affected by

belligerent measures, had perforce to work out his policies towards the warring powers.

Throughout the long months of American neutrality, from August 1914 to April 1917, Wilson, whatever his own pre-dispositions, had to work within limits imposed by American public opinion. That opinion was so divided in its preferences for various belligerents during the first months of the war that any policy for the United States other than a strict neutrality would have been inconceivable. Wilson remarked to the German ambassador, Count Johann von Bernstorff, that 'we definitely have to be neutral, since otherwise our mixed populations would wage war on each other'. More important still, in spite of the attachments of various national and ethnic minorities, and of all the efforts of British, French, and German propagandists in the United States, the predominant American public opinion was consistently neutral before 1917. But Americans, even though they clung doggedly to their traditional isolationism and refused to believe that their vital interests were sufficiently involved in the outcome of the war to justify voluntary intervention, were none the less jealous of their sovereignty and international prestige. In other words, they would tolerate only a certain amount of provocation, and no more. To an extraordinary degree Wilson understood and shared the attitudes of the majority of his fellow-countrymen. Both expediency and conviction dictated policies that were agreeable to the great majority of Americans.

Although Wilson had strong emotional attachments to the Allies, particularly Great Britain, he profoundly admired German contributions to modern civilization. As a sophisticated student of modern history, he well understood that the causes of the war were complex and never imputed exclusive responsibility to either side. He was able to detach emotions from decisions and policies and, self-consciously, to make decisions on the basis of what he considered to be the best interests of America and Europe.

Wilson exercised greater personal control over foreign policy than any other chief of state among the great powers of the world. Constitutionally, as President he was sovereign in the conduct of foreign relations, subject only to the Senate's veto on treaties. Weak Presidents have abdicated their responsibilities to strong secretaries of state or congressional leaders. But Wilson was a 'strong' President. He believed that the people had invested their

Different views of Wilson's conduct.
Above: *The British view, from a* Punch *cartoon. 'Hail Columba! President Wilson (to American Eagle): "Gee! What a dove I've made of you!"'* **Below left:** *A German view. Big Chief Old Serpent letting out a war-cry. The Germans felt Wilson was threatening Berlin.*
Left: *President Wilson is seen here holding up a baseball at a World Series match, 1915. He 'played a part in the fate of nations incomparably more direct and personal than any other man'. Although he was an intellectual and an idealist, in this vital period Wilson understood and shared the attitudes of the majority of his fellow-countrymen*

sovereignty in foreign affairs in him. He not only refused to delegate this responsibility, but insisted upon conducting foreign relations himself. Because he used his full constitutional powers to execute policies that the great majority desired, Wilson not only held the conduct of foreign affairs in his own hands, but was irresistible while doing so. 'It seems no exaggeration,' Churchill later wrote, 'to pronounce that the action of the United States with its repercussions on the history of the world depended, during the awful period of Armageddon, upon the workings of this man's mind and spirit to the exclusion of almost every other factor; and that he played a part in the fate of nations incomparably more direct and personal than any other man.'

Wilson's whole world came tumbling down in the first week of August 1914. Ellen Axson Wilson, his beloved wife since 1885, died on 6th August. Great Britain,

America: The Hope in the West

which he loved, and Germany, which he admired, were already beginning to tear at each other's throats. Near hysteria reigned in Wall Street as a consequence of the disruption of international trade and exchange.

With his customary iron self-control, the President moved confidently and serenely to meet emergencies and establish American neutrality. The formalities were observed easily enough. Wilson proclaimed official neutrality on 4th August and, two weeks later, admonished his fellow-countrymen to be 'impartial in thought as well as in action'.

However, being neutral in the midst of a great war was easier said than done. For example, should the American government permit its citizens to sell vital raw materials and munitions to the Allies when British cruisers prevented the Germans from having access to such supplies? More difficult still, should the government permit American bankers to lend money, which the secretary of state, William Jennings Bryan, called the 'worst of all contrabands', to the belligerents?

Having decided upon a policy of strict neutrality, Wilson, helped by Bryan and the counsellor of the State Department, Robert Lansing, proceeded as systematically and as impartially as possible to be neutral in every circumstance. Hence he permitted the Allies to purchase as much contraband as they pleased, for to have denied them access to American markets and the benefits that flowed from dominant seapower would have been not only un-neutral, but tantamount to undeclared war. For the same reason he permitted American bankers to lend money both to the Allied and German governments.

Wilson followed the rush of the German army through Belgium into northern France and was obviously relieved when the French and British were able to establish a secure defensive line by early autumn. At this point, at any rate, Germany seemed to threaten neither America's vital interests nor her neutral rights. Wilson's main problem in late 1914 was defending American trading rights against British seapower, or, to put the matter more realistically, coming to terms with the British maritime system.

Acting as neutrals always have during wartime, Wilson wanted to keep the channels of commerce to all of Europe open as widely as possible to American ships and goods. Acting as dominant seapowers always have, the British set about to cut off the flow of life-giving supplies from the United States to Germany and Austria-Hungary. Consequently, dispatches about these matters passed frequently between Washington and London, not only during the first months of the war, but as late as

1916. There was much talk of 'freedom of the seas' on the one side and of legitimate belligerent rights on the other. Actually, what sounded like the rhetoric of developing crisis masked the fact that there was substantial goodwill and accommodation on both sides. For their part, the British instituted maritime measures that were not only largely legitimate, but also were based upon precedents established by the United States government itself during the American Civil War of 1861-65. For his part, Wilson, understanding these facts, rejected demands of highly partisan German Americans and American economic interests with a large stake in free trade with Germany for measures to break the British blockade or prevent the Anglo-American trade in contraband.

Having passed through troubles that might have burgeoned into serious Anglo-American crisis, Wilson, at the end of 1914, could view the general state of American relations with the belligerents with some equanimity. There seemed to be no chance of serious conflict with Germany: there were simply no points of contact between the two nations. By Wilson's reckoning, the war would end either in stalemate or, more likely, in an Allied victory. He told a reporter for the *New York Times,* in an off-the-record interview on 14th December 1914, that he hoped ardently for a peace of reconciliation based upon negotiation. But, Wilson added, he did not think that it would 'greatly hurt' the interests of the United States if the Allies won a decisive victory and dictated the settlement.

Between the cruiser and the submarine
The German decision, announced on 4th February 1915, to use an untried weapon, the submarine, in a war against merchant shipping in the English Channel and a broad zone around the British Isles, created an entirely new situation, fraught with peril for the United States. Actually, at this time, the German navy did not possess enough submarines to prosecute an effective campaign, even against Allied merchant ships. But the Germans had compounded the blunder of acting prematurely, largely in bluff, by adding that *neutral* ships might be torpedoed because of the Allied use of neutral flags. It was only the first of a series of blunders by the German admiralty and the high command that would drive the United States into the war.

President Wilson replied to Berlin on 10th February with a stern warning that the United States would hold the German government to a 'strict accountability' and probably go to war if German submarines indiscriminately and illegally attacked American vessels on the high seas.

As it turned out, the gravest German

blunder was to provide the British and French governments with a good excuse for doing what they had already planned to do—severely to tighten their blockade measures. Now they need fear no serious American reprisal. Invoking the ancient right of reprisal, the London and Paris authorities announced on 1st March that, in retaliation against the illegal and ruthless German submarine campaign, they would stop *all* commerce of whatever character to the Central powers, even commerce through neutral ports.

Wilson and Bryan worked hard to arrange an Anglo-American agreement that would provide some protection for American shipping against the cruisers and submarines. Their efforts foundered upon the shoals of the German refusal to give up the submarine campaign except at the price of virtual abandonment by the British of an effective blockade. Wilson was in fact now helpless; he could only acquiesce in the new Anglo-French blockade so long as the sword of the submarine hung over his head.

The President waited in uncertainty all through the early spring of 1915 to see what the Germans would do. There were several attacks against American ships that might have set off a crisis. However, the submarine issue was brought to a head suddenly and dramatically when *U20,* Kapitänleutnant Walther Schwieger, without warning torpedoed the pride of the Cunard Line, the unarmed *Lusitania,* in the Irish Sea on 7th May 1915, killing 128 American citizens among many others.

It was impossible for Wilson to temporize, so violent was the reaction in the United States. Yet what could he do? It was evident after the first shock that a majority of Americans wanted their President to be firm and yet avoid war if possible. This, actually, was Wilson's own intention. In three notes between May and early July, Wilson eloquently appealed to the imperial German government to abandon what was obviously a campaign of sheer terror against *unarmed Allied passenger ships.* In the last note he warned that he would probably break diplomatic relations if the Germans did not abandon that campaign. To each of Wilson's pleas, the German foreign office replied by truculently refusing to admit the illegality of the destruction of *Lusitania.* The impasse was broken by a second incident that came hard on the heels of the *Lusitania* affair—the torpedoing without warning of the White Star liner, *Arabic,* on 19th August (see the previous chapter). Only when they saw that Wilson was on the brink did the Germans yield and promise not to sink unarmed Allied passenger liners without warning. Indeed, Wilson's firmness, and the lack of enough submarines to prosecute

Below: An election truck decorated with Wilson's claim for the trust of his country. In 1916 a wave of neutralist feeling swept the USA and persuaded Wilson to stand as a 'peace' candidate

a decisive underseas campaign, paid even larger dividends in the form of guarantees that the German navy would sink American ships only after making full provision for the safety of human life, and that compensation would be made for all ships and cargoes captured or destroyed.

The subsequent German-American *détente* (encouraged by a temporary abandonment of the submarine campaign in general) set off demands in the United States, primarily by southern cotton producers in deep depression on account of the closing of their central European markets, for action against the total Allied blockade as firm as that taken against the German submarine campaign. Bryan had resigned in the middle of the *Lusitania* crisis, because he feared that Wilson's notes might lead the Germans to declare war against the United States. The new secretary of state, Robert Lansing, did prepare a formidable indictment of the British maritime measure, and Wilson permitted it to go to London on 5th November. But the President had no intention of enforcing the note's demands until German-American differences were clarified.

On the face of it, American relations with Great Britain and Germany had reached

a state of tolerable equilibrium by the end of 1915. The Germans had quietly abandoned their submarine campaign in the North Atlantic, hence there were no incidents in that area to exacerbate German-American relations. For their part, the British had gone to extraordinary (and successful) lengths to support American cotton prices and to come to terms with other American producers who had been hard hit by the Allied blockade. But Wilson and his two principal diplomatic advisers, Colonel House and Lansing, were not reassured as they contemplated potential dangers in the months immediately ahead. The Allies were beginning to arm not only passenger liners but ordinary merchantmen as well, and, apparently, were ordering these ships to attack submarines upon sight. Second, reports from Berlin made it unmistakably clear that there had been only a respite in the submarine campaign, and that the Germans were preparing to use the arming of Allied ships as an excuse for an all-out campaign. So far *ad hoc* solutions had sufficed to preserve the peace, but it now seemed that events might develop which would remove all options. For example, a really ruthless submarine campaign might drive the United States,

willy-nilly, into war, without any other purpose than sheer defence of national rights.

Wilson and House pondered long about the situation in the hope of gaining some initiative and of giving some purpose to American belligerency if it had to come. Sir Edward Grey had said only two months before that his government might be willing to consider a negotiated settlement if the United States would promise to join a post-war league of nations and guarantee to help maintain future peace. Seizing the seeming opportunity offered by Grey's suggestion, Wilson sent House to London in late December 1915 with instructions to work for Anglo-American agreement to co-operate in a drive for peace under Wilson's auspices. If that *démarche* should fail on account of German obduracy, Wilson said, the United States would probably enter the war on the Allied side.

While House was in London opening negotiations, Lansing and Wilson launched their own campaign to get the United States off the submarine hook. The secretary of state, on 18th January 1916, urged the Allies to disarm their merchantmen if the Germans would agree to warn such vessels and evacuate their crews before

VOTE FOR WILSON AND MARSHALL SEABURY AND McCOMBS

WOMEN'S BUREAU
DEMOCRATIC NATIONAL COMMITTEE

FOR PRESIDENT

WOODROW WILSON

WHO BROKE THE MONEY TRUST

WHO KEEPS US OUT OF WAR?

WHO STANDS FOR THE 8 HOUR DAY?

WHO EXTENDED THE PARCEL POST?

WHO GAVE THE FARMER RURAL CREDITS?

VOTE FOR WILSON PEACE WITH HONOR

PROSPERITY PREPAREDNESS

sinking them. Lansing added that his government was contemplating treating armed merchantmen as warships, which would mean that they could not engage in commerce at American ports. The Germans, gleefully agreeing with the secretary of state, announced that submarines would sink all armed merchantmen without warning after 28th February.

Reaction in London to what was called Lansing's *modus vivendi* was so violent that it threatened to wreck House's negotiations. Wilson thereupon hastily withdrew the *modus vivendi*. This action in turn set off a panic in Congress that the United States would go to war to protect the right of citizens to travel on armed ships. Wilson beat back a congressional resolution warning Americans against travelling on armed ships, but he made it clear that only lightly-armed merchantmen would be permitted to use American ports, and, more important, that he did not intend to make a great issue with the German government over armed ships in any event.

There was considerable relief both on Capitol Hill and in Whitehall. In London, Sir Edward Grey and House initialled, on 22nd February 1916, what is known as the House-Grey Memorandum embodying Wilson's plan of mediation.

Colonel House returned to Washington on 5th March in high excitement to tell the President that the British and French were eager to move as rapidly as possible for peace under Wilson's aegis. While Wilson and House were in the midst of planning for the great venture, a German submarine torpedoed a French packet steamer, *Sussex,* in the English Channel on 24th March with heavy loss of life. Reports of ruthless attacks against unarmed merchantmen followed in rapid succession.

After much backing and filling, and mainly in order to pave the way for his mediation, Wilson sent an ultimatum to Berlin on 18th April warning that he would break relations with Germany if she did not agree hereafter to require her submarine commanders to observe the rules of visit and search before sinking all unarmed ships, whether passenger liners or merchantmen. The German admiralty lacked enough U-boats to justify the risk of war with the United States and European neutrals like Holland and Denmark. Consequently, the imperial chancellor, Theobald von Bethmann Hollweg, won the Kaiser's support for submission to Wilson's demand. However, while yielding the Germans reserved the 'right' to resume freedom of decision on the use of submarines if the American government failed to compel the Allies to respect international law in the conduct of their blockade.

The happy settlement of the *Sussex* crisis, coupled with intimations that the Germans were eager for peace talks, spurred Wilson to action to put the House-Grey Memorandum into operation. His first public move was to announce, in an address in Washington on 27th May, that the United States was prepared to abandon its traditional isolationism and join a post-war league of nations. Privately, through Colonel House, he exerted heavy pressure on Grey to put the memorandum's machinery into motion by signalling his government's readiness for Wilson's mediation. Grey responded evasively at first; but Wilson would not be diverted, and then Grey had to tell him frankly that neither the British nor the French governments would consent to peace talks at this time or in the foreseeable future.

Grey's refusal to execute the House-Grey Memorandum, a crushing blow to the President's hopes for an early peace in itself, combined with other developments to cause Wilson to effect what would turn out to be an almost radical change in his policies towards the European belligerents. First, the British government not only refused to relax its controls over American commerce, but, on the contrary, intensified its maritime and economic warfare in the spring and summer of 1916. In retrospect, the new British measures (including search and seizure of American mail on neutral ships and publication in the United States of a 'blacklist' of American firms still doing business with the Central powers) seem trivial when compared with policies in which the Washington administration had already acquiesced. However, Wilson and a majority of Americans resented the new measures as direct affronts to their national sovereignty. Second, the British army's severe repression of the Easter Rising in Dublin in April 1916 not only inflamed Irish Americans, but also caused a tremendous diminution in Great Britain's moral standing throughout the United States. Finally, the German-American *détente* following the *Sussex* crisis sent a wave of neutralism across the country, one so strong that it engulfed the Democratic national convention that re-nominated Wilson for the presidency.

These developments, of course, had their most important impact upon the man in the White House. They convinced him that the American people did not want to go to war over the alleged right of Americans to travel and work on belligerent ships. They forced Wilson to stand as the 'peace' candidate and to accuse his Republican opponent, Charles Evans Hughes, of wanting war. More important, they caused a very considerable hardening of Wilson's attitudes against the Allies, particularly the British. By the early autumn, Wilson believed that the Allies were fighting for victory and spoils, not for a just peace.

Wilson could do nothing, of course, while the presidential campaign was in progress. However, once the voters, on 7th November 1916, invested him with their sovereignty for another four years, Wilson was free to act. And action of some kind seemed to be imperative, for it was growing increasingly evident that both sides were preparing to use desperate measures to break the stalemate.

For the British, these would mean further intensification of economic warfare; for the Germans, it would mean revoking the *Sussex* pledge and launching a wholesale campaign against maritime commerce. The only way to peace and safety, Wilson concluded, was to bring the war to an end through his independent mediation.

Diverted briefly by domestic developments and Germany's own offer to negotiate, Wilson launched his peace bolt on 18th December 1916 by asking the belligerents to state the terms upon which they would be willing to end the fighting. The British and French were stunned and furious. But they were helpless to resist, so dependent had they become upon American credit and supplies for continuation of their war efforts. Then Lansing intervened. Committed emotionally to the Allied cause, he set out to sabotage the President's peace move by encouraging the British and French governments to state such terms as could be won only by a decisive military victory. The Germans, who very much wanted Wilson to force the Allies to the peace table but did not want him meddling once the conference had begun, returned an evasive reply.

Wilson was undisturbed. In mid-January 1917 he launched the second and decisive move in his campaign for peace—high-level, direct, and secret negotiations with the British and German governments to obtain their consent to his mediation. While waiting for their replies, the President went before the Senate on 22nd January to tell the world what kind of settlement he had in mind and the American people would support by membership in a league of nations. The peace to be made, Wilson said, had to be a peace of reconciliation, a 'peace without victory', for a victor's peace would leave 'a sting, a resentment, a bitter memory upon which terms of peace would rest, not permanently, but only as upon quicksand'.

For reasons that are still obscure, the new British cabinet headed by David Lloyd George sent word on 26th January to Wilson that it was prepared to accept the President's mediation. The Austro-Hungarians were desperately eager for peace. But on 31st January Wilson was informed of the German decision to adopt unrestricted submarine warfare. The stage was set for American participation.

America Declares War

It was Lloyd George who once remarked that Europe slithered into war in 1914, and this description, graphically accurate, applies equally well to the entrance of the United States into the World War in 1917. Prior to these separate if similar *dénouements*, neither the Europeans nor the Americans quite knew what they were doing. As previously stated, within weeks of the fateful date of the declaration of war on 6th April, President Woodrow Wilson was asking the belligerents for a peace without victory and hoping to achieve it through his efforts at mediation, while the United States remained outside the war as a neutral power. But then came a series of unexpected military, diplomatic, and political changes, none of them American in origin. Before long, Wilson, to use the description of Senator Henry Cabot Lodge, was 'in the grip of events'. On 6th April 1917 some of the election posters of November 1916 were still up on the billboards, and Americans could ponder the Democratic Party slogans which had helped re-elect the President: 'He Kept Us Out of War'; and 'War in the East, Peace in the West, Thank God for Wilson'. They were not, however, angry with Wilson, for they too had reacted to unforeseen events.

What were these events of early 1917 which moved the President and people? It is easy now to see that, given what had gone before, in January 1917 it would take only a few more blows from the German government to make America abandon her neutrality. Given that government's almost complete lack of understanding of the sensitivities of the American government and people, the wonder is that neutrality lasted as long as it did, that German blunders did not come sooner. It is also curious that Wilson and the American people believed in January 1917 that they still possessed freedom of manoeuvre. The President early that month told his confidant Colonel House 'There will be no war'.

On 19th January 1917 the German government thoughtfully told Ambassador Johann von Bernstorff about the decision to resume unrestricted submarine warfare on 1st February but Bernstorff was to inform the American government, and duly did so, only on 31st January, at 4 pm. It was a crude beginning, this eight hours' notice. Bernstorff had done his best to prevent this stupidity, this tactic of loosing the submarines, which he knew would drive the Americans into war. It was not only the trans-Atlantic munitions trade, or the export of American food (harvests had been poor in 1916), that the Germans were seeking to prevent; they wanted to strangle British economic life by cutting off all imports. They did not have to use so thorough a submarine blockade, which would inevitably affront the Americans, Bernstorff thought. He had cabled his views,

Wild enthusiasm and waving flags on Broadway—America has entered the war

but the German leaders paid no attention.

Bernstorff meanwhile had lowered his stock with the American government and public, and with his own government (he deeply offended the Kaiser), by allowing a peccadillo to get into public print. On a vacation in the Adirondacks with a lady who often entertained him, he posed in a bathing suit for a photograph, with his arms intimately encircling two ladies similarly attired. At the very time when he needed whatever personal influence and dignity he could muster, this photograph found its way into the hands of the Russian ambassador who passed it to the newspapers. Americans snickered at the Bathing Beauty Scandal. Bernstorff was a generally competent diplomat to whom both the American and German governments should have listened. Instead this 'good German' found himself ignored on public matters and laughed at over private ones. 'I am not surprised,' he said upon the break of diplomatic relations when he received his passports. 'My government will not be surprised either. The people in Berlin knew what was bound to happen if they took the action they have taken. There was nothing else left for the United States to do.' In despair he told a press conference that he was through with politics.

After the formal break, two events followed which together pushed the country into war. The first was a clear-cut case of a German submarine sinking a passenger vessel with American citizens aboard. Wilson on 3rd February, when he informed Congress that he was breaking relations, had added that 'I refuse to believe that it is the intention of the German authorities to do in fact what they have warned us they will feel at liberty to do. . . . Only actual overt acts on their part can make me believe it even now'. For two weeks after resumption of unrestricted submarine warfare no incident occurred, no open violation of what Americans liked to believe was one of their principal neutral rights. There was no paralysis of shipping during the period, as American tonnage clearing United States ports dropped only from 1,019,396 in January to 847,786 in February. The day the fatal vessel, the 18,000-ton British liner *Laconia*, sailed from New York harbour, sixty-six ships of all nationalities were in the roadstead, loaded or loading for ports in the zone of war. Wilson spoke again to Congress on 26th February, reporting that 'The overt act which I have ventured to hope the German commanders would in fact avoid has not occurred'. That very moment, however, news of the sinking of the *Laconia* the day before was being flashed to Washington. It was whispered around the House chamber before the President finished his speech, and printed in the country's newspapers the next day.

Three Americans, including two women, had lost their lives. The deaths of the women were not pretty to contemplate: a torpedoing at night, a lifeboat half stove-in as it swung down over the careening hull, this fragile craft itself slowly sinking while it wallowed off into the darkness, Mrs Albert H.Hoy and her daughter Elizabeth standing waist deep in icy water throughout the long night.

This was interpreted as an open challenge, by the German government which authorized it, and by the American government and people who had brought themselves into a frame of mind to oppose it.

The Zimmermann telegram

The second precipitating event came almost immediately when American newspapers on 1st March published the Zimmermann telegram. The *Laconia* disaster had proved that the Germans held no regard for international law and human rights. The Zimmermann telegram showed that they were guilty not merely of legal and moral turpitude but were enemies of the United States, willing to endanger the nation's very existence. In the annals of international stupidity during the 20th century, or any other century, this famous telegram hardly has an equal. It was a German proposal of an alliance to the government of Mexico (an alliance which was possibly to include the Japanese government as well). The Mexicans were to attack the United States during the hostilities now deemed imminent, in exchange for which the Germans promised a return of the 'lost territories' of the Mexican War of 1846-48: Texas, New Mexico, Arizona. The genesis of the proposal is now quite clear. The Americans had been giving Mexico much trouble in the past few years, even to the extent of sending in a punitive military expedition in 1916 under command of General Pershing. The Mexican regime of General Venustiano ('Don Venus') Carranza began to take interest in Mexican-German co-operation, and Don Venus in November made a suggestion, going so far as to offer submarine bases. An assistant in the German foreign office, one Kemnitz, turned the proposal into a project for an alliance. It was so preposterous a project that the German foreign secretary, Zimmermann, should have forgotten it. Instead he picked it up as a great idea.

Zimmermann sent his telegram to Mexico by several means, one of which was through the American embassy in Berlin and thence from Washington to Mexico City by Western Union. Ambassador Gerard transmitted this German message, in its original German code, as part of an arrangement which Colonel House had made, with Wilson's permission, for cable transmission of German messages pertaining to mediation. Ambassador Bernstorff had promised to use the arrangement only for peaceful purposes, but Zimmermann was not put off by that engagement.

The British government intercepted and decoded all three of Zimmermann's transmissions. Under the leadership of Admiral Sir William Reginald Hall, the Admiralty early in the war had set up a code and cipher-cracking operation, which triumphed with the deciphering of Zimmermann's idiotic telegram. Not wishing to show his knowledge of the German code,

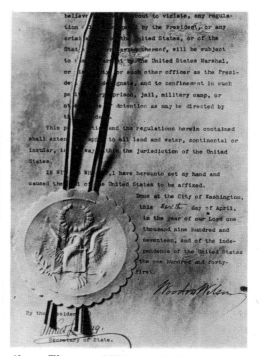

Above: The text of Wilson's declaration of war. Right: Bernstorff, the ladies' man— a diplomat discomfited by scandal

Hall at first was in a quandary about publishing, but ingenuity triumphed. One of his agents in Mexico City procured from the Mexican telegraph office a copy of the still-encoded telegram which Bernstorff had obtained from the American State Department and relayed from Washington. It contained certain small differences from the other intercepts, and upon publication the impression prevailed that someone had stolen or sold a decoded copy of the telegram, getting it from the German legation in Mexico City. The Germans reassured Hall that they were without suspicion by engaging in a lively inquiry with Eckhardt, the German minister in Mexico City, asking how many copies of the decode Eckhardt had made and who had handled them, using of course the same code which Hall had cracked. Hall found it amusing to read that Eckhardt tried to pass the blame off on to Bernstorff in Washington.

No denial

Even after the cat was out of the bag, the telegram published in every American newspaper, it was still possible for Zimmermann in Berlin to quiet the uproar, or at the very least to make the Americans disclose how they obtained the telegram, by baldly denying that he had sent it. President Wilson himself, the author in 1918 of 'open diplomacy', once in a confidential conversation with Colonel House said, admittedly for House's ears only (and, as it turned out, for House's diary), that a man was justified in lying for two purposes, to protect the honour of a lady and to preserve secrets of state. Had Zimmermann but known it, he could have cited the President in support of a diplomatic denial. Secretary Lansing in Washington was certain that Zimmermann would lie his way out, and was incredulous to learn that the German foreign secretary almost at once admitted authorship of the telegram in a burst of truthfulness which was as naïve as the composition which inspired it.

What could the American government do after the publication of the telegram on 1st March? If Wilson does not go to war now, Theodore Roosevelt wrote to Lodge, 'I shall skin him alive'. The Prussian Invasion Plot, as the newspapers labelled the telegram, was transparently clear. Newspapers in the hitherto isolationist Middle West acknowledged the end of neutrality. The Chicago *Tribune* warned its readers to realize now, 'without delay, that Germany recognizes us an enemy', and that the country no longer could hope to keep out of 'active participation in the present conflict'. The Cleveland *Plain Dealer* said there was 'neither virtue nor dignity' in refusing to fight now. The Oshkosh (Wisconsin) *Northwestern*, an authentic voice from the Middle West, said that the telegram had turned pacifists, critics, and carpers into patriots overnight. Zimmermann, as Mrs Tuchman has written, 'shot an arrow in the air and brought down neutrality like a dead duck'.

The rest was anticlimax. The first Russian Revolution of March 1917 forced the abdication of the Tsar and the proclamation of a republic, and removed an embarrassing despotism from the ranks of the Allies, making it easier to say that the Allies were Democracy fighting the Central powers who represented Autocracy. About the same time, U-boats sank four American ships. The presidential decision to arm merchant ships, taken in mid-March, constituting a sort of armed neutrality, had no discernible effect on German policy. The President called a special session of Congress. On the evening of 2nd April 1917, Wilson went before both Houses, duly assembled in the Capitol building in Washington, and as the lights gleamed in the crowded chamber he asked his countrymen for what they were ready to give him. Many Senators had brought small American flags to the House chamber where the President spoke; during the speech they clapped their hands and waved their flags in assent.

British postcard. For Great Britain, America's declaration promised men—and hope

"We are coming, brothers, coming, A hundred thousand strong!"

The New Military Balance

On 6th April 1917 the United States entered the First World War. At the beginning of June General John J.Pershing, the commander-in-chief of the American Expeditionary Force arrived in England for a four-day visit, and then went on to France to began organizing his command. His reception by the British and French was warm to the point of hysteria: the King welcomed him, the crowds cheered and threw roses. The illustrated magazine *The London Graphic* caught the mood and the style of the time by surrounding a photograph of Pershing and his officers with a tabernacle in classical style, in which a luscious symbolic figure of a woman held a laurel wreath over Pershing's head; the caption read: 'Now is the winter of our discontent made glorious summer by this sun of (New) York.' (In fact, Pershing had been born in Missouri.)

The hopes, the great expectations, that were aroused in the British and French peoples by American entry into the war were understandable. The spring and early summer of 1917 saw Allied fortunes at their lowest ebb. The year 1916 had ended with apparently nothing to show for colossal losses but small territorial gains on the Somme and the preservation of Verdun. The expulsion of the Germans from French soil seemed as difficult and as far off as ever. The very real and heavy damage done to German power by the Allied offensives in the late summer and autumn of 1916 was hidden from view.

The third year of the war now unfolded for the Allies a prospect of catastrophe. On 1st February 1917 the Germans began unrestricted submarine warfare. The results of the first three months fully justified German calculations that before the end of the year Great Britain would be unable to prosecute the war because of lack of shipping to transport food, raw materials, and troops: the tonnage sunk rose from 470,000 in February to 837,000 in April. Admiral Jellicoe, the British first sea lord, believed that unless an answer to the submarine could be found—and in his estimation, none was in sight—the war was certainly lost. In March revolution exploded in Tsarist Russia and the Tsar Nicholas II abdicated. Although the Russian army had never fulfilled the hopes of 1914 that it would prove an irresistible steam-roller, it had nevertheless heavily engaged Germany's Austrian ally and brought her to the point of exhaustion, and had also drawn German resources away

Left: US forces arrive in England

from the Western Front. In 1916 General Alexey Brusilov's Offensive had inflicted a smashing defeat in the east on the Central powers. Now Russia was paralysed by revolution, no man could say what help she would bring.

Finally, at the end of April and the beginning of May 1917, the French army, under a new commander-in-chief, General Robert Nivelle, was crushingly, appallingly, repulsed in a general offensive on the Western Front which Nivelle had promised would lead to a swift breakthrough and a rapid, and victorious, end to the war. In the aftermath of this shattering disappointment, all the accumulated war-weariness and exhaustion of the French nation exploded in widespread army mutinies and civil disorders. It was no wonder that the Allied leaders and peoples alike greeted the belligerency of the richest, most industrially powerful nation in the world, with all its unblooded manpower, with somewhat hysterical relief. America brought on to the Allied side a population of 93,400,000 and a steel production of 45,060,607 tons. The human resources went far to make up for the 180 million Russians now perhaps lost to the Allied cause. The industrial power was overwhelming; American steel production alone was nearly three times as great as that of Germany and Austria together. However, all this was only *potential*. How long would it be before American resources, human and industrial, were translated into vast, superbly-equipped armies on the Western Front able to crush down the exhausted and outmatched Germans? In view of the German submarine successes and the manifest unsteadiness of the French army and nation, would there even *be* a Western Front by the time the Americans had deployed their power?

Whatever its enormous long-term importance in 20th-century history, the American entry into the First World War in April 1917 in fact was in itself of far smaller strategic significance at the time than the cheering British and French crowds supposed. There was no progressive transformation of the war—no massive rescue operation. On the other hand, it is certain that without America, the Allies would have lost the war. The clue to this apparent paradox lies in the fact that American help *before* her entry into the war was more vital than many recognize; and American help *after* her entry rather less vital, at least for some fifteen months or so.

The German and Austrian war effort was

Top: Tank Corps recruiting poster. At first the Americans tried to equip military units before sending them to France.
Above: Appeal for the war loan

entirely based on their own industries and technological skill. By the spring of 1915, after a temporary shortage of munitions, Germany had converted her vast chemical industry and her varied and highly modern engineering industries to the production of explosives, propellants, fuses, shells, ammunition, and weapons. Her machine-tool industry—the most modern and inventive in the world except for that of America—had no difficulty in equipping new munitions plants.

Great Britain and France, in sharp contrast, found when they tackled the problem of a massive expansion of war production that their industrial resources were largely out-of-date in equipment and techniques—and that they even lacked completely a whole range of the most modern kinds of industries. Thus, Great Britain and France before the war had been almost entirely dependent on Germany for chemical products, such as dyes, drugs, and photographic processing materials. It was plant that made dyes and drugs that could also easily make explosives. Great Britain had to create a chemical industry from scratch, based on seized German patents. While it was being built up, there was a bottleneck at the very base of shell manufacture—the propellant and the explosive.

British manufacturing industry was still largely mid-Victorian in its types of product, its methods of production, its skills and techniques. Mass-production plant, with lines of automatic or semi-automatic machines, producing all kinds of precision light-engineering work, was hardly known. Before 1914 Great Britain was dependent mostly on Germany, partly on America, for almost all the sophisticated products of the second phase of the industrial revolution—ball-bearings, magnetoes, sparking plugs, cameras, optical goods.

Great Britain therefore lacked both the general and the particular industries to sustain a modern war. Nor could her machine-tool industry equip the vast new factories that had to be created. Machine-tools were—and are—the basic industry of modern technological growth; they are the machines which make machines. The British machine-tool industry was also essentially mid-Victorian; it was small-scale, it made a limited range of tools to order by almost craft methods in small workshops. For the 'modern' kind of automatic or semi-automatic machine for a production-line, it contented itself in peacetime by acting as a distribution agent for American and German imports.

France was in no better case. Thus, American resources and know-how were, from the end of 1914, absolutely essential to the survival of the Allies. It was to America—and to a lesser extent to Sweden and Switzerland—that they looked to supply the specialized sophisticated products that they had imported from Germany. It was on American industry that Great Britain especially depended for shells and other munitions during 1915 and 1916, while Great Britain was still painfully creating her chemical and munitions industries. Even in 1915 a third of all shells issued to the British army were made in North America. In 1916 the debut of the mass British armies in battle was only made possible by shells from America and Canada. As the history of the ministry of munitions expressed it: 'During the early part of 1915, in fact, overseas contractors assumed a place of utmost importance, since upon them the War Office was forced to depend for the bulk of the shell supplies required for the 1916 campaign.'

The Allies were just as dependent on America for their longer-term needs in constructing their own munitions industries. The essential basis of the whole vast programme of national munitions factories, on which Lloyd George's fame as minister of munitions hangs, was the American machine-tool and the American methods and organization it made possible. In 1916, when Great Britain's new war industries were at last getting into full production, *The Times* wrote: 'One of the new factories has grown up on a spot which last November was green fields. Now there are 25 acres covered with buildings packed with machinery. Most of the machines are of American make, and some are marvels of ingenuity.'

The extent of Allied dependence on American technology, and also of their purchases (at the cost of their accumulated overseas investments) is illustrated by the increase in production of certain American industries *before* America began her own war-production programme. Between 1914 and 1917, American exports of iron, steel, and their products to Europe rose four-fold; American explosives production grew ten times between 1913 and 1917. Bernard Baruch, chairman of the US war industries board, wrote: 'Cincinnati is the greatest machine tool manufacturing center in the world. In 1913 the total value of the annual product of the United States was about $50,000,000. During the war period preceding our entrance, our productive capacity was more than doubled, but the expansion took place largely in the output of small and medium-sized machines — machines for the production of shells, rifles, fuses etc.'

It is therefore beyond question that without access to American resources, Great Britain and France would have lacked the material to sustain the war while their own industries were being created, and could not have created the industries at all. This indeed was acknowledged by the

Above left: 'This destroyer is needed to sink Hun submarines' reads the sign on the right. The destroyer was built in seventeen days. Above right: The American commanders of the army and the navy, General Pershing (on the left) and Admiral Sims (on the right)

Above: The first American prisoners to fall into German hands. Below: Loading a troopship for France. As the soldiers, fresh recruits for slaughter, tramp across the dock, girls in Red Cross uniform give each a last gift from the American people and wish them good luck

British history of the ministry of munitions: 'Great Britain was practically dependent upon the United States of America for material for propellant manufacture, for a large proportion of her explosives material. She depended to a considerable extent upon the United States for shell steel and other steel . . . for machine tools.'

Thus America had proved a decisive influence on the course of the First World War long before her own entry into it.

However, by April 1917 the creation of the Allied—especially the British—war industries had been largely completed. Great Britain was now able to supply munitions freely to France and Italy. There was no longer so desperate or so large a need for American shells or machine-tools. The American declaration of war was therefore largely irrelevant and unimportant where Allied war production was concerned. Indeed, the flow of help was reversed once the American armies began to build up in France; it was France and Great Britain who largely equipped the American armies, as they were formed in France. The Americans made the capital mistake of deciding to produce their own designs of artillery pieces and aircraft, instead of adopting French or British designs for which many of their own factories were already producing ammunition or parts. The inevitable teething troubles of new designs were such that the American army received American guns just about in time to fire a salute in celebration of the armistice in November 1918. Not only this, but acute shortage of shipping space made it evidently more sensible to fill ships with men rather than guns, and then equip the men in Europe. So in the event the AEF was given French 75's for its field artillery, French 155-mm guns and howitzers for its medium artillery, and mostly British mortars. The British also supplied machine-guns, steel helmets, and even uniforms. The air component of the United States was equipped with French aircraft.

Obviously the prime fact about American *belligerency*, as opposed to mere industrial availability, was that United States armed forces would henceforth take part in the war. This indeed was the hope that inspired the civilian cheers, when the 1st Division, AEF, landed in France at the end of June 1917. These were the healthy men, from a nation twice as numerous as the British, or the French, who would take over the weight of the fighting from the tired, battle-shaken survivors of three terrible campaigns. Unfortunately, the American declaration of war was by no means followed by a breakneck expansion of the army and its swift deployment in France, such as the British had achieved in 1914-15. The 1st Division was not followed by the 2nd until September; by 31st October 1917

the AEF numbered only 6,064 officers and 80,969 men. Lloyd George has pointed out in his memoirs the poorness of the American performance compared with the British in creating an army: '. . . at the end of six months (after the outbreak of war) the British Expeditionary Force on the Western Front numbered 354,750. The First American Division was put into a quiet sector of the French front on 21st October 1917— nearly seven months after the severance of diplomatic relations with Germany. The tide of American forces in France . . . mounted only in dribbling fashion during these early months. By the end of October it was 87,000; by the end of November, 126,000; and at the beginning of 1918, 175,000. That was nine months after the entry of America into the war. At that stage in our own war effort we had already thrown 659,104 into the various war theatres.'

Thus the United States exerted no military effect at all on the critical year of 1917, when Russia subsided more and more from the war, when Pétain strove to quell the mutinies in the French army and keep it together until such time as the Americans should arrive in force, when the Italians suffered a catastrophic defeat at Caporetto, when the *only* Allied army still capable of an offensive—the British— slogged doggedly forward towards Passchendaele. And, the Germans hoped and expected, 1917 was to be the decisive and final year of the war. For it was their calculation that the American army, as a great force, would never arrive because the U-boats would have destroyed the shipping that might have carried it across the Atlantic; if in fact the war itself had not been ended by the U-boat blockade before the Americans were ready to cross. In 1917 the Americans provided hope, little else to the Allies.

The Americans are not to be entirely blamed for the extreme slowness of their military mobilization. The peacetime American army had been even smaller than the British, and far less prepared for modern war. Whereas the British had at least trained and prepared an expeditionary force of six divisions for a European campaign, and completed all the staff studies about organization and methods necessary for subsequent expansion, the Americans started absolutely from scratch in every way. For example, the size, organization, and ancillary services of the basic infantry division had to be worked out and decided upon, as well as of corps and armies. In peacetime the United States army had numbered 190,000 officers and men spread in small detachments across the face of America and her own overseas dependencies. The very size of America posed its own problems, for before troops

could go aboard the troopships, they had to be concentrated and accommodated near the eastern seaboard. This meant a vast programme of camp construction, on top of other programmes for training camps and training facilities. In France itself port facilities had to be enormously extended, and lines of communication built up from the ports allotted to the Americans to their designated sector in the right-centre of the Allied line, in the Argonne. This entailed major construction work to increase the carrying capacity of the rail links. Colossal supply depots had to be constructed and filled in France. The British had found that supporting an army in another country over twenty-two miles of sea involved enormous rearward services; America had to make war across 3,000 miles of sea. The major bottleneck however was shipping; both for troops and cargoes. The United States mercantile marine had nothing like enough ships available to move the American army across the Atlantic.

Finally, there was a fundamental difference of views between Pershing on the one hand and Haig and Pétain on the other about the employment of American troops. Haig and Pétain at the beginning of 1918 were keenly aware that their armies were seriously under strength and without hope of adequate national reinforcements. They wanted American infantry to fill out their own divisions; they wanted help quickly. Pershing on the other hand (and his government) was resolved to build up

Industry steps up production for America's participation in the war—war workers making steel helmets for doughboys

a completely independent, self-contained American army in France, with its own divisions, corps, and armies. He was not prepared to see Americans swallowed up in Allied formations; he was prepared to wait, for months if need be, until all the artillery and supply services, the higher headquarters and staffs, necessary for an independent force were organized, trained, and equipped. Thus it was that when on 21st March 1918, the Germans launched the first and greatest of a series of titanic offensives on the Western Front, there was only one American division actually in the overstretched and outnumbered Allied line and three divisions in training areas.

The rate of the American build-up in France had been crucial to the calculations of the German high command in deciding on great offensives in the west in the spring of 1918. By November, 1917, when the German decision was taken, unrestricted U-boat warfare had failed in its object of knocking Great Britain out of the war; it had been beaten by the convoy system. Therefore, the Germans had to reckon on the entry into battle, sooner or later, of a mass and entirely fresh American army: certain defeat for Germany and her allies. Therefore, the war must be decided before that mass army arrived. Ludendorff told his colleagues: 'Our general situation requires that we should strike at the earliest moment, if possible at the end of February or beginning of March, before the Americans can throw strong forces into the scale.' In other words, since Russia had finally been knocked out of the war by the Treaty of Brest-Litovsk, the bulk of German strength could be concentrated on France and Great Britain before they could be rescued by their second great ally.

The crisis on the Western Front lasted from 21st March to 18th July, as the German onslaughts fell successively on different parts on the Allied front. Twice the British faced real danger of being driven into the Channel; once there was an acute risk of the French and British being separated; three times the French front was temporarily smashed and the French capital exposed again to possible occupation. In this largest, most violent, and most decisive campaign of the war, the American army played little part. Some units took part in the defence of the Amiens sector after 28th March; the 1st Division carried out a spirited counterattack at Cantigny, near Montdidier, on 28th May; in June the 2nd Division helped the French block the German drive across the Marne, and launched a successful counterattack which led to the recapture of Belleau Wood; units of the 3rd and 42nd Divisions fought defensively in the sector of Château-Thierry. These were very welcome, but hardly decisive contributions to a campaign against 192 German divisions.

What was far more important—indeed decisive—in terms of the issue of the war was the effect of the German offensive on the speed of the American build-up. A week after the Germans attacked on the Somme, on 28th March 1918, Pershing abandoned his somewhat deliberate and pedantic attempt to create an independent American army before entering the conflict, and offered Pétain as a temporary expedient all the troops he had, to use as Pétain wished. So the individual American units saw action under French or British corps and army command, not American. This immediate gesture was one sign of the American realization that the French and British might not last long enough to be rescued; that there was a need for desperate haste in getting American troops over to France and into battle. At the same time, Pershing still remained anxious that his Allies should not rob him of his own independent army by the feeding of Americans into their own divisions. It was only after long arguments between the Allied and American governments and commands, that it was finally agreed, at the beginning of June, that shipping space should be saved by bringing over men—infantry mostly—instead of complete divisions with all their space-occupying equipment. 170,000 combat troops were to come in June and 140,000 in July out of some 250,000 men ready to be transported in each of the two months. New divisions would be formed and equipped in France. These shipments of men were made possible by the British mercantile marine, made available as part of the bargain by the British government by cutting down British imports.

Whereas in March 84,000 Americans had crossed the Atlantic, 118,500 crossed in April, 246,000 in May, 278,800 in June, and 306,703 in July—nearly half of them in British ships. These figures, far higher than the German command had thought possible, spelt defeat for Germany.

On 15th-17th July the last phase of the great German 1918 offensive petered out in failure. On 18th July the French launched a surprise attack, led by massed tanks, from the Forest of Villers-Cotterêts. The attacking troops included two American divisions, each with a strength of 27,000 men, three times as large as a French or German division. The French attack marked the turn of the campaign; from then to the end of the war the Germans were to fight on the defensive.

It was now—and at very long last—that the American military presence in the war proved decisive. The great battles of March to July 1918, which the Allies had won virtually without American help, had left the British, French, and German armies all exhausted, with scant reserves and little hope of reinforcement from the homeland. For the original combatants of the war nothing remained but to break up divisions—to see their armies gradually decrease. A German battalion now numbered on average 660 men. The German gamble on victory had failed: neither the German army nor the German people (hungry, miserable, and despairing after years of blockade) had any further hopes to clutch at. In August, when the British offensive on the Somme (some American units took part), confirmed that the Allies now possessed the initiative, and confirmed also that the morale and discipline of the German army was beginning to disintegrate, there were nearly 1,500,000 Americans in France. The only German reservoir of fresh manpower lay in the 300,000 youths of the 1919 class called up in June. Whereas Allied leaders were planning for a campaign in 1919, whose principal weight was to be borne by a hundred American divisions, for Germany's leaders another year of battle was absolutely unthinkable.

Thus it was that even in the last months of the war, it was the American military *potential*, advertised by their limited offen-

Big guns under construction. But the army only received the new American guns just before the armistice in November 1918

sives at St Mihiel and in the Argonne, rather than the actual fighting achievements of American troops, that affected the outcome of the Great War in 1918. In point of fact, the brunt of the fighting from July to November 1918 was borne by the tired but still dogged British, who took 188,700 prisoners as against 196,000 taken by the French, Belgians, and Americans together.

The American role in the First World War was therefore decisive: decisive industrially between 1914 and 1917, decisive in terms of military potential from midsummer 1918 onwards. It illustrated two facts of enormous importance to the future balance of power in Europe: that Germany was militarily the equal of the British and French empires together; and that Great Britain, the 19th-century 'work-shop of the world', was no longer a first-rank industrial and technological power, no longer able to defend herself and her empire out of her own resources.

5 THE RUSSIAN REVOLUTION

The Last Days of the Tsar

The Russia which entered the First World War in 1914 was a strange mixture of contradictions. The contemporary Western picture was of the 'steamroller', of the mass of Russian peasants, dragged from the ignorance and poverty of backward agrarian conditions to form the six million strong army which Russia was able to mobilize by the first winter of the war. These peasants were both Russia's strength and her fatal weakness.

Less known to the outside world was the new industrial and urban Russia which had grown fast in the last twenty or thirty years before the war, a Russia of coal, steel, and railways, of industrialists and financiers, of lawyers, doctors, and professors, and from 1905, of political parties, professional associations, and even trade unions. Tsarist Russia did not, as is often thought, 'decay' or 'decline': on the contrary, in its last years, it expanded and blossomed in a variety of conflicting forms which imposed an ultimately fatal strain on its structure.

The new Russia could find no place in traditional Tsarist society. Already in 1905 the peasants, urban workers, professional intelligentsia, and even part of the nobility, in uncertain alliance, had shaken the autocracy and compelled it to concede the establishment of a national parliament, the Duma. In theory, this new body represented, however imperfectly, all classes of the nation, but gave the predominant voice to landowners and the wealthier urban elements. The aim of its establishment was to provide a forum in which the government could work with the more influential sections of Russian society to

carry out the reforms which, during the 1905 revolution, were widely felt to be necessary. But as the revolution faded into the past the sense of urgency excited by this task weakened, and the old habits of autocracy reasserted themselves, strengthened by the fear of renewed social violence, by the memory of the Moscow barricades and of rural arson, lynchings, and murders. On the right wing of the Duma, and in the upper house, the State Council, strong groups emerged, on which the government came increasingly to rely for its majority, groups who were concerned to emasculate or indefinitely delay reforms which they feared might open the flood-gates of revolution. This process led among the intelligentsia and on the left wing of the Duma to growing disillusionment with political action and to a helpless and even irresponsible bitterness.

This was the world in which the legend of the 'dark forces' was born. A succession of incompetent or even shady ministers were appointed on the strength of the advice of the 'simple peasant', the self-styled monk, Grigory Rasputin. Seemingly able to cure the congenital haemophilia of the Romanoff heir, the Tsarevich Alexey, and holding an almost hypnotic power over the decadent personalities of the imperial circle, the idea gradually took form, and became widely accepted, that he and 'the German woman' (the Empress, who was by origin a minor German princess) formed the centre of a court clique which was opposed to the war and was even passing secrets to the Germans.

Prince Yusupov, a wealthy young nobleman, who initiated the conspiracy which was to result in Rasputin's murder, described his personal sentiments thus '. . . There was no hope that the Emperor and Empress would understand the

whole truth about Rasputin and dismiss him. What way remained, therefore, to save the Tsar and Russia from that evil genius? Inevitably the thought would run through one's mind: there is only one way —to destroy that criminal "holy man".'

The Tsar overthrown

The murder of Rasputin did nothing to restore the fortunes of the monarchy or increase popular respect for the Tsar. If the removal of her 'friend' lessened the influence of the Tsarina on the nation's affairs, Nicholas showed no inclination to listen to the advice of the more liberal-minded of his ministers; on the contrary, he turned his back on both the government and the Duma and relied on his own imagined authority, exercised primarily through his minister of the interior, Protopopov, who dominated the administration.

Throughout January 1917 the storm of discontent gathered as the war continued to take its toll on the economy. Food shortages and a rapidly rising cost of living resulted in widespread unrest among the industrial workers, particularly in Petrograd and Moscow. There were as many strikes in the first six weeks of 1917 as in the whole of the previous year. But discontent with the monarchy and the conduct of affairs extended far beyond the working-class and the peasantry, into the ranks of the middle class, the progressive deputies to the Duma, the military leaders, and even the Grand Dukes themselves.

In January the Grand Duke Alexander wrote to Nicholas to persuade him to set up a government capable of inspiring confidence in the people. 'The Tsar alone cannot govern a country like Russia', he wrote. Rodzyanko, the chairman of the Duma, warned the Tsar on 20th January that

The Russian Revolution

'very serious outbreaks' were to be expected. Russia wanted a change of government because, he said, 'there is not one honest man left in your entourage; all the decent people have either been dismissed or have left'. But such warnings had no effect on the obstinate and autocratic Tsar. His only reaction to the increasing threat of trouble in the capital was, on 19th February, to place the city under the command of General Khabalov, who was made directly responsible to the Tsar alone for the maintenance of order. The Petrograd garrison was reinforced and equipped with artillery and machine guns. For the first fortnight of February an uneasy peace reigned in the capital; the police and the military appeared to have the situation in hand.

But Rodzyanko knew that the situation was deteriorating, and on 23rd February he told the Tsar he thought a revolution was possible. Nicholas brushed the warning aside and told Rodzyanko that, if the deputies did not watch their words, the Duma would be dissolved. It met, nevertheless, in the Tauride Palace on 27th February, and the government, expecting trouble during the session, stiffened the censorship, arrested all potential troublemakers and braced itself against the popular wrath. Tension in the capital rose. A week later, on 7th March, the Tsar decided to leave Petrograd for the army GHQ in Mogilev.

Next day disorders broke out in the capital which were to lead only a week later to the overthrow of the monarchy. Apparently without any central direction, and initially without any clear political aims, the workers of several large factories in Petrograd came out on strike. Their action was mainly a protest at the breakdown in food supplies, but the nervous reaction of the authorities soon turned industrial and economic unrest into political protest.

Troops were sent immediately to back up the police in the working-class districts of the city, with the result that next day, 9th March, the disturbances spread to the whole city, and protests against the continuation of the war were added to the demand for bread. The central Nevsky Prospect became a mass of marching people, some of whom were now shouting 'Down with the autocracy!'. By the third day, a Saturday, 10th March, a quarter of a million workers were on strike, the city's transport was at a standstill, and the authorities were desperate.

But for Nicholas the situation presented no problem. From the remoteness of Mogilev he cabled Khabalov: 'I order that the disorders in the capital shall be ended tomorrow; they are quite inadmissible at this grave moment of war with Ger-

many and Austria'. But Khabalov, faced with the whole population in revolt, was no longer in a position to carry out his monarch's orders.

It was not that he had scruples about using force to suppress the revolt. The fact was that he could no longer be sure he had the necessary force at his disposal, and that what he had was rapidly slipping out of his control. The normally trustworthy and brutal Cossacks he had sent into action against the crowds had simply been lost among the demonstrators. The police had started to fire on the crowds, only to incense them still further and make them bolder in their resistance to brutality. The wave of arrests had continued, but the protest movement had no obvious outstanding leaders, and Khabalov could not arrest the whole population.

An affair of the capital

What ultimately decided the outcome of the revolt and the collapse of the regime, however, was the defection of the soldiery to the side of the revolution. It began with isolated cases of 'fraternization' between soldiers and demonstrators on the Sunday of 11th March and then spread like wildfire throughout the Petrograd garrison, so that by the Monday evening the whole force of 150,000 men had disintegrated. And when, in despair, Khabalov formed a special detachment of a thousand picked men and sent them into action, they too disappeared among the crowds. Whole regiments revolted, shot their officers, and threw in their lot with the working people, taking their weapons with them. On the Monday evening the workers seized the arsenal, where they found 40,000 rifles which were quickly distributed round the city.

The government was helpless. A decision to have Khabalov declare a state of siege was rendered ineffective by the fact that the authorities no longer controlled a printing press on which the declaration could be produced. The Duma was equally incapable of taking effective action. When Rodzyanko, its chairman, sent the Tsar a message saying that the fate of both the country and the monarchy was in the balance, and that urgent steps must be taken, Nicholas replied on 11th March with an order dissolving the Duma. Though it feared to defy the Tsar outright, the Duma remained in informal session and on 12th March elected a 'Provisional Committee' of twelve members, including representatives of the Progressive Bloc, with Alexander Kerensky, the Socialist Revolutionary, and Chkheidze, the Social Democrat. The Committee assumed the impossible task of 'restoring order'.

On the same day and in the same place — the Tauride Palace — another new body

came into existence. It was the Petrograd Soviet (Council) of Workers' and Soldiers' Deputies, representing in a rough and ready way the interests of the rebelling factory workers, soldiers, and 'democratic and socialist parties and groups'. Such real power as could be said to exist in the capital — and in the country as a whole — was now vested in these two *ad hoc* bodies; the central government and the administration of the country had already collapsed. On the morning of Tuesday, 13th March, the Soviet issued a news sheet — *Izvestya* (News) — bearing a proclamation announcing its existence and calling on the people everywhere to take the conduct of affairs into their own hands. 'We shall fight to wipe out the old system completely and to summon a constituent assembly elected on the basis of universal, equal, secret, and direct suffrage.'

Rodzyanko kept the Tsar informed of the disastrous course events had taken, urging him first to institute reforms and then, when the situation worsened, to abdicate in the interests of the monarchy as an institution. Isolated and deprived of friends and supporters, Nicholas made his decision with surprising speed and lack of emotion. He left Mogilev to return to his capital on 13th March, but was diverted by the revolutionaries to Pskov. There, still in his royal train, on 15th March, he signed a document abdicating the throne in favour of his son Alexey and nominating his brother, the Grand Duke Michael, as regent. But before the two delegates from the Duma could reach Pskov Nicholas had changed his mind and finally handed them a document which said: 'We hereby transmit our succession to our brother, the Grand Duke Michael, and give him our blessing for his accession to the throne of the Russian empire'.

But, after some thought, Michael refused, and with that the Russian monarchy was at an end. It had been overthrown by the ordinary people of the capital with extraordinary little loss of life. Total casualties were estimated at less than 1,500, with less than 200 people killed. As Trotsky later pointed out, the revolution was almost exclusively an affair of the capital. 'The rest of the country simply followed its lead. Nowhere in the country were there any popular groups, parties, institutions, or military units prepared to defend the old regime. Neither at the front nor in the rear was there to be found a brigade or a regiment ready to fight for Nicholas II.'

The same day as Nicholas signed his act of abdication a Provisional Government was set up in Petrograd. But it had to share power with the Soviet, and the conflict between the two bodies was to occupy the next eight months of 1917.

Kerensky's Summer

Alexander Kerensky (left) takes a salute at a military parade. Kerensky, volatile and flexible, was for six months the dominant figure in Russian politics

On 15th March 1917 a large crowd of dishevelled soldiers, enthusiastic intellectuals and students, and glum-looking workers—a typical cross-section of the people who had been demonstrating in the streets of the capital since 8th March—milled around in the large Catherine Hall of the Tauride Palace in Petrograd. They knew that after the prorogation of the Duma by the Tsar on 11th March, a committee of its members had replaced the Tsarist government, which had ceased to exist after failing to control street rioting and the mutiny of a part of the Petrograd garrison.

The leader of the influential liberal Kadets (Constitutional Democrats), and of the parliamentary opposition to the autocratic regime, P.N.Milyukov, addressed the crowd, announcing that a Provisional Government had been set up and giving the names of its members. He was warmly applauded when he said that A.F.Kerensky (the head of the socialist, though non-Marxist, Labour faction of the Duma) had agreed to become minister of justice. Names of other ministers were greeted with surprise and disappointment in the crowd, and Milyukov was asked 'who appointed you?'. He answered that the Government had been appointed 'by the Revolution itself'. The crowd's suspicions were not allayed, and Milyukov was asked what was to become of the dynasty. When he disclosed the plan—which never materialized—to proclaim the infant Alexey Tsar under the regency of his uncle, indignant cries rose from the audience and Milyukov was at pains to point out the necessity of a gradual and orderly transition to a democratic regime. As soon as things were settled, he

The Russian Revolution

said, the people would elect a Constituent Assembly by universal suffrage, and it would decide on the future of Russia. Democratic freedoms would be introduced immediately. This assurance restored the original delirious enthusiasm of the crowd and Milyukov was given an ovation and carried shoulder high from the hall.

Some eight months later, after a turbulent history in which the Provisional Government underwent at least four major reconstructions, only three of its original members remained in office. But the convocation of a Constituent Assembly, to secure a democratic regime for Russia, was still the aim of the government and the polling date was fixed for 28th November.

The footsteps of fate
Yet on 7th November 1917, on the eve of the elections to the Assembly, which could be expected to endorse its policy, the Provisional Government was reduced to a dozen distraught men, huddled in a room of the Winter Palace, with nothing but a group of cadet officers and a women's battalion to defend them from an assault of Red Guards and rebellious sailors led by Bolsheviks. As the approaching steps of the invaders rang through the endless corridors of the Winter Palace, the Provisional Government was asked whether the officer cadets should fight to prevent its falling into the hands of the rebels. The answer was that the Provisional Government would rather yield to force than have blood shed in its defence. And so the ministers were arrested and led off to prison in the Peter and Paul Fortress. The premier, Kerensky, was not among them; a few hours earlier he had left the capital to rally troops to fight the Bolshevik rebellion.

We may well ask what happened in these eight months to reduce the Provisional Government by the beginning of November to this sorry state of isolation and impotence. The Provisional Government was still vested with powers far exceeding those of the last Tsar; it still had under its orders a rudimentary administrative apparatus inherited from the old regime; Kerensky, the prime minister, was supreme commander of all Russian armed forces, at least in name. All political parties, except the monarchists and the Bolsheviks, were in some way represented in the government. And yet the people, whose will and aspirations the Provisional Government claimed to champion, made no move to support it in its hour of trial and Kerensky could not muster the few hundred soldiers needed to suppress the weak and poorly organized Bolshevik rising.

The government which was formed under the wavering and diffident leadership of Prince Lvov in March 1917, combined the highest executive power with full legislative powers; and it soon arrogated to itself the right to interfere with the judiciary. Its claim that it was entitled to act as head of state, replacing the monarch and assuming all his prerogatives, soon brought it into conflict with Finland and other national minorities of the Russian empire.

This concentration of power, the government claimed, was necessary for introducing reforms – such as putting an end to national and religious discrimination – without which no democratic election to the Constituent Assembly was possible. In fact there was more to it than that: the collapse of the monarchy and the promise of every kind of democratic liberty brought about spontaneous changes and threatened a general landslide in the social and legal structures of the country. In order to stem and canalize this revolutionary flood the Provisional Government sought to give a legal form to what were then known as 'the conquests of the Revolution'. But the former revolutionary parties which surfaced from the underground after the Revolution now insisted on 'taking it farther' by destroying every vestige of the 'accursed past' in the shape of state and public institutions, all privileges and prerogatives, and social and army discipline. The popular appeal of these parties, known as the 'revolutionary democracy', was considerable; they dominated the soviets (councils) of workers', soldiers', and peasants' deputies, as well as the trade unions and other rapidly proliferating professional organizations; and they infiltrated the newly formed soldiers' and officers' committees of army units, both at the front and in the rear. Their demands went beyond what the Provisional Government could concede if it was to maintain the fighting capacity of the army and guarantee freedom of decision to the future Constituent Assembly.

It soon became obvious that a certain amount of coercion was necessary to prevent anarchy. For this, however, the Provisional Government lacked both the will and the means of enforcement. The Provisional Government admitted its reluctance to resort to force when, in mid-March, it received the first news of agrarian disorders in the countryside. The government instructed its commissars that force could not be used against looting and rioting peasants: agrarian anarchy was to be prevented by local land committees who were instructed to prepare for the nationalization of land and exhort the peasants to be patient and await the decision of the Constituent Assembly on land reform. Similarly, when told that a mob of soldiers, whose train had been delayed at a station for half an hour, had beaten the stationmaster to death, the Provisional Government ordered the railway authorities to explain to the soldiers that delays were sometimes necessary to prevent collisions and loss of life to passengers. At the same time, the Provisional Government, though it had forbidden them, acquiesced in the unauthorized arrests of former Tsarist officials and army officers; some of them were kept for months in inhuman conditions in the naval fortress of Kronstadt in defiance of government orders.

Disorder in the army
Even if the government had been willing to use force in order to prevent 'revolutionary democracy' from interfering with its administration, it would have found itself without the proper means of doing so. One of the first actions of the Provisional Government had been to disband the police and gendarmerie – bodies which had been guilty of persecuting revolutionaries in the past. Local authorities were told to organize a 'people's militia' for the maintenance of order; but, lacking experience and training, this militia proved to be unequal to the task. There remained the army, but the Provisional Government was unlucky in its relations with the armed forces right from the beginning. In Petrograd, which had a garrison of just under 200,000, the Provisional Government pledged itself in its first proclamation not to transfer any of the units stationed in the capital. This was done to reassure those soldiers who had rebelled against the Tsar and had even killed some of their officers, and who were, therefore, afraid of possible reprisals if they were sent to the front.

The Provisional Government's control over the army was further weakened by the publication on 15th March of the notorious Order No. I of the Petrograd Soviet. This introduced elected soldiers' committees in all units and boldly stated that orders of the Duma Committee were only to be obeyed when they conformed to the instructions of the Petrograd Soviet. Although addressed only to the troops in the capital, Order No. I soon set the pattern for 'revolutionizing' other garrisons and front-line units. It also put the armed forces in the capital virtually under the command of the Soviet, strengthening it against the Provisional Government.

Nor was the Provisional Government successful in its efforts to control the army in the field or in establishing good working relations with the successive supreme commanders whom it appointed. The 'revolutionary democracy' suspected the army, which had played no part in the February Revolution, of a lukewarm attitude to it, and was bent on 'revolutionizing' the rank and file. These efforts, made on the eve of a general offensive agreed upon with the Allies, met with resistance both from GHQ and from officers at the front. A horde of propagandists from Petrograd and other

necessary for an army in the field. Dismissed officers crowded GHQ, where they were joined by others who had lost their commands on the insistence of soldiers' committees infiltrated by Bolsheviks. They were resentful and bitter men looking for leadership in order to stop the process of 'deepening' the Revolution.

The Petrograd Soviet had issued at the end of March an appeal to all warring nations to conclude an early peace renouncing any aggressive war aims. The Provisional Government endorsed this in principle, at the same time assuring the Allies, through the minister of foreign affairs, Milyukov, that Russia would stand by its international obligations. Out of this hardly explicit discrepancy a conflict arose between Milyukov and Kerensky—who felt himself the representative of the Soviet attitude—and this led at the beginning of May to open demonstrations, some demanding and some opposing the resignation of the ministers of foreign affairs and war, Milyukov and Guchkov. Units of the Petro-

revolutionary centres in the rear descended on the troops at the front where they undermined discipline and relations between officers and men.

The first minister of war of the Provisional Government, Guchkov, did nothing to remedy this situation. He himself had fomented discontent and organized sedition against the Tsar before the Revolution, and now, on becoming minister of war, he started a purge of the officers' corps without consideration for the stability so

Above: The armband worn by the followers of Kornilov. Right: German cartoon, July 1917. Nicholas from his prison listens as Lloyd George, President Wilson of the United States, and Ribot, prime minister of France, exclaim: 'We never deal with an autocratic government, never.' Nicholas muses: 'Once these rascals were like brothers to me.' Below: Dutch drawing of Nicholas on his way to Siberia, where the Provisional Government sent him and his family in August 1917

grad garrison took part in one of the demonstrations demanding their resignation. General Kornilov, whom the government had appointed commander-in-chief in Petrograd, had not authorized the demonstration and asked the government to support him and stop the Petrograd Soviet interfering with the troops under his command. Having failed to get satisfaction he resigned his post and returned to the army at the front. His departure coincided with the first ministerial crisis of the Provisional Government. Guchkov and Milyukov resigned, less as a concession to popular clamour than as a result of profound dissensions and divided loyalties inside the government itself. Party ties between Kadet and other liberal ministers proved less binding than the allegiance of some of them to the political masonic organization to which they belonged. Milyukov found himself 'betrayed' by his former deputy party chairman, Nekrasov, who like other Russian masons supported Kerensky. His and Guchkov's departure allowed socialists to enter the cabinet and Kerensky emerged as the initiator of the first coalition government, in which he became minister of war.

DE ROMANOFFS NAAR SIBERIË

The Russian Revolution

Kerensky decided to instil into the army a new revolutionary spirit and a new faith in the justice of the cause for which it was fighting. The supreme commander, General Alexeyev, was dismissed without further ceremony and replaced by General Brusilov, known for his famous offensive in June 1916. Kerensky instituted government commissars attached to various headquarters of the army, who would assist officers in all political matters, including contacts with soldiers' committees, and keep the government informed of the state of the army. The main weapon in Kerensky's arsenal was direct contact with the soldiers at army delegates' conferences and meetings of army units. Mesmerizing them by his eloquence, he impressed on his listeners that they had now become the army of a new-born world. With the proclamation of a 'just peace without annexations or indemnities' by the Revolutionary Democracy of Russia the war, he said, had changed its purpose and had obtained a new historical significance. The soldiers had always readily sacrificed their lives under the knout wielded by the tyrannical, autocratic regime. With how much more enthusiasm would they do so now, Kerensky claimed, as free citizens of a liberated Russia which would lead the world towards a new and happier era. Kerensky's exhortations flattered the other ranks who greeted him with ovations. The officers naturally resented being accused of having used cruel methods in the past to force their men to fight for the unworthy cause of the Rasputin clique: but they were willing to put up with anything which might raise the morale of the army.

When, however, the order for the offensive was given on 26th June, Bolshevik propaganda, supported by a fraternization campaign cleverly carried on by the German high command, proved stronger than Kerensky's oratory; soldiers' committees units at company, regiment, or even divisional level discussed battle orders and questioned their commanders' decisions to take the offensive in a war which supposedly had no aggressive aim. After an initial success, mainly due to patriotic volunteer detachments, the offensive collapsed ignominiously through the defection of whole units. The entire 11th Army deserted the front, lynching its officers, disrupting communications, looting, raping, and burning down whole villages. General Kornilov, who had been transferred from Petrograd to the south-western front, demanded that the government should call off the offensive and reintroduce the death penalty at the front as an emergency measure. In this he was supported by the government commissars attached to the units under his command, in particular by Savinkov, a Socialist Revolutionary (like

Kerensky), and a former leading terrorist. In view of the desperate situation the Provisional Government not only met all Kornilov's demands but appointed him supreme commander-in-chief.

The need for a return to sanity in the army was forcefully impressed on the Provisional Government by the Bolshevik attempt to seize power on 16th July, which coincided with the German break-through in Galicia. The Bolsheviks organized a so-called 'spontaneous' peaceful, armed demonstration under the slogan 'All power to the soviets'. The Soviet and the Provisional Government, unable to rely on the capital's garrison, were faced with a rebellion of armed workers organized as Red Guards and Kronstadt sailors who had invaded the capital at the call of the Bolsheviks. The position of the Provisional Government, however, was quickly restored by the arrival of a few reliable troops from the front. But it had been a narrow escape, and the first coalition government never recovered from the shock.

The abortive Bolshevik coup sharpened the internal dissensions in the government between those who, like Prince Lvov and the Kadets, wanted to strengthen the authority of the government and those who, like Kerensky and the representatives of 'revolutionary democracy', sought to increase the government's popularity by initiating further revolutionary changes. On 20th July Prince Lvov and the Kadet ministers resigned, leaving Kerensky with the task of reconstructing the cabinet. After trying unsuccessfully for a whole fortnight to bridge the differences between the liberal and socialist camps, Kerensky himself resigned on 3rd August, leaving the country virtually without leadership. That same night his deputy, Nekrasov, summoned a memorable joint session of the cabinet and the party leaders in the Malachite Hall of the Winter Palace. After a torrent of speeches it was decided to accept and support a cabinet of Kerensky's choice. He was left free to define his programme, and the ministers were to be free of all control by their party committees and the Soviet.

Except for some changes of personnel, of which the departure of the 'defensist' Menshevik, Tsereteli, was the most important, the second coalition government differed little from the first. Premier Kerensky remained minister of war, but appointed Savinkov, the commissar at Kornilov's headquarters, to be his deputy in charge of the ministry. In practice, delicate political questions were dealt with by an unofficial 'inner cabinet', consisting of Kerensky, the minister of foreign affairs, Tereshchenko, and Nekrasov.

Kornilov himself, on accepting his appointment from a shaky and divided government, demanded that there should be no

Above left: June 1917: Demonstration of soldiers' wives demanding votes for women. *Above right:* Kerensky (centre) at the funeral of cossacks killed in the Petrograd riots, July 1917. They had been recalled from the front to deal with Bolshevik-organized armed workers and sailors. *Below:* Kornilov — determined to restore the fighting capacity of the army

Below: Kerensky. His hesitation won him the mistrust of both the officers' corps and the revolutionaries. *Left:* Delegates from the army in Petrograd. Some, the radicals, have torn the bands off their shoulders to show their scorn for authority. *Right:* July demonstration. The banner says: 'Down with the capitalist ministers. All power to the Soviets'

The Duma in session before (inset) and after the revolution. The trappings of Tsardom, the portrait and the imperial coat of arms had been removed by April

interference with his choice of commanding officers and claimed that as supreme commander he would be responsible only to his conscience and to the nation as a whole. He then urged the government to take the measures which he claimed were indispensable for restoring order in the country and the fighting capacity of the army. These measures, including the death penalty for sedition in the rear, spelled a curtailment of democratic freedoms—for instance freedom of propaganda, which was one of the 'conquests of the revolution' —which were deemed essential by the soviets for free elections. Kerensky hesitated, in spite of pressure from Savinkov who mediated between him and the supreme commander. Kerensky hoped to overcome the split in public opinion between supporters of Kornilov and those of the soviets at a monster debating rally, the Moscow State Conference, in late August. The conference only showed the chasm, presaging the possibility of civil war.

The Kornilov affair

After the failure of the conference, Kerensky decided, without consulting his cabinet, to approach Kornilov through Savinkov, asking for his loyal co-operation in fighting anarchy. He agreed to meet Kornilov's demands. If the publication of the new laws embodying them caused an outbreak of civil disobedience in Petrograd, it was to be suppressed by troops which Kornilov was to send to the capital and put at the disposal of the Provisional Government. A cavalry army corps was concentrated at the approaches to Petrograd on 9th September. Kerensky had not yet, however, put Kornilov's demands before

the cabinet, despite Savinkov's urging. On 8th September he promised to do so that night, when the cabinet was to meet. Shortly before the meeting was due to start, Vladimir Lvov, a former member of the first two Provisional Government cabinets, an unbalanced, excitable, and totally irresponsible character, came to see Kerensky. Lvov had been acting as a self-appointed go-between posing both to Kerensky and Kornilov as a secret emissary of the other. From Lvov's confused and mendacious statement, Kerensky understood that Kornilov was now demanding the resignation of the government and the surrender of all power to him. The idea of a 'Kornilov ultimatum' henceforth dominated all Kerensky's actions at the helm of his foundering government, and was to be the major theme of everything he wrote during the next fifty years. When the cabinet met the same night, Kerensky denounced Kornilov's 'plot' and ultimatum and asked for a free hand to deal with the insubordination of the supreme commander. The ministers who had been given no information of the preceding developments, agreed, but, horrified by the new ordeal threatening Russia, handed in their resignations. Just before the meeting, Kerensky had been communicating with Kornilov by teleprinter, but failed to ascertain whether what he understood Lvov to have reported was correct: he feigned, however, to be in full agreement with Kornilov and promised to join him at GHQ the next day. Instead, after the cabinet meeting, he sent a curt informal telegram dismissing Kornilov from his post and summoning him to Petrograd. Indignantly Kornilov refused to submit and was backed by the overwhelming majority of his senior officers. The conflict had still not been made public and might have been settled, had not a proclamation of the Provisional Government denouncing Kornilov been released to the press prematurely. Kornilov appealed to the country, calling Kerensky's account a complete lie.

Neither Kornilov nor Kerensky disposed of sufficient forces to escalate their exchange of insults into a real trial of strength. The troops sent by Kornilov to Petrograd believed that they were going to support the Provisional Government and were shocked by the announcement of Kornilov's alleged mutiny: they refused to obey marching orders and broke up in confusion. Kerensky was not effectively in control of the capital's garrison; this and the Kronstadt sailors' detachments, ostensibly under the orders of the Soviet, were in fact controlled by the Bolsheviks.

The Kornilov affair petered out ingloriously. Kornilov called the whole thing off and allowed himself to be put under arrest. Kerensky appointed himself supreme com-

mander. A committee of lawyers set up to investigate the alleged mutiny was appalled by the double-crossing and the lack of dignity on all sides, but was unable to complete its work before the collapse of the Provisional Government.

Kerensky is right in referring to the Kornilov affair as the 'prelude to Bolshevism'. But the return of the Bolsheviks to active politics and their final victory in November were made possible not by Kornilov's pressure on the Provisional Government to strengthen its authority, nor by his military measures to back up that pressure, nor even by his angry gesture of insubordination on being suddenly without warning denounced as a mutineer. These actions of Kornilov, who was widely supported by public opinion outside Soviet circles—even by socialists, such as Plekhanov and Argunov—were all brought about by the indecision and procrastination of Kerensky and his closest friends in the cabinet. While conceding in secret negotiations the urgency of the measures demanded by Kornilov, Kerensky seems never to have wanted to implement them and was relieved when he could interpret V.Lvov's incoherent innuendoes as an insolent and arrogant ultimatum by Kornilov, which released him from the promise he had just made to Savinkov to comply with the supreme commander's demands. Kerensky has only himself to blame that both his contemporaries and historians have shown so little sympathy with his behaviour at that critical moment. For after it he was considered by the officers' corps and the Kadets as one who had provoked Kornilov to rise in open rebellion and by the 'revolutionary democracy' as one who had had secret dealings with counter-revolutionary conspirators. Not even the ties binding Nekrasov, Kerensky, and Tereshchenko survived the Kornilov episode, and Nekrasov had to leave the government.

Kerensky's assumption of the highest functions of the state could not restore his popularity nor strengthen his authority. His attempt at establishing a kind of pre-parliament, from appointed representatives of various party and public organizations, led to a final humiliation: when Kerensky demanded full powers from the pre-parliament to deal with the incipient Bolshevik rising, he was rebuffed and told by the representatives of 'revolutionary democracy' that the Bolsheviks could best be fought by the acceptance of a government programme of immediate revolutionary reforms—reforms of a kind which were supposed to be decided by the future Constituent Assembly. Two days after his defeat in the pre-parliament, Kerensky was in flight from the Bolsheviks and the members of his government were incarcerated in the Peter and Paul Fortress.

The Bolsheviks Seize Power

The overthrow of the autocratic Tsarist regime in March (February by the Julian Calender) 1917 was a great victory for the peoples of Russia. In alliance with the army, the working class of Russia fought for and won political freedom. The whole country was covered by a network of 'soviets' (councils) and of committees of soldiers and peasants. Power in the country was divided, but as early as June the Provisional Government had established a dictatorship with the help of the Mensheviks and Socialist Revolutionaries (SRs). Not a single one of the social aims of the revolution had been met. Neither the government of Prince Lvov nor Kerensky's government which followed it gave land to the peasants or rid them of their servitude to the landowners. Workers in the mills and factories continued to be cruelly exploited, their standard of living declined sharply, their wages were cut, and there was hunger in the towns. A country which had been exhausted by the First World War was now thirsting for peace, yet the Provisional Government's policy was to continue the war.

Russia was torn by violent contradictions. The progress of agriculture was held back by the fact that enormous areas remained in the hands of the landowners. At the same time modern industry was developing in the country, with a high level of concentration of production and manpower. The urban working class which amounted to about 20,000,000 of the country's population of over 150,000,000, was organized into trade unions and had learned a great deal about political struggle in the first Russian revolution of 1905.

The Bolshevik Party

The Bolshevik Party, led by Vladimir Ilyich Lenin, directed the struggle of the working class towards the acquisition of power, the solution of the land question, bringing the war to an end, establishing workers' control over production, and nationalizing banks and the more important branches of industry. But this struggle on the part of the workers and peasants came up against bitter resistance from representatives of the ruling classes.

In September 1917 the party of the Russian bourgeoisie, the Constitutional Democrats (Kadets), and the reactionary military circles led by General Kornilov tried to carry out a counter-revolutionary *putsch* and to set up a military dictatorship. In effect, this plot evoked general opposition among the people and rallied the revolutionary forces to the Bolshevik Party. At the beginning of September the Petro-

grad and Moscow soviets of workers' and peasants' deputies passed resolutions proposed by the Bolsheviks. The Moscow Soviet was led by one of the oldest members of the Bolshevik Party, V.P.Nogin, while L.D.Trotsky, who had only recently joined the Party, was elected chairman of the Petrograd Soviet.

The influence of the Bolsheviks in the soviets throughout the country spread rapidly in September and October. The Bolsheviks became the leading element in the soviets almost everywhere.

In the autumn of 1917 the revolution in Russia entered on its decisive stage.

All classes and all social groups in Russian society were drawn into the most far-reaching revolutionary crisis. It was a crisis affecting the whole nation, because it became apparent in all spheres of the nation's life, involving the working people, the ruling classes, and the political parties. With merciless precision Lenin revealed the inevitability of the collapse of a Russian economy dominated by the bourgeoisie and landowners and of the economic policy of the Provisional Government. It was not individual mistakes that brought the government to the brink of disaster. At a time when there was a tremendous growth in the revolutionary activity of the masses all efforts on the part of the Provisional Government to regulate economic life by reactionary bureaucratic means were doomed to failure. The government's whole policy was leading to famine and the disorganization of production, the destruction of economic contacts, and the creation of a state of chaos in the country. To carry out genuinely democratic measures for regulating the economy, to nationalize the banks and syndicates, and control production and demand would have meant taking a step forward—to socialism.

The collapse of the Provisional Government's food policy had an especially serious effect on the condition of the mass of ordinary people. Memories of the March days of 1917, which had started with food riots, were still very fresh in the people's minds. On the eve of the October Revolution the country's food situation worsened considerably as a result of the policy of the Kerensky government which paid no attention to the needs of the people.

The collapse of the Provisional Government's economic policy was seen in its most concentrated form in the breakdown of transport. This was the bloodstream sustaining the country's whole economic life and binding it together into a single organism, and it collapsed with tremendous speed. Towards the end of October 1917

Lenin, on his way to Petrograd to direct the revolution. On 28th October he and the Bolshevik Central Committee finally announced: 'The time is fully ripe'

The Russian Revolution

the minister of transport, A.V.Liverovsky, admitted that the transport situation 'threatened to bring to a halt the major railroads which supplied the country with essential services'.

One very clear sign of the nationwide crisis was the break-up of the ruling parties of Socialist Revolutionaries (SRs) and the Social Democrats (Mensheviks). The formation of left-wing groups among the SRs and Mensheviks, the sharp intensification of conflicts between the leadership of these parties and the rank and file of their members and between the party headquarters and their local organizations, and the enforced rejection by the local committees of SRs and Mensheviks of the slogan of coalition with the bourgeoisie was the direct result of the collapse of those parties' reformist policy. On 4th November the soldiers' section of the All-Russian Central Executive Committee, led by SRs and Mensheviks, demanded peace and the transfer of land to the peasants, but proposed that power should be handed over to 'the democratic majority in the pre-parliament'—that spurious, representative body set up by the Provisional Government.

Traitors to the revolution
From the middle of October 1917 open warfare on the part of all the working people against the Provisional Government became a daily occurrence in the nation's life. The workers everywhere were arming themselves, the number of workers' armed detachments—the Red Guards—increased rapidly, and they developed their contacts and their plans for common action with the garrisons in the major towns. The workers had a tremendously revolutionizing effect on the troops at the fronts, especially on the Western and Northern Fronts. Sailors of the Baltic Fleet declared the Kerensky government to be a government of betrayal of the revolution. Councils of

Below: The Bolshevik Colossus

workers' and soldiers' deputies, regimental and divisional committees, and peasants' organizations proclaimed at the numerous conferences they held that none of the tasks of the revolution could be solved without the overthrow of the Provisional Government and the transfer of power to the soviets. A resolution passed at a congress of soviets of the Vladimir province on 29th October declared the Provisional Government and all the parties which supported it to be traitors to the cause of revolution and all the soviets in the province to be in a state of open and determined warfare with the Provisional Government. This was only one of the moves in this general process of decisive and ruthless warfare between the people and the government. The same resolution was supported by the soviets in Moscow, Ivanovo-Voznesensk, Aleksandrov, Kovrov, Ryazan, and other towns. When a congress of soviets in the Ryazan province decided to hand power over to the soviets immediately, Nikitin, the minister of the interior, demanded that armed force should be used against the people of Ryazan. On 31st October the minister cabled the commander of the Moscow military region: 'Impossible to take counteraction with resources of the civil authority.' But the military commander was also unable to render any assistance, because he had no dependable troops at his disposal. The soviet of the Moscow province proposed that all the soviets in the province should ignore the orders issued by the Provisional Government. The Vladivostok Soviet, some 6,000 miles from Moscow, issued instructions to the effect that failure to obey the soviet's orders would be regarded as a counter-revolutionary act. Soviets in the Urals declared that the main task was to overthrow the Provisional Government.

It was the industrial working class and its party which took the lead in this popular movement. Factory committees sprang up everywhere and quickly gathered strength, and they were everywhere dominated by the Bolsheviks. In Petrograd on 30th October-4th November there took place the first All-Russian Conference of Factory Committees. Ninety-six of the 167 delegates belonged to the Bolsheviks.

Strikes and peasant revolt
The strike movement in the autumn of 1917 was closely connected with the soviets' struggle for power. There were strikes of metal-workers and woodworkers, of chemist-shop assistants and railway workers, of textile workers and miners. A general strike of 300,000 textile workers in the central industrial region (Moscow), which began on 3rd November, affected every branch of life in the region. The workers took control of the plants, occupied

the telephone exchange, mounted guard over the warehouses and offices. It was more than a strike: the workers not only faced up directly to the problem of assuming power, they began to solve it. But in 1917 the strike was only one of many weapons used by the proletariat in its struggle. The Red Guards and the workers' militia, the establishment of factory guards and workers' control, the factory committees and the bold acts of intervention in the management of industrial plants—all these forms of organization and means of struggle gave the working class tremendous possibilities for influencing the course of events and leading them on a nationwide scale.

The strength of the working-class movement was multiplied by virtue of the fact that the industrial workers exercised a tremendous influence over the peasantry and themselves received in return support in the form of a spreading peasant war against the landowners. In September and October 1917 there were something like 2,000 cases in which the peasants took political action, killing the landlords and seizing the land.

'If, in a country of peasants, after seven months of a democratic republic, things could come to the point of a peasant revolt, this demonstrates unquestionably the nationwide collapse of the revolution, the crisis it is in, which has reached unprecedented proportions, and the fact that the counter-revolutionary forces are reaching the limit of their resources,' Lenin wrote in mid-October 1917.

But the peasantry's official representative at the time was the All-Russian Council of Peasants' Deputies, which had been elected at the peasants' congress back in May and had long since lost any right to represent anybody. The executive committee of the All-Russian Council of Peasants' Deputies sanctioned punitive expeditions against the peasants, and supported the policy of hostility to the peasantry pursued by the government (in which the prime minister was the SR Kerensky and the minister of agriculture the SR Maslov). The peasant masses who had risen in revolt against the landowners took decisive action. In the main centres of peasant uprisings the struggle against the landowners acquired, under the influence of the industrial workers, both organization and a clear purpose. The 332 delegates to a peasant congress in the Tver province took a unanimous decision to hand over the land immediately to the management of land committees. The local land committees in the Tambov province seized land belonging to the Church and the landowners and rented it out to peasants who had very little or no land. Similar acts were repeated throughout the country.

Women queuing outside a food-store in Moscow. The bread ration, a pound a day in the spring, was cut to half a pound just before the October Revolution

Government force
How did the Provisional Government reply to these demands by the peasants? It organized punitive expeditions and drew up various legislative proposals providing for eventual reforms, the aim of which was to 'pacify' the peasants and certainly not to satisfy their demand that the land should be handed over to them.

The forces at the disposal of the Provisional Government for undertaking such punitive expeditions were limited, consisting mainly of Cossack and cavalry units. The actions undertaken by the peasants forced the Provisional Government to split up its troops between numerous areas in which there had been uprisings: in the Ryazan, Kursk, Tambov, Kiev, Tula, Saratov, Samara, Minsk, Kazan, Podolsk, Volhynia, and other provinces. Squadrons of Cossacks and cavalry detachments which were dispatched to particular districts became submerged in the vast sea of peasant revolt. Meanwhile, the provincial commissars of the Provisional Government demanded that soldiers be sent to *all* districts to suppress peasant disorders.

But even the local authorities soon realized the futility of using force against the peasantry. In the course of the peasant uprising even those land committees which supported the government's policy were forced to take over the property of the landowners and distribute it among the poorer

Petrograd workers with an armoured car captured from Kerensky's troops. On the fatal night of 7th November Kerensky was searching for loyal troops to support his government

by the landowners. It was this experience which pushed the peasantry to carry out an uprising which, when linked with the struggle of the industrial workers, created the most favourable conditions for the victory of the socialist revolution.

The revolutionary structure

By November 1917 the Bolshevik Party had about 350,000 members. But its strength was to be measured rather by its influence over the many millions of people embraced by the soviets, the trade unions, the factory committees, and the soldiers' and peasants' committees. At a time when an armed revolt was developing on a nationwide scale the task of Lenin's revolutionary party was to take care of the political and military organization of the forces of revolt. At the centre of this preparatory work stood the working class. The Red Guards were acquiring fighting experience, were learning the tactics of street fighting, and were establishing and strengthening their contacts with the revolutionary units in the army. In the districts inhabited by other nationalities the Bolsheviks gained the support of the oppressed peoples, who saw in the victory of a socialist revolution a guarantee of national and social emancipation. Major centres of revolutionary struggle were set up in all these districts and they linked the national liberation movement with the workers' and peasants' movement, bringing Petrograd and Moscow together with the outlying regions in a single revolutionary front. One such centre in central Asia was Tashkent, which as early as September 1917 raised the banner of struggle against the Kerensky government. In the Trans-Caucasus the centre was the industrial city of Baku; in the Ukraine Kharkov and the Donbass; in the Western territories of the country it was Minsk. The Bolsheviks were clearly the dominant force in the decisive places in the country: in the capital, in the industrial centres, on the Western and Northern Fronts, and in the major garrison towns in the interior. The seventy-five Bolshevik newspapers and periodicals which were published in all these regions were a very important organizing force.

The decision to work for an uprising, which was taken at the Sixth Congress of the Bolshevik Party in August 1917, was put consistently into practice. At a meeting on 23rd October, in which Lenin took part, the Central Committee of the Bolsheviks passed a resolution concerning the uprising. This decision did not set a date for the uprising, but it did stress that 'an armed uprising is inevitable and the time for it is fully ripe'. The Central Committee advised all the branches of the party to be guided by this fact and to consider and decide all practical issues with this in

peasants. The Kadets, the SRs, and the Mensheviks tried in every way to minimize the importance of the peasants' struggle, making out that it was just 'wild anarchy' and talking about 'pogroms' and 'disorders'. This falsification of the truth is disproved by the facts: in the main centres of the uprising the peasants transferred the land to the poor peasants in an organized manner. In those places where the SR party obstructed the work of the peasant committees the movement did indeed assume anarchistic forms. But the peasants had thoroughly learned the lessons of the first Russian revolution of 1905. The more advanced forms of peasant protest and revolt (the seizure of arable land and landowners' property) were three or four times as widespread in 1917 as they had been in

1905-07. In the autumn of 1917 between sixty and ninety per cent of all peasant actions included the seizure of land.

As for the proposed reforms, their essence is apparent from the final bill put forward by S.L.Maslov, the minister of agriculture. According to this bill, which was the most 'left-wing' for the Provisional Government, the landowners were to retain the right to own the land. The 'land-lease fund' to be set up under this bill was to take over only 'land not being cultivated by the resources of the owners'. The rent to be paid by the peasants was to go to the landowner.

The whole experience of the eight months during which the Provisional Government was in power demonstrated that without a further revolution the peasantry would not receive any land or rid itself of oppression

mind. The resolution was passed with Zinovyev and Kamenev voting against it. A week later Kamenev wrote an article opposing the decision in the Menshevik paper *Novaya Zhizn* (New Life). L.D. Trotsky voted in favour of the resolution on the uprising, but his later position amounted to delaying the beginning of the revolt until the All-Russian Congress of Soviets, which was to deal with the question of power. This attitude of Trotsky's was subjected to severe criticism by Lenin, who emphasized that to postpone the uprising until the Congress of Soviets would be to give the counter-revolutionary forces an opportunity of organizing themselves and dispersing the soviets.

On 29th October an enlarged session of the Central Committee of the Bolsheviks,

attended by representatives of the Petrograd committee, the Bolsheviks' military organization, factory committees, and trade unions, approved the decision to organize an armed uprising and appointed from its number a Military-Revolutionary Centre composed of A.S.Bubnov, F.E. Dzerzhinsky, Y.M.Sverdlov, I.V.Stalin, and S.M.Uritsky. The leading spirit and organizer of the work of the Military-Revolutionary Committee was Yakov Sverdlov, a thirty-two-year-old Bolshevik who already had behind him seventeen years of revolutionary activity, prison, penal servitude, and seven escapes from deportation. This centre consisting of five men formed part of the Soviet's legal headquarters for the armed uprising – the Military-Revolutionary Committee of the

Petrograd Soviet. A major part in the Committee was played by Bolsheviks N.I. Podvoysky and V.A.Antonov-Ovseyenko, and by the left-wing SR, P.E.Lazimir.

In late October provincial and district conferences and congresses of soviets, factory committees, and army and frontline committees took place throughout the country. History had never before seen such a mass mobilization of popular forces around the working class for a decisive attack on the capitalist system.

Meanwhile, the Provisional Government was trying to regain the initiative. On 1st November it dispersed the soviet in Kaluga, encircled Moscow and Minsk with Cossack troops, and tried to remove the revolutionary units of the capital's garrison from Petrograd. The only effect of these actions was that the revolutionary forces became even more active.

The Military-Revolutionary Committee appointed its own commissars to all units of the Petrograd garrison and to all the more important offices. The revolutionary troops and the Red Guards were brought to a state of readiness for battle. On 6th November the avalanche of popular wrath descended on the government which had betrayed the revolution. On that day the Central Committee of the Bolsheviks organized an alternative headquarters in the Peter and Paul Fortress and took decisions concerning the control of the postal and telegraph services, of the rail junction, and of the food supplies to the capital. The Petrograd garrison and the Red Guards went over to direct military action to bring about the immediate overthrow of the Provisional Government.

The Congress of Soviets

The city of Petrograd is situated on a number of islands, joined together by bridges. Hence the great strategic importance of the bridges. During the day of 6th November units of the Red Guards seized practically all the bridges and defeated efforts on the part of the officer cadets to cut the working-class districts off from the centre. Revolutionary troops occupied the central telegraph office, the central news agency, and the Baltic (Finland) station. Ships of the Baltic Fleet put out from Helsingfors and Kronstadt to come to the help of revolutionary Petrograd.

On the evening of 6th November Lenin left his secret hiding place and arrived at the headquarters of the armed uprising, and under his leadership the uprising developed at much greater speed. Troops of the Military-Revolutionary Committee occupied, on the night of 6th-7th November and the following morning, the telephone exchange, a number of railway stations, and the State Bank. The capital of Russia was in the hands of a people in revolt.

Red Guards outside the Smolny Institute. Inside on 7th November the hall was seething with people. The Congress of Soviets was deciding the future course of the revolution

The Russian Revolution

On the morning of 7th November Lenin wrote his appeal *To the Citizens of Russia,* which announced the transfer of power in the state into the hands of the Military-Revolutionary Committee. This, the first document to emerge from the victorious revolution, was immediately printed and posted up in the streets of Petrograd.

At two thirty-five on the afternoon of the same day the Petrograd Soviet went into session. There Lenin proclaimed the victory of the socialist revolution. In a short, moving speech he defined the main tasks of the revolution: the setting up of a Soviet government, the dismantling of the old state administration and the organization of new, Soviet administration, the ending of the war, a just and immediate peace, the confiscation of the property of the landowners, and genuine workers' control over industrial production.

Throughout the day of 7th November meetings of the party factions from the Congress of Soviets were taking place in the Smolny Institute. Details of the party composition of the second All-Russian Congress of Soviets bear witness to the depth and the extent of the process of Bolshevization among the ordinary people. At the first Congress the Bolsheviks had accounted for only ten per cent of the delegates, but at the second Congress they embraced fifty-two per cent of the delegates. The Bolsheviks carried with them a large group of left-wing SRs—more than fifteen per cent of the delegates, whereas there had been no left-wing SRs at all at the first All-Russian Congress of Soviets. Mensheviks and right-wing SRs of all shades of opinion, who had unquestionably dominated the first Congress of Soviets (eighty-four per cent of the delegates), accounted for only twenty-six per cent of the delegates at the second Congress.

There is no need to produce any more precise evidence to demonstrate the extent to which the *petit-bourgeois* parties had disintegrated; the decline from eighty-four per cent in June 1917 to twenty-six per cent in October is sufficiently clear. All the same, the Bolsheviks did not try to antagonize or isolate the other parties which formed part of the soviets.

The first session of the second All-Russian Congress of Soviets began at 10.40 pm on 7th November and came to an end just after five next morning.

The white-pillared hall of the Smolny Institute was seething with people. Within its walls were to be found representatives of the whole of Russia, of her industrial centres and farming regions, national territories, Cossack regions, and of all the war fronts and garrisons in the interior. It was a representative assembly from the whole of Russia, which had to decide the future course of the revolution.

Sitting on the platform were the downcast leaders of the old Central Executive Committee—Bogdanov, Gots, Dan, Filippovsky—but this was their last appearance as leaders of the supreme organ of the soviets. It was, at the same time, an admission of defeat for their policy of resistance to the popular will and an admission of the legitimacy of the Congress, to which, by the very fact of the official opening, the old Executive Committee was handing over its very reduced authority.

The Congress elected a presidium from among the Bolsheviks and the left-wing SRs, and Dan and his friends departed. Then the work of the Congress began.

There was, in the long stream of speeches, in the heated dispute about the revolution which had taken place, and in the sharp conflict between the political parties, a certain strict logic and system which reflected the relationship of social forces in the vast country stretching out beyond the confines of the Smolny Institute.

The Provisional Government, meeting in the Winter Palace in the centre of Petrograd, was utterly isolated from the country. The palace was defended by detachments of officer cadets, Cossacks, and women's battalions. As the ring of rebel forces drew closer round the Winter Palace, and as the reports from the war fronts grew ever more hopeless, so the speeches of the more conciliatory statesmen became more nervous and their actions became more devoid of logic. By continually walking out of the congress and then coming back to it the Mensheviks and the right-wing SRs tried to disorganize its work. The result of their efforts was very painful for them.

After some noisy demonstrations and much hysterical shouting and appeals the right-wing SRs and Mensheviks succeeded in taking with them out of the congress an insignificant group of people—about fifty of the delegates. At the same time there took place a significant regrouping of forces at the congress. The number of SRs was reduced by seven, but the group of left-wing SRs increased to eighty-one. The Mensheviks disappeared altogether, but the group of Menshevik-internationalists rose to twenty-one. This means that many members of the faction of Mensheviks and SRs did not obey the decision of their leaders to leave the congress, but preferred to switch over to the left-wing groups.

At about ten in the evening of 7th November the revolutionary troops surrounding the Winter Palace went over to the attack for which the signal was a shot fired by the cruiser *Aurora.* The Winter Palace was taken. Antonov-Ovseyenko arrested the members of the Provisional Government and put them in charge of the Red Guards to be taken to the Peter and Paul Fortress.

Pleading
Meanwhile, the forces of the counter-revolution—the Mensheviks, and right-wing SRs, pinned their hopes on the units at the front. During 6th and 7th November General Dukhonin from the General HQ and a representative of the war ministry, Tolstoy, sent messages from Petrograd demanding, begging, and pleading with the commanders of the fronts to send troops as quickly as possible to Petrograd to put down the uprising. The commanders of the South-Western and Rumanian Fronts, where the influence of the conciliators and nationalists seemed to be especially strong, declared that there were no units to be found which were suitable for the job of 'pacifying' Petrograd. And those regiments which they had succeeded by a trick in moving towards Petrograd were held up on the way by the railwaymen, the workers, and revolutionary soldiers. A

Two Soviet paintings of the revolution.
Left: *The signal for revolution—a shot is fired from the cruiser* Aurora. *The attack on the Winter Palace is to begin.* ***Below:*** *'The Inevitable' (by S.Lukin). The Winter Palace has been stormed. The members of the Provisional Government are under arrest. A Red Guard, one of the victors, stands in the throne-room of the Tsars*

strict revolutionary control was set up in Orsha, so that no trains were allowed through to Petrograd. The armoured trains which were sent off for Moscow were held up in Minsk. Vyazma and Gomel not only refused to let troops through but even held up telegrams from the staff of the Western Front.

Contrary to the hopes of the forces of counter-revolution, the soldiers on all fronts came out in defence of the soviets.

At 5.17 am N.V.Krylenko, an officer and a Bolshevik, representing the revolutionary forces of the Northern Front, went up on to the platform of the congress to speak; he was staggering from fatigue. He was soon to be made supreme commander-in-chief of the Russian army. The congress listened with enthusiasm to his statement that a Military-Revolutionary Committee had been set up on the Northern Front,

which had taken over the command and intended to prevent the movement of trainloads of counter-revolutionary troops in the direction of Petrograd. Delegations were continually arriving from the trains sent to Petrograd and declaring their support for the Petrograd garrison.

The first official state document of the socialist revolution—the *Appeal to the Workers, Soldiers, and Peasants*—was drawn up by Lenin. It proclaimed that the Congress of Soviets was taking power into its own hands and that all power throughout the country was passing into the hands of the soviets of workers', soldiers', and peasants' deputies. This was how the main question of the revolution was resolved legally—the soviets' power was established.

The most difficult problems, around which a bitter struggle had been fought throughout the eight months of the

revolution—the questions of peace, land, workers' control, the self-determination of nations, the democratization of the army—were posed and decided openly and straightforwardly in that document.

The *Appeal to the Workers, Soldiers, and Peasants* was approved with only two opposing votes and twelve abstentions. This represented a complete victory for Lenin's idea of transferring all power to the soviets. The first decree approved by the second All-Russian Congress of Soviets was the decree concerning the peace.

Peace

Certain critics were later to assert, quite unfairly, that Russia could have had peace even without the Bolshevik Revolution, and that if it did not come about it was only because of mistakes committed by the governments of the Entente powers and the Provisional Government who did not succeed in seizing the initiative in deciding the question of war or peace.

There can be no question but that the Provisional Government committed plenty of 'mistakes' of every kind. But it was by no means a matter of the weakness of certain individuals or of their personal mistakes. Those mistakes were dictated by the class nature of the policy of the Provisional Government, its loathing of the revolutionary movement and its fear in the face of that movement, and its dependence on the governments of the Entente powers. The growth of this dependence led even to the expulsion from the government of the war minister, A.I.Verkhovsky, who suggested peace with the German bloc so as to concentrate forces against the revolution.

At 9 pm on 8th November the second session of the Congress of Soviets opened. Lenin went up on to the platform. 'Next Lenin, gripping the edge of the reading stand, letting his little winking eyes travel over the crowd as he stood there waiting, apparently oblivious to the long-rolling ovation, which lasted several minutes'—recalls the American journalist John Reed, who was an eye-witness of the events and a participant in them.

'The question of peace is the burning question, the most pressing question of the present time,' Lenin began. The proletarian revolution was not decked out in the flamboyant clothes of beautiful words, nor was it concealed behind noisy manifestoes and impossible promises. It got down in a businesslike way to the great and difficult job of liberating the peoples of Russia and of the whole world from bloody slaughter. There was a note of confidence and firmness in the words of Lenin's decree, which proposed that all the warring peoples and their governments should enter immediately into talks concerning a just peace, without annexations or indemnities.

The Decree on Peace gave legislative form to new principles of foreign policy – the principles of equality and respect for the sovereignty of all peoples, the abandonment of secret diplomacy, and the co-existence of different social systems. The decree was addressed not only to the governments but also to the peoples of the warring nations.

The diplomatic representatives of the Entente powers tried to ignore the Decree on Peace and pretend that the document 'did not exist'. But the decree became the property of hundreds of millions of working people. Evidence of this is to be found in the strikes and demonstrations which swept through many countries of the world at the end of 1917 and in 1918.

The Decree on Peace was approved unanimously by the congress.

The congress turned immediately to the second question: the immediate abolition of landlord property rights. The yearnings of the people, their century-long dreams of being free from the oppression of the landlords were expressed in the Decree on Land.

'Landlord property rights are abolished, immediately and without any compensation,' the decree said. All land was declared to be the property of the whole people. It was made the duty of the local soviets to draw up an accurate account of all property and to organize the strictest revolutionary protection for everything that was handed over to the national economy. There was a special point which proclaimed that the land of the ordinary peasants and Cossacks would not be confiscated. Part of the

decree consisted of the peasants' demands, drawn up on the basis of 242 local peasant demands.

The Decree on Land was approved by a general vote of the delegates, with only one delegate voting against and eight abstaining. Thus the Bolsheviks won a complete victory on this cardinal question of the revolution as well. The peasantry received land from the hands of the victorious urban working class. This turned the alliance between the proletariat and the peasantry into a tremendous force promoting the further progress of the revolution. What the proletariat had failed to achieve in 1905 – to unite its struggle for socialism with the democratic movement of the peasantry for land – was achieved triumphantly in November 1917.

Since it was by its nature an expression of revolutionary democracy, the Decree on Land was put into practice by methods which were both revolutionary and socialist. This is to say, it rid the land of the survivals of serfdom more resolutely and thoroughly than any bourgeois revolution had yet done. By abolishing the private ownership of land the Decree on Land took the first step towards the liquidation of capitalist ownership of banks, industrial undertakings, transport, and so on.

As a result of the agrarian reforms carried out on the basis of the Decree on Land and the subsequent legislation the poor and middle peasants received 540,000,000 acres of land. The big landowners, the royal family and the Church lost all their land – 400,000,000 acres – and the rich

peasants (kulaks) lost 135,000,000 of the 216,000,000 they had owned in 1914.

This revolutionary redistribution of land served as the basis for further reforms in agriculture and for the development of a socialist farming system.

Bolshevik government

Since it enjoyed an overwhelming majority, it was natural that Lenin's party should form the new government. During the Congress the Central Committee of the Bolshevik Party had carried on intensive negotiations with the left-wing SRs about their participation in the government. The left-wing SRs had been members of the Military-Revolutionary Committee and they had – though, it is true, not without some hesitation – taken part in the armed uprising and supported the principal decisions taken by the Congress. But the left-wing SRs were too closely connected with their right-wing colleagues in the party and were too dependent on them in an ideological and organizational sense to be able to make up their minds immediately to join the Soviet government. It was a month later that they took this step.

At this point the Bolsheviks assumed the responsibility for forming a new government. 'We wanted a Soviet coalition government,' Lenin said. 'We did not exclude anyone from the Soviet. If they (the SRs and Mensheviks) did not wish to work together with us, so much the worse for them. The masses of the soldiers and peasants will not follow the Mensheviks and SRs.'

The decree which the Congress passed

*Left: 'The Word of Lenin' by V Liminov, Soviet painter. Soldiers read a news-sheet. Bolshevik propaganda fanned their discontent with the war. Lenin's programme of peace and land, rather than his politics, expressed the longings of the people of Russia. **Below:** 'Working people arise!' by Soviet painter V. Serov. The Bolsheviks exploited working-class discontent*

concerning the formation of a workers' and peasants' government headed by V.I.Lenin became in effect a constitutional document. It determined the name of the new government: the Soviet (Council) of People's Commissars, a name which reflected the fact that the new government was closely linked with the people and had developed out of the soviets. The decree laid down in general terms that the new government was subject to the control of the All-Russian Congress of Soviets and its Central Executive Committee. Thus the decree set out the constitutional principle regarding the responsibility of the workers' and peasants' government to the supreme bodies of the Soviet regime: the Congress of Soviets and the All-Russian Central Executive Committee, which had the right to remove people's commissars.

Once it had proved victorious in Petrograd the revolution spread quickly throughout the country. Immediately after Petrograd, the soviets were victorious in Moscow, where the battles for power were very violent and lasted for five days, ending on 16th November 1917 with the complete victory of the soviets.

In the course of three months the social-ist revolution was victorious throughout the vast country. From the line of the Western Front to the shores of the Pacific Ocean and from the White Sea to the Black Sea. The ways in which the revolutionary power of the soviets was established varied greatly from place to place. In Smolensk, Voronezh, Kazan, Chernigov, Zhitomir, and Kiev the workers and peasants took power only after armed struggle with the counter-revolutionaries. In Minsk, Yaroslavl, Nizhny Novgorod, Samara, Kursk, and Perm the soviets came to power by peaceful means.

At the very beginning of its course the socialist revolution in Russia succeeded in doing what the Paris Commune tried but failed to do. The workers, peasants, and soldiers of Russia set up a new administration, formed their own government at the All-Russian Congress of Soviets, uniting millions of working people, resolved the questions of peace and land, and offered all the peoples of Russia the possibility of national independence.

Such was the victory of the Bolshevik Revolution, which changed the face of the world and had a decisive influence on the fate of mankind.

Soldiers of the revolution, the ragged bootless men who enabled a relatively small party of 350,000 to gain control over a vast country of a hundred and fifty million people

6 BACKS TO THE WALL

The French Army Cracks

By the start of 1917 the war on the Western Front had settled into a state of apparently endless stalemate. For over two years the opposing sides had faced each other across the hardly shifting no man's land of northern France, wearing themselves down in a series of costly and ineffective offensives — Artois, Champagne, Verdun, the Somme. In this prolonged struggle of attrition no nation had suffered more than France. Not only was the war being fought on French soil, with all that this meant in devastation and loss of coal, iron ore, and other industrial resources, but her troops had suffered relatively the highest casualties of any belligerent power, amounting to some two and a quarter million men. As January 1917 dawned, with no promise of decisive - action — let alone victory — in sight, the strain on the nation was beginning to tell. Soldiers and civilians alike were becoming weary and disillusioned. The current mood was expressed by a French officer from general headquarters, Colonel Emile Herbillon. 'The year is opening in a grim atmosphere,' he wrote on the 2nd January 1917. 'Promises and hopes have been followed by too many disappointments.'

Joffre dismissed

All that the Allied war leaders could plan for 1917 was another great Franco-British offensive just as they had ordained for 1915 and 1916. The stage seemed set for a repetition of the great attrition battles of those years. But one significant change had just occurred. Sixty-four-year-old

'Poilus' painted by G.Pierre in 1917

General César Joffre, commander-in-chief of the French army and the main advocate of the attrition strategy, had been replaced. Bulky and imperturbable, 'Papa' Joffre had won enormous prestige as the victor of the Marne in 1914 and since then, at his Chantilly headquarters, had reigned supreme in Allied military affairs. But late in 1916 French deputies, resenting his autocratic powers, had attacked him — ostensibly for his mishandling of the recent Verdun and Somme campaigns and they had virtually forced Aristide Briand, the French prime minister, to dismiss him. With Joffre honorifically created a marshal of France and shunted into the post of the government's military adviser in Paris, General Robert Nivelle was appointed as his successor.

General Nivelle, a dapper, dynamic artilleryman aged sixty, had risen to rapid fame as an army commander at Verdun. 'We have the formula!' he had proclaimed on assuming command. His aggressive spirit and bounding self-confidence had so impressed Briand and his colleagues — now anxiously seeking a leader who would end the impasse on the Western Front — that he was promoted over the heads of France's most senior generals, Ferdinand Foch, Henri-Philippe Pétain, and Edouard de Curières de Castelnau. Nominated commander-in-chief of the armies of the north and north-east, Nivelle caused an immediate stir by brusquely re-shaping the Allied offensive plans for 1917. Now, as at Verdun, he was convinced he had the 'formula' for success, but on a much larger scale. Instead of Joffre's scheme for a combined Franco-British attack on a broad front to take place in February, he prescribed, as

the principal operation, a massive French assault on the thirty-mile Soissons-Rheims sector, flanking the river Aisne, to be launched in April. This was to be supported by British and French attacks designed to contain the German reserves. By this plan, reversing Joffre's aim to let the British take some of the weight off the tired French troops, Nivelle envisaged a spectacular French break-through that might even lead quickly to victory in the west.

Nivelle's formula

Almost a million men were to take part in the main assault — a force commanded by General Micheler, consisting of three armies, the 5th (General Mazel), the 6th (General Mangin), and the 10th (General Duchêne). In support would be 5,000 guns. After a preliminary bombardment the 5th and 6th Armies were to attack and break the German line, and the 10th Army would then advance in the centre to exploit the rupture. The conception ran counter to all current military thinking. It relied on swift, sudden, surprise attack, delivered with overwhelming force and calculated to destroy the main enemy force — as Nivelle emphasized — within forty-eight hours. Considering the formidable power of the defensive as developed by 1917, it was a bold plan by any standards. But seen in relation to the enemy's Soissons-Rheims line it was foolhardy. The terrain was difficult, comprising a series of plateaux and ridges rising 200 feet above the Aisne; and the entire sector, held by the Germans for two years, was honeycombed with elaborate fortifications and bristled with guns and automatic weapons. Yet, dubious as the scheme was, Nivelle obtained approval

for it, in both Paris and London, through sheer persuasiveness and his personal conviction that it would succeed.

From the first, fate seemed to be against Nivelle. In January unprecedented cold descended on the Western Front, hindering offensive preparations, intensifying the troops' hardships as they huddled in their frozen trenches, and depressing still further their already low morale. Then Nivelle's whole plan was jeopardized by a major German withdrawal. In February the Germans began retiring from the ninety-mile Arras-Noyon-Soissons sector (west of the Soissons-Rheims line) to the heavily defended Hindenburg Line. They were thus eliminating a dangerous salient, shortening their front, and breaking contact with the French over a large part of Nivelle's projected field of operations (though a secondary one). Meanwhile they increased the number of their divisions in the Soissons-Rheims line from nine to forty. These moves radically changed the strategic picture; and doubts now arose about the wisdom of Nivelle's scheme. In Paris members of Alexandre Ribot's new government, especially the war minister, Paul Painlevé, received the plan with marked uneasiness. So did some of Nivelle's own generals and, on the British side, commander-in-chief Sir Douglas Haig and his colleagues. But Nivelle, fervently backed by his *chef de cabinet* (chief of staff), the fiery Colonel d'Alenson, refused to modify his main assault plan.

Building false hopes
But as the massive build-up proceeded behind the Aisne's left bank in the continuing wintry weather of March, one element essential to French success—surprise—had already been lost. It was impossible to hide the preparations from the enemy. And among the French troops, faced with yet

another offensive that they had no reason to think would end any differently from previous ones, enthusiasm was at rock-bottom. But here Nivelle scored a psychological triumph. By a concentrated morale-boosting drive he wrought a spectacular change in the army's mood. In anticipation of his promised break-through, apathy disappeared and discipline and bearing noticeably improved. At last, the troops believed, there was a goal worth fighting for: this attack would achieve results. There was striking evidence of the new spirit in letters from the front, as examined by army postal control. In contrast to their earlier gloomy, bitter tone, these now expressed hope and confidence.

Security about the coming offensive was almost non-existent. In the Paris bars and bistros it was discussed openly—and with extravagant optimism. But no such optimism was felt by the French war cabinet, or by an increasing number of Nivelle's officers, senior and junior. Many of these wrote to Painlevé at the war ministry, reporting their misgivings. And so apprehensive were Ribot and his colleagues that, on the 6th April, an emergency top-level council was held at Compiègne (to whose historic Palace Nivelle had just transferred his headquarters) to decide whether the attack should go ahead as planned or not. President Poincaré, ministers, and army chiefs, including Nivelle, assembled in the President's special railway coach at Compiègne station. In a tense discussion almost all present voiced doubts about the operation. Nivelle forcibly argued that it would succeed: he even promised that if his armies had not broken through within forty-eight hours he would call off the assault. Finally, realizing he had no support, he angrily offered his resignation. Amid the general dismay, Poincaré hastened to reassure Nivelle that he had the government's con-

Craonne, April 1917. A painting by François Flameng. It was here in atrocious weather conditions that Nivelle's ill-starred offensive predictably foundered

fidence, and full responsibility for proceeding with the offensive.

The bubble bursts
Nivelle had got his way; and in the sleet-filled dawn of Monday 16th April—a week after a preliminary British attack at Arras—the assault was launched. It turned out to be a disaster. Within a fortnight it had ground to a halt (though local operations continued), broken on the deadly Craonne plateau, the slopes of the Chemin des Dames and the heavily defended heights all along the front. Its failure was evident in the first hours: there were ghastly scenes as French troops struggled against uncut barbed wire and were mown down by withering automatic fire from undestroyed strong-points, and misdirected fire from the French 75s fell among panicking French Senegalese. Poor security, ineffective artillery preparation, and atrocious weather had—quite apart from the basic weakness of the whole conception—all combined to doom the operation from the start. Instead of the promised break-through, Nivelle's troops gained a few miles of ground at the price of almost 200,000 casualties. Their new-found euphoria collapsed like a pricked bubble. The reaction was catastrophic but in the circumstances predictable. In bitter frustration and resentment at their 'betrayal', the men of Nivelle's armies rebelled.

For some six weeks in the spring of 1917 much of the French army was in a state of mutiny. Elements of fifty-four divisions refused to obey orders, demonstrated, deserted, called for peace, brandished red flags, threatened or attempted to march on

Paris and overthrow the government. At the gravest moment, in early June, only two entirely dependable divisions stood between Soissons and the capital sixty-five miles away. The wonder is that the Germans did not take advantage of the situation to launch a counter-attack on the Soissons-Rheims front. Had they done so the course of the war must have been incalculably altered. But equally remarkable is the factor that prevented them from doing this—the maintenance of almost total secrecy which concealed news of the mutinies from the enemy and the French home front, to say nothing of the British high command and government. Such scant information as the Germans received through agents or escaped German prisoners they demonstrably discounted.

Dark episode

The official secrecy over the mutinies has never been relaxed. French military archives are virtually inaccessible and the official French war history *(Les Armées Françaises dans la Grande Guerre)* reveals little detail. Something of the story can be gleaned from contemporary diaries and memoirs; but the fullest and most reliable account comes from Marshal (then General) Philippe Pétain who, as commander-in-chief in succession to Nivelle, was called on to restore order in the demoralized armies. Pétain's record (which he entrusted to Major-General Sir Edward Spears, and which Spears published in his book, *Two Men Who Saved France,* Eyre and Spottiswoode, 1966) throws much light on this dark episode, even to the naming of individual units involved.

The main wave of mutinies lasted from 29th April to 10th June. They reached their height on 2nd June, with seventeen separate outbreaks. Of the 151 incidents recorded (some occurred after the 10th June)

110 were listed as 'grave', and altogether 110 units were affected, mostly in the camps and barracks of the Aisne region behind the Chemin des Dames sector. There were also disorders on over 100 troop trains and at 130 railway stations. The first outbreak took place east of Rheims, where an infantry regiment refused to parade on being ordered back to the line after only five days' rest. On the 4th May a number of infantrymen in the Chemin des Dames area suddenly deserted, and men of a colonial regiment circulated anti-war leaflets and noisily refused to fight. The tempo of revolt now quickened. On the 16th and 17th a Chasseur battalion and an infantry regiment rebelled. On the 19th another Chasseur unit demonstrated, and next day two entire infantry regiments refused to march. Violence had so far been absent; but on the 22nd and 27th, near Tardenois (in the Aisne region), there were two cases of officers being assaulted. On the 28th seven regiments and a Chasseur battalion from five different divisions mutinied. And as the month ended, disorder swept through eight divisions which had fought at Chemin des Dames or were about to move there.

Mutiny spreads

One mutiny was, in Pétain's words, 'conceived in cold blood'. This involved a crack infantry regiment which had fought gallantly at Verdun and since then been in almost constant action until February 1917. Told to stand by for the front, on 27th May it moved from rest quarters to billets near Soissons. On the 29th over 800 men paraded—in excellent order—to protest against making further useless and costly attacks. Rejecting the pleas and threats of their divisional and corps commanders, they recruited more followers with the aim of seizing trains, travelling to

French line-drawing 1917: 'The Grumble'. When Nivelle's offensive yielded only a few miles of ground at a cost of 200,000 casualties the grumble became a mutiny

Paris and putting their demands before the Chamber of Deputies. The officers, who had stood by helplessly, now managed to control the situation. At dawn next day the mutineers were ordered into lorries and driven, still demonstrating, to a quiet area and finally to Verdun. The sequel: courts-martial in which four men were sentenced to death, and the ceremonial stripping of the regiment's colours.

Early June brought more and worse outbreaks. On the 1st one regiment near Tardenois—again with a fine fighting record—was ordered to the front after a brief rest period. Chanting the *Internationale*, the men marched in angry protest to the local town hall. The brigade commander, who tried to stop them, was attacked and his insignia ripped off. The divisional commander intervened but was shouted down. Then the ringleaders freed prisoners from a detention camp and the troops ran wild, overturning lorries and smashing windows. By next evening a 2,000-strong mob was on the march, waving red flags and calling for peace and revolution. On the 3rd the regiment was moved to another camp and the agitation quickly subsided.

Their brief duration was often a feature of these outbursts—even the violent ones. On the 2nd a Chasseur battalion rioted in the same area, opened fire on the commanding officer's quarters and burned the huts of a unit that tried to restrain them. But by nightfall the mutiny had fizzled out and there was no repetition. Meanwhile trouble was rife on leave trains and at railway stations in the rear. Pétain cites two typical cases. At Château-Thierry, on 7th June, police battled with rebellious leave-men from Paris who finally had to be controlled by armed troops. Next day, in a clash at Esternay station, soldiers mobbed and assaulted railway officials who tried to shepherd them back to their trains.

Russian influence

The disorder had now passed its peak, subsiding almost suddenly, like a worked-out fever. From the 10th to the 30th June incidents averaged one a day; and by September had ceased altogether. The whole uprising was essentially a spontaneous protest by desperate and overtried troops rather than a concerted rebellion. Many men saw themselves as strikers, not mutineers. Heinous though this collective indiscipline of an army was in military terms, it should be remembered in mitigation that some mutinying units—among the French army's best—had fought with heroism in previous battles. And the mutinies had their moments of pathos, as when captured rebel formations marched back to face court-martial and the direst penalties with their uniform spruce and their boots shined. French troops already had a list of long-standing grievances over vast and seemingly needless losses, derisory pay, exiguous leave, harsh discipline, wretched welfare conditions. Coming on top of these, the Aisne *débâcle* was the crowning blow. 'The fighting troops were at the end of their tether,' wrote Pétain. A GHQ officer, Lieutenant Henry Bordeaux, reporting on the state of one rear division, observed 'a sort of moral nihilism'. 'It is an army without faith,' he added.

Yet the mutinies were at least encouraged by two external factors. One was the Russian Revolution, which shook the world in mid-March 1917. In France it inspired a wild revolutionary spirit among the two Russian brigades—Russia's small expe-

ditionary force—serving alongside the French. This mood infected many less steadfast *poilus* (French 'Tommies') in the nearby camps—the more so when the Russians, suffering crippling losses in the Aisne offensive, staged their own mutiny. Moved first to bases in the rear, they were then isolated in central France, where they were finally shelled into submission by other Russian troops. The frequent waving of red flags, chanting of the *Internationale,* and calls for revolution by the French mutineers testified to the influence the Russians had on them.

Defeatist campaign

The other factor was more sinister: subversive propaganda spread by civilian agitators in the rear. Active since the previous November (and even earlier) in conjunction with labour troubles in the war plants, it had intensified in the New Year. Military security produced strong evidence of a defeatist campaign being directed at the troops through anti-war tracts and newspaper articles, and illicit meetings and inflammatory speeches in the leave centres. Late in February Nivelle unavailingly requested the minister of the interior, Louis-Jean Malvy, to suppress the traffic and its chief instigators, whom he named. It was only Nivelle's forceful boosting of the troops' morale before the Aisne offensive that damped down the defeatist threat at this crucial moment. But when disorder swept the armies in May, the agitators renewed their assault. They haunted the Paris termini distributing anti-war leaflets to troops in transit; incited them to desert (there were desertion agencies near the stations, where men could obtain civilian clothes); used every means to push the disaffected *poilus* into revolt, including the clandestine dispatch to the army zone of extremist, left-wing news-sheets—like *Le Bonnet Rouge* and *La Tranchée Républicaine*—that defied the censor's ban.

But the anti-war campaign was also being waged against the home front. Playing on the war-weariness of French civilians—and these were almost as spiritless and disillusioned as the soldiers, especially after the hope-shattering fiasco of the Aisne offensive—the saboteurs were provoking labour unrest and infiltrating the war factories with their defeatist-pacifist propaganda. From mid-May—when militant *midinettes* (Parisian working-girls) paraded the Paris boulevards—onwards, demonstrations and strikes became frequent, until by the end of June there were over 170 stoppages in war plants in Paris and the provinces. Sympathizing troops joined in some marches. Occasionally violence erupted, incited by agitators. Beneath the capital's workaday surface there was unwonted tension. Never in the war had

Above: French soldier with wooden crosses sets out to mark graves during the offensive. Left: General Nivelle. It was hoped that his aggressive spirit would end the impasse on the Western Front

national morale been so uneasy. Through the June weeks Ribot's war cabinet met in an atmosphere of constant crisis. The corridors of the Chamber of Deputies buzzed with alarm and pessimism. And in two stormy secret sessions of the Chamber, left-wing members bitterly attacked the government and high command, questioned France's ability to continue fighting and canvassed the possibility of peace. 'The fever is spreading,' wrote President Poincaré. 'Must we await a new victory of the Marne to be healed?'

France's whole war-making capacity was undermined by a grave *malaise.* The superficial unity she had achieved in August 1914—burying her acute political, social, and labour differences in face of the national emergency—was breaking down under the exhausting strain of nearly three years of war. But the particular defeatist-pacifist menace that now threatened her might have been minimized if, at the outset, the government had taken a different decision about national security.

Lukewarm reprisals

Instead of arresting, as intended, some 2,500 potential troublemakers—listed in the police dossier, *Carnet B,* which had been compiled for just this eventuality—the authorities had detained only the known spies, largely on the ground that action against left-wing labour leaders and other suspects might antagonize the workers and impede the call-up. This policy had paid ill. A mixed assortment of pacifists, internationalists, left-wing extremists, Marxists, and anarchists—each with their own pretexts for sabotaging France's war-effort—were left free to disseminate their propaganda. They ranged from Merrheim, the trade union chief, to sponsors of illicit newssheets like Faure, Duval, and Almereyda, and a host of other undesirables, many of them aliens. And behind them were traitors such as the notorious Bolo Pasha, Lenoir and the police chief Leymarie, working directly for Germany. Under the complacent tolerance of Louis-Jean Malvy, minister of the interior, these men operated with almost total immunity. Their task was made easier by continued government reluctance to suppress them for fear of provoking labour disturbances. The treason trials of 1918, bringing Malvy and many lesser fry to justice, were to expose the full extent of the internal danger assailing France.

Pétain to the rescue

How far was the defeatist propaganda responsible for the mutinies? The answer seems to be that while it was not the root cause, it was a strong contributory element. This at least was the verdict of General Pétain, who succeeded Nivelle as commander-in-chief as the troubles were boiling up in mid-May. Nivelle had been dismissed amid a resounding command crisis. Sixty-one-year-old General Philippe Pétain, famous as the saviour of Verdun, was undoubtedly the right man to replace him. Aloof and reserved, he hid beneath his cold exterior an unsuspected warmth: he understood the troops and they trusted him. His method of handling the mutinies was a mixture of sternness and humanity. First he moved ruthlessly to stamp out disorder and punish the ringleaders. He stiffened the faltering authority of his officers. He took vigorous steps to curb the prevalent drunkenness—a potent factor in inflaming the revolts. And he vehemently attacked the 'contamination' from the rear. Furious at the government's failure to suppress the defeatist groups, he bombarded ministers with demands for action, warning them that if the agitation continued he could not answer for the army's recovery. But Pétain knew that much was wrong within the army itself. Thus he set about a whole range of welfare reforms.

Perhaps most effective of all were Pétain's contacts with the troops themselves. Almost daily in these weeks his white-pennanted car left GHQ, Compiègne, on a comprehensive tour of formations. In about a month he covered over ninety divisions. A tall, magisterial figure with his flowing moustache and frosty blue eyes, he addressed officers and men, exhorting, encouraging, explaining his plans for limited operations designed to avoid heavy losses. He talked with individual soldiers, listening sympathetically to complaints and suggestions. The visits were of inestimable value. At last the men felt that someone was caring for their interests, that they counted as human beings. By late summer the French army was well on the way to restoration. The price it had paid for mutiny was not, in the circumstances, high. While many convicted mutineers were sentenced to long terms, of the 412 men condemned to death between May and October, only 55 were executed.

Now the home front remained to be purged. As with Pétain and her army, France providentially possessed the right man for the task. Late in 1917 the elderly Georges Clemenceau emerged from the political wilderness to become prime minister. None of France's previous wartime premiers—René Viviani, Aristide Briand, Alexandre Ribot, and latterly Paul Painlevé—had been able to command a sustained, united war-effort. But Clemenceau was a leader of different calibre. A merciless enemy of all anti-patriotic elements, he feared no party or faction. Having denounced Malvy in the Senate in July, as prime minister he proceeded to liquidate the defeatist cliques, silence the pessimists and doubters, and renew France's bruised and battered fighting spirit. His one aim was victory. 'Home policy? I wage war! Foreign policy? I wage war!' he bluntly stated. 'All the time I wage war!' As 1917 ended, France seemed to have narrowly surmounted her gravest crisis.

Below: The commander-in-chief sympathizes with a soldier's complaint. Pétain handled the mutinies with sternness and humanity, but he knew much was wrong with the army. Bottom: Militant midinettes on the march. Even Parisian working girls were restive

In Flanders' Fields

The name 'Passchendaele' applies, strictly speaking, to the last phase of the 3rd Ypres campaign of July-November 1917. But it is far more usual to find it used as a damning synonym for prolonged battles of attrition in the Flanders mud during the First World War. Half a century later, people are still arguing passionately about whether the offensive should ever have been undertaken in the first place, why it was allowed to go on for so long, and what effect it had on the course of the war as a whole.

On 15th November 1916 General Joseph Joffre, the French commander-in-chief, assembled a conference of the Entente military representatives at Chantilly to determine Anglo-French strategy for the coming year. He and Sir Douglas Haig, the British commander-in-chief, agreed that the attrition battles of the Somme and Verdun in 1916 had left the German army on the Western Front near to breaking point. Joffre feared that the French army could undertake only one more major offensive, but he hoped this would be decisive. He proposed a concerted offensive on all fronts in the spring of 1917 with the British cast for the leading role in the west. In December, however, General Joffre was replaced by the most junior of the French army commanders, General Robert Nivelle, who had persuaded both the French prime minister Aristide Briand and the British prime minister David Lloyd George that he could achieve a complete break-through in under forty-eight hours—a feat which had eluded both sides since September 1914. In Nivelle's plan the French were to strike the major blow on the Aisne sector, while Haig launched diversionary attacks near Arras and took over part of the French line south of the Somme.

Nivelle fails

In February and March 1917 the effective German director of strategy, General Erich Ludendorff, forestalled Nivelle's planned offensive for the spring by withdrawing between fifteen and twenty-two miles on a front of about seventy miles to a strong defensive position known—after the nominal commander—as the Hindenburg Line. Nivelle was reluctant to adjust his aims and—oblivious of the need for surprise—made no secret of his highly ambitious plan. The French offensive began on April 16th in an atmosphere of political and military mistrust between the Allies and lasted until May 7th. It penetrated up to four miles on a sixteen mile front, but this limited success contrasted too sharply with Nivelle's personal promises. Frustrated by failure, the French armies began to disintegrate. Long-festering grievances came to a head in mutinies that broke out in May and June in nearly half the units in the French army. General Henri-Philippe Pétain, the hero of Verdun, who replaced Nivelle on 15th May, quickly restored order, but also dropped strong hints that the French would have to remain largely on the defensive for the rest of the year until they could be backed up by American divisions and more tanks and heavy artillery. Meanwhile, after prolonging the gruelling battle at Arras to shield the French during their offensive on the Aisne, the British had to take a fresh look at the projected Flanders offensive in the light of conditions very different from those that had applied when the Allies had planned their strategy earlier in the year.

On May 4th, the French and British civilian war leaders and their military advisers met at Paris to revise their strategy after Nivelle's failure and the Russian February Revolution. The military chiefs agreed unanimously that offensive operations must be continued on the Western Front. Allied attacks, they believed, had already exhausted a large proportion of Germany's reserves and she must be prevented from throwing her full weight against either Russia or Italy. But, in the words of the chief of the imperial general staff, Sir William Robertson: 'It is no longer a question of aiming at breaking through the enemy's front and aiming at distant objectives. It is now a question of wearing down and exhausting the enemy's resistance. . . . We are all of the opinion that our object can be obtained by relentlessly attacking with limited objectives, while making the fullest use of our artillery. By this means we hope to gain our ends and with the minimum loss possible.' Both the British and French governments gave their approval to these recommendations. Before the seriousness of the French army mutinies began to be revealed to him early in June, the British commander-in-chief, Sir Douglas Haig, was already contemplating a bold stroke in Flanders very different in spirit from the cautious policy outlined above. The British government had laid down in November 1916 that the clearing of German submarine bases from the Flanders coast was a strategic objective of the first importance.

Top left: Gough, the young 'thruster' put in charge of the opening offensive. Top right: Robertson, chief of the imperial general staff. 'It is now a question of wearing down and exhausting the enemy's resistance.' Above: Haig, Joffre, and Lloyd George. Haig and Joffre agreed in 1916 that the Germans on the Western Front were near breaking point. To this misjudgement Haig owed his confidence, and his disastrous persistence in Flanders. Left: 'Canadian gunners in Mud', a painting of Passchendaele by Bastier. 'Passchendaele' assumed the importance of historical myth—a myth of men smothered and helpless in mud, sacrificed for nothing

Backs to the Wall

Haig believed that such a break-through could be achieved from the Ypres salient, assisted by a supporting advance along the coast and an amphibious landing near Ostend. This aim rested on a very optimistic view of weakening German morale and reserves. It also assumed full French co-operation in supporting offensives, and this Pétain – who had just replaced Nivelle – promised on May 18th.

French support crumbles

But on 1st June the picture changed. General Debeney brought Haig a message from Pétain which mentioned euphemistically that 'the French army was in a bad state of discipline' and would not be able to fulfil the promise to attack in support of the opening of the British offensive at Ypres. A week later Pétain himself revealed in more detail the gravity of the situation but added that things were improving – as indeed they were. Thereafter, though hopes of really active French participation faded, Haig remained confident that the British army (assisted by six French divisions) could gain a major victory in Flanders. Lloyd George who, incidentally, knew even less about the breakdown of French discipline than Haig, grew increasingly sceptical about French co-operation. By 13th June he was harrying Robertson with a plan to remove twelve divisions from Haig's command 'to settle the war in Italy'. Robertson, a firm 'Westerner' who usually saw eye to eye with Haig, nevertheless cautioned him against 'large and costly attacks without full co-operation by the French'; and on 13th June he wrote: 'Don't argue that you can finish the war this year, or that the German is already beaten. Argue that your plan [the concentration of all available troops and material on the Western Front] is the best plan – as it is – that no other would be *safe* let alone decisive, and then leave them to reject your advice and mine. They dare not do that'.

Why in these unpropitious circumstances, with even the loyal Robertson urging caution, did Haig decide to launch the Ypres offensive? It had long been apparent to the British commander-in-chief that the French war effort was flagging, so that the collapse of morale after Nivelle's abortive offensive came as no surprise to him. Judging from his diary entries Haig's motives were mixed: he wished to shield and encourage the French, but was also eager to gain a great victory for the British army which had now, at last, become the predominant partner. What needs to be stressed, however, is that the senior French commanders had no enthusiasm for a major offensive in Flanders designed to clear the Channel coast. Pétain, in fact, was opposed to any major

offensive on the Western Front in 1917, and on 19th May he told Sir Henry Wilson – who had been attached to Nivelle's headquarters – that Haig's projected advance towards Ostend was certain to fail. General Ferdinand Foch, chief of the French general staff, was, if possible, even less encouraging and sarcastically referred to the campaign as 'a duck's march'.

Jellicoe's bombshell

The crucial incident, as far as the indecisive British war cabinet committee was concerned, occurred at a meeting on 19th June; namely 'Jellicoe's bombshell'. Not a single member of the committee, consisting of David Lloyd George, Andrew Bonar Law, Sir Alfred Milner, Lord Curzon, and General J.C.Smuts, favoured a major offensive on the Western Front in 1917, but the first sea lord shattered their assumption that time was on their side by declaring that German submarines were taking such a toll of merchant shipping that it would be impossible for Great Britain to continue the war into 1918. The Royal Navy would be in grave difficulty unless the Belgian coast could be cleared by the Army. Although this alarmist prediction suited Haig's own military views, it is very doubtful if he took Jellicoe's warning as seriously as is often supposed. As recently as 7th May Haig had described Jellicoe in a letter to his wife as 'an old woman', and after the meeting on 19th June he noted: 'No one present shared Jellicoe's view, and all seemed satisfied that the food reserves in Great Britain are adequate'. Even more revealingly General Charteris, Haig's chief of intelligence, recorded in his diary on 28th June: 'No one believed this [Jellicoe's] rather amazing view, but it had sufficient weight to make the Cabinet agree to our attack going on.'

The fundamental reason for Haig's determination to launch the Flanders offensive was, it seems clear, neither the necessity to shield the French nor to clear the Channel coast of enemy submarine bases. It was rather his conviction that the Germans were so near to collapse that six months of fighting at the present intensity on the Western Front could end the war that year. His confidence was increased by the auspicious beginning of operations on 7th June, when General Sir Herbert Plumer's 2nd Army – assisted by the explosion of nineteen enormous mines under the German front line – was brilliantly successful in carrying out a limited advance to seize the Messines Ridge and so straighten out the salient south of Ypres.

The interval of fifty-three days which then occurred between this successful preliminary advance and the opening of the main offensive on 31st July was to prove fatal.

Haig's plans were not finally approved until 25th July and then only after the desirability of reinforcing the Italian Front in preference to Flanders had been endlessly debated by the war cabinet. Haig certainly had grounds for the bitter remark that he would have liked such confidence and support as the prime minister had recently given to Nivelle. More important however, as Haig's most recent biographer, John Terraine, has pointed out, Haig had intended even in the preliminary planning stage that there would be a delay of some six weeks between Messines and the main attack. Moreover, as the same author has written, Haig made his 'gravest and most fatal error' in 1917 of entrusting the main role in the Flanders battle to the 5th Army commanded by General Sir Hubert Gough. It could be argued that Gough was the obvious choice for the bold strategy envisaged. He was, at forty-seven, the youngest army commander (whereas Plumer at sixty was by far the eldest); he was a cavalryman and a 'thruster' whereas Plumer – rather like Pétain – was noted for his cautious approach to planning and tactics, and his great concern to minimize casualties. Yet, quite apart from criticisms levelled at Gough and his staff for revising and mishandling Haig's plans, the transfer of command at such a time was bound to cause administrative complications and delays, particularly as the French contingent (General Anthoine's 1st Army) had to be fitted in on Gough's left between the 5th Army and Rawlinson's 4th Army on the coast.

Third Ypres opens

Like so many campaigns of the First World War, the actual operations of Third Ypres – which at last began on 31st July after a fortnight's preparatory bombardment and several postponements at the request of the army and corps commanders – soon ceased to bear much resemblance to the original plan. Essentially Haig had assumed that after eight days the 5th Army would have advanced fifteen miles and would have got control of the Ypres-Roulers-Thourout railway. Only when this was done would the 4th Army begin to attack along the coast, assisted by amphibious landings and, with Gough's support, would turn the German defences. Meanwhile the 2nd Army, after playing only a minor supporting role in the opening days, would advance to the north-east to secure the whole Passchendaele ridge.

This schedule proved to be far too optimistic. The campaign degenerated into a struggle for control of a plateau some sixty metres high. The operation fell into three distinct phases each containing three major actions. In the first phase Gough's 5th Army played the major role, and fought the

'The whole surface of the ground consisted of nothing but a series of overlapping shell-craters, half full of yellow, slimy water. . . . The original roads had almost ceased to exist and it was necessary to lay down corduroy tracks . . . These and the "duck board" walks were daily machine-gunned by low-flying aeroplanes. Every yard of ground had been carefully "registered" by the enemy's guns, and a peculiarly effective form of gas shell, containing "mustard gas", had been evolved . . .' (Brigadier General Baker Carr.) **Above:** *'Void', painted by Wellard.* **Below:** *'Gassed. "In Arduis Fidelis"' by Gilbert Rogers*

battles of Pilckem Ridge (31st July), Gheluvelt Plateau (10th August) and Langemarck (16th August). The British had deliberately thrown away the chance of a surprise attack and they were hampered by driving rain. But despite this the first day, unlike the opening of the Somme battle on 1st July 1916, was far from being a disaster. The main assault was made by fourteen British and two French divisions supported by over 2,000 guns and howitzers on a very wide front of nearly twenty miles. The troops in the centre and to the left managed to reach the third and farthest target lines, and the only real check was suffered on the right of 5th Army's frontage. Here, from the Gheluvelt Plateau, specially trained German divisions made a fierce counter-attack, while the strength of the enemy's counter-bombardment during the battle as a whole showed how little real damage the British army's 'softening-up process' had done. Yet even if GHQ's initial assessment of British casualties at 15,000 was too low, it still compared very favourably with nearly 60,000 on the first day of the Somme.

Unfortunately atrocious weather had already begun to hamper further advance. On the first day the weather had completely prevented the British from using their superior air force for artillery reconnaissance. Far worse, as Colonel Fuller noted at Tank Corps headquarters: 'By July 31st from the Polygone de Zonnebeke through St Julien and northwards past Langemarck the Steenbeck had become a wide moat of liquid mud.' The British were unlucky in that the weather broke on the very first day. But meteorological reports for the previous eighty years could have showed GHQ that Flanders was notoriously wet in August. Rapidly, the swamp expanded, greatly assisted by the bombardment which had effectively destroyed the already precarious drainage system. Tank Corps headquarters daily sent a 'swamp map' to GHQ until instructed not to send any more. It seems unlikely that Haig ever saw these maps, and neither he nor Gough at this stage grasped the full significance of the appalling ground conditions. As early as 4th August General Charteris noted: 'All my fears about the weather have been realised. It has killed this attack. Every day's delay tells against us. We lose, hour by hour, the advantage of attack. . . . Even if the weather were to clear now, it will take days for the ground to harden, if indeed it ever can before the winter frost. . . . I went up to the front line this morning. Every brook is swollen and the ground is a quagmire. . . .'

Although there were some fine days in August, the weather and the terrain dictated the course of operations: Gough's second and third attempts to press forward

Backs to the Wall

Overleaf: 'The Harvest of Battle' by C.R.W.Nevinson. *Normally it took two men to carry a stretcher: by October it took sixteen. Mules and horses sank beneath the mud with their loads. A survivor wrote: '. . . we had often to drink shell-hole water, not knowing what would be at the bottom. Many a lot I helped to pull out of shell holes, where fellows were sinking and could not move'*

(on 10th and 16th August) were thrown back by fierce counter-attacks. In his book *The Fifth Army,* Gough wrote that after 16th August he 'informed the Commander-in-Chief that tactical success was not possible, or would be too costly under such conditions, and advised that the attack should now be abandoned'. This advice was consistent with Lloyd George's prior condition that the attack should be discontinued if casualties were incommensurate with the amount of ground gained. In ignoring this condition and advice, Haig may still have been concerned to assist the French, but another explanation seems more likely. To call off the offensive at this

German prisoner captured in the successful battle of the Messines Ridge, an auspicious opening for Haig's campaign

stage would have entailed surrender to Lloyd George's nagging pressure to divert large forces to Italy. Haig and Robertson were fully agreed that such a move might result in losing the war on the Western Front.

Plumer plans carefully

At the end of August Haig transferred the main role in further operations from Gough to Plumer. This signified a return to a more cautious approach based on concentrating overwhelming artillery cover for each short infantry advance. Contrary to the caricature presented by his extreme critics, Haig did not favour remorseless tactical attrition once the initial attempt at a breakthrough had lost its impetus. Indeed he criticized Gough for ordering too many small attacks on isolated farmhouses and strong points since they were seldom effective and were too costly in lives and

ammunition. It was ironic that although September was to be generally dry, in sharp contrast to August, Plumer spent the first three weeks of it meticulously preparing the next short step forward. The main sector of the offensive was limited to 4,000 yards with four divisions packed into the front line. The depth of the advance was restricted to 1,500 yards when a halt would be made to hold off counter-attacks and to await the ponderous advance of the huge mass of artillery. Plumer, and his chief of staff General Sir Charles Harington, calculated that the Passchendaele-Staden ridge could be cleared by four such limited attacks.

Anzac advance

The first of the three battles of the second phase—that of the Menin Road Ridge on 20th September—resulted in a clear victory. This was essentially an artillery triumph. General Birdwood, who commanded the 1st Anzac Corps in the battle, recalled that it was quite the best artillery barrage the Australians had ever seen. 'Creeping forward exactly according to plan, the barrage won the ground, while the infantry followed behind and occupied all the important points with a minimum of resistance.' The attack began at 5.40 am, and by mid-day the final objectives had been reached. The Germans were unable to counter-attack before 3.15 pm and were successfully beaten off. In bright sunshine British aircraft were able to report nearly four hundred objectives to the artillery. Ludendorff recorded: 'Another terrible assault was made on our lines on September 20th. . . . The enemy's onslaught was successful, which proved the superiority of the attack over the defence. . . .'

Plumer's second offensive—at Polygon Wood on 26th September—closely resembled the Menin Road battle both in its careful preparation and encouraging results. It too was fought in good weather. Prince Rupprecht of Bavaria, commanding the German forces in Flanders, now began to worry about his defensive tactics and the scarcity of reserves. General Charteris, whose optimistic reports fed and fortified the convictions of his chief, noted that the situation at the end of September closely resembled that on the Somme the previous year. 'Now, as then, we had worn down the German resistance to very near breaking point; then as now the weather went against us. It is a race with time and a fight with the weather. One thing is certain, no other army but ours could fight on as we are fighting. D.H. is asking for the last ounce from it and getting a wonderful response.' Encouraged by Plumer's gains and Charteris's assessment of German exhaustion, Haig on 28th September revived the idea that the next advance should be

immediately exploited. 'I am of the opinion that the enemy is tottering, and that a good vigorous blow might lead to decisive results. If we could destroy, or interrupt for 48 hours, the railway at Roulers there would probably be a débâcle, because the enemy would then have to rely on only one railway line for the supply of his troops between Ghent and the sea. . . .'

Plumer's third attack, the battle of Broodseinde on 4th October, followed the same pattern as the previous two: it was a heartening tactical victory but showed no signs of yielding those 'decisive results' which Haig had mentioned to his army commanders. It also marked the zenith of the artillery's contribution to the Third Ypres campaign before casualties, loss of guns, and the sheer impossibility of movement reduced its effectiveness. The Germans suffered particularly heavy casualties in this battle because the British barrage fell on five divisions just as they themselves were forming up to attack. This battle at last afforded the 2nd Army a foothold on the Passchendaele ridge. But a decision now had to be quickly made as to whether to halt the advance, particularly as the amphibious operations against Ostend had by now been abandoned and with them any real hope of reaching the Channel coast that year.

The day after Broodseinde Haig conferred with his army commanders. Charteris noted: 'We are far enough on now to stop for the winter, and there is much to be said for that. Unless we get fine weather for all this month, there is now no chance of clearing the coast. If we could be sure that the Germans would attack us here, it would be far better to stand fast. But they would probably be now only too glad to remain quiet here and try elsewhere. . . . Most of those at the conference, though willing to go on, would welcome a stop.'

Passchendaele—a 'porridge of mud'

The final phase of the campaign from 4th October to 6th November was fought for the almost obliterated village of Passchendaele, and as John Terraine rightly stresses, it 'bore throughout the characteristics which have generally been associated with the whole of it'. After the respite in September rain fell almost unceasingly through October and, with the continuing barrage, destroyed the few remaining signs of roads and tracks. By this time the whole area had reverted to a 'porridge of mud': mules and horses were known to have sunk beneath it with their loads; guns could find no solid ground to fire from; and it took sixteen bearers instead of two to carry each stretcher case the 4,000 yards to the field dressing stations. These conditions characterized the battle of Poelcapelle (9th October), the two battles fought

Above: Desolation after a battle—a strafed wood. **Left:** The dying huddled with the dead, after the battle of the Messines Ridge. **Below left:** A soldier struggles forward. 'Even if the rainfall had been below instead of above the average, the destruction of the drains would have sufficed. . . . The drenching rains simply helped the broken drains to convert a reclaimed marsh into an impassable quagmire' (Lloyd George). By September, Gough wrote, 'Men of the strongest physique could hardly move forward at all and became easy victims to the enemy's snipers. Stumbling forward as best they could, their rifles also soon became so caked and clogged with mud as to be useless.' **Below right:** Reserves waiting in the trenches to advance on the village of Veldhoek

The terrible price of seven miles of mud

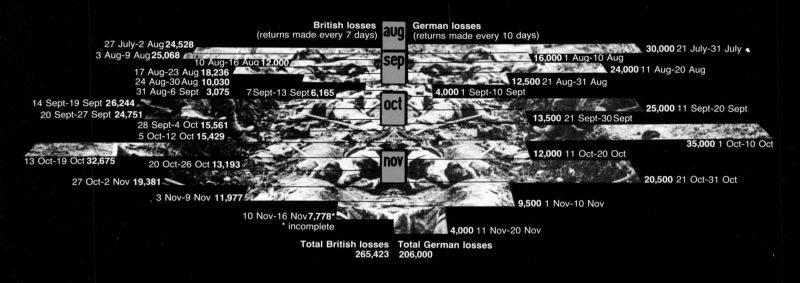

British losses
(returns made every 7 days)

German losses
(returns made every 10 days)

27 July-2 Aug **24,528**

3 Aug-9 Aug **25,068**

10 Aug-16 Aug **12,000**

17 Aug-23 Aug **18,236**

24 Aug-30 Aug **10,030**

31 Aug-6 Sept **3,075**

7 Sept-13 Sept **6,165**

14 Sept-19 Sept **26,244**

20 Sept-27 Sept **24,751**

28 Sept-4 Oct **15,561**

5 Oct-12 Oct **15,429**

13 Oct-19 Oct **32,675**

20 Oct-26 Oct **13,193**

27 Oct-2 Nov **19,381**

3 Nov-9 Nov **11,977**

10 Nov-16 Nov **7,778***
* incomplete

30,000 21 July-31 July

16,000 1 Aug-10 Aug

24,000 11 Aug-20 Aug

12,500 21 Aug-31 Aug

4,000 1 Sept-10 Sept

25,000 11 Sept-20 Sept

13,500 21 Sept-30 Sept

35,000 1 Oct-10 Oct

12,000 11 Oct-20 Oct

20,500 21 Oct-31 Oct

9,500 1 Nov-10 Nov

4,000 11 Nov-20 Nov

Total British losses   **Total German losses**
        265,423   206,000

Above: The struggle of attrition — casualty figures month by month for the British and German armies. Below: Haig's plan of campaign, showing the projected naval attack on the coast and the preliminary engagement at Messines Ridge. Haig did not realize that the customary rainfall in Flanders made an autumn campaign impracticable. Right: What the dead had won: the ground gained by the British between July and November — seven miles

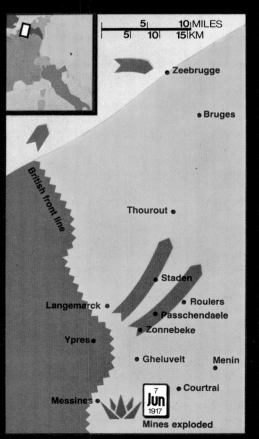

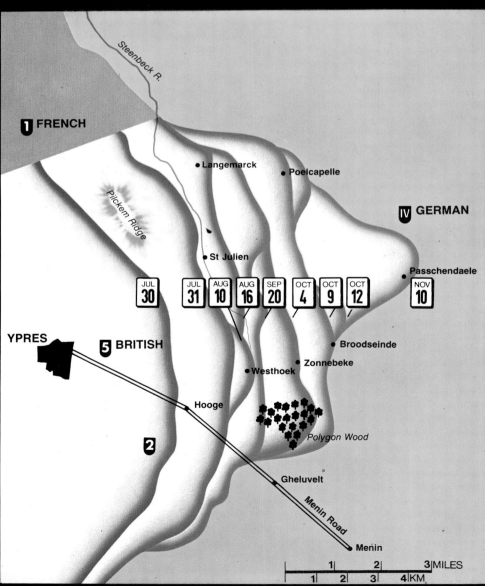

for Passchendaele (12th and 26th October) and the eventual capture of the village by the Canadians on 6th November. For the troops it was, in Terraine's succinct phrase 'a month of dire misery and absolute frustration'. The Germans, as the defenders, at least had less problems of movement, but conditions were not much better for them. Ludendorff did not exaggerate when he wrote: 'It was no longer life at all. It was mere unspeakable suffering.'

Had Haig decided to halt after Broodseinde it is unlikely that even the abominable conditions which characterized much of the fighting in August would have given the campaign its terrible reputation. Even Haig's warmest defenders have been obliged to look beyond the borders of Flanders in order to justify the Passchendaele battles. Thus Charteris wrote on 7th November: 'We have now got to where, with good weather, we should have been in early September, and with two months in front of us to carry on the operation and clear the coast. Now, from the purely local point of view, it is rather a barren victory, and if the home people decide on a defensive next year, it will be almost lives and labour thrown away.' The campaign had pushed out the Ypres salient to a maximum depth of seven miles and ended without capturing the whole Passchendaele-Staden ridge—which had been the first objective. Had Jellicoe's prediction—that Great Britain's ability to continue the war depended on the army clearing the Belgian coast—been well-founded the war would have been lost. Nor did the German IV Army voluntarily retire, as after the Somme campaign, to give the attackers the illusion of victory. Instead the Allies were obliged to defend the Ypres salient through yet another winter while the Germans were reinforced from the Eastern Front. The campaign had failed to realize Haig's hope of inflicting a decisive defeat on the German army.

Defending the disaster
There is a deep-rooted belief that Haig continued to fight at Passchendaele 'to save the French'. Haig's diaries contain several references in the summer to the need to 'encourage the French to keep fighting', and to give the Germans no opportunity to exploit their weakness. That the Germans were not actually planning to attack the French is no reflection on Haig's sincerity, though it was a surprising misjudgement by so experienced a staff officer. For the later phases however, Haig's own diaries reveal that his assessment of French capabilities changed. Thus on 1st September he noted: 'The result of our pressure at Ypres is shown by the slackening of German efforts on the Chemin des Dames, and the comparatively

weak resistance which they have made to the French attack at Verdun. The French army has consequently had the quiet time desired by General Pétain in which to recover from the Nivelle offensive.' Moreover after Pétain had proved reluctant to attack in support of the British in September, Haig wrote to Robertson (on 8th October): 'Though the French cannot be expected to admit it officially, we know that the state of their armies and of the reserve manpower behind the armies is such that neither the French government nor the military authorities will venture to call on their troops for any further great and sustained offensive effort, at any rate before it becomes evident that the enemy's strength has been definitely and finally broken. Though they are staunch in defence and will carry out useful local offensives against limited objectives, the French armies would not respond to a call for more than that, and the authorities are well aware of it.'

Ten years after the campaign Haig asserted that Pétain had repeatedly urged him to attack 'on account of the awful state of the French troops'. But Haig meticulously recorded meetings with all important soldiers and statesmen and there is no suggestion that in his four meetings with Pétain *during the campaign* such a request was even hinted at. Pétain denied the postwar rumour, while Haig never mentioned this crucial piece of intelligence to the British government. Possibly Haig was confusing French requests during the Arras operations in April and May with later events in Flanders.

Counting the cost
It does not seem likely that by prolonging the Flanders offensive Haig gave indirect help to the Allies on other fronts. The Passchendaele phase prevented neither the final collapse of the Russian armies during the autumn of 1917 nor the rout of the Italians at Caporetto towards the end of October. Indeed Ludendorff was actually able to detach several divisions from the Western Front during the British offensive. There is plentiful evidence, including the war memoirs of Prince Rupprecht and Ludendorff, to support Haig's conviction that the Flanders attrition was having a serious effect on the IV Army's morale. But the Allies also suffered severely. Indeed, since the Germans were for the most part defending, and for much of the campaign adopted economical tactics of defence in depth from dispersed strong points, it would not be surprising if the attackers' morale was the more severely strained of the two. Moreover, Haig and his staff (though not Robertson) seem to have underrated the tonic effect on morale of Germany's tremendous victory over Russia

The wounded in a bleak and sodden world. **Above:** *Stretcher-bearers carry a wounded man through mud which reaches their knees.* **Below:** *Wounded German carried on a stretcher by South African Scots*

Below: *Canadian and German 'walking wounded' on their way to a dressing station. They are resting on the devastated ground just outside Passchendaele*

Backs to the Wall

The town of Ypres, its houses ruined and deserted, pitted by huge water-filled shell craters

which became ever more certain as the Flanders fighting dragged on inconclusively. Victory in the east gave the Germans vastly increased numbers – forty divisions were transferred to the Western Front from Russia and Rumania between 1st November and the middle of March and more followed later. And it gave them renewed hope – for a decisive blow in the spring of 1918.

Confusion and controversy over casualty statistics spring not only from gaps in the reliable first-hand sources against which differing estimates can be checked, but also from the different methods used by the belligerents in reckoning their losses. The British total of 245,000 killed and wounded given by the *British Official History* has been widely accepted as approximately correct, though in August 1918 the general staff gave the war cabinet an estimated total of just over 265,000, and Sir Basil Liddell Hart puts it as high as 300,000. The higher of the two German estimates (in their *Official History*) for their IV Army between 1st July and mid-November – covering a much wider front than the Ypres sector – is 202,000 including missing. The *German Medical History,* however, puts the total as low as 175,000. Even if the *British Official History* is accurate for British losses, and the higher German total is on the low side, it would still be impossible to argue that in the gruesome computation of casualties the third battle of Ypres had resulted in a clear gain for the British and French.

Haig misjudges Germany

Although at the time the gradual effects of attrition on enemy numbers and morale was regarded by GHQ as a valid reason for prolonging the battle, Haig himself appears to have been motivated chiefly by his per-

sistent belief that Germany was near to total collapse. The baneful influence of General Charteris in sustaining this illusion has been widely recognized. 'In retrospect,' as one careful historian has written, 'we can say with certainty that General Charteris's estimates of enemy strength and morale were almost criminally optimistic, and that Haig was badly misled in basing his plans upon them.' Well-founded though this criticism is, it would be unjust to make the chief of intelligence a scapegoat for the commander-in-chief. Haig's extremely powerful and self-confident personality could be a source of a weakness as well as of strength: once his mind was made up on a subject he was not easily swayed. In his book *At G.H.Q.,* Charteris, without seeking to denigrate his former commander, cites more than one instance of Haig going well beyond his (already over-optimistic) intelligence reports and predictions. Haig's published papers, while they show clearly the size of the problems he faced also show that he just did not have the critical intelligence needed to judge objectively the enemy's capacity to go on fighting.

Civil-military relations, and Allied co-operation were strikingly defective during the campaign. Lloyd George and the war cabinet committee had little faith in Haig or his plan yet they neither felt able to replace him nor gave him their full support. In turn the commander-in-chief had no confidence in the prime minister and consequently appears to have withheld information about the French mutinies lest it should provide justification for weakening the Western Front. The French war minister and later prime minister, Paul Painlevé, gave Lloyd George stronger assurance than was proper that the French armies could and would give full support to Haig's offensive, and the commander-in-chief

Pétain, similarly made promises which he was reluctant to fulfil. Robertson was perhaps in the least enviable position, for in trying to restrain Lloyd George in his obsession with the Italian front and at the same time caution Haig against attempting too much in Flanders, he earned the former's hostility and the latter's suspicion. Haig did nothing to prevent his removal from office early in 1918.

Tragic waste

In legend, the battles of the Third Ypres campaign appear as nothing but ill-prepared bloodbaths. But they were more than this. Where conditions permitted they were carefully planned and skilfully executed. In particular Plumer's set-piece advances in June and September, and Pétain's operations on the Verdun sector, showed what could be achieved if objectives were strictly limited and superior artillery cover could be concentrated. Yet the Ypres salient was particularly unsuitable for an attempted break-through because of the precarious drainage system, the climate, and the terrain. Indeed, the faint possibility of a break-through to the Channel coast probably depended not only on the complete success of Gough's opening offensive, but also on the simultaneous launching of amphibious operations. Although the latter were carefully planned, the obstacles remained so formidable that it was probably a wise decision to cancel the operation when the land advance failed to make good progress.

The 1914-18 War still retains much of its terrible reputation because, on reflection, so much waste and suffering seem to have been exacted for no sufficient cause. Three years of indecisive slaughter, and the frailty of human judgements combined to produce the tragedy of the Third Ypres campaign in which the heroic endeavour of the troops appeared to yield only negligible results. No one, however, can be certain that the lives lost in Flanders were sacrificed in vain. Also, in changed circumstances – and because he had grown wiser from experience – Haig showed in 1918 that he could fight a more mobile and less costly campaign, culminating in the final victory which he had falsely anticipated in 1916 and 1917. 'Passchendaele', however, transcended the historical reality of an inconclusive campaign and became a potent historical myth. As such its influence reached far beyond 1918. Statesmen and soldiers are activated by such historical myths as well as by present realities. In 1939-45 Churchill and many of his generals had the memory of Passchendaele vividly before them: never again, they were resolved, should British troops be subjected to such a battle of attrition for anything short of national survival.

Caporetto

General Conrad von Hötzendorff, while chief of the Austrian general staff, had an obsession. He was firmly convinced that an all-out offensive against Italy, if properly equipped and timed, would be so effective that she would have to withdraw from the war. He had held this view long before Italy had joined the Allies, and time and again he had urged the old Emperor Franz Josef to let him launch such an attack on Italy. He argued that if she were reduced to military impotence she would more easily resist the temptation to jettison her neutrality in favour of the Allies. Franz Josef, who still believed that the rules governing the conduct of nations must be observed, and that a nation's neutrality must be respected unless she wantonly provoked retaliation, had refused to pander to his chief of staff's whim.

After Italy's entry into the war, Conrad had become more convinced than ever that his plan for a really massive attack on Italy was the only way in which the Italian Front could be eliminated. There is little doubt that if he had had sufficient forces to mount such an offensive without withdrawing the Austro-Hungarian troops on the Eastern Front opposite the Russians, and if he had not had to bow always to the will of the German high command, he would have acted as he proposed. But he had not enough forces; the Germans would not agree to his withdrawing his units

Below: Women leaving their homes in Caporetto. The Austrians had broken through the Italian lines, and soldiers and civilians were crowding down the valleys in headlong flight from the front

Backs to the Wall

on the Eastern Front; and every time he brought the matter up, they maintained that they had no divisions to spare to give him the numbers which he needed.

But the longer the war went on, the more obsessed Conrad became. He flatly refused to believe that the unrestricted U-boat campaign which the Germans were planning, would end the war, as they were insisting it would; and he became such an embarrassment to his colleagues that a month after he last broached the subject—on 23rd January 1917—the new young Emperor Karl, who had succeeded when Franz Josef died in November 1916, replaced him with General Arz von Straussenburg, a much younger man.

Karl did not, however, retire Conrad; he sent him to command the western (Trentino) sector of the Austro-Italian Front.

The Italian Front

The Italian Front stretched from the Swiss-Italian borders in the west to the eastern frontier between Italy and Austria, via the line of the Alps. The eastern frontier more or less followed the course of the River Isonzo. The Isonzo enters the Adriatic Sea west of Trieste, and to get there from its source in the Julian Alps, winds along the eastern edge of the Friulian plain.

Except for about fifteen miles at its southern end, the Isonzo front was guarded by a spur of the main Alpine chain the Julian Alps, which, as it sweeps southwards, broadens out into plateaux and limestone hills. Running more or less parallel with this spur for half its length, the Isonzo cuts its way through a deep and rocky valley, which is separated from the Julian Alps by limestone uplands. Though the slope of these uplands is a fairly gentle gradient, they are deeply incised by a network of valleys and ridges.

South of the town of Tolmino, and rising out of the spur, is what the Italians call the Bainsizza plateau. The word plateau usually describes a flat mountain-top; but the Bainsizza is not flat; it is crossed and recrossed by ridges which rise steeply above the average level.

To the south of the Bainsizza is the Carso plateau, which has been described as 'a howling wilderness of stones, sharp as knives'. Between these two plateaux, but lying to the east, is the Selva di Ternova plateau, which is not so high as the other two, but is densely wooded.

Along the whole length of the front, the Austrians held the high ground and looked down on to the Friulian plain. This meant that unless the Italians attacked only on the fifteen mile coastal strip in the direction of Trieste, everywhere else they would be attacking uphill.

*Above: Two flags of Italian commando troops. **Right:** A trench on the Carso, painted by G.A.Sartorio. The Carso plateau, 'a howling wilderness of stones, sharp as knives', had eventually been taken by the Italians for a terrifying loss of lives and of morale. **Below:** King Victor Emmanuel III meets the Allies at Peschiera in November 1917. It was agreed that the Italian army should stay behind the River Piave to build up its organization and morale. It did so, and a year later the Italians took their revenge for the defeat of Caporetto*

and heavy ammunition. At the vital moment there were not enough guns to press home the advantage, or ammunition supplies would fail.

This situation was partly due to the fact that the switch-over of Italian industry from peace-time to war-time production was difficult and slow; and partly due, particularly as the war developed, to sabotage of the military war-effort by extreme socialists opposed to the war.

In addition, in the pauses between battles, the morale of the soldiers deteriorated. Until after Caporetto, absolutely nothing was done for the leisure entertainment of the troops. The men passed all their time in their dug-outs or tents, with nothing to divert them, and this situation was a breeding-ground for the wildest rumours purporting to describe what was going on behind the fronts. The Italian, with his tremendous attachment to family, grew fearful about his family's welfare, now that he was not there to protect it.

Visitors to the Italian Front, 1917.
Below: *Cadorna (centre). His intolerance prevented him understanding his army.*
Bottom: *Emperors Karl (far left) and Wilhelm II, hoping to knock Italy out of the war*

Eleven battles for seven miles

When the Italians came into the war in May 1915, General Cadorna had thirty-five divisions. This was a respectable force, as far as man-power went, but it was sadly short of artillery. In contrast, the Austro-Hungarians had ten divisions fewer; but were vastly superior in artillery.

Between the two sectors of the front where fighting was possible—at the western end north of Verona, and at the eastern end on the Isonzo—Cadorna deployed his forces. While the 1st and 4th Armies guarded the Venetian plain in the west, the 2nd and 3rd Armies took up positions on the Isonzo, together with the Carnia Group, comprising nineteen battalions of Alpine troops, at the very northern end of the front.

Cadorna decided to make his main effort on the Isonzo front. There were historical as well as military reasons for this. The Austrian provinces east of the Isonzo had once belonged to Italy, and since Italy had been transformed into a united kingdom in 1870, she had been asking for them to be restored to her; while on the military side, Italian pressure here would relieve Austrian pressure on Serbia.

Cadorna's general strategy on the Isonzo was to go forward in a series of what he called offensive bounds. He would attack the Austrians with limited objectives,

pause to consolidate and re-form, and then leap forward again.

The plan, however, did not succeed. Between 23rd June 1915, when he launched his first offensive bound, and 29th August 1917, the Italian armies attacked the Austrians eleven times—the first to eleventh battles of the Isonzo—and by the end of the eleventh battle had gained a maximum of seven miles.

The reasons for so small a return for so great an effort were many and various. Discipline among the higher echelons of officers was faulty, chiefly because Cadorna ruthlessly eliminated any commander who failed to obtain the objectives set him. In the nineteen months before Caporetto he dismissed 217 generals, 255 colonels and 335 battalion commanders. The effect of this was to engender in his senior officers such a sense of insecurity that they became over-cautious, and in their caution failed their commander-in-chief. At the same time it created a lack of contact between the supreme command and the field commanders which had the result of imprisoning Cadorna in an ivory tower by which he was denied all knowledge of the reactions of both officers and men to the war in general and their own problems in particular.

Equally serious, however, was the lack of equipment, and especially of artillery

Backs to the Wall

On the other hand, things were not much better on the Austrian side. The lack of a decisive victory and the extremely hard conditions imposed by the terrain and the weather conditions, particularly in the winter campaigns, had their effect on the morale of the Austrian soldier.

This was especially true after the Italian success, limited though it was, on the Bainsizza sector in the eleventh Isonzo battle of August 1917. After the conclusion of that battle, the Austrian military commanders seriously doubted whether their armies would be able to withstand a twelfth Isonzo battle, should Cadorna decide that the Italian army should launch one.

It was at this point that they recalled the old military adage that the best form of defence is attack. It also came back to them that Conrad had had a plan; and someone remembered that when he had last outlined his plan in detail he had suggested that the Caporetto sector of the Isonzo front should receive the main weight of the Austrian attack, since the Italian line was weakest there. A little elementary intelligence showed that this sector was still the weak link in the Italian Isonzo chain.

However, German help would still be needed, so on 25th August General Waldstatten was despatched to German general

headquarters with instructions to use all his efforts to obtain German approval of and the required assistance for an offensive on the Isonzo.

The German Kaiser informed the Austrian Emperor that he could count on the whole of Germany to crush Italy. His high command had other ideas, but after some argument it was agreed that if Lieutenant-General Krafft von Dellmensingen, an expert in mountain warfare, having inspected the Isonzo at Caporetto, thought such a plan could succeed, then serious German consideration would be given to the proposals.

Dellmensingen went to the Isonzo, looked

Troops and wagons move down a military road in Venezia towards the River Tagliamento. The order for retreat has been given and the Italian army is retiring to lick its wounds after Caporetto

and reported. 'In view of the prevailing difficulties,' he wrote, 'success lies only just on the border of possibility.' This was sufficient for the Germans and practical plans were put in hand.

As it happened, Cadorna had no plans for launching a twelfth battle on the Isonzo. On 20th September he surprised the British and French military missions by telling them that he had abandoned his plans to renew his offensive and was going on to the defensive on the Isonzo—at least for the time being. He gave as his reason the necessity to conserve his supplies of ammunition.

In response to Cadorna's earlier pleas

for artillery, the British and French had just sent a few heavy batteries to Italy 'on loan for the sole purpose of offensive operations'. When they heard that Cadorna intended to abandon the offensive, Lloyd George and his French opposite number Painlevé, in a fit of pique, accused Cadorna of getting the guns under false pretences and ordered them to be withdrawn. All the French batteries were recalled and two out of the three British batteries.

In his memoirs Cadorna explains what caused his decision. The intelligence he had received showed that the Austrians were going to make a tremendous effort to put Italy out of the war, and that they were

going to make this effort soon, and not in the spring of 1918, as German agents in Switzerland were putting it about.

By 6th October forty-three enemy divisions had been identified on the Isonzo front. After this date the intelligence gradually became more precise. There were many troops on the Bainsizza sector and German troops were assembling in the Sava valley, sixty miles east of Caporetto.

On 9th October, the intelligence bulletin said that 'the last week of October might be accepted as the most probable date for the beginning of the enemy offensive'.

On 14th October General Capello, commander-in-chief of the Italian 2nd

Backs to the Wall

Army, on whose sector Caporetto was situated, was ordered to Padua by his doctors for a change of air and rest. This was a blow of the first order, for Capello had the total confidence of his troops, and his absence at a time when they were receiving the full force of the enemy attack could easily place the whole Isonzo front in jeopardy.

A week later Cadorna informed the British director of military operations: 'The attack is coming, but I am confident of being able to meet it. Owing to the very difficult country on the Tolmino sector I am of opinion that an attack there can be checked without difficulty and I am consequently holding that sector lightly. (Caporetto is north of Tolmino.)

In making this fatal decision, Cadorna had made serious errors of appreciation. He had accepted at face value the information given by a Czech deserter that the main attack would be made at Tolmino, and allowed this to colour his appreciation of more detailed information given by Austrian deserters. He had also allowed his knowledge of the Tolmino terrain to underestimate the probable weight of the enemy attack. Most serious of all, because of his confidence, he had failed to send out scouts to the area north of Tolmino—that is, in the neighbourhood of Caporetto—and so did not know that four Austro-German divisions were assembled, one behind the other, in the valley running northward of Plezzo.

The Austrians break through

Cadorna and Capello were two very different characters, and had had several differences of opinion throughout the war. Now they differed again about the plans for countering the enemy attack. Cadorna issued instructions for a defensive attitude with local counter-attacks; Capello favoured an offensive-defensive action, with a large-scale counter-attack, northwest from the Bainsizza.

Disregarding his supreme commander's instructions, Capello deployed his troops in readiness to carry out his own plan, with his three second-line corps *south* of Caporetto.

Though still in a high fever, Capello insisted on returning to his headquarters on the evening of 23rd October, but he grew worse. After dictating orders, he had to retire again. He had been gone only an hour or two, when, at 2 am on 24th October, the artillery of the Austro-German XIV Army on the Tolmino-Plezzo sector, opened fire with gas-shells on the Italian batteries and forward trenches. After two hours there was a two-hour pause. The Italian artillery replied, but after an initial fierceness it weakened and did little harm to the opposing infantry.

*Above: Carving made by an Italian prisoner-of-war depicting the punishments inflicted by the Austrians on Italian-speaking subjects who had deserted to fight against them. The most famous of these was Cesare Battisti. **Left:** A member of the Bersaglieri, crack troops of the Italian army, with his portable bicycle folded on his shoulder*

Soon after the bombardment began, light rain started to fall. Within a short time it changed to a heavy downpour, while on the heights there were snow-storms, and in the bottoms of the valleys thick mist. By dawn visibility everywhere was low.

At 6.30 am the bombardment was resumed with high explosive. From Plezzo down the whole length of the front to the sea, guns of every calibre opened up. Never before on the Isonzo had there been such an intense bombardment, and in a very short time the Italian defences had been reduced to rubble, while men's lungs were seized with a cruel agony which paralyzed their thoughts and actions as their gas-masks let through copious draughts of German poison gas.

And — calamity of calamities at such a time — all communications between commands and advance lines were destroyed.

At 8 am the firing of two giant mines gave the German XIV Army the signal to advance from Plezzo and Tolmino. To his surprise, General Krauss, at Plezzo, met no resistance from the Italians. By 9.30 am the front of the Italian 4th Corps had been pierced.

Meantime, General Stein, just north of Tolmino, had advanced with his divisions. He had been opposite the weakest spot in the Italian front.

In his pre-battle orders, Cadorna had instructed General Badoglio, who was to become famous in the Second World War as Marshal Badoglio, and who was commander of the 18th Corps covering the line from Plezzo to Tolmino, to withdraw his troops to the west bank of the Isonzo. For some reason never subsequently clarified, Badoglio deferred carrying out this order until shortly before the battle began, with the result that only a small force met Stein, and the remainder of the corps was cut off on the east bank.

Stein obliterated this small Italian force, and by doing so opened up a way across the river. By 4 pm he had occupied the village of Caporetto.

Thus, by mid-afternoon a fifteen-mile gap had been punched in the Italian line; and now, on the very first day, in the very sector where Cadorna had not expected an attack, the rot began.

The bogeyman comes

Up to this time the Italians had encountered only Austrians of whom they had no great opinion. In contrast, the reputation of the Germans as fighters was immense. Italian commanders had been wont to use it as a bogeyman to frighten recalcitrant troops into obedience.

Now the Germans were actually here!

When the truth dawned on the Italian troops, their morale, such as it was, snapped completely. In this they were matched by their junior commanders who did not know how to deal with tactics they had not been taught to counter.

The four divisions of General Cavaciocchi's 4th Corps melted away in flight, carrying with them Badoglio's 19th Division. Most of these troops fell prisoner in the next few days.

By nightfall, Krauss was making for Monte Stol, northwest of Caporetto and Stein had the greater part of his divisions on the west bank of the Isonzo. Only south of Tolmino had the Italian forces under General Caviglia held; and as soon as Cadorna heard of the disaster in the north, he ordered them to fall back, too. At the same time he ordered the Duke of Aosta, commanding the 3rd Army, and General Capello to put the defences of the line of the Tagliamento river into a state of readiness with civilian labour, and 'with the utmost speed and maximum secrecy'. He explained that in order to save the 3rd Army and the remainder of the 2nd Army that had held firm, they might have to fall back on that line.

The next morning broke bright and clear, and the sun came out. The situation could be seen a little more clearly now, and Capello, who had returned to take command when the battle began, was forced to inform Cadorna that all positions on 2nd Army's front east of the Isonzo had been lost.

Cadorna ordered the Duke of Aosta to send back the less mobile of the 3rd Army's heavy and medium artillery to the River Piave, in the rear of the Tagliamento line. With the remainder he was to withdraw west of the Carso valley and prepare a line there to cover a general retreat.

At noon, Capello arrived at Cadorna's headquarters at Udine to discuss the situation. He was desperately ill and on the point of collapse. He told Cadorna that in his opinion all contact with the enemy should be broken off and a withdrawal made to the Tagliamento without delay. For once the two men agreed. But Cadorna did not issue the orders for the retreat for another twenty-four hours.

There have been many descriptions given of the flight of the Italian 6th and 27th Corps from Caporetto. Even put baldly and briefly it presents an almost unbelievable situation.

In his *History of the Great War*, C.R.M.F. Cruttwell has written: '400,000 soldiers were going home, with the determination that for them at least the war was ended. The reports of their behaviour are most curious. Having broken contact with the enemy, they were in no hurry; they stopped to eat and drink and pillage. One observer notes their air of "tranquil indifference", another that while they had all thrown away their arms, the troops kept their

Backs to the Wall

gas-masks; nearly as many civilians were fleeing, more wildly, from the face of the enemy, blocking what remained of the road space with their carts and household goods.'

Soldiers and civilians crowded down the valleys, using the only roads by which supplies and reinforcements could have reached them. They held up troops moving over to new lines. They had no thought for honour or country, they who had fought with amazing courage in the eleven battles of the Isonzo.

Yet there was something peculiarly Italian in this mass defection. General Raffaele Cadorna has told the author that his father related that there was no attempt to threaten officers, only a refusal to obey; and that when he himself rode among them, no one lifted a finger against him; on the contrary, as soon as they recognized him they stiffened and saluted.

Vengeance

The retreat, when ordered, took the 3rd Army commanders by surprise. It took the Austrian commander opposite equally by surprise, and he made no attempt to pursue. This was just as well, for there was a certain amount of initial disorder which could have been made worse had the rearguard had to fight.

The retreat of the 2nd Army, however, was extremely chaotic. This was scarcely to be wondered at, in view of the previous headlong flight of half that Army, and the fact that the German commander Berrer did pursue. He succeeded in splitting the 2nd Army irreparably in two.

On the other hand, all was not well with the Austro-Germans. The speed of their advance took them unprepared, and there were no orders which allowed for the full exploitation of the situation. As a result, orders were issued, then changed, and this gave rise to friction which bad staff work did not help to eradicate. In addition, army commanders and divisional commanders began to issue their own orders, and soon, they, too, were in a hopeless confusion.

This helped Cadorna considerably, and by 31st October, he had all his forces, except for the quarter million lost as prisoners, across the Tagliamento, and the German were still so mixed up that he was able to pause and take breath.

With the broad torrent of the river between them and the enemy, the Italian soldiers also took breath—for the first time for a week—and looked about them. What they saw seems to have brought them up short, and soon it was apparent to all observers that a new spirit was beginning to move them. Within a few days an amazing transformation was visible;

military order and discipline were being quickly restored.

But the Germans also recovered, and when they made a large hole in the Tagliamento line, Cadorna decided to withdraw to the line of the River Piave. This further retreat was not without difficulties, but on 9th November all Italian armies stood in good order behind the Piave.

On the same day Cadorna was dismissed and was succeeded by General Diaz.

Throughout the remainder of the winter and the spring of the next year. Diaz regrouped, reinforced, resupplied, and retrained his armies. The lessons of Caporetto were studied and heeded. New tactics were devised, designed to remove the weaknesses of the old which had been responsible for the heavy losses of men and had made Caporetto inevitable.

In June the Germans reopened their offensive. Eight days later it ended in complete victory for the Italians.

In October, Diaz went over to the offensive, and exactly a year to the day from Caporetto, he launched the battle of Vittorio Veneto and inflicted on the Austrians a far worse disgrace than they had inflicted on the Italians on the Isonzo.

Caporetto had been avenged.

Retreat from Caporetto—the weary march of humiliated men. Drawing by Max Gualo

The Home Front: Europe 1917

When war broke out, none of the great powers was really prepared or equipped to wage a protracted war in which the rival blockades would increasingly impose siege conditions on the domestic populations. France, though industrially under-developed, came nearest in 1914 to self-sufficiency, with forty-two per cent of her active population still employed in agriculture; but the balance was totally distorted by the German invasion which involved a loss to France of almost ten per cent of her territory and fourteen per cent of her industrial potential. What France thus lost had to be supplied from outside. As the war dragged on into 1917 the situation became more and more critical. There was little scope for bringing more land under cultivation, and agricultural productivity steadily declined as the soil grew tired and the men who once had worked in order to cultivate it were slaughtered.

Great Britain had been prodigal in her neglect of agriculture in the pre-war years, so that she had to depend on imports for four-fifths of her wheat and forty per cent of her meat, and relied on Austria and Germany for almost all of her beet sugar. For the island nation more than any other, trade was life: the unrestricted submarine campaign launched by Germany on 1st February 1917 threw the whole Allied war effort into dire jeopardy.

Submarine warfare

Before the war Germany had efficiently developed her agricultural and industrial resources and in 1914 was producing two-thirds of her own food and fodder requirements. Through scientific inventiveness and the use of *Ersatz* ('substitute') materials she was able to overcome many immediate shortages. The initial advantage was Germany's, but as the war continued that advantage slowly, implacably, wasted away. It was as vital to Germany that her submarine campaign should achieve a quick kill as it was to the Allies to ward off that fate.

By Easter 1917 German submarines were doing such deadly business that one out of every four ships sailing out of British ports was doomed to destruction. Disruption in basic imports meant scarcity, high prices, profiteering, and austerity. Life in Great Britain and France took on the hue of battleship grey: 'Paris is no longer Paris,' a contemporary lamented; *l'année des privations* ('the year of privations'), was how another described 1917. Day and night were reversed. Once the streets had been filled, during the day, with breathless bustle; now they were deserted—for everyone had work to do, whether in a munitions factory or the local forces canteen. At night there was now complete darkness where once there had been a constellation of lights, and the sounds of steam-hammers and factory machinery where once there had been total silence. And the night was full of the noise of rumbling convoys and the long, ominous-looking trains that carried munitions or delivered the shattered bodies of soldiers straight to the sidings at the military hospitals.

Although the strain on civilian morale was severe, the crisis point in Great Britain was limited to a few anxious weeks in the summer of 1917 when it seemed likely that the entire war effort might founder. Then the last-minute adoption of the convoy system eased the situation. But in France hardship and social strains were more intense, and these, added to the terrible slaughter at the battle of Verdun, the previous year, created a condition in which a complete collapse of morale was always a possibility—a collapse which would have struck the foundations of the whole Allied effort.

Shortages everywhere

The first real shortages, and first queues appeared in Great Britain in the early months of 1917. The press described the kind of scene which became common everywhere: at Wrexham a farm-wagon laden with potatoes 'was surrounded by hundreds of clamouring people, chiefly women, who scrambled on to the vehicle in the eagerness to buy. Several women fainted in the struggle and the police were sent for to restore order'.

In December 1916 David Lloyd George took over the government. He appointed a food controller who established himself amid the splendour of Grosvenor House where the suggestive flesh of the famous Rubens paintings was covered up to protect the morals of the girls recruited as typists for the new ministry. A scheme of voluntary rationing, whereby each citizen was to restrict himself to four pounds of bread, two-and-a-half pounds of meat, and three-quarters of a pound of sugar a week was announced on 3rd February—two days, it may be noted, after the start of unrestricted submarine warfare. At the beginning of May a Royal Proclamation on the saving of grain was read on successive Sundays in churches and chapels throughout the land, and a special food economy

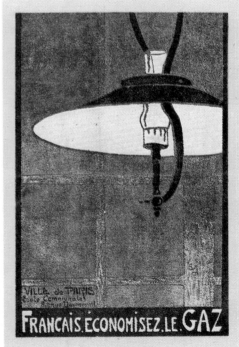

Top: British poster stigmatizes indolent luxury. But upper- and middle-class families did turn to substitute foods.
Above: A French poster appeals for economy in the use of gas lighting

Above: French peasant women harvesting the potato crop in place of their menfolk who had gone to the front. The real brunt of the war was borne by the peasantry and their bitterness against their urban compatriots introduced a new and dangerous tension into France in 1917.
Centre: British appeal for economy in face of the U-boat menace. By Easter 1917 one of every four ships sailing out of British ports faced destruction by German submarines.
Right: Austrian appeal for nickel, copper and brass to feed the guns.
Below: Pineapples with everything? They were cheaper than potatoes in Great Britain in February 1917

campaign was mounted. Some shops and local authorities established their own rationing schemes and these were reinforced by statutory food control committees formed throughout the country. Margarine, fats, milk, and bacon became very scarce. Sugar and butter were practically unobtainable. Even 'Government Control Tea'—often likened to sweepings off the floor—was very hard to get. Towards the end of the year there was a 'meat famine', followed by meat rationing early in the new year. Upper and middle-class families turned to substitute dishes. To them shepherd's pie still seemed something of an outrage: 'but mummy, it's a particularly nasty piece of shepherd', lamented a little boy in one of the many cartoons which concentrated on the food situation. For working-class families the biggest hardship was the steep rise in the price of bread: to make matters worse bread was 'Government Bread' whose various strange ingredients tended to go bad in warm weather.

Bombs, strikes and scandals

To ram home the consequence of their submarine blockade the Germans unleashed the heaviest civilian bombing raids of the entire war: the underfed, war-weary citizens of London took to the tubes for shelter. Across the Channel there was little bombing in 1917 but in other respects France did not fare so well. During the harsh winter of 1916-17 coal supplies gave out. This was the topic upon which French cartoons concentrated: in one a lackey is depicted bowing obsequiously before the coalman—'Coal,' he says, indicating a richly carpeted stairway, 'take it up by the main staircase.' In various parts of the country coal wagons were forcibly commandeered by members of the public. *Pâtisseries* were closed, and restaurant menus subject to severe restriction. Because of flagrant profiteering, the government encouraged the founding of co-operative and civic restaurants and industrial canteens with *prix fixe* ('fixed price') menus. The cost of living had gone up by at least eighty per cent since 1914, causing special hardship to the million or so refugees from the German-occupied areas scattered throughout the main centres of population.

Farmers and many small tradesmen were able to do well for themselves (American troops became a particularly good source of quick profit) but many bakers, adversely affected by government price control, went bankrupt. The salaried middle class suffered severely from the rising cost of living, while sections of the working classes, protected by government minimum wage laws, did not do too badly.

The February and October revolutions in Russia, by which eventually a major coun-

Berlin in 1917. The public parks lose their flowerbeds and take on the appearance of allotments. All food was desperately scarce

try was lost to the Allied cause, spread a tremor of excitement throughout the working-class movement in Great Britain and France, though war weariness and the high cost of living were probably sufficient to account for the great outbreak of industrial unrest which characterized 1917. In France there were 689 strikes involving 293,810 strikers (compared with only 98 strikes and 9,344 strikers in 1916). In Great Britain the 'May strikes', breaking out on the 10th of the month and lasting for a fortnight, caused such dislocation of war production that on 13th June the government appointed commissions of enquiry into industrial unrest. The commissioners for the north-east declared that 'the high price of staple commodities have undoubtedly laid a severe strain upon the majority of the working classes, and in some instances have resulted in hardship and actual privation'.

Other commissions noted food prices and profiteering as the main grievances. In Great Britain the political structure, reactivated by Lloyd George, just managed to survive the test, though there were

Bread ration book for itinerant German. A bad harvest in 1916 further added to decay in German agriculture induced by war

bitter struggles between politicians and military leaders. In France there was a succession of political scandals, some dangerously tainted with defeatism. By the end of the year three prime ministers had resigned: Aristide Briand in March, Alexandre Ribot in September, and Paul Painlevé in November. Only the accession on 15th November of the seventy-six-year-old Clemenceau gave promise of any restoration of leadership and stability.

The razor and the noose

In her use of submarine warfare Germany just failed to slash open the jugular vein of the Allied powers. But if the German weapon against the Allies was the razor, the Allies weapon against the Germans was the noose – and it was already applying slow strangulation. There were no bloodstains but the life was being squeezed from the German nation. As the war continued, so Germany's initial advantage disappeared: food imports from neutral countries came to a halt, and whatever requisitions Germany might make from conquered territories these fell far short of redressing the balance. By the winter of 1916-17 the German people were already suffering hardships beyond anything endured in Great Britain or France. Yet, while the Allied press did occasionally carry stories of shortages and hunger in Berlin, they more usually concentrated on praising the thoroughness of Teutonic organization, setting it up as an example for the Allies to follow. In fact, even since August 1916 when the dominion of General Erich Ludendorff (the new quartermaster general) and General Paul von Hindenburg

(the new chief-of-staff) had been established, Teutonic organization was not doing too well against the vested interests which were stronger in the loose confederation known as the German empire than in more homogeneous countries like Great Britain and France. Part cause, more symptom, of Germany's troubles was the bad harvest of 1916: for all the pre-war advances farming was now in decay because of a shortage of farm workers and, thanks to the blockade, of a shortage of fertilizers and farm implements.

No men, no trains

The problem upon which the new military rulers concentrated was that of Germany's manpower shortage, staggeringly revealed in a census of 1916 which showed that although there were a million more women and thousands more children in employment, total numbers in productive employment were three-and-a-half million less than before the war. The 'Hindenburg Programme' of December 1916 was basically intended to surmount the manpower problem. Under the terms of a law of 5th December every male German citizen aged between seventeen and sixty not on active service, was to be drafted into 'Patriotic Auxiliary Service'. Because of the resistance of employers, who were as reluctant to employ women as they were to release their skilled men, and because there were many routes through which wealthier citizens could escape their obligations (by, for instance, joining some voluntary wartime committee), the law was not very successful. The early months of 1917 revealed the 'Hindenburg Programme' to be falling far short of its targets. Manpower was the topic of the moment, rather as coal was in France and austerity food in Great Britain: one German cartoon pictured two ageing spinsters lamenting, 'If only compulsory female service would come – then perhaps the marriageable age would also be extended to fifty years.'

Undue attention to manpower concealed the chaos which was developing in German transport. Before the war German imports had come inland from the North Sea ports by river and canal: now, with these ports blockaded, the main transport burden lay on the rail connections to the Ruhr and Silesian coalfields, to the iron deposits of occupied France, and to the food-stores of the east. Trains simply began to go missing as the various state and local authorities raided them for the provisions they needed. Close on the heels of the transport crisis there followed a widespread coal deficiency.

Poor German production figures – thirty to forty per cent less than before the war by 1917 – revealed not so much inefficient leadership as the weariness of an underfed people. Etched deep into the German consciousness was the bitter 'Turnip Winter' of 1916-17 when in place of potatoes the people ate fodder beets—and there was not always a lot else to eat. For Germans it was not a question of the imposition of rationing—for two years they had had cards for bread, fats, milk, meat, and butter—but a question of whether the ration to which they were officially entitled would in fact be obtainable. At the beginning of 1917 men were subsisting on a basic ration of a quarter of a loaf of bread (200 grams) per day, and less than a quarter of a pound of fats per week; the procurement of other

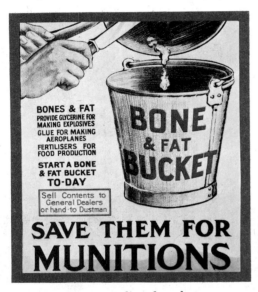

British poster appealing for what was once considered refuse. Only in wartime was the value of such commodities fully appreciated

commodities was difficult and sporadic. Total German consumption of meat in 1917 was one quarter of what it had been in pre-war years, and what was available was most inequitably distributed.

Throughout the year schoolchildren and women's organizations collected kitchen waste, coffee-grounds, hawthorn fruits, kernels of fruit, acorns and chestnuts, stinging nettles, pine cones, green leaves (as fodder), paper waste, rubber waste, cork and cork waste, tin waste, metals, parts of bulbs, bones, bottles, celluloid, rags and tatters, photographic silver residues, platinum (from discarded sets of teeth, or from jewellery), gramophone records, women's hair. Most notorious example of all of German thoroughness was the conversion of dead horses into soap. This prompted the Allied atrocity story that Germany was building 'corpse-conversion factories' to make soap from dead soldiers.

To the pains of hunger and squalor was added anger over profiteering and black

marketeering. Price control, in the hands of over a thousand separate agencies, was totally inadequate. 'The black market,' said a speaker in the Reichstag, 'has become the one really successful organization in our food supply system'. The famous memorandum from the Neukölln municipal council to the war food department, pirated in the left-wing press, revealed clearly what was happening. Big firms, using their economic power, or access to desirable commodities, were directly cornering food for their own employees; occasionally municipalities were able to do likewise, creating conditions of bitter local rivalry, and a complete breakdown of any pretence at food distribution. The memorandum predicted that from 'shortage and famine' the country would go to 'catastrophe'.

Even those allowed extra rations by virtue of their heavy manual work were getting less than half the necessary intake of calories. By late 1917 milk was practically unobtainable. Scarcity of soap brought a new menace: lice. The toll in disease and premature death was heavy. Death among those under five increased by fifty per cent in 1917; deaths from tuberculosis doubled. On 16th April the government had planned a reduction in the meagre bread ration. Working-class opinion was not mollified by announcements in various localities that such extras as sauerkraut, barley groats or smoked herring (one quarter of a herring per week) would be made available, and the proposed cut was met by the first wave in what, as in France and Great Britain, was to prove a year of strikes. Altogether nearly two million working days were lost, compared with less than a quarter of a million in 1916 and 42,000 in 1915. In the German navy, bottled up in its own ports, frustration, privation, and bitterness were at boiling point. Sailors, as well as workmen and food rioters, participated in the second wave of strikes which broke out in June.

German morale crumbles

Social and industrial troubles, naturally, bubbled over into politics. The political crisis of July began with various vague promises of reform: if the workers had no bread, then they must have political rights—that was the argument of politicians. It ended with the resignation of the chancellor, Theobald von Bethmann Hollweg. But conditions got worse, especially for the farmers—who had earlier done reasonably well, but who were now subject to food searches, regulations, and enforced slaughter of their stock—officials, who in some cases were, literally, worked to death, and the salaried middle class. Relatively speaking the upper strata of the industrial working class did better, because in official circles the industrial worker was valued

more highly than any other class in the community, except the military. One bitter middle-class comment was typical: 'A family with two munitions workers normally enjoyed not only extra rations but a higher purchasing power than the family of a professor (whose war value, if he was a physiologist, was limited to the writing of articles proving the scientific adequacy of wartime standards of nutrition).'

The blockade, on both sides, brought home to the civilian populations some of the grim truths of war. From governments it brought, in a curious way, certain positive responses. Minimum wage laws and

Poster glibly assuring Germans that their army would win the freedom of the seas. Yet the Allied blockade strangled the country

social welfare, designed to meet some of the grievances of the industrial worker were now seen to be as vital to the nation's survival as the man in the trenches. France was sorely tried. One more bloody reverse on the field of battle might well have been sufficient to let loose civil disorder. But on the whole civic loyalty in Great Britain and in France withstood the test. It was in Germany, apparently the efficient, disciplined nation, that the pressures of economic warfare exposed the selfishness of the employers, the jealousies of the different localities, the class antagonisms, and the hollow façade of the parliamentary structure.

In January 1918 Germany was hit by the third and mightiest wave of strikes. Subsiding before the priority needs of the last great German offensive, it was, nonetheless, a clear sign that while Britain and France had, by a hair's breadth, managed to survive their worst year, 1917, the existing German system was approaching collapse and revolution.

The Struggle for the Sea-lanes

Whereas in 1915-16 the German naval and military 'Hawks' had been subdued by the political 'Doves' over the prosecution of unrestricted U-boat warfare, at the beginning of 1917 the renewed tussle in Berlin ended in success for the 'Hawks'. They guaranteed victory within six months—despite the likelihood of the USA entering the war on the Allied side. Accordingly orders were issued to resume unrestricted warfare on 1st February; and three days later President Wilson broke off diplomatic relations. Meanwhile, on 16th January, the German foreign minister had sent via Washington to the ambassador in Mexico City the message still known as the 'Zimmermann Telegram'. It promised to Mexico that in return for alliance with Germany the 'former lost territory' of the southern states of the USA would be restored to her. This astonishing *gaucherie* was intercepted and deciphered in London, and was passed to the American ambassador, Walter Page, at a carefully chosen moment. The indignation it aroused in America made active intervention certain, and on 6th April the USA declared war on Germany.

In actual fact, the claims put forward by the German 'Hawks' were by no means as fantastic as they may now appear, and for the first four months it seemed quite likely that they would be fulfilled. In 1916 the U-boat fleet had more than doubled (from 54 to 133) and only twenty-two had been sunk. Allied and neutral shipping losses rocketed from 386,000 tons in January 1917 to the colossal total of 881,000 tons in April—a figure which, if maintained for a few more months, would have brought a German victory. The chief burden of countering the U-boat campaign naturally fell on the British navy, and as the many and varied antidotes adopted had failed to prove effective the dispute over whether convoy should be introduced grew hotter. The Admiralty, supported by a good deal of Merchant Navy opinion, considered that the disadvantages, such as lengthened 'turn-round' of ships, outweighed the possible advantages. But the Ministry of Shipping was confident that such arguments, which were in fact supported by wholly misleading Admiralty statistics regarding the relation between losses and safe arrivals of ships, were false. Lloyd George, the prime minister, took the same view. At the end of April he forced the Admiralty to try convoy, and the recommendations of the Atlantic Convoy Committee, which was set up in May and produced a comprehen-

sive scheme early in the following month, were at once adopted. Admiral W.S.Sims, commander of the US Naval Forces in Europe, was also a strong supporter of convoy, and with the help of the American destroyers, which soon began to operate from Queenstown (now Cobh) in southern Ireland, the experiment proved wholly successful. Not only did shipping losses decline sharply after April, but sinkings of U-boats increased from twenty in the first half of the year to forty-three in the second half. However, the confrontation between Lloyd George and the Admiralty caused a considerable loss of confidence in the Board on the part of the political leaders. In July therefore Lloyd George appointed Sir Eric Geddes first lord in place of Sir Edward Carson, who had consistently supported the sea lords' views on the convoy issue; and in December Geddes abruptly dismissed Admiral Sir John Jellicoe, the first sea lord.

A barrage of mines

Though the introduction of convoy was without doubt the most important factor in surmounting the crisis, it would be misleading to ascribe it entirely to that measure. The conflict between minelayer and minesweeper was now at its height, and in the autumn the British at last had available an efficient mine—copied from the Germans. The Straits of Dover were the crucial area, since unless both the long-range High Seas Fleet U-boats working from the German North Sea bases and the smaller boats based on Zeebrugge and Ostend could pass through the English Channel they would be forced to take the much longer route round the north of Scotland to reach their operational areas in the western approaches to the British Isles. In consequence the British concentrated a great effort on creating an impenetrable barrage of mines and nets, with surface vessels patrolling constantly overhead, in the Dover Straits. Though these measures gradually took effect, in 1917 U-boats made no less than 250 successful transits through the English Channel, mostly at night and on the surface. Not until the end of the year, by which time the barrage had been provided with night illumination, did it become really

German sailors take aim for mines—the U-boats' most dangerous enemy. They accounted for forty-eight known losses throughout the war

The U-boat campaign

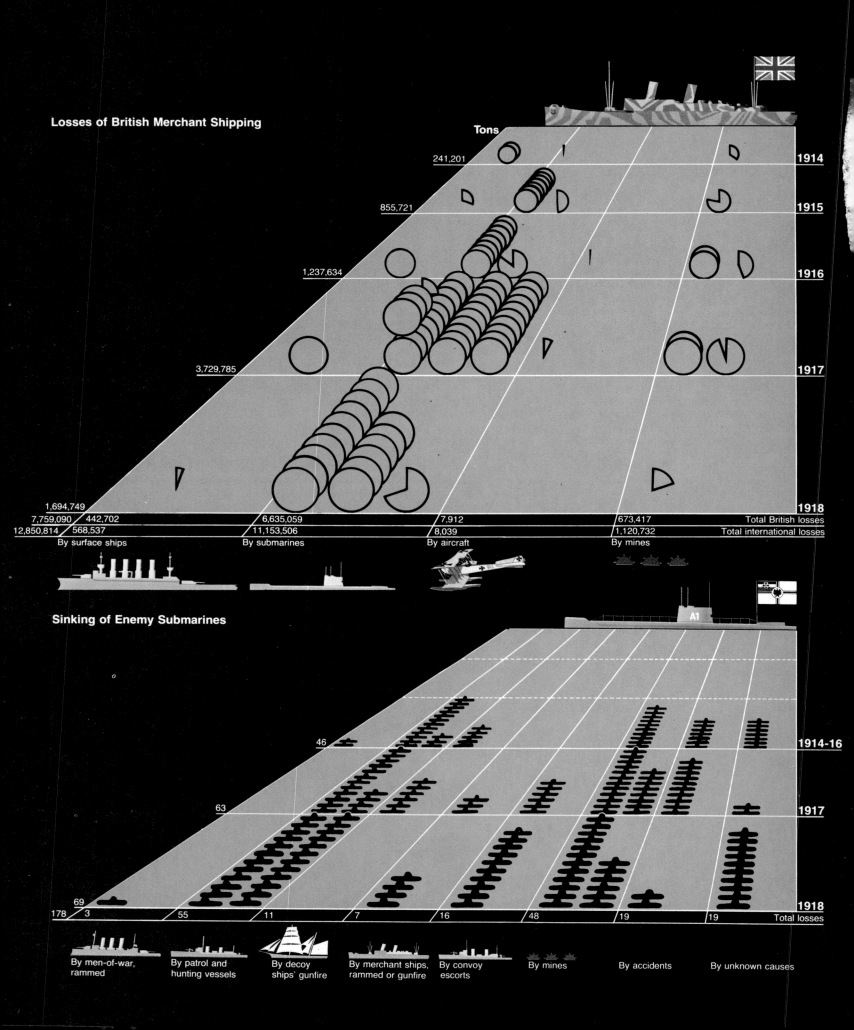

Losses of British Merchant Shipping

Tons

	1914	241,201
	1915	855,721
	1916	1,237,634
	1917	3,729,785
	1918	1,694,749

7,759,090	442,702	6,635,059	7,912	673,417	Total British losses
12,850,814	568,537	11,153,506	8,039	1,120,732	Total international losses
By surface ships		By submarines	By aircraft	By mines	

Sinking of Enemy Submarines

A1

	1914-16	46
	1917	63
	1918	69

| 178 | 3 | 55 | 11 | 7 | 16 | 48 | 19 | 19 | Total losses |
| By men-of-war, rammed | By patrol and hunting vessels | By decoy ships' gunfire | By merchant ships, rammed or gunfire | By convoy escorts | By mines | By accidents | By unknown causes |

Left: A victim of the German blockade — a steamer torpedoed by a U-boat. In April 1917 the U-boats sunk 881,000 tons of Allied shipping. If this success had continued a few months longer, Germany might have won the war. **Far left:** *Balance sheet of the German blockade by U-boat: figures for the losses in Allied merchant shipping (above) and the losses in German submarines (below), 1914-18*

The Struggle for the Sea-lanes

dangerous for U-boats to attempt the short passage. Nor was minelaying confined to the narrow waters of the Channel. The British discovered, from deciphered messages, the routes used by the U-boats to pass in and out of the Heligoland Bight, and hundreds of mines were laid to catch them at the beginning or end of their patrols. The Germans did not, of course, take the strengthening of the Dover Barrage and the obstruction of the U-boat routes lying down. Their minesweeping service struggled hard to keep the channels to and from the North Sea bases clear, while their surface ships several times attacked the vessels patrolling the Dover minefields. But although the British patrols sometimes suffered quite heavy losses, the Germans could not reverse the current trend, which showed all too plainly that the passage of the Straits was becoming unacceptably hazardous.

Of all the many anti-submarine measures adopted in 1917 the mine, with twenty U-boats sunk, was by far the most successful U-boat killer. Surface ship or submarine patrols sank sixteen enemies, convoy escorts and Q-ships (decoys) each sank six, and about a dozen were lost through accidents of one sort or another. Yet although the total sinkings in 1917 (sixty-three) were nearly three times greater than in the previous year, new construction more than kept pace with losses. At the end of the year the U-boat fleet of 142 was actually greater by nine than it had been twelve months earlier; and many of the new boats were of improved types. Plainly, then, the battle was as yet far from won by the Allies.

Blocking the blockaders

To turn back to the German scene, the entry of the USA into the war enabled the Allied naval-economic blockade to be tightened to a stranglehold. German merchant ships which had long sheltered in American ports were seized; and — more important still — there was no longer any question of American firms trying to send contraband goods to Germany, or of American merchant ships running the British blockade to reach Scandinavia or Dutch ports with such cargoes. Almost overnight on 6th April 1917 Allied control of seaborne traffic became worldwide and complete. To make matters worse for Germany the 1917 harvest was again bad, largely because of the lack of imported fertilizers; and civilian food rations were cut to a level at which it was no longer possible to remain in good health. Furthermore, there was now an acute shortage of many metals, and in consequence the equipment of the armed forces began to suffer. The renowned discipline of the German people had not yet weakened seriously, but by the end of 1917

it was becoming plain that unless the shortages of every kind, and sheer hunger, were alleviated in the fairly near future a collapse was likely on the home front.

By the beginning of 1918 some 5,000 mines had been laid in the Dover Barrage, but U-boat transits none the less continued — in March there were twenty-nine. The British were especially anxious to put the Flanders U-boat bases out of action — if the army could not capture them. Indeed the terribly costly prolongation of the 3rd battle of Ypres into the autumn of 1917 must be ascribed partly to Admiralty pressure to capture Ostend and Zeebrugge. When that offensive had plainly failed the earlier idea of a blocking operation was resurrected, and after several false starts it was carried out on the night of 22nd-23rd April. Although at the time the British believed that Zeebrugge had been effectively blocked, it is now clear that this was not so. Despite the great gallantry with which the attack was carried out (no less than eleven Victoria Crosses were awarded to participants) by early May the U-boats could work their way round the blockships. And the attack on Ostend, though repeated on 10th May, was a total failure on both occasions.

Germany feels the pinch

With the U-boats forced increasingly to use the long route round the north of Scotland the possibility of laying a gigantic minefield between the Orkneys and the Norwegian coast was raised. As the distance was some 250 miles, and the depth of water was in places far greater than the Straits of Dover, this was an undertaking of a very different order from the blocking of the twenty-mile-wide Straits. In July 1917 a new American mine was ready for mass production, and the decision was taken to go ahead. The US Navy carried out the lion's share of the laying, often in very bad weather. By the end of the war 56,000 American and 13,000 British mines had been laid in this Northern Barrage. Unfortunately, many of the American mines exploded prematurely, and there was always a gap at the eastern end in Norwegian territorial waters — which the U-boats were not slow to exploit. Though this barrage probably did make U-boat passages to their operational areas slower and more dangerous, the results achieved (three U-boats possibly sunk and another three damaged) were hardly commensurate with the effort involved.

The Mediterranean had until 1918 been a happy hunting ground for U-boats, which had sunk merchant ships with almost complete impunity. The Austrian submarine fleet totalled twenty-seven boats, most of them ex-German, and they were reinforced by German boats sent out periodically

Backs to the Wall

through the Straits of Gibraltar to work from Cattaro (now Kotor) or Pola. Hence arose the attempt to construct yet another barrage—across the Straits of Otranto—to block the routes to and from the Adriatic bases. Once again mines, nets, and surface and air patrols were all used; but with very little success. It was without doubt the introduction of convoy which defeated the Mediterranean U-boats. Of the ten sunk in those waters in 1918 at least half can be attributed to convoy escorts. One of the most interesting of these successes was the capture of Karl Dönitz from UB.68 on 4th October 1918, since he was to command Germany's U-boat fleet in the Second World War.

In July 1918 the Germans made a last desperate attempt to pass U-boats down-Channel to attack the troopships which were bringing an ever increasing flood of American soldiers to the Western Front. Of the six boats sent out only three returned home, and two of them were severely damaged. The last west-bound transit took place in August, and at the end of that month the Germans accepted that only the long northern route remained open to them. Meanwhile, a mine barrage had been laid off the east coast of England, where U-boats had previously achieved considerable successes; and more mines were laid in the Heligoland Bight. It was at this time that the British laid the first magnetic mines, off the Flanders bases, which were now virtually useless to the Germans. Also in August a heavy attack was made on the morale of the U-boat crews by publishing the names of 150 officers, most of them captains of boats, known to have been killed or captured. Recent analysis of this list shows how well-informed were the Admiralty's anti-submarine and intelligence departments.

Submarine death toll

On 25th October Admiral Reinhard Scheer, commander of the High Seas Fleet, recalled all U-boats from the sea routes with a view to their taking part in a final sortie by his fleet. There were twenty-three at sea at the time. Nine days later all possibility of carrying out that desperate plan was eliminated by widespread mutinies among Scheer's major warships; but the U-boat crews remained loyal to the end. A condition of the armistice terms signed at Compiègne on 11th November was that all surviving U-boats should be surrendered.

There is no doubt at all that in 1918

Allied anti-submarine forces inflicted a heavy defeat on the U-boats. Though seventy new ones had been built, sixty-nine were sunk, and total strength declined from 142 to 134. The convoy escorts and surface ship patrols between them accounted for thirty-four enemies; but mines, with eighteen U-boats destroyed, again proved very effective. Air escorts and patrols sank few, if any, enemies; but they played an increasingly important part by reporting U-boats' positions and forcing them to remain submerged. Of all the varied weapons in the armoury of the Allied anti-submarine forces the mine was, taking the war as a whole, much the most effective, with forty-eight successes to its credit. The depth charge with thirty came second, the torpedo with twenty third, and the ram with nineteen fourth. But the sinkings achieved by the U-boats totalled the immense figure of 11,153,506 tons out of total losses by all nations from all causes of 12,850,814 tons. The British Merchant Navy was by far the heaviest sufferer, and the 7,759,090 tons lost was no less than thirty-seven per cent of its pre-war total tonnage. The loss of 178 U-boats was perhaps a small price to pay for the amount of shipping destroyed.

As to the Allied blockade of the Central powers, by August 1918 the civilian ration in Germany was reduced below 2,000 calories daily, resistance to disease had been much lowered by malnutrition, and the death rate was rising very sharply. Perhaps the best indication of the effect of the blockade on the German people is the fact that during the four years 1915-18 civilian deaths exceeded by 760,000 the number which pre-war statistics indicated as probable. Though the German armies were as thoroughly defeated on land as their U-boats were at sea, and the so-called 'stab in the back' by the civil population's collapse is a fiction of German militaristic imagination, it is nonetheless true that the blockade inflicted great suffering on the German and Austrian people. In Great Britain and France, though rationing of food was made increasingly stringent after 1916, there was no comparable degree of suffering; nor did the war industries of the Allied nations suffer difficulties such as the shortage of raw materials caused in Germany. Thus there is a good deal of truth in the saying that the Allied victory of 1918 was achieved through 'the triumph of unarmed forces', as well as by the successes of the fighting services on land, at sea, and in the air.

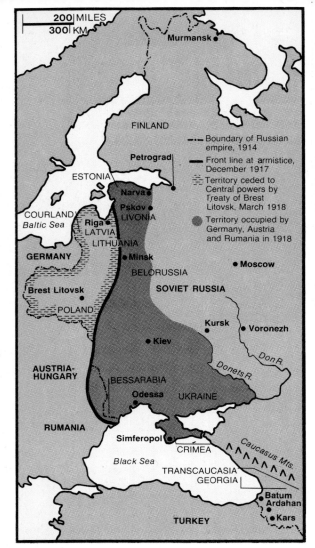

Far left: *The humiliation of Russia by the Central powers. By the terms of a 'dictated' peace Russia lost Poland, Courland, Riga, and parts of Lithuania and Bessarabia. Then the Germans and Austrians moved in to occupy the Ukraine.* **Above:** *Germans and Russians sign the ceasefire in December 1917.* **Left:** *Skoropadsky, Hetman of the Ukraine, talks to the Kaiser. Germany signed a separate peace treaty with the Ukraine—but Skoropadsky had not the power to fulfil his promise to supply Germany with badly needed food.* **Below:** *Captured Cossack guerrilla leaders being interrogated by German officers in Tiflis*

The Treaty of Brest Litovsk

No more than eight months separated the victorious peace settlement imposed on Russia by Kaiser Wilhelm's Germany at Brest Litovsk from Germany's capitulation at Compiègne. For eight months her rulers could dream that at last a decisive turning point had been reached in the war and that the most far-ranging aspirations would now be fulfilled—plans for establishing a ruling position for Germany throughout the world. The great power on Germany's eastern border, Russia, had been abased and compelled to sign a separate peace and her vast territory, seized by revolution and debilitated by civil war, appeared to be an easy prey.

The Peace of Brest Litovsk had wider implications than its effect on German-Russian relations. On 3rd March when Sokolnikov signed the treaty as Soviet representative it seemed that more had happened than the mere winning of the first round in the war; most contemporaries thought the balance had definitely shifted

in favour of Germany and the Central powers. It looked as if willingness to risk a fight on two fronts had paid off. It seemed to have justified those military circles that favoured expansion and adventure.

The fanfares of triumph in Berlin and Vienna inevitably caused serious alarm among the Allies. Wheat from the Ukraine would make the sea blockade of the Central powers impotent, and there was reason to fear the transfer of huge contingents from the German and Austro-Hungarian armies to the French and Italian theatres before the American Expeditionary Force could arrive. In some Allied countries voices were again raised, suggesting that it would be better to reach a compromise than face a long drawn out war. The spokesmen for the national liberation movements among the suppressed peoples of Austria-Hungary were worried, and with reason.

The road from the ceasefire signed in December 1917 to the Treaty of Brest Litovsk was neither short nor easy. Each

Above: A professional revolutionary on his way to talk peace with a Prussian general—Trotsky sets off for Brest Litovsk. The Germans knew that Russia could not stop their armies; but Trotsky looked for a revolution in Germany that would cripple her military might

side needed time to analyse the actions of the other in order to clarify its expectations of what peace might bring. The Central powers, and in particular their economies, were on the verge of complete exhaustion. Ludendorff admits in his memoirs that he was waiting for a 'miracle', for a revolution in Russia to eliminate from the war an enemy whose endless territory had been swallowing up division after division. The problem of making peace on the Eastern Front was a double-edged one. As good a balance as possible had to be struck between the expansionist ambitions of some circles, particularly military ones, and more realistic intentions to bite off only as much as the Central powers could chew. Russia's withdrawal from the war had helped to spark off a highly unwelcome surge of discontent and revolutionary unrest in Austria-Hungary and Germany, which would be fanned by the conclusion of a palpably annexationist treaty.

Among the foremost exponents of a relatively realistic line were Richard von Kühlmann, first secretary in the German foreign office, and the Austrian foreign minister, Count Czernin. It would be wrong of course to imagine that there was any idyllic measure of agreement between Berlin and Vienna about the approach to peace with Russia. Early in December Czernin threatened to sign a separate treaty if necessary, regardless of Berlin's policy. This he hoped would eliminate the influence of extremist circles in Germany whose exaggerated demands were likely to prevent any peace settlement with Russia — a settlement which the Danubian monarchy needed even more urgently than its ally. Czernin seems to have realized that the insatiability of the German imperialists outran their real capabilities. This does not mean, however, that he was prepared to abandon all plans of annexation; he agreed with Kühlmann that Poland, Lithuania, Courland, and the greater part of Livonia should stay in the hands of the Central powers.

In Petrograd, similarly, the views of the Soviet government about the peace problem were slowly changing. The Bolsheviks had gone into the revolution with the slogan of 'peace without annexations or indemnities', a policy of dissociation from both sides in the war and rejection of the aims of both great power alliances. Refusing to fight on, the Soviet government 'declared war on war'. It nevertheless made intensive efforts to avoid being identified in its peace offers with either side in the battle and proposed terms to all the contestants. Even after signing a ceasefire with the Central powers — who in view of their military, economic, and domestic political plight were in no position to reject any proposals out of hand — tion to reject any proposals out of hand —

the revolutionary government in Petrograd continued to urge the Allies to join in the negotiations. It was reluctant to embark on a separate peace and its spokesmen went so far as to get the German negotiators to undertake that there would be no transfers of troops from the Russian to the Western Front. Indeed, even after the Brest negotiations had been broken off in February 1918 and the German offensive had started, the Bolsheviks appealed for help to the Allied missions in Russia.

Revolutionary hopes

Not even the Bolshevik Party was untouched by disagreements about the whole complex of issues involved in making peace with the Central powers. One wing of the party, and similarly one wing of the coalition partners in the government and in the Central Executive Committee of Soviets, was sharply opposed to the conclusion of the Brest Litovsk Treaty. Bukharin, as leader of the Left Communists, declared that the first proletarian state in the world must not sign an agreement which would betray the revolutionary movement in the other countries and repress the rising wave of revolutionary action. Similar arguments were used by the Left Socialist Revolutionaries, who were anti-German and pro-Allied in their sympathies. Without a close familiarity with the political theories then prevailing in Soviet Russia it is hard to understand how these ideas of a 'revolutionary war' could have been used in protest against the Brest negotiations — especially since the Russian army had virtually disintegrated.

It must be admitted that there were many illusions and unrealistic, though revolutionarily optimistic, assessments of the situation on the Soviet side. One illusion was that the curtain was about to go up on a pan-European, if not worldwide, revolution arising from the extraordinary intensification of political, class, and social antagonisms and conflicts brought about by the war. Even before the victorious October Revolution in Russia, Lenin had formulated his theory of the 'prologue', the theory that the Russian events would be a spark setting fire to a revolutionary conflagration throughout the main industrial countries of Europe — all of which were involved in the war — and above all in Germany. The spate of demonstrations and manifestations that followed the opening of negotiations in Brest Litovsk, both in Germany and still more in Austria-Hungary, seemed to bear out this expectation, and this was bound to influence decision-making quarters in Soviet Russia.

The first few weeks of negotiation, in December 1917 and January 1918, gave no indication of the slightest approximation of views between the two sides. On the

contrary it became ever more clear that the real dictator at the conference was not Kühlmann, the titular head of the German delegation, but the brutal Prussian general Max Hoffmann, a spokesman of the most extreme imperialist and militarist circles in Germany. His extempore outbursts, culminating in the famous moment when he banged the table with his fist and demanded that the remaining Baltic territories should be evacuated by the Russians and taken under German 'protection', caused a crisis in the negotiations.

From January 1918 the Soviet peace delegation was headed by Trotsky, who shared Lenin's view that from a purely military standpoint Soviet Russia had no chance at all in a conflict with the Central powers. He agreed that a treaty must be signed as soon as Germany presented an ultimatum, and before leaving for Brest he assured Lenin that he had no intention of putting over a doctrine of 'revolutionary war'. But at the same time Trotsky considered that the radical mood of the population had made the home front of the Central powers so unstable that their armies would be incapable of launching an effective anti-Soviet offensive. It was therefore his policy to postpone the conclusion of an agreement until it might appear plain that the Central powers were not only determined, but actually able, to start large-scale military operations against Russia. When the German ultimatum was delivered, then, he declared the standpoint of the Soviet government to be 'neither peace nor war'; with that, the Soviet delegation went back to Petrograd.

The subsequent course of events fully bore out Lenin's attitude, which had previously failed to win majority support. The German and Austrian armies of intervention advanced without meeting serious obstacles, and the assumption that there would be a revolutionary upheaval inside Germany proved false. Soviet historians have recently considered the question of the magnitude of the opposition put up by improvised Red Army units and some at least now take the view that the much-vaunted victories of Narva and Pskov were isolated phenomena compared with the general abandonment of positions by the army. At the Seventh Congress of the Bolshevik Party Lenin ruefully described the capture by the enemy of railway stations which no one attempted to defend. 'Yes, we shall live to see worldwide revolution,' he remarked. 'But so far it is only a pretty fairy-tale, a most attractive fairy-tale.' Not that Lenin had ceased to believe in the forthcoming world revolution, but he recognized that revolution in Europe was not probable at that moment.

During the night of 23rd-24th February 1918 the Central Executive Committee of the Congress of Soviets ended a lively debate by voting 116 to 84 in approval of the earlier decision of the Bolshevik Party's Central Committee to accept the German peace ultimatum. A telegram in these terms was immediately despatched to the German headquarters, where meanwhile fresh and still stiffer conditions had been drafted. For Trotsky's previous reply had caused consternation among the German politicians. At the meeting of the Imperial Council called to seek a way out of the unexpected situation ('Are we to go running after the Russians, pen in hand?' Kühlmann had exclaimed) the state secretary had proposed taking note of Trotsky's declaration and awaiting further developments. Kühlmann felt obliged to take account of domestic reaction and to avoid needless exacerbation of the anti-war mood of the masses by any aggressive prolongation of the war. But as usual in such moments of decision, it was the intransigent, expansionist, and annexationist views of the general staff that won the day, demanding the formal signature of a treaty incorporating further annexations. The same quarters were even playing with the idea of continuing the war, overthrowing the Bolsheviks, and setting up a new 'national' government of supporters of the monarchy to guarantee pro-German policies for the future—for the whole German offensive had virtually become a technical problem of organization rather than one of military strategy. German military circles were well aware that the Soviet government was 'inwardly hostile' to them.

After making a declaration that he was signing the document not as a negotiated peace treaty but as a *Diktat* under the pressure of *force majeure,* the Soviet representative put his name to the list of demands presented by the Central powers and by Germany in particular. The hostilities between the Central powers and Soviet Russia were formally at an end. For the temporary victors, the booty was enormous. Russia gave up so-called Congress Poland, Lithuania, Courland, Riga, and part of Belorussia pending a decision by the Central powers about the fate of these lands; in the Caucasus Kars, Ardahan, and Batum fell to Turkey; some million square kilometres with a pre-war population of forty-six million was ceded. Reparations totalling three thousand million roubles in gold were imposed on Russia.

The Treaty of Brest Litovsk had an immediate effect, of course, on the course of the war elsewhere. So far events had not been dominated by revolution, but by the war itself, whose general course determined the pattern and outcome of happenings that seemed to be only marginally connected with it. It is not surprising,

then, that so many voices were raised immediately after the signing of the treaty, especially in the Allied countries, accusing the Soviet government of being a lackey to Germany. The dictated settlement was quoted as evidence that Lenin and his Bolsheviks, far from being a defeated party obliged by circumstances to swallow humiliating peace terms, were in fact the instrument and partner of Germany and of its general staff in their fight for world domination. Even in Soviet Russia itself, indeed, not everyone saw the force of Lenin's argument that Russia had to sign the Treaty of Brest Litovsk because she had at this point to give way before superior force since she lacked the military strength to defend herself.

Bread at bayonet point

It soon became apparent, however, that the Brest Litovsk Treaty involved deep and insuperable contradictions which made co-operation between the parties impossible. The contrast in attitudes toward the peace, toward its short-term and long-term aims alike, condemned the agreement to failure before the signatures were even dry. Representatives of two social systems, one imperial and nationalist, the other proletarian and internationalist, based their attitudes on doctrines which promised ultimate results on an international scale. Germany, the undoubted leader of the Central powers, had a rapacious and undisguised desire to become the leader of Europe and so lay the foundations of world domination. The Soviet government, on the other hand, sought to be a beacon for pan-European, if not worldwide, revolutionary upheavals. Both aims were at the time unrealistic. Germany failed to foresee all kinds of developments latent in the situation of the moment, Russia paid no attention to anything except that its partner in the newly signed peace treaty would not be its partner for long. A relationship founded on such a basis was practically doomed to be short-lived and could not even furnish a practicable *modus vivendi* for forces which, however antagonistic to each other, continued to recognize to some extent a certain appreciation of the realities of power and the basic purposes of the other side. So the Treaty of Brest Litovsk could not outlast the First World War.

It was the Central powers, and especially Germany, who were the first to realize (and that very speedily) that the optimism they had invested in the treaty, loudly proclaimed on the home front as the *Brotfrieden* or Bread Peace, was built upon sand. The only hopes that were fulfilled were those associated with the freeing of part of their troops. By June 1918 there were over 200 divisions on the Western Front and only 40 on the Eastern. This

transfer made possible the Germans' spring offensive, which the Allies required the utmost effort to withstand; for the Allies victory and peace now seemed distant indeed, a prospect for 1919 at the earliest.

The German hope that failed most completely was that of turning Russia, particularly the Ukraine, into an economic hinterland for the supply of food and raw materials to the Central powers, so that the catastrophic effects of the Allied blockade would be removed. Germany made a secret agreement with the Viennese government about economic policy in the eastern areas previously belonging to Russia. Since December a special office had also been set up under the former state secretary Helfferich not only to do the preparatory work, particularly on the economic and financial side, for the impending peace treaty, but in the long run to lay the ground for the complete domination of Russia's food and raw material supplies, by German industry. The meeting of 16th May 1918 held between leaders of German economic and industrial life, showed that the permanent influence of Germany in Russia was to rest, above all, on the bayonets of the German army and the assistance of the entire military machine. But Germany's ruling circles had overestimated her strength and they mistook a temporary pattern of power for a valid foundation of long-term policy. The idea of basing economic exploitation on a military apparatus proved quite ineffective even during the course of 1918; the classic instance of this was the experience that befell the Austro-Hungarian occupying forces in the Ukraine.

The Ukrainian Central Council led by Hetman Skoropadsky had induced the Central powers without any difficulty to sign a separate peace recognizing its independent status, and the Brest Litovsk Treaty incorporated a commitment on the part of the Soviet government to come to terms with the Central Council too. But who was there to make peace with? The German politicians were well aware that they were treating with a fictitious government fully justifying Trotsky's sarcastic remark that the only territory the Central Council ruled over was the suite its delegates occupied in the Brest Litovsk hotel. In fact on the day before the signature of the separate peace with the Ukraine the entire Central Council had to flee from Kiev. The treaty was nevertheless signed, such was the beguiling effect of the delegates' 'personal guarantee' to deliver 'at least one million bushels of grain' to the Central powers.

Military requisitioning of grain in the countryside took too many soldiers and was ineffective anyway, while for normal trade relations there were not the most elementary economic conditions. The occupying power was unable to carry out any commercial acquisition of grain because its own militarized industry was incapable of furnishing capital or consumer goods in exchange, and had too few roubles for ordinary purchases in the villages.

Between the German and Austrian purchasing organizations there arose with increasing frequency not merely rivalry but mutual deception and fraud. In Kiev the German representatives were forever complaining that their Austrian colleagues were unfairly outbidding them, in violation of their agreement. The Austrians, moreover, exploited the more favourable communications between their own country and the Ukraine in order to seize the lion's share of the grain purchases, such as they were. In mid-May 1918 the German military inspectors reported that a mere 4,000 tons of grain had been exported to Germany to date, whereas Austria had procured 25,000 tons from the Ukraine. In all, the German and Austro-Hungarian conquerors were only able to squeeze out of the Ukraine about a fifth of the expected quantities of foodstuffs and agricultural products. In absolute terms the procurements were pretty sizeable, but they looked small in comparison with the conquerors' requirements and, indeed, with the hopes invested in the conquest of the Ukraine's 'black earth' belt. German officers and diplomats based on Kiev came gradually to the conclusion that the Central Council's authority was 'not to be taken seriously', for it showed itself incapable of organizing even the foundations of a viable economy. Ironically enough, one of the major problems of implementing the *Brotfrieden* in the Ukraine was rail transport. Although the Central powers had acquired among other things the whole hard-coal minefield of the Donets, they had to import 80,000 tons of coal month by month from Germany to keep transport going.

Hopes of economic profit from Soviet Russian deliveries likewise fell far short of expectations. The commercial attaché in Moscow, Lista, found that the Soviet government was putting a number of obstacles in the way of trade with Germany. In the summer of 1918 a practical barter operation was started up, but it remained small in scope and had no serious effect on Germany's food and raw material shortages. Nor did the forced surrender of part of Russia's gold reserve demanded by the Protocol of 27th August 1918, which supplemented the Brest Litovsk Treaty with provisions concerning reparation for German property nationalized or confiscated in Soviet Russia.

German political plans for Russia's future also underwent an interesting development after the Brest Litovsk Treaty, under the influence of extreme annexationist views, especially those represented by the military clique around General Ludendorff. To be fair, these views were not shared by some of the more sober civilian politicians like Kühlmann who (it has been said), when it came to argument over eastern policy, 'must always have felt doomed to defeat in any dispute with Ludendorff'.

Foretaste of Nazism

In recent years the attention of historians has been drawn not only to the nature of German aims at the beginning of the First World War, but also to a detailed examination of German objectives in the east after the signing of the Brest Litovsk Treaty. The subject is all the more important because of the number of similarities, in scope and strategy, between the annexationist aims of that period and those of Nazi Germany formulated a quarter of a century later at the zenith of the *Wehrmacht*'s successes. In both periods we find the same limitless and overweening rapacity, together with the crudest contempt for the basic rules of international life: the respect for treaties and for the rights of other countries. The appetite of the German high command ranged from Finland and the Baltic to Murmansk, from the Ukraine and the Crimea to the Caucasus, Georgia, and Baku. These ideas were fully supported by the still decisive influence of the court in the First World War; Wilhelm II was delighted by the *élan* of his generals. Objections raised against such flagrant violation of the recently concluded peace settlement were imperiously dismissed as 'fear politics', on the grounds that 'peace with Russia can only last as long as they are afraid of us'. In the spring of 1918, pursuing this strategy of fear, German troops crossed the arbitrarily fixed frontiers and entered the central Russian districts of Voronezh and Kursk, lending aid in money and arms to the Cossack leader Krasnov on the Don. Ludendorff even toyed with the idea of setting up a 'South-Eastern League', covering the whole area between the Don and the Caucasus, under German surveillance.

The policies of Ludendorff and the high command in the Crimea, after the peninsula had been occupied in the summer of 1918 by German troops from the Ukraine, were the very prototype of Nazi ambitions to establish a German enclave there. The original plan was to assign a certain influence on the Crimea to Germany's ally Turkey, as her Pan-Ottoman enthusiasts, remembering the former glories of the Ottoman empire, wished; but this plan soon collapsed. Instead, the Kaiser's headquarters started to think about a 'State of Crimea and Tauris', perhaps in federa-tion with the Ukraine; under this plan the Crimea, of course, was to be settled mainly by German colonists from the Caucasus, the Volga basin, Bessarabia, and so on. Germany would be given sole use of the port of Simferopol and exercise a dominating economic influence over this whole artificial entity. The purpose of this fantastic plan was evidently to guard the Ukraine from the rear and ensure its obedience to German orders. This is clear, for example, from Ludendorff's argument that it was in the interests of the *Reich* 'that there should exist on the Black Sea a state under chiefly German influence to serve as a buttress to our significant economic interests in the East'.

These wide-ranging militarist plans for the east were of course quite out of proportion to Germany's military means at the time and merely put further strains upon them as the situation developed. They were in the strictest sense 'boundless', as leading officials of the *Wilhelmstrasse* described them. In order to 'secure' existing territorial gains and hopes of further spheres of influence, these plans always required involvement in more and more distant regions. In the case of the Caucasus they even led to a conflict of interests within the camp, between Germany and Turkey. For in addition to her immediate territorial gains under the Brest Litovsk settlement Turkey was already trying, exactly in German style, to enlarge her own sphere of influence at Russian expense to the north of the Caucasus, where she proposed to set up a chain of vassal buffer-states. Berlin, however, did not intend to make way for these ambitions. For Germany regarded Transcaucasia as a bridge for further penetration into Central Asia; she wanted to 'use an opportunity which occurs perhaps once in many centuries'. Ludendorff was personally disposed at the beginning to leave the Turks a free hand in the Caucasus. But he soon swung round to the opposite policy, in its extreme form as usual, and proposed sending 'small forces' into Transcaucasia. These he described as mere 'training units' for a future Georgian army, yet in the same breath he defined their role as similar to that of the German expeditionary force in Finland – a force which took on a decisive role in the civil war there.

In June 1918 Ludendorff explained Germany's expansionist aims in the Caucasus quite pragmatically. He stressed the importance of securing rich mineral deposits and supplies for Germany's war economy. He hoped it would be possible to form a native army to fight side by side with Germany against Russia and to create another 'Caucasian Bloc', possibly in alliance with the above-mentioned 'South-Eastern League' and with various Cossack

Below: The arrival of the first delivery of Russian gold to Berlin. Reparations totalling three thousand million roubles in gold were imposed on Russia, but neither this nor the requisition of wheat from the rich lands of the Ukraine made any real difference to the war economies of Austria-Hungary and Germany

and other states to the south-east of Russia. The German militarists gave willing support, especially in arms, to the most dubious local and tribal leaders who now converged on Berlin with offers of collaboration (a 'Kalmuk Prince' amongst them); they were to accept German protection after their artificial states had been set up with the help of German bayonets. This fully accorded with Wilhelm's idea of breaking up the Russian state into four tsardoms—the Ukraine, Transcaucasia and the whole South-East, Great Russia (Muscovy), and Siberia. Such a programme of course, if ever attempted, would mean further protracted warfare with Russia.

The real loser—Germany

The real victor to emerge from the Peace of Brest Litovsk was not Germany, who had dictated its brutal conditions, but Soviet Russia, who had accepted them with all the humiliation they involved. Lenin's tactics of prevarication and temporary retreat brought their expected reward. They gave Soviet Russia the necessary time for consolidation at a critical stage. The economic gain the Central powers had anticipated from a separate peace remained, despite the best efforts of the occupying powers to purchase or requisition goods, far below the expected levels. The 35,000 wagons of corn and other foodstuffs and raw materials sent out of the occupied area, mainly the Ukraine, in the course of six months'

exploitation were not enough to make any appreciable difference to the war economies of Germany and Austria-Hungary.

The treaty also spelt defeat for the Central powers in another and equally sensitive field. Multitudes of prisoners returned to Germany and Austria-Hungary after experiencing the revolution in Russia; they returned with very different scales of values and concepts than those they had had when they put on uniform in 1914. They were glad to be back home, of course —but not to get back into uniform and resume fighting. They became a source of infection in the army and doubtless accelerated its collapse as the Russian revolution itself and the dissemination of the politics and ideology, especially peace propaganda, that went with it undoubtedly did. The Austro-Hungarian army, like the state it served, broke up into its national components. In November 1918 German regiments started to set up military councils which took part in the revolutionary movements on German soil.

In November, too, the Soviet government denounced the Treaty of Brest Litovsk and Germany undertook to cancel it by signing peace terms at Compiègne. The time when she could enforce the conditions of a dictated peace had passed. The Soviet government no longer had to fear the possibility of German intervention. And official Berlin could no longer hope to maintain its hold in Russia with bayonets; it could not even maintain relations with

the Soviet government when, under the impact of revolution at home, the very German soil was shaking under its feet.

The surprise and anxiety caused in the Allied countries by the signature of a separate peace in 1918 had a kind of epilogue in the fears aroused among some of the new post-war states of central Europe at the thought of a possible German-Soviet *rapprochement*. But these fears were groundless at the time when they occurred. The Brest Litovsk Treaty had left too sour a taste behind it to serve as a suitable psychological model for future policy. Besides, external circumstances had changed too much. When the November revolution broke out in Germany it seemed as if the moment which the Bolsheviks had prophesied, the moment of pan-European revolution, was finally approaching. Only gradually was it seen with sufficient clarity that none of the revolutionary outbursts in the rest of Europe had been powerful enough to overturn the existing structure of society. No link in Europe's social chain had been as weak as Tsarist Russia. The German-Soviet treaty later signed at Rapallo, some aspects of which were anticipated as early as 1920, was in no way a continuation of the Brest Litovsk pattern; it was not a *Diktat* but a treaty between equal partners. It implied a new approach to international problems and it signalled the creation of a new and more permanent constellation of forces.

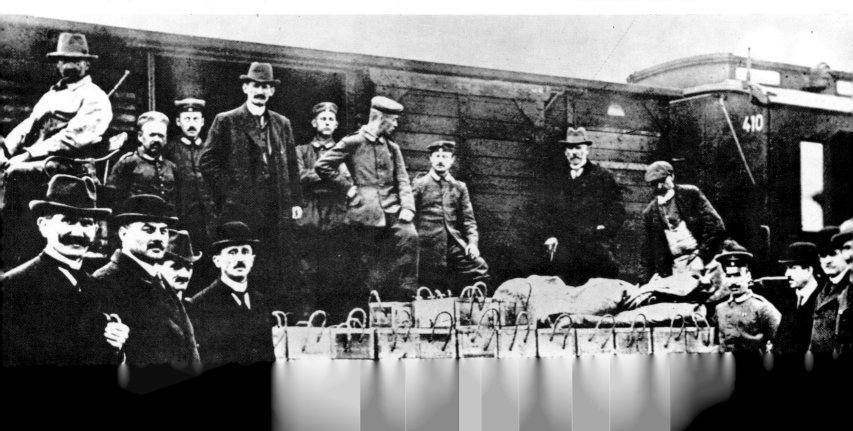

Germany's Last Throw

By the end of 1917, Europe was on the verge of bankruptcy—but a bankruptcy far more vitiating than one declared in some centre of commercial law, for it was of blood and spirit, of manhood and human hopes. Three and a half years of war had bled the nations white. France alone had provided the burying-ground for two million men: in the Ypres Salient and at Loos in 1915, at Verdun and on the Somme in 1916, and as a result of the Nivelle and Passchendaele Offensives of 1917.

Grim despondency was the mood which dominated the peoples of the warring nations—not yet plunged into defeatism, but unable to perceive the means of victory. All Europe—indeed the whole world—was hypnotized by that appalling spectacle known as the Western Front.

To its embittered inhabitants, the Front was known as 'The Sausage Machine'; for it was fed with live men, churned out corpses, but remained firmly screwed in place. This was its keynote—frustration and deadlock; it was a massive block to the progress of humanity, robbing it of happiness, ending so many lives in futile and inconsequential agony. From the Belgian coast near Nieuport down in a straggling curve to Beurnevisin on the Swiss border, the trench lines and the strips of shattered earth between and behind them, lay smeared across the land like the trail of a gigantic snail.

Along it, all day and every day, Death was present—and at night the working parties went out to court it. From dusk until just before dawn they were out, hacking at the earth to carve connecting trenches between isolated posts or even between shell-holes which could be used by machine-gunners, driving iron screw-pickets or wooden stakes into the ground to support lines of hastily-draped wire, lying close to enemy trenches all night in order to overhear their conversation; perhaps leaping into them, and after a few minutes' nightmarish activity with bomb and bayonet, dragging back to their own lines some whimpering, blood-smeared prisoner for the sake of a few morsels of incoherent military intelligence.

Draped on the wire belts were the bodies of the men killed during those white, nerve-racked, back-breaking nights. Some were killed by rifle-bullets as they crawled over the ground carrying coils of wire, some caught by scything machine-gun fire as they stood to fix the wire, some bombed by prowling patrols as they worked, hearing above their own exertions only the last few footfalls of the oncoming enemy, or the soft thud of the grenade as it landed at their feet. The entire trench system from the Channel to the Swiss frontier was dug, fortified, and held by pain and death.

At any hour of the day or night, death or mutilation could come from the guns. In winter, the shells would burst on the ice-hard ground with devastating violence, slivers of steel sighing or screaming as they sped through the frost-laden air to clatter on the ground, or to thud dully into animate or inanimate obstruction. Each type of gun had its own noise, each type of shell its own evil. German 77-mm field artillery spat 'whiz-bangs' which arrived with the noise of giant fire-crackers; 5·9s threw out their shells with vicious barks, the shells whining and growling over the valleys and ridges before ending their lives with vicious, ill-tempered crashes. Heavy guns pounded the back areas with shells that roared overhead like express trains and smashed to earth with tremendous and awful effect: and every now and then *Minenwerfer*—huge trench-mortars—would cough their black burdens into the air, to wobble uncertainly in terrifying parabolas.

The infantry hated the artillery. They hated its wantonness, its random, murderous power: above all their defencelessness against it. It was like a primitive god, uncertain, inconsistent, and unjust.

As 1917 died, a battle was fought in a sector of the British front known as the Flesquières Salient which typified the bitterness and the fury, the bravery and the squalor, the resolution and the waste of all the trench fighting which had taken place along the Western Front since it had first been formed. From just before dawn on 30th December until the early afternoon of 31st December the men of the British 63rd Division fought to hold a derisory hillock called Welsh Ridge, under attack from two and a half divisions of the German II Army. For thirty hours, the sector was a cauldron of fire, of bursting shell and erupting bomb, of drifting smoke and creeping gas, of savage bayonet attack and counter-thrust, laced throughout with the dry rattle of machine-gun fire.

And at the end, less than a mile of trench had changed hands. One thousand four hundred and twenty British soldiers and nearly two thousand Germans had died, and four thousand men of both sides were wounded or missing; and ironically, those who had been driven back found themselves in far better and stronger positions

Left: An echo of 1914. The speed of the German advance brought war once more to the open field. Right: German tank man

than those which they had originally occupied, while the victors were so exposed to hostile fire and counter-attack that they quickly abandoned their gains.

There was little other fighting along the Western Front on that last day of 1917 – sporadic sniping, routine shelling, a few lengths of trench blown in by mortar fire. It is probable that the average daily 'wastage' of some two thousand men of all nationalities due to action or sickness caused by the conditions in which they lived, was maintained.

As light began to fail, the armies stood to. Flares and starshell rose into the sky with the evanescence and sinister loveliness of tropical plants; the crater-studded, moon-like waste vibrated spasmodically to the percussion of desultory shell-fire and explosion. More men were killed, more were wounded, more died. As midnight approached there were sounds of music and singing along the German and Austrian trenches, and there was a little mild celebration among the British.

Just south of the Ypres Salient a battalion of the Royal Sussex Regiment were in the line, and a group of junior officers drank healths together, and stared out across the snowy miles at the lines of casual flares, rising, floating, dropping. One of them was Edmund Blunden, the poet, who wrote of the scene: 'The writing on the night was as the earliest scribbling of children, meaningless; they answered none of the questions with which the watcher's eyes were painfully wide. Midnight; suc-

cessions of coloured lights from one point, of white ones from another, bullying salutes of guns in brief bombardment, crackling of machine-guns small on the tingling air; but the sole answer to unspoken but importunate questions was the line of lights in the same relation to Flanders as at midnight a year before. All agreed that 1917 had been a sad offender. All observed that 1918 did not look promising at its birth.'

Yet, in fact, 1918 was to bring the end of the conflict, and despite the atmosphere of horror and waste which mere mention of the year 1917 evokes in European memories, two events had occurred during the twelve previous months which would dangle the golden prize of victory first before the eyes of the Central powers, then of the Allies.

In March 1917 had begun the Russian Revolution. It did not immediately release German and Austrian divisions from the Eastern Front – indeed the Russian General Brusilov was to launch yet another offensive there – but it was obvious to the German rulers that by early 1918 they should be able to concentrate their strength in the west. In order to expedite the Russian collapse, the German government even allowed the passage of Lenin across the country ('in a sealed carriage, like some dangerous bacillus' as Churchill was to describe the episode), for they knew that if they were to grasp their chance of victory, they must do it quickly. Germany's chance was *now*, for in April 1917 had

German artillerymen haul field guns into position during the opening of what Ludendorff hoped would be Germany's final offensive. This was to knock out the Western Allies before American troops could arrive in force

occurred another event which might well serve to snatch victory from her; America had entered the war, and her vast potential of men and materials would undoubtedly tip the scales against the Central powers if given time to do so. So it became a race – *against* time for Germany, *for* time for Great Britain and France.

Race against time

To nobody was the reality of this situation more clear than to the first quartermaster-general of the German forces, Erich Ludendorff. Since August 1916, this large, rather stout, typically Teutonic soldier had been virtual dictator of Germany, for there was no doubt that although his great friend and admirer Hindenburg held the higher rank – chief of the general staff of the field army – Ludendorff's was the guiding brain and personality.

Ludendorff had realized for some time that between the end of the British 1917 offensive and the summer of 1918, Germany must win the war; otherwise the arrival of the American armies would tip the balance against the Central powers and all their hopes and ambitions would be tumbled in the dust.

The decision must be forced in the west,

and on 11th November 1917, he had presided at a conference held at Mons to decide how it could be brought about. Present at the conference were the chiefs of staff of the groups of armies nominally commanded by the Crown Prince and Prince Rupprecht of Bavaria, but it is noteworthy that neither of these two exalted personages were invited, and neither were the Kaiser himself nor Hindenburg—even though both of them were in the neighbourhood. The subject of discussion was deemed of too great an importance for any but strictly professional soldiers.

The main, broad issue first to be decided was whether to launch an attack westwards against the British-held sector of the front, or southwards against the French. The disadvantage of the first was that if the British retreated, they would do so across old battlefields and the desolation and waste intentionally created by the Germans when they retreated to the Siegfried Line (known to the Allies as the Hindenburg Line). This would undoubtedly hamper the attackers, and the British were likely to prove difficult enough to dislodge from the first line of trenches, without giving them the advantage of successive lines to protect them as they fell back.

On the other hand, the French to the south had almost unlimited space into which they could retreat, thus bulging out the trench line until even Ludendorff's reinforcement from the Russian front would not provide sufficient numbers to hold the line of advance—especially with ever-lengthening lines of communication. A successful onslaught on Verdun might dislodge the eastern hinge of the French army—with enormous effects on French morale and probably on Franco-American co-operation (for the newly-arriving Americans were stationed in that area)—but as Ludendorff presciently remarked, the British might not feel themselves compelled to send assistance to the French so far away from their own areas of interest, and he would then be faced with mounting another large-scale offensive in Flanders.

He eventually summed up the conclusions of the conference in the following words: 'The situation in Russia . . . will, as far as can be seen, make it possible to deliver a blow on the Western Front in the New Year. The strength of the two sides will be approximately equal. About thirty-five divisions and one thousand heavy guns can be made available for *one* offensive: a second great simultaneous offensive, say as a diversion, will not be possible.

'Our general situation requires that we should strike at the earliest moment, if possible at the end of February or beginning of March, before the Americans can throw strong forces into the scale.

'We must beat the British.

'The operations must be based on these conditions.'

There were to be many more conferences, many more planning sessions before final directions could be issued, but eventually on 21st January, 1918, Ludendorff gave his final decisions with regard to the direction and scope of his great offensive.

Ludendorff's plans

He would greatly have liked to attack the Allied line along its northernmost fifty miles—from just south of Armentières up to the coast—in converging attacks on each side of the Ypres Salient which would meet near Hazebrouck and cut the vital north-south railway which fed the Allied armies, then turn north and drive the British into the sea. Two schemes, code-named St George 1 and St George 2, were drawn up on these lines but reluctantly Ludendorff came to the conclusion that they would be too dependent upon the weather. He had no desire to engulf his armies in virtually the same mud as that which had absorbed the force of the British attacks in 1917.

South of this area, the British held the thirty-five-mile front covering Béthune and Arras along the Vimy Ridge in great strength, and although his staff produced plans Valkyrie and Mars to push them off it, Ludendorff was well aware of the tenacity of British infantry when well dug in.

However, from Arras down past St Quentin to la Fère was a stretch of line held by the British 3rd Army in the north (down to Flesquières) and their 5th Army (down to la Fère) which seemed to promise very well indeed. Not only was it likely to be thinly manned in view of the fact that the British had only just taken over the most southern stretch from the French (thus extending existing forces) but opposite it was his own immensely strong and capaciously excavated Hindenburg Line—surely the best place in which to concentrate his force and launch his attack. Accordingly, his staff produced an overall plan under the code-name St Michael, which was then sub-divided into three sections, numbered downwards from the north.

The left flank of the St Michael 3 attack lay therefore on the banks of the Oise where it flowed through la Fère. As that river flowed on across the lines, it could conveniently continue as the left flank of the attack in that area, and then four miles on behind the British lines lay the Crozat Canal—which again would act as a line upon which his southern attack group could rest and guard its flank, while the remainder of the XVIIIth Army (the main force chosen for the opening of the offensive, under General von Hutier) broke the British front on each side of St Quentin and flooded forward until it reached the concave line of the Somme between Ham and Péronne. This would be the flank of the whole offensive, and Hutier's duty would be to see that no counter-attacks broke through to upset the balance of the attack to the north, to be borne by General von der Marwitz's II Army (St Michael 2) and General von Below's XVII Army (St Michael 1). These two armies would drive forwards until they reached, respectively, Albert and Bapaume, and on that line they would swing north and obtain a decision.

As Ludendorff knew only too well the vanity of man's proposals and the myriad accidents which can overset them, he also had plans drawn up for offensives along all the rest of the front from la Fère south and east as far as the Verdun Salient, naming them with an odd mixture of classical and religious fervour, Archangel, Achilles, Roland, Hector, Castor, and Pollux.

But the main emphasis was to be on Michael—with perhaps some assistance from Mars to the north and Archangel to the south.

The offensive opens

As early as the beginning of February, British Intelligence had garnered sufficient information for the staffs to be able to make a fairly accurate assessment of Ludendorff's plans; not that there was much they could do to protect the most immediately threatened area around St Quentin and la Fère, for there was hardly enough labour available to make good the front-line trenches just taken over from the French (who, after the Nivelle Offensive, had been so occupied with their own internal troubles that they had been content—so far as battle was concerned—merely to observe the gigantic conflicts in the Ypres Salient and do little else even to strengthen their own defences).

General Sir Hubert Gough, commanding the twelve infantry and three cavalry divisions of the British 5th Army, had thus been able only to strengthen the forward zone as far as its occupiers could manage in night working parties, the main battle zone immediately behind (varying in depth up to four thousand yards depending on the lie of the land) so far as fatigue parties from the units 'resting' could manage, and the rear zone only insofar as his labour force (consisting mostly of Chinese coolies) could construct roads along which material could be brought for the more urgent work farther forward.

Given time, Gough's men would undoubtedly have constructed defences comparable to those along Vimy Ridge, but no amount of labour—nothing short of a fairy wand—could have prepared the neces-

Backs to the Wall

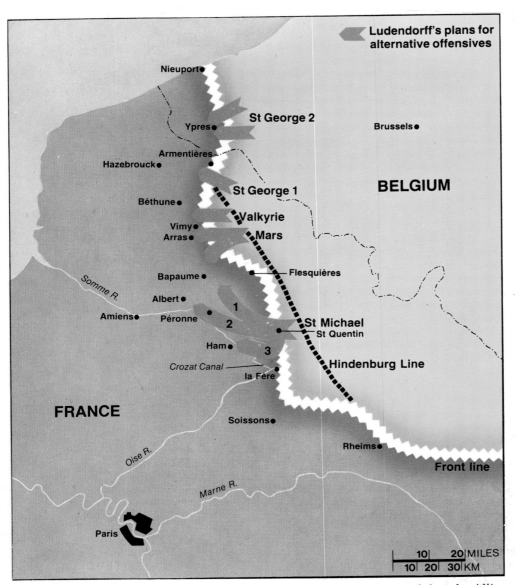

Map labels: Ludendorff's plans for alternative offensives · Nieuport · Ypres · St George 2 · Brussels · Armentières · Hazebrouck · St George 1 · BELGIUM · Béthune · Valkyrie · Vimy · Mars · Arras · Flesquières · Bapaume · Albert · 1 · Amiens · Péronne · 2 · St Michael · St Quentin · Ham · 3 · Crozat Canal · la Fère · Hindenburg Line · Somme R. · FRANCE · Soissons · Oise R. · Rheims · Front line · Marne R. · Paris · 10 20 MILES · 10 20 30 KM

The alternative plans Ludendorff considered for the blow which was to defeat the Allies

sary defences in a few weeks. But the men of the 5th Army did what they could, and awaited the onslaught with that mixture of resignation and bitterness which by now typified the front-line soldier's attitude to the war, to his commanders, and to his probable fate.

Just before five o'clock on the morning of Thursday 21st March, 1918, began the most concentrated artillery barrage the world had known. Nearly 6,000 German guns opened fire almost simultaneously along the forty-mile stretch between the Sensée river and the Oise, and when 2,500 British guns answered, the additional noise was hardly noticed even by the men who fired them.

Tons of steel and high explosive fell with shattering force upon the 5th Army forward and battle zones, and as the men crouched

deafened and dazed in their trenches or staggered drunkenly towards control points, the ground rocked and heaved under them and the air filled with the taint of lethal and lachrymatory gas.

In the battle zone gun positions, battery and brigade headquarters, telephone exchanges, and road junctions collapsed or split apart under the weight and volume of fire, ammunition dumps blew up in towering mushrooms of flame and destruction, laboriously-laid signal wires were ripped apart and cannon were pounded into unrecognizable lumps of metal. For forty miles the eastern horizon was a line of leaping red flame, with dulled reflection beneath a sheet of fog which covered the southernmost of the British positions near the Oise.

For four and a half hours this barrage of

fire continued, sweeping back and forth across the forward and battle zones, obliterating the trenches, blasting the control organizations and tearing up what flimsy obstructions the British troops had been able to lay down. And at 9.40 am the German infantry rose to their feet and stormed forward.

The main assault troops moved fast as they had been recently trained to do, generally with rifles slung—relying for effect upon the ample supplies of stick-bombs they all carried, and upon the effect of the light machine-guns and flame-throwers which accompanied each section. Where aided by the fog, they passed quickly through the forward positions, evading the known strong-points and redoubts, leaping across the trenches, racing ahead to reach the remains of communications centres and artillery batteries in the battle zone. Behind them the second and third waves mopped up—sometimes by merely directing dazed and bleeding prisoners to the rear, sometimes completing the havoc of the guns with bayonet and rifle butt. Then they followed the first wave on into the battle zone.

Their fortunes varied inversely with their distance from the Oise, where the fog was thickest. Along the banks of the river where the fog had originated and was slowest to disperse, German infantry were right through the battle zone by early afternoon; but around St Quentin and to the north the British were able to hold on, though at a terrible price; of eight British battalions in one part of the front line only fifty men survived to reach the battle zone, and no indication of the fate of two whole battalions of the King's Royal Rifle Corps was found until months later, when the few survivors were discovered in a German prison-camp, recovering from their wounds.

Farther north still, towards the Flesquières Salient, the British infantry were proving the value of Ludendorff's forecast of their tenacity. Here the fog had not been so thick and had dispersed by 10.30 am; and the British were also fighting in trenches which had been their own responsibility for some time. The result was that by the end of the day, in the far north all positions had been held, down as far as St Quentin the battle zone had been entered but not penetrated by the Germans, and only in the extreme south had it been overrun. Here, by evening, the line was back to the Crozat Canal, and Hutier's southern flank had done all it had been asked.

That night, the Kaiser presented the Iron Cross with Golden Rays to Hindenburg (the last occasion had been to Blücher in 1814), Ludendorff and General von Kuhl (chief of staff to Rupprecht of Bavaria) coolly and dispassionately studied their maps, while on the field of battle, streams

British defenders watch the advancing Germans appear through the mist. Fog aided the German attackers. Near the banks of the Oise they broke right through the battle zone on the first day of the offensive. But where the fog dispersed the British clung on grimly—for both sides knew that if the Germans did not win the war in the spring of 1918, they would lose it

of British soldiers made their way surreptitiously back towards their own lines from positions in which they had been isolated, while the German attackers rested after their vast labours and prepared themselves for ordeals still to come.

During the days which followed, the pattern of the opening hours of the offensive was repeated, with the British positions in the north holding fast but those in the south being forced back as Hutier's advance pressed relentlessly forward against ever-weakening obstruction. By the evening of the second day, the British in the south had been flung back over the Somme almost as far up as Péronne, and positions north towards Flesquières had perforce been abandoned in order to keep some form and shape of a defensive line. It was as though a door was being forced open, hinged on Flesquières and with its outer edge

swinging ominously back towards Amiens.

But this movement, of course, opened a gap in the wrong direction so far as Ludendorff was concerned. He had no wish—or perhaps more important, no plans—for a break-out to the south-west, despite the fact that it could lead towards Paris. His plans were for a break-out to the north and, with this in mind, he tried to shift the weight of his attack to the Michael 1 section, along the Cambrai-Bapaume road, in order to smash the door off its hinge. Gradually, between the Salient and the Sensée Canal, the weight of this attack forced the defences to yield until a bulge formed anchored on the Arras defences in the north and the Flesquières Salient in the south, and it seemed as though these two positions were iron spikes driven into the ground, each anchoring the end of a flexible and slightly elastic cable; but it seemed that

the Michael 1 offensive could not break it.

All through Saturday 23rd March, the pressures everywhere continued and under it the defences in the south crumbled, the 5th Army slowly but surely disintegrated. Reeling with weakness and fatigue, the troops fought on until they were killed, or retreated until they dropped unconscious—and inevitably contact with the forces holding to the north was lost. At 7 am the following day the six battalion commanders of the Royal Naval Division holding the tip of the Flesquières Salient, having apparently lost contact with higher command and concluding—as they watched the gaps on either flank widen—that their position was fast becoming untenable, decided that in order to avoid annihilation, they must withdraw. The Salient was evacuated and the iron spike wrenched from the ground.

The Great Retreat had begun.

SEGITSETEK A BÉKÉÉRT VALÓ KÜZDELEMBEN!

JEGYEZZETEK HADIKÖLCSÖNT

7 THE DEFEAT OF THE CENTRAL POWERS

The Collapse of Germany's Allies

Throughout the First World War most military leaders in London and Paris assumed that the prime task of the British and French armies was to defeat the Germans on the Western Front. Victory, they believed, would come only after a long war of attrition, in which the German army would be bled to death by endless attacks across the shell-scarred fields of France and Flanders. To these 'Westerners' the struggle against Germany's allies—Austria-Hungary, Turkey, and Bulgaria—was at best a tiresome sideshow and at times a dangerous distraction, ravenously consuming both men and munitions. Yet, from the first, the Western strategy had its critics on either side of the Channel. 'Why', they asked in effect, 'pit thousands of men against heavily fortified positions in a theatre of operations selected by the Germans themselves for their main effort? If there is deadlock between the huge armies on the Western Front, then surely a decision should be sought elsewhere, by striking at Germany's vulnerable partners so as to isolate the principal enemy and turn the natural fortress of central Europe from the rear?' This policy was broached in the first winter of war; and yet it was not until September 1918 that the Allies managed, almost as an afterthought, to put it into practice effectively.

Not all the delay stemmed from the obduracy of the Westerners. The differing importance of Germany's partners to the various Allied governments led to confusion, and even suspicion, in their counsels. To the Italians, for example, the war remained a last chapter in the *Risorgimento*, with the Austrians no less an

Left: Hungarian War Loan appeal

enemy than in the days of Cavour and Garibaldi; and the nationalists in Rome regarded Turkey and Bulgaria as insignificant adversaries, less of a danger to Italy's aspirations than her nominal ally, Serbia (who also aspired to win influence in Dalmatia). The French, too, could not neglect the Austrian threat in northern Italy, for there was always a possibility of a Napoleonic campaign in reverse, with a joint Austro-German army sweeping across Lombardy and making for Lyons and the heart of France (a strategic project which was actually proposed by the Austrian chief-of-staff to the German high command in 1916). Although the French had clearly defined ambitions in Syria, they had in general little interest in Turkish affairs, but there was far greater concern in Paris than in London for the 'Army of the Orient', that supremely cosmopolitan force which, under French command, had been gathered at Salonika to succour the Serbs and keep the Bulgarians out of Greece.

The British, by contrast, became increasingly convinced as the war continued that Turkey was second only to Germany among their enemies. Each successive Turkish affront rankled: the sanctuary afforded to the *Goeben* and *Breslau* in 1914; the gullies of Gallipoli, silent with the humiliation of vain endeavour; and the ominous lists of prisoners from Mesopotamia dying in Turkish camps. On the other hand, in London, Austria-Hungary and Bulgaria seemed of little account. There was a tendency to leave the Habsburg empire to the Italians, for it was assumed—at least until Caporetto—that fifty-two divisions and 5,000 guns concentrated on so small a front as the Isonzo would, sooner or later, crack the Austrian defences. And, although the London press

made much of Bulgarian atrocities in Macedonia, a Gladstonian-Liberal sympathy with the Bulgarians lingered on at Westminster, where the war was notoriously slow to shatter the enchantment of lost illusions. The prospects of entering Sofia in triumph held little appeal compared with the glory of liberating Jerusalem or of humbling the Turk in his capital on the Bosphorus.

The changes in the British attitude are clearly illustrated by the evolution of Lloyd George's ideas on general strategy. Even before becoming prime minister in December 1916, Lloyd George had convinced himself that the surest method of defeating Germany was by 'knocking away the props' afforded by her allies. But his priorities for destruction varied with the fluctuations of the war: thus in December 1914 he wanted an inter-Allied force from the Balkans to advance up the Danube; by January 1917 he had come to favour a joint offensive in northern Italy, with supporting attacks on the Bulgarian positions in Macedonia; but six months later he emerged as a latter-day Crusader, seeking Jerusalem as a Christmas gift for the British people, and triumphs in Turkey continued to fire his imagination until the final collapse of 1918. He maintained that, if the Turks were forced by defeat in Palestine to make a separate peace, the Allies could insist on occupying Constantinople and its hinterland and thus roll up the map of German-dominated Europe from its south-eastern tip. Few military advisers agreed with him; but Lloyd George was not to be inhibited by the disapprobation of brass-hat pundits.

The instrument chosen by Lloyd George in June 1917 to fulfil his wishes in Palestine was General Sir Edmund Allenby, who

had gained a striking success for British arms at Arras that spring, but had subsequently fallen out of favour with Haig. Allenby was a soldier of personality, a physical and moral giant. His predecessor as commander of the army in Egypt, Sir Archibald Murray, had lost nearly six thousand men in the last assault on the olives and cactus-hedges of Gaza; and Allenby, weary of the wastage on the Western Front, was determined to avoid all such costly attacks on the heavily fortified positions along the Palestinian coastal plain. He had the cavalryman's instinctive liking for a war of movement. At the end of October 1917 he struck at Beersheba, in the Judaean hills, twenty miles east of Gaza, breaking through the Turkish lines and swinging round so as to take Gaza from the sand-dunes on the flank of its defences. A rapid pursuit carried the advance fifty miles up the coast to the port of Jaffa. With rain falling night after night, so that the army was forced to rely on mules and donkeys for transport along the mud-caked tracks, Allenby himself pressed forward from Beersheba north-

westwards to Jerusalem. On 9th December the city, which had been in Muslim hands for over 600 years, fell; and the victory was hailed in London as the most impressive conquest yet achieved by British troops in the war. Yet the Turkish army, bolstered by a leavening of German officers and specialist units, was still far from beaten. Heavy rain prevented any further British advance. In February 1918 Jericho was taken; but Allenby, who was forced to send sixty battalions back to France after the German spring offensive, had to mark time all that summer, improvising an army of British, Australian, New Zealand, and Indian divisions which, supplemented by Lawrence's 'Arab Legion', would be capable of striking a decisive blow in the autumn.

Across the Mediterranean, the Allies in Salonika were also preparing to go over to the offensive. Maurice Sarrail, the politically ambitious general who had presided like a proconsul over the 'Army of the Orient' since its inception in October 1915, was recalled by Clemenceau in December 1917. His post was offered to General

Franchet d'Esperey, an 'Easterner' by conviction and a soldier who knew from his enterprising travels before the war the Balkans and central Europe better than any other high-ranking Frenchman. But Franchet d'Esperey was reluctant to relinquish his command on the Oise and the Aisne at this crucial hour in what he regarded as a personal duel with Hindenburg. It was accordingly General Guillaumat whom Clemenceau sent to Salonika, with the hard task of reconciling the British, Serbian, Greek, and Italian commanders, long estranged from the French by Sarrail's slights and pinpricks. He restored some of the confidence of this much despised army, but before launching an offensive he was summoned back to a Paris menaced by the Germans on the Marne; and Franchet d'Esperey, whose Army Group had sustained a reverse on the Chemin des Dames, was peremptorily sent east as Guillaumat's successor.

Although totally different in appearance and physique, Franchet d'Esperey had much in common with Allenby: the same liking for independence in command, the

Austrian POWs after Vittorio Veneto

same sudden eclipse on the Western Front, the same broad strategic sweep of the mind, the same conviction that, after years of entrenchment, the hour of the cavalry was at hand and that fast-moving squadrons could turn tactical success into final triumph. Like Allenby, he combined a volcanic temper with the personal magnetism which lifts the spirit of a downcast army; and, again like Allenby, his determination to achieve victory was hardened by the tragic loss in battle of an only son. When he landed at Salonika on 17th June 1918 he bluntly told the group of officers assembled to greet him, 'I expect from you savage vigour'. His British subordinates, struggling with the unfamiliar pentasyllabic surname, promptly dubbed their new commander 'Desperate Frankie'. It was an apt nickname; for, within nineteen days of arriving in Macedonia, his energy and drive had produced plans for an offensive to smash the Bulgarians and carry the war back to the Danube, nearly three hundred miles to the north.

The proposed Balkan offensive was discussed at a meeting of the supreme war council at Versailles on 3rd July, which was attended by the French and British prime ministers and their principal military advisers. The plan came under attack not only from the die-hard Westerners, who disliked any enterprise which might draw troops away from France, but from Lloyd George as well, primarily because he feared that it would divert men and material from Allenby in Palestine. A sub-committee of inter-Allied military representatives studied the project in detail and, on 3rd August, gave it their support, provided that it did not interfere with operations on the Western Front or require extensive re-routing of shipping in the Mediterranean. The British government was, however, still reluctant to give its consent, while the chief of the imperial general staff, Sir Henry Wilson, remained positively hostile to any operations in the Balkans. A curious situation thus developed: General Milne, the commander of the British Salonika Army, was confident of success and informed Lloyd George that 'an offensive here at the psychological moment may have more than local effect';

and he therefore made preparations for an attack which London was reluctant to authorize. In great secrecy but, in this instance, with cautious British backing, Allenby too was putting the final touches to plans which bore some resemblance to those contemplated in Macedonia.

Franchet d'Esperey wished to attack on 15th September and Allenby on 18th September. Not until 4th September did Lloyd George, overruling General Wilson's objections, finally give his approval to the Balkan offensive. He came firmly down on the side of the Easterners after a visit to London by General Guillaumat who, drawing on his own experience of the Macedonian Front, was able to assure the prime minister that a resolute attack would sap the war-weary Bulgarians' will to resist. Characteristically, once Lloyd George had decided to give his backing to Franchet d'Esperey, he reverted to his earlier argument for a comprehensive knocking aside of all the 'props'; and he insisted that every effort should be made to induce General

The Defeat of the Central Powers

Diaz, the Italian commander-in-chief, to take the offensive against the Austrians along the river Piave. Marshal Foch, watching his armies in France roll the Germans slowly northwards, was also eager for a simultaneous Italian attack, but Diaz refused to move until he had some clear evidence that Austria-Hungary was on the verge of disintegration. As recently as the middle of June the Austrians had crossed the Piave in force and, although they had been repulsed with heavy casualties, the Italians were taking no risks. They could not afford a second Caporetto.

The cancer of defeat

The bonds binding Germany's partners to the government in Berlin were under considerable strain even before the joint Allied offensives. The sentiment for peace was probably most widespread in Bulgaria, as Guillaumat and Milne had perceived. Such industry as the country possessed was harnessed by German managers to the German war machine. A few businessmen in the towns made fat profits from German contracts, but for hundreds of workers there was nothing but hard work and low wages. With agriculture hit by the absence of able-bodied peasants, there was a threat of starvation. Moreover, the casualties suffered by the small kingdom in the combined campaigns of the bitter Balkan Wars and the two-year struggle in Macedonia had eliminated a higher proportion of the active population than in either Germany or France. The Bulgarians had made enormous sacrifices without gaining a single tangible reward; and, with the example of their fellow-Slavs in Mother Russia to look to, it was hardly surprising that many of the younger generation were thinking in terms of revolution.

Turkish disaffection took a different form. The Germanophile leaders, Enver and Talat, were still in power in Constantinople but, since the collapse of Russia, they had been solely interested in acquiring territory in Armenia and the Caucasus. Reinforcements—often only raw recruits—were sent to the Tigris to meet the danger from General Marshall's Mesopotamian Army, toiling northwards from Baghdad with the thermometers registering 110°F. for days on end; but few Turkish levies (and even less equipment) found their way to Palestine. There the commander was General Liman von Sanders, the greatest German expert on Turkish affairs, whose flair for organization had saved Gallipoli in 1915. However von Sanders could do little with an army which was short of food and plagued with typhus and malaria. Morale had declined considerably during the winter and spring; and in June 1918 Liman gloomily reported to Berlin that his effective strength was less than the

number of deserters who had slipped away in the previous three months. There was no threat of revolution in the Ottoman empire; but a mood of apathy and surrender pervaded almost every unit on the Palestine Front. More and more Liman was forced to rely on his German 'Asia Corps'; for, of the beys, only General Mustafa Kemal was still willing to offer spirited resistance.

The oldest of Germany's allies, Austria-Hungary, was no less tired of war than Bulgaria and no more able than Turkey to prevent desertion in large numbers among the reluctant conscripts, especially those from Czech, Slovak, or South Slav districts. The Emperor Karl (who came to the throne on Franz Josef's death in November 1916) did not conceal his desire for peace and there was a movement to break all bonds with Germany even among the more intransigent Hungarians. Everyone dreaded another winter of privation. But it is easy to exaggerate the demoralization in the Dual Monarchy. The Italians were wise to treat their adversaries along the Piave with respect; for, although the 'Imperial and Royal Army' was short of supplies, short of food, and deployed for internal security as well as for external war, the hard core of professional soldiery was steeled by two centuries of tradition and discipline. In the old battle zone at the head of the Adriatic the Army still offered strong resistance: it was among the scattered units who were in the Albanian mountains, or struggling back from the Ukraine, or policing the Serbian lands, that the cancer of defeat consumed the will to fight. And it was in this very area of south-eastern Europe that the Allies struck their first blow.

Early on 14th September five hundred guns began to pour shells on the Bulgarian positions along eighty miles of mountain and ravine in Macedonia; and on the following morning Serbian, French, and Senegalese infantry stormed the heights of a broken formless ridge known as the Dobropolje, more than 7,000 feet above sea-level. It was a dramatic start to Franchet d'Esperey's offensive; and it took both the Bulgarians and their German advisers completely by surprise, for no one anticipated an attack across such grim terrain. At first the Bulgarians resisted fanatically and the French were forced to use flame-throwers against their emplacements, but after three days of fierce fighting several Bulgarian regiments were on the verge of mutiny, and the Serbs were able to thrust an arrow-head fifteen miles into the enemy position, threatening the supply depot in the small town of Gradsko and the vital artery of the Vardar valley.

On 18th September, fifty miles to the east, the British and Greeks launched their assault on the hump of hills above Lake Doiran, where concrete casements and concrete machine-gun nests protected the frontier of the Bulgarian homeland. Twice in 1917 the British had sought to win these three miles of scrub and rock, looming over lake and trenches like some miniature Gibraltar. Now they tried once more to scale 'Pip Ridge' and the 'Grand Couronné', while a Cretan division moved round the lake to cut communications. But, though the South Wales Borderers reached the last defences, courage and enterprise could not carry the Grand Couronné. And yet, after two days' fighting, a strange silence settled on the ridges and ravines. Cautiously the British and Greeks advanced. They found the emplacements abandoned. On German orders, the Bulgarians had pulled back into the Balkan mountains rather than risk being cut off by Franchet d'Esperey's columns from the west.

There followed nine days of hectic pursuit. The French and the Serbs advanced up the Vardar valley, covering twenty-five miles in a day, with no regular rations, 'in rags and bare-footed', reported one French general. A French colonial cavalry brigade of Spahis from Morocco, led by General Jouinot-Gambetta (a hard-riding and hard-swearing nephew of the radical statesman of the 1870's), swung left from the line of advance and, by crossing some of the worst country in the Balkans, succeeded in seizing the key town of Skoplje on 28th September, while the main body of Serbs and French were still thirty miles to the south. At the same time, the British began to penetrate the valleys of Bulgaria, with the RAF obliterating the enemy columns, caught on impossible roads through the rocky ravines. The cascade of bombs turned the retreat into a rout; although barely noticed at the time, it was the first real victory of air power. With riots in four Bulgarian towns and local soviets striking Leninist attitudes, the Bulgarian high command asked for an armistice. Peace delegates waited on Franchet d'Esperey at Salonika; and on 30th September Germany's least powerful ally withdrew from the war. The British entered Sofia and a battalion of the Devonshire Regiment reached the Danube at Ruse.

The Salonika Armistice terms included the occupation of strategic points in Bulgaria and the use of Bulgarian railways. It was thus possible to isolate Turkey and march overland on Constantinople from the west and from the north. Accordingly, while Franchet d'Esperey continued to pursue German and Austro-Hungarian units through Serbia, General Milne was ordered from London to concentrate the bulk of the British Salonika army against

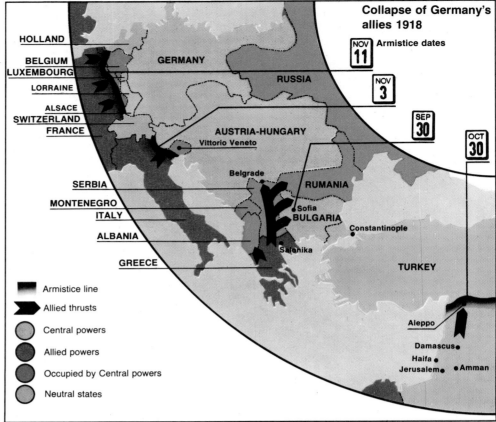

HOLLAND

BELGIUM
LUXEMBOURG

LORRAINE

ALSACE
SWITZERLAND
FRANCE

GERMANY

RUSSIA

AUSTRIA-HUNGARY
Vittorio Veneto

Belgrade

SERBIA

MONTENEGRO
ITALY

ALBANIA

GREECE

RUMANIA

Sofia
BULGARIA

Constantinople

Salonika

TURKEY

Aleppo

Damascus
Haifa
Jerusalem   Amman

NOV 11   Armistice dates
NOV 3
SEP 30
OCT 30

Armistice line

Allied thrusts

Central powers

Allied powers

Occupied by Central powers

Neutral states

Turkey 'with a view to helping her surrender', as Lloyd George wrote. Yet it may be doubted if these dispositions were necessary, for the Turks had already been defeated in Palestine and were on the verge of collapse in Mesopotamia as well.

Allenby opened his offensive in Palestine on 18th September, the same day as Milne. Elaborate deception had convinced Liman von Sanders that the main British attack would come from the east, beyond Jordan. But the blow fell on the coastal plain of Megiddo, where the cavalry broke through to the hills under a fierce artillery bombardment. As in Macedonia, heavy bombing threw the Turkish rear into confusion and Liman himself narrowly avoided capture in a daring cavalry raid on his headquarters at Nazareth. With Lawrence's Arabs helping in the east, the Turks and the German 'Asia Corps' were thrown back towards Damascus and Aleppo. An impressive roll of captured cities graced the war communiqués— Haifa and Acre on 23rd September, Amman on 25th September, Damascus itself on 2nd October. The French, far more interested in Syria than in Palestine, took a hand in the operation on 7th October, when their naval forces seized Beirut; but the victory was Allenby's, and it was his divisions which pursued the Turks relentlessly northwards to Aleppo.

With General Marshall pressing along the Tigris towards Mosul (whence he, too, could have advanced on Aleppo), realization of defeat slowly penetrated the palaces of Constantinople. At last on 13th October Sultan Mahmud VI plucked up the courage to dismiss Enver and Talat, and on the following day the new grand vizier, Izzet, sought an armistice. The Turks, however, made contact, not with Allenby, but with the commander-in-chief of the British Mediterranean Fleet, Admiral Calthorpe. It was, accordingly, at Moudros—the island base in the Aegean established by the British before the Dardanelles expedition—that the Turkish armistice was duly signed on 30th October. All fighting in the Middle East officially ceased on the following day; and on 12th November an Allied naval squadron sailed up the Dardanelles, past the rusting wrecks on the Gallipoli beaches, to anchor below the Golden Horn in Constantinople.

While Turkey was seeking peace, the war against Austria-Hungary was entering its final phase. But one Allied commander, at least, was in no mood for peace. With the towns of Serbia falling into his hands throughout October, Franchet d'Esperey was confidently preparing to march on Berlin by way of Belgrade, Budapest, Vienna, and Dresden. Spurred forward by Napoleonic notions of grandeur, he reported on 19th October that French guns had been

heard on the Danube for the first time in 109 years. Belgrade was liberated on 1st November and with one Serbian army following the French into southern Hungary and a second one marching on Sarajevo, the wheel of war had come full circle.

Yet the final blow against the Habsburgs came, not from the French and the Serbs, but from the enemy they had despised since Metternich's day; for the Italians, fearing that peace might break out before they had avenged Caporetto, went over to the offensive at last on 24th October. With British and French support, they launched a furious attack on the Piave, which cost them 25,000 men in sixty hours of grim fighting. On 30th October the Austrian line caved in, and squadrons of cavalry and armoured cars took the Austrian headquarters at Vittorio Veneto (the name subsequently given to the whole battle). Already the Austrians were suing for peace and fighting ceased on 3rd November. In ten days the Italians had no less than half a million dispirited prisoners.

A last tragi-comedy was played out on 7th November in Belgrade. The newly-independent Hungarian government did not consider itself bound by the Italian armistice, which was signed by representatives of the old order. The Hungarian Liberal, Count Mihaly Károlyi, accordingly travelled to Belgrade, confident that he would obtain generous treatment for his country from the spokesman of republican France. Károlyi asked that Hungary might be occupied by the French, British, Italians, and Americans and not by the east European peoples or by 'colonial troops'. But Franchet d'Esperey brusquely turned aside his requests. By the Belgrade Armistice more than half of the old Hungarian kingdom was occupied by Allied soldiery, including Serbs, Rumanians, and

Czechs. The revenge of the 'subject nationalities' was complete—but it was not without significance for the future that they owed their newly found status to the favours dispensed by a French general.

The successes gained by the Allied armies from Salonika and Cairo and Baghdad were soon eclipsed in the public eye by the humbling of Germany; and only Italy among the great powers regarded a victory against one of Germany's allies as the crowning glory of the war. With the coming of peace, private disputes hardened into an open controversy which was sharpened by the publication of military and political memoirs: some writers insisted that final victory had come when it did only because German might was vanquished on the fields of France and Flanders; others argued that the rapidity with which Germany's collapse followed the fall of her partners fully vindicated Lloyd George's policy of 'knocking away the props'. In the bitterness of this debate, the achievement of the soldiers and airmen in the distant theatres of war was sometimes misrepresented or denigrated. All too frequently people forgot that Germany's allies were no less the declared enemies of Great Britain and France than the government in Berlin; and it was hardly possible for their military potential to be ignored, especially when they were already in occupation of so much Allied territory. The great merit of the offensives of Allenby and Franchet d'Esperey was that they formed part of a general strategy for enveloping Germany, while disposing of her partners with a limited use of manpower and resources. Militarily they are of particular interest, for they combined the tactical employment of both the oldest and newest instruments in a war of movement, cavalry and aircraft.

The Break-up of the Habsburg Empire

Top: Czech elements of the Austrian navy demonstrating their support for the new Czechoslovak Republic during a parade in Prague. The Habsburg empire, nationalists averred, had been rotten, inhuman, and ready for liquidation.
Above: Emperor Karl I and Empress Zita of Austria-Hungary on the occasion of their coronation as King and Queen of Hungary. Crown Prince Franz Josef Otto stands with them. Karl had come into an unenviable inheritance—an empire overstrained by war

Like most important events in this century, a general European war had been discussed often enough. But when it happened, it took everyone by surprise. There were scenes of wild enthusiasm in Vienna when war was declared; they took place as well in Berlin, Paris, St Petersburg, London. It is doubtful whether anyone realized what they were in for.

The involvement of Austria-Hungary in the Balkans was one of the principal causes of the First World War; the war became, in its turn, one of the main reasons for Austria's dissolution.

The long, tremendously demanding war brought out the weaknesses of all the great powers: it helped to destroy the Habsburg empire. The empire's political and social structure was more complex than that of any other European state, and more sensitive to strains put on it by the war.

The army, which took the full brunt of it, reflected the national composition of the empire. It was multinational even among its senior ranks. The language of command was German and it consisted of some sixty words only: otherwise the troops spoke the language they found most convenient. The army offered a tempting career for young Poles and Czechs as well as Germans and Hungarians: Croatia supplied some of its most famous commanders. On the whole, it gave a good account of itself during the hostilities. When the war ended, the battlelines manned by the Austro-Hungarian armies ran through enemy territory.

It was not on the battlefields that the army did badly. The declaration of war gave the military authorities new powers. By an imperial edict, high treason, offences against the Emperor and the members of the house of Habsburg, disturbances of public order, and acts of sabotage were withdrawn from civil and placed under military jurisdiction. In addition, the military had complete administrative control over the 'zones of war', often extending far behind the battle-lines. While exercising their new powers, the soldiers assumed that army methods could be used in regard to the civilian population, and they often exceeded the limits of good sense and sometimes of legality. But worse than that, for almost two years after the outbreak of the war, the Army high command waged a relentless struggle with the civil government and administration. The military in fact wanted to take over the running of the country. They found their match in the Hungarian prime minister, Count István Tisza, who successfully protected the Hungarian part of the monarchy. There was no

politician of the same stature as Tisza in Austria, where the military came near to victory.

Though in the end the high command concentrated first on the conduct of the war, it had succeeded in further undermining the political stability of the Austrian part of the monarchy. In order to show the incompetence of the civil authorities, the military exaggerated and generalized isolated instances of treason. By treating harshly the guilty and innocent alike, they made new enemies for the Austrian state.

Hungary keeps its corn

At the same time as the struggle between the civil and the military authorities was taking place, the Austrian parliament was in recess; it had not been meeting when the war broke out, and it was not summoned again until May 1917. In spite of its many deficiencies and circumscribed powers, the Reichsrat (parliament) embodied the unity of the Austrian lands. It brought politicians of many nationalities from distant towns and regions into contact with each other, with the government, and with the court. It was a constant reminder of the diversity of the Habsburg lands and of the many difficulties involved in running them as a more or less unitary state. It had been a civilizing influence which disappeared at a crucial time.

The political life in Austria—the Hungarian parliament in Budapest continued meeting—became fragmented after the outbreak of the war more than was necessary. The lack of contact with the capital, the scarcity of reliable political information, the chicanery, especially in the case of the Slav peoples, of the military, all combined to produce an atmosphere in the provincial towns that was not really conducive to good political sense. The war did not improve relations between the two parts of the monarchy, Austria and Hungary, nor between the monarchy and her allies, Germany and Italy. Tisza, the Hungarian prime minister until June 1917, a politician as obstinate as he was shrewd, defended Hungary, usually successfully, against every attempt at interference from Vienna. Perhaps too successfully. In September and October 1916 the two meetings of the council of ministers for both Austria and Hungary dealt with no other problems but food supplies. The Austrians had become convinced that the Magyar magnates, led by István Tisza, the men who had the political power as well as the corn, were holding out on them. This was at the time when the effects of the Allied blockade were

The Defeat of the Central Powers

making themselves felt in the central empires; an Austrian later said that he could forgive the blockade imposed by the enemy but not by the Hungarians.

It may be that the ties of a prosperous economy were the strongest link holding together the peoples of the empire and that as the economy grew weaker and was transformed from an economy of plenty into one of scarcity those ties were loosened. The peoples of the empire found no appeal in Hindenburg's grim slogan *Durchhalten!* —see it through. They were not ready to go as far in making sacrifices as their German comrades in arms.

Indeed, from the very beginning of the war, the relations between Vienna and Berlin left a lot to be desired. Immediately after the outbreak of hostilities, when the Germans concentrated most of their forces in the west, the Austrian high command was left in charge of a larger section of the Eastern Front than it had foreseen. The Austrians complained at once and loudly: the German ambassador to Vienna, for his own part, kept on reporting on the 'spirit of Sadowa'—the Austrian desire to revenge their defeat by the Prussians almost half a century ago—in Austrian ruling circles.

Vienna's war-time association with Berlin was never smooth and sometimes stormy: the relations between Vienna and Rome ended in disaster. On the outbreak of the war Italy, a member state of the Triple Alliance, remained neutral; in May 1915 the Italians joined Great Britain, France, and Russia and attacked their former allies. Italy was finally won over by the side that had more to offer: she had been promised large chunks of Austrian territory by the Allies. The tortuous negotiations the Italians had conducted with the two sides before the outbreak of the war broke the health of an Austrian ambassador to Rome, and the temper and the career of the Austrian foreign minister. Before his resignation in January 1915, Count Berchtold said that he would rather fight the Italians than negotiate with them.

Death of an emperor

At the beginning of the third and so far bleakest winter of the war, the emperor Franz Josef died in Vienna on 21st November 1916. His death had a deeply depressing effect on the monarchy; crowned heads came to Vienna for the last time, to attend his funeral. The empire survived Franz Josef by less than two years.

His nephew, Archduke Karl, who succeeded Franz Josef as Karl I, was twenty-nine years old. He was handsome, slight, impressionable; like the German Kaiser, he had a fondness for fast changes from one splendid uniform into another. His spontaneous boyish gaiety and readiness to experiment might have become assets in

more peaceful times. He entered an unenviable inheritance. After the formidable, paternal figure of Franz Josef, Emperor Karl appeared, and was, insubstantial. When he was crowned the king of Hungary in Budapest the Crown of St Stephen came down over his eyes, covering half his face.

Soon after his accession, Emperor Karl and his new foreign minister, Count Czernin, began to explore the possibilities of peace. The Emperor's good intentions did not compensate for his inexperience. He conducted the negotiations partly behind the back of his own foreign minister as well as his allies: when Karl's private negotiations were revealed his foreign minister resigned, the Emperor had to apologize to Berlin, and his country became tied to Germany more firmly than ever.

In the same reforming spirit Karl summoned the Austrian parliament in May 1917, and proclaimed an amnesty for political prisoners. Again, those good ideas went wrong. The concessions were not backed up by any comprehensive plan for political reform and, anyway, they came too late.

Throughout the war, the attention of everyone in Austria-Hungary was riveted to the events on the Eastern Front and in Russia: the Germans were taking care of the war in the west and it was therefore of much less consequence for the Austrians. In March 1917 the revolution in Russia made a profound impression on them, and on their rulers in particular. They were haunted by the threat of a revolution. When Lenin came into power on 7th November 1917, and when he started putting into practice his peace policy, the Austrians were more frightened than relieved. Some of the units released from the Eastern Front in the winter of 1917-18 were kept at home, to maintain internal order: the prisoners-of-war returning from Russia were given an elaborate screening treatment, so that they would not infect their fellow-citizens with Bolshevik doctrines.

Despite the extensive strike movement in Austria-Hungary early in 1918, the main threat to the Habsburg order did not come from a Russian-Bolshevik type of social revolution. The social unrest stimulated by the Bolshevik victory made itself felt mainly among the two top nations of the empire—the Germans and the Hungarians. With their national aspirations either satisfied or absent, the cause of national independence took second place to social reform. For the rest of the Habsburg peoples—the Poles, the Czechs, the South Slavs, the Rumanians, the Italians—national independence was the first aim.

It had not always been so. Before the war, the politicians had been fully occupied by their party and national politics: both were very absorbing and parochial pursuits. The outbreak of the war broadened

Hungarian soldiers of the Austrian army in leisurely occupation of a road junction in Prague, October 1918. The Habsburg empire meekly conceded nationalist demands

their horizons while depriving them of their usual pastimes. All kinds of political plans were spun in the war-time isolation and gloom of the provincial towns.

The Italians in South Tyrol and Dalmatia and the Rumanians in Transylvania had Italy and Rumania to look to, and both countries eventually joined the ranks of Austria's enemies. The task of the Italian and the Rumanian politicians in the Habsburg monarchy was therefore comparatively simple, and most of them gradually transferred their sympathies to their own national kingdoms during the war. For those Serbs who liked the idea of being its subjects, there was the kingdom of Serbia—but there existed the alternative, properly developed only during the war, of a united kingdom of all the South Slavs: the Serbs, the Croats, the Slovenes. The position of the Poles, divided among the three powers—Austria, Germany, and Russia—was the most tragic because they were engaged in a fratricidal fight. But it had the advantage that they could not help ending up on the winning side.

The Czechs, with their powerful industry and recently developed, though very articulate, national life, had at first no assets on their side. Whether they liked it or not, they were very much a part of the fabric of the Habsburg state. If the Italians received South Tyrol and a large part of the Dalmatian coast, or if the Rumanians took away Transylvania from the Habsburgs, the monarchy could have survived without much trouble. Perhaps even the amputation of Galicia or Croatia would not have proved fatal. But without Bohemia and Moravia the Habsburgs could not have survived as the rulers of a great power.

As in every other province of the empire, the beginnings of the Czech movement for independence were small and unorganized. A few exiles abroad, a few sympathizers at home: none of the national movements possessed an organization, after the outbreak of the war, that could approach the strength and the efficiency of, say, Lenin's revolutionary organization in Russia.

The Serbs and the Croats of Dalmatia gave the anti-Habsburg movement its first, and most numerous, group of political exiles. Most of them had Italian as their second language, and all of them had the example of the unification of Italy before their eyes. Ante Trumbić and Fran Supilo (a Croat leader of the Serb and Croat coalition working for the union of the South Slavs) had left for Italy a few days before Austria-Hungary declared war on Serbia. After that they moved from one Allied capital to another, propagating the idea of South Slav unity, raising funds, recruiting volunteers. They were staggered when they got to know, by accident in Petrograd, of the Allied promise to Italy, as part of the terms of the Treaty of London which committed Italy to war, of a large part of Dalmatia. Their activities suffered from isolation from their home country.

The Czech exiles, on the other hand, were careful to keep their lines of communication with Austria-Hungary open. They claimed to represent their people at home, a claim that became true only towards the end of the war, and they developed an intensive anti-Habsburg publicity. They announced that the Habsburg empire was rotten, inhuman, and ready for liquidation; that it was dominated by the military who, in their turn, were nothing but tools of Berlin and its expansionist plans. The Czech political exiles were fortunate in having Thomas Masaryk for their leader. Masaryk, born in the Moravian-Slovak border area, was a university professor and politician, sixty-four years old when the war started. He was also the founder of one of the smallest of the Czech political parties. During the war, he mobilized the few Slovak exiles and the many Slovak immigrants in America for the fight, with the Czechs, against the Habsburg monarchy. By no means a revolutionary before the war, Masaryk maintained that the Central powers could not win against the combined forces of France, Russia and, especially, of the British empire. Masaryk disapproved of the pro-Russian sympathies of the Czechs: he tended to rely instead on the support for his plans of the Western powers.

By the end of 1917, Masaryk and his

Triumphant Masaryk enters Prague surrounded by the Czech Legionaries he had raised in Russia, France, and Italy, together with Czech and Slovak officers of the Austrian army

Czechoslovak National Council, based on Paris, had successfully organized Czech and Slovak military units in Russia, France, and Italy: they had made the Allied governments take note of their plans for the break-up of the Habsburg empire. They kept in touch with the secret revolutionary society in Prague, informing the Czechs at home of their successes abroad.

The end of an empire
After the failure of the attempts at separate peace with Austria towards the end of the year 1917, and under the impression of military necessity in the spring of 1918 the governments of the Allied powers began recognizing the claims of the Czechs, the South Slavs, and the Poles to independent states. They sanctioned the break-up of the Habsburg empire before it took place.

Nevertheless, inside the monarchy the anti-Habsburg national movements had been gaining support since the spring of 1917. The ties that had bound the peoples to the monarchy were gradually loosened; the plans entertained by a few visionary politicians in September 1914 received a broad political support four years later. The peoples of the Habsburg empire entered the war with one kind of 'nationalism' and left it with another. At the end of the war, nothing but completely independent states could satisfy them.

It was too late when, on 16th October 1918, the Austrian premier made a proposal for the transformation of Austria into a federal state. The previous attempts at reform by Emperor Karl had been less broadly based and they did not have the

desired effect. After the re-opening of the Reichsrat in May its work was impeded by violent scenes; the pre-war *Kameraderie* of the deputies had disappeared. The amnestied political prisoners increased the ranks of the anti-Habsburg politicians. Anyway, at one point in the months after the Russian Revolution, Emperor Karl seems to have lost the little self-confidence he may have possessed. In the last months of the war, as he was growing more bewildered, his political actions were becoming more and more erratic. His loss of nerve affected every level of the official hierarchy of the Habsburg state. Sometime before the end of the war, its rulers lost conviction in their right to govern. The informal document of abdication which Karl signed on 11th November 1918 contained no trace of his desire to carry on the burden of the government: 'Since I am filled now, as before, by unchangeable love for all my nations, I will not place my person as an obstacle to their free evolution . . .'

At the time, the empire existed no more. The double-headed eagles had been taken down from official buildings; the imperial anthem was no longer sung; the whole machinery of the Habsburg state had disappeared. The Serbs, Croats, and Slovenes were busy building a united state under the Karageorgević dynasty; the Rumanians and the Italians joined their own national kingdoms; the Poles were trying to amalgamate three disparate provinces into one republic; the Czechs and the Slovaks were building their common state. The Hungarians and the Austrians had to come to terms with their new insignificance.

Ludendorff's Defeat

Ludendorff was making a bid for final victory. At the end of 1917 he had decided that he must knock the French and, above all, the British out of the war before the promised American reinforcements could arrive and turn the tide once and for all in the Allies' favour. On 21st March 1918 the greatest bombardment the world had ever seen started up on the Western Front. In heavy fog the German assault troops stormed through the British strongpoints from St Quentin to la Fère, and in the following days they pushed the British back over the old hard-fought battleground of the Somme. Ludendorff's plan, St Michael, envisaged a complete breakthrough down from Arras through the Flesquières Salient to St Quentin and la Fère. On 24th March, while the Germans pushed through to north and south, the British started to withdraw from the Flesquières Salient, the last point they held south of Arras on the old front line. But Arras, contrary to German plans, stayed firm as the British front line retreated. It was as though a door hinging on Arras was swinging open.

As a result of the mutual respect which existed between the British and French commanders-in-chief, Sir Douglas Haig and General Philippe Pétain, French divisions had been hastily flung into the gap left as the door opened, and after a conference held at Doullens, on 26th March, the Allied armies had an overall commander-in-chief in the person of General Ferdinand Foch. It was to prove a happy choice, and in the existing circumstances the British could only gain from this apparent surrender of their independence; reserves could only flow towards them—at least until this vast emergency was over.

By 29th March reserves were coming up from the south to fill the gaping holes in the British line—which now ran from Arras down through Albert, Villers Bretonneux, and Cantigny—and it was also evident that the steam was going out of the German attack. Many factors contributed to this—inevitable casualties, accumulated fatigue in the surviving assault troops, the ever-lengthening lines of communication, and the foreseen difficulties of moving men and supplies forward across the enormous confusion of the old Somme battlefields.

But there was another reason, illustrated by an entry in the diary of a German officer, Rudolf Binding: 'Today the advance of our infantry suddenly stopped near Albert. Nobody could understand why. Our airmen had reported no enemy between Albert and Amiens . . . our way seemed entirely clear. I jumped into a car to investigate.

'As soon as I got near the town I began to see curious sights. Strange figures which looked very little like soldiers . . . were making their way back out of the town. There were men driving cows before them in a line: others who carried a hen under one arm and a box of notepaper under the other. Men carrying a bottle of wine under their arm and another one open in their hand. Men who had torn a silk drawing-room curtain from its rod . . . more men with writing paper and notebooks. Evidently they had found it desirable to sack a stationer's shop. Men dressed up in comic disguise. Men with top hats on their heads. Men staggering.'

Ludendorff's dream vanishes

Three and a half years of grim austerity had led to this. As the front of the German advance crept out of the battle area into the line of villages which had until a few days before been inhabited by civilians—grown rich on commerce with the British troops—it seemed to the Germans that they had stumbled into Aladdin's cave. All were affected, officers and men, rich and poor alike, for the wealth of Prussia had been unable to buy during the last years the booty which now lay around them for plunder. Binding himself writes, almost with hysteria, of 'smearing our boots with lovely English boot-polish . . .'

And together with this understandable but uncontrollable lust for trivial comforts and luxuries which had been for so long denied them, drunkenness now joined to check the German armies. Fear and battle had dried the moisture from the soldiers' bodies quicker than the desert sun—and after a week living on scummy water from the bottom of shell-holes foul with cordite and decomposition, the troops found themselves in deserted villages whose houses still held wine-stocked cellars. To those few who could remember, the scenes stirred memories of the great sweep to the Marne in 1914.

And so the March offensive petered out. In all, it won from the Allies some 1,200 square miles of territory, vast quantities of stores, over 90,000 prisoners, and 1,000 guns; it had also presented the victors with nearly fifty extra miles of front to hold, none of which could possibly be as strongly fortified, as defensible, or even as comfortable as the Hindenburg Line from which it had started.

With the halting of St Michael (and also the failure of a brief attack aimed at smashing away the door-hinge at Arras)

Above: French prisoners captured in the opening stages of the German offensive.
Left: Canadian Highlanders on the march painted by Eric Kennington

The Defeat of the Central Powers

Ludendorff realized that his dream of a break-through in the southern half of the British front was fast vanishing—but there were still other schemes produced by his staffs, notably the St George attacks, which had attracted him when they had first been presented to him in December. These plans proposed attacking the Allied line along its northernmost fifty miles—from south of Armentières to the coast—in offensives on each side of the Ypres Salient, which would meet near Hazebrouck and then turn north and drive the British into the sea. Ludendorff had originally rejected them because of the uncertainty of the weather—he had no desire to engulf his armies in the Flanders mud as the British had done in 1917.

March 1918, however, had proved an exceptionally dry month and the ground was likely to be firm—so as many men as could be spared from the coalescing fronts between Albert and Cantigny were withdrawn, the German artillery train hurriedly transferred north, and the plans examined for converging attacks on the Ypres Salient.

However, it soon became evident that insufficient numerical strength was available for so grand a project, and only the southern half of the blow could be launched. Even this was limited to a twelve- instead of a thirty-mile front, and at the suggestion of one of Ludendorff's more sardonic staff officers the code-name was changed from St George to Georgette.

While the German general staff busied itself with the organization of this second act of their offensive, the Allies—severely shaken but thankfully aware of the passing of their most immediate peril—held a series of rapid and salutary post-mortems, which resulted firstly in the dismissal of the unfortunate Sir Hubert Gough, and secondly in the further strengthening of General Foch's position. The agreement reached at Doullens was superseded by the following announcement: 'General Foch is charged by the British, French, and American governments with the co-ordination of the action of the Allied armies on the Western Front. To this end all powers necessary to secure effective realization are conferred on him. The British, French, and American governments for this purpose entrust to General Foch the strategic direction of military operations.'

There were certain reservations with regard to tactical direction in the final passages of the agreement, but the Allies were at last obtaining for themselves the immense advantage of a single supreme commander—which the Central powers had enjoyed for many months. Another most hopeful factor was the presence of two American generals at the conference, Generals Pershing and Bliss.

It was tacitly admitted that in the circumstances the sooner American troops were in action the better; and that General Pershing's natural desire for the American army to fight solely as a national army under his own command might in days of such emergency be modified to allow separate American divisions to be fed piecemeal into the front wherever the Allied requirements were greatest.

According to legend, General Pershing made a high-flown speech ending 'I come to tell you that the American people will esteem it a great honour that our troops should take part in the present battle. . . . There is at the moment no other question than that of fighting. Infantry, artillery, aeroplanes, tanks, all that we have is yours. Dispose of us as you wish. . . . The American people will be proud to take part in the greatest and finest battle in history.'

Apart from the fact that no American aeroplanes, artillery, or tanks had as yet arrived in Europe (in the event, none arrived before the Armistice), a study of Pershing's character reveals that it is most unlikely that he would ever indulge in such verbal histrionics. It is far more likely that whatever he said approximated far more closely to General Bliss's remark.

He had said: 'We've come over here to get ourselves killed; if you want to use us, what are you waiting for?'

Despite its mordant note, few speeches have ever afforded greater relief. Munitions for the front were ready and to hand, but only America could replace the lost legions – and within a week American engineers were working on the defence lines and taking part in repelling German attacks on British positions.

It was, of course, problems of manpower which most deeply worried Sir Douglas Haig, the British commander-in-chief during the days immediately following the last spasms of the St Michael offensive – and the condition of some of the divisions which had been involved in it. Five of these divisions he removed from the line and replaced by rested divisions from the northern sector – transferring the battered remnants of the 9th, 19th, 25th, 34th, and 40th Divisions to a quiet section between the Ypres-Comines Canal and la Bassée; as neighbours on their right flank, they should have had the 1st and 2nd Portuguese Divisions, but as it happened, shortly after the arrival of the British divisions from the south, the 1st Portuguese left the line and as no replacements seemed to be forthcoming the 2nd Portuguese thinned themselves out to occupy the spaces left vacant by their compatriots.

On 7th and 8th April, Armentières to the north and the area around Lens to the south were deluged in mustard gas, and at 3 am on the 9th the opening of Georgette

was signalled by an intense bombardment from Ludendorff's 'battering train', followed shortly after 8 am by a violent onslaught by the infantry of nine full-strength German divisions. The main weight of the attack fell upon the Portuguese sector, and pausing only long enough to remove their boots, the troops fled to the rear, several of them assisting their passage by commandeering the bicycles of the British 11th Cyclist Battalion who had been rushed up to hold the gap.

The remainder of the morning was a wild confusion of attack and counter-attack, as every available British unit was hastily flung into the breach, but by evening the Germans had stormed forward for six miles as far as the banks of the River Lawe, behind which the Highlanders of the 51st Division waited in grim anticipation of the next morning's battle.

As it happened, the main weight of the next day's attack was directed by Ludendorff farther to the north than the Highlanders' positions. In the first onslaught, only half of Georgette had been delivered (against the northern flank of the British 1st Army, commanded by Sir Henry Horne) and now it was time for the southern flank of Sir Herbert Plumer's 2nd Army to take the brunt of the attack. As the Ypres Salient was a part of the 2nd Army's responsibility, both the men and their beloved commander were well used to the horrors and vicissitudes of battle.

All day long the battle raged (again the attackers were aided at first by thick fog in the Lys valley) but unlike the previous day – and unlike the previous weeks of the March offensive – the British line remained unbroken as it went slowly back; it was yielding ground quite methodically, and just as methodically exacting an enormous price in German blood for every inch it gave. Armentières and Erquinhem, Messines and Ploegsteert, all fell into German hands that day – to the dismay and astonishment of many armchair strategists weaned on the belief that to lose ground was to lose the battle – but already Plumer sensed his command of the situation was secure, and this was confirmed on 12th April when Sir Douglas Haig extended his sector southwards so that the whole British defence would be directed by one man.

Plumer's sector thus resembled a gigantic reversed S from the right bank of the Coverbeek stream north of Ypres, right around the Ypres Salient through Poelcapelle to the Passchendaele Ridge of fearful memory; back across the Wytschaete Ridge, and around in the first twelve miles of the bottom curve of the S as far as Merville. It was a line won at dreadful cost during three and a half years of slaughter and agony, and every yard of the northern sector in the Salient

itself had been the site of deeds recorded in some British regimental history – and with a refreshing realism Plumer decided to withdraw from it in order to shorten his line and accumulate reserves for the defence of Béthune and Hazebrouck.

As a result, when Ludendorff again shifted his attack north to probe for a weak spot, his opening bombardment fell on empty trenches, and to attack the new British line his infantry had to advance down the open face of the deserted ridge, while their support artillery tried to heave its way over two miles of churned mud.

Georgette bogged down. A week after that first storming success against the Portuguese, the battle of the Lys began to show the same signs of stagnation as those which had heralded the halting of the St Michael offensive. Although the attacking troops still made progress – and Baillieul fell into their hands a smoking ruin on 15th April – they were tired, their supplies were arriving late and were inadequate, while all the time the defences against which they battered, grew stronger. The defensive crust, in fact, had been given time to harden, and Ludendorff's chance of a break-through was vanishing. On 16th April, violent but unsuccessful German attacks were launched to the south against the left flank of Sir Henry Horne's army, but on 19th April a lull descended on the entire front.

French divisions now came up to take over the line from Méteren to Wytschaete, and the five British divisions most severely mauled on the Lys – including the 19th and 25th which had been brought up from Flesquières after their battering during St Michael – were transferred south to a quiet section of the French front along the Chemin-des-Dames, where it was confidently believed that they would enjoy ample facilities for rest and recovery.

The British hold fast

During the whole of the recent crises, the new Allied commander-in-chief General Foch had been indomitably and sometimes infuriatingly optimistic whatever happened. His invariable reaction to every piece of news, however alarming, had been ' 'Bon!' until on one occasion Haig's patience had worn thin and he slapped the table and retorted 'Ce n'est pas bon du tout!' – but nonetheless Foch's attitude of supreme confidence and energy played some considerable part in the battle.

But Ludendorff, on the other side of the line, had been growing increasingly depressed. Despite the gains in territory, booty, and prisoners – vast in comparison with those of any Allied offensive on the Western Front – he had nevertheless failed to attain the type of sweeping victory which had attended his efforts on the

The Defeat of the Central Powers

Eastern Front, and which he knew would be necessary if the Central Powers were to win the war. However loudly the German press might proclaim his genius as a military commander and however striking the gains might look on the maps and in the balance sheets of the stores depots, the cold fact remained that a large number of his finest soldiers had been killed and those that were left had to hold fifty more miles of line than when St Michael began.

He had, he began to feel, been mistaken in attacking the British section of the front, however sound his reasoning had appeared when the decisions were made, and on 17th April he instructed his staff to prepare plans for yet another large-scale offensive, this time against the French, in the area adjacent to the southern edge of the now moribund St Quentin attack. It was here that the original line of the Western Front had curved around from roughly north-south to west-east, before beginning its sixty-mile straight run to Verdun.

There were still two battles to be fought against the British, however, the last spasms of Georgette and St Michael. On 24th April thirteen German tanks led an attack which finally succeeded in taking Villers Bretonneux though the town only remained in German hands a matter of hours, a combined British and Australian attack retaking it during the following night. And on 25th April a violent German attack captured Mont Kemmel from the French troops who had just taken it over from the exhausted British.

But again, gaps torn in the Allied lines were not exploited. Plumer poured his accumulated reserves like cement into the line, the line hardened and set, and nothing Ludendorff could do could break it; in any case, his attentive and slightly bulbous gaze was now fixed on the scene of his next offensive which, abjuring both religion and the classics and placing his trust in history, he had now christened 'Blücher'. Perhaps he hoped for an Iron Cross with Golden Rays for himself.

When the men of the British divisions transferred south for a well-earned period of rest and recuperation first arrived in the delightful Champagne country, blossoming now in the warm spring sunshine, the contrasts from the drab mists and mud of the Flanders plain had been to them a blissful revelation. The verdant countryside was broken by hills among which nestled charming villages untouched by war, and if the trenches were shallow and insanitary to a degree which only French troops could have tolerated, they were nevertheless so screened in foliage as to resemble more the brambled hideouts of childhood games than the fortifications

of more adult pursuits. Not that this mattered, for this was a cushy front.

At first.

But after a week the men began to wonder, for in addition to glorious weather May brought an increasing feeling of tension coupled with an almost imperceptible daily increase in the amount of German shell-fire. And if the troops felt uneasy, the battalion commanders were soon horrified to discover the manner in which their men were disposed along so shallow a defensive line.

Unfortunately, there was nothing which could be done about this, for these British divisions were now in the command area of the French 6th Army, under the command of General Duchesne, whose choleric disposition was such that he fiercely resented criticism even from superior officers of his own nationality. When suggestions for changes in disposition came from subordinates, and when the subordinates were British—and those moreover who had recently and disgracefully retired in front of German attacks—then they met with flat rejection, worded in the most insulting terms. When the British staff remonstrated further, he dismissed them with a basilisk stare and breathed a curt *'J'ai dit!'*

All troops in Duchesne's sector, British and French alike, were thus herded compactly up into front lines of dubious protective value, and when, despite Duchesne's repeated announcements that no German attack was imminent, the opening bombardment of Blücher fell upon them at 1 am on the morning of 27th May, it trod them into the ground with an obliterative effect even greater than the opening barrage of St Michael. At 3.40 am German Storm Troops began to move forward behind the wall of their own bursting shells, through scenes of carnage and destruction beyond the imagination of Hieronymus Bosch.

By mid-day they were across the Aisne—Duchesne had delayed blowing the bridges until too late—and by evening German spearheads had reached the Vesle on both sides of Fismes. The following morning they crossed the river and surged onwards towards the Marne, at the same time broadening the base of their advance to threaten the rail centre of Soissons—thus advancing twelve miles in one day, a feat long considered impossible upon the Western Front.

An attack launched in conditions which applied in France between 1914 and 1918 has been aptly compared to the overturning of a bucket of water on a flat surface. Unless action is taken with extraordinary rapidity and decision in the first vital seconds, attempts to dam or channel the floods are of no avail, and

there is nothing to do but wait until the waters lose their impetus and reach the limit of their dispersion.

This happened with Blücher. Day after day the German tide flooded southwards, until on 30th May troops of General von Böhn's VII Army reached the Marne, with Paris lying fifty miles away straight up the corridor between the Marne and the Ourcq. But however entrancing this view may have been to the Kaiser and the Crown Prince (both following their armies some fifty miles to the rear), to Ludendorff and his staff two ominous facts were emerging which thoroughly dampened their spirits. Firstly, the map now showed a huge bulge depressingly similar to those lately and abortively formed by their own efforts to the north; and secondly, their troops were now passing through the Champagne country and the reports coming back from the front indicated that all ranks were appreciating the contents of French cellars far more than the need to press forward; and *Feldpolizei* dispatched to restore order far too often succumbed to temptation themselves.

Thus Blücher, too, lost impetus and died—and one of the most significant facts about the halting of the tide occurred on 1st June at Château-Thierry, when for the first time a German attack was met and firmly repulsed by American troops. It had taken rather longer than had been expected for General Pershing to augment his promises made at Doullens, but now the 2nd American Division was in action and American troops were to take part in all the battles still to come.

The Black Day of the German army

It was now that the essential book-keeping behind warfare began to reveal the true state of affairs. There was no denial of the fact that, so far as possession of real estate in France was concerned, Germany had made vast gains during the past few weeks, to the direct loss of the Allies—but the cost had been excessive. Ludendorff's strength in divisions on paper was little less than it had been at the beginning of St Michael, but the average battalion strengths had been reduced by this time from 807 to 692—despite the arrival of 23,000 recruits of the 1899 class, and some 60,000 men withdrawn from rail, transport, and other supply services. Moreover, the quality of the battalions was distinctly lower than at the beginning of the year, for the simple reason that Ludendorff had creamed off the best men to form his Storm Troop units; these had inevitably suffered the highest casualties, as they had both led every attack and then been flung in to hold any gaps.

Now, therefore, his best men were gone and in their place were the unfit, the very

1 German supply wagons choke a road on the Somme. The difficulties of moving war-weary troops and their supplies forward across the old battlefields sapped the impetus of the German offensive. 2 French troops take cover as one of their tanks is hit. 3 Artist's impression of German tank attack on Villers Bretonneux. 4 Men of a New Zealand division support British tanks during the counter-offensive. In the background, captured German guns

The Defeat of the Central Powers

Top: Bespectacled German soldier surrenders during the counter-offensive. With his best men dead, Ludendorff replaced them with the unfit, the very young, and the middle-aged. Above: Men of a Lancashire regiment pose excitedly in German headgear

young and the middle-aged, and that irreducible proportion of men in every army which normally manages to occupy the safest and most lucrative positions, and who are therefore most aggrieved when circumstance forcibly exchanges their comfort for danger. This undesirable faction had already been responsible for some ugly incidents; desertion had increased, troops had failed to return from leave, and many of those who did return as far as the railheads behind the lines, now joined up with others as sullen and mutinous as themselves to roam the back areas, defying the *Feldpolizei*, raiding

stores and generally spreading confusion.

On the Allied side, however, once American troops joined the line, the manpower problem was solved. Not only did Pershing's command form an apparently inexhaustible supply of young, fit, eager —and, most important of all—inexperienced and therefore confident soldiers, but their very presence in such visible abundance spread optimism through the Allied armies, who, despite the vast bulges on the maps, regained during the early summer of 1918 that feeling of certain victory which had been missing since the days of Verdun and the Somme.

There were to be two more attempts by Ludendorff to break out of the net in which his armies seemed to be caught—one at Noyon, between the St Michael and Blücher bulges, and the second on the eastern flank of the Chemin-des-Dames bulge—a double-pronged attack aimed at isolating Rheims; but the Allies were now in growing strength and well able to absorb and counter Ludendorff's everweakening blows.

On the morning of 18th July, after a violent cloudburst, the first stage of the Allied counter-attack opened under command of General Mangin on the western flank of the Chemin-des-Dames bulge, aimed at cutting the German supply route down to Château-Thierry. Three hundred and forty-six Renault tanks took part in the opening phase, and although these broke down within a matter of hours, they gave essential aid during the first break-through—and the menace of the flank attack was enough to bring Ludendorff hurrying back from a conference in the north.

The following day, American divisions attacked in the south of the bulge, and Ludendorff—acutely conscious of the exposed position of his troops at the bottom of the sack—authorized, and indeed organized, a retreat; that he was still a competent soldier is shown by the fact that despite another Allied flank attack, this time from the east, he managed to wedge open the jaws of the trap west of Soissons and west of Rheims, until by 4th August most of his men were back behind the line of the Aisne and the Vesle, and the sack formed by Blücher had vanished.

But on 8th August, British, Canadian, and Australian divisions, supported by almost the whole of the British Tank Corps—604 tanks in all—struck at Ludendorff's line in front of Amiens, in an attack stretching from the Ancre in the north, down across the Somme and past Villers Bretonneux to the Luce. The blow had been elaborately and most efficiently prepared and was, almost ironically, aided on this occasion by nature who provided the Allies with fog—almost the first time an

Allied attack had been so favoured.

All the way along the attack front, the first thrusts were successful and the tanks proved an immense success in supporting the infantry, who whenever a machine-gun post gave trouble lay down and waited for one of the mastodon shapes of their armoured protection to lumber forward and crush the opposition. By that evening, fifteen miles of the German front had been stove in and British Whippet tanks and infantry, with their Dominion comrades, were seven miles in advance of their startline.

Ludendorff was shocked when, on the following day, he appraised the results of the fighting on 8th August—but not so much by the loss of territory, of material, or even of men; the Allies had lost far more in all these categories every day for over a week during the March offensive, but they had not lost the war. It was an entirely different loss which spelled out to him the presage of doom. It was the loss of spirit.

According to the reports on his desk, six German divisions had collapsed that day in scenes unprecedented in German military legend. Companies had surrendered to single tanks, platoons to single infantrymen, and on one occasion retreating troops had hurled abuse at a division going forward resolutely to buttress the sagging line, accusing them of blacklegging and 'toadying to the Junkers'.

'8th August was the Black Day of the German army . . .' he wrote afterwards, and history has justified the comment.

On 8th August began the Allied advance to the Rhine.

From then on, the front was never quiet. Whatever shortcomings may have in the past blemished Foch's planning, in the summer of 1918 his doctrine of the continual offensive brought success—so long as attacks were switched as soon as the defensive crust in front hardened.

On 11th August the battle of Amiens was called off after an advance of ten miles, but two days before, the French army under General Debeney had attacked and taken Montdidier, while the following day General Humbert's French 3rd Army —one stage farther south—advanced towards Noyon and liberated Lassigny in fighting which lasted until the 16th. And on the 18th, Mangin's army struck on Humbert's right, and took the Aisne heights on the 20th.

Each attack was broken off as soon as it lost its initial impetus, by which time another attack had been launched near enough to the previous one to profit from its success—and again continued only until resistance stiffened to such a point that further attacks would be unprofitable.

So it was to continue. On 21st August the British 3rd Army, under General Sir Julian Byng, attacked north of Albert (an

Ludendorff's Defeat

Below: Ludendorff's desperate gamble. He had decided it was imperative to knock the French and above all the British out of the war, before the promised American reinforcements could arrive and turn the tide, once and for all, in the Allies' favour

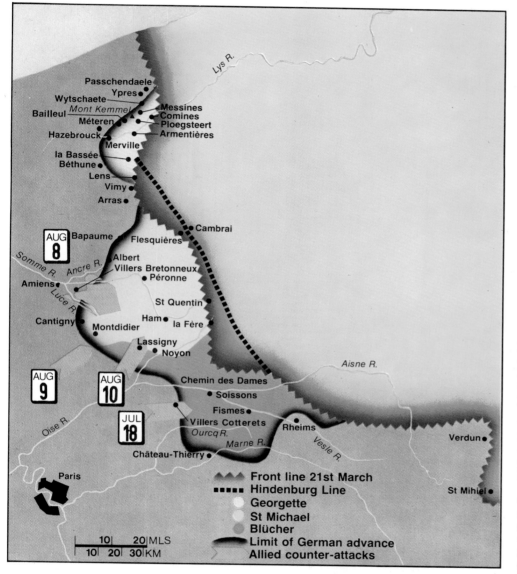

Front line 21st March
Hindenburg Line
Georgette
St Michael
Blücher
Limit of German advance
Allied counter-attacks

turn and lever away the defensive positions on each flank as these came under frontal attack. With admirable organization, reserve divisions came up through the gaps created, leap-frogged through the remnants of the assault divisions and drove even deeper into the complex of trenches and dug-outs, wire belts and tunnels which all Germany had confidently expected to withstand any onslaught.

All day long German troops had fought from the defences of their famous line with much of the skill and ardour which had distinguished them in the past—their defeat was due mainly to fog, to the offensive spirit of the Americans and the Australians, and the spirit of victory which animated the British; and possibly to German luck, which had changed.

For although no one realized it then, that afternoon Germany had lost the war.

Under the accumulating strain, Ludendorff's nerve had cracked, and at four o'clock that afternoon he had suffered a minor stroke while staying—appropriately —at the Hôtel Britannique, in Spa. He had gone there to attend another of the eternal conferences to which he was of late always being summoned, in order to convince politicians from home that his plans for victory were developing well.

That evening, pale and shaken, he visited his superior and constant ally Hindenburg in the suite below his own, and admitted that he could see no way out of the impasse into which Germany had been manoeuvred; and sadly, Hindenburg —as ever—agreed with his chief subordinate. An armistice must be asked for, and the staff must immediately commence drawing up movement orders for a planned withdrawal of the army, together with as much of the heavy materials of war as could be moved, back to the western frontier of Germany. There they would present to the world a spectacle of an unbeaten force still capable of defending their honour and the fatherland.

That two men in such high position in the world could be so divorced from reality that they could believe their position was such that the Allies would agree to this, merely exemplifies the lack of political common sense which permeated the entire military conduct of the war, on both sides. In the event, the Allied powers exacted a surrender as unconditional as the one they were to exact twenty-seven years later, though the actual terms agreed to were less demonstrative of Allied victory.

The conditions of the Versailles Treaty may well have been harsh and ungenerous, but German memories might not have been so short if their own country had been subjected to some of the physical damage which had been inflicted upon France, and affected future French attitudes to war.

attack buttressed by 200 tanks salvaged from the battle of Amiens), and the following day Rawlinson's 4th Army struck a few miles to the south, between Albert and the Somme. By that evening the front was back running along the edge of the old Somme battlefields across which the flower of British manhood had gone to its death two years before, and twenty-four hours later both Byng's and Rawlinson's troops were three miles farther forward!

23rd August was thus an even blacker day for the German army than had been 8th August and there was to be no respite for them until an armistice was signed. Throughout the remaining days of August and the opening week of September, the Allies beat a continual tattoo on the German line, and by 9th September almost the entire territorial gains of the Ludendorff spring offensive had been lost, a hundred thousand German soldiers had

entered Allied prison-camps, many more had been killed or wounded, and—most ominously of all—had deserted.

Two days later the American attack on the St Mihiel Salient opened and within two days this perpetual thorn in French flesh had vanished, 14,500 German prisoners and 443 German guns lay behind American lines, and Pershing was regrouping his forces for a vast offensive northwards through the Argonne.

But there was still one slender hope in Ludendorff's mind—that the concrete fastnesses of the Hindenburg Line might give him some respite; he thus watched the opening moves of the attack on it with great anxiety. It began with a fifty-six-hour bombardment, launched on a five-division front by British, American, and Australian divisions. Again, fog aided the attackers, allowing the British to cross the St Quentin Canal almost unseen, then to

259

The Road to Armistice

Germany's unlimited submarine warfare had in fact been a military as well as a political gamble. In the short run, the military gamble seemed to come off, for the results of the first four months were far above expectations. It was only later in 1917 that Allied counter-measures made the number of German submarine successes decline sharply.

Politically, however, submarine warfare was one unmitigated failure from the outset. It brought the USA into war, and with its entry, the defeat of Germany. American participation in the war infused the war-weary Western nations with new hopes, while it discouraged correspondingly the Central powers who were no less sick of the war, in particular the Slav nationalities in Austria-Hungary. Their hearts had never been in a war which had started as a 'punitive action' against an independent Slav nation—Serbia.

By the spring of 1917 the situation in the Dual Monarchy had become so desperate for the ruling German and Hungarian groups that the new Emperor Karl took to heart a deeply pessimistic memorandum by his chief minister, Count Czernin, on the urgent necessity to make peace very soon, and passed it on to Matthias Erzberger, a leading member of the German Catholic Centre Party. Erzberger was deeply impressed. In Germany disillusionment about submarine warfare, and political unrest under the stress of the war reached a new intensity in the summer of 1917. Even the SPD (the Social Democratic Party), smarting under the sharp attacks by the USPD (the Independent Social Democratic Party), their left-wing breakaway, was becoming restive and threatened for the first time to vote against the war credits. It was in this situation that Erzberger and the SPD took the parliamentary initiative to relieve somehow the domestic pressure by attacking Chancellor Bethmann Hollweg. Philipp Scheidemann and Friedrich Ebert, the two outstanding leaders of the loyal Socialists, criticized both the over-optimistic assessment of submarine warfare and the chancellor's refusal to come out for a peace of moderation, and demanded political reform in Prussia. On 4th and 6th July Erzberger joined the fray in the central committee of the Reichstag. Erzberger declared the submarine warfare a failure and suggested that the Reichstag should pass a resolution declaring itself in favour of a peace without annexations.

The result was shattering, and Erzberger initiated one of the most extraordinarily muddled political affairs in Germany, the so-called crisis of July 1917. In it aspects of foreign and domestic policy were inextricably mixed—submarine warfare, war aims, war credits, reform of the franchise in Prussia and of the political structure in the Reich, the fear of the Majority Socialists that they would be outmanoeuvred by the left-wing USPD. The main results of the crisis were a vote of the Prussian ministry for equal franchise in Prussia (11th July), Bethmann Hollweg's fall (12th July), the Peace Resolution of the Reichstag (19th July), and the uncertain beginnings of parliamentary government in the Reich.

Since early 1917 Bethmann Hollweg had been in favour of reforming the Prussian franchise in order to appease the working class and to strengthen the majority leaders of the SPD against the USPD. His success in carrying a reluctant Prussian ministry with him on 11th July was, however, only a Pyrrhic victory for it incensed the high command against him even more. Ludendorff and Hindenburg hurried to Berlin and threatened to resign, if equal franchise and the Peace Resolution, as drafted by an informal committee of the three new majority parties (Centre, Progressive Party, and Majority Socialists), were accepted. The Kaiser, on the other hand, did not want to come to a decision without consulting the Crown Prince, whose views were consistently reactionary and Pan-German. The Crown Prince took the unusual step of consulting the leaders of the political parties. To his surprise, he found that all of them, except the Progressives, were against the chancellor: the Conservatives and National Liberals thought he made too many concessions to the Left and was too weak in pursuing vigorous war aims; the Centre Party and the SPD felt he had become a liability because of his ambiguity over war aims and because it was in any case he who had led Germany into war.

The Crown Prince presented his father triumphantly with the result of his soundings. In a hectic atmosphere of confusion the Kaiser dismissed the chancellor, before Ludendorff and Hindenburg had time to storm in and confront their sovereign with their resignation. When they arrived, the Kaiser merely told the surprised generals: 'He is gone.' Thus Bethmann Hollweg was felled by a strange alliance. That he had incurred the enmity of the conservative and military element could not astonish anybody. But the Centre Party and the SPD turned against him at the very moment when he had adopted their programme of domestic reform

Two faces of Peace. **Above:** *Gloom in Berlin—its streets full of demobilized men.* **Left:** *Jubilation in London at the signing of the Treaty of Versailles*

Above: The men in the middle while Imperial Germany crumbled. 1. Ludendorff, who rose from Quartermaster General to virtual military dictator. 2. Michaelis, the civilian front-man. 3. Hertling, his conservative successor. 4. Prince Max of Baden, last Imperial chancellor

and relatively moderate war aims. On the other hand, if Bethmann Hollweg had gained the support of a Centre-Left coalition in the Reichstag and had fought for his new moderate line, defying the will of his sovereign, it would have amounted to revolution by German standards.

Some German historians recently make out Bethmann Hollweg's fall as the beginning of parliamentary democracy in Germany. But it was a very curious beginning, for the 'victory' of parliament had been achieved in a most haphazard and unexpected way, over a chancellor who was about to collaborate with the new majority. Bethmann Hollweg's fall solved nothing. The parliamentary parties were unable even to nominate any successor, let alone one who would suit them. Out of continuing malaise and confusion emerged the new chancellor, Georg Michaelis, a non-political non-entity, who only ushered in the dictatorship, barely veiled, of Ludendorff and the army high command. On 19th July the Reichstag did vote the Peace Resolution, after it had been modified and accepted by Ludendorff and Michaelis. But even the Peace Resolution, if looked at in the light of the general concept of German war aims in the First World War, was far from being a straightforward and honest declaration of the intention to return to the *status quo*. Whatever propaganda value it may have had was destroyed by the new Chancellor's notorious rider that he accepted it, 'as I understand it', and by the violent reaction of the Right against the 'weaklings' in Parliament.

The immediate effects on the constitution of Bethmann Hollweg's fall were negligible. The committee of the majority parties, which had drafted the Peace Resolution, did keep together during sessions of the Reichstag. But their tortuous debates on reforms only demonstrated painfully their utter inability to reach any positive conclusions at all, except for the pious wish for some modification of the constitution which would create the impression that a peaceful parliament had come to power. Far from being revolutionaries, they wanted neither the republic nor genuine democracy, nor a peace on the basis of the *status quo,* so long as Germany was powerful. In the days following the signing of the Treaty of Brest Litovsk coupled with the apparently successful German offensive in the west, even the outwardly moderate appearance of the new majority faded away. The Treaty of Brest Litovsk was carried in the Reichstag by a huge majority. Only the USPD voted against it; the Majority Socialists meekly abstained.

The only perceptible result of the whole crisis of July 1917 in political terms was the appointment of one Prussian minister, two secretaries and two under-secretaries of state in the central government of the Reich, who were representatives of the political parties in favour of domestic reforms. Even these modest gains, however, were more than offset by the fact that most of the freshly appointed party politicians stood on the conservative wing of their respective parties, and by Ludendorff's unproclaimed yet effective dictatorship. If parliamentary government started in Germany in July 1917, it did so only in outward appearance; more than ever before parliament served as a fig leaf for a regime which remained autocratic and undemocratic.

Fear of the Socialists

The progress of the Russian Revolution and its repercussions on Germany made that delicate and artificial structure less and less tenable. The influence of radical groups on the left, in particular of the USPD and, to a lesser extent, of the Spartacists (the followers of the Socialist Karl Liebknecht), increased amongst Berlin workers and sailors of the fleet, whereas the Pan-German element rallied in the 'Vaterlandspartei' (Fatherland's Party), a combination of various right-wing organisations. Under the leadership of Tirpitz, the proto-Fascist element in Germany thus found its first powerful organizational form.

While war went on without hope of peace, the increasing polarization of political forces in Germany weakened the empire from within. The extreme Right was dissatisfied with the formal conces-

sions to the moderate Left, and mistrusted them as a halfway-house to revolution and Socialism. The extreme Left rightly feared that small political changes were only made in order to forestall genuine reform and to patch up the regime, which remained intrinsically undemocratic.

In autumn 1917 these tensions came into the open for the first time when they brought about the downfall of Michaelis. For all his political inexperience, the new chancellor was intelligent and open-minded enough to realize that Germany would never be able to conclude peace on the basis of German war aims. This is why he demanded, at a crown council on 11th September, that Germany give up claims on Belgium in order to facilitate peace. His act of political independence and relative shrewdness did not endear him to the generals or the Kaiser, who dropped him at the first opportunity.

During the days of the Peace Resolution there had been an agitation among sailors of the German battle fleet in favour of a peace without annexations, which they found most strongly championed by the USPD. There were arrests and courts-martial among the sailors; five were

Illustration from British propaganda leaflet dropped over the German lines: a jovial German prisoner savouring one of the delights of captivity

German plenipotentiaries, displaying white flags, arrive in the French lines to hear Allied armistice conditions. The surrender was later concluded in Foch's railway coach

sentenced to death, two of them actually executed. When he was attacked in the Reichstag by leaders of the USPD on 9th October, the chancellor created the impression that he wanted the USPD banned. The majority parties, no friends of the USPD, baulked, because they feared the chancellor would turn next against them. In a turbulent session of the Reichstag the parties clearly expressed their lack of confidence in the chancellor. The high command did nothing to keep Michaelis, and the Kaiser did not want to antagonize the parties who once again had to vote the war credits. Less than three weeks later, Michaelis was dismissed.

His successor was Count Hertling, seventy-three years old and half-blind. He had been one of the leaders of the Centre Party in the Reichstag before the war, and Bavarian prime minister since 1912. Although he was a party politician, he had not been nominated by the majority parties, nor was he their representative. Hertling, a staunch Conservative throughout his political life, was willing enough to appease the majority parties by agreeing to their political demands, especially the reform of the franchise in Prussia, but he definitely felt himself to be the servant of the crown, not dependent on parliament. The reform of the Prussian franchise made, indeed, no progress under Hertling. As for German war aims, the high command succeeded in committing the new chancellor to their programme. The Germans decided to pin down the Austrians, with whom they were at that time conferring, to staying in the war until all the German war aims had been accomplished. The conference with the Austrians took place on 6th November.

One day later the Bolsheviks seized power

from the Provisional Government in Russia.

From now on the domestic situation in Germany became hopeless. While internal polarization continued, the parliamentary façade disguising Ludendorff's dictatorship had been strengthened a little by appointing Payer, a south German Progressive, vice-chancellor under Hertling. The south German, non-Prussian element apparently was destined to save the Reich from its impending catastrophe. But following developments showed that the ostentatious prominence of south German Liberals and Catholics at the top of the government did not alter the policy of the Reich. When President Wilson announced his Fourteen Points for peace, January 1918, Hertling rejected them out of hand, whenever they affected Germany. During the great strike of the metal workers in Berlin, which spread to other German cities in the last days of the same month, the government did not budge an inch to meet the political demands of the striking workers. In spring 1918 even the pretence had gone that parliament ruled Gemany, when Erzberger, during the debate on the Treaty of Brest Litovsk, declared it perfectly compatible with the demands of the Peace Resolution, following in fact the guidance of Ludendorff.

Thus, the German Reich drifted unreformed into its next political crisis in the autumn of 1918. Now Germany was even more exhausted, her people even more embittered than in summer 1917. The last illusions about submarine warfare, the miracle in the east and German offensives in the west were definitely gone. The Allied counter-offensives of July and August 1918 had, at last, destroyed even Ludendorff's hopes of winning the war.

In autumn 1918 the end of the war came,

where it had started — in the Balkans. At the end of September the Allied Army of the Orient smashed the Macedonian front and Bulgaria sued for peace. Turkey was tottering, Austria-Hungary was on the brink of political decomposition. It was only a matter of weeks before Turkey and the Dual Monarchy would leave the war. However firm the German front might keep in the west, Allied troops would be able to invade Germany from the south and south-east within a few months.

On 28th September, when Ludendorff learned of Bulgaria's collapse, it was not difficult for him to foresee the chain of future events. It was only now that he admitted military defeat.

Yet, typically, Ludendorff, the military dictator at the end of his tether, blamed chiefly the forces of the Left for the coming débâcle. On 1st October he explained to his closest collaborators in the army high command, why it had become necessary to have a parliamentary government. He had asked the Kaiser, 'to include also those circles in the government to whom we owe chiefly our present situation. . . . Let them now make that peace, which has to be made. Let them now bear the consequences of what they have done to us'. The famous 'stab-in-the-back' legend was invented as a face-saving device by Ludendorff even before Germany laid down her arms.

In a desperate effort to save what could be saved Ludendorff ordered parliamentary government into existence in Germany and coupled it with the demand for an immediate armistice, before the German Western Front broke as well. Hertling, honest Conservative to the last minute, refused to become chancellor of a parliamentary government and resigned. After a few days of hurried search, the last imperial chancellor was found. Again, he was not chosen by the now 'victorious' parliamentary forces. He was not even a party politician or a member of any parliament, but the member of a south German dynasty, Prince Max von Baden, who had a reputation for liberal leanings. There was a certain historic logic and justice in this choice: Baden and her Grand Duke had been Bismarck's most important agent and ally in 1870-71 when he was founding the Second Empire. Now, in its dying days, a member of the same dynasty was called to save the Reich and the monarchy. Prince Max was half successful. It was beyond his power to keep the monarchy, because the Kaiser stubbornly clung to his throne, when hardly any one, even in Germany, wanted him there any more. But he managed to preserve the Reich and its social order by a most liberal interpretation of the Constitution and by ingeniously handing over power on 9th November to another south

'Work ceased in shops and offices, as news of the armistice spread . . . Omnibuses were seized, and people in strange garments caroused on the open upper deck. A bonfire heaped against the plinth of Nelson's column in Trafalgar Square has left its mark to this day. Total strangers copulated in doorways and on the pavements. They were asserting the triumph of life over death. The celebrations ran on with increasing wildness for three days, when the police finally intervened and restored order.' A.J.P.Taylor: *English History, 1914–1945* (OUP)

Above: After the armistice, German troops enter Berlin, accompanied by cheering children. *Left:* French soldier's reunion with his wife and child. *Below:* Armistice celebrations in Paris. *Right:* London goes wild. Buses became carnival-floats as Londoners celebrated the end of war

The Road to Armistice

German, Friedrich Ebert, the conservative SPD leader from Heidelberg.

On 3rd October Prince Max was appointed chancellor. Payer remained vice-chancellor, while several members of the Reichstag joined the cabinet, among them Scheidemann for the SPD and Erzberger for the Centre Party. The political changes were institutionalized on 26th October, when the Reichstag voted an amendment to the constitution, which made the chancellor dependent on the confidence of parliament. Parliamentary government had been formally introduced for the first time in the Reich. Germany, by a simple vote in parliament, had become a *'Volksstaat'*, although for the time being the monarchy remained.

Yet political progress had not been spontaneous. It had only been effected with one eye to threatening unrest from inside and another to certain military defeat from outside. Wilson had made it clear in his note of 23rd October that he did not want to conclude a negotiated peace with the old autocratic regime in Germany. The constitutional changes of 26th October were the German response. With disturbing flexibility Germany had suddenly donned parliamentary democracy in the hope of some tactical advantage; less than fifteen years later she was to divest herself of this alien political structure, the adoption of which, after all, had not apparently brought the advantages Germany had hoped for.

Once Ludendorff had made up his mind that the war was lost, he was in a hurry. He got his way without serious trouble on the domestic front by hastily installing the Prince Max-Scheidemann-Erzberger government on 3rd October. But it was more difficult to convince the political leadership of the urgent need for an armistice. Their reluctance was understandable, because the majority parties did not want the responsibility for having surrendered. It was only after hard pleading on the part of Ludendorff and a special session of leading members of the Reichstag on 2nd October to whom an officer of the general staff explained the catastrophic military situation, that the political leadership gave in once more to the pressure of the generals. On 3rd October 1918 the new government under Prince Max officially asked for an armistice.

'November criminals'

Even in the hour of defeat Germany tried to make the best of a bad situation. The note asking for an armistice also indicated Germany's willingness to conclude peace on the basis of Wilson's Fourteen Points, and it was addressed not to the Allies, Great Britain and France, but to the United States. Wilson's Fourteen Points,

The Defeat of the Central Powers

scorned only nine months ago, now became the saving plank for the Reich. The choice of the American President as addressee of the German note was a very clever move, because it appealed to his ambition to bring peace to the world.

Meanwhile, fighting went on, submarine warfare as well as the battles on land. The German armies, retreating under pressure on the Western Front, practised the policy of 'scorched earth'—systematic destruction —on French and Belgian soil. At Wilson's demand Germany made an end to submarine warfare, but protested that she had done nothing contrary to international law on her Western Front. At the last minute, the armistice demanded by Germany seemed to be in danger. In his third note to Germany of 23rd October, Wilson had pointed out that the only form of armistice acceptable to the United States and the Allied powers was one which would make it impossible for Germany to renew hostilities. Now Ludendorff brusquely reversed his position again. He suddenly found that Germany's military position turned out not to be so gloomy as he had first thought, and it would be better for Germany to perish than conclude peace on dishonourable terms. Ludendorff spoke for a certain segment of Germany's political leaders, who toyed with the idea of a last-minute *levée en masse* for the defence of the Fatherland to the last ditch. Even Walter Rathenau joined the chorus in demand for an end worthy of *Götterdämmerung*. A phrase went round, which Goebbels was to take up one generation later in a similar situation: 'Better an end in terror than terror without end!'

This time it was the civilian government that resisted the temptation of a heroic demagogic gesture. Collective suicide was not practical policy for a nation of sixty-five million people, as one minister put it. Ludendorff was relieved of his post on 26th October and thus happily escaped the formal responsibility for concluding the armistice. He fled abroad incognito to hibernate in neutral Sweden, in wait for better times, in which he could stage his comeback. Ludendorff's successor was yet another south German, General Groener. Hindenburg remained as formal head of the German army.

Whatever doubts may have lingered in German minds about the necessity of laying down arms, they were definitely destroyed by events inside and outside Germany. On 27th October Emperor Karl of Austria-Hungary threw up the sponge and announced to the German Kaiser his intention to sue for peace. Austria-Hungary fell apart, and so did her army. On 3rd November Austria signed an armistice which put her roads and railways at the disposal of the Allies. Germany lay practically open to invasion through Bohemia and Tyrol into Silesia, Saxony, and Bavaria. To wage war on foreign soil was one thing, to have the destructions of modern warfare on sacred German soil was another.

This explains why the spontaneous, quasi-revolutionary movement of soldiers and workers to end the war started at the periphery of the Reich, in Bavaria and Saxony. It became even more urgent for the ruling groups to avoid a crushing defeat in the west and to effect an orderly retreat into the Reich. This alone could prevent a genuine social revolution.

But some kind of revolution was already in the offing when on 29th and 30th October sailors of the battle fleet refused to join in a last naval battle. From then on there existed in Germany two competing movements for ending the war quickly, an official one from above and a popular one from below. The official one sought an early armistice in the hope of preserving the political and social *status quo*. It was supported by approximately the same kind of alliance that had supported the war: the army high command, the bureaucracy, industrialists, and the majority of the Reichstag. The popular one hoped, by ending war through revolutionary pressure, for the establishment of democracy and— very vaguely—of some kind of socialism. Although the movement from above had started earlier, on 28th September, Wilson's delaying tactics resulted in the movement from below overtaking the official one. The revolutionary upsurge reached Berlin and its culminating point on 9th November, the armistice was concluded near Compiègne only two days later.

The victory of the German revolution was more apparent than real. Even the democratic wing of the parliamentary establishment was not rewarded for its self-effacing loyalty to the Reich. After Erzberger had played Ludendorff's game and signed the armistice on 11th November 1918, he and his friends were denounced 'November criminals' by the extreme Right. Erzberger himself was murdered in 1921, less than twelve years before the Weimar Republic was strangled by the same political forces who had dreamed first of Germany's bid to become a world power and then to stage national suicide when they saw they had miserably failed.

The Treaty of Versailles

The Germans surrendered to the Allies on 11th November 1918. Seven months later they signed the Treaty of Versailles, accepting new frontiers and stern penalties. During those seven months the victorious powers debated, both openly and secretly, every aspect of the future of Germany. Was it to be split up into small, separate states? Was it to be crippled economically? Was it to be deprived of territory? Was it to lose its empire in Africa and the Pacific? Was it to be prevented from ever having a powerful army, navy, or air force again? These were some of the questions on which every public figure, and most private people, held strong opinions, and argued over during the seven months between the military cease-fire and the signature of the treaty.

Yet the peace conference did not decide all of these issues. Many had been determined beforehand. During the war itself each side had worried continuously over the post-war settlement. Every nation had its dreams, its hopes, its secret agreements, and its publicly proclaimed aspirations. France was pledged to take back the provinces of Alsace and Lorraine which Germany had annexed in 1870. Great Britain was determined to absorb as much of the German colonial empire as possible. As early as 1915 Italy had been promised Austrian, Turkish, and German territory in return for entering the war on the side of the Allies. Serbia was promised parts of Bosnia and Albania; Russia was promised Constantinople; the Jews were promised a 'National Home' in Palestine; the Arabs were promised independence from the Turks; and the Poles were offered the restoration of an independent Poland.

Woodrow Wilson, the President of the United States, had, in January 1918, offered *all* subject peoples the right of 'self-determination'. This gave an impetus to many ambitious nationalists, to Czechs and Slovaks, to Serbs, Slovenes, and Croats, to Ukrainians, to the Baltic peoples, to the Rumanians inside Austria, to the Armenians inside Turkey, indeed, to a hundred groups, however small, who saw in 'self-determination' a chance, however slim, of statehood. Even the young Vietnamese Communist, Ho Chi-Minh, asked the Paris Peace Conference to liberate his people from the 'curse' of French imperial rule. But most of the small nationalities, like Ho Chi-Minh's, were doomed to be disappointed. Wilson's idealism shone like a beacon to the dispossessed; but to the French and the British, with their large empires and many subject peoples, and

with their own hopes of territorial gain, 'self-determination' was a theme to be dampened down wherever it conflicted with their own ambitions.

The 'war for human liberty'

Wilson believed that the war was the 'final war for human liberty'. He therefore wished to infuse the peace treaties with his own concept of liberty. For him, the central issue was that of national dignity: the right of people to be independent, with secure frontiers and unavaricious neighbours. When he spoke to Congress in February 1918 Wilson made it clear that, in his and the American view: 'Peoples are not to be handed about from one sovereignty to another by an international conference or an understanding between rivals and antagonists. National aspirations must be respected; peoples may now be dominated and governed only by their own consent. "Self-determination" is not a mere phrase. It is an imperative principle of action, which statesmen will henceforth ignore at their peril.'

Great Britain and France had little faith in self-determination. As a vague, idealistic liberal concept, they approved it in their public utterances, but during the heat of battle they had to consider other pressures besides liberal sentiment. At various moments in the war the Allied position was precarious. New allies had to be found. But neutrals do not easily agree to join in a war which they see to be one of terrible carnage, both on land and sea, involving the suspension of peaceful trade and industry, hardships in daily life, and, above all, the ever-present risk of defeat, occupation, humiliation, and national ruin.

The pledges made during the war had thus one dominating purpose, to persuade the uncommitted and the uncertain that it was in their full interest to support the Allied cause. Once that support had been forthcoming, the Allies could hardly go back on their promises. Where they did so, as in the case of Italy, they created a sense of grievance which had widespread repercussions. Italy had been promised, by Great Britain, France, and Russia, a share in any partitions of Turkish or German territory in Africa and the Near East. She was promised also the Austrian provinces of the Trentino, the South Tyrol, Gorizia,

Right: 'We Germans in foreign lands protest against the seizure of our property' —protest in Berlin against the treaty. Germany had to agree to the sale of German property in Allied countries

The Defeat of the Central Powers

and Istria, the Dalmatian coast and control over Albania. But most of these promises were unfulfilled. Albania became fully independent. The Dalmatian coast vent to Yugoslavia. Great Britain and France kept all Germany's African colonies for themselves, and gained all the benefits of the Turkish collapse. At the peace conference all Italy's protestations were in vain. Although she emerged from the peace treaties with her territory enlarged, she had become an unsatisfied nation, anxious to see a further revision of the treaty frontiers. Within a few years Mussolini was exploiting this sense of deprivation. He demanded the fulfilment of what Italy had been promised. But immediately the peace conference ended the world sought only to be done with alarms and crises, wars and arguments. At Paris, from January to June 1919, any claim could be made with impunity, for the six months of the conference was essentially a period when every nation pressed for as much as it dared to claim, and urged its claims with passion. But once the treaties were signed, any call for revision was made to seem an incitement to aggression, and the word 'revisionist' quickly became synonymous with 'troublemaker', even when the power demanding revision was a former ally.

In one case the war-time pledges could be easily ignored. For in 1917 the Russian Bolsheviks renounced the secret treaties and declared that they would not accept any of the territorial gains promised to Russia. As a result, the Anglo-French promise of Constantinople to the Tsar could lapse. But even so, the strategic waterway from the Black Sea to the Mediterranean was not to return easily into Turkish hands. From 1918 to 1924 the 'Zone of the Straits' was occupied by an Allied force, and for six years a British High Commissioner was the effective ruler of the former Turkish capital. Only the military successes of Kemal Ataturk made it possible for Turkey to retain Anatolia intact, and, although deprived of all her Arabian, Syrian, and Mesopotamian territory, to survive as a robust national state.

The spoils of war
The secret treaties were not the only complications confronting the peace-makers when they reached Paris. Territory had changed hands at every stage of the war, and it proved difficult to dislodge claimants who were already in possession of what they claimed. During the conference Woodrow Wilson criticized the Australian Prime Minister, William Hughes, for insisting that Australia should keep control of German New Guinea, which Australian troops had occupied as early as 1914, within a month of the outbreak of war. Did Hughes really intend, questioned Wilson, to flout

the opinion of the civilized world by annexing territory? Would she let it be said that she took part of the German empire as the spoils of war? Was Australia proposing to make a profit out of Germany's defeat, to impose her rule on aborigines, to take over valuable mineral rights, to extend her sovereignty as far north as the equator? To all of which Hughes replied acidly: 'That's about it, Mr President.'

The Australians were not alone in insisting upon the maxim of 'what we have, we hold'. Japan pressed vigorously for control over the Chinese port of Tsingtao, a German possession which the Japanese had occupied in 1914, after a month's hard fighting. To the chagrin of the Japanese, the peace-makers forced them to return Tsingtao to China. As a result, the Japanese, like the Italians, felt cheated of a 'fruit' of victory, and looked for a chance to redress the balance. The Japanese invasion of China in 1937, like the Italian invasion of Albania in 1939, was in part a legacy of the frustrations of the peace conference. Other victor nations were less frustrated. No one dislodged the New Zealanders from German Samoa, the South Africans from German South West Africa, the British from German East Africa, or the Australians from New Guinea. Even the Japanese were allowed to retain control of most of Germany's vast Pacific island empire, which included over two thousand islands and covered three million square miles. Great Britain and France partitioned the German territories of Togoland and the Cameroons between them; the Italian occupation of the former Turkish Dodecanese Islands was made more secure; Cyprus, occupied by Great Britain under nominal Turkish suzerainty for forty years, was transformed into a permanent British possession. The areas of Turkey conquered in October 1918 remained firmly under the controlling hands of their conquerors—the British in Palestine, Transjordan, and Iraq, the French in Syria and Alexandretta, the Arabs in the Yemen and the Hejaz.

Such were the many territorial gains which were made during the course of the war. Most were criticized at the peace conference, particularly by Woodrow Wilson. But all survived the peace-making, and became a part of the new world order. Some even survived the Second World War; South Africa still rules German South West Africa; Australia still controls German New Guinea; New Zealand still occupies Samoa. Japanese control over Germany's Pacific Islands north of the equator passed, in 1945, not back to Germany, but on to the United States, the third imperial power to come into possession of the islands and atolls which stretch in a broad band out from the coast of China across three thousand miles of ocean.

The new map of Europe
When the victor powers met in Paris they had to consider more than the promises which each ally had made, and the existence of new possessions which particular Allies had every intention of making permanent. They had also to take into account the people who, even before the war was ended, had proclaimed themselves independent. There were many such people, each determined to keep the territory which they claimed as the basis of permanent national frontiers. Thus the Czechs and Slovaks had declared their complete severance from Austria-Hungary before the Austro-Hungarian surrender; and they were insisting upon a new state which would include the historic frontiers of Bohemia, thereby placing over two million German-speaking people within their proposed territory. The South Slavs had also declared themselves an independent state, ruling over territory in which were to be found Hungarian, Italian, and Austrian minorities. These frontiers were of course still open to negotiation and change. But the Allies had for most of the war given support to all enemies of Austria-Hungary. In April 1915 they promised the future Serb state a part of the Adriatic coast and the Austro-Hungarian provinces of Bosnia and Dalmatia. They might strive to create 'ideal' frontiers, excluding minorities and satisfying conflicting claims and promises, but since the same territories were often occupied by different nationalities this was no easy matter, even from the point of view of abstract national geography.

As a result the frontiers in existence before the conference met tended to become the permanent ones. The pre-conference frontiers had been established by the subject peoples of Germany, Austria-Hungary, and Turkey. As the conference was made up of those who had fought these three empires in the war, the likelihood was that the pre-conference frontiers would, in the main, be allowed to survive—as indeed they were. When the Paris Peace Conference met a new map of Europe had already come into existence, drawn by new nations upon the ruins of the German, Austrian, and Turkish empires. The victor nations did not redraw the old map of Europe; instead, they fussed and argued over the new one. The conference obtained many marginal modifications; but the map which they saw in January was in most respects the same one which they were to agree upon in June.

Woodrow Wilson obtained some verbal changes in the war-time decisions. Instead of Germany's colonies being described as integral parts of the empires which conquered them, they were given the name of 'Mandates'. The new owners were then

The World after Versailles

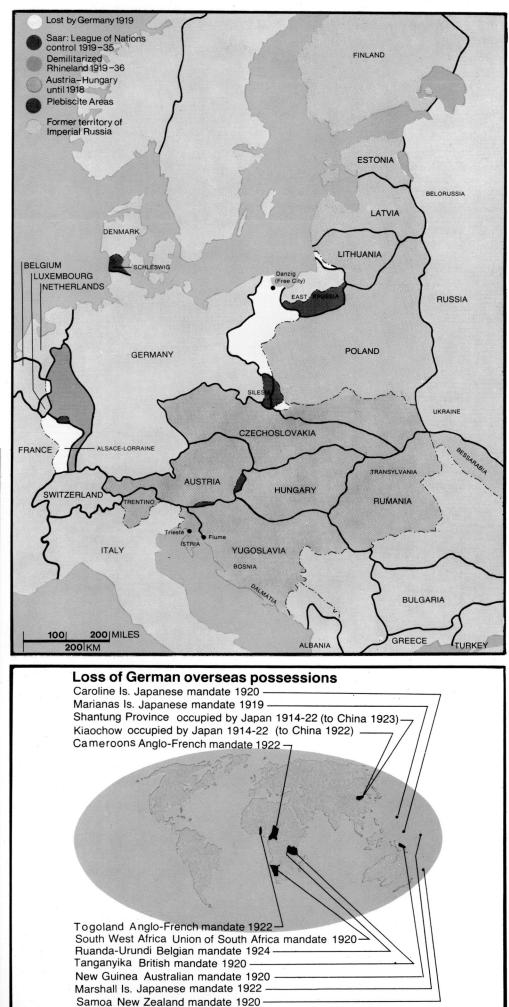

Below: Europe before 1914, dominated by Germany, Austria-Hungary, and Tsarist Russia. **Right:** Europe after the peace treaties. From the Austro-Hungarian empire have come three new states, Austria, Hungary, and Czechoslovakia. The Austrian-ruled South Slavs have joined the old kingdoms of Montenegro and Serbia in the new state of Yugoslavia. Italy and Rumania have gained large chunks of Austro-Hungarian territory. Poland has been re-formed from Russian, Austrian, and German territory. Amongst other changes, France has regained Alsace-Lorraine, and Greece has gained Bulgaria's Aegean coastline.
Bottom left: The break-up of the Turkish empire. Turkey kept only her northern, Turkish, territory. In Arabia the Hejaz and Yemen (and later Saudi-Arabia) became independent Arab kingdoms. **Bottom right:** What happened to Germany's colonies

Legend (top map):
- Lost by Germany 1919
- Saar: League of Nations control 1919–35
- Demilitarized Rhineland 1919–36
- Austria–Hungary until 1918
- Plebiscite Areas
- Former territory of Imperial Russia

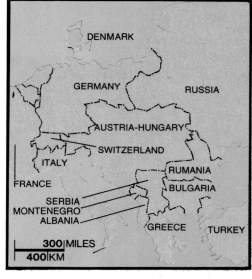

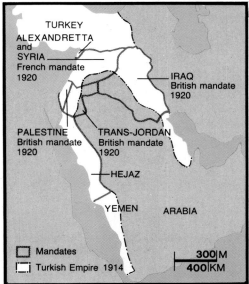

Mandates
Turkish Empire 1914

Loss of German overseas possessions

Caroline Is. Japanese mandate 1920
Marianas Is. Japanese mandate 1919
Shantung Province occupied by Japan 1914-22 (to China 1923)
Kiaochow occupied by Japan 1914-22 (to China 1922)
Cameroons Anglo-French mandate 1922

Togoland Anglo-French mandate 1922
South West Africa Union of South Africa mandate 1920
Ruanda-Urundi Belgian mandate 1924
Tanganyika British mandate 1920
New Guinea Australian mandate 1920
Marshall Is. Japanese mandate 1922
Samoa New Zealand mandate 1920

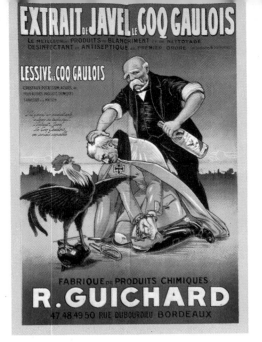

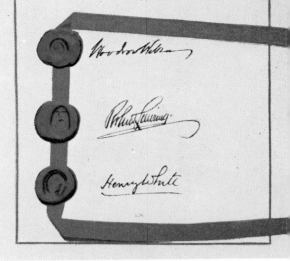

in theory responsible to the League of Nations, a world organization designed by Wilson to secure permanent peace and the just settlement of all international disputes, and which was transformed in 1945 into the United Nations. But the 'Mandates' remained securely under the powers who obtained them. The new League of Nations was also to safeguard the rights of minorities: and, this being so, minorities were allowed to remain in Poland, Czechoslovakia, Rumania, and Yugoslavia. Yet when persecution and discrimination began, the League was powerless to intervene.

Conditions of armistice

The main barrier to a well-balanced treaty was built before the peace conference. When Germany, Austria, Bulgaria, and Turkey each surrendered, they did so by signing armistice agreements with the Allies. These agreements contained sets of conditions, on the acceptance of which the Allies agreed to stop the fighting. The armistice conditions were severe, and had to be carried out immediately. As a result of this, long before the Paris Peace Conference began, they had irrevocably altered the map, and the mood of Europe. Much of what politicians later denounced and historians criticized in the peace treaties was in fact created by the armistices.

The atmosphere at the time of the drafting of the armistice agreements was an atmosphere of war: the guns still roared, the fighting was still savage, the outcome was still uncertain. The terms were therefore harsh. It was necessary for the Allies to ensure that the armistice agreements were not tricks, brief halts engineered to obtain the breathing space necessary for recuperation and renewed fighting. Each armistice agreement was intended to make absolutely certain that the fighting capacity of the enemy was utterly broken. This they did. As a result, when the Paris Peace Conference opened, Germany, Austria, Bulgaria, and Turkey had already been treated with a severity which was both intentional, effective, and by its nature largely irrevocable.

The first armistice to be signed was with Bulgaria, on 29th September 1918. The Bulgarians were desperate for peace: their armies in Greece and Serbia were in retreat, while a large corps of Bulgarian mutineers was marching on Sofia, the capital. They therefore agreed to evacuate all Serbian and Greek territory which their troops still occupied, and which they had hitherto claimed for themselves. A month later, on 30th October, the Turks, two-thirds of whose Palestinian army had been taken prisoner, the remnant of which was in retreat, signed their armistice. They were obliged to accept the use of their

Below: 'The Surrender of the German High Seas Fleet' — part of the armistice agreement. Above: Advertisement for a bleach, typical of French feelings. Clemenceau uses it to wash out the Kaiser's crimes

American signatures to the Treaty of Versailles (the American representatives signed it but Congress refused to ratify it). Wilson's utopian idealism left its mark on the final form of the treaty

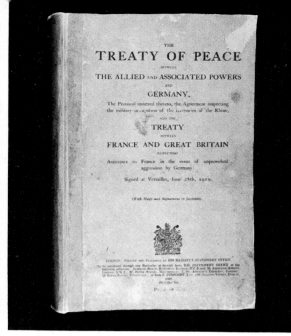

The transcript of the treaty sold in Great Britain. The British negotiators, in particular Lloyd George, had tried to temper the French demand for revenge and a crippled Germany—but in vain

British press poster after Versailles. The press had been a powerful agitator of patriotic emotion during the war. Its power to whip up hatred was less welcome to the men trying to create a fair peace

The stamp of a new nation—Czechoslovakia, which had declared its independence from the Habsburg empire during the last months of the war, and to whom the treaty gave generous frontiers

capital, Constantinople, as an Allied naval base; to surrender the Black Sea port of Batum and the oilfields of Baku, both of which they were occupying; and to surrender all garrisons in Arabia, the Yemen, Syria, Mesopotamia, and Cilicia. The surrender of these garrisons was to be followed by immediate French and British occupation; the obvious prelude to political control.

On 3rd November the Austrians, beaten back on the Italian front, signed an armistice which was similarly decisive. Italian troops were allowed to occupy the territory which they claimed, and the Allies obtained the right to move at will along every line of communication throughout the Austro-Hungarian empire. The new nations had already proclaimed themselves. The Allied presence provided them with a firm guarantee that they would survive. They were thus two months old before the peace conference met.

'Reparation for damage done'

But it was towards Germany that the armistice was most severe. The total collapse of Bulgaria, Turkey, and Austria was taken for granted once the Allied military advances had begun. But Germany was believed to be stronger and more resilient than her allies. On 12th September, speaking at Manchester, Lloyd George, the British prime minister, insisted that 'Prussian military power must not only be beaten, but Germany herself must know that'. With the Allied armies reinforced by fresh, enthusiastic troops from the United States, and the German trench fortifications in Flanders broken, such a double aim seemed feasible. But a month later Sir Douglas Haig, the commander-in-chief of the British forces in France, sounded a warning note. On 19th October he returned to London from France to tell the war cabinet that all was not well. The American army, he claimed, 'is disorganized, ill-equipped, and ill-trained. . . . It has suffered severely through ignorance of modern war'. As for the French army, it seemed 'greatly worn out'. The British army, he concluded, 'is not sufficiently fresh or strong to force a decision by itself' and the war would go on, in Haig's view, well into 1919. All this pointed to the need for a severe armistice, which would deprive the Germans of any opportunity of hitting back once they had agreed to surrender. The war cabinet felt that if the armistice terms were comprehensive, they would serve as 'pledges for the fulfilment of our peace terms'.

On 11th November the fourth and last armistice of the war was signed. Germany accepted total defeat. Lloyd George's conditions were fulfilled: all military power was broken, and the German people were presented with a document both comprehensive and severe. Of the thirty-four clauses, the following give a picture of how much Germany had to agree to, not to make peace, but merely to bring an end to war.

Immediate evacuation of the invaded countries — Belgium, France, Luxembourg, *as well as Alsace-Lorraine.*

Surrender in good condition by the German Armies of the following equipment —

5,000 guns
25,000 machine guns
3,000 trench mortars
1,700 aeroplanes

5,000 locomotives and 150,000 wagons, in good working order, with all necessary spare parts and fittings, shall be delivered to the Associated Powers. . . . 5,000 motor lorries are also to be delivered in good condition.

To surrender . . . all submarines at present in existence . . . and

6 battle-cruisers
10 battleships
8 light cruisers
50 destroyers of the most modern types

Evacuation by the German Armies of the districts on the left bank of the Rhine. These districts . . . shall be administered . . . under the control of the Allied and United States Armies of Occupation.

By signing this armistice, Germany abandoned all hopes of territorial gain; even of retaining Alsace-Lorraine. She also agreed to accept a four-word financial condition: 'Reparation for damage done.' The interpretation of what was meant by these four words proved a major point of argument during the treaty negotiations, and poisoned the international atmosphere for twenty years, giving Adolf Hitler a powerful lever against the western democracies. The four words that the Germans, at the moment of defeat, accepted without discussion, provoked the most bitter discussion of the inter-war years.

The idea of 'reparation for damage done' was not a new one. Germany had imposed such reparations on France in 1870, even though the fighting took place on French soil. Nor was there any doubt that the 'damage done' by Germany in France and Belgium was severe. Some small damage was done by Allied aeroplanes dropping bombs on Germany, but this was offset by the many more German air-raids, particularly on London, and by the German naval bombardment of undefended seaside towns on the east coast of Great Britain. The amount of damage done by Germany was immense, and little of it was made necessary by the dictates of war. In German-occupied France nearly 300,000 houses were completely destroyed. Six thousand factories were stripped of their machinery, which was sent to Germany. The textile mills of Lille and Sedan were smashed. Nearly 2,000 breweries were destroyed. In the coal mines around Roubaix and Tourcoing 112 mineshafts were blown in, and over 1,000 miles of underground galleries flooded or blocked. During their retreat, the Germans burned and looted on a massive scale, destroying over 1,000 miles of railway line, blowing up 1,000 bridges, looting thousands of houses, and stripping churches. During the four years of occupation the Germans took away half a million cows, half a million sheep, and over 300,000 horses and donkeys. These were the acts of vandals. And in the military sphere too it was France and Belgium, not Germany, that suffered most. After the war the French had to pull up over 300,000,000 metres of barbed wire, and fill in over 250,000,000 cubic metres of trenches. Much agricultural land was rendered useless because so many shells had fallen on it; some remained dangerous for many years because of unexploded shells and the leakage of poison gas from unused canisters.

The British were equally determined to secure reparation. The Germans had torpedoed five hospital ships during the war; an action which inflamed the public and created an atmosphere in which the demand for high reparations flourished. The German U-boats had taken a cruel toll of merchant shipping. They had sunk thousands of unarmed ships mostly without warning. The British lost nearly 8,000,000 tons of commercial shipping; and many of the crews had been left to drown. Among the Allied nations, France, Italy, and the United States lost between them 2,000,000 tons of shipping; among neutrals Norway lost over 1,000,000 tons, Denmark, Holland, and Sweden over 200,000 tons each. No nation had been spared the deliberate terror of submarine war. The Allies had not, of course, sat idly by to watch these losses. The blockade of Germany was rigorously enforced, and as a result as many as 500,000 German civilians probably died of starvation. But in the moment of victory these victims of war's all-pervading cruelty did not seem to compensate for what the Allies had suffered. Nations use victory to settle the debt which they feel is owed to them; the other side of the account is ignored. The demand for reparations combined the physical damage that had been done with the psychological need to have tangible evidences in the form of gold, that the 'enemy' would make amends. Rudyard Kipling, who had lost a son in the fighting, expressed this feeling in a bitter poem (he wrote it in 1917 when the reparations issue was being discussed in public):

These were our children who died for our lands: they were dear in our sight.
We have only the memory left of their home-treasured sayings and laughter.
The price of our loss shall be paid to our hands, not another's hereafter.
Neither the Alien nor Priest shall decide on it. That is our right.
But who shall return us the children?

That flesh we had nursed from the first in all clearness was given
To corruption unveiled and assailed by the malice of heaven
By the heart-shaking jests of Decay where it lolled on the wires —
To be blanched or gay-painted by fumes — to be cindered by fires —
To be senselessly tossed and retossed in stale mutilation
From crater to crater. For this we shall take expiation.
But who shall return us the children?

'Squeeze the German lemon'

During the British general election held before the treaty negotiations began, the public cried out for heavy reparations. Almost every responsible politician tried to soften the public mood. But one, Sir Auckland Geddes, told an eager audience in London that 'we would squeeze the German lemon till the pips squeaked' and even Lloyd George, tired out by the strains of electioneering, told a large meeting at Bristol that the Germans 'must pay to the uttermost farthing, and we shall search their pockets for it'. These were not his true views. He had begun, from the day the war ended, to adopt a moderate stance. He feared most of all that if Germany were humiliated too much by the treaty it would go Bolshevik, and not a single clause would be fulfilled, nor a penny of reparations paid.

In secret Lloyd George pressed his colleagues to adopt a certain leniency towards Germany, to send food to the starving millions in Germany and Austria, to think in terms of a peace free from vindictive clauses. But the public did not approve of such liberal sentiments. As Winston Churchill, who was then minister of munitions, recorded: 'The Prime Minister and his principal colleagues were astonished and to some extent overborne by the passions they encountered in the constituencies. The brave people whom nothing had daunted had suffered too much. Their unpent feelings were lashed by the popular press into fury. The crippled and mutilated soldiers darkened the streets. The returned prisoners told the hard tale of bonds and privation. Every cottage had its empty chair. Hatred of the beaten foe, thirst for his just punishment, rushed up from the heart of deeply injured millions. All who had done the least in the conflict were as

might be expected the foremost in detailing the penalties of the vanquished. . . . In my own constituency of Dundee, respectable, orthodox, life-long Liberals demanded the sternest punishment for the broken enemy. All over the country the most bitter were the women, of whom seven millions were for the first time to vote. In this uprush and turmoil state policy and national dignity were speedily engulfed.'

Like Lloyd George, Churchill urged a moderate treaty. He too feared that harsh terms would force Germany into the Bolshevik embrace. But when Lloyd George reached Paris in January 1919, he found the French determined to obtain maximum reparations, and the sternest possible treaty.

At the peace conference Lloyd George was handicapped by the moods and utterances of the general election: the anti-German moods, continuing fierce, meant that in any moderation he urged he had to keep one eye on his own public opinion, which, when it felt that he was exercising undue leniency, could, and did, protest; while the bravado of the election speeches, vivid in French minds, meant that when Clemenceau, the French prime minister, urged severity he could always refer to Lloyd George's public statements as support for his own contentions. Although Lloyd George tried, throughout the negotiations, to control the evolution of the treaty, he began from a position of weakness from which he was unable fully to recover, and which obstructed many of his efforts to obtain a viable peace.

At Paris Lloyd George was the leading advocate of moderation. He sought to act as if he were above national antagonisms. He tried to be the arbiter of conflicting passions. But the House of Commons would not let him forget in what tone the election had been fought. When it became clear the reparations were being calculated on the basis of what Germany 'could' pay, rather than on what she 'ought' to pay, 370 Coalition Conservatives sent a petulant telegram, reminding him of what they and the electorate expected, and ending: 'Although we have the utmost confidence in your intention to fulfil your pledges to the country, may we, as we have to meet innumerable inquiries from our constituents, have your renewed assurance that you have in no way departed from your original intention?'

Within a week of receiving this challenge Lloyd George returned to London, and on 16th April 1919 rebuked the House of Commons for its impatience. He reminded MPs that he was having to settle the fate of five continents in Paris; that ten new states had to be brought into existence; that territorial, military, and economic questions had all to be decided upon, and that 'you are not going to solve these problems by telegram'. He reminded them that, even if mistakes were made, the League of Nations, which was being set up as part of the treaties, would be able to make the necessary adjustments later. He made it clear to his critics that if they insisted upon terms which the League were ultimately to judge unduly severe, those terms would be modified. For an hour Lloyd George cajoled, threatened, appealed to, and won over his listeners: '. . . and when enormous issues are dependent upon it, you require calm deliberation. I ask for it for the rest of the journey. The journey is not at an end. It is full of perils, perils for this country, perils for all lands, perils for the people throughout the world. I beg, at any rate, that the men who are doing their best should be left in peace to do it, or that other men should be sent there. . . .

'We want a stern peace, because the occasion demands it. But its severity must be designed, not to gratify vengeance, but to vindicate justice. . . .

'[It is the duty of] statesmen in every land, of the Parliaments upon whose will those statesmen depend, of those who guide and direct the public opinion which is the making of all—not to soil this triumph of right by indulging in the angry passions of the moment, but to consecrate the sacrifice of millions to the permanent redemption of the human race from the scourge and agony of war.'

Lloyd George as moderator

Lloyd George returned to Paris. But although he appeared to have convinced the House of Commons that leniency was needed, he was unable to convince the French. They made some concessions, abandoning their hopes for the creation of a separate Rhineland State, and for a Polish annexation of Danzig, but in general French desires were met. The treaty as finally published had a vindictive tone about it.

In a memorandum which Lloyd George wrote while at the peace conference, he declared that his concern was to create a peace for all time, not for a mere thirty years. A short peace might be possible if punitive measures were taken against Germany. But unless the Germans were placated, they would go Bolshevik, and Russian Bolshevism would then have the advantage, according to Lloyd George, 'of the organizing gift of the most successful organizers of national resources in the world'. The initial shock of war would pass, and then, wrote Lloyd George: 'The maintenance of peace will depend upon there being no causes of exasperation constantly stirring up either the spirit of patriotism, of justice, or of fairplay to achieve redress. . . . Our Peace ought to be dictated by men who act in the spirit of judges sitting in a cause which does not personally engage their emotion or interests, and not in a spirit of a savage vendetta, which is not satisfied without mutilation and the infliction of pain and humiliation.'

This was utopian. Yet Lloyd George was convinced that he was right. He went on to criticize all clauses which might prove 'a constant source of irritation', and suggested that the sooner reparations disappeared the better. He deprecated putting Germany under alien rule, fearing that by doing so 'we shall strew Europe with Alsace-Lorraines'. He emphasized that the Germans were 'proud, intelligent, with great traditions', but that those under whose rule they would be placed by the treaty were 'races whom they regard as their inferiors, and some of whom, undoubtedly for the time being, merit that designation'. These arguments fell upon

The German delegation to Versailles. They had been forced to accept not only humiliating losses, but blame for causing the war

The Defeat of the Central Powers

stony ground: the French could not understand Lloyd George's sudden conversion to what they could only describe as imbecilic pro-Germanism. Clemenceau replied icily to Lloyd George's memorandum that 'if the British are so anxious to appease Germany they should look . . . overseas . . . and make colonial, naval, or commercial concessions'. Lloyd George was particularly angered by Clemenceau's remark that the British were 'a maritime people who have not known invasion', and countered angrily that 'what France really cares for is that the Danzig Germans should be handed over to the Poles'.

These bitter exchanges were symptomatic of a growing rift in Anglo-French relations. For Clemenceau, the treaty was perhaps the best chance that France would have of designing effective protection against a Germany that was already almost twice as populous as France, and must therefore be shown by deliberate, harsh action that it would not pay to think of revenge. For Lloyd George, the treaty was an opportunity to arbitrate for Europe without rancour, and to create a continent whose future problems could be adjusted without malice. Great Britain, by supporting the League of Nations, would be willing to help in the process of adjustment. Clearly it was the treaty that would first need to be altered: Lloyd George did not fear that. For him the treaty was not a sacred instrument but a pliable one. It was obvious from his comments while it was being drafted that he would not be content to see it become the fixed rule of the new Europe.

At Paris Lloyd George opposed strenuously, but in vain, the transfer to Poland of areas predominantly German. His protest was a forceful one, yet it was not forceful enough to break the French desire for the reduction of German territory. 'I am strongly averse,' Lloyd George wrote, 'to transferring more Germans from German rule to the rule of some other nation than can possibly be helped. I cannot conceive any greater cause of future war than that the German people, who have certainly proved themselves one of the most vigorous and powerful nations in the world, should be surrounded by a number of small states, many of them consisting of people who have never previously set up a stable government for themselves, but each of them containing large masses of Germans clamouring for reunion with their native land. . . . [These proposals] must, in my judgement, lead sooner or later to a new war in Eastern Europe.'

The Treaty of Versailles was not as vindictive as France had hoped; nor was it as moderate as Lloyd George desired. It was certainly not as utopian as Woodrow Wilson envisaged. A study of its clauses reveals great concern for detail, an often

punitive attitude, and very little account taken of the personal hardships and political discontent which the clauses might arouse. Thus Austria and Germany were forbidden, by Article 80, to unite, a future possibility which the British foreign secretary, A.J.Balfour, had regarded as a sensible solution which might soften the blow of defeat. Article 100 took away from Germany the entirely German city of Danzig, turning it into an isolated 'Free City' within the 'customs frontiers' of Poland, and depriving all its citizens of German nationality. Under Article 118 Germany renounced all her 'rights, titles and privileges . . . whatever their origin' outside Europe. This meant that even purely commercial concessions, freely negotiated before 1914, were lost. All Germany's colonies were taken from her, together with 'all movable and immovable property in such territories'; even the property of the German school at Shanghai was given to the French and Chinese governments. All pre-war German trading agreements were declared null and void, and the patient, innocent, costly efforts of German businessmen in China, Siam, Liberia, Egypt, and Morocco were entirely undone. Article 153 laid down that 'All property and possessions in Egypt of the German empire and the German states pass to the Egyptian government without payment'; and Article 156 transferred to Japan all German state submarine cables in China 'with all rights, privileges, and properties attaching thereto'.

The military clauses were as one would expect. The size of the German army was limited to 100,000 men. Germany was forbidden to import any arms or munitions. Compulsory military training was abolished. Universities and sporting clubs were forbidden to 'occupy themselves with any military matters'. They were specifically forbidden to instruct or exercise their members 'in the profession or use of arms'. All fortresses in the Rhineland were to be dismantled. At sea, Germany was restricted to six battleships, six light cruisers, twelve destroyers, and twelve torpedo boats. She was allowed not a single submarine. Her naval personnel were limited to 15,000 men. All warships under construction were to be broken up.

One clause was a dead letter from the moment it was signed. Under Article 227 the Allies announced the trial of the Kaiser 'for a supreme offence against international morality and the sanctity of treaties'. He was to be tried by five judges, an American, an Englishman, a Frenchman, an Italian, and a Japanese. It was their duty 'to fix the punishment which it considers should be imposed'. Despite the British public's keenness to 'hang the Kaiser', Lloyd George felt that such a solution was a

mistake. When, therefore, the French began to demand the return of the Kaiser from Holland, Great Britain refused to give France any support. The Kaiser remained safely in exile, cultivating his garden.

'War guilt'

The most controversial clause in the Treaty of Versailles was Article 231, the notorious 'War Guilt' clause against which successive German governments argued in vain, and which even many British politicians thought too extreme. The Article read: 'The Allied and Associated Governments affirm and Germany accepts the responsibility of Germany and her allies for causing all the loss and damage to which the Allied and Associated Governments and their nationals have been subjected as a consequence of the war imposed upon them by the aggression of Germany and her allies.'

How had this clause come into being? What made the Allies so anxious to get Germany to accept responsibility for 'all the loss and damage'? Why was 'the aggression of Germany' referred to so bluntly?

The War Guilt clause originated before the end of the war. The Supreme War Council, meeting under the leadership of Clemenceau and Lloyd George at Versailles on 4th November 1918, had drafted a note to President Wilson, explaining to him the need for reparations from Germany. The note began: 'They (the Allied governments) understand that compensation will be made by Germany for all damage caused to the civilian population of the Allies by the invasion by Germany of Allied territory. . . .'

As Germany had never denied invading Belgium, Luxembourg, or France, this clause was a fair one: a statement of acknowledged fact. But someone at the meeting pointed out that as the clause stood, while Germany would have to pay for damage done from the Channel to the Vosges, there was nothing in this wording to enable any economic compensation to go to the non-continental allies, the USA, India, Australia, Canada, or even Great Britain, and that certainly the Dominions, who had played such a large part, not only in providing men but also materials, would resent their exclusion from money payments. The clause would therefore need redrafting. The new draft cut out 'the invasion by Germany of Allied territory' and replaced it by 'the aggression of Germany'. Aggression was a word that could cover a much wider sphere: it could be claimed that every aspect of war costs was involved. But it was also a condemnatory word. Invasion had been admitted; aggression had not. The justification in German eyes for the invasion was self-defence; aggression was a word pregnant with moral disapproval, allowing of no subtle interpretation; spelling, all too clearly, guilt.

Lloyd George's personal assistant recalled in 1931: 'I remember very distinctly discussing with L.G. the interpretation to be put upon the question of "restoration" or "reparations". His view was—"We must make it clear that we cannot charge Germany with the costs of the war. . . . She could not possibly pay it. But she must pay ample compensation for damage and that compensation must be equitably distributed among the Allies and not given entirely to France and Belgium. Devastated areas is only one item in war loss. Great Britain has probably spent more money on the war and incurred greater indirect losses in, for instance, shipping and trade, than France. She must have her fair share of the compensation."

'He then instructed me to prepare a form of words. . . . I did so. . . . I remember thinking, after the draft had been taken by L.G., that it did not cover adequately the point that compensation was due to all the Allies. . . . I therefore revised it to read "damage to the civilian population of the allies by the aggression of Germany by land, air and sea".'

Thus was written the clause which most aggravated Anglo-German relations between the wars, made the task of appeasement with Germany so difficult, and made the Germans feel that, whatever concessions Great Britain made, whatever gestures of friendship she volunteered, in reality her policy was dictated by an explicit belief in German guilt.

The reparations clauses were the most often criticized part of the treaty. Yet the total demand of £24,000,000,000 was whittled away at a series of international conferences, until finally, at Lausanne in 1932, reparations were brought to an end. Great Britain was paying off her war debts to the United States until the end of the 1960's; Germany stopped paying for the war over forty years ago.

The new frontiers

The treaty's most lasting clauses were those which created new frontiers. They were also the most defensible. Many were established, not by Allied insistence, but as a result of plebiscites, in which the inhabitants were asked where they wanted to go. The plebiscites in East Prussia resulted in the province remaining entirely German. In two border areas of Austria the inhabitants voted to remain Austrian. The people of the Saar, after fifteen years of League of Nations supervision, voted to return to Germany, and were reincorporated into Hitler's Reich—this, his first territorial acquisition, was a positive gain made possible only because of the treaty which he was always denouncing. In Silesia the plebiscite results were indecisive, and this rich industrial region was therefore divided between Germany and Poland. The

Danes of Schleswig voted to leave Germany: the sole plebiscite to go wholly against the German interest.

The lands which Germany lost outright were Alsace-Lorraine, a German war gain of 1871, and territory in the east which went to Poland. Germany had helped destroy Polish independence at the end of the 18th century, and had annexed Polish territory during the three partitions: now that territory was returned to the recreated Polish state, and with it a corridor which gave Poland an outlet on the Baltic Sea. The Germans later made a great fuss about this corridor. But its inhabitants were mostly Poles, and Poland, after over a hundred years of subjugation, was entitled to a measure of security.

The greatest frontier changes arose from the disintegration, in the last weeks of the war, of the Austro-Hungarian empire. Czechoslovakia had proclaimed itself an independent state; the treaties gave it a generous frontier. Yugoslavia did likewise, fulfilling the Slav dream of a new South Slav kingdom; and the Allies were again generous, though not allowing the port of Fiume to go to the new state. The Poles obtained territory from both Germany and Austria, and the Allies, eager to see Poland as a bastion between Bolshevik Russia and the west, encouraged an eastern frontier drawn very much at Russia's expense. Yet even here, Lloyd George was reluctant to see Poland push too far east or west, and

The Defeat of the Central Powers

PEACE AND FUTURE CANNON FODDER

The Tiger: "Curious! I seem to hear a child weeping!"

Prophetic cartoon—Clemenceau leaving the conference, which had met to ensure peace, hears one of the children it had doomed to become a soldier in 1940 weeping at his fate

British control, four independent states—Iraq, Transjordan, Saudi Arabia, and the Yemen. A fifth state, the Jewish national home in Palestine, remained under British rule for nearly thirty years, but was then partitioned between Arabs and Jews. The Armenians, too, were given a state of their own: but when the Turks destroyed it in 1922 the Allies did nothing to intervene. Over a million Armenians were murdered by the Turks during the war; but the Allies made no efforts to protect them after the war. Soviet Russia provided a haven for some, in the Soviet Republic of Armenia. Others fled to Europe as refugees, stateless, without a national patron.

Out of the collapse and Bolshevization of Russia emerged four new independent states—Finland, Latvia, Lithuania, and Estonia. The Caucasian states also declared their independence; and the Allies encouraged Georgia to maintain its sovereignty. But when Stalin sent Soviet troops into the land of his birth, the Allies accepted the fall of Georgian independence.

The German problem

Of the four empires shaken by the war only the German empire survived; it had lost one eastern province and restored Alsace-Lorraine to France, but its sovereignty was secure. As the Kaiser had abdicated before the end of the war, Germany became a republic; but alone of the defeated nations it preserved its territorial unity. The treaty restrictions were irksome, but made no serious inroads on national sovereignty, and, if anything, provided a powerful stimulus to German nationalism. The Treaty of Versailles may have created Hitler; it also preserved as a state the country in which he was to make his mark.

Neither the defeat of Germany nor the Treaty of Versailles solved the German problem. Germany was still the country with the largest population in Europe. The day after the treaty was signed Austen Chamberlain, the chancellor of the exchequer, wrote to his sister: 'So Peace is signed at last . . . Will the world have rest? . . .

'Even the old Germany would not, I think, rashly challenge a new war in the West, but the chaos on their Eastern frontier, and their hatred and contempt for the Poles, must be a dangerous temptation. . . .'

If the First World War was fought to prevent Germany from creating hegemony in Europe it failed. Germany was weakened, but not so weakened that it could not rise within a generation to threaten the balance of world power once again. The Empires of old Europe had been swept away. The provisions of the victorious peacemakers failed to fill the vacuum—millions had died in vain.

it was left to Polish military action, not any Allied treaty, to secure parts of the Ukraine, Belorussia, and Lithuania for the new Poland. To Rumania the Allies allotted the primarily Rumanian districts of Austria-Hungary, principally Transylvania. Bulgaria, an 'enemy' power, lost her outlet on the Aegean Sea, which went to Greece; but her full independence, secured from Turkey not ten years before the war began, was not tampered with. Austria lost only one basically Austrian province, the South Tyrol, which went to Italy. The nation with the most convincing grievance was Hungary; large communities of Hungarians found themselves inside Czechoslovakia, Rumania, and Yugoslavia.

But once again, Hungarian independence was secured, and although Hungary extended her frontiers when in alliance with Hitler, she returned to her 1919 borders in 1945; and they survive to this day.

What was the balance sheet of the peace treaties? Out of the collapse of the Austro-Hungarian empire emerged three independent states—Czechoslovakia, Hungary, and Austria; and three states gained from the old empire territory filled mostly with their fellow-countrymen—Poland, Yugoslavia, and Rumania. Two states, Austria and Hungary, felt deprived of territory; the other four were well satisfied.

Out of the collapse of the Ottoman empire emerged, after a brief period of

Balance Sheet of the First World War

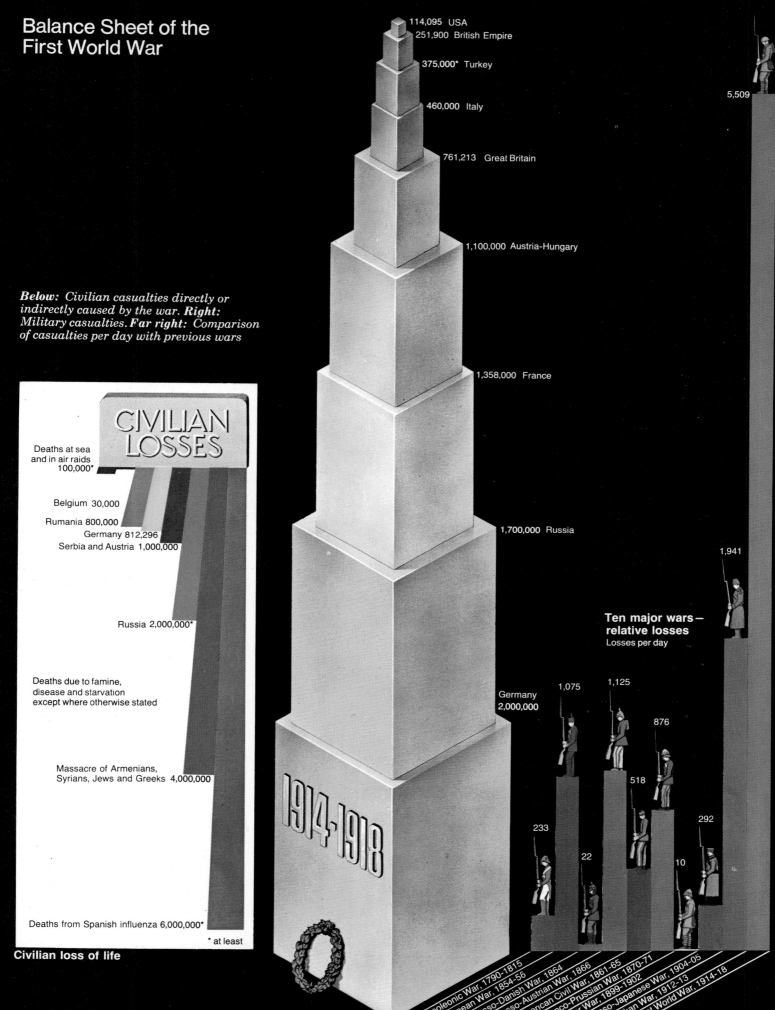

Below: Civilian casualties directly or indirectly caused by the war. *Right:* Military casualties. *Far right:* Comparison of casualties per day with previous wars

CIVILIAN LOSSES

Deaths at sea and in air raids 100,000*

Belgium 30,000

Rumania 800,000

Germany 812,296

Serbia and Austria 1,000,000

Russia 2,000,000*

Deaths due to famine, disease and starvation except where otherwise stated

Massacre of Armenians, Syrians, Jews and Greeks 4,000,000

Deaths from Spanish influenza 6,000,000*

* at least

Civilian loss of life

114,095   USA
251,900   British Empire
375,000* Turkey
460,000   Italy
761,213   Great Britain
1,100,000 Austria-Hungary
1,358,000 France
1,700,000 Russia
Germany 2,000,000

1914·1918

Military loss of life

Ten major wars — relative losses
Losses per day

5,509
1,941
1,125
1,075
876
518
292
233
22
10

Napoleonic War, 1790-1815
Crimean War, 1854-56
Prusso-Danish War, 1864
Prusso-Austrian War, 1866
American Civil War, 1861-65
Franco-Prussian War, 1870-71
Boer War, 1899-1902
Russo-Japanese War, 1904-05
Balkan War, 1912-13
First World War, 1914-18

Index

Index

Index

Acknowledgments

This book has been compiled from material contained in the *History of the 20th Century* partwork published by BPC Publishing Ltd. Pictures were obtained from the following sources:

Herman Axelbank; Chris Barker; Bavarian Army Museum, Munich; Derek Bayers; Earl Beatty; Berliner Illustrierte; Bibliothek für Zeitgeschichte, Stuttgart; Bibliothèque Nationale, Paris; Bradford City Library; Brown Brothers; Commando 1a Divisione; Carabinieri Pastrengo, Milan; Camera Press; Culver Pictures; Coll. René Dazy; Domenica del Corriere; Will Dyson/Odhams Ltd; E. C. Armées; Editions Rencontre; Fine Arts Publishing Co. Ltd; Martin Gilbert; Hartingue/ Viollet; Heeresgeschichtliches Museum, Vienna; Historical Research Unit; Robert Hunt Library; Huntingdon Hartford; L'Illustration; Illustrazione Italiana; Imperial War Museum; Das Interessante Blatt; International Institute of Social History; Kladderadatsch; Photothèque Laffont; Leach Heritage of the Air Collection; London Express; Lords Gallery; Mansell Collection; Moro, Milan; George Morrison; Musée de l'Armée, Invalides; Musée de la Guerre, Paris; Museo Aeronautico Caproni di Taliedo; Museo Bersagliere, Rome; Museo di Storia Contemporeanea, Milan; Museo Storico dei Granatieri, Rome; Museo Storico Italiano Della Guerra, Rovareto; Musée Royal de l'Armée, Brussels; National Army Museum, Sandhurst; National Gallery of Canada; National Museum of Ireland, Dublin; National Portrait Gallery; Nerbini; New Ireland Assurance Co; New York Public Library; Novosti; Gerard Oriol; Paul Popper; Press Association; Princip Museum Sarajevo; Radio Times Hulton Picture Library; S.C.R. Photo Library; Simplicissimus; Smithsonian Institute, Washington (Henry Beville); Snark International; Alan Spain; SPB Prague; Sphere; Staatsbibliothek, Berlin; Strato Maggiore Aeronautica, Rome; Südd-Verlag, Munich; Syndication International; Tate Gallery; Oscar Tellgmann; Topix; Tretyakov Gallery, Moscow; Ulk/Tasiemka; Ullstein; USIS; US Navy Dept; Vhú Prague; Roger Viollet; Der Welt Spiegel; Wehrgeschichtliches Museum, Rastatt.